Lecture Notes in Computer Science 11195

Commenced Publication in 1973
Founding and Former Series Editors:
Gerhard Goos, Juris Hartmanis, and Jan van Leeuwen

W0080053

More information about this series at http://www.springer.com/series/7407

Salah A. Al-Sharhan · Antonis C. Simintiras
Yogesh K. Dwivedi · Marijn Janssen
Matti Mäntymäki · Luay Tahat
Issam Moughrabi · Taher M. Ali
Nripendra P. Rana (Eds.)

Challenges and Opportunities in the Digital Era

17th IFIP WG 6.11 Conference on
e-Business, e-Services, and e-Society, I3E 2018
Kuwait City, Kuwait, October 30 – November 1, 2018
Proceedings

 Springer

Editors
Salah A. Al-Sharhan
Gulf University for Science and Technology
   (GUST)
Hawally, Kuwait

Antonis C. Simintiras
Gulf University for Science and Technology
   (GUST)
Hawally, Kuwait

Yogesh K. Dwivedi
Swansea University
Swansea, UK

Marijn Janssen
Delft University of Technology
Delft, The Netherlands

Matti Mäntymäki
University of Turku
Turku, Finland

Luay Tahat
Gulf University for Science and Technology
   (GUST)
Hawally, Kuwait

Issam Moughrabi
Gulf University for Science and Technology
   (GUST)
Hawally, Kuwait

Taher M. Ali
Gulf University for Science and Technology
   (GUST)
Hawally, Kuwait

Nripendra P. Rana
Swansea University
Swansea, UK

ISSN 0302-9743   ISSN 1611-3349   (electronic)
Lecture Notes in Computer Science
ISBN 978-3-030-02130-6   ISBN 978-3-030-02131-3   (eBook)
https://doi.org/10.1007/978-3-030-02131-3

Library of Congress Control Number: 2018957282

LNCS Sublibrary: SL1 – Theoretical Computer Science and General Issues

This Springer imprint is published by the registered company Springer Nature Switzerland AG
The registered company address is: Gewerbestrasse 11, 6330 Cham, Switzerland

Preface

This book presents the proceedings of the 17th International Federation of Information Processing (IFIP) Conference on e-Business, e-Services, and e-Society (I3E), which was held in Kuwait City, Kuwait, from October 30 to November 1, 2018. The annual I3E conference is a core part of Working Group 6.11, which aims to organize and promote exchange of information and co-operation related to all aspects of e-business, e-services, and e-society (the three Es). The I3E conference series is truly interdisciplinary and welcomes contributions from both academics and practitioners alike.

The central theme of the 2018 conference was "Challenges and Opportunities in the Digital Era" and although the framework of the I3E was maintained with the core of papers related to e-business, e-services, and e-society, those that touched upon wider opportunities and challenges in the digital era were welcome. Consequently, the aim of the conference was to bring together a community of scholars for the advancement of knowledge regarding the adoption, use, impact, and potential of social media across e-business, e-services, and e-society along with the business models that are likely to prevail in the digital era.

The conference provided an ideal platform for knowledge advancement and knowledge transfer through fruitful discussions and cross-fertilization of ideas with contributions spanning areas such as e-business, social media and networking, big data and decision-making, adoption and use of technology, ecosystems and smart cities, modeling and artificial intelligence, behaviors and attitudes toward information, and information technology and education. The call for papers solicited submissions in two main categories: full research papers and short research-in-progress papers. Each submission was reviewed by two knowledgeable academics in the field, in a double-blind process. The 2018 conference received 99 submissions from academics worldwide. The final set of 53 full papers submitted to I3E 2018 appear in these proceedings.

The success of the 17th IFIP I3E Conference was a result of the enormous efforts of numerous people and organizations. Firstly, this conference was only made possible by the continued support of WG 6.11 for this conference series and for selecting GUST to host I3E 2018, and for this we are extremely grateful. We are privileged to have received so many good-quality submissions from authors across the globe and the biggest thank you must go to them for choosing I3E 2018 as the outlet for their current research. We are indebted to the Program Committee, who generously gave up their time to provide constructive reviews and facilitate enhancement of the manuscripts submitted. We would like to thank Gulf University for Science and Technology (GUST) and the College of Business Administration for hosting the conference as well as the Kuwait Foundation for the Advancement of Sciences (KFAS), and That Al Salasil Bookstore for supporting the conference. Finally, we extend our sincere gratitude to everyone involved in organizing the conference, to our esteemed keynote speakers, and to Springer LNCS as the publisher of these proceedings, which we hope will be of use for the continued development of research related to the three Es and social media in particular.

August 2018

Salah A. Al-Sharhan
Antonis C. Simintiras
Yogesh K. Dwivedi
Matti Mäntymäki
Luay Tahat
Marijn Janssen
Issam Moughrabi
Taher M. Ali
Nripendra P. Rana

Organization

Conference Chairs

Salah Al-Sharhan   Gulf University for Science and Technology (GUST), Kuwait

Antonis Simintiras   Gulf University for Science and Technology (GUST), Kuwait

Program Chairs

Salah Al-Sharhan   Gulf University for Science and Technology (GUST), Kuwait

Antonis Simintiras   Gulf University for Science and Technology (GUST), Kuwait

Yogesh K. Dwivedi   Swansea University, UK

Matti Mäntymäki   University of Turku, Finland

Marijn Janssen   Delft University of Technology, The Netherlands

Nripendra P. Rara   Swansea University, UK

Luay Tahat   Gulf University for Science and Technology (GUST), Kuwait

Issam Moughrab   Gulf University for Science and Technology (GUST), Kuwait

Taher Mohammad Ali   Gulf University for Science and Technology (GUST), Kuwait

Organization Chairs

Ahmed ElMelegy   Gulf University for Science and Technology (GUST), Kuwait

Yasean Tahat   Gulf University for Science and Technology (GUST), Kuwait

Khiyar Abdallah   Gulf University for Science and Technology (GUST), Kuwait

Khalid Kisswani   Gulf University for Science and Technology (GUST), Kuwait

Nada Al Masri   Gulf University for Science and Technology (GUST), Kuwait

Dhoha Al Saleh   Gulf University for Science and Technology (GUST), Kuwait

Ahmed ElMorshidy   Gulf University for Science and Technology (GUST), Kuwait

Mohammad Al Najem	Gulf University for Science and Technology (GUST), Kuwait
Mohammad Ouakouak	Gulf University for Science and Technology (GUST), Kuwait
Gertrude Hewapathirana	Gulf University for Science and Technology (GUST), Kuwait
Saeed Askary	Gulf University for Science and Technology (GUST), Kuwait
Shobhita Kohli	Gulf University for Science and Technology (GUST), Kuwait

Conference Administrator

Nabae Asfar	College of Business Administration, Gulf University for Science and Technology (GUST), Kuwait

I3E 2018 Keynote Speakers

H. Raghav Rao	The University of Texas San Antonio, USA
Saad Al Barrak	Executive Chairman of ILA Group

I3E 2018 Program Committee

Salah Al-Sharhan	GUST, Kuwait
Antonis Simintiras	GUST, Kuwait
Yogesh K. Dwivedi	Swansea University, UK
M. P. Gupta	IIT Delhi, India
Fawaz Al-Anzi	Kuwait University, Kuwait
Naser Abu-Ghazaleh	GUST, Kuwait
Khaled El-Mawazini	GUST, Kuwait
Omar Mouzakkir	GUST, Kuwait
Jean Paul Arnaout	GUST, Kuwait
Matti Mantymaki	University of Turku, Finland
Marjin Janssen	Delft University of Technology, The Netherlands
Luay Tahat	GUST, Kuwait
Issam Moughrabi	GUST, Kuwait
Taher Mohammad Ali	GUST, Kuwait
Nripendra P. Rana	Swansea University, UK
Ahmed ElMelegy	GUST, Kuwait
Yasean Tahat	GUST, Kuwait
Khiyar Abdallah	GUST, Kuwait
Nada Al-Masri	GUST, Kuwait
Dhoha Al-Saleh	GUST, Kuwait
Ahmed El-Morshidy	GUST, Kuwait
Mohamad Al-Najem	GUST, Kuwait
Gertrude Hewapathirana	GUST, Kuwait

Contents

Mobile Application Adoption Predictors: Systematic Review of UTAUT2 Studies Using Weight Analysis

Kuttimani Tamilmani[✉], Nripendra P. Rana, and Yogesh K. Dwivedi

School of Management, Emerging Markets Research Centre (EMaRC), Swansea University Bay Campus, Swansea SA1 8EN, UK
kuttimani.tamilmani@gmail.com, ykdwivedi@gmail.com,
{n.p.rana,y.k.dwivedi}@swansea.ac.uk

Abstract. Mobile phone subscriptions are the largest form of consumer technology adopted across the world. Despite their potential, the research is very scant in understanding various predictors of consumer adoption towards mobiles technologies in particular mobile applications. This study intend to fulfil this purpose through weight analysis on mobile application adoption based studies that utilized UTAUT2 model. Studies needed for weight analysis were located through cited reference search method in Scopus and Web of Science bibliographic databases. The results of weight analysis revealed performance expectancy/perceived usefulness, trust and habit as best predictors of consumer behavioural intention to mobile applications adoption whereas behavioural intention was the best predictor of use behaviour. There were also two promising predictors with perfect weight of one such as perceived risk on behavioural intention and habit on use behaviour. Further steps of this research involves meta-analysis to develop comprehensive conceptual model concurrent with weight analysis results for empirical evaluation on various mobile applications.

Keywords: UTAUT2 · Weight analysis · Systematic review

1 Introduction

Marketing is an indispensable business function that serves as lifeline for any organisations survival since its core objective is to attract and retain customers to generate revenue [1]. Recent years has seen rapid explosion of mobile devices (mdevices) with a number of unique mobile subscribers reaching 5 billion in 2017 encompassing two thirds of global population elevating mobile to the highest scale of consumer technology worldwide [2]. Apart from providing entertainment to user's, mobile devices such as smartphones and tablets improves their productivity through plethora of mobile apps [3]. Examples of such applications include but are not limited to project management (slack), shopping (Amazon), business card (camcard), news organizer (flipboard), health/fitness (fitbit), note taking (evernote), transportation (uber), payment (square) and so on [4]. Unlike traditional advertising medium such as newspapers, televisions, magazine and radio, the unique characteristics of mobile platform enable

© IFIP International Federation for Information Processing 2018
Published by Springer Nature Switzerland AG 2018. All Rights Reserved
S. A. Al-Sharhan et al. (Eds.): I3E 2018, LNCS 11195, pp. 1–12, 2018.
https://doi.org/10.1007/978-3-030-02131-3_1

marketers to reach right consumers anytime anywhere. This phenomenon is popularly referred as mobile advertising [5, 6]. The continuous advancement of wireless communication and network technologies such as 3G, 4G and 5G will make mobile advertising a popular form of advertising medium in the near future. The market research firm Statista's report reveals companies spend a whopping 105.95 billion USD on mobile advertising in 2017 and it is expected to reach 175.64 billion in 2020 [7]. However, despite the rise in mobile technologies, a research on Fortune 500 companies' mobile websites for their mobile readiness revealed just one-quarter of them had mobile-responsive websites and majority of the companies were unprepared [8].

Given the preceding discussion on centrality of mobile advertising in marketing function to organisations, it would be impeccable to evaluate various predicators of consumer intention to adopt/use IT enabled mobile applications. The extended unified theory of acceptance and use of technology (UTAUT2) is the most comprehensive research model in the IS arena as on date in understanding various predictors influencing individuals to accept and make use of information technologies [see 9 for review]. Despite UTAUT2 model recent introduction in the year 2012, it has already garnered more than 3000 citations in Google Scholar alone spanning from IS field and beyond emphasising on its predictive ability. Thus, the objective of this study is to undertake weight analysis on consumer adoption/diffusion research of various mobile applications using UTAUT2 theory to evaluate the cumulative performance of various predictors. The study involves following steps to fulfil the objective:

- Locate empirical studies that utilized UTAUT2 model in understanding consumer intention/use behaviour of mobile applications.
- Conduct weight analysis of the empirical studies to understand the significance and insignificance of various relationships and their performance.
- Represent the predictors of consumer adoption to mobile applications in the form of sundial.

The next section of this paper describes the research method employed in this study; Sect. 3 presents the findings of weight analysis and systematic literature review followed by discussion in Sect. 4 and conclusion in Sect. 5.

2   Research Method

Since the purpose of this study is to synthesize the existing research findings on consumer adoption of mobile applications, a combination of "systematic review", "citation reference search" and "weight-analysis" approach were deemed appropriate [10–12]. Cited reference search for Venkatesh et al. [9] article in Scopus and Web of Science database from March 2012 to March 2017 resulted in 1,320 papers (823 from Scopus; 497 from Web of Science). On further scrutiny, we found 452 citations were common in both databases resulting in 868 unique citations for UTAUT2. Out of 868 articles, 16 empirical studies were found pertinent to mobile applications with relevant data for weight analysis. Weight analysis determines indicative predictive power of an independent variable over dependant variable. A weight is ratio between the number of times an independent variable found as significant predictor of dependant variable

(a) to the total number of times an independent variable is examined as a predictor of dependant variable (b) and thus is calculated using formula (a)/(b) [13].

3   Findings

This section presents and explains the findings from the systematic review and weight analysis

3.1   Literature Synthesis

The 16 mobile applications related studies included ten different countries: Malaysia was the most studied country with four empirical examination; whereas Jordon, China and the USA with two examinations each emerged as the second most studied countries. This is followed by six countries in third position such as Mozambique, France, Bangladesh, Portugal, Chile and the UK with one study each. Six major themes emerged based on the technology examined: (1) Mobile payments as a broader theme was the most examined technology with nine studies. Out of nine studies, six directly examined mobile payments, whereas three studies examined technologies such as NFC payments, mobile wallet and remote mobile payment to broadly fall under mobile payment classification. (2) Mobile banking was the second most popular technology examined with three studies, and finally the remaining four themes: (3) Mobile Apps

Table 1. Summary of mobile application studies

SN	Author name	D.V	Technology Examined	Country
1	Alalwan et al. [18]	UB	Mobile Banking	Jordon
2	Baptista and Oliveira [19]	UB	Mobile Banking	Mozambique
3	Hew et al. [14]	BI	Mobile Apps	Malaysia
4	Jia et al. [19]	BI	Mobile Payment	China
5	Jia et al. [20]	BI	Mobile Payment	China
6	Koenig-Lewis et al. [21]	UB	Mobile Payment	France
7	Mahfuz et al. [22]	UB	Mobile Banking	Bangladesh
8	Morosan and Defranco [23]	BI	NFC Payments	USA
9	Oliveira et al. [24]	BI	Mobile Payment	Portugal
10	Qasim and Abu-Shanab [25]	BI	Mobile Payment	Jordon
11	Ramírez-Correa et al. [14]	UB	Mobile Internet	Chile
12	Shaw [26]	BI	Mobile Wallet	USA
13	Slade et al. [27]	BI	Remote Mobile Payment	UK
14	Teo et al. [28]	BI	Mobile Payment	Malaysia
15	Wong et al. [15]	BI	Mobile TV	Malaysia
16	Wong et al. [16]	BI	Mobile Advertising	Malaysia

LEGEND: BI: Behavioural Intention; **D.V:** Independent Variable; **UB:** Use Behaviour

[14]; (4) Mobile Internet [15]; (5) Mobile TV [16] and 6) Mobile advertising [17] were examined on one instance each. It was also found that only five studies employed Use behaviour (UB) as their outcome/dependant variable with all having behavioural intention (BI) as their immediate antecedent whereas BI was the most operated outcome/dependant variable with 11 studies (see Table 1).

3.2   External Variables

Thirteen out of sixteen studies employed UTAUT2 constructs in combination with external variables. Whereas the remaining three studies (i.e. Jia, Hall [20]; RamírezCorrea, Rondán-Cataluña [15]; Wong, Wei-Han Tan [16] adapted only UTAUT2 based constructs in understanding consumer intention to use various mobile applications. Table 2 presents findings of external variables analysis across thirteen

Table 2. Summary of external variables

SN	External constructs	Frequency	Citations
1	Trust	5	Alalwan et al. [18]; Jia et al. [21]; Qasim and Abu-shanab [26]; Shaw [27]; Slade et al. [28]
2	Perceived risk	2	Koenig-lewis et al. [22]; slade et al. [28]
3	Perceived security	2	Morosan and Befranco [24]; oliveira et al. [25]
4	Innovativeness	2	Oliveira et al. [25]; wong et al. [17]
5	Exposure	1	Jia et al. [21]
6	Information searching	1	Jia et al. [21]
7	Knowledge	1	Koenig-lewis et al. [22]
8	General privacy	1	Morosan and Defranco [24]
9	System-related privacy	1	Morosan and Defranco [24]
10	Compatibility	1	Oliveira et al. [25]
11	Behavioural intention to recommend	1	Oliveira et al. [25]
12	Network externalities	1	Qasim and Abu-shanab [26]
13	Self-efficacy	1	Shaw [27]
14	Informal learning	1	Shaw [27]
15	Perceived transaction speed	1	Teo et al. [29]
16	Perceived transaction convenience	1	Teo et al. [29]
17	Mobile skilfulness	1	Wong et al. [17]
18	Website quality	1	Mahfuz et al. [23]
SN	*External moderators*	*Frequency*	*Citations*
1	Hofstede cultural moderators	2	Baptista and Oliveira [19]; Mahfuz et al. [23]
2	Educational level	1	Hew et al. [14]

studies to reveal eighteen unique external constructs and two unique external moderators. Trust was the most frequently utilised external construct with five studies followed by the second most used external constructs such as perceived risk, perceived security and innovativeness that were used on two occasions each. In addition, there were 14 more external constructs like: (1) exposure, (2) information searching, (3) knowledge, (4) website quality, (5) general privacy, (6) system-related privacy, (7) behavioural intention to recommend, (8) compatibility, (9) network externalities, (10) informal learning, (11) self-efficacy, (12) perceived transaction convenience, (13) perceived transaction speed and (14) mobile skilfulness that were used on one instance each. The hypothesis from all external constructs to consumer behavioural intention/use behaviour of various mobile applications were positive apart from perceived risk and system related privacy variable that were hypothesized negatively to BI. A (-) sign in Table 3 indicates the negative path relationship among the independent and dependant variable in examining consumer adoption of mobile applications. Finally, the two external moderators: Hofstede's cultural moderators and educational level were used together on three instances with two studies the former one was the most used.

4 Weight-Analysis

4.1 Coding Independent and Dependent Variables

This study employed generalized coding scheme adapted from Jeyaraj et al. [13] to uniformly code findings between various independent and dependant variables. The coding template was organised into 'rows' and 'columns'. Each row represents one of the 16 studies, whereas each column represents the path relationship between an independent and dependant variable. The intersection points between studies in "row" and path relationship in "column" represent the significance of the particular path relationship corresponding to that study. The coding scheme has four different values: (1) '+1' in the case where the path relationship examined was significant and hypothesized in positive direction; (2) '−1' in the case where the path relationship examined was significant and hypothesized in negative direction; (3) '0' in the case where the path relationship examined was insignificant; and (4) "Blank" when the relationship was not studied [13]. The thorough examination of 16 articles uncovered 63 unique path relationships employed among 31 independent and 12 dependent variables. However, the findings of this study is limited only to 31 path relationships on two dependant variables i.e. behavioural intention (comprising 27 independent variables) and use behaviour (comprising four independent variables) (see Table 3).

Since the objective of this study is to understand various predictors of consumer behavioural intention and use of mobile applications.

4.2 Consumer Mobile Applications Predictor's Findings

Table 3 presents the summary on weight-analysis findings of 16 studies mobile application studies. An independent variable is termed as well-utilized when examined by researchers in five or more studies and termed as experimental variable in case of less than five examinations. Furthermore, the independent variable qualifies as the best predicator of dependant variable when they are used in five or more studies (welluti-lized) and have a weight of 0.80 or more. On the other hand, independent variable can be considered as a promising predicator when it is used in less than five studies (experimental) and have perfect weight of one [12].

Table 3 lists 27 independent variables on behavioural intention and four on use behaviour in understanding consumer adoption towards mobile applications. There were eight well-utilized independent variables/predictors (examined five or more instances) of behavioural intention such as performance expectancy/perceived usefulness (exam-ined 16 times), effort expectancy/perceived ease of use (examined 14 times), social influence (examined 12 times), facilitating conditions (examined 9 times), hedonic motivation/perceived enjoyment (examined 9 times), price value (examined 7 times), habit (examined 7 times) and trust (examined 7 times). Out of eight well-utilized pre-dictors the best predictors of behavioural intention are the one with weights $\geq$ 0.80 which are performance expectancy/perceived usefulness (0.81), trust (0.80) and habit (1.00). However, some independent variables, despite being used more than five times, yielded non-significant results consistently to emerge as the worst predictors of con-sumer behavioural intention towards mobile payment with weight < 0.80. The label of worst predictors may not necessarily appeal to the well utilized predicators having weight in between the range of 0.80 and 0.50 such as social influence (0.67), facilitating conditions(0.78) and hedonic motivation/perceived enjoyment (0.78) are worth of future examination [13].

Instances of worst predictors with weight < 0.50 comprise effort expectancy/perceived ease of use (0.43) and price value (0.29). Furthermore, there were 19 experimental variables used in understanding consumer behavioural intention towards mobile payment. Out of nineteen experimental variables only three variables: 1) perceived risk, 2) perceived security and 3) innovativeness were examined on two instances each with rest sixteen variables were examined on once instance each. The discussion is restricted to experimental variables examined more than one instance. Perceived Risk emerged as the promising predicator with weight of one.

There were four independent variables in understanding consumer use behaviour towards mobile applications. Among the four, behavioural intention was the only well utilized and best predictor with significant values on all five occasions. The remaining three: 1) facilitating conditions (examined 4 times, significant 3 times), habit (examined 2 times, significant 2 times) and website quality (examined 1 times, significant 1 times) are experimental variables. Habit emerged as the promising predicator with weight of one among experimental variables examined more than one instance. Figure 1 presents sundial of consumer mobile applications adoption predictors and their corresponding weight. Surprisingly none of the sixteen studies on consumer mobile applications employed UTAUT2 moderator's relationships in their original form.

Table 3. Weight analysis summary approach adapted from Jeyaraj et al. [13]

SN	Independent Variable	DV	Sig (a)	In-Sig	Total (b)	Weight (a/b)
1	Performance expectancy/Perceived Usefulness	BI	13	3	16	0.81
2	Effort expectancy/Perceived ease of use		6	8	14	0.43
3	Social Influence		8	4	12	0.67
4	Facilitating Conditions		7	2	9	0.78
5	Hedonic motivation/Perceived enjoyment		7	2	9	0.78
6	Price Value		2	5	7	0.29
7	Habit		5	0	5	1
8	Trust		4	1	5	0.8
9	Perceived Risk(-)		2	0	2	1
10	Perceived security		1	1	2	0.5
11	Innovativeness		1	1	2	0.5
12	Informal learning		1	0	1	1
13	Online shopping habit		0	1	1	0
14	Mobile shopping habit		1	0	1	1
15	Cell phone Usage habit		0	1	1	0
16	Mobile payment usage habit		1	0	1	1
17	Masculinity Vs Femininity		0	1	1	0
18	Information searching		1	0	1	1
19	General privacy		0	1	1	0
20	System-related privacy(-)		1	0	1	1
21	Compatibility		1	0	1	1
22	Power distance		0	1	1	0
23	Uncertainty avoidance		0	1	1	0
24	Website quality		0	1	1	0
25	Network externalities		1	0	1	1
26	Perceived Transaction Convenience		0	1	1	0
27	Perceived Transaction Speed		1	0	1	1
28	Behavioural Intention	UB	5	0	5	1
29	Facilitating Conditions		3	1	4	0.75
30	Habit		2	0	2	1
31	Website quality		1	0	1	1

Legend: D.V: Independent Variable; In. Sig: Number of insignificant path values; Sig (a): Number of significant path values

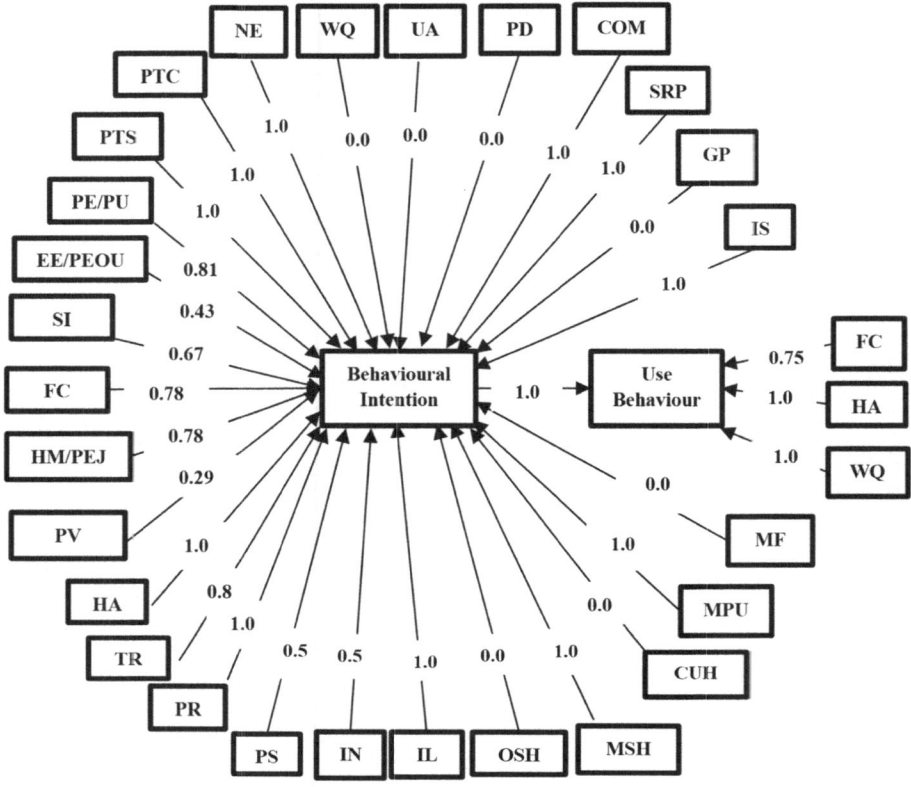

[LEGEND: **CUH:** Cell Phone Usage Habit; **COM:** Compatibility; **EE/PEOU:** Effort Expectancy/Perceived Ease Of Use; **FC:** Facilitating Conditions; **GP:** General Privacy; **HA:** Habit; **HM/PEJ:** Hedonic Motivation/ Perceived Enjoyment; **IL:** Informal Learning; **IS:** Information Searching; **IN:** Innovativeness; **MF:** Masculinity Vs Femininity; **MPU:** Mobile Payment Usage Habit; **MSH:** Mobile Shopping Habit; **NE:** Network Externalities; **OSH:** Online Shopping Habit; **PR:** Perceived Risk; **PS:** Perceived Security; **PTC:** Perceived Transaction Convenience; **PTS:** Perceived Transaction Speed; **PE/PU:** Performance Expectancy/ Perceived Usefulness; **PD:** Power Distance; **PV:** Price Value; **SI:** Social Influence; **SRP:** System-Related Privacy; **TR:** Trust; **UA:** Uncertainty Avoidance; **WQ:** Website Quality.]

Fig. 1. Consumer mobile applications adoption predictors a Sundial

5   Discussion

Literature synthesis reveals the deployment of UTAUT2 theory to understand consumer adoption of six different mobile applications in ten different countries underscoring generalizability of UTAUT2 theory across various technological and cultural contexts. Utilitarian value based mobile applications were the most studied with mobile payments (9 studies) and mobile banking (3 studies) together comprising 12 out of 16 studies. The findings revealed that only five (around 31%) studies employed UB as endogenous variable whereas the remaining 11 studies comprising (69%) employed BI as endogenous variable. This pattern is comprehensible since popular mobile applications are still evolving and it is difficult to measure actual consumer use of these technologies, in such cases BI can be good indicator of future technology use. However, Wu and Du's [30] meta-analysis on BI and UB caution the researchers notion of considering BI as surrogate of UB as it's not appropriate for studies to report user behaviour without assessing actual system usage. In addition, they caution all stakeholders in research community should be circumspect of such studies not investigating user behaviour but only behavioural intention [30].

The two independent variables of technology acceptance model (TAM) i.e. perceived usefulness similar to performance expectancy (16 studies) and perceived ease of use (14 studies) similar to effort expectancy emerged as the most utilized variables emphasising TAM's dominance in individual adoption research. However, the most frequently used predicators does not necessarily translate into best predictors [13]. For instance, effort expectancy, despite being the second most examined independent variable on 14 instances, was significant on just six occasions with weight of 0.43 to become the worst predictor of consumer behavioural intention to mobile applications. Surprisingly price value the latest addition to the UTAUT2 model was the worst predicator of BI with lowest weight of 0.29 among relationships that are examined five or more times. A meta-analytic study on price value construct found the construct inappropriate to examine mobile applications that are available to users free of cost as they were prone to insignificant results in determining consumer adoption to those technology [31]. Researchers need compelling reason to include the worst predicators as independent variables in evaluating consumer adoption towards mobile payment. On the other hand, researchers should continue using four best predictors in understanding consumer adoption of mobile applications three of them performance expectancy/perceived usefulness (0.81), trust (0.80) and habit (1.00) were on behavioural intention, whereas behavioural intention (1.00) the fourth and final one was on use behaviour all having weights of ≥ 0.80. Moreover, there were only two promising predictors with perfect weight of one used more than one instance such as perceived risk (1) and habit (1). Adoption to innovative product such as mobile applications that are entirely new to market can involve great element of risk. However, UTAUT and TAM, the most popular theoretical models in understanding individual technology adoption, have often overlooked constructs such as perceived risk, privacy concerns and trust [21]. Weight analysis finding confirms the notion of Koenig-Lewis et al. [21] with trust emerging as best predicator and perceived risk as promising predicator of consumer adoption to mobile applications. Researchers should continue using promising predicators in future studies to enable more testing and ascertain their suitability as the best predicator.

As far as habit is concerned, it emerged as best predictor of behavioural intention and promising predictor of use behaviour. HA → BI path was the most examined habit based relationship with all five significant instances and the remaining two significant relationships were for the path HA → UB. UB is less utilized as dependant variable of HA than BI, since HA → UB is better hypothesis in understanding consumer adoption of well-established and mature technologies, whereas BI is better predictor of habit and subsequent UB for new and rarely used technology applications such as our case under investigation i.e. mobile applications [32]. Moreover this belief is strengthened through meta-analysis study that focussed on habit construct which revealed habit as not an optimal construct to examine technology users at early stage of adoption where sufficient time hasn't elapsed in using technologies to form habit [33].

6 Conclusion

This paper aimed to understand the predictors of consumer adoption to mobile application through weight analysis. The results of weight analysis divulged the most/least/best/worst and promising predictors of consumer adoption for mobile applications and provided comprehensive review on this subject. The results also revealed that more than 80% of the studies employed external variables since UTAUT2 and other popular technology acceptance theories have disregarded predictors such as trust (best predictor) and perceived risk (promising predictor) in consumer adoption for mobile applications. Moreover, none of the studies employed UTAUT2 moderating variables due to the complexity of their relationship amongst various constructs. In addition, despite being the most frequently used predictor; effort expectancy produced the most insignificant results. This calls for researchers to be more cautious while operationalizing their constructs from existing theory/model to make necessary adaptations or omit irrelevant constructs depending upon context rather than having obligation to replicate all the constructs in underpinning model/theory. Despite precautionary measures taken for coding and analysis the findings of the study is not without its limitations. The studies involved for weight analysis were limited only to two databases such as Web of Science and Scopus restricting the number of empirical studies. Future weight analysis should include a large number of studies from wider range of databases to minimize publication bias. Although weight analysis is good indicator on significance of predictors it does not take sample size into consideration like meta-analysis to provide true effect size. Thus, the next stage of this research is as follows: (1) to conduct meta-analysis and develop research model in combination with weight analysis; (2) to collect data on selected mobile applications through questionnaires; and (3) to analyse the collected data and empirically examine the research model through statistical techniques.

References

1. Srivastava, R.K., Shervani, T.A., Fahey, L.: Marketing, business processes, and shareholder value: an organizationally embedded view of marketing activities and the discipline of marketing. J. Mark. **63**, 168–179 (1999)
2. Gsmaintelligence. (2017). Global Mobile Trends 2017. Retrieved from: https://www.gsmaintelligence.com/research/?file=3df1b7d57b1e63a0cbc3d585feb82dc2&download, Last accessed 2018/05/01
3. Keith, M.J., Thompson, S.C., Hale, J., Lowry, P.B., Greer, C.: Information disclosure on mobile devices: Re-examining privacy calculus with actual user behavior. Int. J. Hum Comput Stud. **71**(12), 1163–1173 (2013)
4. Patel, S.: 21 Apps to Boost Productivity, Accountability, and Success. Retrieved from: https://www.entrepreneur.com/article/244945, Last accessed 2018/05/10

5. Maneesoonthcrn, C., Fortin, D.: Texting behaviour and attitudes toward permission mobile advertising: an empirical study of mobile users'acceptance of sms for marketing purposes. Int. J. Mob. Mark. **1**(1), 66–72 (2006)
6. Yang, K.C.: Exploring factors affecting consumer intention to use mobile advertising in Taiwan. J. Int. Consum. Mark. **20**(1), 33–49 (2007)
7. Statista.: Mobile advertising spending worldwide from 2010 to 2020 (in million U.S dollars) https://www.statista.com/statistics/303817/mobile-internetadvertising-revenue-worldwide/. Accessed 20 May 2018
8. McCorkindale. T., Morgoch, M.: An analysis of the mobile readiness and dialogic principles on Fortune 500 mobile websites. Public Relat. Rev. **39**(3), 193–197 (2013)
9. Venkatesh, V., Thong, J.Y., Xu, X.: Consumer acceptance and use of information technology: extending the unified theory of acceptance and use of technology. MIS Q. **36**(1), 157–178 (2012)
10. Venkatesh, V., Thong, J.Y., Xu, X.: Unified theory of acceptance and use of technology: a synthesis and the road ahead. J. Assoc. Inf. Syst. **17**(5), 328–376 (2016)
11. King, W.R., He, J.: A meta-analysis of the technology acceptance model. Inf. Manag. **43**(6), 740–755 (2006)
12. Dwivedi, Y.K., Rana, N.P., Jeyaraj, A., Clement, M., Williams, M.D.: Reexamining the unified theory of acceptance and use of technology (UTAUT): towards a revised theoretical model. Inf. Syst. Front. 1–16 (2017). https://doi.org/10.1007/s10796-017-9774-y
13. Jeyaraj, A., Rottman, J.W., Lacity, M.C.: A review of the predictors, linkages, and biases in IT innovation adoption research. J. Inf. Technol. **21**(1), 1–23 (2006)
14. Hew, J.-J., Lee, V.-H., Ooi, K.-B., Wei, J.: What catalyses mobile apps usage intention: an empirical analysis. Ind. Manag. Data Syst. **115**(7), 1269–1291 (2015)
15. Ramírez-Correa, P.E., Rondán-Cataluña, F.J., Arenas-Gaitán, J.: An empirical analysis of mobile Internet acceptance in Chile. Inf. Res. **19**(3), 1–19 (2014)
16. Wong, C.-H., Wei-Han Tan, G., Loke, S.P., Ooi, K.-B.: Mobile TV: a new form of entertainment? Ind. Manag. Data Syst. **114**(7), 1050–1067 (2014)
17. Wong, C.-H., Tan, G.W.-H., Tan, B.-I., Ooi, K.-B.: Mobile advertising: the changing landscape of the advertising industry. Telemat. Inform. **32**(4), 720–734 (2015)
18. Alalwan, A.A., Dwivedi, Y.K., Rana, N.P.: Factors influencing adoption of mobile banking by Jordanian bank customers: extending UTAUT2 with trust. Int. J. Inf. Manage. **37**(3), 99–110 (2017)
19. Baptista, G., Oliveira, T.: Understanding mobile banking: The unified theory of acceptance and use of technology combined with cultural moderators. Comput. Hum. Behav. **50**, 418–430 (2015)
20. Jia, L., Hall, D, Sun, S.: The effect of technology usage habits on consumers' intention to continue use mobile payments. In: Proceedings of the 20th Americas Conference on Information Systems, Savannah, AIS (2014)
21. Jia, L., Hall, D., Sun, S.: Trust building in consumer learning process and its effect on consumers' behavioral intention toward mobile payments. In: Proceedings of Twenty-first Americas Conference on Information Systems, Puerto Rico (2015)
22. Koenig-Lewis, N., Marquet, M., Palmer, A., Zhao, A.L.: Enjoyment and social influence: predicting mobile payment adoption. Serv. Ind. J. **35**(10), 537–554 (2015)
23. Mahfuz, M. A., Hu, W., Khanam, L.: The influence of cultural dimensions and website quality on m-banking services adoption in bangladesh: applying the UTAUT2 model using PLS. In: WHICEB (2016)
24. Morosan, C., DeFranco, A.: It's about time: Revisiting UTAUT2 to examine consumers' intentions to use NFC mobile payments in hotels. Int. J. Hosp. Manag. **53**, 17–29 (2016)

25. Oliveira, T., Thomas, M., Baptista, G., Campos, F.: Mobile payment: Understanding the determinants of customer adoption and intention to recommend the technology. Comput. Hum. Behav. **61**, 404–414 (2016)
26. Qasim, H., Abu-Shanab, E.: Drivers of mobile payment acceptance: the impact of network externalities. Inf. Syst. Front. **18**(5), 1021–1034 (2016)
27. Shaw, N.: The mediating influence of trust in the adoption of the mobile wallet. J. Retail. Consum. Serv. **21**(4), 449–459 (2014)
28. Slade, E., Williams, M., Dwivedi, Y., Piercy, N.: Exploring consumer adoption of proximity mobile payments. J. Strat. Mark. **23**(3), 209–223 (2015)
29. Teo, A.-C., Tan, G.W.-H., Ooi, K.-B., Hew, T.-S., Yew, K.-T.: The effects of convenience and speed in m-payment. Ind. Manag. Data Syst. **115**(2), 311–331 (2015)
30. Wu, J., Du, H.: Toward a better understanding of behavioral intention and system usage constructs. Eur. J. Inf. Syst. **21**(6), 680–698 (2012)
31. Tamilmani, K., Rana, N.P., Dwivedi, Y.K., Sahu, P.G., Roderick, S.: Exploring the role of 'price value' for understanding consumer adoption of technology: a review and meta-analysis of utaut2 based empirical studies. In: Twenty-Second Pacific Asia Conference on Information Systems, Japan (2018)
32. Ouellette, J.A., Wood, W.: Habit and intention in everyday life: the multiple processes by which past behavior predicts future behavior. Psychol. Bull. **124**(1), 54–74 (1998)
33. Tamilmani, K., Rana, N. P., Dwivedi, Y. K.: Use of 'Habit' is not a habit in understanding individual technology adoption: a review of UTAUT2 based empirical studies, forthcoming. In: Proceedings of IFIP WG 8.6 Working Conference - Smart Working, Living And Organising 25th June, Portsmouth, UK (2018)

The Role of Social Networks in Online Marketing and Measurement of Their Effectiveness – The Case Study

Hana Mohelska and Marcela Sokolova(✉)

Faculty of Informatics and Management, Department of Management, University of Hradec, Hradec Kralove 3, Rokitanskeho 62, Kralove, Czech Republic
{hana.mohelska,marcela.sokolova}@uhk.cz

Abstract. This paper is devoted to online marketing tools and primarily focuses on the use of social networks and measuring their effectiveness. The theoretical part briefly presents the topic of online marketing and selected tools. The next section deals with the case study that analyses the use of social networks on a particular project, including measuring the efficiency of social networks by comparing the planned and actual state according to the selected metrics. In conclusion, there is a discussion on the results obtained and the possible directions, which would increase the efficiency of social networks, i.e. online marketing, are outlined. The results of assessing the current state of online marketing for the surveyed project in 2017, by comparing the planned and actual metric values, largely fail to meet the targets. With measuring social networking tools, the planned numbers of website visits and social networking orders didn't reach their planned values. Regarding the number of fans on individual social networks, the planned status was only achieved with the Pinterest and Instagram social networks.

Keywords: Online marketing · Social networks · Efficiency measurement Facebook · Twitter · Instagram

1 Introduction

The rapid development of information and communication technologies, in which, the Internet plays an important role, has been an important trend in the recent years. Nowadays, only a few people can imagine life without Internet. The possibilities of using the Internet include real-time communication between people, access to a wide range of information and services and it has a great potential mainly for entrepreneurship, even for businesses that normally operate outside the Internet. Today, the vast majority of businesses are presented on the Internet. Thanks to online marketing, they have a better chance of entering people's awareness and increasing their sales.

The present time brings enhanced possibilities of marketing communication through the Internet. Communication on the Internet is characterized by a number of positive characteristics, particularly through the ability to accurate target, personalize, interact and measure, and all with relatively low costs [1, 2].

S. A. Al-Sharhan et al. (Eds.): I3E 2018, LNCS 11195, pp. 13–20, 2018.
https://doi.org/10.1007/978-3-030-02131-3_2

2   Objective and Methodology

The submitted study's aim was to evaluate the current state of online marketing for the selected project. An assessment of the current state of online marketing was carried-out in 2017 on three major tools - social networks, PPC advertising and e-mailing – this paper primarily focuses on social networking findings.

2.1   The Analyzed Project Presentation

The case study for the demonstration of measuring social networking effectiveness was carried-out on a selected start-up project. It is an exclusive platform that connects the selected designers and enthusiasts who love original design and can appreciate creative work. Within this project, it currently exhibits around 500 designers from around the world. So far, the project works mainly within the Czech Republic and Slovakia.

2.2   Social Networking Efficiency Measurement

The tools were evaluated in 2017 by comparing planned and actual metric values. The evaluation data was obtained from Google Analytics, Google AdWords, MailChimp, and the project's website [3, 4].

3   Theoretical Background - Online Marketing Tools

The marketing definition from Kotler's point of view states that marketing is a science and an art to discover, create and deliver value that meets the needs of the target market. Marketing identifies unfulfilled needs and requirements. It defines, measures and quantifies the scope of the selected market and the potential profit. It precisely determines which market segments the company can maintain best, it designs and promotes appropriate products and services [5, 6].

The Internet provides companies with new opportunities and benefits from a marketing perspective. These include, for example, the provision of important information, a new sales channel and the promotion of business activities and products around the world, the ability to customize the offer via database information on the number and frequency of site visitors and many others. Linking Internet and marketing therefore creates a significant area [7–9].

3.1   Electronic Commerce

Active marketing and the sale of goods and services on the Internet is referred to as ecommerce. Thanks to the Internet, today's world is characterized by inter-connection, which brings new methods, such as identifying or searching for customers, how to distribute products more effectively, or how to communicate more effectively with large groups of customers [10, 11].

The main factors that have influenced the development of e-commerce, include the following four factors: (1) Digitization and networking; (2) Rapid Internet development; (3) New forms of trading; (4) Adapting products to customer needs.

E-business. E-business includes all electronic information exchanges via electronic platforms (intranet, extranet, Internet) to conduct business activities. The Internet and other technologies help businesses to conduct their business activities faster, more accurately and in a greater time and space range [12, 13].

E-commerce. E-commerce is a more specific term that includes sales and purchasing processes using electronic communication. Electronic markets are used to represent market venues and vendors use them to offer their products and services online. Ecommerce includes e-marketing and e-purchasing (the "shopping" site of e-commerce) [12, 14].

E-marketing. E-marketing or electronic-marketing is the "selling" e-commerce site and involves communication, sales promotion and sales of goods and services through the Internet. It represents the effort of the company to inform on the products and services, to promote them and to sell them [12, 15].

3.2   Online Marketing Elements

SEO. SEO, i.e. website optimization for search engines or optimization of searchability on the Internet, is an abbreviation of the Search Engine Optimization in English. A more detailed definition of SEO is explained by SEO consultant Pavel Ungr, who says SEO is the process of influencing the visibility of the website in the unpaid part of the search engine results. Generally speaking, the higher and the more often the web appears in the search engine results, the more visitors the web can get from the Internet search engine. SEO can target different types of search including images, local search, videos, academic information, news, or narrower search in specific fields [16, 17].

Link-building. Link-building is an activity that aims to establish a partnership where reference is made in the form of a link, text or image, leading to the promotion of websites in places where potential customers look for them. The authority of website is created during link-building [18].

Content marketing. Content marketing means regular creation and the sharing of quality free-of-charge content among listeners who share it and it will be useful to them or entertain them. Quality content related to the company's business scope will attract potential customers who will become more interested in the company. Then, they can become customers and if customers are satisfied, the customers become returning clients. By publishing high-quality educational content, the company gains the confidence of customers who want to do business with it [19].

Copywriting. Copywriting is a creative activity that creates gentle and engaging advertising and marketing texts that sell products and services [20].

Conversion rate optimization. Optimizing the conversion rate means adjustments to the website to increase the conversion rate. Conversion is an indication of a fact when a web visitor becomes a customer, most often it includes an order [20].

Social networks. Social networks are an online social media where users create and share a variety of content, such as photos, videos, personal experiences and opinions. Companies on social networks create content and communicate with potential customers to promote brands and marketing goals [1, 20].

PPC advertising. PPC is the abbreviation for the english term "Pay Per Click". This is a business model when the advertiser pays for every click on the ad.

E-mailing. Newsletter is an English term for an electronic newsletter regularly sent to logged-in subscribers and it belongs to a modern, inexpensive and effective marketing tools. Everyone, who receives a newsletter, is a potential customer. At the same time, it also serves for the dissemination of the company's awareness and its further growth [21, 22].

3.3   Measurement and Evaluation of Online Marketing Tools

Online marketing is a powerful tool due to the possibility of accurate monitoring of target customers. The advantage of online activities is that they are relatively easy to measure.

The metrics of different tools and campaigns are also different depending on the given goals to be achieved. The most significant metrics include site traffic, conversions, i.e. desirable site visitor's actions, average time spent on the site, the number of pages visited by the user, the site instant exit rate and others. The metrics need to be analyzed using the tools for that purpose. The most common metrics tracking tool on the web is Google Analytics, then Google AdWords tool for PPC advert, e-mailing such as MailChimp, on social networks like Facebook, the Facebook Insights tool is used.

4   Assessing the Current State of Social Networking as an Online Marketing Tool - The Case Study

The tools were evaluated by comparing planned and actual metric values in 2017. The evaluation data was obtained from Google Analytics, Google AdWords, MailChimp, and the project's website.

To measure the effectiveness of the social networking tool, the following table (Table 1) lists the number of visits and the number of orders that are made from individual social networks. Website traffic through social networking channels was estimated to 8,593 visits in 2017 and accounted for 14.16% of the total traffic. By clicking through the social networks, 28 conversions were carried out in the form of orders for design products. What is important here is the fact that none of the social networks have been financially subsidized, so they are only organic unpaid results.

The comparison of the planned and actual state is used to evaluate this tool. The following table (Table 2) shows that the estimated number of site visits and the number of social networking orders scheduled was far from being achieved.

An important social networking tool metric is also the number of fans who express interest from a potential customers' point of view. The next table (Table 3) lists the scheduled and actual numbers of fans on each social network. Fulfilment of the planned values were carried-out only on the Pinterest and Instagram social networks.

Table 1. Website traffic from social networks and number of orders leading from social networks in 2017. (Google Analytics, customized processing)

Social Network	Traffic	Share of total traffic	Number of orders	Share of total orders
Facebook	6271	72.98%	11	39.29%
Pinterest	1914	22.27%	7	25.00%
Instagram	102	1.19%	2	7.14%
LinkedIn	88	1.02%	6	21.43%
Twitter	88	1.02%	2	7.14%
Tumblr	1	0.01%	0	0%

Table 2. Scheduled and actual number of visits and orders from social networks in 2017. (Google Analytics, project website, customized processing)

	Social networks
Scheduled visits	50000
Visits	8464
Planned number of orders	500
Number of orders	28

Table 3. Social networks – fan number values in 2017. (Facebook.com, Pinterest.com, Instagram.com, Twitter.com, Linkedin.com, customized processing)

	Facebook	Pinterest	Instagram	Twitter	LinkedIn
Fan schedule plan for 2017	130000	3500	1500	1500	50
Fans at the beginning of 2017	112570	2516	699	1150	5
Fans at the end of 2017	115396	3521	1956	1270	23

However, for all social networks, the number of fans had a growing character (Fig. 1), also reflecting the work of a social networking specialist, who tried to influence these numbers with their activity on social networks.

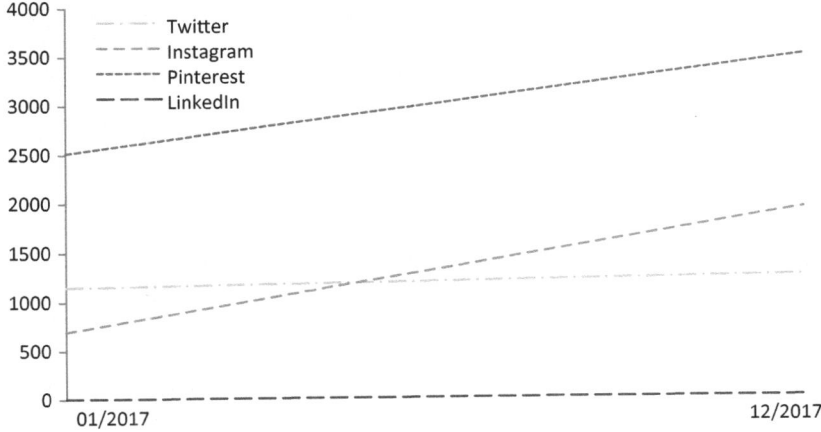

Fig. 1. Development of fan numbers on the following social networks - Pinterest, Instagram, Twitter and LinkedIn in 2017. (customized processing)

The social networking tool is used extensively within the scope of the project, in terms of the number of social networks on which it operates. From the point of view of shared network contributions, broader sharing options could be used - a broader type of content, or a wider focus on target groups, their interests, and so on.

5   Discussion

The aim of the submitted study was to evaluate the current state of online marketing for the selected project. Firstly, the project was introduced, subsequently an assessment of the current state of the use of social networking in online marketing in 2017 was carried-out concerning three important tools - social networks, PPC advertising and emailing - the paper's focus was primarily on social networks. Based on data from Google Analytics, Google AdWords, and MailChimp, the scheduled and actual metric values for each tool were compared.

The assessment results for the current state of online marketing of the project under review in 2017, by comparing the scheduled and actual metric values of the three selected tools largely failed to reach their targets.

With measurements of social networking tools, the scheduled number of website visits and social networking orders didn't reach their expected values. Regarding the number of fans on individual social networks, the planned status was only achieved by the Pinterest and Instagram social networks.

Within PPC advert measurement it was discovered that the estimated number of visits and clicks on adverts were only fulfilled for the campaign on the awareness of the brand in the content network (for the Czech Republic and Slovakia). The planned number of orders resulting from the PPC ad click wasn't reached by any of the campaigns carried-out.

When measuring e-mailing, it was discovered that the planned number of newsletter subscribers wasn't reached by one target group. The lack of content and capacities were the reason why the other target groups failed to meet the planned number of newsletters sent. The estimated average rate of opening newsletter was fulfilled only for designers in the Czech Republic and Slovakia, and the estimated average click-through rate in the newsletter was reached only for the target group of design lovers in the Czech Republic and Slovakia. The planned numbers of orders resulting from the newsletter click-out were not reached for one target group.

We consider the value of the number of orders on the web as the most important metric as it brings profit to a business. Nevertheless, the values of the planned order numbers didn't reach the planned target in any of the measured tools, on the contrary, these values are very distant to the planned state. Low order values are attributed to different purchasing behavior as they are higher priced products. The reason for not achieving the planned situation is also the fact that more financial investments and capacities were originally planned for the planned activities and the metric values.

So, it is important to realize that the project under consideration as a start-up conceals a great deal of human capacity and total commitment to the given project. In order to achieve business and marketing goals for 2018, it is also necessary to invest sufficient funds to enable the implementation of planned communication activities. The project should continue to focus on presenting its brand, designers and products offline as today's trends show that being online is not as competitive as it used to be. The project could also focus on events in Slovakia, where the design area is experiencing a boom. Due to the high prices of the offered design products, it could also target products with lower value to make them more accessible to a wider range of customers.

6 Conclusion

At the time of the boom of information and communication technologies, it is important for each organization to use the potential which is offered to them, because that's the only way they can compete in a competitive battle.

Sufficient efforts and financial investment in meaningful communication activities will later return to the organizations in the form of satisfied customers and increased profitability.

Acknowledgments. The paper was written with the support of the specific project 6/2018 grant "Determinants of cognitive processes impacting the work performance" granted by the FIM UHK and thanks to help of students Aneta Machačková.

References

1. Karlíček, M., Král, P.: Marketingová komunikace: jak komunikovat na našem trhu. Grada, Praha (2011)
2. Mohelská. H., Sokolová, M.: Smart, connected products change a company's business strategy orientation. Appl. Econ. **48**(47), 4502–4509 (2016)
3. Grant, R.M.: Contemporary Strategy Analysis: Text and Cases, 7th edn.,vol. xvi, 926 p. Wiley, Hoboken, NJ (2010)
4. Grappone, J, Gradiva, C.: Search Engine Optimization: An Hour a Day, 3rd edn. 408 p. Wiley Publishing, Indianapolis, Indiana (2011)
5. Kotler, P.: Marketing v otázkách a odpovědích. CP Books, Brno (2005)
6. Sokolová, M , Zubr, V. Innovation as a Requirement for Business Competitiveness - Czech Republic Case Study. Advanced science letters. American Scientific Publishers (2015). https://doi.org/10.1166/asl.2016.6694
7. Kotler, P., Keller, K.L.: Marketing Management. Grada, Praha (2007)
8. Strauss, J., E-Ansary, A., Raymond, F.: E-Marketing - 4. Prentice Hall, New Jersey (2005)
9. Charlesworth, A.: Internet Marketing: A Practical Approach. Routledge (2011)
10. Chaffey, D., et al.: Internet Marketing. Strategy, Implementation and Practice. Redwood Books Limited. Trowbridge (2000)
11. Boon-Long, S., Wongsurawat, W.: Social media marketing evaluation using social network comments as an indicator for identifying consumer purchasing decision effectiveness. J. Direct, Data Digit. Mark. Pract. **17**(2), 130–149 (2015). https://doi.org/10.1057/dddmp. 2015.51
12. Kotler, P.: Moderní marketing: 4. evropské vydání. Grada, Praha (2007)
13. Yadav, M., Kamboj, S., Rahman, Z.: customer co-creation through social media: the case of 'Crash the Pepsi IPL 2015'. J. Direct Data Digit. Mark. Pract. **17**(4), 259–271 (2016). https://doi.org/10.1057/dddmp.2016.4

14. Dhami, G.A.: A. measuring the impact of security, trust and privacy in information sharing: a study on social networking sites. J. Direct Data Digit. Mark. Pract. **17**(1), 43–53 (2015). https://doi.org/10.1057/dddmp.2015.32
15. Leonhardt, J.M.:Tweets, hashtags and virality: marketing the affordable care act in social media. J. Direct Data Digit. Mark. Pract. **16**(3), 172–180 (2015). https://doi.org/10.1057/dddmp.2015.4
16. Ungr, P.: Definice: Co je SEO – optimalizace pro vyhledávače? http://blog.bloxxter.cz/definice-co-je-seo/. Accessed 27 Jan 2017
17. Landers, B.: The measure of SEO success is revenue, not your Google website ranking. Air Cond. Heat. **251**(3), 24–24 (2014)
18. Podstavec, F.: Co je linkbuilding a kdo je linkbuilder? http://www.podstavec.cz/co-jelinkbuilding-a-kdo-je-linkbuilder/. Accessed 27 Jan 2017
19. Content marketing. Copyblogger. http://www.copyblogger.com/content-marketing/. Accessed 01 Feb 2017
20. Mencák, T.: Online marketing v praxi – Online marketing mix (přednáška) Hradec Králové, CS Technologies, s.r.o., UHK, (2016)
21. Finklestein, R.: 49 marketingových tajemství pro zaručené zvýšení prodeje. Computer Press, Brno (2010)
22. Newsletter. Adaptic. http://www.adaptic.cz/znalosti/slovnicek/newsletter/. Accessed 03 Feb 2017

Learning Time Analysis - Case Study in the IT Sector in the Czech Republic

Vaclav Zubr$^{(\boxtimes)}$ (iD) and Hana Mohelska$^{(\boxtimes)}$ (iD)

Faculty of Informatics and Management, The University of Hradec Kralove,
Hradec Kralove, Czech Republic
{vaclav.zubr, hana.mohelska}@uhk.cz

Abstract. For learning organisations, acquiring knowledge is one of the key activities. Then for example, the acquired knowledge will allow organisations greater flexibility or a strategic advantage. As small and medium-sized organisations in the Czech Republic are of great importance from the employment of people viewpoint, this survey is focused on education in these organisations. The aim of this study is to evaluate learning time in small and medium-sized organizations in the Czech Republic and to compare the learning time of general staff and managers in these organizations. When comparing results with foreign studies, it can be argued that the results obtained correlate with each other and are satisfactory. In this study, there was a statistically significant difference found between people who are learning at least 1–10 h per month and those who are not. At the same time, the positive influence of learning on the evaluation of some dimensions was found.

Keywords: IT sector · Learning time · Small and medium-sized organizations
General staff learning · Managers' learning

1 Introduction

The definition of a "learning organisation" has been described by several authors over the years. For example, a learning organisation is defined in the book of The Fifth Discipline by Peter Senge as: "… an organisation whereby people continually improve their abilities and achieve the results they truly desire where they find support, new and dynamic models of thinking where collective thinking and inspiration are very welcome, and where people still learn how to learn [14]."

From other sources, a learning organisation can be characterised as an organisation that acquires knowledge and innovates fast enough to survive and prosper in a rapidly changing environment, supports continuous employee education, critical thinking as well as risk-taking in the application of new ideas, as well as the dissemination of new knowledge for an organisation in order to incorporate them into day-to-day activities [3]. Learning then becomes an integral part of the whole work process. Work and learning are interconnected in the process of continual improvement. A learning organisation doesn't rely on learning as a by-product of routine work but is actively supported, facilitated and rewarded. Interaction between individuals is then a key aspect of organisational learning [1, 17].

Published by Springer Nature Switzerland AG 2018. All Rights Reserved
S. A. Al-Sharhan et al. (Eds.): I3E 2018, LNCS 11195, pp. 21–29, 2018.
https://doi.org/10.1007/978-3-030-02131-3_3

According to several studies, more factors are involved in good functioning of the learning organisation concept (management, learning communities, inner compliance, empowering individuals, organising culture, self-development, teamwork, sharing information, creating knowledge, building reliable learning dimensions and innovation or facilitating leadership) [19]. Learning is one of the basic activities for the learning organisation concept and can be carried out at individual, group or organisational levels [18].

Organisational learning is the result of an interactive and interdependent process. This type of learning is based on organisational memory (past knowledge and experience) and is carried out through common knowledge and mental models of individual company members. Individuals and groups in the organisation are articles through which organisational learning takes place [8, 9].

1.1   Small and Medium-Sized Organizations in the Czech Republic

The importance of small and medium-sized organizations in the Czech Republic is relatively high given the high percentage of people they employ (more than 70% of employees in the private sector) [5].

Small and medium-sized organizations are defined as organizations that employ up to 250 people. In detail, small and medium-sized organizations can be divided into small enter-prises (also micro-companies) with 1 to 9 employees, small organizations with 10 to 49 employees and medium organizations employ between 50 and 250 people [4, 5].

1.2   Measurement of Learning Organisation

We can use a large number of tools to measure and diagnose learning organisations. The used tool depends on the different definitions of the learning organisation. The definition of learning organisation by Marsick and Watkins [15] is also one of these tools (Tables 1 and 2).

Table 1. Seven learning organisation dimensions

No of dimension	Name
1	Create continuous learning opportunities
2	Promote inquiry and dialogue
3	Encourage collaboration and team learning
4	Create systems to capture and share learning
5	Empower people toward a collective vision
6	Connect the organisation to its environment
7	Provide strategic leadership for learning

Source: own processing by [7, 9]

According to Marsick and Watkins, there are seven dimensions that characterise the learning organisation culture. Individual dimensions then represent the efforts of organisations to create learning opportunities for all employees, the effort to create a platform supporting dialogues, reactions and experiments among members, team learning, vision sharing or strategic leadership [12].

All dimensions are interconnected, which can aggravate statistical evaluation of analyses [16]. When comparing organisations with dimensions, we can see a correlation between dimensions and knowledge and financial performance [9, 13].

In the Czech Republic, the topics of introducing a learning organisation and the level of learning in organisations haven't been significantly addressed yet. The missing data about learning situation in organizations can lead to worsen market position of the organization. Therefore the aim of this study is to evaluate learning time in small and medium-sized organizations in the Czech Republic and to compare the learning time of general staff and managers in these organizations. According to the published foreign studies [16], using the Dimension of a Learning Organisation questionnaire seems to be satisfying tool to evaluate the level of learning in organizations. To maintain the validity of this study it was conducted the cross-section questionnaire survey with using the Dimensions of a Learning Organization questionnaire.

2 Methodology

At the beginning of the research, an in-depth data analysis was carried out analysing articles from books and journals searched using web databases (Web of Science, Scopus, Sage Journals, Emerald Insight, Science Direct, Wiley Online Library, Taylor & Francis, etc.) with related issues. Based on the synthesis of the obtained data, the search keywords were chosen: learning organisation, learning organisation performance, building a learning organisation, DLOQ, Dimensions of a learning organisation questionnaire study, etc.

To comparison this study with published foreign studies [16] a cross-section questionnaire survey was conducted between December 2017 and February 2018. This survey was focused on small and medium-sized organizations in the IT sector in the Czech Republic. The respondents were sent a questionnaire via e-mail addresses obtained from the Albertina Business and Marketing Database [2]. The size of the organization and the sector of activity were selected as a business selection criterion. The business sectors were entered by the CZ-NACE code, the predominant activity, specifically [10]:

J – Information and communication activities – 62.0 – Activities in the Information Technology field – 62.01 – Programming - 62.02 – Information Technology Consultancy - 62.03 – Computer Equipment Management – 62.09 – Other IT activities

For this survey, a Dimension of a Learning Organisation questionnaire was selected in a 21-issue questionnaire version focusing on the 7 dimensions of a learning organisation [9]. Thanks to its expansion, this questionnaire is easily comparable to foreign studies. This questionnaire also provides adequate measurement results with its focus on the seven dimensions of a learning organisation. To maintain the validity of the questionnaire, the questionnaire was translated by two independent translators from English into Czech and then back to English. At the same time, retaining the meaning of the questionnaire was considered. For each dimension, Cronbach confidence coefficient was calculated using IBM SPSS Statistics Version 24. The Alpha coefficient ranged from 0.683 to 0.860 for each dimension. Overall, the value of the coefficient was 0.933. The calculated values of the Cronbach coefficient appear to be satisfactory (the coefficient higher than 0.7 is "satisfactory") [6]. Individual dimensions were assessed by the respondents on the 6-point Likert scale.

In order to verify the clarity of the questionnaire, a pilot study was initially carried out. This pilot study was attended by a total of 20 students from the combined form of follow-up Master's degree in Information Management. The final version of the questionnaire was created using "docs.google.com". In total, 2,884 respondents were addressed. Approximately 250 of the e-mail addresses no longer existed, 25 respondents are not currently in business.

The obtained data was analysed using Microsoft Excel 2016 and IBM SPSS Statistics version 24 using descriptive statistics, parametric and non-parametric tests at confidence levels $\alpha = 0.01$ and $\alpha = 0.05$.

3   Results

In order to verify the questionnaire understands, a pilot study was carried out involving 20 students from the combined form of Master's degree in Information Management at the Faculty of Informatics and Management in Hradec Králové. These respondents are employed in the following areas: software development, telecommunications, IT, electronics production, internet sale, sales, law, health, advertising, government, work with children, transport and logistics, sports, energy and heating. The data from the pilot study was evaluated using Microsoft Excel 2016 and the IBM SPSS Statistics version 24 statistical programme.

After evaluating the pilot survey, information on the organisation's size and the position in the organisation was added to the questionnaire.

Table 2. Cronbach alpha for each dimension

Dimension	Cronbach α
D1: Creating opportunities for systematic learning	0.721
D2: Support for polling and dialogue	0.860
D3: Encourage team learning and collaboration	0.761
D4: Creating systems for capturing and sharing learning	0.683
D5: Motivating people for a collective vision	0.796
D6: System interfaces	0.765
D7: Strategic guidance for learning	0.791
Total	0.933

Source: own processing

Using the Cronbach alpha reliability indicator, the reliability of each dimension was determined. All dimensions except dimension 4 met the required reliability value, total reliability is relatively high ($\alpha = 0.933$). Although dimension 4 (Creating systems for capturing and sharing learning) didn't reach 0.7 value, it's significantly close to this value (0.017 difference), so this value can also be considered satisfactory.

A total of 2,884 respondents from small and medium-sized companies from the Czech Republic with a focus on information technology activities were addressed. The study was attended by a total of 201 respondents (return on questionnaires was 6.97%). Organisations employing up to 10 employees (32.3%), up to 50 employees (45.3%) and 250 employees (22.4%) were represented in the study. General staff accounted for 35.8% of the respondents and managers accounted for 64.2% of the respondents. The respondents were made up of 137 men and 64 women. The largest age group were respondents aged 39 (6.0%), then 38 years (5.5%) and 47 years (5.0%). Regarding the distribution of respondents to age groups, the 31–40 years age group (37.8%) were represented most, followed by 57 respondents in the 41–50 years age group (28.4%) and 32 respondents in the 51–60 years age group (15.9%). In terms of education, respondents with a university education (72.1%) were represented most, followed by secondary school graduates (20.9%).

The respondents reported employment time in the organisation up to five years (32.8%), followed by 11–15 years (21.4%). Only two respondents worked in organisations for a longer time - one respondent for 31 years and the other for 36 years.

When comparing the evaluation of individual questions, one can say that none of the questions received less than half of the points. The respondents rated the worse questions 10 and 11: "My organisation creates systems to measure the difference between actual and expected performance" with an average rating of 3.386 and "My organisation makes all evaluations available to all employees" with an average rating of 3.236. The greatest indecision through the evaluation by respondents was expressed at question 20: "In my organisation, managers look for opportunities for further education.", when they identified two values on the Likert scale from which the average was calculated.

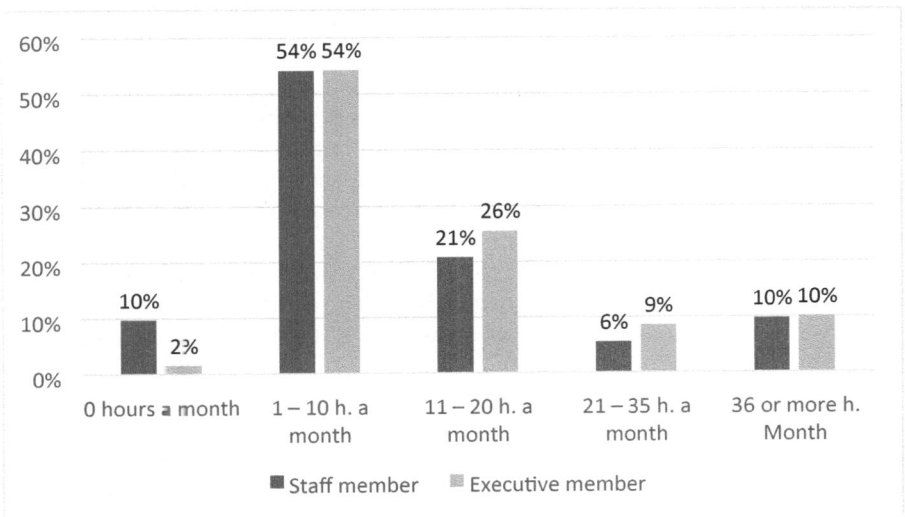

Fig. 1. Training time (per month) by worker's position (Source: own processing)

The majority of respondents devote from 1 to 10 h per-month to education that's related to employment. On average, employees spend 13 h on education. The relationship between the training time and job position is shown in Fig. 1.

Table 3. Comparison of respondents' responses with different intensity of education

	Average of D1	Average of D2	Average of D3	Average of D4	Average of D5	Average of D6	Average of D7
0 h a month	2.741	3.463	3.778	3.148	3.111	3.370	3.296
1–10 h a month	4.482	4.346	4.125	3.557	4.335	3.888	4.280
11–20 h a month	4.396	4.444	4.347	3.493	4.403	3.948	4.462
21–35 h a month	4.600	4.578	4.444	3.622	4.622	4.078	4.378
36 or more h Month	5.100	4.725	4.167	3.550	4.442	4.400	4.667

Source: own processing

The differences between managers and ordinary staff members are noticeable in the case where employees don't learn. The poorer attitude of ordinary staff members in regard to education could be justified by insufficient motivation for further education or by the fact that the organisation doesn't require further training. For dimensions 3, 4, and 5, the statement asserts that positive dimension ratings are growing up to 35 h per-month while investing more time in education per-month is slightly declining. The T-test reveals a statistically significant difference between people devoting "0 h" a month to education and the other groups of respondents who devote to education ("1–10 h" $p = 0.00028$; "11–20 h" $p = 0.00025$; " 21–35 h" $p = 0.000092$; "more than 36 h" ($p = 0.00074$, $\alpha = 0.01$).

4   Discussion

The extension of the learning organisation concept in the Czech Republic hasn't been described yet. This paper is focused on evaluation of the learning organisation concept in Information Technology organisations registered in the Czech Republic.

Overall, nearly the study consisted of 70% men and approximately 30% women. This result was expected with respect to the field chosen for the study and is in-line with the reported male/female statistics in the IT sector [11].

When comparing the learning time of the ordinary staff members and managers, it's clear that managers learn more than regular staff. The managers' higher education is probably directly related to their higher assessment of the individual learning organisation dimensions (Fig. 1).

If we compare the learning time per-month with the average assessment of the individual dimensions, we find that there is a statistically significant difference ($p = 0.00074$) between non-learning staff and the employees who learn 36 or more hours per-month at the materiality level of $\alpha = 0.01$. At the same time, for dimensions 3, 4, and 5, positive dimensional ratings are growing up to 35 h per-month, while investing more time in education per-month slightly decreases (Table 3). If employees were learning more than 36 h per-month, training could eventually take place at the expense of employment, which may have resulted in lower dimensions evaluation.

If we compare the average results of each dimension, we see that all dimensions correlate very closely with one another, which is consistent with Watkins, O'Neil [16].

Table 4 below shows an example of studies conducted abroad, along with an average rating score for each dimension. The total number of respondents in the comparative studies was N = 2854.

Table 4. Comparing DLOQ results with other studies

Study author	N	D1	D2	D3	D4	D5	D6	D7
Watkins and Marsick	389	3.94	3.91	3.98	3.50	3.74	4.00	4.13
Selden	142	5.01	4.05	4.09	3.44	3.83	4.17	4.49
McHargue	264	4.16	4.15	4.33	3.78	4.20	4.35	4.73
Lien Yang, Li	79	3.97	4.05	4.00	4.13	4.08	4.01	4.26
Hernandez	906	3.94	4.16	4.01	4.09	4.21	3.96	4.27
Maria	628	4.05	4.08	3.84	3.96	3.79	3.98	4.21
			4.35	4.32	3.13	4.15	3.99	4.42
			4.09	**4.01**	**3.86**	**3.99**	**4.04**	**4.29**
Zubr			**4.39**	**4.19**	**3.52**	**4.33**	**3.94**	**4.33**
Ellinger	208	4.12	4.04	4.13	3.70	3.93	4.19	4.26
Milton. Watkins	37	4.26						
Weighted average		**4.06**	**201**	**4.45**				

Source: own processing by [16]

5   Conclusion

The aim of this study was to evaluate learning time in small and medium-sized organizations in the Czech Republic and to compare the learning time of general staff and managers in these organizations. To obtain the results we used the Dimensions of a Learning organization questionnaire according to other published studies. This questionnaire was distributed via e-mail between the general staff and managers of small and medium-sized organizations in IT sector in the Czech Republic. If we compare this study's results with studies already conducted, we can say that the results obtained from organisations from the IT sector in the Czech Republic are satisfactory. The results obtained in 5 of 7 dimensions are higher than the weighted average of foreign studies that have been conducted. Compared to the weighted average of results, it can be concluded that organisations in the IT sector in the Czech Republic meet most of the learning organisation's dimensions better than organisations in foreign studies. Higher ranking of organisations should give organisations a greater strategic advantage [16]. Organisations in the Czech Republic only have a lower average score in two dimensions. Specifically, Dimension 4 "Creating systems for learning and sharing learning" and Dimension 5 "System interfaces". There was no statistically significant difference between the individual dimensions of the learning organisation concept (p = 0.658,

$\alpha = 0.05$) when comparing the average value from the comparative studies with the completed study in the Czech Republic. The training period per month has a positive impact on the evaluation of individual dimensions.

When assessing individual dimensions of the learning organisation, the differences between managers and ordinary staff members were observed. In the follow-up research, it would be appropriate to analyse several small and medium-sized organisations to look for a larger sample of management as well as ordinary staff members. At the same time, it would be useful to mutually compare DLOQ results across the various fields of action.

Acknowledgement. The paper was written with the support of the specific project 6/2018 grant "Determinants of Cognitive Processes Impacting the Work Performance" granted by the University of Hradec Králové, Czech Republic and thanks to help of students Majid Ziaei Nafchi.

References

1. Adamec, J.: Základní principy koncepce učící se organizace a jejich přijímání (2010). http://emi.mvso.cz/EMI/2010-02/07%20Adamec/Adamec.pdf
2. Albertina for business and marketing (2018). http://www.albertina.cz/?gclid=Cj0KCQiAzrTUBRCnARIsAL0mqcz2seJjjxmISfi7QlvHHAwN-ZnZrWpd4Botnujmtq08Zio1vx0BfBMaAu-bEALw_wcB
3. BusinessDictionary.com: Learning organization (2015). http://www.businessdictionary.com/definition/learning-organization.html
4. Czech Statistical Office: Malé a střední podniky (jejich místo a role v české ekonomice) (2005). https://www.czso.cz/csu/czso/cri/male-a-stredni-podniky-jejich-misto-a-role-vceske-ekonomice-2005-rhybfgzbj0
5. Czech Statistical Office: Malé a střední firmy v ekonomice ČR v letech 2003–2010 (2013). https://www.czso.cz/documents/10180/20534676/116111a.pdf/9c378e0f-d77a-4f21bf3e-e4ed35cb1122?version=1.0
6. Institute for Digital Research and Education: What does Cronbach's alfa mean? (2017). https://stats.idre.ucla.edu/spss/faq/what-does-cronbachs-alpha-mean/
7. Jamali, D., Sidani, Y., Zouein, C.: The learning organisation: tracking progress in a developing country. A comparative analysis using the DLOQ. Learn. Organ. **16**, 103–121 (2009). https://doi.org/10.1108/09696470910939198
8. Marquardt, M.J.: Building the Learning Organisation. Davies-Black Publishing, Palo Alto (2002)
9. Marsick, V.J., Watkins, K.E.: Demonstrating the value of an organisation's learning culture: the dimensions of the learning organisation questionnaire. Adv. Dev. Hum. Resour. **5**, 132–151 (2003). https://doi.org/10.1177/1523422303251341
10. NACE: 62.0 Činnosti v oblasti informačních technologií (2018). http://www.nace.cz/nace/62-0-cinnosti-v-oblasti-informacnich-technologii/
11. National centre for women and information technology (2018). https://www.ncwit.org/
12. Norashikin, H., Safiah, O., Fauziah, N., Noormala, A.: Learning organisation culture, organisational performance and organisational innovativeness in a public institution of higher education in malaysia: a preliminary study. Procedia Econ. Financ. **37**, 512–519 (2016). https://doi.org/10.1016/S2212-5671(16)30159-9

13. Qawasmeh, F., Al-Omari, Z.: The learning organisation dimensions and their impact on organisational performance: orange jordan as a case study. Arab Econ. Bus. J. **8**, 38–52 (2013). https://doi.org/10.1016/j.aebj.2013.11.005
14. Senge, P.: The Fifth Discipline: The Art & Practice of Learning Organization. Doubleday, New York (2006)
15. Watkins, K.E., Marsick, V.J.: Sculpting the Learning Organisation: Lessons in the Art and Science of Systematic Change. Jossey-Bass, San Francisco (1993)
16. Watkins, K.E., O'Neil, J.: The dimensions of the learning organisation questionnaire (the DLOQ): a nontechnical manual. Adv. Dev. Hum. Resour. **15**, 133–147 (2013). https://doi.org/10.1177/1523422313475854
17. Yadav, S., Agarwal, V.: Benefits and barriers of learning organisation and its five discipline. IOSR - JBM **18**, 18–24 (2016). https://doi.org/10.9790/487X-1812011824
18. Zubr, V.: E-learning as part of a learning organisation. In: Double-Blind Peer-Reviewed Proceedings of the International Scientific Conference Hradec Economic Days 2016 1240-1246. University of Hradec Kralove, Hradec Kralove (2016)
19. Zubr, V., Mohelska, H., Sokolova, M.: Factors with positive and negative impact on learning organisation. In: Double-Blind Peer-Reviewed Proceedings of the International Scientific Conference Hradec Economic Days 2017 980-985. University of Hradec Kralove, Hradec Kralove (2017)

Acceptance and Use of Mobile Devices and Apps by Elderly People

Blanka Klimova[✉]

Faculty of Informatics and Management, Department of Applied Linguistics,
University of Hradec Kralove, Rokitanskeho 62, 500 03 Hradec Kralove,
Czech Republic
blanka.klimova@uhk.cz

Abstract. Currently, there is an increase in the number of older generation groups. These demographic changes obviously cause serious social and economic problems. Therefore, there is a need to prolong an active life of elderly people, who want to lead active, fulfilling and quality life in a sense of their inclusion, socialization and independence. This can be achieved not only by continuous support from their family members, but current trends show an important role of information and communication technologies (ICT) in this process. The purpose of this study is to explore the acceptance and use of mobile technology, specifically mobile devices and applications by elderly people, both from the technical and sociological point of view. The methods used in this study include a method of literature review of available sources, a method of comparison and evaluation of the findings from the selected studies on this topic. The findings show that although there is a number of mobile apps for the elderly on the market, they do not usually meet specific needs of these people such as their physical and cognitive impairments or relevant technical specifications of mobile device designed for this group of people. In addition, since the use of mobile technologies by elderly people is quite a new field of research, there are almost no research studies which would prove acceptance of these mobile apps. Therefore, there is a need of vast and detailed research in this area and also find a solution to this complex technological and sociological issue.

Keywords: Mobile devices · Mobile applications · Older people
Acceptance · Use

1 Introduction

Ageing is becoming a big social issue nowadays. In 2000, the number of people at the age of 65+ in the world reached 12.4% and this number is expected to grow to 19% by 2030 [1]. In developed countries, this number of older adults forms 24% and it should rise to 33% by 2050 [2]. In Europe the population group aged 65+ represents 18% of the 503 million Europeans, which should almost double by 2060 [3]. Compared to the world's data, this trend of aging population causes additional problems such as increased costs on the treatment and care about this elderly people [4, 5].

Therefore, there is a need to prolong an active life of elderly people, who want to lead active, fulfilling and quality life in a sense of their inclusion, socialization and

Published by Springer Nature Switzerland AG 2018. All Rights Reserved
S. A. Al-Sharhan et al. (Eds.): I3E 2018, LNCS 11195, pp. 30–36, 2018.
https://doi.org/10.1007/978-3-030-02131-3_4

independence. This can be achieved not only by continuous support from their family members, but current trends show an important role of information and communication technologies (ICT) in this process. They are also known under the common name as gerontechnology because they try to meet the needs of aging society [6, 7].

Furthermore, socio-scientific positions are used to develop a range of research that deals with the relationship between ICT and groups defined by gender, life cycle phases, or specific needs. An example is a study by Lubas et al. [8], which focuses on design and implementation of mobile applications (apps) that thanks to their construction enable their alternative form of communication to children with autistic disabilities to be tailored to their specific needs and to compensate for their communication barrier. The dynamic relationship between technology and aging is being systematically developed and becoming a narrowly defined area of interest. It uses social science theory to identify everyday ICT-related practices or needs, whose satisfaction requires a degree of user competencies or needs, whose satisfaction may be via ICT improved. Rogers et al. [9] in Technology and Aging offer thematic areas in the everyday life of seniors that require research:

> "...we address the extent to which older adults use new technologies, factors to consider in the adoption of technology (e.g., attitudes), the influence of technology design on older adults' performance (e.g., design of input devices), and ways to optimize training for older adults in using new technologies (e.g., age-specific instructional designs). We then review emerging areas of research that may direct the focus of human factors research in the next decade. These areas of research include ubiquitous computing (e.g., home monitoring systems), health care technologies (e.g., telehealth), robotics (e.g., Nursebot), and automated systems (e.g., cruise control). Finally, we consider opportunities and challenges to human factors research as the field continues to address the questions of optimizing technology for older adult users." (p. 131)

An essential feature of this approach is the emphasis on optimizing technologies to adapt their design to the needs of aging users, which may not only have the nature of reduced capabilities and health restrictions [9]. Further studies show that the processes of digitalization and automation of public services may represent a hindrance for the elderly in their availability. Technological solutions often fail to take into account the specific (e.g., sensory) abilities of the elderly. The practical problems that arise from it are then attributed to blaming this class of actors for incompetence and other stereotyping and stigmatization. Criticism of this practice has highlighted the problem of technological normativity, which is the accompanying effect of socio-technical systems [10]. The authoritativeness and nobility of technological solutions that require unconditional adaptation from human actors is no longer obvious. Equal status of technical and human factors is developed using concepts of socio-technical systems, networking theory/material semiotics [11–14].

Although in the area of designing technological solutions in the last two decades, the user-centred research trend (UCD) has emerged, there is often no senior among model users. For this reason, already in 2001, a group of American researchers identified the UCD research strategy as "senior-centred research" that was applied to the design of medical information portals, for which the senior part of the population is quantitatively predominant clientele [15].

The purpose of this study is to explore the acceptance and use of mobile technology, specifically mobile devices and applications by elderly people, both from the technical and sociological point of view.

2 Findings and Discussion

As research shows, elderly people are nowadays more digitally literate, especially those parents of baby boomers, and 80% of them have access to the Internet [4, 16, 17]. Furthermore, there is an increasing number of those elderly people who own and use mobile devices, such as a mobile phone. For instance, 78% of older people at the age of 65+ own a mobile phone in the USA, as well as in the UK [18]. In the Czech Republic, it is 91% [19]. In fact, currently mobile devices seems to be more exploited than the desktop computers [20]. For example, 84% of elderly people in the Czech Republic (in 2014, 65+ seniors formed 17.4% of total population) use mobile phones every day [21], thus being even more passionate users than teenagers. The National Action Plan for active aging for the period of 2013–17 [22], approved by the Czech government in 2013, reflects the regional implementation strategy of the Madrid International Action Plan. Among others, it also pays attention to lifelong education. As stated by Sak and Kolesarova [23], current generation of seniors is the last to be literate in culture and the first to be changing quality of life with the help of a computer, the Internet and a mobile phone, thus crossing the generation gap between the culture and cyber-culture.

Although almost all people, including elderly population, own a mobile phone and some of them even use a smartphone, the number is still low. The reason of such a low number of elderly users is that a construction of these smartphones does not meet the specific needs of elderly people who require a mobile phone that is easy to use, provides safety and security, and is relatively cheap (e.g. [24, 25]). Thus, specific needs of this group when using a mobile phone must be addressed. These are as follows [26–29]:

- *Healthcare and monitoring the state of health needs:* At present, there is an increasing number of elderly people who exploit the so-called mobile healthcare, i.e. remote care service due to the limitation of aged care resources. This remote care service might include, for example, obtaining information on their health, receiving reminders for scheduled visits, medication instructions, or consulting a doctor at a distance [30].
- *Social Needs:* Most elderly people live on their own and want to be in contact with their loved ones and friends. They also want to use the technologies their children like using.
- *Leisure and sales needs:* Personal leisure (entertainment or self-education) is important for senior citizens in what constitutes their free time occupation. They can also do shopping via mobile phones, order meals or play computer games in order to maintain quality of their life in case they are not able to go out regularly.
- *Safety and privacy needs:* This is considered as the most critical aspect for senior citizens. The user's activity must be monitored by using presence sensors and be analyzed with consideration to different scenarios.

On the basis of the older people's needs, the following apps seem to be the most suitable for them:

- *Applications which convert the smartphone into a simpler and safer senior's mobile phone.* Elderly people follow rooted stereotypes and archetypes, which is reflected in the use of mobile phones as well. They want their new, modern smartphones to possess the designs of old-fashioned land lines, with similar keypad and features in order to conduct all their daily tasks. In addition, they want to feel safe when they are home alone. Such an application which can meet these requirements is, for example, Kcala Phone Launcher [31].
- *Application and use of mobiles for healthcare or monitoring the state of health.* Elderly people use mobile applications for monitoring their state of health or obtaining information about healthcare. This is especially true for people suffering from dementia or diabetes [32, 33].
- *Applications focused on entertainment* [34], *education and improvement of cognitive functions.* Playing games help elderly people to spend their time in an entertaining way. In addition, it develops their memory, socializing and it has a positive impact on their psyche and overall state of health [35]. Some research studies [16] also prove that playing games can assist in the delay of Alzheimer's disease symptoms and other dementias.

However, since the use of mobile technologies by elderly people is quite a new field of research, there are almost no research studies which would prove acceptance of these mobile apps in the areas of the needs described above (cf. [36, 37]).

For example, in the Web of Science 167 articles were found on the acceptance of mobile apps by the elderly (consult Fig. 1). The first one appeared already in 1996. However, most of the articles on the research issue started to be published after 2010 [38]. The topic of the majority of studies relates to health monitoring and assisted living technologies. This is not surprising since elderly people are mainly concerned at this age in maintaining their health conditions. The number of articles on the pure exploration of elderly people and their acceptance of technologies was relatively scarce.

In the Czech Republic, there is no such research study, which would explore the acceptance and the use of mobile apps for the maintenance and improvement of quality of life for elderly people, specifically in the area of physical and cognitive activities, which as research studies show, can be maintained with an appropriate intervention. So far, there have been just a few projects, which, however, only focused on the use of the Internet by elderly (e.g., [39–41]). The similar situation can be observed in other European countries. Therefore, there is a need of vast and detailed research in this area and also find a solution to this complex technological and sociological issue.

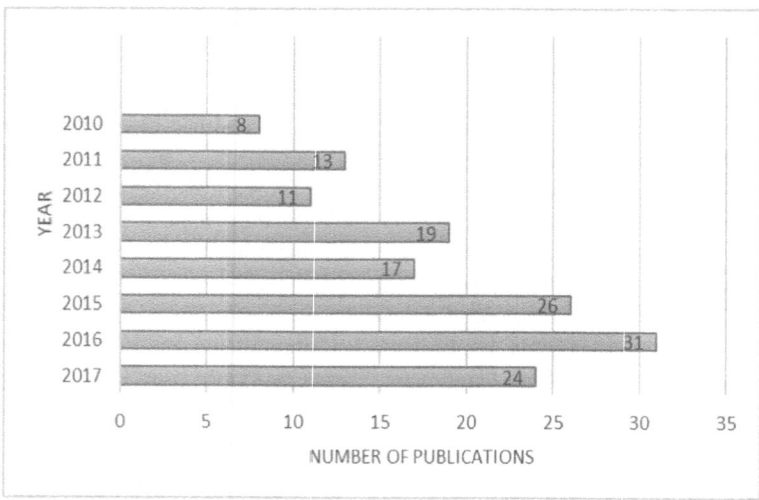

Fig. 1. An overview of the number of publications on the research topic in the Web of Science, authors' own processing based on the data from the Web of Science [11].

3 Conclusion

Generally, there seem to be a number of mobile apps for the elderly on the market. However, they do not usually meet specific needs of these people such as their physical and cognitive impairments or relevant technical specifications of mobile device designed for this group of people. In addition, since the use of mobile technologies by elderly people is quite a new field of research, there are almost no research studies which would prove acceptance of these mobile apps. Therefore, there is a need of vast and detailed research in this area and also find a solution to this complex technological and sociological issue.

Acknowledgments. This study is supported by the SPEV project 2104/2018, run at the Faculty of Informatics and Management, University of Hradec Kralove, Czech Republic. The author thanks Josef Toman for his help with the data collection.

References

1. Vafa, K.: Census bureau releases demographic estimates and projections for countries of the World.   http://blogs.census.gov/2012/06/27/census-bureau-releasesdemographic-estimates-and-projections-for-countries-of-the-world/. Last accessed 29 Jan 2018
2. World population ageing 2013. UN, New York (2013)
3. Petterson, I.: Growing Older. Tourism and Leisure Behaviour of Older Adults. Cabi, Cambridge (2006)
4. Klimova, B., Maresova, P., Kuca, K.: Non-pharmacological approaches to the prevention and treatment of Alzheimer's disease with respect to the rising treatment costs. Curr. Alzheimer Res. **13**(11), 1249–1258 (2016)

5. Maresova, P., Klimova, B., Kuca, K.: Alzheimer's disease: cost cuts call for novel drugs development and national strategy. Ceska Slov. Farm. **64**(1–2), 25–30 (2015)
6. Plaza, I., Martin, L., Martin, S., Medrano, C.: Mobile applications in an aging society: status and trends. J. Syst. Softw. **84**, 1977–1988 (2011)
7. Klimova, B., Valis, M.: Smartphone applications can serve as effective cognitive training tools in healthy aging. Front. Aging Neurosci. **9**, 436 (2018)
8. Lubas, M., Mitchell, J., De Leo, G.: User-centered design and augmentative and alternative communication apps for children with autism spectrum disorders. Sage Open **4**(2), 2158244014537501 (2014)
9. Rogers, W.A., Stronge, A.J., Fisk, A.D.: Technology and aging. Rev. Hum. Factors Ergon. **1**(1), 130–171 (2005)
10. Garrety, K., Badham, R.: User-centered design and the normative politics of technology. Sci. Technol. Human Values **29**(2), 191–212 (2004)
11. Pfaffenberger, B.: Social anthropology of technology. Annu. Rev. Anthropol. **21**(1), 491–516 (1992)
12. Callon, M.: Actor-network theory—the market test. Sociol. Rev. **47**(1_suppl), 181–195 (1999)
13. Latour, B.: Reassembling the Social: An Introduction to Actor-Network-Theory. Oxford University Press (2005)
14. Law, J.: Actor network theory and material semiotics. In: The New Blackwell Companion to Social Theory, pp. 141–158 (2009)
15. Kwahk, J., Smith-Jackson, T.L., Williges, R.C.: From user-centered design to senior-centered design: designing internet health information portals. In: Proceedings of the Human Factors and Ergonomics Society Annual Meeting, pp. 580–584. SAGE Publications, Los Angeles, CA (2001)
16. Heart, T., Kalderon, E.: Older adults: are they ready to adopt health-related ICT? Int. J. Med. Inform. **82**, e209–e231 (2013)
17. Wu, Y.H., Damnee, S., Kerherve, H., Ware, C., Rigaud, A.S.: Bridging the digital divide in older adults: a study from an initiative to inform older adults about new technologies. Clin. Interv. Aging **10**, 193–201 (2015)
18. Pew Research Center.: The demographics of device ownership. http://www.pewinternet.org/2015/10/29/the-demographics-of-device-ownership/. Last accessed 29 Jan 2018
19. Šimonová, I., Klímová, B., Poulová, P., Pražák, P.: The use of ICT devices by older people with a special focus on their type and respondents' age – a Czech case study. Educ. Gerontol. **43**(12), 641–649 (2017)
20. StatCounter.: Mobile and tablet internet usage exceeds desktop for first time worldwide. http://gs.statcounter.com/press/mobile-and-tablet-internet-usage-exceedsdesktop-for-first-time-worldwide. Last accessed 29 Jan 2018
21. Czech Statistical Office.: Temer tri ctvrtiny Cechu jsou online. [Almost three fourths of the Czechs are online.] http://www.czso.cz/csu/tz.nsf/i/temer_tri_ctvrtiny_cechu_jsou_online_20141202. Last accessed 13 Apr 2018
22. Narodni akcni plan podporujici pozitivni starnuti pro obdobi let 2013 az 2017 [The National Action Plan for active aging for 2013–17 period]. http://www.mpsv.cz/files/clanky/14540/NAP_2013-2017_070114.pdf. Last accessed 29 Jan 2018
23. Sak, P., Kolesarova, K.: Sociologie stáří a seniorů, 1st edn. Grada, Praha (2005)
24. Glasscock, N.F., Wogalter, M.S.: Evaluating preferences for mobile phone features. In: Proceedings of the Human Factors and Ergonomics Society 50th Annual Meeting. USA: San Francisco (2006)

25. Mallenius, S., Rossi, M., Tuunainen, V.K.: Factors affecting the adoption and use of mobile devices and services by elderly people – results from a pilot study. http://citeseerx.ist.psu.edu/viewdoc/download?doi=10.1.1.130.2463&rep=rep1&type=pdf. Last accessed 29 Jan 2018
26. Chen, K., Chan, A.H.S.: Cell phone features preferences among older adults: a paired comparison study. Gerontechnology 13(2), 184 (2014)
27. Gao, J., Koronios, A.: Mobile application development for senior citizens. http://www.pacisnet.org/file/2010/S05-03.pdf. Last accessed 13 Apr 2018
28. Hameed, K.: The application of mobile computing and technology to health care services. Telemat. Inform. 20, 99–106 (2003)
29. Lapinsky, S.E.: Mobile computing in critical care. J. Crit. Care 22, 41–44 (2007)
30. Bujnowska-Fedak, M.M., Pirogowicz, I.: Support for e-health services among elderly primary care patients. Telemed. J. E-Health 20(8), 696–704 (2014)
31. Lipertova, M.: Koala Phone Launcher: promente smartphone na mobil pro seniory. [Koala Phone Launcher: convert the smartphone into a mobile phone for elderly people.] http://svetaplikaci.tyden.cz/koala-phone-launcher-promente-smartphone-namobil-pro-seniory/. Last accessed 29 Jan 2018
32. Amstrong, N., Nugent, C., Moore, G., Finlay, D.: Using smartphones to address the needs of persons with Alzheimer's disease. Ann. Telecommun. 65, 485–495 (2010)
33. Mangialasche, F., Kivipelto, M., Andrieu, S., Coley, N., Ngandu, T., Van Charante, E.M., et al.: Use of new technology to improve dementia prevention: the healthy aging through internet counseling in the elderly (HATICE) project. Alzheimer's Dement. J. Alzheimer's Assoc. 9(4), 881 (2013)
34. Vanden Abeele, V.A., Van Rompaey, V.: Introducing human-centered research to game design: designing game concepts for and with senior citizens. In: Proceedings of CHI 06 Extended Abstracts on Human Factors in Computing Systems. ACM, New York (2006)
35. Gerling, K.M., Schulte, F.P., Masuch, M.: Designing and evaluating digital games for frail elderly persons. http://dl.acm.org/citation.cfm?id=2071501. Last accessed 13 Apr 2018
36. Hedman, E., Ljotsson, B., Lindefors, N.: Cognitive behavior therapy via the Internet: a systematic review of applications, clinical efficacy and cost-effectiveness. Expert Rev. Pharmacoecon. Outcomes Res. 12, 745–764 (2012)
37. Klimova, B., Simonova, I., Poulova, P., Truhlarova, Z., Kuca, K.: Older people and their attitude to the use of information and communication technologies – A review study with special focus on the Czech Republic (Older people and their attitude to ICT). Educ. Gerontol. 42(5), 361–369 (2016)
38. Web of Science. http://apps.webofknowledge.com/Search.do?product=WOS&SID=C2TMWq9F8rnnGhDVklU&search_mode = GeneralSearch&prID = da7f67df-a1b9-4a62-b29d93c351c42a43. Last accessed 29 Jan 2018
39. AU3V ČR.: Dlouhodobý záměr seniorského vzdělávání na vysokých školách na období 2008–2015 [Long-term plan of senior education at universities for the period of 2008–2015] (2007). http://au3v.vutbr.cz/soubory/DZ_AU3V_CR.doc. Last accessed 29 Jan 2018
40. Mannova, B., Bicik, J.: Projekt SEN-NET (older people in network). http://www.csvs.cz/konference/NCDiV2006_sbornik/Mannova.pdf. Last accessed 29 Jan 2018
41. Rain, T., Svarcova, I.: Internet and seniors. J. Effic. Responsib. Educ. Sci. 3(2), 79–85 (2010)

Evaluation of the Effectiveness of the Use of a Mobile Application on Students' Study Achievements – A Pilot Study

Blanka Klimova[1(✉)] and Pavel Prazak[2]

[1] Department of Applied Linguistics, Faculty of Informatics and Management,
University of Hradec Kralove,
Rokitanskeho 62, 50003 Hradec Kralove, Czech Republic
blanka.klimova@uhk.cz
[2] Department of Informatics and Quantitative Methods, Faculty of Informatics
and Management, University of Hradec Kralove,
Rokitanskeho 62, 50003 Hradec Kralove, Czech Republic
pavel.prazak@uhk.cz

Abstract. At present, mobile learning (m-learning) seems to be a well established methodology at the institutions of higher learning. Most recently, smartphone apps started to be a popular part of m-learning. The purpose of this article is to evaluate mobile application effectiveness on students' study achievements in the Course of English taught at the Faculty of Informatics and Management in Hradec Kralove, Czech Republic. The results of this study confirm that learning via the smartphone app is effective. However, the content of the mobile app has to be adapted to students' needs in order to make them motivated to use the app. Therefore, the whole pedagogical process should be well planned, react to students' immediate needs and implement appropriate teaching and learning methods, which can contribute to the positive learning outcomes.

Keywords: M-learning · Mobile applications · English · Effectiveness
Study achievements

1 Introduction

Currently, mobile devices are important part of educational process and they are used in the so-called mobile learning (m-learning), which can be defined as *learning across multiple contexts, through social and content interactions, using personal electronic devices* [1]. Thus, m-learning can take any form of learning with the help of a mobile device, which can be done at anytime and anywhere when the learner needs it [2]. In this way, mobile devices are revolutionary because they transcend the boundaries of the structural status of classrooms and lecture halls and their associated modes of communication – they do not have to be confined to one particular place and time in order to be effective [3].

Nearly all students nowadays own mobile devices and about half of them own more than one [4]. The most exploited mobile devices among young people seem to be

© IFIP International Federation for Information Processing 2018
Published by Springer Nature Switzerland AG 2018. All Rights Reserved
S. A. Al-Sharhan et al. (Eds.): I3E 2018, LNCS 11195, pp. 37–44, 2018.
https://doi.org/10.1007/978-3-030-02131-3_5

mobile phones, respectively smartphones. In fact, about 90% of young people aged 18–29 years own a smartphone [5]. This has been confirmed also by other research studies [2, 6].

M-learning is natural continuation of the well-established eLearning methodology, which has been used at the University of Hradec Kralove (UHK) since 1999. All eLearning courses are created in a virtual learning environment Blackboard Learn. Both methodologies, i.e. m-learning and eLearning, are part of the so-called blended learning (BL). BL can be defined as a combination of traditional, face-to-face teaching and online learning [7], which means that in addition to their face-to-face classes, students are provided with their online complement so that they could revise and practice the material taught at school. Students have no problems with this type of study and they are well equipped with mobile devices (i.e., laptop, smartphone or tablet) as research shows [8, 9]. Almost all students own one mobile device and three quarters have even two mobile devices [10].

This is also true for students who attend English language classes at the Faculty of Informatics and Management (FIM) of UHK. Their face-to-face classes are also supported by eLearning courses in which materials from these classes and additional exercises for revising and practicing at home are available. At present, there are about 30 eLearning courses designed and actively used only for English language learning at FIM.

However, as it has been indicated above, students now tend to use their mobile phones, respectively smartphones for learning. Therefore, also English language teaching (ELT) has to face to challenge and in the winter semester of 2017 a pilot course introducing learning with smartphone application (app) was conducted. This was performed within an English language course.

The purpose of this article is to evaluate mobile application effectiveness on students' study achievements in the Course of English.

2   Materials and Methods

Participants

Altogether 33 students attended the English language course in the winter term of 2017. They were all full-time students of Management of Tourism in their third year of study at FIM. Their level of English according to CERF (2018) was B2. During the semester, however, two students left the course, and thus, only 31 students completed the whole course. Out of 31 students 19 students, who had access to the app compatible with their smartphone operating system, also used a smartphone with a special mobile app tailored to their needs as a supporting tool to their face-to-face classes. 12 students served as a control group. The course lasted from 26 September till 12 December 2017 and classes were held regularly once a week for 90 min.

Study Design

The first method used in this study was a needs analysis since the proposed mobile app should have satisfied and enhanced both students' learning and study achievements.

The needs analysis was based on the SWOT (strengths, weaknesses, opportunities and threats) self-evaluation and was conducted during the first introductory lesson.

Secondly, on the basis of the data from the needs analysis, a mobile app was designed and gradually developed. The described mobile app consists of two application parts and one server part. The first application part is designed as a web interface for the teacher (Fig. 1) and the second application part is presented with a mobile app for students (Fig. 2). This app is intended now only for the Android operating system and it is available for free at Google Play store. The reason was the ratio of students who use the Android operating system on their smart devices. The app itself then enabled to use its statistics since it can collect all user data and distribute it to the server part for subsequent research and evaluation by the teacher.

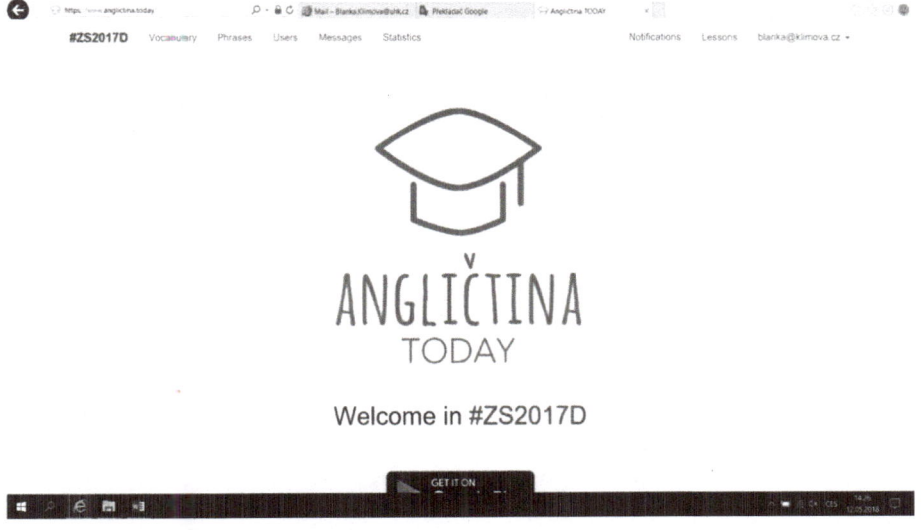

Fig. 1. Teacher interface

Thirdly, methods of analysis and evaluation of the results of students' achievement tests were used. including a statistical analysis. The pass mark for doing the final achievement test was 50%, i.e., 30 points. All the results were recorded and statistically analyzed. A group of 31 students was randomly assigned into two independent groups. The research group, whose size was $n1 = 19$, used a mobile application in their learning. The second group, the size of which was $n2 = 12$, did not use the app and was a controlled group. The following hypothesis was set.

H: Students who use mobile apps in their studies have significantly higher learning outcomes than students who do not use this app.

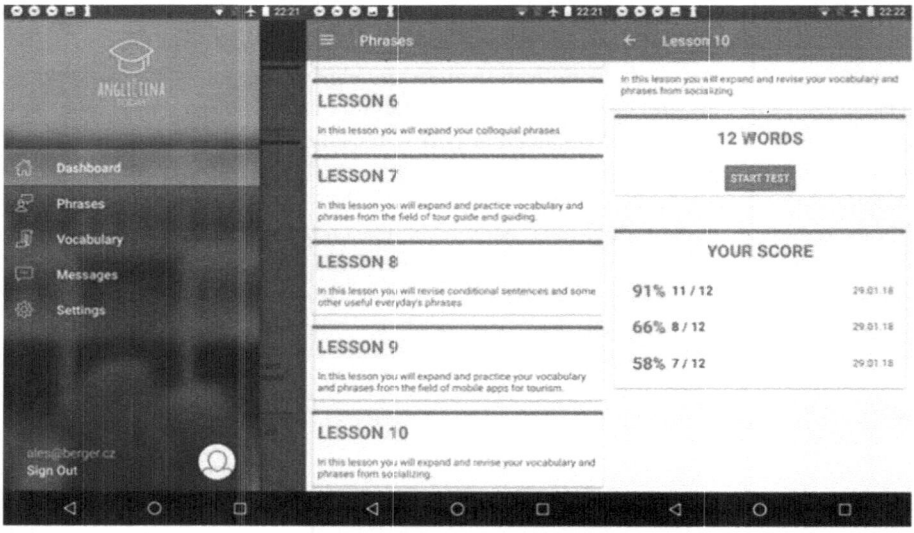

Fig. 2. Mobile app screens

3   Results

The results of the needs analysis showed that students' biggest weakness was learning and retention of English vocabulary. This finding is also reflected in other research studies [11, 12].

Therefore, the newly developed smartphone app was targeted at and tailored to the development and practicing of new English words and phrases. Altogether, there were ten parallel lessons of vocabulary and phrases. The content of the lessons was physically completed with words and phrases by the teacher. The students had to translate the word or the phrase from their native language into English. Each lesson was done as a test and consisted on average of 15 new words and 10 new phrases. The selected words and phrases were those discussed in the face-to-face classes and focused on their field of study, i.e., tourism. The teacher was encouraging students to use the mobile app and practice new words and phrases discussed in class through notifications in their mobile app twice a week (Fig. 3).

Students' results of the final achievement test were statistically analyzed at the beginning of the year of 2018. A box diagram of the results of the two groups is shown in Fig. 4 and Table 1. It demonstrates that the students of the experimental group achieved the higher results as it was expected.

However, this observation was further confirmed by the calculation (Table 1). Due to the small ranges of the two sets in the pilot study, it is not possible to use the parametric t-test to compare the mean values obtained from the tests. Thus a non-parametric Mann-Whitney U test with a p-value estimated from approximation by

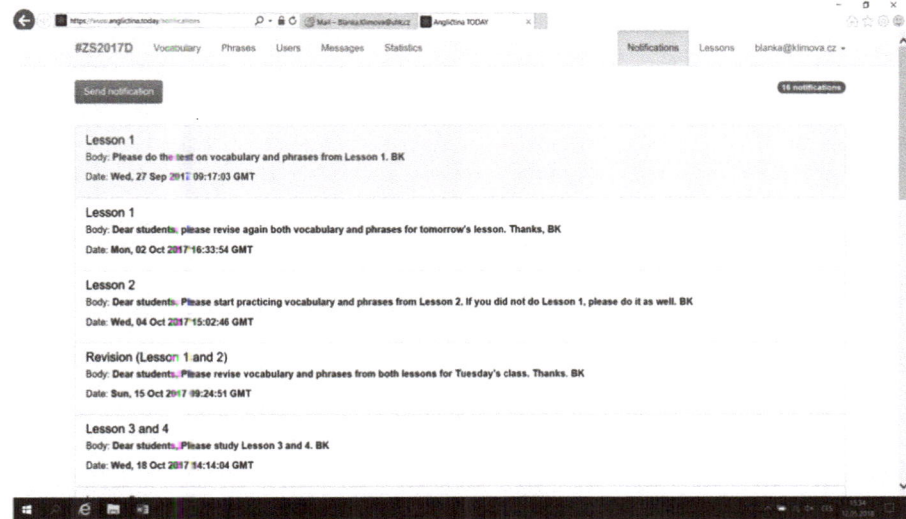

Fig. 3. Teacher's notifications sent to students via the smartphone app

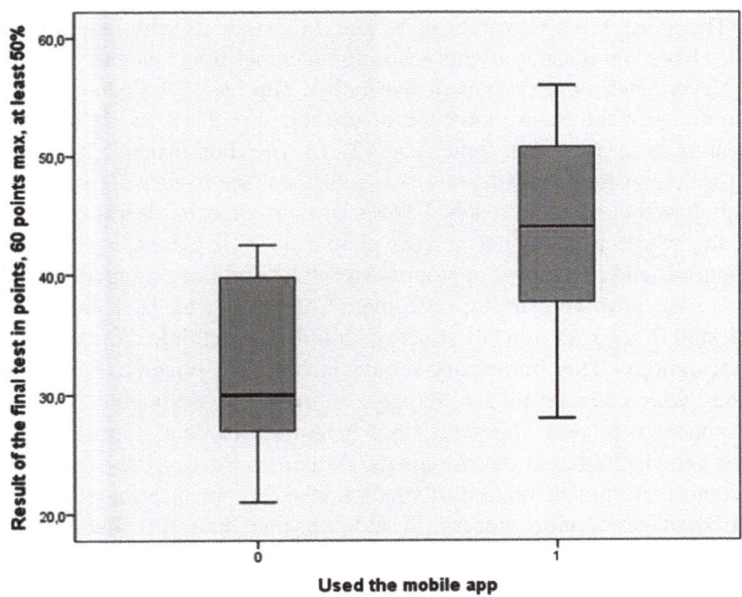

Fig. 4. A box diagram of students' results

Table 1. Results from Mann-Whitney U test

Test statistics[a]	
	Result of the final test in points, 60 points max, at least 50%
Mann-Whitney U	27,500
Wilcoxon W	105,500
Z	−3,512
Asymp. Sig. (2-tailed)	,000
Exact Sig. [2 * (1-tailed Sig.)]	,000[b]

[a]Grouping Variable: Used the mobile app
[b]Not corrected for ties

normal distribution and continuity correction was used. According to the result of this test, the hypothesis H can be assumed at the significance level of 0.01. Specific results of the SPSS calculation can be found in Table 1.

4   Discussion

The results of the statistical analysis confirm that learning via the smartphone app is effective. Therefore, the set hypothesis is true, i.e., students who use mobile apps in their studies have significantly higher learning outcomes than students who do not use this app. Nevertheless, the content of the mobile app has to be adapted to students' needs in order to make them motivated to use the app. This has been confirmed by other research studies on this topic, e.g. [2, 13–16]. For instance, the findings by Lopuch [15] demonstrate that students who enhanced face-to-face classroom education with an app-based curriculum reached 165% of their expected learning achievement.

Thus, the whole pedagogical process should be well planned, react to students' immediate needs and implement appropriate teaching and learning methods, which can contribute to the positive learning outcomes. Churchill et al. [17] propose a special learning design framework as a key strategy for utilizing multiple affordances of mobile learning technology. This framework should include and integrate at least four core components, which are resources, activity, support and evaluation. Especially, the activity component is very important since it requires students to engage with intellectual and knowledge-based developments. Celik and Yavuz [18] expand that a guided and controlled implementation of smartphones can enhance the effectiveness and quality of language learning process. In addition, they state that mobile apps should correspond to the level of the students' language knowledge and should be designed by experts (cf. [19]).

The limitation of this case study consists in the small subject sample, which is connected with piloting this tailored-made mobile app.

5 Conclusion

The results of this study indicate that m-learning via a smartphone app can be effective and serve as an appropriate complementary method to other forms of course delivery, especially face-to-face teaching.

Future research should focus on the effectiveness of mobile apps for learning with bigger sample sizes, as well as extending the mobile app for the Apple's platform and iOS.

Acknowledgments. This study is supported by the SPEV project 2104/2018, run at the Faculty of Informatics and Management, University of Hradec Kralove, Czech Republic. The authors thank Ales Berger for his help with the data collection.

References

1. Crompton, H.: A historical overview of mobile learning: toward learner-centered education. In: Berge, Z.L., Muilenburg, L.Y. (eds.) Handbook of Mobile Learning, pp. 3–14. Routledge, Florence, KY (2013)
2. Teodorescu, A.: Mobile learning and its impact on business english learning. Procedia Soc. Behav. Sci. **180**, 1535–1540 (2015)
3. El-Hussein, M.O.M., Cronje, J.C.: Defining mobile learning in the higher education landscape. Educ. Technol. Soc. **13**(3), 12–21 (2010)
4. Cheung, S.K.S.: A case study on the students' attitude and acceptance of mobile learning. In: CCIS 2014, pp. 45–54. Springer, Heidelberg (2015)
5. Smith, A.: Record shares of Americans now own smartphones, have home broadband. http://www.pewresearch.org/fact-tank/2017/01/12/evolution-oftechnology/. Last accessed 8 May 2018
6. Klimova, B., Poulova, P.: Mobile learning and its potential for engineering education. In: Proceedings of 2015 IEEE Global Engineering Education Conference (EDUCON 2015), pp. 47–51. Tallinn University of Technology, Estonia, Tallinn (2015)
7. Frydrychova Klimova, B.: Blended learning. In: Mendez Vilas, A., et al. (eds.) Research, Reflections and Innovations in Integrating ICT in Education, pp. 705–708. FORMATEX, Spain (2009)
8. Klimova, B.: Evaluation of the blended learning approach in the course of business english – a case study. In: Huang, T.-C., Lau, R., Huang, Y.-M., Spaniol, M., Yuen, C.-H. (eds.) SETE 2017. LNCS, vol. 10676, pp. 326–335. Springer, Cham (2017). https://doi.org/10.1007/978-3-319-71084-6_37
9. Frydrychova Klimova, B., Poulova, P.: Forms of instruction and students' preferences - a comparative study. In: Cheung, S.K.S., Fong, J., Zhang, J., Kwan, R., Kwok, L.F. (eds.) ICHL 2014. LNCS, vol. 8595, pp. 220–231. Springer, Cham (2014). https://doi.org/10.1007/978-3-319-08961-4_21
10. Klimova, B., Poulova, P.: Mobile learning in higher education. Adv. Sci. Lett. **22**(5/6), 1111–1114 (2016)
11. Lee, P.: Are mobile device more useful than conventional means as tools for learning vocabulary? In: Proceedings of the 8th International Symposium on Embedded Multicore/Manycore SoCs, pp. 109–115. IEEE (2014)

12. Wu, Q.: Designing a smartphone app to teach English (L2) vocabulary. Comput. Educ. **85**, 170–179 (2015)
13. Bidaki, M.Z., Naderi, F., Ayati, M.: Effects of mobile learning on paramedical students' academic achievement and self-regulation. Futur. Med. Educ. J. **3**(3), 24–28 (2013)
14. Elfeky, A.I.M., Masadeh, T.S.Y.: The effect of mobile learning on students' achievement and conversational skills. Int. J. High. Educ. **5**(3), 20–31 (2016)
15. Lopuch, M.: The effects of educational apps on student achievement and engagement. http://www.doe.virginia.gov/support/technology/technology_initiatives/elearning_backpack/institute/2013/Educational_Apps_White_Paper_eSpark_v2.pdf. Last accessed 8 May 2018
16. Sandhya, K., Smith, J., Asha, J.V.: Mobile learning apps in instruction and students achievement. IJIM **11**(1), 143–147 (2017)
17. Churchill, D., Fox, B., King, M.: Framework for designing mobile learning environments. In: Churchill, D., Lu, J., Chiu, T., Fox, B. (eds.) Mobile Learning Design. Lecture Notes in Educational Technology. Springer, Singapore (2016)
18. Celik, O., Yavuz, F.: The effect of using mobile applications on literal and contextual vocabulary instruction. IJLT **0**(0), 126–136 (2018)
19. Pikhart, M.: Managerial communication and its changes in the global intercultural business world. In: SHS Web of Conferences, vol. 37, p. 01013 (2017)

Digital Payments Adoption Research: A Review of Factors Influencing Consumer's Attitude, Intention and Usage

Pushp P. Patil[✉], Nripendra P. Rana, and Yogesh K. Dwivedi

Emerging Markets Research Centre (EMaRC), School of Management,
Swansea University Bay Campus, Swansea SA1 8EN, UK
pushpppatil@gmail.com,
{n.p.rana, y.k.dwivedi}@swansea.ac.uk

Abstract. Digital payment methods (DPMs) are evolving fast but they are yet to be widely adopted particularly in the developing countries. An initial review of literature suggests that several studies have already been conducted on this topic for understanding antecedents of digital payments adoption. However, only a few studies have examined this emerging topic in the context of developing countries. The aim of this submission is to identify antecedents of consumer adoption and usage of digital payments methods. The results of this literature analysis suggest that constructs related to technology acceptance model (TAM) and unified theory of acceptance and use of technology (UTAUT) along with trust and risk are the most frequently examined constructs for determining consumer's behavioural intention to use and usage of DPMs. The findings from this work can help researchers selecting factors for inclusion in the future empirical works on this topic.

Keywords: Adoption · Cashless payments · Construct mapping
Digital payments · Meta-analysis · Mobile payments

1 Introduction

The adoption and use of emerging digital devices and applications (i.e. mobile and other handheld devices, Near Field Communication (NFC), mobile wallets, P2P apps, quick response code and wearable) complemented with Internet connectivity are gradually shifting various activities from the real world to a virtual world [6, 25, 26, 35]. Consumers are also moving towards changing their payment method from cash and cheque based system to contactless devices [26].

There are several benefits such as potential to bring financial inclusion by offering financial services to the unbanked masses and improve their lives for better, enhancing transparency in financial transactions, reducing tax envision and improving public welfare and delivery systems of digital payment methods (DPMs) to various stakeholders and consumers. Despite of several benefits DPMs such as mobile payments have not yet widely adopted as expected in both developed and developing countries except for few countries such as Kenya and Philippines where mobile payments are readily accepted due to relative lack of penetration of formal banking system [3, 26, 40].

© IFIP International Federation for Information Processing 2018
Published by Springer Nature Switzerland AG 2018. All Rights Reserved
S. A. Al-Sharhan et al. (Eds.): I3E 2018, LNCS 11195, pp. 45–52, 2018.
https://doi.org/10.1007/978-3-030-02131-3_6

The slow adoption of DPMs by consumers provides motivation and relevance to undertake research in this area. However, several studies have conducted to examine factors influencing mobile payments adoption largely in the context of developed countries and there are some in developing countries context [25, 26]. [26] study presented an initial review and attempted to identify limitations of existing work and research gaps that need further attention by researchers in this area. This review also identified dominant theories and models utilised in this domain [26, 27]. However, this review did not present a detailed analysis of antecedents of consumer's attitude, intention, usage, continuance intention and satisfaction. Such review and analysis would help to unearth inconsistencies in existing research as well as help to discover well tried and tested antecedents for examining adoption and usage of digital payment methods. The aim of this study is, therefore, to undertake review and analysis of factors/constructs employed by existing studies on consumer adoption of digital payments methods.

The remaining sections of this article is structured as follows: Sect. 2 describes literature search and analysis method. The results are then presented in Sect. 3. Finally, Sect. 4 presents a brief concluding discussion and future research directions.

2 Literature Search and Analysis Method

As this work is focused on analyzing findings reported in existing studies, first step for this study was to identify relevant work published on digital payment methods/systems adoption. A keyword based search was considered appropriate to identify studies relevant to digital payment methods, which was achieved by utilizing the following keywords in the Scopus database: "Digital Payment" OR "Cashless Payment" OR "Mobile Payment" AND "Adoption" OR "Acceptance" OR "Diffusion" OR "Usage" OR "Intention" OR "Success" OR "Satisfaction". This search resulted in 109 studies, but after initial screening it was found that some studies were not relevant to consumer adoption to digital payments, which reduced total number of studies to 80. However, some of these 80 articles (mainly conference papers) were not accessible through researcher's library, hence total number further reduced to 75 studies. Articles found were mainly on the adoption of mobile payment systems hence, for this paper term, "digital payment systems" mainly refers to mobile payment and have less relevance with any other form of digital payment system. The articles were deemed appropriate for inclusion in this study if the data collection of research took place among consumers or the studies developed conceptual model to be empirically tested on consumers at later stage.

Construct mapping was conducted to identify various independent variables (IVs) employed to determine influence of different dependent variables (DVs) such as behavioural intention (BI), usage (U), satisfaction and continuance intention. This was achieved by collecting the information regarding name of IVs and DV along with types of relationships (significant, insignificant or conceptual) reported between them, which we utilized to conduct analysis and mapping of constructs examined in existing works.

A detailed screening of search outputs suggests that existing studies have mainly examined issues related to mobile payments, Mobile Payment Devices (Smartphones),

NFC, [34] adoption Contactless Mobile Payments and QR Mobile Payment System. This suggests that other forms of digital payments yet to be examined such as banking cards, mobile wallets, bank pre-paid cards etc. Hence, the term digital payments in this paper is largely represent mobile payments and may have less relevance for any other form of digital payments.

3 Results

Constructs analysis undertaken in this study suggests that many constructs/factors/IVs have been utilised to determine different DVs (including attitude, behavioural intention (BI), adoption, usage and satisfaction) of digital payment methods. The IVs employed in existing studies belong to several dominant adoption and diffusion theories and models including Technology Acceptance Model (TAM), Innovation Diffusion Theory (IDT), Unified Theory of Acceptance and Use of Technology (UTAUT) and extended UTAUT (UTAUT2). The review presented below demonstrates that the focus of existing empirical studies was on examining consumers' intention to adopt/use digital payment methods and very few attempted to explain usage behaviour and satisfaction.

3.1 Antecedents of Consumer Attitudes Towards Adoption of Digital Payment Methods

A total of six studies have examined the role of different IVs on consumer attitude towards digital payment methods. These IVs include: Compatibility [17, 39], Confidence and Facility of Use [17], Individual Mobility [12, 17, 33, 39], Perceived Ease of Use [12, 17, 29, 33], Perceived Security [17, 33], Perceived Usefulness [12, 17, 33, 39], Personal Innovativeness [39] and Subjective Norm [17, 33].

3.2 Antecedents of Behavioural Intention

PU from TAM was utilised by 22 studies to determine BI, which included 20 studies with significant effect [2, 5, 14, 41, 44] and two studies with non-significant effect [16, 27]. The role of other constructs similar to PU from alternative theories have also examined. For example, Performance Expectancy (PE) from UTAUT examined by eight studies [1, 22, 36, 37] and Relative Advantage from IDT by three studies [20, 43]. This suggests that usefulness of digital payment methods for consumers plays a vital role in influencing their BI to adopt such emerging applications. The role of the PEOU has also been tested on BI by 15 studies, which include 11 studies with significant effects [2, 7, 14, 44] and four studies with non-significant effects [15, 18, 24, 27]. A total of six studies examined the role of Effort Expectancy (EE) (similar to PEOU), but only one study [1] reported significant effect on BI and remaining five studies [22, 28, 36, 37] found non-significant effect.

The remaining two IVs (i.e. Social Influence (SI) and Facilitating Conditions (FC)) from UTAUT are tested by relatively fewer number of studies. Only 10 studies examined role of SI on BI, which includes nine with significant effect [1, 23, 28, 36, 37, 43] and remaining one study [15] reported non-significant result for this. Only three studies examined role of FC on BI with only one study reporting significant [22] and remaining three [24, 36] with non-significant results.

The role of additional constructs (namely, habit, price value (PV) and hedonic motivation (HM)) from the UTAUT2 are also less often tested. Three studies reported significant [22, 36, 44] and one non-significant effects of Habit on BI. PV examined by only two studies [24, 37] and both reported non-significant influence on BI. HM or perceived enjoyment has been examined by four studies with two [15, 22] reporting significant and other two [24, 36] with non-significant effects on BI. The role of attitude has also been tested by five studies [12, 17, 33, 39], all with significant effect on BI. Five studies [20, 27, 46] have examined and reported significant effect of Cost/Perceived Cost on BI but only one such study [43] has reported non-significant effect of this construct.

Trust, risk and innovativeness have also been examined by digital payment adoption studies for determining their influence on BI. The role of Trust has been examined by 10 studies and majority (i.e. nine) of them [25–28, 37, 42, 43] have reported its significant influence on BI. In contrast [33] have found non-significant influence of trust on BI. 18 studies have tested the effect of Risk on BI, which include 15 studies [2, 15–17, 20, 24, 36, 37] with significant influence and in the remaining three [13, 21, 27] with non-significant effect of this construct. Only seven studies examined the role of innovativeness and they all [17, 21, 24, 32, 36, 38, 43] have its significant influence on BI.

Other IVs that have been utilised to explain BI include information security [1, 7, 24, 44], privacy concerns [22], knowledge [15], positive emotions [41], self-efficacy [21], subjective rules [17], network externalities [28] and adoption reediness [38].

3.3 Antecedents of Use/Usage Behaviour

This literature review suggests that only four studies [4, 6, 11, 15, 39] have examined usage behaviour of digital payment methods. These four studies examined role of several IVs such as risk [4, 6, 11], BI [11, 15, 39], PEOU [4], PU [4, 39], fee/cost [4, 39], and knowledge [15] for significantly influencing usage or actual behaviour of using digital payment methods.

3.4 Antecedents of Satisfaction

Only two studies [19, 45] have tested the role of some antecedents for explaining satisfaction gained from using digital payment methods. [45] study suggests that flow, system and service quality has a significant effect on determining satisfaction from using mobile payment systems, where information quality had insignificant effect. [19] examined the effects of post usages privacy protection perception, post usages social influence and post usages perceived mobility on satisfaction. The results from this study suggest that amongst three IVs only post usages perceived mobility significantly explained satisfaction [19]. However, none of the existing work has examined effects of actual or self-reported usage on satisfaction, which is an important consideration.

3.5   Antecedents of Continuance Intention

Like satisfaction, only two studies [45] examined antecedents of continuance intention. [45] examined the role of flow, satisfaction and trust and found that all three constructs had a significant influence on continuance intention. [46] study suggests that flow, performance expectancy and trust had a significant influence on continuance intention.

4   Concluding Discussion, Limitations and Future Research Directions

This study conducted a review of digital payments antecedents used to explain consumer attitude, intention, usage and satisfaction. The following salient points emerged from this literature analysis:

- Several studies have examined behavioural intention of consumers to adopt DPMs but very few studies attempted to examine usage. In early stages of digital payments adopters were very few so it was appropriate to focus on determining intention than actual usage behaviour. However, penetration and adoption of digital payments are now increasing so it is important to focus on usage/use behaviour.
- Theories and models, which are only partially utilised, suggest that theory testing and extension is weak in this emerging area of study. For example, not all constructs from UTAUT or UTAUT2 have been utilised. Mainly PE and EE have been tested followed by SI and very few studies tested the role of FC. For adequate contribution to theory as much as possible, all elements of a theory should be included in the empirical work.
- TAM is tested by several studies. This is a parsimonious model and good for applying in organisational settings but less suitable for examining complex domain such as consumer adoption of DPMs, where issue is not just limited to usefulness and ease of use but there are also other concerns such as trust, security, privacy, risks, anxiety and self-efficacy. Therefore, it is important to apply a more comprehensive theory in this domain.
- Attitude has been examined by a number of studies and found significant, which means it is a relevant construct but guiding theories such as TAM, UTAUT, UTAUT2 don't have this construct. However, a recent modification of UTAUT [8–10, 30, 31] has demonstrated that attitude plays a central in UTAUT model. Future studies recommended to adopt a simpler yet comprehensive UTAUT [8, 9] or other such alternative for guiding model for their empirical work.
- It is also important that future studies should also consider examining satisfaction and continuance intention as these aspects have not been examined yet, but they are vital for growth and sustainability of digital payments ecosystem.
- Existing studies have mainly examined mobile payment methods. Future studies should also focus on examining other forms of digital payment methods for a holistic development of digital payments ecosystems and emerging FinTech applications.

This review was based on literature search using only Scopus database, so studies that are not indexed in this database may have been excluded. Future Literature reviews should consider other databases to address the limitations of this study. This study has provided only descriptive review of factors. Future studies should consider undertaking meta-analysis of existing results for estimating cumulative effect size to overcome problem of inconsistences and errors, which can help to formulate robust conclusions about influence of different factors.

References

1. Alshare, K., Mousa, A.: The moderating effect of espoused cultural dimensions on consumer's intention to use mobile payment devices. In: Proceedings of the 35th International Conference on Information Systems, pp. 1–15 (2014)
2. Andreev, P., Pliskin, N., Rafaeli, S.: Drivers and inhibitors of mobile-payment adoption by smartphone users. Int. J. E-Bus. Res. **8**(3), 50–67 (2012)
3. Augsburg, C., Hedman, J.: Value added services and adoption of mobile payments. In: Proceedings of the 16th International Conference on Electronic Commerce, 5–6 August 2014. ICEC, Philadelphia (2014)
4. Berrado, A., Elfahli, S., El Garah, W.: Using data mining techniques to investigate the factors influencing mobile payment adoption in Morocco. Paper presented at the 2013 8th International Conference on Intelligent Systems: Theories and Applications (2013)
5. Chandrasekhar, U., Nandagopal, R.: Mobile payment usage intent in an Indian context: an exploratory study. Asian J. Inf. Technol. **15**(3), 542–552 (2016)
6. De Kerviler, G., Demoulin, N.T., Zidda, P.: Adoption of in-store mobile payment: are perceived risk and convenience the only drivers? J. Retail. Consum. Serv. **31**, 334–344 (2016)
7. Di Pietro, L., Mugion, R.G., Mattia, G., Renzi, M.F., Toni, M.: The integrated model on mobile payment acceptance (IMMPA): an empirical application to public transport. Transp. Res. Part C: Emerg. Technol. **56**, 463–479 (2015)
8. Dwivedi, Y.K., Rana, N.P., Jeyaraj, A., Clement, M., Williams, M.D.: Re-examining the unified theory of acceptance and use of technology (UTAUT): towards a revised theoretical model. Inf. Syst. Front., 1–16. https://doi.org/10.1007/s10796-017-9774-y (2017a)
9. Dwivedi Y.K., Rana N.P., Janssen, M., Lal, B., Williams, M.D. Clement, R.M.: An empirical validation of a unified model of electronic government adoption (UMEGA). Gov. Inf. Q., **34**(2), 211–230 (2017b)
10. Dwivedi, Y.K., Rana, N.P., Chen, H., Williams, M.D.: A meta-analysis of the unified theory of acceptance and use of technology (UTAUT). In: Nüttgens, M., Gadatsch, A., Kautz, K., Schirmer, I., Blinn, N. (eds.) TDIT 2011. IAICT, vol. 366, pp. 155–170. Springer, Heidelberg (2011). https://doi.org/10.1007/978-3-642-24148-2_10
11. Hongxia, P., Xianhao, X., Weidan, L.: Drivers and barriers in the acceptance of mobile payment in China. In: 2011 International Conference on e-Business and e-Government (ICEE), pp. 1–4. IEEE, May 2011
12. Hossain, R., Mahmud, I.: Influence of cognitive style on mobile payment system adoption: an extended technology acceptance model. In: 2016 International Conference on Computer Communication and Informatics (ICCCI), pp. 1–6. IEEE, January 2016
13. Huang, Y., Liu, W.: The impact of privacy concern on users' usage intention of mobile payment. In: 2012 International Conference on Information Management, Innovation Management and Industrial Engineering (ICIII), vol. 3, pp. 90–93. IEEE, October 2012

14. Kim, Y., Park, Y.J., Choi, J.: The adoption of mobile payment services for "Fintech". Int. J. Appl. Eng. Res. **11**(2), 1058–1061 (2016)

15. Koenig-Lewis, N., Marquet, M., Palmer, A., Zhao, A.L.: Enjoyment and social influence: predicting mobile payment adoption. Serv. Ind. J. **35**(10), 537–554 (2015)

16. Li, H., Liu, Y., Heikkilä, J.: Understanding the factors driving NFC-enabled mobile payment adoption: an empirical investigation. In: PACIS, p. 231 (2014)

17. Liébana-Cabarillas, F., Muñoz-Leiva, F., Sánchez-Fernández, J.: Influence of age in the adoption of new mobile payment systems. Revista Brasileira de Gestão de Negócios **17**(58), 1390 (2015)

18. Liu, B.: Understanding consumers' intention to use mobile payment services: the perspective of University students in Northern Jiangsu area. In: Proceedings of Second International Conference on Business Computing and Global Informatization (BCGIN), pp. 257–260. IEEE, October 2012

19. Lu, J., Wei, J., Yu, C.S., Liu, C.: How do post-usage factors and espoused cultural values impact mobile payment continuation? Behav. Inf. Technol. **36**(2), 140–164 (2017)

20. Lu, Y., Yang, S., Chau, P.Y., Cao, Y.: Dynamics between the trust transfer process and intention to use mobile payment services: a cross-environment perspective. Inf. Manag. **48**(8), 393–403 (2011)

21. Makki, A.M., Ozturk, A.B., Singh, D.: Role of risk, self-efficacy, and innovativeness on behavioral intentions for mobile payment systems in the restaurant industry. J. Foodserv. Bus. Res. **19**(5), 454–473 (2016)

22. Morosan, C., DeFranco, A.: It's about time: revisiting UTAUT2 to examine consumers' intentions to use NFC mobile payments in hotels. Int. J. Hosp. Manag. **53**, 17–29 (2016)

23. Musa, A., Khan, H.U., AlShare, K.A.: Factors influence consumers' adoption of mobile payment devices in Qatar. Int. J. Mob. Commun. **13**(6), 670–689 (2015)

24. Oliveira, T., Thomas, M., Baptista, G., Campos, F.: Mobile payment: understanding the determinants of customer adoption and intention to recommend the technology. Comput. Hum. Behav. **61**, 404–414 (2016)

25. Patil, P.P., Rana, N.P., Dwivedi, Y.K., Abu-Hamour, H.M.J.: The role of trust and risk in mobile payments adoption: a meta-analytic review. In: Proceedings of Pacific Asia Conference on Information Systems, Japan (2018)

26. Patil, P.P., Dwivedi, Y.K., Rana, N.P.: Digital payments adoption: an analysis of literature. In: Kar, A.K., Ilavarasan, P.V., Gupta, M.P., Dwivedi, Y.K., Mäntymäki, M., Janssen, M., Simintiras, A., Al-Sharhan, S. (eds.) I3E 2017. LNCS, vol. 10595, pp. 61–70. Springer, Cham (2017). https://doi.org/10.1007/978-3-319-68557-1_7

27. Phonthanukitithaworn, C., Sellitto, C., Fong, M.: User intentions to adopt mobile payment services: a study of early adopters in Thailand. J. Internet Bank. Commer. **20**(1), 1–29 (1970)

28. Qasim, H., Abu-Shanab, E.: Drivers of mobile payment acceptance: the impact of network externalities. Inf. Syst. Front. **18**(5), 1021–1034 (2016)

29. Rana, N.P., Dwivedi, Y.K., Williams, M.D.: A meta-analysis application for synthesizing findings of existing research on citizen adoption of e-Government. Inf. Syst. Front. **17**(3), 547–563 (2015)

30. Rana, N.P., Dwivedi, Y.K., Lal, B., Williams, M.D., Clement, M.: Citizens' adoption of an electronic government system: towards a unified view. Inf. Syst. Front. **19**(3), 549–568 (2017)

31. Rana, N.P., Dwivedi, Y.K., Williams, M.D., Weerakkody, V.: Adoption of online public grievance redressal system in India: toward developing a unified view. Comput. Hum. Behav. **59**, 265–282 (2016)

32. Sam, K.M., Chatwin, C.R., Zhang, J.X.: Adoption of near field communication for mobile payment: evidence from Macau. In: 2014 IEEE International Conference on Industrial Engineering and Engineering Management (IEEM), pp. 1121–1125. IEEE, December 2014

33. Schierz, P.G., Schilke, O., Wirtz, B.W.: Understanding consumer acceptance of mobile payment services: an empirical analysis. Electron. Commer. Res. Appl. 9(3), 209–216 (2010)

34. Shin, S., Lee, W.J.: The effects of technology readiness and technology acceptance on NFC mobile payment services in Korea. J. Appl. Bus. Res. 30(6), 1615 (2014)

35. Sivathanu, B.: Adoption of digital payment systems in the era of demonetization in India: an empirical study. J. Sci. Technol. Policy Manag. (2018). https://doi.org/10.1108/JSTPM-07-2017-0033

36. Slade, E.L., Dwivedi, Y.K., Piercy, N.C., Williams, M.D.: Modeling consumers' adoption intentions of remote mobile payments in the United Kingdom: extending UTAUT with innovativeness, risk, and trust. Psychol. Mark. 32(8), 860–873 (2015)

37. Slade, E., Williams, M., Dwivedi, Y., Piercy, N.: Exploring consumer adoption of proximity mobile payments. J. Strat. Mark. 23(3), 209–223 (2015)

38. Thakur, R., Srivastava, M.: Adoption readiness, personal innovativeness, perceived risk and usage intention across customer groups for mobile payment services in India. Internet Res. 24(3), 369–392 (2014)

39. Tian, Y., Dong, H.: An analysis of key factors affecting user acceptance of mobile payment. In: 2013 Second International Conference on Informatics and Applications (ICIA), pp. 240–246. IEEE, September 2013

40. World Economic Forum: Mobile financial services development report. http://reports.weforum.org/wp-content/pdf/mfsr-2011/wef-mfsd-report-2011.pdf (2011)

41. Wu, J., Liu, L., Huang, L.: Exploring user acceptance of innovative mobile payment service in emerging market: the moderating effect of diffusion stages of WeChat payment in China. In: PACIS, p. 238, June 2016

42. Xin, H., Techatassanasoontorn, A.A., Tan, F.B.: Exploring the influence of trust on mobile payment adoption (2013)

43. Yang, S., Lu, Y., Gupta, S., Cao, Y., Zhang, R.: Mobile payment services adoption across time: An empirical study of the effects of behavioral beliefs, social influences, and personal traits. Comput. Hum. Behav. 28(1), 129–142 (2012)

44. Zhong, J., Dhir, A., Nieminen, M., Hämäläinen, M., Laine, J.: Exploring consumer adoption of mobile payments in China. In: Proceedings of International Conference on Making Sense of Converging Media, p. 318. ACM, October 2013

45. Zhou, T.: An empirical examination of continuance intention of mobile payment services. Decis. Support Syst. 54(2), 1085–1091 (2013)

46. Zhou, T.: Understanding the determinants of mobile payment continuance usage. Ind. Manag. Data Syst. 114(6), 936–948 (2014)

Motivations Affecting Attitude Towards Information: Development of a Conceptual Model

Daniele Doneddu[1,2]([envelope])

[1] School of Management, Swansea University, Swansea SA1 8EN, UK
d.doneddu@swansea.ac.uk
[2] SCIENTIA Group, Swansea, UK

Abstract. Electronic word of mouth (eWOM) plays an important part in our everyday life. When seeking information online through eWOM, our attitude towards specific information is inevitably affected by a wide range of factors and motives. Identifying and studying how motivations to seek eWOM affect our attitude towards said information may play a role to help us devise strategies to deal with new products, services and technologies as they are released in to the wild and get exposure to consumers. The aim of this research is to develop a model to study how certain specific motivations may affect the attitude individuals hold towards eWOM information. This paper develops a set of hypotheses to help evaluate how motivations affects the information seeker's attitude towards the information. Future empirical research will test the proposed hypotheses to advance our understanding of the role of motivations when seeking eWOM information.

Keywords: Electronic word of mouth · eWOM · Attitude towards information
Information seeking · Motivations

1 Introduction

The advent of the Internet, social media and the advancements in e-commerce-type transactions (and related security technologies development) have provided traditional word of mouth communication with the new, powerful approach of electronic word of mouth (eWOM), to greatly support the process of information seeking. Ismagilova et al. [1] provide a thorough and comprehensive compendium on eWOM, starting with a new and improved definition: "the dynamic and ongoing information exchange process between potential, actual or former consumers regarding a product, service, brand or company, which is available to a multitude of people and institutions via the Internet" (p. 18).

The eWOM related research field is now being populated with a substantial body of empirical evidence that shows the significant impact eWOM has within consumer behaviour and information process behaviour. In particular, in previous studies significant evidence has been produced showing the impact of eWOM on information adoption [2], intention to buy [3], information overload [4], and change in consumer's attitude [5].

© IFIP International Federation for Information Processing 2018
Published by Springer Nature Switzerland AG 2018. All Rights Reserved
S. A. Al-Sharhan et al. (Eds.): I3E 2018, LNCS 11195, pp. 53–59, 2018.
https://doi.org/10.1007/978-3-030-02131-3_7

Most of the studies on eWOM communications paid attention on changes in consumer's attitude towards products [5], brands [6] or website [7]. However, the existing literature has not thoroughly identified and investigated which factors affect attitude towards information. Additionally, a limited number of studies has investigated how motivations to search for online information affect consumer's attitude towards information. Since consumers' attitude can influence consumers' decision making and, as a result, sales [8], the study of the factors affecting consumers' attitude has importance from both theoretical and managerial perspectives. The identification and study of how motivations to seek eWOM affect our attitude towards said information may play a role to help us devise strategies to deal with new products, services and technologies as they are released in to the wild and get exposure to consumers. As a result, the aim of this research is to develop a model to study how certain specific motivations may affect the attitude individuals hold towards eWOM information.

Previous studies found that motivations to engage in eWOM can affect frequency of eWOM communications and intention to buy. However, the impact of motivations to seek information on consumer's attitude towards information has, to the best of the author's knowledge, so far not been investigated. In-depth understanding of factors affecting consumer's attitude can improve information adoption, intention to buy and, as a result, level of sales. In light of the potential substantial impact of such factors on information adoption, intention to buy and resulting sales, the development of a conceptual model on motivations to seek information and attitude towards information will advance understanding of information processing.

The aim of this paper is to present a conceptual model of the relationships between motivation to seek eWOM communications (e.g. social approval, social interaction benefit, risk reduction, reduction of search time and effort, and getting product (usage) information) and attitude towards information. The rationale of this paper is that different motivations can influence consumer's attitude towards information. The following section explores the key literature on attitude and motivations to seek eWOM communication. Next, the conceptual model and hypotheses are presented. Finally, the paper is concluded and directions for future research are outlined.

2 Literature Review

Attitude is defined as an evaluation of an entity with some degree of disfavour or favour [9]. Existing studies on eWOM communications found that eWOM communication can influence reviewer's attitude towards products [10], brands [6], websites [7]. Researchers found consumers' attitude to be influenced by different factors, such as: source credibility, message format, quality, type of message, volume, valence, extremity, and subjectivity [10–13]. There is, however, a lack of studies that have investigated how motivations to seek eWOM can influence consumer's attitude.

Previous studies found that there are several motivation for seeking eWOM communication, such as risk reduction, social approval, reduction of search time and effort, getting product (usage) information and social interaction benefits [14, 15]. Some researchers also investigated the connection between motivations to seek eWOM and behavioural intentions/ consumers behaviour. For example, Hennig-Thurau et al. [14]

investigated the motivations for consumers to retrieve other consumers' online articulations, and their impact on consumer buying and communication behaviour. Furthermore, again Hennig-Thurau et al. [16] studied the motives of consumers' online articulations and their resulting behaviour (frequency of platform visits, number of comments).

Scholars call for further investigation on the effect of motivations on consumers' behaviour [14]. Thus, the focus of this research, which emphasises its original contribution to knowledge enhancing the theory of information processing, is to investigate the effect of motivations to seek eWOM communications on perceived attitude towards information, an aspect which has not been studied before.

3   Conceptual Model

This section discusses each of the constructs of the proposed research model and presents the proposed hypotheses. The research model (see Fig. 1) is based on the framework proposed by Henning-Thurau et al. [14], which identified the main motivations for people to seek information online.

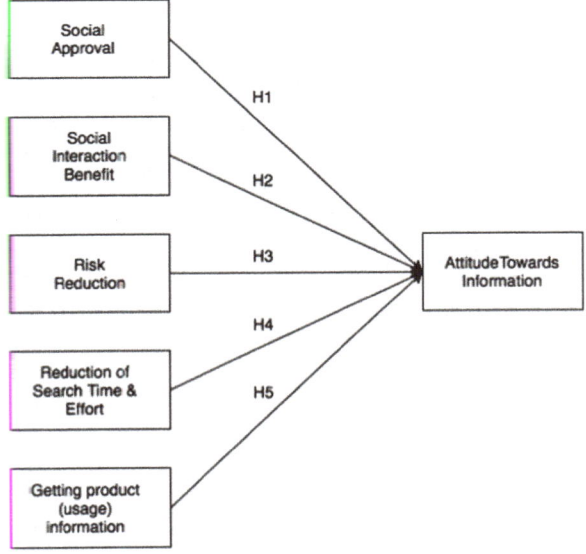

Fig. 1. Proposed research model

3.1   Social Approval

According to Hennig-Thurau et al. [14], social approval is connected to information search process for the social function of consumption. Individuals search for eWOM communication in order to buy a product/service which is accepted by other people. Furthermore, using eWOM communications individuals can compare their existing ideas about a product/service with other people or receive other individuals' approval of the purchase decision [14, 17]. Previous studies found that social approval is one of the motivations for people to search for articulations of others online [14, 18–21]. It was also found that social approval influence consumer's behaviour online [14, 19]. As a result, it is proposed that:

H1: Social approval has a positive effect on consumer's attitude towards eWOM communications.

3.2   Social Interaction Benefits

By using the Internet individuals can have a sense of belonging to a community by looking for other consumers' postings on online eWOM platforms. When investigating motivations to search information about product/services, online previous studies found that the benefits of social interaction motivate consumers to seek eWOM and affect online consumer behaviour [15, 22]. The following hypothesis is proposed:

H2: Social interaction benefit has a positive effect on consumer's attitude towards eWOM communications.

3.3   Risk Reduction

Individuals use eWOM communication to decrease the perceived risk in decision making [23]. Previous studies found that people rely on interpersonal sources of information when they perceived a purchase as risky [24]. eWOM information gives people an opportunity to get clarification and feedback which will decrease their decision making uncertainly about a product or service. As a result, using information from eWOM communication allows receiver of this information to build confidence in purchase decision and reduce perceived risk of the purchase [25]. Previous studies found that risk reduction is one of the main motivations for people to read online information from others on Internet [14, 19, 22, 23, 26–28]. It was also found that risk reduction influences consumers' behaviour online [14]. As a result, the following hypothesis is proposed:

H3: Risk reduction has a positive effect on consumer's attitude towards eWOM communications.

3.4   Reduction of Search Time and Effort

Individuals use eWOM communication to reduce search time and effort in making purchase decisions [23]. High volume of available information online and a wide range of products/services can make consumers face difficulties when it comes to know all the available alternatives [17]. eWOM can be a convenient way to obtain necessary buying-related information with time reduction on searching activities. Previous studies found that reduction of search time and effort is an important motivation for people to seek information using eWOM communications and it has an impact on consumer behaviour online [14, 15, 19, 22, 29]. Thus, the following hypothesis is proposed:

H4: Reduction of search time and effort has a positive effect on consumer's attitude towards eWOM communications.

3.5   Getting Product (Usage) Information

Individuals read eWOM communication to receive product-related information [14]. By using eWOM communications people can get information about new products/services and learn how to use them. It was examined by previous studies that getting product (usage) information influences people to seek for information online [22, 23], which could lead to a change in attitude towards eWOM communications.

Thus, it is proposed that:

H5: Getting product (usage) information has a positive effect on consumer's attitude towards eWOM communications.

4   Conclusion

The aim of this research is to develop a conceptual model to study how certain specific motivations may affect the attitude individuals hold towards eWOM information. Based on the framework proposed by Hennig-Thurau et al. [14], this paper develops a set of hypotheses to help evaluate how motivations affects the information seeker's attitude towards the information. Investigating the impact of motivation on attitude towards information is important for marketers. It has been previously shown that attitude towards eWOM communications affects information usefulness, which in turn affects information adoption and intention to buy [30]. Understanding how motivations can lead to a positive or negative attitude towards information will help to gain a greater understanding of eWOM communications by investigating determinants of attitude towards eWOM information, which will lead to the development of better marketing strategies. The findings from this study will lead to a richer understanding of the factors which affect consumer's attitude towards information and this research will therefore advance current understanding of the role of motivations to seek eWOM in an information seeking situation. The next step for this research is to validate the proposed hypotheses as follows: (1) data collection using questionnaires (2) Structural equation modelling to be used to test hypothesised relationships among constructs, using the SPSS® Amos software from IBM®.

References

1. Ismagilova, E., Dwivedi, Y.K., Slade, E., Williams, M.D.: Electronic Word of Mouth (eWOM) in the Marketing Context: A State of the Art Analysis and Future Directions. Springer (2017)
2. Cheung, R.: The influence of electronic word-of-mouth on information adoption in online customer communities. Glob. Econ. Rev. **43**, 42–57 (2014)

3. Tsao, W.-C., Hsieh, M.-T., Shih, L.-W., Lin, T.M.: Compliance with eWOM: the influence of hotel reviews on booking intention from the perspective of consumer conformity. Int. J. Hosp. Manag. **46**, 99–111 (2015)
4. Furner, C.P., Zinko, R.A.: The influence of information overload on the development of trust and purchase intention based on online product reviews in a mobile vs. web environment: an empirical investigation. Electron. Mark. **27**, 211–224 (2017)
5. Huang, G.-H., Korfiatis, N.: Trying before buying: the moderating role of online reviews in trial attitude formation toward mobile applications. Int. J. Electron. Commer. **19**, 77–111 (2015)
6. Sandes, F.S., Urdan, A.T.: Electronic word-of-mouth impacts on consumer behavior: exploratory and experimental studies. J. Int. Consum. Mark. **25**, 181–197 (2013)
7. Chih, W.-H., Wang, K.-Y., Hsu, L.-C., Huang, S.-C.: Investigating electronic wordof-mouth effects on online discussion forums: the role of perceived positive electronic word-of-mouth review credibility. Cyberpsychol. Behav. Soc. Netw. **16**, 658–668 (2013)
8. Cheung, C.M., Thadani, D.R.: The impact of electronic word-of-mouth communication: a literature analysis and integrative model. Decis. Support Syst. **54**, 461–470 (2012)
9. Eagly, A.H., Chaiken, S.: The advantages of an inclusive definition of attitude. Soc. Cogn. **25**, 582–602 (2007)
10. Ladhari, R., Michaud, M.: eWOM effects on hotel booking intentions, attitudes, trust, and website perceptions. Int. J. Hosp. Manag. **46**, 36–45 (2015)
11. Jeong, H.-J., Koo, D.-M.: Combined effects of valence and attributes of e-WOM on consumer judgment for message and product: the moderating effect of brand community type. Internet Res. **25**, 2–29 (2015)
12. Lee, J., Park, D.-H., Han, I.: The effect of negative online consumer reviews on product attitude: an information processing view. Electron. Commer. Res. Appl. **7**, 341–352 (2008)
13. Lee, M., Rodgers, S., Kim, M.: Effects of valence and extremity of eWOM on attitude toward the brand and website. J. Curr. Issues Res. Advert. **31**, 1–11 (2009)
14. Hennig-Thurau, T., Walsh, G., Walsh, G.: Electronic word-of-mouth: Motives for and consequences of reading customer articulations on the Internet. Int. J. Electron. Commer. **8**, 51–74 (2003)
15. Khammash, M., Griffiths, G.H.: 'Arrivederci CIAO. com, Buongiorno Bing. com'— Electronic word-of-mouth (eWOM), antecedences and consequences. Int. J. Inf. Manag. **31**, 82–87 (2011)
16. Hennig-Thurau, T., Gwinner, K.P., Walsh, G., Gremler, D.D.: Electronic word-ofmouth via consumer-opinion platforms: what motivates consumers to articulate themselves on the Internet? J. Interact. Mark. **18**, 38–52 (2004)
17. Han, S.M.: Motivations for Providing and Seeking eWOM: A Cross Cultural Comparison of US and Korean College Students. ProQuest (2000)
18. Huang, L., Shao, J., Wang, W.: Research on the relationships between hotel internet word-of-mouth and customers' behavior intention based on trust. In: 2013 6th International Conference on Information Management, Innovation Management and Industrial Engineering (ICIII), pp. 250–254. IEEE (2013)
19. Kim, E.E.K., Mattila, A.S., Baloglu, S.: Effects of gender and expertise on consumers' motivation to read online hotel reviews. Cornell Hosp. Q. **52**, 399–406 (2011)
20. Matta, V., Frost, R.: Motivations of electronic word-of-mouth communications by reviewers: a proposed study. SSRN Electron. J. (2011)
21. Yap, K.B., Soetarto, B., Sweeney, J.C.: The relationship between electronic word-ofmouth motivations and message characteristics: the sender's perspective. Australas. Mark. J. (AMJ) **21**, 66–74 (2013)

22. Burton, J., Khammash, M.: Why do people read reviews posted on consumer-opinion portals? J. Mark. Manag. **26**, 230–255 (2010)
23. Goldsmith, R.E., Horowitz, D.: Measuring motivations for online opinion seeking. J. Interact. Advert. **6**, 2–14 (2006)
24. Bansal, H.S., Voyer, P.A.: Word-of-mouth processes within a services purchase decision context. J. Serv. Res. **3**, 166–177 (2000)
25. Ha, H.-Y.: The effects of consumer risk perception on pre-purchase information in online auctions: brand, word-of-mouth, and customized information. J. Comput. Mediat. Commun. **8**, JCMC813 (2002)
26. Akyüz, A.: Determinant factors influencing eWOM. Mediterr. J. Soc. Sci. **4**, 159 (2013)
27. Awad, N.F., Ragowsky, A.: Establishing trust in electronic commerce through online word of mouth: an examination across genders. J. Manag. Inf. Syst. **24**, 101–121 (2008)
28. Zhang, Y., Lv, T.: Analysis of the relationship between involvement and the internet word-of-mouth. In: 2010 2nd IEEE International Conference on Network Infrastructure and Digital Content, pp. 1018–1024. IEEE (2010)
29. Munzel, A., Kunz, W.H.: Creators, multipliers, and lurkers: who contributes and who benefits at online review sites. J. Serv. Manag. **25**, 49–74 (2014)
30. Erkan, I., Evans, C.: The influence of eWOM in social media on consumers' purchase intentions: an extended approach to information adoption. Comput. Hum. Behav. **61**, 47–55 (2016)

Motivations to Seek Electronic Word of Mouth Communications and Information Adoption: Development of a Conceptual Model

Daniele Doneddu[✉]

School of Management, Swansea University, Swansea SA1 8EN, UK
d.doneddu@swansea.ac.uk

Abstract. Electronic word of mouth (eWOM) plays an important part in our everyday life. eWOM communications have been shown to affect the adoption of information, thus affecting the information seeker's decision-making. Identifying and studying how motivations to seek eWOM affect information adoption can prove beneficial in aiding new product, services and, in general, technology strategy development and adoption. This research aims at developing a model to investigate how certain specific motivations may affect the adoption of information sought through eWOM. This paper develops a set of hypotheses to help evaluate how motivations affect the information seeker's adoption of the information sought, based on the moderating effect of gender. The paper improves on the knowledge of factors affecting information adoption and the impact of gender, and thus help advance our understanding of consumer behaviour online and information processing. Future empirical research will test the proposed hypotheses to advance our understanding of the role of motivations when seeking eWOM information.

Keywords: Electronic word of mouth · eWOM · Information adoption
Information seeking · Motivations

1 Introduction

Consumers face difficulties when making online purchase decision due to limited information about the products/services provided by sellers [1]. Thus, more consumers use electronic word of mouth communications in their decision making process.

eWOM is defined by Ismagilova et al. [2] as "the dynamic and ongoing information exchange process between potential, actual or former consumers regarding a product, service, brand or company, which is available to a multitude of people and institutions via the Internet" (p. 18). eWOM communications have significant impact on consumers and their behavior and it has received much attention from researchers. It was found that eWOM can affect individuals' information adoption [3, 4] which could influence attitude towards product or services [5, 6], intention to purchase [7, 8] and result in sales [9, 10]. It is therefore important to investigate consequences and factors affecting information adoption, as it will advance understanding of consumer behaviour.

The majority of studies investigated factors affecting consumers' information adoption, such as source credibility [3] and quality [11] of the message, to name but a

S. A. Al-Sharhan et al. (Eds.): I3E 2018, LNCS 11195, pp. 60–66, 2018.
https://doi.org/10.1007/978-3-030-02131-3_8

few. However, here is a lack of research and evidence of how motivations to receive eWOM communications can influence information adoption. Previous research found that motivations to receive eWOM can influence intention to buy, intention to engage in eWOM and frequency to platform visits [12]. Nevertheless, the influence of consumers' motivations - to receive eWOM - on information adoption has not been studies by previous research. It is important to know the factors affecting information adoption, as it will help advance the understanding of consumer behavior and serve marketers in their endeavors to develop strategies to influence consumers' purchase decision in turn influencing the level of sales. Thus, the aim of this research is to investigate how motivations to receive eWOM will influence information adoption by developing a conceptual model to advance the understanding of information processing.

The rest of the paper is structured as follows. Next section explores the key literature on information adoption and motivations to receive eWOM communication. The subsequent section introduces the conceptual model and presents the related hypotheses. Finally, the paper is concluded and directions for future research are outlined.

2   Literature Review

Information adoption is the extent to which people accept and use eWOM communication in making purchase decisions [3, 13]. Studies on eWOM communications investigated that eWOM communications can influence information adoption [14–16]. Scholars identified different factors which can affect information adoption, such as source credibility argument strength, information comprehensiveness, information consistency, quality, source attractiveness, homophily and valence [11, 15–18]. However, none of the studies investigated how motivations to seek eWOM communication can affect information adoption.

Researchers identified several main motivations for consumers to seek eWOM communications such as risk reduction, social approval, reduction of search time and effort, getting product (usage) information and social interaction benefits [6, 19–21]. It was found by previous studies that motivations to receive eWOM communications affect consumer behaviour [12, 20], for example, consumers' intention to buy and communication behaviour resulting in frequency of platforms visits and number of comments.

Studies on eWOM communication call for further examination of the impact of motivations to receive eWOM communications on consumer's behaviour [20]. As a result, this paper focuses on the effect of specific motivations to receive eWOM communications on information adoption. This has not been researched before; shedding some light on the relationships investigated will help to enhance the theory of information processing.

3   Development of the Conceptual Model

This section introduces and discusses each of the constructs of the proposed research model. The proposed conceptual model is based on Hennig-Thurau et al. [20] framework of motivations to receive eWOM and proposes that motivations influence information adoption and are moderated by gender (Fig. 1).

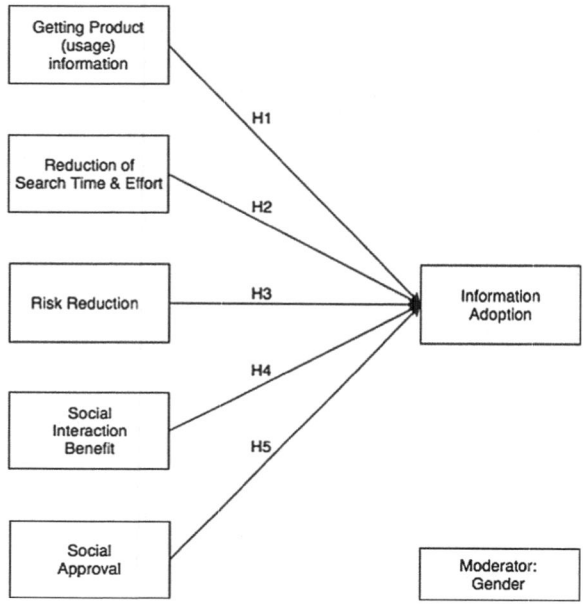

Fig. 1. Proposed research model

3.1   Getting Product (Usage) Information

According to Hennig-Thurau et al. [20] people seek eWOM information in order to get product-related information. Due to the fact that eWOM is provided by people who bought and used the product, receivers of information find it more relevant in comparison with information provided by companies. Individuals can obtain information about new products and services, solve problems associated with using products/services and learn how to consume the products [22]. Since it was found by previous studies that motivations to seek eWOM can results on consumer's behavior, the following is proposed:

H1: Getting product (usage) information has a positive effect on consumer's information adoption.

3.2 Reduction of Search Time and Effort

Nowadays consumers are faced with a high volume of available information online and a wide range of available products and services. Consumers might, as such, experience difficulties in knowing all the alternatives available to them [23]. eWOM communications can help consumers get the needed buying-related information with a reduction of time on search activities. Researchers investigated that reduction of search time and effort motivates people to receive information using eWOM communications and can influence their behaviour online [6, 20, 24]. As a result, it is proposed that:

H2: Reduction of search time and effort has a positive effect on consumer's information adoption.

3.3 Risk Reduction

Consumers rely on eWOM communications to minimise the perceived risk associated to making buying decisions [19]. eWOM communications provide individuals with clarification and feedback opportunities and minimise uncertainty before buying and using particular products or services [25]. Researchers found that risk reduction is one of the main motivations for people to receive eWOM communications and that risk reduction also influences consumers' online behaviour [6, 20, 26, 27]. Thus, the following hypothesis is proposed:

H3: Risk reduction has a positive effect on consumer's information adoption.

3.4 Social Interaction Benefits

Previous studies found that social interaction benefit motivates people to seek eWOM communications, as individuals can participate in other consumers' shopping experience and derive a sense of belonging to an online community [20, 21, 27]. Furthermore, it was found that social interaction benefits influence online behaviour [20]. Thus, the following it proposed:

H4: Social interaction benefit has a positive effect on consumer's information adoption.

3.5 Social Approval

Consumers have a motivation to seek information through eWOM communications to buy products or services accepted by other individuals. Additionally, by using eWOM communications consumers can become aware of a social image of a product or a service, as well as compare their thoughts and opinions about them with other individuals [20, 23]. Researchers on eWOM communications found that social approval plays an important role for people's motivation to look for eWOM of others on Internet [6, 20, 28]. Studies found that social approval can influence consumers' behaviour on Internet [6, 20]. As a result, it is proposed that:

H5: Social approval has a positive effect on consumer's information adoption.

3.6 Gender

Number of studies found that there are gender differences in internet use [29] and information processing [6, 30, 31]. For example, Bem [30] investigated that men and women use different cognitive attributes for information encoding and problem solving. Another study conducted by Meyers-Levy [31] found that men focus on concrete, objective cues such as form and physical attributes, while women pay more attention to the message content and react to more subtle cues in messages. Kim et al. [6] found that men and women have different motivations to seek eWOM communications. So, based on the previous studies the following hypothesis is proposed:

H6: Gender has a moderating effect on the impact of motivations to seek eWOM on information adoption

4 Conclusion

This study aims to develop a conceptual research model in order to examine how motivations to receive eWOM communication affect information adoption based on moderating effect of gender. Through the application of the framework proposed by Hennig-Thurau et al. [20] this study developed a set of hypotheses which aim to examine how consumer's motivation to receive eWOM influence their information adoption as well as the role gender plays in it. Studying the influence of motivations on information adoption has important implications for both theory and practice. It will improve current state of knowledge of factors affecting information adoption and the impact of gender, which will advance theory of information processing. Thus, it will help researchers to advance the knowledge and understanding of consumer behaviour online. Marketers can use this study to develop better marketing strategies to influence information adoption, which will influence consumers purchase decisions, ultimately resulting in increased sales [32].

The next steps to be undertaken in order to validate the proposed hypotheses will be to collect information online using questionnaires and to apply structural equation modelling to analyse the collected data using the IBM® SPSS® Amos software.

References

1. Dimoka, A., Hong, Y., Pavlou, P.A.: On product uncertainty in online markets: theory and evidence. MIS Q. **36**, 395–426 (2012)
2. Ismagilova, E., Dwivedi, Y.K., Slade, E., Williams, M.D.: Electronic Word of Mouth (eWOM) in the Marketing Context: A State of the Art Analysis and Future Directions. Springer (2017)
3. Lis, B.: In eWOM we trust. Bus. Inf. Syst. Eng. **5**, 129–140 (2013)
4. Teng, S., Wei Khong, K., Wei Goh, W., Yee Loong Chong, A.: Examining the antecedents of persuasive eWOM messages in social media. Online Inf. Rev. **38**, 746–768 (2014)

5. Jeong, H.-J., Koo, D.-M.: Combined effects of valence and attributes of e-WOM on consumer judgment for message and product: the moderating effect of brand community type. Internet Res. **25**, 2–29 (2015)

6. Kim, E.E.K., Mattila, A.S., Baloglu, S.: Effects of gender and expertise on consumers' motivation to read online hotel reviews. Cornell Hosp. Q. **52**, 399–406 (2011)

7. Bartikowski, B., Walsh, G.: Attitude contagion in consumer opinion platforms: posters and lurkers. Electron. Mark. **24**, 207–217 (2014)

8. Baber, A., Thurasamy, R., Malik, M.I., Sadiq, B., Islam, S., Sajjad, M.: Online wordof-mouth antecedents, attitude and intention-to-purchase electronic products in Pakistan. Telemat. Inform. **33**, 388–400 (2016)

9. Baek, H., Ahn, J., Oh, S.: Impact of tweets on box office revenue: focusing on when tweets are written. ETRI J. **36**, 581–590 (2014)

10. Kim, S.H., Park, N., Park, S.H.: Exploring the effects of online word of mouth and expert reviews on theatrical movies' box office success. J. Media Econ. **26**, 98–114 (2013)

11. Aghakhani, N., Karimi, J.: Acceptance of implicit and explicit eWOM: a factor based study of social networking sites (2013)

12. Hennig-Thurau, T., Gwinner, K.P., Walsh, G., Gremler, D.D.: Electronic word-ofmouth via consumer-opinion platforms: what motivates consumers to articulate themselves on the Internet? J. Interact. Mark. **18**, 38–52 (2004)

13. Sussman, S.W., Siegal, W.S.: Informational influence in organizations: an integrated approach to knowledge adoption. Inf. Syst. Res. **14**, 47–65 (2003)

14. Cheung, R.: The influence of electronic word-of-mouth on information adoption in online customer communities. Glob. Econ. Rev. **43**, 42–57 (2014)

15. Shuang, Y.: Effects of information quality and source credibility on EWOM adoption in context of virtual community. In: 2013 International Conference on Management Science and Engineering (ICMSE), pp. 194–200. IEEE (2013)

16. Wang, X., Teo, H.-H., Wei, K.K.: Simultaneity and interactivity of the effects of communication elements on consumers' decision making in eWOM systems. J. Electron. Commer. Res. **16**, 153 (2015)

17. Bansal, H.S., Voyer, P.A.: Word-of-mouth processes within a services purchase decision context. J. Serv. Res. **3**, 166–177 (2000)

18. Chang, H.H., Wu, L.H.: An examination of negative e-WOM adoption: brand commitment as a moderator. Decis. Support Syst. **59**, 206–218 (2014)

19. Goldsmith, R.E., Horowitz, D.: Measuring motivations for online opinion seeking. J. Interact. Advert. **6**, 2–14 (2006)

20. Hennig-Thurau, T., Walsh, G., Walsh, G.: Electronic word-of-mouth: motives for and consequences of reading customer articulations on the Internet. Int. J. Electron. Commer. **8**, 51–74 (2003)

21. Khammash, M., Griffiths, G.H.: 'Arrivederci CIAO. com, Buongiorno Bing. com'— Electronic word-of-mouth (eWOM), antecedences and consequences. Int. J. Inf. Manag. **31**, 82–87 (2011)

22. Bickart, B., Schindler, R.M.: Internet forums as influential sources of consumer information. J. Interact. Mark. **15**, 31–40 (2001)

23. Han, S.M.: Motivations for Providing and Seeking eWOM: A Cross Cultural Comparison of US and Korean College Students. ProQuest (2000)

24. Munzel, A., Kunz, W.H.: Creators, multipliers, and lurkers: who contributes and who benefits at online review sites. J. Serv. Manag. **25**, 49–74 (2014)

25. Silverman, G.: Secrets of Word-of-Mouth Marketing: How to Trigger Exponential Sales Through Runaway Word of Mouth. AMACOM, Division of American Management Association (2011)

26. Awad, N.F., Ragowsky, A.: Establishing trust in electronic commerce through online word of mouth: an examination across genders. J. Manag. Inf. Syst. **24**, 101–121 (2008)

27. Burton, J., Khammash, M.: Why do people read reviews posted on consumer-opinion portals? J. Mark. Manag. **26**, 230–255 (2010)

28. Huang, L., Shao, J., Wang, W.: Research on the relationships between hotel internet word-of-mouth and customers' behavior intention based on trust. In: 2013 6th International Conference on Information Management, Innovation Management and Industrial Engineering (ICIII), pp. 250–254. IEEE (2013)

29. Pope, N., Brown, M., Forrest, E.: Risk, innovativeness, gender, and involvement factors affecting the intention to purchase sport product online. Sport Mark. Q. **8**, 25–34 (1999)

30. Bem, S.L.: Gender schema theory: a cognitive account of sex typing. Psychol. Rev. **88**, 354 (1981)

31. Meyers-Levy, J.: The influence of sex roles on judgment. J. Consum. Res. **14**, 522–530 (1988)

32. Sharma, R., Morales-Arroyo, M., Pandey, T.: The emergence of electronic word-of-mouth as a marketing channel for the digital marketplace. J. Inf. Inf. Technol. Organ. **6**, 41–61 (2012)

Performance Evaluation of Post-quantum Public-Key Cryptography in Smart Mobile Devices

Noureddine Chikouche[1,2]([✉]) [ID] and Abderrahmen Ghadbane[2]

[1] Laboratory of Pure and Applied Mathematics,
University of M'Sila, M'Sila, Algeria
chiknour28@yahoo.fr
[2] Computer Science Department, University of M'Sila, M'Sila, Algeria

Abstract. The classical public-key schemes are based on number theory, such as integer factorization and discrete logarithm. In 1994, P.W. Shor proposed an algorithm to solve these problems in polynomial time using quantum computers. Recent advancements in quantum computing open the door to the possibility of developing quantum computers sophisticated enough to solve these problems. Post-quantum cryptography (PQC) is resistant against quantum attacks. The aim of this paper is to evaluate the performance of different post-quantum public-key schemes for constrained-resources smart mobile devices; and to give a comparison between the studied post-quantum schemes in terms of computational time, required memory, and power consumption.

Keywords: Post-quantum cryptography · Public-key encryption
Public key signature · Performance · Mobile devices

1 Introduction

The classical public-key algorithms used today to secure user data and networking communications (e.g. Internet, mobile, etc.) are based on number theory. For example, the RSA cryptosystem is based on integer factorization problem, and the Diffie-Hellman scheme is based on discrete logarithm problem. In 1994, Shor [31] proposed an algorithm to solve these problems in polynomial time using quantum computers.

In 2015, the National Security Agency (NSA) [27] announced that it is working with several partners to develop quantum-resistant encryption algorithms. In 2016, the NIST (National Institute of Standards and Technology) [29] has started the process of developing, evaluating, and standardizing one or more public-key post-quantum cryptographic algorithms. It's crucial to re-evaluate the existing cryptographic schemes which are used to protect information, and to improve quantum-safe cryptography.

The quantum computing is not a future project but it already exists in the real-world. The D-Wave Systems Inc. [11] was the first company that commercialises products based on quantum computing principles that are being used by some of the important advanced organizations, including Google and NASA Ames. In 2017, this company developed the D-Wave 2000Q system which is a quantum annealer that has

S. A. Al-Sharhan et al. (Eds.): I3E 2018, LNCS 11195, pp. 67–80, 2018.
https://doi.org/10.1007/978-3-030-02131-3_9

up to 2048 qubits and 5600 couplers. It can solve larger problems in various areas, such as machine learning, financial analysis, optimization and security. In security, this quantum computer can carry out factoring integers, detects computer viruses and network intrusion.

Nowadays, there are various classes of post-quantum public-key cryptography, including:

- **Code-based cryptography:** The classic example is McEliece cryptosystem based on Goppa codes [25]. It uses error correcting codes to generate public key from private matrices with intentionally added errors. It is employed in the construction of diverse cryptographic schemes and it does not need any cryptographic processor.
- **Lattice-based cryptography:** The most basic lattice problem is the shortest vector problem (SVP), given an arbitrary basis of lattice, the goal is to find the shortest nonzero vector in it. NTRU scheme [19] is one of the most interesting lattice-based variants.
- **Multivariate-based cryptography:** It uses a set of multivariate polynomial equations that are based on the multivariate quadratic (MQ) Problem. One of its many interesting schemes is Rainbow public-key signature scheme which was proposed by Ding and Schmidt [13] in 2005.
- **Hash-based cryptography:** It is based on so-named one-time signature (OTS), a single key pair must only be used once. it requires a cryptographic hash function to create a public-key signature. For example, Winternitz onetime signature (W-OTS) [14] that relies on collision resistance, which means that using the same private-key to sign multiple documents will not yield a similar signature.
- **Isogeny-based cryptography:** This category was introduced as a solution to breaking elliptic curve cryptography by Shor's algorithm. Isogeny problem is to find the isogeny mapping between two elliptic curves with the same number of points. NIST [6] stated that not enough analysis has been done prove the claimed security.

Post-quantum cryptography (PQC) is resistant against quantum attacks and its computational complexity is of type NP-hard problem. Recently, there are several security protocols based on PQC have been presented, such as [7–9, 24]. In the context of smart mobile technology, to secure user data and mobile communication, it is crucial to implement efficient cryptographic primitives. In the other hand, the most important problem is the limitation of resources, storage, processing, and power.

The aim of this paper is to survey the post-quantum public-key algorithms in regards to their efficient in smart mobiles. We evaluate their performance in terms of computational time, required memory, and power consumption. Moreover, we compare the different PQC in terms of performance and security.

The rest of this paper is structured as follows: Sect. 2 presents related works. Section 3 presents post-quantum encryption schemes. Section 4 presents post-quantum signature schemes. The experimental results is detailed in Sect. 5. We discuss of obtained results in Sect. 6. Finally, conclusion has been presented in Sect. 7.

2   Related Works

An important number of studies have been realised in order to present efficient implementation of post-quantum cryptography in constrained resource devices. In the rest of this section, we introduce some research efforts in this area.

Eisenbarth et al. [15] investigated the efficient software implementation of McEliece scheme on embedded systems, low-cost 8-bit AVR microprocessor and a Xilinx Spartan-3AN FPGA. Hayes [17] evaluated different implementation possibilities for McEliece, Niederreiter, and their variants. In addition, He evaluated the performance of the schemes using various types od codes on smartcard class microcontrollers and a range of FPGAs. Wang et al. [34] improved the previous implementations of Niederreiter encryption scheme in terms of efficiency and security level by presenting a new implementation using binary Goppa codes in FPGA.

About the implementation of PQC on mobiles devices, Tayoub et al. [33] implemented NTRU scheme and other classical public-key schemes on Android mobiles, and evaluated their performances in terms of timing and memory occupation. In 2016, Boledovič and Varga [4] implemented McEliece encryption scheme in messenger application of Android operating system by using Bouncy castle provider.

3   Post-quantum Encryption Schemes

Post-quantum encryption scheme is used to safeguard the confidentiality of stored and exchanged information. It consists of three processes: key generation, encryption, and decryption. The key generation process creates a key pair consisting of a public and a private key. The public-key is used to encrypt a plaintext and the private-key, to decrypt a ciphertext. Various post-quantum encryption schemes subsequently designed are presented below.

3.1   McEliece Scheme

In 1978, McEliece [25] introduced the first public key cryptosystem (PKC) based on coding theory. The security of McEliece scheme is based on the problem of computational dual decoding syndrome. Let C[n, k, t] be a binary linear code, where n is length, k is dimension which stands as a generator matrix G. C can correct up to t errors.

The McEliece encryption scheme is defined as follows:

Key Generation:

- Generate three private matrices, a generator matrix $G' \in \mathbb{F}_2^{k \times n}$ of a binary Goppa code C, a permutation matrix $P \in \mathbb{F}_2^{n \times n}$ and an invertible matrix $S' \in \mathbb{F}_2^{k \times k}$,
- Compute the public-key matrix $G = S^0 G^0 P$, which is another valid generator matrix,
- The private-key is (S^0, G^0, P, A(.)), where A(.) is a polynomial-time decoding algorithm,
- The public-key is (G, t).

Encryption: To encrypt a message $m \in \mathbb{F}_2^k$

- Generate an error vector $e \in \mathbb{F}_2^n$ of weight wt(e) $\leq t$,
- Compute the codeword $c \in \mathbb{F}_2^n$ where c is mG and the plaintext is $m \in \mathbb{F}_2^k$,
- The cryptogram $c^0 = c \oplus e$.

Decryption: To decrypt a cryptogram c^0

- Compute $z = c^0 P^{-1}$,
- $y = A(z)$,
- Output $m = yS^{0-1}$.

3.2   Niederreiter Scheme

Niederreiter encryption scheme [28] introduced the dual version of McEliece encryption scheme. This variant is based on the syndrome decoding $SD-$ problem using the parity check matrix. The important advantage of this scheme compared to McEliece is reduction of the public-key size from $k \times n$ to $n \times (n-k)$. The Niederreiter encryption scheme is defined as follows:

Key generation:

- **Parameters:** $n, t \in N$, where $t < n$
- Generate a parity check matrix $H' \in \mathbb{F}_2^{(n-k) \times n}$ of a binary linear C,
- Generate a permutation matrix $P \in \mathbb{F}_2^{n \times n}$,
- Generate an invertible matrix $Q \in \mathbb{F}_2^{(n-k) \times (n-k)}$,
- **Private-key:** $(Q, H^0, P, A(.))$ with $A(.)$ a decoding algorithm until $\frac{d}{2}$ errors,
- **Public-key:** $H \in \mathbb{F}_2^{(n-k) \times n} := QH'P$ and t integer $< \frac{d}{2}$.

Encryption: To encrypt message m

- decode m to error vector $e \in \mathbb{F}_2^n$ with wt(e) = t,
- $c^0 := H^{\tau}e$,
- output ciphertext c^0.

Decryption: To decrypt cryptogram c^0

- $Q^{-1}c^0 := Q^{-1}QH^0(Pe)$,
- compute $P^{-1}(Pe)$,
- encode e into message m.

3.3   McE Kobara-Imai Scheme

Kobara and Imai [23] proposed modified versions of McEliece scheme that can be proven to be semantically secure against adaptive chosen-ciphertext attacks (CCA2). In addition, their conversion γ (Algorithm below) uses the entropy in the error vector, to decrease the overhead of data further.

The McE Kobara-Imai scheme (Kobara-Imai conversion γ for the McEliece scheme) is defined as follows:

Encryption: To encrypt a message m

- $r := Rand$,
- $y1 := Gen(r) \oplus (m$ k $Const)$ where $Gen(.)$ is a random number generator and $Const$ is a public constant,
- $y2 := r \oplus Hash(y1)$,
- $(y5$ k $y4$ k $y3) := (y2$ k $y1)$,
- $z \leftarrow Conv(y4)$ where $Conv(.)$ a constant weight encoding function,
- Output the cryptogram $c := y5$ k $y2G \oplus z$.

Decryption: To decrypt a cryptogram c

- $c := y5kc^0$,
- $y3 := Decrypt_{Mceleice}(c0)$,
- $y3G \oplus y0$,
- $y4 := Conv^{-1}(z)$,
- $(y2$ k $y1) := (y5$ k $y4$ k $y3)$,
- $r := y2 \oplus Hash(y1)$,
- $(x\tilde{\ }kConst^0) := y1 \oplus Gen(r)$,
- if $Const^0 == Const$ return $x := x\tilde{\ }$,
- else return $\perp$.

3.4   NTRU Encryption Scheme

The NTRU cryptosystem was published by Jeffrey Hoffstein and Jill Pipher and Joseph Silverman in 1998 [19] and it was standardised by IEEE in 2008. NTRU uses a public parameter N to specifies the size of the polynomials used, a large modulus q and a smaller modulus p. The sender creates a pair of a public and a private key by generating two polynomials f and g, where f is invertible modulo both p and q.

The NTRU encryption scheme is defined as follows:

Key Generation:

- **Parameters:** N, q, p, where N and p prime, $gcd(p, q) = gcd(N, q) = 1$
- randomly choose two private polynomials f and g in the ring
- **Private key:** consists of the polynomials f and $f_q := f^{-1} \bmod p$
- **Public key:** $h := p * f_q * g \bmod q$ where $f_q := f^{-1} \bmod q$

Encryption: To encrypt a message m

- generate a random polynomial r
- $c := p * r * h + m \bmod q$
- The cryptogram is the polynomial c

Decryption: To decrypt a cryptogram c

- $a := f * c$ where the coefficients of a lie between $q/2$ and $q/2$
- $b := a \bmod p$
- $m := f_p * b \bmod p$
- output m

4 Post-quantum Signature Schemes

The digital signature scheme is a cryptographic primitive that provides publickey message authentication. It consists of three processes, key generation, signature generation, and signature verification. The key generation process creates a key pair consisting of a public and a private key. The private-key is used to sign a document and to generate a signature when the public-key is used to verify this signature. In this section, we present four important post-quantum digital signatures: Niederreiter CFS, NTRUSign, Rainbow, and XMSS.

4.1 Niederreiter-CFS Signature Scheme

A signature scheme based on the Niederreiter encryption scheme was introduced by Courtois, Finiasz and Sendrier in [10]. The idea of the Niederreiter-CFS scheme is to frequently hash the message, randomized by a counter of bit-length i, until the output is a ciphertext that can be decrypted. To determine the error vector, the signer uses his corresponding private key, and with the current value of the counter, the error vector will then serve as a signature. This signature scheme has the following parts:

The Niederreiter-CFS signature scheme is defined as follows:

Signature: To sign the document d

1. $i \leftarrow i + 1$,
2. $s^0 := A(Q^{-1}h(h(d)ki))$,
3. if no x^0 was found go to 1 else output $(i, x^0 P)$.

Verification: To verify the $(i, x^0 P)$

- $s^0 = Hx^0 T$,
- $s = h(h(d)ki)$,
- If s^0 and s equals, then the signature is valid.

4.2 NTRU Signature Scheme

The NTRU Signature scheme, also known as NTRUSign was presented in [18], it's based on the GGH signature scheme. NTRUSign includes mapping a message to a random point in 2 N-dimensional space, with N being a parameter, and solving the closest vector problem (CVP) in a lattice which is related to the NTRUEncrypt lattice problem.

The NTRU signature scheme is defined as follows:

Key Generation:

- pick two short polynomials h and f in ring R,
- find (F, G) with $f * g - g * F = q$,
- **Private key:** (f, g, F, G),
- **Public key:** $h := g * f^{-1} \bmod q$ with f is invertible in R_q.

Signature: To sing the document d

- $t := 0$
- Repeat

  1. $t := t + 1$,
  2. $\mu := Hash(dkt) \in R_q$,
  3. $(x, y) := (0, \mu) \begin{pmatrix} G & F \\ -G & f \end{pmatrix}$,
  4. $s := -x * f - y * g$,

- until k$(s, s * h - d)$k $\leq N$,
- return (s, t).

Verification: To verify (d, s, t)

- $\mu := Hash(dkt)$,
- if k$(s, s * h - d)$k $\leq N$ then the signature is valid.

4.3   Rainbow Signature Scheme

In 2005, Ding and Schmidt [13] proposed a public-key signature scheme named Rainbow, which is based on the idea of Oil and Vinegar variables. The idea of Oil and Vinegar variables is one way to create easily invertible multivariate quadratic systems.

The Rainbow signature scheme is defined as follows:

Key Generation:

- **Private key:** Two invertible affine maps L_1 and L_2 and the map $F = (f_{v1+1}(x), ..., f_n(x))$. The number of components of F is $m = n - v1$,
- **Public key:** The composed map $P(x) = L_1 \circ F \circ L_2$.

Signature: To sign a document d

- $h := hash(d)$,
- $x := L_1^{-1}(h)$,
- $y := F^{-1}(x)$ where $F^{-1}(x)$ means finding one pre-image of x,
- $z := L_2^{-1}(y)$,
- output: the signature z.

Verification: To verify z

- $h^0 := P(z)$,
- $h := hash(d)$,
- if $h^0 = h$ then the signature is valid.

4.4   XMSS Scheme

The eXtended Merkle Signature Scheme (XMSS) was proposed by Buchmann et al. [5] in 2011. It is a hash-based digital signature system that is a variant of the Merkle tree scheme and it is forward secure. Recently, IETF has published XMSS as informational RFC (RFC 8391).

The XMSS signature scheme is summarized as follows:

Key Generation:

- **Private key:** It consists of a cryptographic *seed* for a pseudorandom function, *PRNG*. Using *PRNG* function, create the WOTS Key pair and the leaf index i corresponding to the next W-OTS keys to be used,
- **Public key:** It contains bitmasks and the root node value used in the transitional levels of the hash tree.

Signature:

- *input:* message M, the private-key sk and the index i,
- use the ith W-OTS key pair to sign ith message,
- The signature $(\sigma, i, Auth)$ consists of the W-OTS signature σ, index i, and the leaf node authentication path $Auth$,
- the authentication path contains the hash values of H different nodes in the XMSS tree,
- the contained leaf index i in the XMSS private-key is updated.

Verification:

- input: a signature $(\sigma, i, Auth)$, a message M and the XMSS public-key,
- verify the W-OTS signature σ using the corresponding W-OTS public key,
- verify the authentication path by traversing the tree using $Auth$ to obtain P_H,
- If P_H is equal to the root node value in the public-key, the signature is valid.

5   Performance Evaluation

In this section, we present the developing environment of different post-quantum schemes in smartphone and the obtained experimental results.

5.1   Developing Environment

Android smartphones are the most used mobiles. Android is an operating system based on Linux kernel and other open-source software; written in Java, C and other programming languages. It was developed by Google for mobile devices. In this work, we develop an PQC benchmark set with the studied schemes by using two cryptographic providers: FlexiProvider [16] and Spongy Castle [32] which is a repackage of Bouncy Castle for Android platform. This performance evaluation is based on the running time, required memory, and power consumption for each studied scheme.

For the evaluation of the timing and the memory usage, we used the methods of java.lang.System and java.lang.Runtime classes, respectively. To measure the energy consumption of the three processes of each scheme, we used Batterystats which is a tool included in the Android framework that collects battery data on smartphones.

We benchmarked the performance of the previously studied schemes on smartphone Samsung Galaxy A5, model SM-A500H which is equipped with Exynos 7880 Octa-core 1.9 GHz processor, an internal memory with 3072 MB capacity, and a battery with a capacity of 3000 mAh. The Android version installed was 6.0.1 Marshmallow.

5.2   Experimental Results

NIST [6] recommends that all data that has to stay secure for more than 10 years should use a minimum of 128-bits security level. Table 1 describes different parameters used for each scheme with 128 security.

Table 1. Parameters for post-quantum schemes at the 128 bits security level

Scheme	Category	Parameter	References
McEliece McE Kobara-Imai Niederreiter Niederreiter CFS	Code-based	$(n = 4096, k = 3604, t = 41)$	[2]
NTRU (Encry and Sign)	Lattice-based	APR2011_439	[22]
Rainbow	Multivariate-based	$v1 = 36, o1 = 21, o2 = 22$	[30]
XMSS	Hash-based	xmss- sha2 10 256	[20]

Table 2. Computation speed and consumption energy in encryption schemes

Scheme	Timing (ms)			Energy (mAh)
	KeyGen	Encryption	Decryption	
McEliece	320313	11	364	18.3
McE Kobara-Imai	64478	134	463	6.3
Niederreiter	27046	157	475	0.6
NTRUEncry	4052	47	70	0.3

Table 2 presents the running time (key generation, encryption and decryption) and energy consumption of different encryption schemes. We mention that the measure of consumption energy is for all parties of each scheme.

Table 3. Computation speed and consumption energy in signature schemes

Scheme	Timing (ms)			Energy (mAh)
	KeyGen	Signature	Verification	
Niederreiter-CFS	63115	>1 h	>1 h	–
NTRUSign	4052	262	491	6.3
Rainbow	855157	276	77	42
XMSS	352714	486	199	18

Table 3 presents the running time (key generation, signature generation and signature verification) and energy consumption of different digital signature schemes.

For each post-quantum scheme, the required space in terms of pair key, ciphertext (in encryption schemes) or signature (in signature schemes) and memory usage (RAM) is showed in Table 4.

Table 4. Required space for each scheme

	Scheme	Pair key(kB)		Ciphertext	Memory
		Private key	Public key	or signature (Byte)	usage (MB)
Encryption	McEliece	1851.61	1802.05	512	33.57
	McE Kobara-Imai	256.29	218.264	512	9.20
	Niederreiter	40.074	216.744	62	2.76
	NTRUEncry	0.67	0.59	604	0.22
Signature	Niederreiter-CFS	40.07	216.74	–	–
	NTRUSign	0.67	0.59	604	49.01
	Rainbow	156.24	136.359	82	4.82
	XMSS	2.264	0.063	2499	5.61

6 Discussion

In this work, we evaluate three variants of schemes based on coding theory, McEliece, McE Kobara-Imai, Niederreiter, and Niederreiter CFS. McEliece encryption scheme has high-speed encryption process compared to other postquantum schemes. Moreover, it is easy to implement as it does not need any cryptographic processor. However, McEliece scheme consumes an important amount of energy (18.3 mAh). McE Kobara-Imai which is the CCA2 secure conversion of McEliece scheme, led to slower results because of the added steps to the encryption procedure. Niederreiter scheme performs better than the McEliece one when it comes to the timing of the decryption process. It generates the lowest ciphertext sizes, 8 times smaller than any other encryption scheme, which make it the best scheme when storing or transmitting the ciphertext. Moreover, McE Kobara-Imai scheme and Niederreiter scheme consume less amount of energy. The Niederreiter-CFS signature was the worst performing scheme on the signing process, it used a lot of computational resources and therefore is not suitable for mobile devices (Table 5).

In the other hand, code-based schemes requires large key sizes especially the McEliece scheme with an astounding 3.8 MB for a key pair. To avoid this limitation, quasi-cyclic and quasi-dyadic variants [1, 26] were designed to offer much lower key sizes. In addition, the generation of pair key is slower than NTRUEncry. We notice that the code-based cryptography has been recommended by Post-Quantum Crypto Project of Europe because it "has been studied since 1978 and has withstood attacks very well" [12].

Table 5. Advantages and disadvantages of each studied scheme

Scheme	Advantages	Disadvantages
McEliece	– Very fast encryption process	– Very large key sizes – High memory usage and energy consumption
McE Kobara-Imai	– More secure McEliece variant	– Large key sizes
Niederreiter	– Lowest cipher text size	– Large key sizes
Niederreiter CFS		– Resource-intensive signature generation process – Large key sizes
NTRUEncrypt	– Very fast execution – Lowest key size – Lowest memory usage and energy consumption	– Somewhat large cipher text sizes
NTRUSign	– Very fast execution (signature generation) – Lowest key size	– High memory usage and energy consumption (signature generation)
XMSS	– Small key sizes	– Somewhat large signature sizes
Rainbow	– Very fast signature generation and verification – Signature size	– Long key generation process – High energy consumption

When we compared the code-based schemes to the NTRUEncrypt scheme we found that NTRUEncrypt offers a balanced execution speeds for encryption and decryption processes and requires the lowest amount of memory in RAM when performing the operations of encryption and decryption. Moreover, the key length of NTRUEncrypt is smaller, which is suitable with limited resources of mobiles phones. In addition, NTRUEncrypt scheme uses the least amount of energy. NTRUSign scheme is fast in signature generation process and consumes less energy compared to other post-quantum signature schemes. However, NTRUSign is slow in signature verification and it occupies the biggest space of RAM memory (49 MB).

The NTRU cryptosystem has been broken by recent attacks that use special structures of the rings used in those schemes. Recently, Bernstein et al. [3] proposed a new variant of NTRU, called "NTRU Prime" to avoid the weaknesses of NTRU, and proved that it is IND-CCA2 secure. They submitted this work to NIST's "Post-Quantum Cryptography Standardization Project".

The Rainbow signature scheme provided the shortest signature, 7 times smaller than the NTRUSign and 31 times smaller than the XMSS scheme. It is fast and fairly similar to the NTRUSign scheme in signing operation. Unfortunately, it is the worst scheme in terms of key pair generation time, key pair size, and consumption energy. In security, Rainbow scheme is still uncertain.

The verification speed of XMSS was good. It has small private- and publickey and consumes less energy. However, it provides the biggest signature among post-quantum signature schemes and its signing speed is very slow. Concerning the security of

XMSS, Hülsing et al. [21] presented a multi-target attack against hash-based signature schemes like SPHINCS and XMSS.

Based on our experimental results and discussion, we summarized the advantages and the limitations of each tested scheme in 5.

7   Conclusion

In this work, we have presented results of performance benchmarks of implemented different post-quantum schemes on smart mobile devices. Based on the experimental results, we have compared the studied schemes from the viewpoints of computational time, required memory, and power consumption.

In code-based cryptography, the encryption operation is faster than other PQC and it seems to have the most important security, but it uses large keys. Recently, it was improved to generate small key sizes. The optimisation of de-cryption operation and the minimization of the consumption energy are further studies.

NTRUEncrypt and NTRUSign schemes gave the best results compared to other schemes, it should be noted that NTRUSign uses some improvement for memory consumption when generating digital signatures. The Rainbow scheme is very fast and it generates the lowest signature sizes, but it takes too long to generate its key pair which lead to great energy consumptions. The XMSS scheme has lower key sizes, and acceptable signature generation speeds, however the generated signature is too big and could use some optimizations in that regard. The most posed problem in NTRU, Rainbow, and XMSS schemes is the security, there are various detected attacks in these schemes in the last years.

Finally, we mention that the selection of the post-quantum scheme depends on its performance, its security, and the context in which it will be used.

References

1. Berger, T.P., Cayrel, P.-L., Gaborit, P., Otmani, A.: Reducing key length of the McEliece cryptosystem. In: Preneel, B. (ed.) AFRICACRYPT 2009. LNCS, vol. 5580, pp. 77–97. Springer, Heidelberg (2009). https://doi.org/10.1007/978-3-642-02384-2_6
2. Bernstein, Daniel J., Chou, T., Schwabe, P.: McBits: fast constant-time code-based cryptography. In: Bertoni, G., Coron, J.-S. (eds.) CHES 2013. LNCS, vol. 8086, pp. 250–272. Springer, Heidelberg (2013). https://doi.org/10.1007/978-3-642-40349-1_15
3. Bernstein, D.J., Chuengsatiansup, C., Lange, T., van Vredendaal, C.: NTRUPrime: reducing attack surface at low cost (2017). https://ntruprime.cryp.to/papers.html
4. Boledovi̇c, A., Varga, J.: Practical implementation of McEliece cryptosystem on Android. In: 16th Central European Conference on Cryptology (CECC 2016) (2016)
5. Buchmann, J., Dahmen, E., Hülsing, A.: XMSS - a practical forward secure signature scheme based on minimal security assumptions. In: Yang, B.-Y. (ed.) PQCrypto 2011. LNCS, vol. 7071, pp. 117–129. Springer, Heidelberg (2011). https://doi.org/10.1007/978-3-642-25405-5_8
6. Chen, L., et al.: Report on post-quantum cryptography (2016)

7. Chen, R., Peng, D.: A novel NTRU-based handover authentication scheme forwireless networks. IEEE Commun. Lett. **22**(3), 586–589 (2018)
8. Chikouche, N., Cherif, F., Cayrel, P.L., Benmohammed, M.: RFID authentication protocols based on error-correcting codes: a survey. Wirel. Pers. Commun. **96**(1), 509–527 (2017)
9. Cho, J.Y., Griesser, H., Rafique, D.: A McEliece-based key exchange protocol for optical communication systems. In: Baldi, M., Quaglia, Elizabeth A., Tomasin, S. (eds.) WCS 2017. LNEE, vol. 447, pp. 109–123. Springer, Cham (2018). https://doi.org/10.1007/978-3-319-59265-7_8
10. Courtois, Nicolas T., Finiasz, M., Sendrier, N.: How to achieve a McEliece-based digital signature scheme. In: Boyd, C. (ed.) ASIACRYPT 2001. LNCS, vol. 2248, pp. 157–174. Springer, Heidelberg (2001). https://doi.org/10.1007/3-540-45682-1_10
11. D-Wave Systems Inc.: The D-Wave 2000Q quantum computer: technology overview (2017). http://www.dwavesys.com/
12. Daniel, A., Lejla, B., et al.: Initial recommendations of long-term secure postquantum systems. PQCRYPTO. EU. Horizon **2020 ICT-645622** (2015)
13. Ding, J., Schmidt, D.: Rainbow, a new multivariable polynomial signature scheme. In: Ioannidis, J., Keromytis, A., Yung, M. (eds.) ACNS 2005. LNCS, vol. 3531, pp. 164–175. Springer, Heidelberg (2005). https://doi.org/10.1007/11496137_12
14. Dods, C., Smart, N.P., Stam, M.: Hash based digital signature schemes. In: Smart, Nigel P. (ed.) Cryptography and Coding 2005. LNCS, vol. 3796, pp. 96–115. Springer, Heidelberg (2005). https://doi.org/10.1007/11586821_8
15. Eisenbarth, T., Güneysu, T., Heyse, S., Paar, C.: MicroEliece: McEliece for embedded devices. In: Clavier, C., Gaj, K. (eds.) CHES 2009. LNCS, vol. 5747, pp. 49–64. Springer, Heidelberg (2009). https://doi.org/10.1007/978-3-642-04138-9_4
16. FlexiProvider homepage. https://www.flexiprovider.de/. Accessed 2 March 2018
17. Heyse, S.: Post quantum cryptography: implementing alternative public key schemes on embedded devices. Ph.D. thesis, Ruhr-University Bochum, Germany (2013)
18. Hoffstein, J., Howgrave-Graham, N., Pipher, J., Silverman, Joseph H., Whyte, W.: NTRUSign: digital signatures using the NTRU lattice. In: Joye, M. (ed.) CT-RSA 2003. LNCS, vol. 2612, pp. 122–140. Springer, Heidelberg (2003). https://doi.org/10.1007/3-540-36563-X_9
19. Hoffstein, J., Pipher, J., Silverman, Joseph H.: NTRU: a ring-based public key cryptosystem. In: Buhler, Joe P. (ed.) ANTS 1998. LNCS, vol. 1423, pp. 267–288. Springer, Heidelberg (1998). https://doi.org/10.1007/BFb0054868
20. Huelsing, A., Butin, D., Gazdag, S., Rijneveld, J., Mohaisen, A.: XMSS: eXtended Merkle Signature Scheme. RFC 8391 (May 2018). https://www.rfc-editor.org/rfc/rfc8391.txt
21. Hülsing, A., Rijneveld, J., Song, F.: Mitigating multi-target attacks in hash-based signatures. In: Cheng, C.-M., Chung, K.-M., Persiano, G., Yang, B.-Y. (eds.) PKC 2016. LNCS, vol. 9614, pp. 387–416. Springer, Heidelberg (2016). https://doi.org/10.1007/978-3-662-49384-7_15
22. Jarvis, K., Nevins, M.: ETRU: NTRU over the Eisenstein integers. Des. Codesand Cryptogr. **74**(1), 219–242 (2015)
23. Kobara, K., Imai, H.: Semantically secure McEliece public-key cryptosystems -conversions for McEliece PKC -. In: Kim, K. (ed.) PKC 2001. LNCS, vol. 1992, pp. 19–35. Springer, Heidelberg (2001). https://doi.org/10.1007/3-540-44586-2_2
24. Li, D., Chen, H., Zhong, C., Li, T., Wang, F.: A new self-certified signature schemebased on NTRUSing for smart mobile communications. Wirel. Pers. Commun. **96**(3), 4263–4278 (2017)
25. McEliece, R.J.: A public-key system based on algebraic coding theory. Technical Report DSN Progress Report 44, Jet Propulsion Lab (1978)

26. Misoczki, R., Barreto, Paulo S.L.M.: Compact McEliece keys from goppa codes. In: Jacobson, Michael J., Rijmen, V., Safavi-Naini, R. (eds.) SAC 2009. LNCS, vol. 5867, pp. 376–392. Springer, Heidelberg (2009). https://doi.org/10.1007/978-3-642-05445-7_24
27. National security agency: cryptography today (2015). https://www.nsa.gov/ia/programs/suitebcryptography/
28. Niederreiter, H.: Knapsack-type cryptosystems and algebraic coding theory. Probl. Control. Inform. Theory **15**(2), 159–166 (1986)
29. NIST: post-quantum cryptography standardization (2016). https://csrc.nistgov/projects/post-quantum-cryptography
30. Petzoldt, A., Bulygin, S., Buchmann, J.: Selecting parameters for the rainbow signature scheme. In: Sendrier, N. (ed.) PQCrypto 2010. LNCS, vol. 6061, pp. 218–240. Springer, Heidelberg (2010). https://doi.org/10.1007/978-3-642-12929-2_16
31. Shor, P.: Polynomial-time algorithm for prime factorization and discrete logarithmson a quantum computer. In: Proceedings of the 35th Annual Symposium on Foundations of Computer Science, vol. 124 (1994)
32. Spongy Castle Homepage. https://rtyley.github.io/spongycastle/. Accessed 2 March 2018
33. Tayoub, W., Somia, L., Chikouche, N.: Implementation of public-key cryptographic systems on embedded devices (case: Computation speed). In: The First International Symposium on Informatics and its Applications (ISIA 2014) (2014)
34. Wang, W., Szefer, J., Niederhagen, R.: FPGA-based niederreiter cryptosystem using binary goppa codes. In: Lange, T., Steinwandt, R. (eds.) PQCrypto 2018. LNCS, vol. 10786, pp. 77–98. Springer, Cham (2018). https://doi.org/10.1007/978-3-319-79063-3_4

Investigating Dual Effects of Social Networking Sites

A. K. M. Najmul Islam[1(✉)], Matti Mäntymäki[1], Aaron W. Baur[2(✉)],
and Markus Bick[2]

[1] Turku School of Economics, University of Turku, Turku, Finland
{najmul.islam,matti.mantymaki}@utu.fi
[2] ESCP Europe Business School Berlin, Berlin, Germany
{abaur,mbick}@escpeurope.eu

Abstract. This paper investigates the dual effects (i.e. benefits and dangers) of a social networking site (SNS). Our dependent variables are subjective vitality and addiction. We employ self-determination theory (SDT), specifically the concepts of autonomous and controlled motivation and hypothesize that social enhancement and enjoyment represent autonomous motivation and contributes to subjective vitality while voyeurism and exhibitionism represent controlled motivation and contribute to SNS addiction. We test our hypotheses with data from 289 student Facebook users using Partial Least Squares (PLS). The results suggest that both social enhancement and enjoyment predict subjective vitality. In contrast, exhibitionism is the sole predictor of SNS addiction while voyeurism has no effect.

Keywords: Social networking sites · Addiction · SNS addiction
Subjective vitality · Voyeurism · Exhibitionism · Enjoyment

1 Introduction

Social networking sites (SNSs) have become a prominent venue for social interaction. Nearly 80% of the Internet users use social networking sites such as Facebook, the Russian vKontakte or the Chinese equivalent Renren. The most popular SNS, Facebook, has more than 2 billion users globally.

SNSs offer their users various ways for communication, social interaction and self presentation (Mäntymäki and Islam 2014, 2016). Good social relationships and interaction with other people support one's psychological well-being. Considering the number of SNS users globally, it is particularly interesting to investigate to what extent SNS use supports user's psychological well-being (Islam et al. 2018). For example, receiving positive feedbacks on posted content may increase an individual's self-esteem and well-being (Valkenburg et al. 2006).

The IS research is traditionally emphasized performance improvement as the main benefit of IT use (Davis 1989; DeLone and McLean 2003; Venkatesh et al. 2012). The performance improvement has traditionally been conceptualized as (work) efficiency gains. In addition, due to the proliferation of hedonic IS and consumer use of IT the

S. A. Al-Sharhan et al. (Eds.): I3E 2018, LNCS 11195, pp. 81–101, 2018.
https://doi.org/10.1007/978-3-030-02131-3_10

hedonic outcomes have gained increasing interest (Turel and Serenko 2012; Van der Heijden 2004; Venkatesh et al. 2012).

However, individual's psychological well-being as an outcome of IT use, particularly in the SNS context, has thus far received only limited attention in prior IS research. To fill this research gap, we explore what increases individuals' subjective vitality (i.e., an aspect of well-being) in an SNS use context. In practice, we argue that social enhancement and enjoyment are the two drivers of subjective vitality.

At the same time, there is an increasing awareness that the accelerated sharing caused by the pervasive use of social networking sites is not entirely positive but is also related to adverse phenomena such as voyeurism, exhibitionism (Munar 2010), and addiction (Andreassen et al. 2012). Prior IS research suggested that hedonic systems like SNSs, games, etc. would be more addictive than utilitarian system (Turel and Serenko 2012). In general, technology producing thrills or filling socio-psychological voids in users' lives are more addictive than others (Young 2010). By participating in an SNS, an individual fills his/her social voids and experiences thrills, and thus he/she becomes addicted to the SNS (Turel and Serenko 2012).

Turel and Serenko (2012) found that majority of prior technology addiction research investigated the consequences of technology addiction. Technology addiction can affect adversely on individual, organizational, and societal levels. Possible technology addiction outcomes include productivity losses (Yellowless and Marks 2007), health problems (Block 2008), worsening academic performance (Kuss and Griffiths 2011), and additional treatment costs (Xu et al. 2012). There is a lack of research on understanding antecedents/determinants of technology addiction (Turel and Serenko 2012). To fill this second research gap, we explore factors that might contribute to SNS addiction. As a result, we place voyeurism and exhibitionism motivations as factors driving SNS addiction.

To recap, SNS use can bring both benefits and dangers to the users. Therefore, this paper examines the dual effect of SNS use. In doing so, we extend the scope of IS research from examining only either benefits (DeLone and McLean 2003; Venkatesh et al. 2012) or dangers (Turel et al. 2011; Xu et al. 2012) towards a parallel investigation of both positive and negative side of IT use (Mäntymäki and Islam 2016).

The remainder of this paper is organized as follows. In Sect. 2 we present the theoretical foundations. Section 3 is dedicated to hypotheses development and Sect. 4 presents the research method. Section 5 presents data analysis results and discussions. Finally, Sect. 6 discusses limitations and future research.

2 Theoretical Foundations

2.1 Subjective Vitality

The concept of vitality has been theorized as an important idea within diverse theoretical frameworks (Ryan and Deci 2008). According to the Oxford English Dictionary, an individual with vitality has vigour and liveliness, a general energy for life. When vital, individuals experience a sense of enthusiasm, aliveness, and energy available to the self (Ryan and Fredrick 1997).

As one cannot, in principle, directly measure the energy available to the self, Ryan and Fredrick (1997) suggested exploring vitality as a subjective variable. In relation to this, Akin (2012) defined subjective vitality as the subjective experience of being full of energy and alive. Furthermore, subjective vitality is considered as an aspect of eudaimonic well-being, as being vital and energetic is part of what it means to be fully functioning and psychologically well (Ryan and Deci 2001).

Prior research on psychology and medicine has empirically found that subjective vitality is robustly associated with both behavioural and health outcomes (e.g., Pennix et al. 2000; Ryan and Deci 2008; Thayer 1996). This assertion has been supported by neuroscientific research that has shown that when experiencing vitality, specific configurations in the brain are activated (Barrett et al. 2004). Consequently, subjective vitality has been linked to other positively toned and energized states such as feelings of vigour (McNair et al. 1971), calm energy (Thayer 1996), and activated positive affect (Watson and Tellegen 1985). Vital individuals have been found more active and productive and possess better abilities to cope with stress and challenges (Ryan and Deci 2008). In addition, vital individuals are less vulnerable to illness, have better mental health as well as are more resilient to physical and viral stressors (Pennix et al. 2000; Ryan and Deci 2008).

Ryan and Deci (2008) argued subjective vitality as a complex and dynamic outcome that is influenced by social and psychological factors. They pointed that social events could leave even a well-nourished person feeling excited and energized, or alternatively stressed, angelic, and drained. As SNSs have become an integral part of people's social life, it is important for IS researchers to investigate what factors influence individual's subjective vitality in the SNS use context.

Prior psychology literature conceptualized subjective vitality in two ways: individual difference level (Ryan and Frederick 1997) and state level (Nix et al. 1999). In this paper, we have adopted the state level conceptualization of subjective vitality (i.e., the energy felt during SNS use). Consequently, we define subjective vitality as the subjective experience of being full of energy and alive during SNS use.

Although the concept of subjective vitality has never been explored in IS research, we argue that it can be linked to several IS constructs. We suggest two research directions for IS researchers related to subjective vitality. First, IS researchers may explore the outcomes of subjective vitality. For example, subjective vitality may improve individuals' productivity in an organization, and ability to innovate with IT. Second, examining the antecedents of subjective vitality such as design features of the IT artifact or user motivation would be meaningful for IS researchers.

2.2 Addiction

The concept of addiction is frequently used in clinical and behavioural science (Marlatt et al. 1988). Addiction is defined as a repetitive habit pattern that increases the risk of disease and/or associated personal and social problems, often experienced subjectively as "loss of control" [that] continues despite volitional attempts to abstain or moderate use (Marlatt et al. 1988, p. 224).

Addiction has six symptoms as suggested by prior literature (Brown 1993; Griffiths 2005; Andreassen et al. 2012). These are: (1) Salience: meaning that the activity dominates thinking and behaviour; (2) Mood modification: meaning that the activity modifies/improves mood; (3) Tolerance: meaning that an increasing amount of activity is required for the purpose of remaining satisfied; (4) Withdrawal: meaning that when the activity is discontinued or suddenly reduced, the individual experiences panic, anxiety, agitation, or other unpleasant feelings; (5) Conflict: meaning that the activity causes conflicts in relationships, in work/studies, and other activities; (6) Relapse: meaning that the tendency to revert to earlier patterns of the activity after abstinence or control.

Since the early 1990s, psychology researchers have been investigating the phenomenon of technology dependencies or technology addictions (Kubey and Csikszentmihalyi 2002). Technology addictions are a type of behavioural addiction that does not involve any external chemical substance (Marks 1990). These addictions mainly occur when human interacts with machines (Widyanto and Griffiths 2006). They can be classified either as passive (e.g., radios, televisions, etc.) or active (e.g., computer games, Internet, online forums, SNSs, etc.), and include inducing and reinforcing features which may contribute to promote addictive tendencies (Griffiths 1995). This implies that Internet addiction or problematic use of the Internet can be viewed as a type of active technology addictions. Internet addictions like other behavioural addictions are often manifested through the six symptoms (salience, mood modification, tolerance, withdrawal, conflict, and relapse) that have been described above.

In psychology and clinical psychology (Andreassen et al. 2012; Cheung et al. 2013), SNS addiction falls under the broad category of problematic use of the Internet. Diverse terminologies have been used in prior literature in order to refer problematic use of the Internet such as "Internet Addiction Disorder", "Pathological Internet Use", "Problematic Internet Use", "Excessive Internet Use", "Compulsive Internet Use", Cyberspace Addiction, Online Addiction, Net Addiction, Internet Addicted Disorder, and High Internet Dependency (Widyanto and Griffiths 2006; Douglas et al. 2008; Cheung et al. 2013). Altogether, as pointed out by Turel et al. (2011), the issue of problematic use of IT is relatively new in the IS literature, and scientific understanding of this issue is still evolving.

Young (1996) conducted the first ground-breaking research study on the problematic use of Internet. Following this, several researchers defined Internet addiction. For example, Mitchell (2000, p. 632) defines Internet Addiction Disorder as "the compulsive overuse of the Internet and the irritable or moody behaviour when deprived of it". Rice (2005) defined Internet Addiction as a proclivity toward compulsive use of the Internet that interferes with one's ability to lead a normal life. Shapira et al. (2003) conceptualized problematic Internet use as an impulse control disorder in which an individual experiences rising tension or arousal before Internet use and a sense of relief or pleasure after completion of the behaviour. Internet addiction is characterized by one's inability to control his/her dependence on the Internet, leading to feelings of distress and functional impairments of daily activities (Shapira et al. 2000). Beard (2005) defined it as an individual's psychological state, which includes both mental and emotional states, as well as their scholastic, occupational and social interactions, is impaired by the overuse of the medium.

To sum up, all these definitions capture one or more symptoms of behavioural addictions. This accords with the suggestions to conceptualize addiction using six core symptoms of behavioural addictions (e.g., Charlton and Danforth 2007; Davis et al. 2002; Young 1998). Following this, we conceptualize SNS addiction as the degree of a user's psychological dependency on the SNS, and the magnitude of the associated behavioural addiction symptoms.

2.3 Motivations

Social Enhancement

Social enhancement is the value that an individual derives from gaining acceptance and approval from other SNS members, and the enhancement of one's social status within his/her community (Dholakia et al. 2004). Building one's accurate perceptions of the self is important for his future mental health (Taylor and Brown 1989). Individuals generally want to see themselves and be seen by others in a positive light, and thus they employ different strategies to enhance their social image (McCaslin et al. 2010). Recognition from others has been found as one of the driving forces behind joining virtual communities (Hars and Ou 2002).

Horvath and Morf (2010) argued that narcissists and genuine self-esteemed individuals follow different strategies for social enhancement. Narcissists exploit self-enhancement opportunities primarily by augmenting self-ratings on positive traits while nonnarcissists self-present themselves more moderately and use more socially accepted discounting of negative traits. In this paper, we conceptualize social enhancement as a non-narcissistic tendency to present accurate image of oneself in an SNS platform.

Prior IS research has successfully used the concept of image, a variable similar to social enhancement (Moore and Benbasat 1991; Venkatesh and Davis 2000). It has been found that individuals' technology usage behaviour is motivated by image (e.g., Venkatesh and Davis 2000).

Hedonic Motivation

Due to the advent of systems such as computer and console games, virtual worlds and SNSs, hedonic uses of IS have become increasingly important. Hedonic systems aim to provide self-fulfilling values such as fun, and pleasure to the users. Hence, the focus on motivational drivers of system use has shifted from extrinsic to intrinsic reflections, such as perceived enjoyment (Van der Heijden 2004; Turel and Serenko 2012). Intrinsic motivation refers to the activity spawned by the pleasure of action (Ryan and Frederick 1997) and drives voluntary activity done for no apparent reinforcement other than the process of performing the activity per se (de Charms 1968).

Prior IS literature has successfully used the concept of intrinsic motivation. Venkatesh (2000) found intrinsic motives are important for system use decisions. Van der Heijden (2004) even found perceived enjoyment (i.e., an intrinsic motivation) as more important than perceived usefulness in predicting intention to use hedonic systems. Perceived enjoyment was also found important predicting habit and engagement in SNS usage context (Turel and Serenko 2012). Based on these findings, we decided to use perceived enjoyment as the proxy of hedonic motivation. We conceptualize perceived enjoyment as the extent to which the activity of using an SNS is perceived to be enjoyable in its own right (Davis et al. 1992).

Voyeurism

Traditionally, the concept of voyeurism has referred to the sexual interest in or practice of spying on people who are naked or who are engaged in sexual activities, or other actions that are usually considered private in nature (Hirschfeld 1938).

The most extreme behavioural manifestations of voyeurism are clinically regarded as abnormal sexual behaviour. American Psychiatric Association's (APA) Diagnostic and Statistical Manual of Mental Disorders (DSM-IV 1994) offers the following psychiatric diagnostic criteria for voyeurism:

A. Over a period of at least 6 months, recurrent, intense sexually arousing fantasies, sexual urges, or behaviors involving the act of observing an unsuspecting person who is naked, in the process of disrobing, or engaging in sexual activity.
B. The person has acted on these sexual urges, or the sexual urges or fantasies cause marked distress or interpersonal difficulty.

Today, as pointed out by Calvert (2000), voyeurism does not necessarily include sexuality. In the context of media use, Calvert (2000, p. 2) defines voyeurism as "the consumption of revealing images of and information about other's apparently real and unguarded lives, often yet not always for purposes of entertainment but frequently at the expense of privacy and disclosure, through the mass media and Internet." Many everyday activities such as watching reality TV can be driven by voyeuristic motives without any sexual connotation. In this paper, we conceptualize voyeurism as pleasure derived by accessing others' private content in SNSs (Metzl 2004).

Exhibitionism

Exhibitionism refers to self-disclosure "process of making the self, known to others" (Jourard and Lasakow 1958, p. 91). With regard to exhibitionism, the self-disclosure is not driven by building trust to develop interpersonal relationships (see e.g. Joinson et al. 2008). Rather, the self-disclosure is driven by one's narcissistic tendency (Ames et al. 2006; Brunell et al. 2011; Carpenter 2012) to demonstrate superiority and to seek for admiration from other people in order to build a desirable self-image. To this end, Oxford English Dictionary defines exhibitionism as an extravagant behaviour that is intended to attract attention to oneself and Webster's Ninth Collegiate Dictionary defines it as the act of practice of behaving so as to attract attention to oneself.

As a psychological trait in the general population, exhibitionism is not overtly negative or harmful like for example manipulation of others or hostility. Rather, it indicates extraversion and low impulse control (Panek et al. 2013). Furthermore, exhibitionism is considered as a first order-component of narcissistic personality (Ames et al. 2006; Raskin and Terry 1988). A combination of self-absorption, vanity, superiority, and exhibitionistic tendencies that illustrates the features of self-love and theatrical selfpresentation is labeled grandiose exhibitionism (Ackerman et al. 2011).

Exhibitionism is diagnosed with the following criteria (DSM-IV 1994):

A. Over a period of at least 6 months, recurrent, intense sexually arousing fantasies, sexual urges, or behaviours involving the exposure of one's genitals to an unsuspecting stranger.
B. The fantasies, sexual urges, or behaviours cause clinically significant distress or impairment in social, occupational, or other important areas of functioning.

People's self-disclosure in SNSs can be driven by exhibitionism as a narcissistic trait (Carpenter 2012). In this paper, we do not consider exhibitionism as a psychopathological condition but conceptualize it as a pleasure derived from disclosing private information online in order to gain superiority.

3   Hypotheses Development

3.1   The Bright Side: Social Enhancement and Perceived Enjoyment as Predictors of Subjective Vitality

Prior psychology research differentiated between autonomous and controlled motivations (Ryan and Frederick 1997). An individual can be motivated to act in a particular way by external compulsion (i.e., controlled motivations) or out of inwardly endorsed motives such as personal interests or values (i.e., autonomous motivations). Intrinsic motivations have been regarded as autonomous by definition, which means that they are experienced as emanating from one's self, whereas extrinsic motivations vary in the degree to which they are autonomous versus controlled (Deci and Ryan 1991).

We argue that social enhancement and hedonic motivations are autonomous. Actions for enhancing social status and enjoyment in SNSs are self-determined. Koopmans and Sremac (2011) pointed that presenting authentic self is autonomous. Based on this, it is logical to assume that the act of enhancing self or building one's appropriate image is autonomous. Prior IS research also suggested enjoyment as an intrinsic motivation (Van der Heijden 2004) and hence it is autonomous by definition (Ryan and Frederick 1997). Individuals act with an internal perceived locus of causality in SNSs in order to gain social enhancement, and enjoyment (Deci and Ryan 1991).

When people are intrinsically motivated or autonomously extrinsically motivated, they will feel their energy enhanced (Nix et al. 1999). Consequently, it is logical to assume that social enhancement and enjoyment may enhance an individual's subjective vitality. Based on this we propose the following two hypotheses.

H1. Social enhancement positively influences subjective vitality

H2. Enjoyment positively influences subjective vitality

We also argue that the other two motivations: exhibitionism and voyeurism are controlled motivations and hence these would not have any influence on subjective vitality. Voyeuristic people look for content that they cannot otherwise see in an SNS. These people do so due to their curiosity or comparing themselves with others to maintain self-esteem. Exhibitionist people look for opportunities to show that they are superior to others by presenting a possible self-image in an SNS. They do such activities because of a pressure to maintain self-esteem. Both voyeuristic and exhibitionistic behaviours are governed by a regulatory process within an individual that is experienced as a pressure or demand. Prior psychology research suggests that behaviours that are executed because of pressure or demand are controlled in nature (Nix et al. 1999). Thus, exhibitionism and voyeurism are controlled form of behaving and are not likely to enhance subjective vitality (Deci and Ryan 1991).

3.2   The Dark Side: Voyeurism and Exhibitionism as Predictors of Addiction

Prior psychiatric literature suggests that exhibitionism and voyeurism are addictive sexual behaviours (Coleman-Kennedy and Pendley 2002; Roller 2004). Following this, we argue that the exhibitionistic and voyeuristic motivations would make individuals addicted to the SNS.

Prior IS research on addiction suggests that excessive use of IS may develop habit which eventually lead to addiction (Turel and Serenko 2012). Following this finding, we argue that voyeuristic and exhibitionistic individuals use SNSs heavily and thus these people become addicted. The logical basis of this argument is that voyeurism cannot exist without disclosure whereas exhibitionists require an audience. Both types of individuals depend on each other (i.e., control each other) in an SNS platform. Both types of individuals require acceptance from each other to raise their self-esteem (Silverstein 1996). In the process of gaining acceptance from others, exhibitionistic people spend huge amount of time to constantly post contents while voyeuristic people spend huge amount of time to constantly consume contents posted by others. Eventually, many people start to post contents publicly over real friends (Kuss and Griffiths 2012). Similarly, many individuals start to consume contents of unknown people. Spending hours in an SNS can lead to significant behavioural and psychological problems. For instance, they might feel a compulsion to use the SNS to meet their exhibitionistic and voyeuristic needs. Consequently, we propose the following two hypotheses.

H3. Voyeurism positively influences addiction to SNS

H4. Exhibitionism positively influences addiction to SNS

We also argue that the autonomous motivations: social enhancement and enjoyment are not expected to influence addiction. Addictive behaviours are compulsive. It means that an addict performs his addictive behaviour because he experiences an irresistible urge to do it. The addict performs the act repeatedly and unable to stop it. The act is not something that the addict does out of his/her self-choice. This implies that autonomous motivations are not expected to influence addiction. Koopmans and Sremac (2011) pointed that addiction might be incompatible with autonomy as addiction is often been equated with loss of control, powerlessness, and unmanageability.

3.3   Controlling for Habit

Prior IS literature found habit (i.e., the extent to which people tend to perform behaviours automatically because of learning) as a significant determinant of addiction (Turel and Serenko 2012). Consequently, we decided to control the effect of habit on addiction and subjective vitality in this paper. Figure 1 below summarizes the hypothesized relationships.

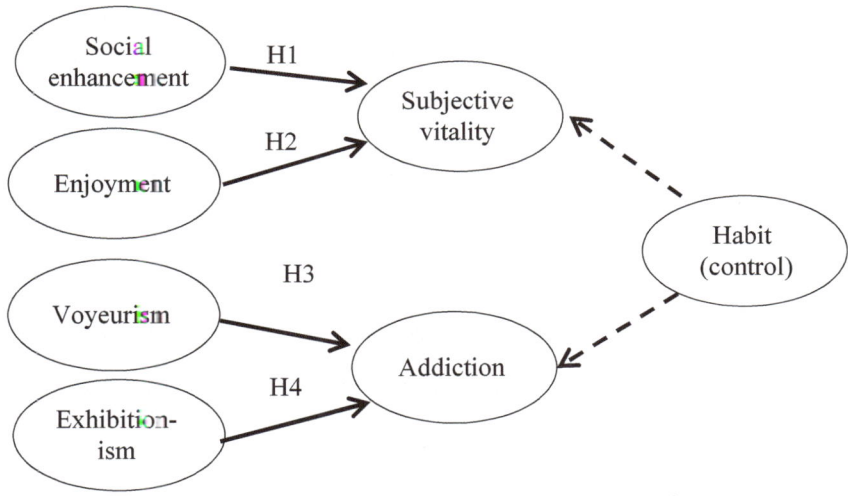

Fig. 1. The research model

4 Study Design

4.1 Instrument Development

The items were measured using five-point Likert scale, with answer choices ranging from "Strongly disagree (1)" to "Strongly agree (5)". Items were adopted from the prior literature with minor changes in wording reflecting the target context. The measures of habit were adapted from Limayem et al. (2007). The measures of social enhancement and enjoyment were adapted from Dholakia et al. (2004) and Davis et al. (1992) respectively. The measures of exhibitionism were adapted from Ames et al. (2006) while the measures of voyeurism were adapted from Nabi et al. (2006) and Bagdasarov et al. (2010). Finally, the measures of subjective vitality and addiction to SNS were adapted from Bostic et al. (2000) and Andreassen et al. (2012) respectively.

After the questionnaire was drafted, it was first sent to two senior scholars for a review. Based on their comments, some items were adjusted to make the wordings more precise. The final questionnaire items are shown in Table 1.

4.2 Data Collection

The data was collected with an online survey among student of a Finnish university. The respondents were randomly selected from a sample that in turn was randomly selected from student database. The survey was sent to altogether 1,500 respondents. Altogether 289 usable responses were received. This yielded to a response rate of 19.27%. 68% of the respondents were female.

To investigate the possible non-respondent bias, we ran a series of independent samples t-tests. The respondents were first divided into two groups based on the median date of completion of the survey and then compared their responses on subjective

Table 1. Construct items' averages, standard deviations (std.), and loadings

Construct	Item	Mean	Std.	Loading	P value
Habit (Limayem et al. 2007)	HABIT1: Using Facebook has become automatic to me	3.53	1.31	0.888	<0.001
	HABIT2: Using Facebook is natural to me	3.57	1.13	0.880	<0.001
	HABIT3: When I want to stay in touch with my friends, using Facebook is an obvious choice for me	3.55	1.20	0.806	<0.001
Social enhancement (Dholakia et al. 2004)	SOC1: Using Facebook helps me to impress other people	2.31	1.05	0.816	<0.001
	SOC2: Using Facebook helps me to express myself	2.75	1.18	0.832	<0.001
	SOC3: Using Facebook helps me to feel important	2.23	1.04	0.844	<0.001
	SOC4: Using Facebook helps me to project a desired image of myself	2.55	1.19	0.825	<0.001
Subjective vitality (Bostic et al. Bostic et al. 2000)	SV1: When I use Facebook, I feel alive	1.79	0.98	0.809/0.822	<0.001
	SV2: When I use Facebook, I don't feel very energetic	2.56	1.17	0.299	<0.001
	SV3: When I use Facebook, sometimes I feel so alive I just want to burst	1.72	0.78	0.844/0.843	<0.001
	SV4: When I use Facebook, I have energy and spirit	1.95	0.91	0.860/0.854	<0.001
	SV5: When I use Facebook, I feel I am fully living	1.59	0.82	0.830/0.843	<0.001
Addiction to SNS (Andreassen et al. 2012)	ADDICT1: I spend a lot of time thinking about Facebook or plan use of Facebook	1.51	0.80	0.672/0.706	<0.001
	ADDICT2: I feel an urge to use Facebook more and more	1.45	0.76	0.817/0.809	<0.001
	ADDICT3: I use Facebook in order to forget about personal problems	1.33	0.77	0.567	<0.001
	ADDICT4: I have tried to cut down on the use of Facebook without success	1.66	1.05	0.634	<0.001
	ADDICT5: I become restless or troubled if I am prohibited from using Facebook	1.57	1.01	0.772/0.795	<0.001
	ADDICT6: I use Facebook so much that it has a negative impact on my studies/work	1.53	0.94	0.806/0.803	<0.001

(*continued*)

Table 1. (*continued*)

Construct	Item	Mean	Std.	Loading	P value
Exhibitionism (Ames et al. 2006)	EXHIBIT1: I really like to be the center of attention on Facebook	2.19	1.11	0.776	<0.001
	EXHIBIT2: I am apt to show off on Facebook if I get the chance	2.13	1.14	0.739	<0.001
	EXHIBIT3: I get upset when people don't comment/put a like on my posts in Facebook	2.77	1.40	0.851	<0.001
	EXHIBIT4: I get into a bad mood if people don't comment/put like on my posts on Facebook	1.93	1.16	0.720	<0.001
Enjoyment (Davis et al. 1992)	HED1: Using Facebook is enjoyable	2.98	0.99	0.864	<0.001
	HED2: Using Facebook is pleasurable	3.23	0.99	0.898	<0.001
	HED3: Using Facebook is fun	3.42	0.95	0.852	<0.001
	HED4: Using Facebook is exciting	2.68	1.01	0.717	<0.001
	HED5: Using Facebook is interesting	3.29	0.98	0.832	<0.001
Voyeurism (Nabi et al. 2006; Bagdasarov et al. 2010)	VOYEUR1: I enjoy viewing Facebook because it helps me get a peek into other's private moments	2.78	1.25	0.744	<0.001
	VOYEUR2: I like Facebook because it provides access to other people's information	2.64	1.25	0.798	<0.001
	VOYEUR3: I like Facebook because people don't know that I am accessing their information	2.36	1.36	0.865	<0.001
	VOYEUR4: I like watching people when they don' t know that they are being watched	2.14	1.22	0.858	<0.001
	VOYEUR5: I get satisfaction out of watching others when they are unaware	1.64	0.99	0.778	<0.001

Note: Items in Italic were removed due to low loadings

vitality, addiction, habit, social enhancement, voyeurism, exhibitionism and enjoyment (Armstrong and Overton 1977). The test did not reveal any statistically significant differences between the early and late responses, supporting the notion that non-response bias was not a major concern in our study.

4.3   Data Analysis

Partial least squares (PLS) approach with WarpPLS was utilized in the analysis. PLS is a second-generation regression method that combines confirmatory factor analysis with linear regression, and this makes it possible to run the measurement and structural models simultaneously. A rule of thumb for the required sample size in PLS is that the sample should be at least ten times the most complicated multiple regressions in the model (Barclay et al. 1995). The sample size in this paper fulfils this criterion well.

We followed Gefen and Straub's (2005) procedure to test convergent and discriminant validity. Convergent validity indicates the extent to which the items of a scale that are theoretically related are also related in reality. Convergent validity is ensured by comparing the item loadings, composite reliability (CR), and average variance extracted (AVE) values. Fornell and Larcker (1981) recommended path-loading values at least 0.7 to be acceptable. Based on this criterion, SV2 from subjective vitality construct was removed. Similarly, ADDICT3, and ADDICT4 have been removed from addiction construct. From Table 2, we observe that all the constructs have composite reliability values between 0.855 and 0.920, fulfilling the recommended value proposed by Nunnally (1978). Finally, all AVE values exceed the threshold of 0.5 as recommended by Fornell and Larcker (1981).

Table 2. Correlations between latent variables and squared root of average variance extracted

Construct	AVE	CR	ENJ	SE	EXHIBIT	VOYEUR	SV	ADDICT	HABIT
ENJ	0.697	0.920	**0.835**						
SE	0.688	0.898	0.463	**0.829**					
EXHIBIT	0.598	0.855	0.385	0.608	**0.773**				
VOYEUR	0.656	0.905	0.251	0.373	0.433	**0.810**			
SV	0.706	0.906	0.429	0.368	0.276	0.173	**0.841**		
ADDICT	0.633	0.873	0.238	0.405	0.492	0.305	0.261	**0.796**	
HABIT	0.737	0.894	0.576	0.438	0.398	0.321	0.321	0.387	**0.859**

Note: Average variance extracted (AVE), Composite reliability (CR), Enjoyment (ENJ), Social enhancement (SE), Exhibitionism (EXHIBIT), Voyeurism (VOYEUR), Subjective vitality (SV), Addiction (ADDICT), Habit (HABIT)

Discriminant validity refers to whether the items measure the construct in question or other (related) constructs (Gefen and Straub 2005). We verified discriminant validity using correlation matrix and factor analysis. Table 2 shows the correlation matrix with the square root of AVE values presented diagonally. The square root of the AVE value for the variables is consistently greater than the off-diagonal correlation values, suggesting satisfactory discriminant validity between the variables (Fornell and Larcker 1981). The "item to latent variable correlation" values obtained from the confirmatory factor analysis are shown in Table 3. It shows that all items have cross-loadings coefficients lower than the factor loading on their respective assigned latent variable, suggesting that discriminant validity on the item level is met for all the constructs (Gefen and Straub 2005).

Overall, these tests of validity and reliability provided us with a high degree of confidence with the measures used in testing our research model.

5   Results and Discussions

5.1   PLS Results

The test of the structural model includes estimates of the path coefficients, which indicate the strengths of the relationships between the dependent and independent variables, and the R-square values, which represent the amount of variance explained by the independent variables. Figure 2 shows the results of the hypothesized structural model.

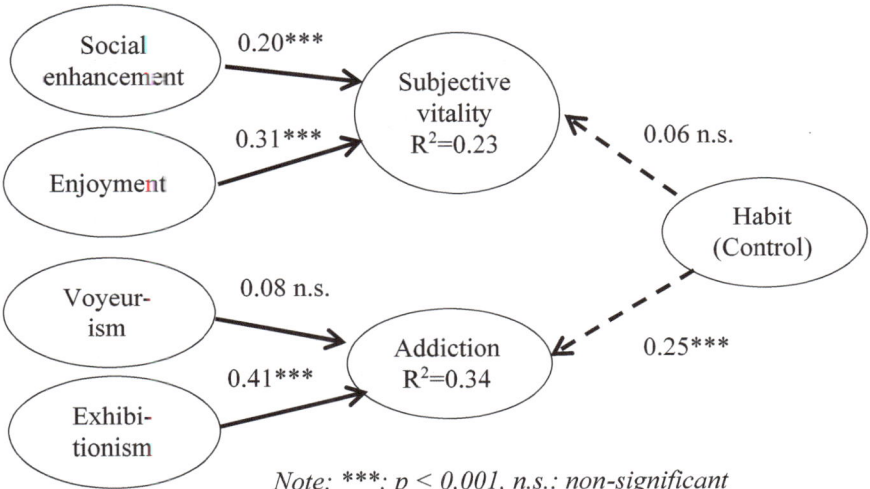

Note: ***: p < 0.001, n.s.: non-significant

Fig. 2. PLS results

As hypothesized, social enhancement ($\beta = 0.20$, $p < 0.001$) and perceived enjoyment ($\beta = 0.31$, $p < 0.001$) had significant effect on subjective vitality after controlling the effect of habit on it. The explained amount variance of subjective vitality by its predictors was 23%

Exhibitionism ($\beta = 0.41$, $p < 0.001$) had significant influence on addiction after controlling the influence of habit on it. Interestingly, voyeurism ($\beta = 0.08$, ns) had no-significant influence on addiction. Taken together, the determinants explained 34% of the variance in addiction.

5.2   Key Findings

We point out to two observations that we think are the most interesting. First, we found that both social enhancement and enjoyment influence subjective vitality. This finding implies that an accurate presentation of one's image and enjoyment experienced by communicating and interacting with peers in an SNS improves one's subjective vitality. For example, when one receives positive feedback for the content he/she has posted (e.g., pictures, profile information, etc.), it may influence his/her subjective vitality. It also provides him/her pleasure. Additionally, surfing around in SNS for a while may offer a refreshing break and help one to feel more energetic.

Second, we found that exhibitionism significantly predicted addiction to SNS while controlling for the influence of habit. This may imply that exhibitionists frequently post content and check how many people comment or 'like' in their updates. In doing so, they may feel an urge to use the SNS more and more and eventually develop addiction. Interestingly, we also found that individuals' voyeuristic behaviours had non-significant influence on addiction to SNS. The reason behind the non-significant relationship can be explained by the fact that the SNS under investigation (i.e. Face-book) contains more features to support exhibitionistic behaviours and fewer features to support voyeuristic behaviours. Features like updating status, check-in, posting photos, etc. that supports exhibitionistic behaviours can be accessed easily in both desktop and mobile versions of Facebook. These features are integrated in mobile devices in such a way that individuals can execute these features with just few taps. In contrast, voyeuristic activities like finding a person from outside of one's friend list and viewing his/her content require much effort. Recently, Facebook has introduced the Graph Search feature that has eased the process of finding and accessing the content on Facebook. However, the Graph Search feature has not been included yet in the Facebook applications for mobile devices. Additionally, it is still not available for all (e.g. Finnish) Facebook users. Nevertheless, the Graph Search will most likely con-siderably increase the voyeuristic value of Facebook.

5.3 Theoretical Implications

Our study has three theoretical implications for IS research. First, we advance the understanding of dual effect of IT. Prior IS research has mostly investigated either the positive (e.g. DeLone and MacLean 2003) or negative (e.g. Turel et al. 2011) effect of IT use. However, in this study we have shown that hedonic systems such as SNSs may lead to both positive and negative individual-level consequences. To this end, we included a benefit related variable (i.e., subjective vitality), and a danger related variable (i.e., addiction) in our research model as the dependent variables and examined their predictors.

Second, we accumulate the understanding of addiction in the SNS context. Prior IS research mostly implied that SNS enjoyment shapes habitual behaviour, which in turn leads to addiction (Turel and Serenko 2012). We found that exhibitionism is a sig-nificant predictor of addiction to SNSs after controlling the influence of habit. In fact, we found that the influence of exhibitionism on addiction was much stronger than that of habit.

Finally, drawing the concept of autonomous motivation (Deci and Ryan 1991), we hypothesized and empirically found that both social enhancement and enjoyment are significant predictors of subjective vitality. Despite its importance, prior IS research did not put enough effort investigating the concept of subjective vitality. We suggest future research investigating other autonomous motivations that influence subjective vitality.

Table 3. Item to latent variable correlations

Items	Enjoyment	Social enhancement	Exhibitionism	Voyeurism	Subjective vitality	Addiction	Habit
HED1	**0.864**	0.420	0.338	0.228	0.391	0.273	0.493
HED2	**0.898**	0.366	0.320	0.188	0.381	0.203	0.535
HED3	**0.852**	0.356	0.302	0.169	0.335	0.198	0.538
HED4	**0.717**	0.446	0.314	0.264	0.352	0.203	0.360
HED5	**0.832**	0.358	0.336	0.211	0.335	0.118	0.460
SOC1	0.333	**0.816**	0.552	0.305	0.255	0.397	0.306
SOC2	0.476	**0.832**	0.508	0.263	0.341	0.331	0.397
SOC3	0.369	**0.844**	0.471	0.271	0.340	0.300	0.365
SOC4	0.357	**0.825**	0.488	0.401	0.284	0.318	0.385
EXHIBIT1	0.331	0.522	**0.776**	0.257	0.240	0.407	0.322
EXHIBIT2	0.252	0.481	**0.739**	0.243	0.168	0.284	0.301
EXHIBIT3	0.360	0.512	**0.851**	0.425	0.271	0.416	0.375
EXHIBIT4	0.237	0.358	**0.720**	0.408	0.163	0.414	0.223
VOYEUR1	0.352	0.364	0.479	**0.744**	0.252	0.246	0.328
VOYEUR2	0.271	0.335	0.353	**0.798**	0.151	0.208	0.246
VOYEUR3	0.146	0.271	0.348	**0.865**	0.088	0.244	0.258
VOYEUR4	0.126	0.239	0.260	**0.858**	0.113	0.239	0.248
VOYEUR5	0.143	0.318	0.333	**0.778**	0.112	0.300	0.226
WB1	0.359	0.304	0.249	0.123	**0.822**	0.165	0.267
WB3	0.374	0.332	0.271	0.154	**0.843**	0.265	0.288
WB4	0.362	0.344	0.243	0.136	**0.854**	0.226	0.259
WB5	0.348	0.257	0.165	0.169	**0.843**	0.218	0.266

(continued)

Table 3. (*continued*)

Items	Enjoyment	Social enhancement	Exhibitionism	Voyeurism	Subjective vitality	Addiction	Habit
ADDICT1	0.264	0.363	0.394	0.240	0.217	**0.768**	0.341
ADDICT2	0.162	0.325	0.373	0.252	0.208	**0.839**	0.267
ADDICT5	0.203	0.289	0.442	0.234	0.177	**0.787**	0.315
ADDICT6	0.134	0.314	0.361	0.244	0.228	**0.788**	0.312
HABIT1	0.437	0.356	0.342	0.327	0.268	0.379	**0.888**
HABIT2	0.599	0.408	0.356	0.270	0.315	0.309	**0.880**
HABIT3	0.444	0.366	0.327	0.226	0.242	0.307	**0.806**

5.4   Practical Implications

Our study has three practical implications. First, it should be remembered that IT may have dual effects on individuals. Using an SNS may both improve user's subjective vitality but also create addiction. In addition, to identifying the psycho-social predictors such as the variables employed in this study, understanding the dual effect of SNS's use requires also understanding the use patterns and use context. For example, taking short breaks from work and surfing SNSs may improve individual's subjective vitality, however, spending hours or frequent SNS surfing might lead to addiction. We hope that organizational and governmental decision-makers pay increased attention to the potential dual effects of IT in general and SNS in particular. We hope that the decision makers consider the possibility that the increased IT use is not mechanistically positive, and that all uses are not equally beneficial, or harmful.

Second, we found that individual's exhibitionistic behaviours cause addiction. SNSs contain many features for performing exhibitionistic behaviours. For example, status updates, pictures, likes and comments are some of the features that exhibitionists might utilize to show off. (Mäntymäki and Islam 2016; Islam et al. 2018). To reduce the risk of addiction, we slightly provocatively suggest that SNS providers and their legislative regulators would consider whether the exhibitionistic appeal of SNSs could be constrained. For example, the number of status updates or photos per day or month could be limited to a certain maximum to reduce the adverse effects and time spent on SNSs.

Finally, we found that an SNS use can be a source of subjective vitality improvement as it affords portraying one's appropriate image and offers hedonic value. Based on this finding, we suggest organizations that have categorically banned, and occasionally even tried to prevent SNS use in the workplace to reconsider this decision.

6   Limitations and Future Research

Our study has a number of limitations that may serve as the avenue for future research. First, the research was cross-sectional. The beliefs of the users regarding a system will change as the users gain experience of a target system but such changes cannot be captured with the type of cross-sectional study undertaken. Thus, longitudinal research is necessary to overcome the issue. Second, the study has been conducted using a single SNS (Facebook) in a single Finnish university. Hence, generalizing the findings directly to other user groups or other SNSs is not an appropriate course of action. Third, we included only a few drivers of subjective vitality and addiction. Future studies could incorporate a more extensive set of drivers of subjective vitality and addiction. Finally, yet we focused on subjective vitality and addiction to capture the dual effect of SNS use, these two constructs are by no means an exhaustive presentation of the possible positive and negative outcomes. Thus, future research could aim at identifying additional positive and negative outcomes of SNS use.

References

Ackerman, R.A., Witt, E.A., Donnellan, M.B., Trzesniewski, K.H., Robins, R.W., Kashy, D.A.: What does the narcissistic personality inventory really measure? Assessment **18**(1), 67–87 (2011)

Akin, A.: The relationship between Internet addiction, subjective vitality, and subjective happiness. Cyberpsychology Behav. Soc. Netw. **15**(8), 404–410 (2012)

Ames, D.R., Rose, P., Anderson, C.P.: The NPI-16 as a short measure of narcissism. J. Res. Pers. **40**, 440–450 (2006)

Andreassen, C.S., Torsheim, T., Brunborg, G.S., Pallesen, S.: Development of a Facebook addiction scale. Psychol. Rep. **110**(2), 501–517 (2012)

Armstrong, J.S., Overton, T.: Estimating nonresponse bias in mail surveys. J. Mark. Res. **14**, 396–402 (1977)

Bagdasarov, Z., Greene, K., Banerjee, S.C., Krcmar, M., Yanovitzky, I., Ruginyte, D.: I am what I watch: Voyeurism, sensation seeking, and television viewing patterns. J. Broadcast. Electron. Media **54**(2), 299–315 (2010)

Barclay, D., Higgins, C., Thompson, R.: The partial least squares (PLS) approach to causal modeling: personal computer adoption and use as an illustration. Technol. Stud. **2**(2), 285–324 (1995)

Barrett, J., Della-Maggiore, V., Chouinard, P.A., Paus, T.: Mechanisms of action underlying the effect of repetitive transcranial magnetic stimulation on mood: behavioral and brain imaging studies. Neuropsychopharmacology **29**, 1172–1189 (2004)

Beard, K.: Internet addiction: a review of current assessment techniques and potential assessment questions. CyberPsychology Behav. **8**(1), 7–14 (2005)

Brown, R.I.F.: Some contributions of the study of gambling to the study of other addictions. In: Eadington, W.R., Cornelius, J. (eds.) Gambling behavior and problem gambling, pp. 341–372. University of Nevada Press, Reno (1993)

Block, J.J.: Issues for DSM-V: internet addiction. Am. J. Psychiatry **165**(3), 306–307 (2008)

Bostic, T.J., Rubio, D.M., Hood, M.: A validation of the subjective vitality scale using structural equation modeling. Soc. Indic. Res. **52**, 313–324 (2000)

Brunell, A.B., Staats, S., Barden, J., Hupp, J.M.: Narcissism and academic dishonesty: the exhibitionism dimension and the lack of guilt. Pers. Individ. Differ. **50**(3), 323–328 (2011)

Calvert, C.: Voyeur nation: media privacy, and peering in modern culture. Westview Press, Boulder (2000)

Carpenter, C.J.: Narcissism on Facebook: self-promotional and anti-social behaviour. Pers. Individ. Differ. **52**(4), 482–486 (2012)

Charlton, J.P., Danforth, I.D.W.: Distinguishing addiction and high engagement in the context of online game playing. Comput. Hum. Behav. **23**(3), 1531–1548 (2007)

Coleman-Kennedy, C., Pendley, A.: Assessment and diagnosis of sexual addiction. J. Am. Psychiatr. Nurses Assoc. **8**(5), 143–151 (2002)

Davis, F.D.: Perceived usefulness, perceived ease of use, and user acceptance of information technology. MIS Q. **13**(3), 319–340 (1989)

Davis, F.D., Bagozzi, R.P., Warshaw, P.R.: Extrinsic and intrinsic motivation to use computers in workplace. J. Appl. Soc. Psychol. **22**(14), 1111–1132 (1992)

Davis, R.A., Flett, G.L., Besser, A.: Validation for a new scale for measuring problematic internet use: implications for pre-employment screening. Cyberpsychology Behav. **5**(4), 331–345 (2002)

De Charms, R.: Personal Causation: the Internal Affective Determinants of Behaviour. Academic Press, New York (1968)

Deci, E.L., Ryan, R.M.: A motivational approach to self: integration in personality. In: Dienstbier, R. (ed.) Nebraska Symposium on Motivation. Perspectives on motivation, vol. 38, pp. 237–288. University of Nebraska Press, Lincoln (1991)

DeLone, W.H., McLean, E.R.: The DeLone and McLean model of information systems success: a ten year update. J. Manag. Inf. Syst. **19**(4), 9–30 (2003)

Dholakia, U.M., Bagozzi, R.P., Pearo, L.K.: A social influence model of consumer participation in network- and small-group-based virtual communities. Int. J. Res. Mark. **21**, 241–261 (2004)

Douglas, A.C., Mills, J.E., Niang, M., Stepchenkova, S., Byun, S., Ruffini, C., Lee, S.K., Loutfi, J., Lee, J.-K., Atallah, M., Blanton, M.: Internet addiction: meta-synthesis of qualitative research for the decade 19996-2006. Comput. Hum. Behav. **24**, 3027–3044 (2008)

Fornell, C., Larcker, D.F.: Evaluating structural equation models with unobservable variables and measurement error. J. Mark. Res. **18**(1), 39–50 (1981)

Gefen, D., Straub, D.: A practical guide to factorial validity using PLS-Graph: tutorial and annotated example. Commun. Assoc. Inf. Syst. **16**(5), 91–109 (2005)

Griffiths, M.D.: Technological addictions. Clin. Psychol. Forum **95**, 14–19 (1995)

Griffiths, M.D.: A "components" model of addiction within a bio-psychosocial framework. J. Subst. Use **10**, 191–197 (2005)

Hars, A., Ou, S.: Working for free? Motivations for participating in open-source projects. Int. J. Electron. Commer. **6**(3), 23–37 (2002)

Hirschfeld, M.: Sexual Anomalies and Perversions: Physical and Psychological Development, Diagnosis and Treatment, (new and revised) edn. Encyclopaedic Press, London (1938)

Horvath, S., Morf, C.C.: To be grandiose or not to be worthless: different routes to self-enhancement for narcissism and self-esteem. J. Res. Pers. **44**, 585592 (2010)

Islam, A.K.M.N., Mäntymäki, M., Benbasat, I.: Duality of self-promotion on social networking sites. Inf. Technol. People (2018). (In press)

Joinson, A.N., Paine, C., Buchanan, T., Reips, U.: Measuring self-disclosure online: Blurring and non-response to sensitive items in web-based surveys. Comput. Hum. Behav. **24**(5), 2158–2171 (2008)

Jourard, S.M., Lasakow, P.: Some factors in self-disclosure. J. Abnorm. Soc. Psychol. **56**(1), 91–98 (1958)

Koopman, F., Sremac, S.: Addiction and Autonomy: are addicts autonomous? Nova Prisut. **9**(1), 171–188 (2011)

Kubey, R., Csikszentmihalyi, M.: Television addiction is no mere metaphor. Sci. Am. **286**, 74–80 (2002)

Kuss, D.J., Griffiths, M.D.: Addiction to social networks on the Internet: a literature review of empirical research. Int. J. Environ. Public Health **8**(9), 3528–3552 (2011)

Kuss, D.J., Griffiths, M.D.: Social networking on the Internet: from pastime to excess and addiction. Ment. Notes **6**(3), 26–28 (2012)

Limayem, M., Hirt, S.G., Cheung, C.M.K.: How habit limits the predictive power of intention: the case of information systems continuance. MIS Q. **31**(4), 705–737 (2007)

Marks, I.: Behavioural (non-chemical) addictions. Br. J. Addict. **85**(11), 1389–1394 (1990)

Marlatt, G., Baer, J., Donovan, D., Kivlahan, D.: Addictive behaviors: etiology and treatment. Annu. Rev. Psychol. **39**, 223–252 (1988)

McCaslin, M.J., Petty, R.E., Wegener, D.T.: Self-enhancement and theory-based correction processes. J. Exp. Soc. Psychol. **46**, 830–835 (2010)

McNair, D., Lorr, M., Droppleman, L.: Profile of Mood States. Ed ITS/Educational and Industrial Testing Service, San Diego (1971)

Metzl, Jonathan M.: Voyeur nation? Changing definitions of Voyeurism, 1950–2004. Harv. Rev. Psychiatry **12**(2), 127–131 (2004)

Moore, G.C., Benbasat, I.: Development of an instrument to measure the perception of adopting an information technology innovation. Inf. Syst. Res. 2(3), 192222 (1991)

Mitchell, P.: Internet addiction: Genuine diagnosis or not? The Lancet 355(9204) (2000)

Munar, A.M.: Digital exhibitionism: the age of exposure. Cult. Unbound 2, 401422 (2010)

Mäntymäki, M., Islam, A.K.M.N.: Voyeurism and exhibitionism as gratifications from prosuming social networking sites. In: Proceedings of the 22nd European Conference on Information Systems (ECIS2014), Tel Aviv, Israel, 9–11 June 2014 (2014)

Mäntymäki, M., Islam, A.K.M.N.: The Janus face of Facebook: positive and negative sides of social networking site use. Comput. Hum. Behav. 61(8), 14–26 (2016)

Nabi, R.L., Stitt, C.R., Halford, J., Finnerty, K.L.: Emotional and cognitive predictors of the enjoyment of reality-based and fictional television programming: an elaboration of the uses and gratifications perspective. Media Psychol. 8(4), 421–447 (2006)

Nix, G.A., Ryan, R.M., Manly, J.B., Deci, E.L.: Revitalization through self-regulation: the effects of auton omous and controlled motivation on happiness and vitality. J. Exp. Soc. Psychol. 35, 266–284 (1999)

Nunnally, J.C.: Psychometric Theory. McGraw Hill, New York (1978)

Panek, E.T., Nardis, Y., Konrath, S.: Mirror or megaphone?: How relationships between narcissism and social networking site use differ on Facebook and Twitter. Comput. Hum. Behav. 29(5), 2004–2012 (2013)

Penninx, B.W.J.H., Guralnik, J.M., Bandeen-Roche, K., Kasper, J.D., Simonsick, E.M., Ferrucci, L.: The protective effect of emotional vitality on adverse health outcomes in disabled older women. J. Am. Geriatr. Soc. 48(11), 1359–1366 (2000)

Raskin, R., Terry, H.: A principal-components analysis of the narcissistic personality inventory and further evidence of its construct validity. J. Pers. Soc. Psychol. 54(5), 890 (1988)

Rice, M.: Online addiction. Beijing Rev. 48(46), 32–33 (2005)

Roller, C.G.: Sex addiction and women: a nursing issue. J. Addict. Nurs. 15, 53–61 (2004)

Ryan, R.M., Frederick, C.: On energy, personality, and health: Subjective vitality as a dynamic reflection of well-being. J. Pers. 65, 529–565 (1997)

Ryan, R. M., Deci, E.L.: To be happy or to be self-fulfilled: a review of research on hedonic and eudaimonic well-being. In: Fiske, S. (ed.), Annual Review of Psychology, vol. 52, pp. 141–166. Annual Reviews, Inc., Palo Alto (2001)

Ryan, R.M., Deci, E.L.: From ego depletion to vitality: theory and energy findings concerning the facilitation of energy available to the shelf. Soc. Pers. Psychol. Compass 2(2), 702–717 (2008)

Shapira, N.A., Goldsmith, T.G., Keck Jr., P.E., Khosla, U.M., McElroy, S.L.: Psychiatric features of individuals with problematic internet use. J. Affect. Disord. 57, 267–272 (2000)

Shapira, N.A., Lessig, M.C., Goldsmith, T.D., Szabo, S.T., Lazoritz, M., Gold M.S., Stein, D.J.: Problematic Internet use: Proposed classification and diagnostic criteria. Depress. Anxiety 17 (4), 207–216 (2003)

Silverstein, J.: Exhibitionism as countershame. Sex. Addict. Compulsivity, 3(1), 33–42 (1996)

Taylor, S.E., Brown, J.D.: Illusion and well-being: a social psychological perspective on mental health. Psychol. Bull. 103(2), 193–210 (1989)

Thayer, R.E.: The Origin of Everyday Moods. Oxford University Press, New York (1996)

Turel, O., Serenko, A.: The benefits and dangers of enjoyment with social networking websites. Eur. J. Inf. Syst. 21(5), 512–528 (2012)

Turel, O., Serenko, A., Giles, P.: Integrating technology addiction and use: an empirical investigation of online auction users. MIS Q. 35(4), 1043–1051 (2011)

Van der Heijden, H.: Acceptance of hedonic information systems. MIS Q. 28(4), 695–704 (2004)

Valkenburg, P., Peter, J., Schouten, A.: Friend networking sites and their relationship to adolescents' well-being and social self-esteem. CyberPsychology Behav. 9, 584–590 (2006)

Venkatesh, V.: Determinants of perceived ease of use: integrating control, intrinsic motivation, and emotion into the technology acceptance model. Inf. Syst. Res. **11**(4), 342–365 (2000)

Venkatesh, V., Davis, F.D.: A theoretical extension of the technology acceptance model: four longitudinal field studies. Manag. Sci. **46**(2), 186–204 (2000)

Venkatesh, V., Thong, J.Y.L., Xu, X.: Consumer acceptance and use of information technology: extending the unified theory of acceptance and use of technology. MIS Q. **36**(1), 157–178 (2012)

Watson, D., Tellegen, A.: Toward a consensual structure of mood. Psychol. Bull. **98**, 219–235 (1985)

Widyanto, L., Griffiths, M.D.: Internet addiction: a critical review. Int. J. Ment. Health Addict. **4**, 31–51 (2006)

Xu, Z., Turel, O., Yuan, Y.: Online game addiction among adolescents: motivation and prevention factors. Eur. J. Inf. Syst. **21**, 321–340 (2012)

Young, K.S.: Internet addiction: the emergence of a new clinical disorder. Paper presented at the 104th annual meeting of the American Psychological Association, Toronto, Canada (1996)

Young, K.S.: Internet addiction: the emergence of a new clinical disorder. CyberPsychology Behav. **1**, 237–244 (1998)

Young, K.: Internet addiction over the decade: a personal look back. World Psychiatry **9**(2), 91–91 (2010)

Yellowlees, P. M., Marks, S.: Problematic internet use or internet addiction? Comput. Hum. Behav. **23**(3), 1447–1453 (2007)

Do Business Ecosystems Differ from Other Business Networks? The Case of an Emerging Business Ecosystem for Digital Real-Estate and Facility Services

Matti Mäntymäki[✉], Hannu Salmela, and Marja Turunen

Turku School of Economics, University of Turku, 20014 Turku, Finland
{matti.mantymaki,hannu.salmela,marja.turunen}@utu.fi

Abstract. The concept of ecosystem emanates from ecology and subsequently has been broadly used in business studies to describe and investigate complex interrelationships between companies and other organizations. However, it is widely known that borrowing constructs from natural sciences to social sciences, or vice versa, can be problematic. For example, the use of the ecosystem concept outside its original domain has received criticism. To better understand the essence, applicability and boundaries of the business ecosystem concept, this study conducts a conceptual analysis of a set of concepts used to describe business networks. To this end, we analytically comparing business ecosystem with other prominent concepts, namely industry, population, cluster, inter-organizational network and value network. We then present an illustrative case of an emerging business ecosystem of digital services for real-estate and facility services and scrutinize the applicability of the focal concepts for our case. The results indicate a need for increased conceptual clarity when describing business networks. The results indicate a need for conceptual clarity when describing business networks. We conclude with a synthesis and discuss under what circumstances using the business ecosystem concept may add value for research and practice. The paper contributes to the business ecosystem literature by clarifying the similarities and differences between business ecosystem and other concepts used to describe business networks.

Keywords: Business ecosystem · Cluster · Network · Industry
Value network · Collective consciousness · Digitalization · Conceptual analysis

1 Introduction

The term ecosystem has diffused outside its original domain in natural sciences (Autio and Thomas 2014; Mäntymäki and Salmela 2017). In biology, an ecosystem, or ecological system, typically denotes a unit of biological organization made up of all the organisms in a given area, thus forming a "community". Organisms within a community interact with the physical environment so that the flow of energy leads to characteristic trophic structure and material cycles within the system (Odum 1966).

© IFIP International Federation for Information Processing 2018
Published by Springer Nature Switzerland AG 2018. All Rights Reserved
S. A. Al-Sharhan et al. (Eds.): I3E 2018, LNCS 11195, pp. 102–116, 2018.
https://doi.org/10.1007/978-3-030-02131-3_11

The specific focus of this paper is the use of the ecosystem metaphor in describing business networks (cf. Aarikka-Stenroos and Ritala 2017). The literature has coined concepts such as business ecosystems (Peltoniemi and Vuori 2004), innovation ecosystem (Oh et al. 2016), software ecosystems (Hyrynsalmi et al. 2016), service ecosystem (Vargo and Lusch 2010), product ecosystem (Frels et al. 2003), and platform ecosystem (Ceccagnoli et al. 2012), to name but a few. The widespread use of the ecosystem metaphor implies that has been viewed to provide some value-added for researchers. At the same time, however, the use of ecosystem metaphor has also been criticized and the accuracy of the metaphor questioned (Hyrynsalmi 2015; Oh et al. 2016). Boulding (1956) holds that analysing tools, such as conceptualizations of organization need to be at the same level of the complexity with the phenomena in question. To foster this element, we apply Turunen (2015) view of organizing which maintains that all conceptualization of are embedded in organizational consciousness which we take along in this paper.

The purpose of this paper is to understand (1) what is a business ecosystem and (2) how does the concept of business ecosystem relate to other similar concepts, including what role cross-organizational collective consciousness plays in the ecosystem concept. In this paper, we focus on five widely discussed concepts that have been used to describe business networks, i.e. groups of inter-connected organizations, namely industry, population, inter-organizational network, cluster and value network.

Based on our analysis we argue that concepts industry and population emphasize competitive relationships between firms, whereas an inter-organizational network and a cluster place more emphasis on collaboration. In this respect, an ecosystem is a more diverse concept, presuming both collaborative and competitive relationships, which generate intertwined awareness processes such as collective consciousness (Turunen 2015), which draws on social sciences, particularly from psychology and sociology.

This study contributes to the literature by demonstrating that there is an overlap between the business ecosystem concept and other similar concepts. This is particularly so in the use of these concepts by practitioners. For researchers, our study shows a clear need for more fine-grained conceptual and theoretical analyses of the business ecosystem concept. We further conclude that additional scrutiny of the ecosystem metaphor and its value-added for theorizing and for managerial communication is needed.

The paper proceeds as follows: after the introductory section, we present a discussion of the business ecosystem concept. Thereafter, the present a set of related constructs used to depict business networks and analyse how they converge with, and diverge from, the business ecosystem construct. The paper concludes with a synthesis of the analysis and suggestion for future research.

2   The Business Ecosystem Concept

The business ecosystem concept was coined by Moore (1993). His seminal article debates capability coevolution around innovation with distinct stages towards a shared future and accruable profit model of business ecosystem:

*...a business ecosystem [...] crosses a variety of Industries [...], companies coevolve capa-
bilities around a new innovation: they work cooperatively and competitively to support new
products, satisfy customer needs, and eventually incorporate the next round of innovations.
Every business ecosystem develops in four distinct stages: birth, expansion, leadership, and
self-renewal – or, if not self-renewal, death. [...] While the centre may shift over time, the role
of the leader is valued by the rest of the community. Such leadership enables all ecosystem
members to invest towards a shared future in which they anticipate profiting together."* (Moore
1993, p. 76)

Moore (1996) further defines ecosystem as an economic community supported by a
foundation of interacting organizations and individuals:

*"This economic community produces goods and services of value to customers, who are
themselves members of the ecosystem. The business ecosystems are characterized by a large
number of loosely interconnected participants who depend on each other for their mutual
effectiveness and survival."* (Moore 1996, p. 26)

In their business ecosystem conceptualization, Iansiti and Levien (2004, pp. 8–9)
put more emphasis on networks. Accordingly, an ecosystem is essentially as an
analogy to describe modern business networks. They also acknowledge the using
biological analogies in business literature can be a controversial issue and further argue
that "the analogy between evolved biological systems and networks of business entities
is too often misunderstood." Iansiti and Levien (2004, p. 5). Authors further lament that
their use of the term ecosystem is probably closer to the biological term community but
they use the term ecosystem to highlight that they are discussing a complex system and
working with a biological analogy.

Based on subsequent literature on business ecosystems, such systems appear to
have at least three characteristic features:

1. Members of an ecosystem are highly interconnected. Interconnectedness refers to
   the fact that the success or failure of a member of an ecosystem affects the other
   members.
2. A business ecosystem often includes a keystone that "regulates ecosystem health"
   (Moore 1993, p. 8). The keystone is typically an actor that is able to support and
   orchestrate the activities that take place within the ecosystem.
3. Ecosystems are complex systems Peltoniemi and Vuori (2004). As described by
   Cowan (1994, p. 1), complex systems "contain many relatively independent parts
   which are highly interconnected and interactive." Lewin in turn (Lewin 1999)
   further laments that complex systems are systems whose properties are not fully
   explained by an understanding of its constituent parts. (Lewin 1999). Thus, complex systems can be informed by the process research (James 1977), (Tsoukas and
   Chia 2002) of collective interaction (Kimble 2008).

While the characteristic features of #1 and #3 are somewhat congruent, the second
one raises a question: how can a complex, interconnected, system be regulated by one
actor? This appears to be one of the internal tensions related to the concept of business
ecosystem. On the other hand, co-operation in business ecosystem creates a common
awareness that in turn helps to manage diversity and complexity.

In software business, the ecosystem concept has been used to depict business
networks built around a key player such as Apple. The core of Apple's ecosystem is the

App Store. For customers, the App Store is a software marketplace where Apple acts as a gatekeeper and trust provider. For application developers, such as providers of different mobile games, Apple provides the development tools and a distribution channel via its App Store. For Apple, the App Store is a means to generate additional revenue but also a mechanism to significantly extend its value proposition beyond hardware and the core software that is pre-installed in its products.

3 Comparison of Industry, Population, Cluster, Interorganizational Network, Value Network, and Business Ecosystem

One way to seek a better understanding of the ecosystem is to compare it with other similar concepts used in prior research. In the following, we shall present and compare an ecosystem with five such concepts: industry, population, inter-organizational network, value network and cluster. While the first two assume relationships between firms as primarily competitive, the last three bring the collaborative relations into the surface.

3.1 Industry

Perhaps the most traditional concept used in describing and classifying companies' environment is industry. Generally speaking, an industry consists of companies or networks of companies that provide similar product or service offerings to same markets. Porter defines the concept industry as follows (Porter 1980, p. 32):

> "Structural analysis, by focusing broadly on competition well beyond existing rivals, should reduce the need for debates on where to draw industry boundaries. Any definition of an industry is essentially a choice of where to draw the line between established competitors and substitute products, between existing firms and potential entrants, and between existing firms and suppliers and buyers."

The underlying theme in the concept is that competitive relations define borders for industry. Industries can be treated as entities, having attributes of their own. For instance, because of structural differences, some industries may be more profitable than others (Porter 1980). The dynamics inside the industry is largely explained by forces of competition.

The idea of an industry as a competitive marketplace does not exclude collaboration completely, but it is seen as an exception, labelled with terms such as strategic alliances or co-opetition (Bengtsson and Kock 2000; Hamel et al. 1989).

Industries are also complex systems, even if no collaborative relations are taken into consideration. For example, in hypercompetitive industries, companies need to rely on complex strategic manoeuvring in order to capitalize on new opportunities in the marketplace faster than their competitors (D'Aveni 1994). However, as the industry players focus on their own competition, there does not emerge cross-organizational collaboration or collective awareness among industry players.

A company can belong to industries of different levels, for example game developers belong to game industry but on a more generic level also to software industry. When industry concept is applied to computer and mobile game providers, the emphasis is on competitive relations: game providers compete over same customers' (players') time and money. They also compete with other forms of current and future forms of entertainment. In the industry concept, platform providers like Apple are seen as distribution channel firms, whose negotiation power decreases profit margins of game providers. By leaving the collaborative relations behind, industry and industry analysis brings forth the competitive ones – which may be sufficient to explain many complex phenomena in the gaming industry.

3.2 Population

Population is a theoretical concept used in analysing variability of organizations over time (Hannan and Freeman 1989). Here the classification of companies is based on a number of attributes, such as the size of the organization, organizational form, and strategy. As an example, small, family owned companies that focus on niche markets can be seen as one population.

The purpose of this classification is to explain variance and dynamics between organizations. Hannan and Freeman describe the approach as follows (Hannan and Freeman 1989, p. 13):

> "The population ecology perspective concentrates on the sources of variability and homogeneity of organizational forms. It considers the rise of new organizational forms and the demise of transformation of existing ones. In doing so, it pays considerable attention to population dynamics, especially the processes of competition among diverse organizations for limited resources such as membership, capital, and legitimacy."

A basic assumption underlying the population concept is that competition in markets will favour those populations of companies that have the characteristics needed in new situations. Hence, "there are strong parallels between processes of change in organizational populations and in biotic populations" (Hannan and Freeman 1989, p. 13).

Population ecology acknowledges that sometimes organizations form communities, i.e. organizations that collaborate with each other. Hence, survival could take place at the level of communities, rather than at the level of populations of similar companies.

This idea is not, however, included in the analysis. The power of population ecology is in explaining, why some populations of independent firms succeed in competition while others vanish.

Overall, population ecological models demonstrate, that complex phenomena behind birth and growth of new types of companies and demise of existing ones can be explained with competitive relationships. It can be concluded that those companies who can best leverage the ecosystem reap the best benefits.

In mobile and computer game business, an example of population is the emergence, growth, and typically also decline of a certain types of game developers. While the companies compete with one another, they also share the destiny of their competitors, in particular the ones which are most similar to them. The population ecology model explains, how new types of companies emerge to markets, thus causing existing companies to suffer from shrinking markets.

For example, the rapid growth and success of freemium games from game companies such as Supercell's Clash of Clans or King's Candy Crush Saga took markets from established game companies relying on traditional pricing. This may also have contributed to the birth of a new type of population: small and medium-sized game companies offering freemium games (cf. Koskenvoima and Mäntymäki 2015). Hence, by using long time frames, population ecology model explains many "ecology" type of phenomena – purely with competitive relations.

3.3   Inter-organizational Network

Research on business networks or inter-organizational networks takes a completely opposite approach. Research focuses on such entities, where inter-relationships of companies are seen as predominantly collaborative. Because of a wide variety of collaborative forms, giving an exact definition for an inter-organizational network is difficult. Nevertheless, Provan et al. (2007, p. 482) provide the following characterization of an inter-organizational network:

> "... we make no effort to try to offer an all-encompassing definition of an interorganizational network. Rather, we focus instead on one specific type of network that has been frequently discussed but only infrequently researched, namely, a whole network consisting of multiple organizations linked through multilateral ties. A whole network is viewed here as a group of three or more organizations connected in ways that facilitate achievement of a common goal. That is, the networks we discuss are often formally established and governed and goal directed rather than occurring serendipitously" (Kilduff and Tsai 2003).

A characteristic feature of an inter-organizational network is that it comprises several independent organizations. Like all groupings of organizations, also inter-organizational networks evolve, but such evolution can be treated as conscious and goal-directed. For example, Ring and Van de Ven (1994) have proposed a process framework that focuses on formal, legal, and informal socio-psychological processes by which parties jointly negotiate, commit to, and execute their relationship.

The idea of competition within a network is not completely absent. For instance, the governance processes described by Ring and Van de Ven (1994) need to ensure both efficient and equitable outcomes. They will also need to be able to deal with conflicts as they arise. While the concept of inter-organizational network does not deny conflicts of interest, the primary emphasis is on collaborative ties between individual organizations. This suggests that inter-organizational collaboration does not hit the potential which is available.

It is perhaps surprising; how few are the examples of software companies engaging in genuinely collaborative network relations that would involve three or more organizations. In computer and mobile games, collaboration between game companies and movie producers can, perhaps, be seen as an example of such a collaboration. Collaboration in open-source forums, or digital platforms, can sometimes fulfill some requirements of an inter-organizational network. But traditionally the relationships have been arms-length relations without shared governance or formal contracts.

3.4 Cluster

The term cluster emanates from the works of Porter (1990) on nations' competitive advantage. Cluster has a strong conceptual linkage to industry as a cluster is a part or a representative of an industry (Dayasindhu 2002; Porter 1990; Tallman et al. 2004). Porter (2000) defines cluster as follows:

> *"a geographically proximate group of interconnected companies and associated institution in a particular field, linked by commonalities and complementarities."* (Porter 2000, p. 16)

The concept of cluster offers a vehicle to explain why large numbers of companies operating in a same market are concentrated on certain geographical locations. With the term cluster Porter (1990) refers to a phenomenon linked to geographic concentrations of national industries which origin from vertical or horizontal relationships between companies. Locality is considered a key characteristic of a cluster as companies in a cluster as companies in a cluster are often located in a single city or region (Porter 1990; Scheel 2002; Tallman et al. 2004). Cluster has a strong conceptual linkage to industry as a cluster is a part or a representative of an industry (see e.g. Dayasindhu 2002; Tallman et al. 2004).

Porter (1990) sees intense competition within a cluster as its main driving force as competition forces companies to increase the standard of their operations in order to remain competitive. Intense competition can be due to bargaining power of customers who may be interact with several companies within the cluster. These interactions in turn accelerate exchange of information and diffusion of innovations. Collaboration and interaction build up not only cross-organizational awareness but consciousness fields (Turunen 2015) in the cluster.

In software business, physical proximity of companies operating in a certain field is almost a norm due to the positive network externalities. Silicon Valley is perhaps the best-known example of a geographical concentration of software companies. But there are also other countries, like India, China, Russia, Ireland and Israel, who have strong concentrations of software development (Carmel and Tija 2009). The emergence of gaming industry in Finland can also be seen as a good example of a cluster: Interest of capital investors, support from the government, and availability of programmers specialized (and interested) in games, are examples of cluster effect. While companies don't necessarily collaborate extensively (as they often are competitors), they still seem to benefit from the mere existence of other similar companies in the same region.

3.5 Value Network

The value network concept emphasizes the intangible capabilities of the network. Normann and Ramirez (1993) maintain that business should not focus on the positioning the fixed set of activities along the value chain only but focus on the *value creating system* itself. While Normann and Ramirez addressed the systems view, Christensen and Roosenbloom (1995) set the stage for value network concept from the attacker's position in the competitive arena. According Christensen (2013), value network extends beyond the product categories and focuses on the context i.e. the value network of a firm to excel on the competition. Christensen defines value network as a context of competitive arena on immaterial values:

> *"The collection of upstream suppliers, downstream channels to market, and ancillary providers that support a common business model within an industry. When wouldbe disruptors enter into existing value networks, they must adapt their business models to conform to the value network and therefore fail at disruption because they become co-opted." Christensen* (2013, p. 296)

The boundaries of the value network are determined as a unique definition of the product performance and on the cost structure to meet the customer preferences, according Christensen (2013, p. 54).

While both Normann and Ramirez (1993) and Christensen (2013) focused on firms, Allee (2003) definition of value networks is applicable for any organizations, not only those on the competitive arena. She maintains that the key of the value network is the exchange of intangible assets between individuals, groups and organizations:

> *"A web of relationships that generates both tangible and intangible value through complex dynamic exchanges between two or more individuals, groups or organizations. Any organization or group of organizations engaged in both tangible and intangible exchanges can be viewed as a value network, whether private industry, government or public sector."* (Allee 2003, p. 268)

Allee emphasized the importance of revealing the hidden network patterns behind business processes with an analytical tool to define, map, and analyze the participants, transactions (Williamson 1989) and tangible and intangible deliverables that together form a value network. As a result, value network can be seen as a conceptual tool to describe the social, technical and intangible resources between individuals, groups and organizations in highlighting the context outside the firm boundaries. It is also a predictive tool to analyze and explain company performance (Christensen 2013) in competitive landscapes, for instance to explain why well-established, large companies fail. The main contribution to the conceptual analysis is that value network moves away from the linear model, which the other concepts maintain. Individuals, groups and organizations negotiate of value constellations. Thus, they are due to transformations and disruptions which may put one backwards or aside of the linear time that accrues the from the past and the future of multiple members of the network. Thus, value network might face cyclical or other trajectories in addition to linear development.

Collective consciousness is accommodated in the value network. In fact, it becomes fostered in the interrelations between individuals, groups and organizations. Indeed, the contributors of value network concept mention the benefits of collective consciousness explicitly, such as Normann (2001) and Allee (2003). For instance, Allee (2003) maintains that "collective consciousness provides a new transformative shift towards understanding the more complex layers of the system and new avenues for connecting together with other players" i.e. collaboration in the intangible areas of value creation.

For software business, advances in digital technologies, for example in sensor technology and Internet of Things (IoT) (cf. Mian et al. 2016) enable the creation of new value networks and business models for established, mature businesses and simultaneously challenges the existing logics for value creation.

4 Synthesis

We scrutinized the results from the literature and business cases and present them into a synthesis of our conceptual analysis of business ecosystem, industry, and population. We derive directly from the definitions described in the above sections. After that we provide a generic description of the applicability of a concept, which is not directly related to the definition. Table 1 below presents a synthesis of our conceptual analysis of business ecosystem, industry, and population.

The first and perhaps the clearest difference can be found in the ways of which the concept defines the group of companies that constitute the environment. As a result, the borders for an industry are defined by established and potential competitors (Porter 1990), for population by variability and homogeneity of organizational forms (Hannan and Freeman 1989), for inter-organizational network by multilateral ties between organizations (Provan et al. 2007), and for cluster geographical proximity (Porter 2000). An ecosystem can be seen as a large number of loosely interconnected participants from various industries, who depend on each for their mutual effectiveness and survival (Moore 1996).

Concerning to the nature of ties, we find the concepts falling into three groups. In industries and populations, companies are connected primarily through competitive relationships (Hannan and Freeman 1989; Porter 1990). In inter-organizational networks, primary relationships between companies are seen as collaborative (Provan et al. 2007). For clusters and ecosystems, ties can be both collaborative and competitive. Within a cluster, organizations' competitive and collaborative regional relationships assist them in global competition (Porter 2000). In value networks and in ecosystems, it is an explicit assumption that companies within work cooperatively and competitively (Moore 1996).

In terms of sources of transformation, competitive forces are central in the evolution of industry, population and cluster. Industry evolution is directed by several competitive forces (Porter 1990), the growth and demise of populations results from competition over access to limited resources such as membership, capital and legitimacy (Hannan and Freeman 1989), and the destiny of regions is an outcome of global competition (Porter 1990). At the opposite end, the evolution of inter-organizational networks are seen to result from negotiations that are formally governed and goal directed (Provan et al. 2007). In between are ecosystems - and value networks-, where transformation is seen as contingent upon new customer needs and/or new product and service innovations, leading to reforms in ecosystems (Moore 1996) with the distinction of value networks where reforms may be initiated in several parts of the network depending on the negotiated value (Allee 2003).

Overall, a strength of the business ecosystem concept is that it acknowledges both collaborative and competitive relationships. Hence, the concept enables simultaneous analysis of transformation, both within networks but also in the markets where they operate. At the same time, however, the concept itself becomes more complex: Defining borders of an ecosystem is more difficult, because the relationships defining an ecosystem are manifold. Hence, the ecosystem lens can also lead to an overly complex view of reality, in particular if collaborative (or competitive) ties between companies are insignificant. Furthermore, business ecosystem concept provides the

Table 1. Concepts depicting business networks

	Industry	Population	Inter-organizational network	Cluster	Value network	Business ecosystem
Definition of group borders	Established and potential competitors; firm borders	Homogeneity of organizational forms; firm borders	Multiple organizations linked through multilateral ties; network borders	A geographically proximate group; distance border	Exchange of intangible assets between individuals, groups and organization; borders of experienced value constellations of network	Loosely connected firms who depend on each other for their mutual effectiveness and survival; an entity and a system with borders
Primary relationship between firms	Competition; including latent competition	Competition; among diverse organizations forms	Collaborative ties that facilitate reaching a common goal	Loose collaborative ties within a region that assist in global competition	Competition and collaboration in value creation	Competitive and collaborative ties
Sources of transformation and change	Selection through competition; large number of competitive factors; 'The best fit wins'	Selection through competition; competition for limited resources; 'The strongest benefiter wins'	Formally, established governance processes between network parties; 'The best network wins'	Selection of most viable regions through global competition; 'The strongest collaborator/adapter wins'	System's capacity to create tangible and intangible value constellations beyond product components. Ability to generate value from intangible resources. 'The best negotiator wins'	New products and customer needs incorporate the next round of innovations; 'The dominant player attracting contributors, such as platform player wins'
Applicability	Explaining success and viability of individual companies	Explaining success and viability of populations of companies	Explaining evolution and success of inter-organizational networks	Explaining success of geographic regions	Explaining success and failures of companies and new products. Predictive analysis.	Explaining simultaneous evolution/disruption of markets and networks
Existing Business cases	Games industry	Supercell's Clash of Clans or King's Candy Crush Saga	Collaboration between game companies and movie studios	Silicon Valley; Seattle region	Hard disk manufacturer in 'Innovators dilemma'	Apple, Amazon, Facebook, Alibaba

most opportunities to produce viable collective consciousness fields because many actors try to make sense of the larger system. However, on a conceptual level, an ecosystem draws on biology, as explained earlier, and consequently does not imply a term of collective consciousness. These consciousness fields focus attention and feed in mechanisms and opportunities for leveraging the complexity of the terrain. However, using the vocabulary of and drawing conceptually from natural sciences in social sciences may inhibits tapping the potential of the complexity present in e.g. the business cases presented above.

5   The Case of an Emerging Business Ecosystem for Digital Real-Estate and Facility Services

In order to delineate the similarities and differences between the different concepts described above the present an initiative that is aimed to become a business ecosystem for digital real-estate and facilities services.

The concrete activities within initiative take place under a industry-academia research and development program that is funded by Business Finland – The Finnish Funding Agency for Technology as well as the companies and universities participating the program.

The purpose of the program is to develop end-user services using IoT, sensor technology, face recognition, artificial intelligence etc. as well as to identify potential use cases and develop business models for these services. The activities within the project are divided into four thematic entities, titled well-being, intelligent restaurant, data-asservices and empathetic building. The thematic entities are led by the companies participating the research program. Table 2 below contains a brief description of the network of participants.

Table 2. Description of the emerging business ecosystem

Dimension	Description
Definition of group borders	Participating institutions, companies, and research s, and financing institutions
Primary relationship between firms	Collaborative and competitive ties. In the beginning of the endeavor, the relationships are intense and loose
Sources of transformation and change	The collective platforms of sharing information, which engage partners of the network to challenge the old models and adopt new ones. High quality collective consciousness fields and working methods
Applicability	Explaining collaboration of diverse organizations and individuals with partly shared and competitive/diverse motives. Business ecosystem a benchmark and desired end state
	Ecosystem metaphor an important part of the discourse within the program participants

When scrutinized through the different concepts used to describe business networks discussed in the prior sections, we see that certain concepts are more insightful to describe the emerging ecosystem for digital real-estate and facility services.

First, the industry concept does not apply directly very well, because the industry consortium comprises companies from both real estate and facility as well as ICT sectors. On the other hand, the industry concept has certain relevance in the early state of the program where the participating companies operate mostly based on the dominant logics of their respective industries.

The concepts highlighting the collaborate relationships between the players such as inter-organizational network, cluster and value-network have certain value in describing the relationships between the participants. The population concept in turn builds upon the assumption that the players homogenous which significantly limits the applicability of the population concept in our case.

The business ecosystem concept has certain fit to our case as the relationship between the players is essentially co-opetitive. On the other hand, at least in its current formative stage, there is no clearly dominant player that characterize an ecosystem.

As a result, we conclude that value network appears to have the best fit to our case in its present state. Value network does not assume the existence or emergence of a dominant player. The lack of a clear dominator may on one hand increase the need for additional negotiation and thus slow down the development activities. On the other hand, it forces the participants to articulate their needs and intentions and take responsibility of the course of action. Table 3 below provides a summary of the analysis.

6   Discussion

Compared to the related concepts investigated here - industry, population, inter-organizational network, cluster, and value network - the concept of business ecosystem appears to enable the analysis of both collaborative and competitive relationships. The need for the concept is often argued on the basis that economy and competition has changed and collaborative arrangements are becoming increasingly significant due to globalization and digitalization.

Our analysis of the concepts suggests that all six concepts provide partially distinct perspective to and emphasis on business networks. We further pointed out the system complexity might be a relevant dimension to classify business networks. Using theoretical and conceptual tools that can explain the research problem with a minimal complexity is generally considered a virtue in research. At the same time, however, overly simple tools and concepts are often insufficient in finding solutions for highly complex problems (Boulding 1956). For example, inter-organizational collaboration generates different levels and qualities of attention (Teece 2010) such as collective awareness and collective consciousness. This in turn, can accommodate dealing with highly complex levels issues and problems, including innovations, sustainability and ethics (Turunen 2015). Therefore, managerial decision makers' tolerance to educate themselves on complexity may be worthwhile.

Table 3. Applicability of different concepts to describe the emerging ecosystem for digital real-estate and facility services

Concept	Applicability	Description
Industry	Partial explanation power. Omits part of the system	The program focuses on real estate and digitalization industries. The current stage of the affairs cannot be described accurately with the industry concept
Population	Problems due to the ontological differences of the domains vs. biology and social sciences	Population does not apply to the Program except of strong and dominant players such as big firms or set up of coordination
Inter-organizational network	Leaves out the heterogeneity of the actors i.e. organizations, for instance motives	The players form a network and sub-networks. However, there is no strong mutual dependency (at the early stage of the program)
Cluster	Partial explanation power. Geography is not relevant	The constellation of the players involved has no clear geographical dimension. The players represent different businesses (real estate, ICT)
Value network	Good explanation power. Does not accrue in explaining the system	The dynamics of a value networks are to a certain degree visible. Participants collaborate and negotiate of value constellation. Interactions in the value network create collective consciousness
Business ecosystem	Problems due to the ontological differences of the domains vs. biology and social sciences	Co-opetition between players. A dominant player is missing

The same applies also to managers who are making strategic decisions. The key question in selecting a perspective is how significant collaborative arrangements are in a given industry. If collaborative arrangements are business critical, belonging to the right network(s) can make a difference. However, if barriers for leaving and joining ecosystems are low and multi-homing in several ecosystems in parallel is possible, the classical competitive industry perspective can be more valuable in strategic decision making.

Our analysis implies that the ecosystem concept appears to fit particularly well to situations where there is a focal firm or platform leading the network (Iansiti and Levien 2004; Teece 2010; Autio and Thomas 2014). This is the case with global players such as Alibaba, Apple and Amazon where the network consists of a very large number of actors and is being led and coordinated by a single leading firm (cf. Hyrynsalmi et al. 2016). On the other hand, in the absence of a clear dominant player, tools and concepts such as value network that put emphasis on inter-organizational collaboration such as value network may offer more insightful descriptions. For instance, as stated by Allee (2003), value network analysis can lead to profound shifts in perception of problem situations and mobilize collective action to implement change.

Like any other piece of research, this study suffers from a number of limitations. First, we focused only a limited set of concepts. Future research should thus incorporate e.g. platform and alliance in the analysis. Second, we have focused on business ecosystems on a general level. However, there are presumably different types of business ecosystems. Future studies could thus identify different types of business ecosystems.

References

Aarikka-Stenroos, L., Ritala, P.: Network management in the era of ecosystems: Systematic review and management framework. Ind. Mark. Manag. **67**, 2336 (2017)

Allee, V.: The Future of Knowledge: Increasing Prosperity Through Value Networks. Routledge, London (2003)

Autio, E., Thomas, L.: Innovation ecosystems. In: The Oxford handbook of innovation management, pp. 204–288 (2014)

Bengtsson, M., Kock, S.: Coopetition" in business networks—to cooperate and compete simultaneously. Ind. Mark. Manag. **29**(5), 411–426 (2000)

Boulding, K.E.: General system theory – the skeleton of science. Manag. Sci. **2**(3), 197–208 (1956)

Carmel, E., Tija, P.: Offshoring Information Technology: Sourcing and Outsourcing to a Global Workforce. Cambridge University Press, Fourth Printing, Cambridge (2009)

Ceccagnoli, M., Forman, C., Huang, P., Wu, D.J.: Cocreation of value in a platform ecosystem! The case of enterprise software. MIS Q., 263–290 (2012)

Christensen, C.: The Innovator's Dilemma: When New Technologies Cause Great Firms to Fail. Harvard Business Review Press, Boston (2013)

Christensen, C.M., Rosenbloom, R.S.: Explaining the attacker's advantage: technological paradigms, organizational dynamics, and the value network. Res. Policy **24**(2), 233–257 (1995)

Cowan, G.A.: Conference opening remarks. In: Cowan, G.A., Pines, D., Meltzer, D. (eds.) Complexity: Metaphores, Models, and Reality, pp. 1–4. Westview (1994)

D'Aveni, R.A.: Hypercompetition: managing the dynamics of strategic maneuvering. Free Press, New York (1994)

Dayasindhu, N.: Embeddedness, knowledge transfer, industry clusters and global competitiveness: a case study of the Indian software industry. Technovation **22**(9), 551560 (2002)

Frels, J.K., Shervani, T., Srivastava, R.K.: The integrated networks model: explaining resource allocations in network markets. J. Mark. **67**(1), 29–45 (2003)

Hamel G., Doz Y.L., Prahalad C.K.: Collaborate with your competition and win. Harv. Bus. Rev. **67**(1), 133–139 (1989)

Hannan M.T., Freeman J.: Organizational Ecology. Harvard University Press, Cambridge (1989)

Hyrynsalmi, S.: Letters From the War of Ecosystems (doctoral dissertation). University of Turku, Finland (2015)

Hyrynsalmi, S., Suominen, A., Mäntymäki, M.: The influence of developer multihoming on competition between software ecosystems. J. Syst. Softw. **111**, 119–127 (2016)

Iansiti, M., Levien, R.: Strategy as ecology. Harv. Bus. Rev. **82**(3), 68–81 (2004)

James, W.: A Pluralistic Universe. Harvard University Press, Harvard (1977)

Kilduff, M., Tsai, W.: Social Networks and Organizations. Sage, Thousand Oaks (2003)

Kimble, H.J.: The quantum internet. Nature **453**(7198), 1023 (2008)

Koskenvoima, A., Mäntymäki, M.: Why do small and medium-size freemium game developers use game analytics? In: Janssen, M., Mäntymäki, M., Hidders, J., Klievink, B., Lamersdorf, W., van Loenen, B., Zuiderwijk, A. (eds.) I3E 2015. LNCS, vol. 9373, pp. 326–337. Springer, Cham (2015). https://doi.org/10.1007/978-3-319-25013-7_26

Lewin, R.: Complexity: Life at the Edge of Chaos. University of Chicago Press, Chicago (1999)

Mäntymäki, M., Salmela, H.: In search for the core of the business ecosystem concept: a conceptual comparison of business ecosystem. In: 9th International Workshop on Software Ecosystems (IWSECO 2017), p. 103 (2017)

Mian, S.Q., Mäntymäki, M., Riekki, J., Oinas-Kukkonen, H.: Social sensor web: towards a conceptual framework. In: Dwivedi, Yogesh K., Mäntymäki, M., Ravishankar, M.N., Janssen, M., Clement, M., Slade, Emma L., Rana, Nripendra P., Al-Sharhan, S., Simintiras, Antonis C. (eds.) I3E 2016. LNCS, vol. 9844, pp. 479–492. Springer, Cham (2016). https://doi.org/10.1007/978-3-319-45234-0_43

Moore, J.F.: Predators and prey: a new ecology of competition. Harv. Bus. Rev. **71**(3), 75–83 (1993)

Moore, J.F.: The Death of Competition: Leadership and Strategy in the Age of Business Ecosystems. Harper Business (1996)

Normann, R.: Reframing Business: When the Map Changes the Landscape. Wiley, New York (2001)

Normann, R., Ramirez, R.: From value chain to value constellation: designing interactive strategy. Harv. Bus. Rev. **71**(4), 65–77 (1993)

Odum, E.P.: The strategy of ecosystem development. Science **164**(81), 262–270 (1966)

Oh, D.S., Phillips, F., Park, S., Lee, E.: Innovation ecosystems: a critical examination. Technovation **54**, 1–6 (2016)

Peltoniemi, M., Vuori, E.: Business ecosystem as the new approach to complex adaptive business environments. In Proceedings of eBusiness Research Forum, vol. 2, pp. 267–281 (2004)

Porter, M.E.: Competitive Strategy: Techniques for Analyzing Industries and Competitors. The Free Press, Macmillan Publishing Co., New York (1980)

Porter, M.E.: The competitive advantage of nations. Harv. Bus. Rev. **68**(2), 73–93 (1990)

Porter, M.E.: Location, competition, and economic development: local clusters in a global economy. Econ. Dev. Q. **14**(1), 15–34 (2000)

Provan, K.G., Fish, A., Sydow, J.: Interorganizational networks at the network level: a review of the empirical literature on whole networks. J. Manag. **33**(3), 479–515 (2007)

Ring, P.S., Van de Ven, A.H.: Developmental processes of cooperative interorganizational relationships. Acad. Manag. Rev. **19**(1), 90–118 (1994)

Scheel, C.: Knowledge clusters of technological innovation systems. J. Knowl. Manag. **6**(4), 356–367 (2002)

Tallman, S., Jenkins, M., Henry, N., Pinch, S.: Knowledge, clusters, and competitive advantage. Acad. Manag. Rev. **29**(2), 258–271 (2004)

Teece, D.J.: Explicating dynamic capabilities: the nature and microfoundations of (sustainable) enterprise performance. Strat. Manag. J. **28**(13), 1319–1350 (2007)

Teece, D.J.: Business models, business strategy and innovation. Long Range Plan. **43**(2–3), 172–194 (2010)

Tsoukas, H., Chia, R.: On organizational becoming: rethinking organizational change. Organ. Sci. **13**(5), 567–582 (2002)

Turunen, M.: Toward a Consciousness-Based View of Organizing. Aalto University, pp. 1–220. Unigrafia: Helsinki (2015)

Vargo, S.L., Lusch, R.F.: From repeat patronage to value co-creation in service ecosystems: a transcending conceptualization of relationship. J. Bus. Mark. Manag. **4**(4), 169–179 (2010)

Williamson, O.E.: Transaction cost economics. In: Schmalensee, R., Willig, R.D. (eds.) Handbook of Industrial Organization. Elsevier (1989)

Strategic Positioning in Big Data Utilization: Towards a Conceptual Framework

Milla Wirén and Matti Mäntymäki[✉]

Turku School of Economics, University of Turku, 20014 Turku, Finland
milla.wiren@utu.fu, matti.mantymaki@utu.fi

Abstract. This paper introduces a conceptual framework for strategic big data utilization. We discuss big data through (i) its origins (where and how does the data accumulate), (ii) its constitution (what is the nature of the data), and (iii) its applications (how and why can the data be processed and utilized). Based on this conceptual analysis, we argue for three continua that can guide the process of making strategic decisions regarding the utilization of big data. We further use these continua as a foundation for proposing a conceptual framework for strategic data use and strategic positioning. The conceptual framework facilitates understanding the firm-specific possibilities that emerge from aligning the overarching business goals with the opportunities emerging from big data.

Keywords: Big data · Strategy · Big data utilization

1 Introduction

Big data has become a richly researched phenomenon from the perspectives of its accumulation (Brynjolfsson and McAfee 2012), attributes (Chen et al. 2012), implications (Newell and Marabelli 2015; Zuboff 2015; Yoo 2010) and individual applications (Davenport et al. 2012; Varian 2010). At the same time, there are increasing calls for integrating the information systems, or digital strategy with the overarching business strategy (Bharadwaj et al. 2013). However, maybe reflecting the fundamentally amorphous nature of the phenomenon labelled big data (Constantiou and Kallinikos 2015), the discussions under the same label suffer from a level of amorphousness where the origins, constitution, threats, possibilities and utilization are somewhat conflated. As argued by Zuboff (2015), the abundance of definitions for the concept of big data suggests that understanding the phenomenon is still suffering from a lack of sufficient conceptual clarity.

We ground our approach on a threefold conceptualization of big data: the phenomenon can be explored by zooming into its origins, emergence and accumulation; from the viewpoint of addressing its attributes, nature and constitution; or from the perspective of outcomes, emerging both through deliberate utilization and from unintended implications. Our focus lies in the third vantage, explicitly in the part of the deliberate, strategic level utilization of the big data.

Previous discussions about this third vantage of big data, its outcomes, are either focused on specific business applications or use cases such as customer relationship management (McAfee et al. 2012), predictive maintenance (Wang et al. 2017), or game

S. A. Al-Sharhan et al. (Eds.): I3E 2018, LNCS 11195, pp. 117–128, 2018.
https://doi.org/10.1007/978-3-030-02131-3_12

analytics (Koskenvoima and Mäntymäki 2015). The practitioner-oriented advices pivot primarily on the need of employing capable data scientists and on the need of making decisions based on data driven knowledge (Davenport et al. 2012; McAfee and Brynjolfsson 2012; Schildt 2017). Another avenue within this third vantage is the critically tinged stream of literature assessing the implications of the phenomenon of big data (Zuboff 2015; Newell and Marabelli 2015), however while we acknowledge a set of insights derived from those approaches, our focus is not on the unintended implications. Instead, we address another gap: research providing strategic directions for the use of big data is largely absent in the literature. We argue that to reap the strategic benefits of big data, data-driven decisions need to be underpinned by knowledge of how do the specific choices regarding big data utilization reflect and fit the overall business strategy.

To address this void in the literature, we draw on Newell and Marabelli (2015) and Zuboff (2015) to categorize the sources of big data into five types. We thereafter categorize big data into two types based on its constitution (Constantiou and Kallinikos 2015). In practice, we take the aforementioned threefold approach and identify the phenomenon labelled big data through (i) its origins (where and how does the data accumulate), (ii) its constitution (what is the nature of the data), and (iii) its applications (how and why can the data be processed and utilized). Distinguishing between these three vantages is important for the sake of conceptual clarity, because conflating the three vantages in the descriptions threatens to muddle the conceptual understanding of the complex phenomenon.

As a result of this conceptual analysis, we argue for three questions that can guide the process of making strategic decisions regarding the utilization of big data. We further use these questions as a foundation for proposing a conceptual framework for strategic data use and strategic positioning. In addition, the proposed framework facilitates positioning the data-use related firm-specific choices into a wider context of strategic tradeoffs that allow assessing the level of alignment between the overarching business goals of the firm and its choices related to utilization of big data.

The remainder of the paper is structured as follows: we begin by outlining and continuing the discussions (Constantiou and Kallinikos 2015; Tilson et al. 2010; Zuboff 2015) delineating and crystallizing the phenomenon labelled big data and its impacts on strategizing. In sum, we view big data from the three vantages of its origins, constitution and use, with the emphasis on the last part. Then we continue by identifying three continua along which the firms need to position their strategic approaches in regards to utilizing big data. Subsequently, we propose a framework to support strategic utilization of big data and conclude by recapping the contributions and providing future research avenues.

2   Big Data: Origins, Constitution and Utilization

According to Zuboff (2015), as most discussions of big data are accompanied by efforts of defining it, a satisfactory definition of the phenomenon loosely given the label seems to not yet exist. The origins of the concept are often traced to the 2001 paper by Laney at Gartner (Gartner and Laney 2001), where the qualitative changes in data and its accumulation were defined by three v's, volume, velocity and variance. Subsequent definitions have introduced for example additional v's, like veracity, variability, visualization, value to name a few (Newell and Marabelli 2015), blurring the definition further. For the sake of conceptual clarity, here we identify the phenomenon through three vantages: origins, constitution and use.

With respect to the origins of big data, Newell and Marabelli (2015) propose a category of two (human-digital interaction, e.g. social media and internet searches and signals from embedded sensors), whereas Zuboff (2015) identifies three more sources (computer-mediated digital economic transactions, corporate and government databases, and surveillance systems) to present altogether five source categories. Here we utilize the more comprehensive categorizing by Zuboff to ground our approach.

The human-digital interaction refers to the traces people leave when utilizing the digital devices by e.g. browsing the web, using social networking sites and navigation services, or storing online fitness activities recorded by wearable devices. Especially when using mobile digital devices, we are creating data harnessed also by embedded sensor technology tracking for example our location (Abbas et al. 2014) or even the intensity of our discussions (Greene 2014). The developments in sensor technology are quite notable: it is for example possible to detect from a distance whether the driver of a car driving by is under the influence of alcohol (Hewitt 2014), or even to monitor brainwaves (Sundaresan 2017), each of these applications resulting in creating data in numerous forms. Equally notable are the sensor technology developments underpinning the Industry 4.0 scenarios (Gilchrist 2016; Hermann et al. 2016; Kagermann 2015) in the industrial setting, and in the creation of the so called internetof-everything, the development of smart gadgets and equipment for both industrial and domestic use. These developments in the sensor technology have also an impact on the third data source identified by Zuboff (2015), the surveillance systems (Lyon 2015), taking additional advantage of the increasingly ubiquitous cameras and satellites.

These three types of data sources represent the new forms of data creation, where the data being harvested is far from uniform or categorized at the outset. In contrast, the fourth source, government or corporate databases, is old and as such, mostly reliant on *a priori* categorizing the desired data, including its form. This means that the type of data originating from these more traditional sources is qualitatively different to the data resulting from the more contemporary sources of big data: for example, a governmental health related database contains only such information of the citizens that someone at some point has deemed pertinent to ask and store. The fifth identified source, the traces of digital transactions (Varian 2010) falls in between these categories, as a part of that data is predefined and -categorized, consisting of alphanumerical information, whereas a part of that data is mere imprints of the events and actions accompanying the transaction processes.

In terms of the constitution of big data, Constantiou and Kallinikos (2015) detail the diversity of the types of data being accumulated. Part of the data is pre-categorized and alphanumerical (like the data in governmental databases, for example), but more notable are for example the images, location specific data, audio signals and social network system tokens, such as Facebook "Likes", resulting from the newer types of data creation. In contrast to such data that has long been used in business intelligence (i.e. harvested by firms to facilitate decision-making by seeking out answers to predefined questions), these new forms of data do not result from *a priori* planning and categorizing the specific type of data needed for specific business purposes but accumulates as a trace of all types of digital activities (Chen et al. 2012). This type of data is not "sorted in the way in" (Weinberger 2007), but instead requires advanced analytical and processing capabilities in distilling the meaningful from the noise.

To recap, the sources of big data can be categorized into five types, and the constitution of data can be reduced into two types based on prior literature. However, similar typologies focusing on the uses of big data are largely absent in the literature. To address this void in the extant literature, we argue for three questions that can guide both data use related theorizing and strategically exploiting the potential of big data.

3 Three Continua of Strategic Utilization of Big Data

The first continuum stretches between generalizability and personalization. It pertains to the expected value generation of data: do we want to use the data in seeing patterns and trends, or do we want to be able to predict the actions of an individual, be it human or machine? The second continuum relates to our access to data, and consists of the polar ends of proprietary and networked sources of data: can we source all data through our own efforts, or do we need data from external sources? The third continuum relates to the level of investments we are willing to make in our data processing capabilities: is our business primarily in refining the raw data, or in utilizing the refined data?

Next, each of these continua is explored in more detail, followed by a synthesizing framework that can provide starting points for strategic data use.

3.1 Utility: Generalizability vs. Personalization

The first strategic question in thinking about the potential use of the enablers of big data is: does the business benefit more from understanding general trends and patterns, or from being able to understand the behavior of an individual, be it a human, a process or a machine? The answers to this question form a continuum along which the firm can position itself.

A furniture retail firm was struggling with staffing issues in their physical stores – the customers peaked seemingly at random, which meant that the store was constantly either overstaffed or understaffed in regards to the customer needs. The firm hired a consultancy specialized in data analysis, and after some twists and turns, it was found out that the customer peaks correlated with local weather patterns: customers kept pouring in the day after it had rained and poured outside. While the data revealing this insight did not enable analyzing the causes of this, it however helped the firm in its staffing issues: a year later the personnel costs were notably smaller, and the turnover rate of sales on the peak days was notably better.

This example captures nicely the potential of big data in identifying patterns and creating generalizable preferences. The massive amounts of data about seemingly unrelated issues processed with algorithms enables seeking and seeing correlations. In industrial setting, such correlations can be found between error logs and for example specific type of use or location, thus helping in designing predictive maintenance protocols.

However, while these correlations and patterns reveal a lot about the aggregated tendencies, they do not yet yield information about the individual dispositions. Newell and Marabelli (2015) highlight the issue with an example from the field of insurance. Based on comparing the accident logs with the information about the drivers of those vehicles, young male drivers, as a group, drive more recklessly than other groups. However, this information cannot be used as grounds for charging young men more for their car insurance, because that risks discriminating against such young men who drive safely.

This leads towards the other end of the continuum; the use of big data in personalization, also dubbed as little – or small – data by some authors (Boncheck 2013, Newell and Marabelli 2015). Continuing with the insurance example, it is possible to gather data from the driving behavior of an individual with equipment fitted into the vehicle (e.g. use of gas, brakes, speed, acceleration) or through identifying a passing car by means of surveillance equipment (cameras, road sensors) and a connection to for example license plate registries. This data can then be compared to the general data about what type of driving typically leads to accidents, and from those correlations it is possible to derive a personalized prediction about the likelihood of a specific individual having an accident. That information can then be used in allocating a risk premium or offering a discount on the insurance, as for example some companies already do (Progressive N/A).

In social media marketing, the recent case of Cambridge Analytica (Cadwallar and Graham-Harrison 2018) highlights other applications of personalized insights extracted from big data. By first harvesting vast masses of Facebook "likes" from diverse individual and connecting that data to the results of the online personality quizzes of those same individuals, it has been possible to deduce for example the political opinions of people based on their "liking" Kitkat or Harley Davidson (Kosinski et al. 2013). This means that through analyzing the "likes" of an individual, it is possible to create fairly accurate predictions of the preferences of that individual, which then in turn enables microtargeting of ads, personalized marketing. Additionally, in the industrial side this approach enables monitoring a specific piece of equipment and predicting its maintenance and service needs. Comparing the general error log data with the data about how specific environmental circumstances and use of that equipment correlate with that data, and then analyzing the accumulated data of the environment and use of a specific piece of equipment enables estimating the need for servicing of that specific piece of equipment.

To sum, while from the technical perspective of harvesting and analyzing data this use-related distinction can be to a degree neglected, understanding the business utility of big data is an essential strategic choice.

3.2   Access: Proprietary vs Networked Data

The question facilitating the positioning along the second continuum of data access is: to what extent is it possible to ground the strategic decisions of the firm on the internally generated (operational) data, and to what extent is access to external data sources necessary for strategic purposes?

The second continuum is underpinned by the insight that data required and generated in the process of firm activities (stored often in diverse CRM and ERP solutions), and the data needed in strategic business related decisions should be seen as two distinct types of data as defined by its use. The first type of data is operational, necessary in and generated as a side product of the operations of the firm, but it is the second type of data that is required in strategic decisions. The important distinction to understand is that while the underlying data sets (including generating, storing and processing the data) may be the same, the use of that data is different depending on whether it is used for operational or strategic purposes. In our second dimension, the question is about the tightness of the coupling between these two uses of data.

At the one end of this continuum, it is possible for the firm to exploit the data it generates for the operational purposes also in strategic decisions to the degree where it is not necessary for the firm to source data externally. An example can be found from traditional heavy machinery industries where the main economic logic is that of economies of scale, and the competitive advantage results from superior cost-efficiency. In that context the data generated by the operations, including operative costs like fuel, material, downtime of machinery and personnel can be utilized in identifying factors that increase the costs and thus diminish the bottom line. What follows is that from the business perspective, such decisions that reduce the costs are directly aligned with the low-cost strategy, and as such, strategic. In these contexts, the benefits from big data emerge from the capability of the firm to process its operational data also in its strategic pursuits of low costs.

In this realm, the only external information required is the buying and selling prices of the relevant markets. The required data sources are primarily internal, related to the operations of the firm, however the technological advances in sensor technology and connectivity mean that in order to exploit the potential of big data fully in this context, it may be necessary to retrofit the mechanical pieces of equipment with such systems that enable the more comprehensive monitoring of all operation related processes and resulting costs.

At the opposite end of this continuum this connection between the internally generated data and the data required for strategic decisions is decoupled. The firm may or may not generate data for its operational purposes, but the business decisions are highly dependent on data from external sources. Shipyards serve well to illustrate this position at the other far end of the continuum. Shipyards operate in the nexus of on the one hand the ship owners and carrier lines, and on the other hand the multitude of subcontractors responsible for designing, constructing and implementing diverse systems, ranging from the heavy machinery like the engines to the interior design, electrical systems and various navigating related solutions. In short, the shipyards can be envisioned as a type of platform where the diverse needs of the ship owners and operators meet the diverse offerings in the field of maritime engineering. In order for this platform to create value, it needs access to several external sources of data, related to not only the contemporary technological advances in the maritime engineering, but also to the drivers of competitive value in the shipping industry, the overarching regulatory and environmental developments in the maritime industries, and the overall market trends and ecosystems in global maritime transportation industries.

In these types of settings, the value from big data emerges from the capabilities geared towards creating appropriate data collaboration relationships grounded on strategic insights about which types of big data have strategic value, where do such types of big data originate from, and how and by whom should the volumes of heterogeneous data be processed. This last type of capability leads towards the third continuum in the conceptual framework of strategic data use.

3.3   Investments: Raw vs Refined Data

The third continuum assesses the optimal tradeoff between the investments on the requisite data-processing capabilities and the expected value returns of those invest-ments: can the firm create value from possessing such sophisticated data-processing capabilities that enable dealing with the raw data, or does the value emerge only from wielding refined data?

The third continuum can be approached through looking at the diverse stages of making sense of the masses of data. Each stage is accompanied with specific requirements, in other words investments in specific types of data-processing capa-bilities. This translates into strategic decisions, where the required investments in data-processing capabilities in different stages of data analysis can be weighed against the business goals: in short, where is the firm-specific cut-off point where the benefits of having such capabilities in-house outweigh the costs of the requisite investments.

As previously discussed, the big data consists of both pre-categorized alphanu-merical data, and uncategorized, highly heterogeneous data. This means that the pro-cessing of the latter type of data has to begin with rendering the data uniform enough to be processed together: ultimately this underpins the notion of digitalization, which means that the diverse types of data signals are digitized, made into bits (binary digits) (Tilson et al. 2010) that can then be processed by various digital technologies. So, the first set of data processing capabilities are such technologies that facilitate digitizing of previously heterogeneous data.

However, the subsequent mass of digital data is still amorphous and unorganized. Unlike traditional data already gathered based on predefined categories, this mass of data needs to be categorized. This is the second stage of data processing, where the artificial intelligence, i.e. sophisticated algorithms are necessary, because processing the vast amounts of data isn't a feasible task for human capabilities. However, this has two pre-requirements: first of all, the firm needs to have the resources needed in developing or accessing the requisite algorithmic capabilities, and secondly, the firm needs to have the human capabilities required in delineating the desired categories then filled with the sorted data – even the most sophisticated algorithms function only based on what they are coded to do, based on the categories they are programmed to identify.

In the third stage, the algorithms are equally necessary. When the unorganized noise of big data is first digitized and then categorized, the artificial intelligence can be used in finding patterns and correlations within or in between the diverse categories. It is here that the business benefits begin to emerge. However, what is still needed, especially on the human side, is the fourth stage, the capability of understanding how and why certain patterns and correlations could have business value, what is the strategic importance of the unearthed insights.

The strategic positioning of the firm in this third continuum emerges through asking the question of whether our competence lies in the first three, or in the fourth stage – or maybe the competitive advantage is a result of having the requisite capabilities in all stages. Amazon is an example of a firm that has invested heavily on capabilities spanning the whole continuum, there are data analyzing firms exploiting the business potential of focusing on the first two stages, whereas for most of the businesses the value of big data derived insights begins to emerge only when the results of the third stage of analysis are combined with the specific strategic needs and ambitions of the firm identified with the fourth stage capabilities.

This third continuum has also another dimension, related to the discussion in the context of the second continuum. Many firms generate masses of operational data that they may or may not use in the strategic decision-making. In the case where the operational data does not carry business value for the focal firm, it might however carry business value to another actor. This means that one of the offerings a firm could consider would be selling (or sharing) the data it generates, either as raw or refined, depending on the emphasis on the data analyzing capabilities in-house. So, ultimately a firm has four choices in regards to data collaboration, depending on its choices in data analysis capabilities, its evaluation of the strategic value of its internally generated data, and its evaluation of its strategic external data needs.

First, if the firm has invested little in the data analyzing capabilities, it can sell (or share) such internally generated raw data it regards of little strategic importance to itself and acquire such refined external data it deems having strategic business value. The other three options presume a level of internal data analyzing capabilities. The firm can still sell (or share) raw data with little value to itself but acquire such raw data it deems valuable and possesses the capabilities to analyze. With adequately sophisticated analyzing capabilities, the firm can sell its data in an already refined form and acquire raw data it then processes to meet its needs – or the needs of its customers, if the firm is in the actual business of data analyzing. Finally, the firm can also acquire refined external data, and in turn offer refined internally generated data. This last option requires a crystallized understanding of the specific data needs in both the strategic actions of the business itself, and in the businesses of the data collaborators.

3.4   Conceptual Framework: Starting Points for Strategic Big Data Utilization

Traditional data gathering processes result from predefined data needs answered by gathering pre-categorized data to answer premeditated questions. As a result, the data in traditional corporate and governmental databases is relatively homogeneous (alphanumerical), structured, and it fills a predefined purpose. In contrast, the big data generated from the sources of human-digital interaction, surveillance systems, sensors and partly digital transactions is highly heterogeneous and trans-semiotic (including not only text and numbers, but also image, sound and activity tokens), and un- or semistructured, and its accumulation is not only a result of purposeful data collection but a residue of the actions and interactions within the digital realm.

Tackling these issues emerging from the origins and constitution of big data leads towards our conceptual framework. To begin with, can the firm benefit from making the heavy investments required in having the capabilities spanning the whole continuum or should it focus on a specific set of data processing capabilities? In addition, as the raw data is in itself useless, how does the firm ensure the adequate access to the other stages of data processing capabilities, if its position on this continuum is narrow? Furthermore, what is the level of coupling between the internally generated operational data and the data required for strategic purposes: i.e. is possible to rely of proprietary data alone or is external data needed, and if so, should it be raw or refined – and with whom and how should the data collaboration agreements be sketched?

Ultimately, however, the aforementioned questions need to be aligned with the anticipated business utility of data: in terms of the business goals of the firm, is it necessary to glean personalized insights or can most value be derived from generalizations? To sum, these choices can be envisioned as a three-dimensional matrix, depicted below (Fig. 1).

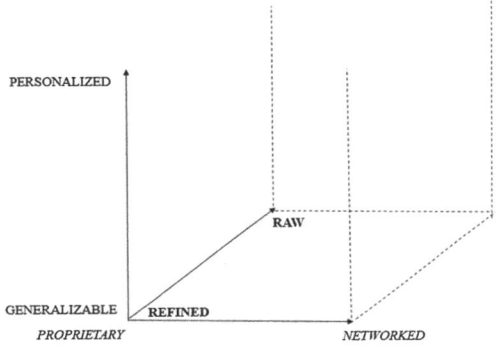

Fig. 1. Conceptual framework of strategic data use

In the nexus where the utility of the data is realized from generalizable insights, access to data is proprietary, and the investments on data processing capabilities are primarily based on dealing with refined data, the strategic data use is still quite traditional, merely enhanced by the efficiency enabling facets of data and automation. However, as soon as the strategic aspirations move onwards on any of the dimensions, the changes in the data use become more profound, increasing both the potential benefits of harnessing big data, and the risks, costs, and complexities in handling the big data. This means that moving onwards on any of these dimensions should be firmly grounded on the overarching strategic choices and business goals of the firm, which subsequently implies that the optimum position along each continuum is highly firm specific, dependent on both the endogenous capabilities and dispositions, and the exogenous environmental elements.

4 Discussion

4.1 Contributions

As its chief contribution to the literature on the strategic potential of big data, the present paper has put forward a framework for strategic utilization of big data. In doing so, the paper responds to the call for research on big data and decision-making (Abbasi et al. 2016). Moreover, this research also continues the discussion initiated by Constantiou and Kallinikos (2015) who highlighted the changes in the strategic contexts resulting from big data: we acknowledge the inevitable changes and go further in exploring the subsequently emerging choices regarding the strategic approaches to utilizing data. Furthermore, we heed the call (Bharadwaj et al. 2013) for the need of digital business strategy where the strategic choices of data use are embedded in the overarching business strategy. As our contribution, we present the conceptual framework identifying the questions underpinning the deliberate data use, which enables assessing the alignment between the overall business goals of the firm and its big datarelated choices.

The framework has both theoretical and practical value. In terms of theorizing, it provides a possible way of categorizing the discussions concerning the third vantage of big data, the deliberate use of big data. For practice, our framework highlights that the further from the nexus of generalizable, proprietary and refined data use the ambitions of the firm in terms of data are, the bigger the complexities, required investments and potential rewards are – and the less the firm can rely on traditional methods of using big data as a subset of business intelligence. Furthermore, understanding these strategic choices of data use can serve as a basis for differentiation through developing analytical capabilities and insights (Abbasi et al. 2016).

4.2 Limitations and Future Research

Like any other, the present study is not without limitations. We thus suggest future research addressing the limitations and shortcomings of the present study.

First, due to the conceptual nature of the present study, we cannot provide first-hand empirical evidence of the applicability of our framework. As a result, future research should empirically scrutinize the framework, including also the firm-dependent guidelines for assessing the optimum position along the continuums.

Second, due to space limitations, we have not discussed role of analytics and business intelligence (cf. Chen et al. 2012). Future research should investigate and elaborate on the analytical capabilities, tools and processes needed to obtain the desired business impact of each type of big data use presented in our framework.

Third, in addition to analytical capabilities, tools and processes, the strategic choices presented in and guided by our framework are likely to have ramifications on the firm level but also the network-level business model. We thus suggest future research focusing on how utilizing different types of big data should manifest in the business model and vice versa (cf. Woerner and Wixom 2015), including the network-level effects.

And finally, the big data driven changes to the strategic choices and decision-making processes are by no means limited to the questions of data use. The research on these changes is nascent, with ample room for further scholarly contributions.

References

Abbas, R., Michael, K., Michael, M.G.: The regulatory considerations and ethical dilemmas of location-based services (LBS) a literature review. Inf. Technol. People **27**(1), 2–20 (2014)

Abbasi, A., Sarker, S., Chiang, R.H.: Big data research in information systems: toward an inclusive research agenda. J. Assoc. Inf. Syst. **17**(2) (2016)

Bharadwaj, A., El Sawy, O.A., Pavlou, P.A., Venkatraman, N.V.: Digital business strategy: toward a next generation of insights **37**(2), 471–482 (2013)

Boncheck, M.: 05/03, 2013-last update, Little Data Makes Big Data More Power-ful [Homepage of Harvard Business Review]. https://hbr.org/2013/05/little-data-makes-big-data-mor. Accessed 21 Feb 2018

Brynjolfsson, E., Mcafee, A.: Race against the machine: how the digital revolution is accelerating innovation, driving productivity, and irreversibly transforming employment and the economy. Brynjolfsson and McAfee (2012)

Cadwallar, C., Graham-Harrison, E.: 03/17, 2018-last update, How Cam-bridge Analytica turned Facebook 'likes' into a lucrative political tool [Homepage of The Guardian]. https://www.theguardian.com/technology/2018/mar/17/facebook-cambridge-analytica-kogan-data-algorithm?CMP=share_btn_tw. Accessed 18 March 2018

Chen, H., Chiang, R.H., Storey, V.C.: Business intelligence and anaytics: from big data to big impact. MIS Q., 1165–1188 (2012)

Constantiou, I.D., Kallinikos, J.: New games, new rules: big data and the changing context of strategy. J. Inf. Technol. **30**(1), 44–57 (2015)

Davenport, T.H., Barth, P., Bean, R.: How big data is different. MIT Sloan Manag. Rev. **54**(1), 43 (2012)

Gartner, Laney, D. Last update, 3D data management: Controlling data volume, velocity and variety [Homepage of Gartner], [Online] (2001). https://blogs.gartner.com/doug-laney/files/2012/01/ad949-3D-Data-Management-Controlling-Data-Volume-Velocity-and-Variety.pdf. Accessed 21 Feb 2018

Gilchrist, A.: Introducing Industry 4.0, pp. 195–215. Springer (2016)

Greene, B.: 02/02, 2014-last update, How your boss can keep you on a leash [Homepage of CNN], [Online]. http://edition.cnn.com/2014/02/02/opinion/greene-corporatesurveillance. Accessed 15 Jan 2018

Hermann, M., Pentek, T., Otto, B.: Design principles for industrie 4.0 scenarios, 2016. In: 49th Hawaii International Conference on System Sciences (HICSS), pp. 3928–3937. IEEE (2016)

Hewitt, J.: 06/17, 2014-last update, Engineers create the first laser breathalyzer, for driveby DUI enforcement [Homepage of Extremetech], [Online]. https://www.extremetech.com/extreme/184050-engineers-create-the-first-laser-breathalyzer-for-drive-bydui-enforcement. Accessed 10 Jan 2018

Kagermann, H.: Change Through Digitization—Value Creation in the Age of Industry 4.0. Management of Permanent Change. pp. 23–45. Springer (2015)

Koskenvoima, A., Mäntymäki, M.: Why do small and medium-size freemium game developers use game analytics? In: Janssen, M., et al. (eds.) I3E 2015. LNCS, vol. 9373, pp. 326–337. Springer, Cham (2015). https://doi.org/10.1007/978-3-319-25013-7_26

Kosinski, M., Stillwell, D., Graepel, T.: Private traits and attributes are predictable from digital records of human behavior. Proc. Natl. Acad. Sci. U.S.A. **110**(15), 5802–5805 (2013)

Lyon, D.: Surveillance After Snowden. Wiley (2015)

McAfee, A., Brynjolfsson, E., Davenport, T.H., Patil, D., Barton, D.: Big data: the management revolution. Harvard Bus. Rev. **90**(10), 60–68 (2012)

Newell, S., Marabelli, M.: Strategic opportunities (and challenges) of algorithmic decision-making: a call for action on the long-term societal effects of 'datification'. J. Strateg. Inf. Syst. **24**(1), 3–14 (2015)

Pariser, E.: The Filter Bubble: What the Internet is Hiding from You. Penguin UK (2011)

Progressive, N/A-last update, Snapshot discount system [Homepage of Progres-sive Casualty Insurance Company], [Online]. https://www.progressive.com/auto/discounts/snapshot/. Accessed 21 Feb 2018

Schildt, H.: Big data and organizational design–the brave new world of algorithmic management and computer augmented transparency. Innovation **19**(1), 23–30 (2017)

Sundaresan, S.: 04/05, 2017-last update, Don't speak, just think: The technology that turns thoughts into text [Homepage of World Economic Forum], [Online]. https://www.weforum.org/agenda/2017/04/technology-that-could-turn-your-thoughts-intotext/. Accessed 10 Jan 2018

Tilson, D., Lyytinen, K., Sorensen, C.: Desperately seeking the inrastructure in IS research: conceptualization of "digital convergence" as co-evolution of social and technical infrastructures. In: 2010 43rd Hawaii International Conference on 2010a System Sciences (HICSS), pp. 1–10. IEEE (2010)

Varian, H.R.: Computer mediated transactions. Am. Econ. Rev. **100**(2), 1–10 (2010)

Wang, J., Zhang, L., Duan, L., Gao, R.X.: A new paradigm of cloud-based predictive maintenance for intelligent manufacturing. J. Intell. Manuf. **28**(5), 1125–1137 (2017)

Weinberger, D.: Everything is Miscellaneous: The Power of the New Digital Disorder. Macmillan (2007)

Woerner, S.L., Wixom, B.H.: Big data: extending the business strategy toolbox. J. Inf. Technol. **30**(1), 60–62 (2015)

Yoo, Y.: Computing in everyday life: a call for research on experiential computing. MIS Q. **34**(2), 213–231 (2010)

Zuboff, S.: Big other: surveillance capitalism and the prospects of an information civilization. J. Inf. Technol. **30**(1), 75–89 (2015)

Understanding the Value of MOOCs
from the Perspectives of Students:
A Value-Focused Thinking Approach

Shang Gao[1(✉)], Ying Li[2], and Hong Guo[3]

[1] School of Business, Örebro University, Örebro, Sweden
shang.gao@oru.se
[2] School of Business Administration, Zhongnan University of Economics
and Law, Wuhan, China
liying0912@qq.com
[3] School of Business Administration, Anhui University, Hefei, China
homekuo@gmail.com

Abstract. This study aims to identify the values of MOOCs in education from students' perspective in China. The value of Massive Open Online Course (MOOCs) can be seen as the benefits associated with the use of MOOCs in education. To address this, we employed the Value-Focused Thinking (VFT) approach to identify the values of MOOCs with university students in China. Twenty active students of MOOCs were interviewed in China. Based on the data collected from the interviews, we developed a means-ends objective network describing the value of MOOCs in education. According to the results, efficiency in learning, effectiveness in learning, convenience of learning, learning experience of MOOCs, and usability of MOOCs were identified as the fundamental objectives to maximize values of MOOCs in education.

Keywords: Massive Open Online Course (MOOCs) · The value-focused
Thinking (VFT) approach · Means-ends objective network · Value

1 Introduction

Massive Open Online Courses (MOOCs) can be seen as a technology enhanced innovation in online distance learning of higher education. MOOCs are defined as digitized materials offered freely and openly for educators, students and self-learners to use and reuse for teaching, learning and research [18]. More and more universities are offering MOOCs to their students. MOOCs use information technology to support interactions between the instructors and students, which may lead to enhanced learning outcomes. Since MOOCs are regardless of time and location, MOOCs provide students a new channel of acquiring educational resources. With the open environment, MOOCs enable a diverse group of learners to collaborate and learn together. MOOCs offer through platforms (e.g., Coursera, edX) on which allow students across the world to participate in the course. Many students have completed MOOCs successfully.

Although MOOCs are getting increasingly popular, there has been an ongoing debate about the educational values of MOOCs [7]. For instance, the high dropout rate

S. A. Al-Sharhan et al. (Eds.): I3E 2018, LNCS 11195, pp. 129–140, 2018.
https://doi.org/10.1007/978-3-030-02131-3_13

of participants is one of the major challenges of MOOCs [6]. Hew and Cheung [11] studied reasons why students sign up for MOOCs and why students drop the courses. They identified the following main reasons for dropping out MOOCs: lack of incentives, failure to understand the content material, having no one to turn to for help, and having other priorities to fulfill. The lack of a social environment that facilitates sustained student engagement has also been identified as a reason for high dropout rate [1]. Moreover, another criticism of MOOCs is the insufficient pedagogical approaches that are applied to design and run MOOCs [20]. Furthermore, individual's learning styles also have strong impact on the learning outcomes of MOOCs [9]. Some students may prefer to have face-to-face classroom teaching. These students may not be interesting in taking MOOCs. Last but not least, some teachers may have a lack of trust in technology associated with MOOCs [8]. Most previous research tended to focus on the adoption of MOOCs [10], and teaching and learning in MOOCs from a pedagogical perspective [12]. However, few studies tended to focus on the values of MOOCs from students' perspective. The purpose of this research is to identify the values of MOOCs from students' perspective. The research question of this research is: what are the values of MOOCs from the perspectives of students. To address this, we employed the value-focused thinking (VFT) to identify the values of MOOCs with university students in China. This is helpful to make the use of MOOCs with maximized values.

The rest of the paper is organized as follows. We present the literature review in Sect. 2. Section 3 illustrates the research method. Section 4 describes the application of the methodology and results of this study. We discuss the findings of the study in Sect. 5. Section 6 concludes this research and points out some future research directions.

2 Literature Review

The literature related to this research is discussed in this section.

2.1 Online Learning

Online learning is defined as learning that takes place partially or entirely over the Internet [17]. Online learning provides an alternative way in delivering knowledge. Online learning is designed to enhance the quality of learning experiences and outcomes [17]. Online learning has become popular because it enables learners to have flexible access to knowledge regardless of time and location. Previous studies have been carried out to study online learning from different perspectives. For instance, the authors [25] investigated the learners' perspectives of online learning. Some studies focused on the adoption of online learning (e.g., [13, 19]).

MOOCs can be seen as a form of online learning. Most MOOCs consist of relatively short video lectures and related content while feedback is managed either with peer-review and group collaboration or by automation [2]. MOOCs have two major features: open access to anyone, anywhere with Internet access [16, 26], and scalability, in which courses are designed to support an indefinite number of learners [21].

2.2   Research on MOOCs

There are some existing research works on MOOCs. For instance, the author investigated the adoption of MOOCs from the perspective of the institutional theory in China [10]. In [11], the authors studied motivations and challenges of using MOOCs. In [4], the authors studied the value of delivering MOOCs from key stakeholders' perspectives in Caribbean. Six stakeholders were interviewed in [4]. However, none of he interviewees had experience with MOOCs before. In [2], the authors explored factors that enhance an individual' intention to continue using MOOCs

The success of MOOCs in education depends on the users' adoption of MOOCs. The sustainability of MOOCs is associated with the participation from key stakeholders involved in MOOCs (e.g., students and instructors). It is important to understand the benefits, weaknesses of MOOCs in educational settings. On one hand, the identified benefits and weaknesses are the important factors for the adoption of MOOCs. On the other hand, these benefits and weaknesses are also able to provide some insights for further development of MOOCs. This motivated us to further study the value of MOOCs in China.

To our knowledge, the literature on the usage of MOOCs in China is still developing and lacks comprehensive studies and empirical evidences. This research draws attention to value-focused thinking (VFT) to investigate the value of MOOCs from the perspectives of students in China. This research aims to complement and extend existing research by focusing on the value of MOOCs in the Chinese context. Furthermore, it is a continuing effort in studying the potential factors to enable students to use MOOCs, which would potential contribute to the existing research on the adoption of MOOCs.

3   Research Methodology

The value focused thinking approach [15] provides a method to identify values and structure the identified values systematically. Values are defined as principles used for evaluation by customers [15]. Values that are of concern are made explicit by the identification of objectives. An objective is a statement of something that one desires to achieve [15]. VFT approach can result in a means-ends objective network which can represent fundamental objectives and means objectives.

VFT is a decision technique developed by [15] where values are the primary focus of the decision-making process. VFT is designed to focus the decision-maker on the essential activities that must occur prior to solving a decision problem [14]. In this study, we aim to get insights of the essential activities that must occur to maximize the value of MOOCs in education from students' perspectives. Therefore, it is believed that VFT is an appropriate approach to address the research question. The VFT approach has been applied to the research in information systems, such as creativity in understanding users' privacy and security concerns with SNS [5], understanding the values of mobile technology of education [24], the values of live game streaming [27], and strategic implications of mobile technology [22].

The VFT approach is chosen to answer the proposed research question 'what are the values of MOOCs from perspectives of students?' as the approach helps identify value objectives.

The application of the VFT methodology in exploring students' perspectives on the value of MOOCs in higher education can lead to a more comprehensive information collection which can result in an improved level of understanding of the value of MOOCs in education. The VFT approach is designed to identify what is important and how this can be achieved as it focuses on what the decision-maker cares about [14, 22].

In this study, we employed VFT approach as follows (see Fig. 1):

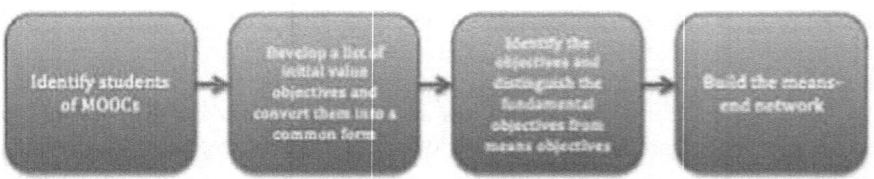

Fig. 1. Steps of VFT approach

- Step 1: Identify users of MOOCs. Getting information and insights from the users of MOOCs is significant to assure the accuracy of the values and objectives.
- Step 2: Develop a list of the initial value objectives and convert them into a common form. Several techniques such as wish lists, problems and shortcomings, alternatives can help conclude the possible objectives from the insights and make them easier to comprehend.
- Step 3: Identify the objectives and distinguish the fundamental objectives from means objectives. Fundamental objectives are the ends that decision makers valued in a specified context, while means objectives are methods to reach the ends. In the process of distinguish means objectives from fundamental objectives and build their relationships, Keeney suggested using the question "why is that important" [15]. For each value objectives, the question will result into two types of possible responses. One is that this objective is one of the essential reasons for interest in the situation, and it is the fundamental for decision making. That is called fundamental objective. Another response is that the objective is important because of its implication for other objective, which is called means objective [24].
- Step 4: Build the means-end network on the basis of the third step. The network provides a model describing the specified relationships between fundamental objectives and means objectives. According to this, analysts could find out how fundamental objectives can be achieved via means objectives. And the relationships presented in the network can help analysts to better understand the complex value system of decision makers.

4 Application of the Methodology

4.1 Data Collection

Data collection was done with students in different universities in one province in China. We invited students from different universities to participate in this study. As a result, a total of 20 students agreed to participate in this research. The VFT approach was applied to uncover the values of MOOCs in China from students' perspective. Interview questions were emailed to the participants two days before the scheduled interviews (see Sect. 4.3 for the questions).

4.2 Subjects

Twenty respondents participated in this research were university students in different majors and aged from 19 to 24 years old. They had taken MOOCs at the university before and had some experience with MOOCs. Therefore, it is believed that these participants could precisely comprehend our research questions and express their felling about MOOCs, such as benefits, limitations and weaknesses.

4.3 Identifying the Value Objectives

Following the VFT approach, we interviewed the participants with the probing questions below:

What are the benefits of using MOOCs, and why is that important?
What problems have you faced in using MOOCs?
What encourage you to finish a MOOC?
If you have a chance to develop a MOOC, what features or functions do you want to add?

Using these questions, we collected an initial list of value objectives about MOOC. On the base of these initial list, we used the "Why is that important" test to explore and distinguish means objectives and fundamental objectives. The "Why is that important" test introduced subjects to think critically about the relationships between value objectives. The subjects need to think the essential reason why he or she uses MOOC. Until the subject said "I think the objective is important because itself is important", the test is done and the fundamental objectives have been identified.

Using the "means-ends" chain theory, the relationships between these value objectives had also been found out. The specific steps are as follows:

When one respondent mentioned "I think the reason why MOOC is attractive to me is that it gives me an opportunity to get access to the elite courses in famous schools", the researchers then asked "Why access to the elite courses is important to you in MOOC learning?" Respondents answered that "Elite teacher often has a more widely horizon than ordinary teachers in the same subject, they can use many cases or models to help us better understand the course materials.. In MOOC class, I not only have a chance to join these elite courses, but also can choose them on my own." The researchers then asked, "Why do you think having an opportunity to choose a course is important?" Respondents said "Learning behavior varies from person to person, and different teaching methods fit different learners. The traditional way of teaching is that students only have to accept the teacher who arranged by school and his/her methods. While in MOOCs, students have opportunities to make their own study plans by select different courses and teachers." The researchers asked "Why making a learning plan by yourself is important?" Respondents replied "Because I could be more efficient in my own learning pace". "Why is efficiency important?" Respondents answered "The efficiency of learning is intrinsically important."

In this example, after coding the interview content, the means-end chain is as follows: "Maximize participation of educational resources", "Maximize alternative of courses", "Maximize customized learning", "Maximized efficiency in learning". In the chain, the last "Maximized efficiency in learning" will be recognized as the basic fundamental objectives, and other value objectives are means objectives which use to achieve the fundamental objectives.

As the research data came from the dictation of the respondents, and each of them had his/her own way of expression, this may result in some misunderstanding. On the other hand, the data identification process could also been influenced by the subjectivity of researchers to a certain extent. In order to minimize the influence of subjectivity of researchers and increase the reliability of this research, another researcher had been invited to participate in the step of identification and classification of the value objectives.

Two researchers firstly conducted coding of six interviews, and identified fundamental objectives and means objectives from the interview material independently. Then the coding results had been compared, with 90% of the coding in the same. Some ambiguities caused by oral and written expression had been discussed. After an agreement was reached, one researcher coded the remaining interview material. Once the interview material coding in the previous step has been completed, three researchers reviewed all the coding results, merging duplicate values and removing the extra values. The results of the identification of value objectives were showed in Table 1.

4.4   Identifying the Value Objectives

We have identified fundamental objectives and means objectives and their relationships in Sect. 4.3. The developed Means-Ends objective network is presented in this section (see Fig. 2). In the Means-Ends objective network, every means-end relationship has at least been mentioned by four respondents. This is to assure built Means-Ends objective network obtain main and common relationship [23].

5   Discussion on the Findings

This study used a qualitative research approach to understand the values of MOOCs in education from students' perspectives (e.g., what do students expect with MOOCs in education), and developed a means-ends objective network that depicts these values and their relationships.

This paper contributed to previous literature. Firstly, to our knowledge, our study was one of the first studies that formally investing the values of MOOCs. Second, our study contributed to the existing literature on using value-focused thinking approach to

Table 1. The results of the identification of value objectives Fundamental

Objectives:
Maximize efficiency in learning
Example: Maximize time self-management
Maximize progress self-management
Maximize effectiveness in learning
Example: Maximize acquisition of knowledge
Maximize understanding of learning materials
Maximize convenience of learning
Example: Minimize time/location constrains for learning
Enable studying in fragmented time
Maximize learning experience of MOOC
Example: Maximize assistance from others
Maximize support from Internet
Maximize usability of MOOC
Example: Maximize ease of use of MOOC service
Maximize ease of search/navigation on MOOC platform
Means objectives:
Maximize utilization of information technology
Example: Maximize the presentation of course content with multi-media tools
Students' learning data can be collected in the background and be analyzed
Maximize interaction in learning
Example: Improve the interaction experience between students and instructors
Improve the interaction chance among students
Enable online testing
Example: Students can take test anytime and anyplace
Instructors can organize more quizzes, exams during the course
Maximize immediate feedback
Example: Maximize students' ability to get immediate answer
Maximize instructors' ability to offer real-time question/answering
Maximize virtual collaboration among students
Example: Maximize ability of collaborative learning tools
Maximize collaborative learning chance among students
Maximize coverage area and connection speed of Internet
Example: Maximize Internet access points
Maximize Internet connected speed
Minimize learning equipment threshold
Example: Enable MOOC learning in a low-cost computer
Enable MOOC learning in a low-cost mobile device
Maximize accessibility of MOOC resource
Example: Maximize access to MOOC services at any time
Maximize access to MOOC services at any place

(continued)

Table 1. (*continued*)

Means objectives:
Maximize information sharing/communication
Example: Maximize exchange of information among students
Maximize the communication of students and instructors
Maximize student involvement in learning
Example: Maximize students participation in learning
Minimize aloneness brought by online learning
Maximize flexibility in time arrangement
Example: Enable students arrange their learning time in demand
Maximize flexibility in learning schedule
Example: Enable students arrange their learning schedule in demand
Minimize cost of learning
Example: Minimize cost of purchasing course resource
Minimize other cost during MOOC learning
Maximize participation of educational resources
Example: Maximize the participation of instructors in MOOC
Maximize the participation of institutions in MOOC
Maximize alternative of courses
Example: Maximize varieties of MOOC courses (category, complexity) for students to choose
Maximize customized learning
Example: Enable students learn at their own pace
Provide personalized learning plan for each student
Enhance usability of user-interface
Example: Maximize ease of user guidance
Maximize ease of MOOC service
Minimize language barrier
Example: Provide mother language courses for students
Provide mother language subtitles for foreign students
Maximize accuracy of course search
Example: Maximize ease of course search engine
Enable users view course comments from others
Maximize social recognition
Example: Provide a MOOC course certification after finish learning
Maximize the influence of MOOC course certification

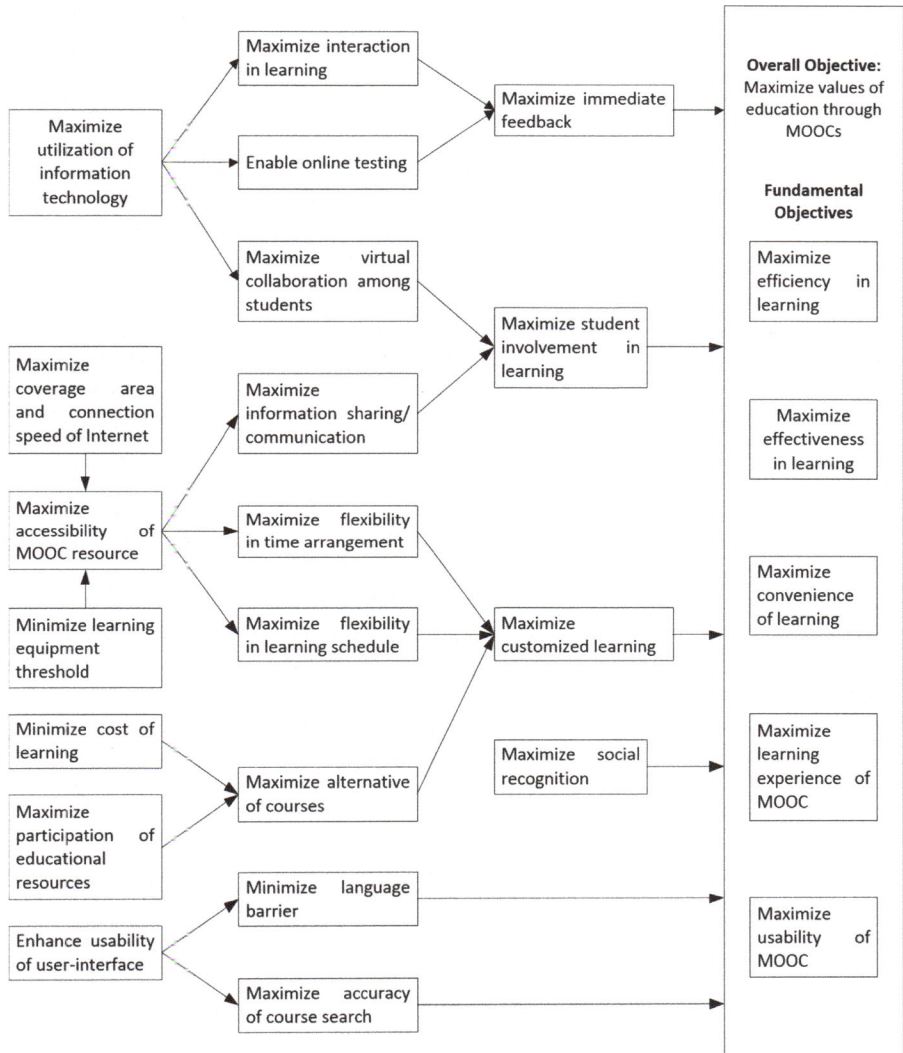

Fig. 2. Means-ends objective network

explore the values of innovational services. Lastly, we added new evidences of how students expect to benefit from using MOOCs in the competitive learning environment.

According to the results, a total of 25 objectives were derived from the collected data in the interviews. Efficiency in learning, effectiveness in learning, convenience of learning, learning experience of MOOCs, and usability of MOOCs have been identified as the five fundamental objectives to maximize values of MOOCs in education. Twenty means objectives were identified as important objectives to realize the derived five fundamental objectives.

The developed means-ends objective network also revealed some problems with MOOCs. For instance, students would like to have more interactions with teachers. There is limited contact between students and teachers. This is consistent with one of the findings in [4]. The authors indicated that teachers' active presence on MOOCs was needed [4]. The issue with the active engagement of teachers on MOOCs needs to be addressed. The university management team needs to find out a solution to encourage teachers' active engagement on MOOCs. Some students also indicated that better Internet connectivity and coverage on campus was needed to maximize the value of MOOCs. The university can make further investment to upgrade the broadband and network infrastructure on campus.

Another critical issue with MOOCs is the financial issue. Who is going to fund the hours instructors spent in developing MOOCs. Teaching a MOOC requires major commitment and distracts the instructors from their usual campus responsibilities. Concerning the sustainability of MOOCs, It is important for universities to obtain the revenue to operate MOOCs.

The results also provided some insights for decision makers at universities. In [3], the author argued that the use of VFT can improve decision making over traditional thinking. It is believed that the findings of this study would have impact to decision makers in the management and development of MOOCs. For instance, decision makers at university can get a better understanding of university students' expectation to maximize the value of MOOCs at an educational setting. Consequently, decision makers can assess the strengths and weaknesses of operating MOOCs to make further plans and investments in developing MOOCs in higher education. Furthermore, it can also help universities develop guidelines for students to take MOOCs.

6   Conclusion and Future Research

This study identified the value of MOOCs in education from the perspectives of students using VFT approach. It targeted university students since they were one of the key stakeholders with MOOCs. The results indicated that efficiency in learning, effectiveness in learning, convenience of learning, learning experience of MOOCs, and usability of MOOCs were identified as the fundamental objectives to maximize values of MOOCs in education in China.

We are also aware of some limitations of this study. The sample size of this study was quite small. Therefore, the generalizability of the results to other users remains to be determined. Secondly, the participants of this study were mainly between 19 to 24 years old. Although they can represent students of MOOCs to some extent, they may not reflect the total population of MOOCs' students in China.

We plan to refine the means-ends objective network by including other key stakeholders (e.g., teachers) views' on the value of MOOCs in the future. Furthermore, we also plan to identify the value of MOOCs in education from students' perspectives in some other countries.

References

1. Adamopoulos, P.: What makes a great MOOC? An interdisciplinary analysis of student retention in online courses (2013)
2. Alraimi, K.M., Zo, H., Ciganek, A.P.: Understanding the MOOCs continuance: the role of openness and reputation. Comput. Educ. **80**, 28–38 (2015)
3. Barclay, C.: Using frugal innovations to support cybercrime legislations in small developing states: introducing the cyber-legislation development and implementation process model (CyberLeg-DPM). Inf. Technol. Dev. **20**(2), 165–195 (2014)
4. Barclay, C., Logan, D.: Towards an understanding of the implementation & adoption of massive online open courses (MOOCs) in a developing economy context. In: Proceedings Annual Workshop of the AIS Special Interest Group for ICT in Global Development, pp. 1–14 (2013)
5. Barrett-Maitland, N., Barclay, C., Osei-Bryson, K.-M.: Security in social networking services: a value-focused thinking exploration in understanding users' privacy and security concerns. Inf. Technol. Dev. **22**(3), 464–486 (2016)
6. Clow, D.: MOOCs and the funnel of participation. In: Proceedings of the Third International Conference on Learning Analytics and Knowledge, pp. 185–189. ACM (2013)
7. Conole, G.G.: MOOCs as disruptive technologies: strategies for enhancing the learner experience and quality of MOOCs. Revista de Educación a Distancia (39) (2013)
8. Ekberg, S., Gao, S.: Understanding challenges of using ICT in secondary schools in Sweden from teachers' perspective. Int. J. Inf. Learn. Technol. **35**(1), 43–55 (2018)
9. El-Hmoudova, D.: MOOCs motivation and communication in the cyber learning environment. Proced. Soc. Behav. Sci. **131**, 29–34 (2014)
10. Gao, S., Yang, Y.: An empirical study on users' adoption of MOOCs from the perspective of the institutional theory. Int. J. Netw. Virtual Organ. **16**(4), 377–388 (2016)
11. Hew, K.F., Cheung, W.S.: Students' and instructors' use of massive open online courses (MOOCs): motivations and challenges. Educ. Res. Rev. **12**, 45–58 (2014)
12. Hill, P.: Online educational delivery models: a descriptive view (2014)
13. Huang, J.-H., Lin, Y.-R., Chuang, S.-T.: Elucidating user behavior of mobile learning: a perspective of the extended technology acceptance model. Electron. Libr. **25**(5), 585–598 (2007)
14. Keeney, R.L.: Creativity in decision making with value-focused thinking. Sloan Manag. Rev. **35**(4), 33 (1994)
15. Keeney, R.L.: Value Focused Thinking - a Path to Creative Decisionmaking. Harvard University Press, Cambridge, US (1992)
16. Martin, F.G.: Will massive open online courses change how we teach? Commun. ACM **55**(8), 26–28 (2012)
17. Means, B., Toyama, Y., Murphy, R. et al.: Evaluation of evidence-based practices in online learning: a meta-analysis and review of online learning studies (2009)
18. OECD: Giving knowledge for free: the emergence of open educational resources (2007)
19. Park, S.Y., Nam, M.W., Cha, S.B.: University students' behavioral intention to use mobile learning: Evaluating the technology acceptance model. Br. J. Educ. Technol. **43**(4), 592–605 (2012)
20. Rizzardini, R.H., Gütl, C., Chang, V. et al.: MOOC in Latin America: implementation and lessons learned. In: Uden, L., Tao, Y.H., Yang, H.C., Ting, I.H. (eds) The 2nd International Workshop on Learning Technology for Education in Cloud, pp. 147–158. Springer, Netherlands (2014)

21. Robinson, A.C., Kerski, J., Long, E.C., et al.: Maps and the geospatial revolution: teaching a Massive Open Online Course (MOOC) in geography. J. Geogr. High. Educ. **39**(1), 65–82 (2015)
22. Sheng, H., Nah, F., Siau, K.: strategic implications of mobile technology: a case study using value-focused thinking. J. Strateg. Inf. Syst. **14**(3), 269–290 (2005)
23. Sheng, H., Nah, F.F.H., Siau, K.: Value-focused thinking and its application in MIS research. J. Database Manag. **18**(3), I–V (2007)
24. Sheng, H., Siau, K., Nah, F.F.-H.: Understanding the values of mobile technology in education: a value-focused thinking approach. ACM SIGMIS Database **41**(2), 2544 (2010)
25. Song, L., Singleton, E.S., Hill, J.R., et al.: Improving online learning: student perceptions of useful and challenging characteristics. Int. High. Educ. **7**(1), 59–70 (2004)
26. Terras, M.M., Ramsay, J.: Massive open online courses (MOOCs): Insights and challenges from a psychological perspective. Br. J. Educ. Technol. **46**(3), 472–487 (2015)
27. Yang, X., Gao, S.: Understanding the values of live game streaming: a ValueFocused thinking approach. In: 16th Wuhan International Conference on EBusiness (WHICEB 2017), Wuhan, China, May 26–27, pp. 394–401. Association for Information Systems (2017)

Is Ecosystem Health a Useful Metaphor? Towards a Research Agenda for Ecosystem Health Research

Sami Hyrynsalmi[2] and Matti Mäntymäki[1(✉)]

[1] University of Turku, Turku, Finland
matti.mantymaki@utu.fi
[2] Pervasive Computing, Tampere University of Technology, Pori, Finland
sami.hyrynsalmi@tut.fi

Abstract. The term ecosystem has been widely adopted outside its original domain in biology, for example in business and engineering studies. Ecosystem health is a derivative metaphor used to describe the success of the ecosystem. In this paper, we describe the key shortcomings of ecosystem health research. We put forward two key postulates of ecosystem health. Based on these postulates we present a research agenda for ecosystem health.

Keywords: Business ecosystem · Software ecosystem · Ecosystem health

1 Introduction

The term 'ecosystem' has been widely adopted outside its original domain in biology, for example in business and engineering studies. Prior studies have introduced terms including 'business ecosystems' (Peltoniemi and Vuori 2004), 'innovation ecosystems' (Oh et al. 2016), 'mobile application ecosystems' (Hyrynsalmi et al. 2016), 'service ecosystems' (Vargo and Lusch 2011), 'product ecosystems' (Frels et al. 2003), among others. The widespread use implies that the ecosystem analogy has been viewed to provide value-added for research. At the same time, the use of ecosystem analogy has also been criticized (see for example Oh et al. 2016; Hyrynsalmi et al. 2015a, Mäntymäki and Salmela 2017).

In biology, an ecosystem, or ecological system, typically denotes a unit of biological organization made up of all the organisms in a given area, thus forming a "community". Organisms within a community interact with the physical environment so that the flow of energy leads to characteristic trophic structure and material cycles within the system (Odum 1966). *Ecosystem health* is an analogy used to describe business ecosystems. According to Ianisiti and Levien (2004a, p. 5), ecosystem health is a crucial concept in business ecosystem research: *"if the ecosystem is healthy, individual participants will thrive; if the ecosystem is unhealthy, individual participants will suffer"*.

Up to date, with one notable exception (Hyrynsalmi et al. 2018), very few studies have critically evaluated applicability of the ecosystem health analogy outside the biological domain, for example with respect to business or software. To address this

S. A. Al-Sharhan et al. (Eds.): I3E 2018, LNCS 11195, pp. 141–149, 2018.
https://doi.org/10.1007/978-3-030-02131-3_14

void in prior literature, this study aims to concretize the critique presented by Hyrynsalmi et al. (2018) towards a research agenda. As a result, the purpose of this paper is to *(i)* critically discuss the applicability of the ecosystem health analogy in business research, *(ii)* address the key challenges related to the use of the ecosystem health analogy, and *(iii)* put forward a research agenda to address these challenges.

The remaining of the study is structured as follows. Section 2 previews the extant literature on software ecosystem health. Section 3 defines the starting hypotheses and drivers for the ecosystem health research renewal. In addition, it discusses on various countermeasures against the seen issues. Section 4 lists the research actions proposed and Sect. 5 concludes the study.

2 Ecosystem Health as a Metaphor

In addition to different biology inspired analogies such as rainforest or jungle, research on business networks has used the 'business ecosystem' analogy by Moore (1993, 1996), and its derivatives—such as 'software ecosystem'—as a crucial conceptualizations for today's business networks. A key characteristic that distinguishes natural ecosystems from artificial ecosystems such business ecosystems is actor's consciousness of the existence of the ecosystem and the actors involved in the ecosystem ecosystems (Moore 1993). The fact that actors are conscious of the ecosystem allows then to also evaluate the health of the ecosystem and adapt their behaviour intentionally.

In this paper, we view software ecosystem as a subset of the more generic business ecosystem concept (Hyrynsalmi et al. 2015a). There are several different kinds of software ecosystems (SECO) focusing on the software producing companies and their networks (Jansen et al. 2009; Manikas and Hansen 2013a), mobile ecosystems formed by the companies producing hardware and software for new era smartphones (Basole 2009), and even mobile application ecosystems comprise the relationships of mobile application marketplaces, their content producers i.e. application developers, and users (Hyrynsalmi et al. 2014; Suominen et al. 2014). Furthermore, the software ecosystem concept includes non-commercial open-source ecosystems built on shared code repositories (e.g., OSGi ecosystem), commercial open-source projects (e.g., WebKit) as well as platform ecosystems revolve around global players such as Amazon, Facebook, and Alibaba and utilize the focal company's interface to customers and brand.

To illustrate the difference between business and software ecosystem, Manikas and Hansen (2013) pointed out that in a software ecosystem, the relationships between the actors are based on a shared software technology or a software platform (Manikas and Hansen 2013a). Based on these considerations, we conceptualize, software ecosystems are business ecosystems where software constitutes a focal part of the unit of exchange.

Software ecosystem as research area is relatively young, first publications dating back to the first decade of the 2000s (Jansen and Cusumano 2013). The term and conceptualization emanate from Moore's (1993, 1996) work on business ecosystems. According to Moore (1993), a business ecosystem is a complex network of organizations and individuals that are involved in the creation or delivery of a service or a product. The business ecosystem concept has hitherto become critical for both scholars as well as for practitioners to understand and describe today's business networks. Due to the potentially simultaneous cooperation and competition as well as abundance of organizations involved in the network (cf. Mäntymäki and Salmela 2017; Hyrynsalmi et al. 2017), business ecosystem are often complex systems.

It is not surprising that business ecosystems are nowadays seen everywhere, from retail (Moore 1993) to telecommunication (Basole 2009), and from small ecosystems orchestrated by a single company to massive software-based value-chains consisting of hundreds of thousands of independent vendors (Hyrynsalmi 2014). According to Moore (1993) a key characteristic of a business ecosystem is the survival of an individual actor depends on the whole network. The survival of the ecosystem is turn contingent upon the individual actors' own choices and agency (Moore 1993). Since then, the literature has examined and put forwards conceptualizations for the well-being of business ecosystems (e.g. Iansiti and Levien 2004a, b; Hyrynsalmi et al. 2015; da Silva Amorim et al. 2017; Alves et al. 2018).

Iansiti and Levien (2004a) derived three health measures from biological ecosystems for business ecosystems: *productivity*, *robustness* to external shocks, and *niche creation* that helps the ecosystem to renew. Iansiti and Levien are (2004a) describe these three measures as follows:

Productivity of business ecosystems can be measured as e.g. return on capital invested or economic value-added created from tangible and intangible assets in producing goods or services. This refers to a biological ecosystem's ability e.g. create biomass from inputs such as sunlight.

Robustness, in its simplest form, refers to the survival rate of ecosystem's members, either in relation to other ecosystems or over time. Robustness means that the ecosystem can face and survive from the changes of the environment.

Niche Creation in the context of business ecosystems refers to ability to create value by putting new functions into operation and increasing meaningful diversity in ecosystem through that. Diversity gives ecosystem potential for productive innovation and indicates its ability to absorb shocks from outside.

In his analysis of ecosystem health literature, Jansen (2014) noted the lack of operationalisations for ecosystem health. To address this issue, Jansen (2014) presented the OSEHO, a health model for open-source ecosystems. It is based on health characteristics defined by Iansiti and Levien (2004a). However, while Jansen's approach is holistic, the model is only applicable for the open-source software ecosystem and thus it cannot be used to evaluate the multitude of different types of software ecosystems.

Ben Hadj Salem Mhamdia (2013) extended the Iansiti's and Levien's (2004a) model and measured the health of an ecosystem with *robustness*, *productivity*, *interoperability*, *satisfaction of stakeholders* and *creativity*. However, the model is built on an interpretation that only firms located in the same country would create a business ecosystem or a software ecosystem. Similarly, den Hartigh, Tol and Visscher (2006) presented a model and measured well-being of an ecosystem based on their co-location in the same country. These interpretations and measures presented for the health of an ecosystem are not compatible with the more traditional interpretation where businesses are required to cooperate instead of being nearly located.

In addition, Hyrynsalmi et al. (2015) as well as Manikas and Hansen (2013b) have presented models for ecosystem health assessment. Hyrynsalmi et al. (2015) adapted a process-like view on ecosystem health assessment. However, the work is based on summarizing extant literature and did not presented any empirical validation to support the models.

Manikas and Hansen (2013b) divided software ecosystem health into three components: the health of software, actors and orchestration. This approach diverges from other conceptualizations and thus provides a novel perspective to study ecosystem health but lacks operationalization and thus also empirical validation. Furthermore, the model measures the health of software through the healthiness of components and platforms. However, instead of a shared platform, software ecosystem can be based on a common standard (cf. Jansen and Cusumano 2013; Knodel and Manikas 2015).

Finally, some existing critique have presented towards the current models. For example, Hyrynsalmi (2016) presented a critique towards unclear terminology and required redefining the concept. Hyrynsalmi et al. (2018) continue the critique by noting that *(i)* it is not clear for whom ecosystem health measures are meant to (e.g., should they be used by ecosystem orchestrators or customers), *(ii)* whether the measures are proactive or only reactive, and *(iii)* emphasizing that the natural evolution of an ecosystem (c.f. Plakidas et al. 2016; Teixeira et al. 2017) has not been taken into account in most of the ecosystem health metrics. However, neither of those works proposed any concrete steps to improve the current status quo.

3 Key Shortcomings of Prior Ecosystem Health Literature

In this section, we elaborate on the key issues related to ecosystem health that, in our view, prior research has not sufficiently addressed. To this end, we put forward two key postulates of ecosystem health.

> *Key postulate 1: Due to the scattered use of the terms 'ecosystem' and 'ecosystem health' both concepts have become muddled and meaningless.*

The concepts *business ecosystem* and *business ecosystem health* are often used as labels for systems or networks under empirical investigation without sufficient consideration and argumentation whether the entity under investigation is an ecosystem. With respect to this issue, Hyrynsalmi et al. (2015) claim that after the labelling has been done, the ecosystem or ecosystem health aspect is often forgotten. This in turn has led to a situation where a multitude of easy-to-collect measures are proposed for assessing the ecosystem health. Thus, in the current discourse, a very diverse set of entities are labelled and empirically treated as ecosystems. Consequently, more or less every aspect of the so-called ecosystem can be used to measure ecosystem health. (Hyrynsalmi et al. 2015b; Seppänen et al. 2017.)

As an example of the easy-to-collect measures for ecosystem health, a number of prior studies have proposed using lines of code as a productivity measure of a software ecosystem (cf. Hyrynsalmi 2014 for a summary). However, the number of code lines has been considered an insufficient metric of productivity for decades (Jones 2000). For example, comparing different programming languages is hard and work needed to write a single line of code varies a lot between different kinds of tasks as well as environments. Moreover, productivity should capture an ecosystem's ability to *"transform technology and other raw materials of innovation into lower costs and new products"* (Iansiti and Levien 2004a, p. 3). It is thus questionable whether the number of source code lines meaningfully captures the productivity of an ecosystem.

To address these issues, we hold it is important to move towards establishing a baseline for ecosystem health, i.e. defining what being healthy means in the context of software ecosystems. A potential step to this direction would be to study major software ecosystems—such as Google Play ecosystem and Symbian ecosystem—that exist currently and have already become extinct. The extant literature has focused only on the existing software ecosystems and omitted the studies of departed ecosystems, i.e. *ecosystem post-mortems* (c.f. Hyrynsalmi et al. 2015a; da Silva Amorim et al. 2017). This could potentially help better understand what *health* means and whether absence of health leads into ecosystem death.

Key postulate 2: Existing frameworks to analyse software ecosystem health have been designed to describe certain ecosystem sub-types but have limited value for identifying general properties of business or software ecosystems.

According to (Hyrynsalmi et al. 2015a), current research has treated different software ecosystems as a homogenous group and omitted the rich diversity of different ecosystem types. For example, when Wnuk et al. (2014) tested the ecosystem health framework by Jansen (2014), they used a tool designed for general type open-source ecosystems while their case study focused on a hardware-dependent software ecosystem.

4 Towards a Research Agenda for Software Ecosystem Health

In this section, we build on our two key postulate and move towards putting forward a research agenda for software ecosystem health. To this end, we describe four directions for future research activities.

Study of extinct and dying ecosystems. We propose future research taking a lifecycle perspective to ecosystem health. While there are studies analysing the reasons for the fall of the Symbian mobile ecosystem (e.g. West and Wood, 2013), there is a lack of research examining specifically how ecosystem health measures evolved during the ecosystem life. To address this void, future research could look into other ecosystems potentially approaching the terminal stage and examine how the situation look like through the current measures of ecosystem health and what kind of weak signals, if any, might predict the decline of an ecosystem. This type of research could be conducted e.g. with case study methodology.

Study of healthy ecosystems. We propose an analysis of software ecosystems that are in the different phases of their lifecycles while still considered to be growing. The focus of the research is specifically on existing health measures as well as identifying signals, incidents, and contingencies that may predict the success of an ecosystem. This would help to create a more comprehensive picture of the usefulness of different ecosystem health metrics. In addition, by combining the results of this line of inquiry with insights from the studies of extinct ecosystems, it would be possible to evaluate the usability and relevance of different metrics in different stages of ecosystem lifecycle.

Conceptualization of ecosystem health. We propose conceptual research focusing on ecosystem health. As pointed out by Hyrynsalmi et al. (2015a, 2018), there is an evident need for increased conceptual clarify with respect to business ecosystems and ecosystem health.

Ecosystem taxonomy construction. As discussed in Sect. 3, we propose building a general business ecosystem taxonomy. This would help to make sense in the vast field of ecosystems as well as to characterize relationships and connections between different types of ecosystems. The underlying idea behind the taxonomy is that that there are certain characteristics that are similar between certain types of ecosystems. Thus, by creating the ecosystem taxonomy and identifying measures that can be applied to study the health of different ecosystems, the taxonomy could help select the most usable health measures for each type of ecosystem. Figure 1 below provides an illustrative example of an ecosystem taxonomy.

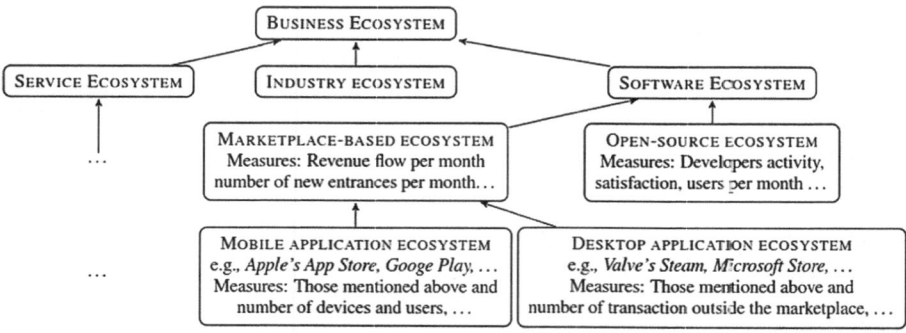

Fig. 1. A partial, simplified, example of an ecosystem taxonomy.

Figure 2 summarizes the proposed research lines as well as their expected impacts to the redefining the field of ecosystem health research. The present study is subject to a number of threats. First, it is possible that each ecosystem should be treated as a snowflake. That is, each ecosystem is unique enough that no common characteristics can be identified. Keeping in mind that there is a limited number of ecosystems available – and the number of competitive ecosystems that a single market support is limited (Hyrynsalmi et al. 2015a) plausibility of the snowflake hypothesis needs to be carefully evaluated.

Second, it is not clear whether the current or even new metrics have predictive or only explanatory value. That is, software ecosystem metrics might turn out to be useful tools for explaining the past issues but lack have predictive power to evaluate the possible future development. Therefore, it is important for the ecosystem health research field to focus also on empirical studies exploring the limits of different metrics.

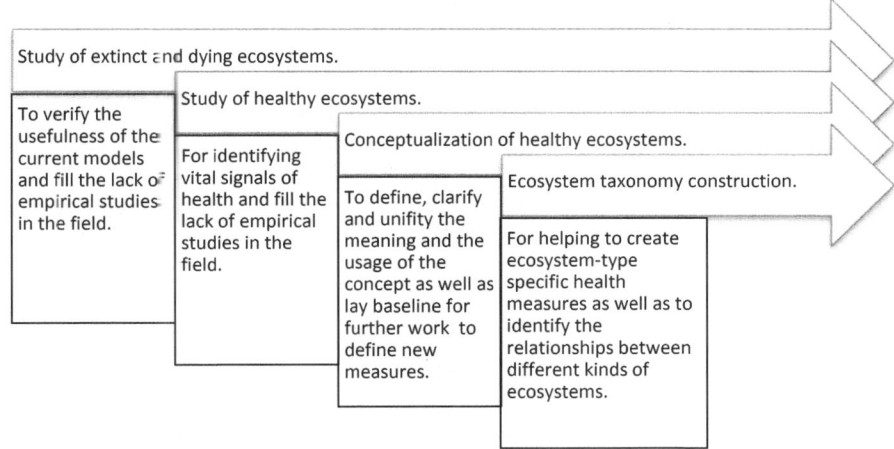

Fig. 2. Proposed four directions and their expected impacts for advancing ecosystem health research

5   Conclusions

This study has presented two key postulates of ecosystem health research and put forward a research agenda to study ecosystem health. To this end, we have put forward two key postulates:

- *#1: Due to the scattered use of the terms 'ecosystem' and 'ecosystem health' both concepts have become muddled and meaningless,* and
- *#2: Existing frameworks to analyse software ecosystem health have been designed to describe certain ecosystem sub-types but have limited value for identifying general properties of business or software ecosystems.*

In addition, based on those two postulates, we proposed four research directions that should be advanced in order to restart ecosystem health research. Our points of departure to the most of the previous studies are our proposals to focus on ecosystem-type specific health measures, and to study also extinct ecosystems. The former would help us to define better-fitting measures for a case at hand. The latter would help us to evaluate whether the proposed measures are useful for predicting the future development and forecasting the fate of an ecosystem based on the health measures.

References

Alves, C., Oliveira, J., Jansen, S.: Understanding governance mechanisms and health in software ecosystems: a systematic literature review. In: Hammoudi, S., Śmiałek, M., Camp, O., Filipe, J. (eds.) ICEIS 2017. LNBIP, vol. 321, pp. 517–542. Springer, Cham (2018). https://doi.org/10.1007/978-3-319-93375-7_24

da Silva Amorim, S., et al.: How has the health of software ecosystems been evaluated? A systematic review. In: Proceedings of the 31st Brazilian Symposium on Software Engineering, pp. 14–23. ACM (2017)

Basole, R.C.: Visualization of interfirm relations in a converging mobile ecosystem. J. Inf. Technol. 24(2), 144–159 (2009)

Ben Hadj Salem Mhamdia, A.: Performance measurement practices in software ecosystem. Int. J. Prod. Perform. Manag. 62(5), 514–533 (2013)

Frels, J., Shervani, T.A., Srivastava, R.K.: The integrated network model: explaining resource allocations in network markets. J. Mark. 67(1), 29–45 (2003)

den Hartigh, E., Tol, M., Visscher, W.: The health measurement of a business ecosystem. In: van Eijnatten, F.M. (ed.) Proceedings of the European Network on Chaos and Complexity Research and Management Practice ECCON 2006 Annual Meeting: "Organisations as Chaordic Panarchies"—Towards Self-Transcending Work Holarchies, Bergen aan Zee, The Netherlands, pp. 1–39 (2006)

Hyrynsalmi, S.: Letters from the War of Ecosystems—An Analysis of Independent Software Vendors in Mobile Application Marketplaces. University of Turku, Finland, TUCS Diss. No 188 (2014)

Hyrynsalmi, S., Seppänen, M., Suominen, A.: Sources of value in application ecosystems. J. Syst. Softw. 96, 61–72 (2014)

Hyrynsalmi, S., Seppänen, M., Nokkala, T., Suominen, A., Järvi, A.: Wealthy, healthy and/or happy—what does 'ecosystem health' stand for? In: Fernandes, João M., Machado, Ricardo J., Wnuk, K. (eds.) ICSOB 2015. LNBIP, vol. 210, pp. 272–287. Springer, Cham (2015a). https://doi.org/10.1007/978-3-319-19593-3_24

Hyrynsalmi, S., Suominen, A., Mäntymäki, M.: The role of developer multi-homing and keystone developers in mobile ecosystem competition. Acad. Manag. Proc. 1(14157), 2015b (2015b)

Hyrynsalmi, S., Suominen, A., Mäntymäki, M.: The influence of developer multi-homing on competition between software ecosystems. J. Syst. Softw. 111, 119127 (2016)

Hyrynsalmi, S.: To redefine ecosystem health, or not to redefine? A view of scientific knowledge on the "software ecosystem health" concept. In: Proceedings of the European Workshop on Software Ecosystems 2015, pp. 47–51 (2016)

Hyrynsalmi, S., Mäntymäki, M., Baur, Aaron W.: Multi-homing and software firm performance. In: Kar, A.K., et al. (eds.) I3E 2017. LNCS, vol. 10595, pp. 442–452. Springer, Cham (2017). https://doi.org/10.1007/978-3-319-68557-1_39

Hyrynsalmi, S., Ruohonen, J., Seppänen, M.: Healthy until otherwise proven: some proposals for renewing research of software ecosystem health. In Proceedings of the First Software Health Workshop. ACM (2018)

Iansiti, M., Levien, R.: The Keystone Advantage: What the New Dynamics of Business Ecosystems Mean for Strategy, Innovation, and Sustainability. Harvard Business School Press, USA (2004a)

Iansiti, M., Levien, R.: Strategy as ecology. Harv. Bus. Rev. 82(3), 68–78 (2004b)

Jansen, S.: Measuring the health of open source software ecosystems: moving beyond the project scope. Inf. Softw. Technol. 56(11), 1508–1519 (2014)

Jansen, S., Cusumano, M.A.: Defining software ecosystems: a survey of software platforms and business network governance. In: Software Ecosystems: Analyzing and Managing Business Networks in the Software Industry, Chapter 1, pp. 13–28. Edward Elgar, USA (2013)

Jansen, S., Finkelstein, A., Brinkkemper, S.: A sense of community: a research agenda for software ecosystems. In: 31st International Conference on Software Engineering—Companion Volume, ICSE-Companion 2009, pp. 187–190. IEEE (2009)

Jones, C.: Software Assessments, Benchmarks, and Best Practices. Addison-Wesley Information Technology Series. Addison-Wesley Longman Publishing Co. Inc., USA (2000)

Knodel, J., Manikas, K.: Towards a typification of software ecosystems. In: Fernandes, João M., Machado, Ricardo J., Wnuk, K. (eds.) ICSOB 2015. LNBIP, vol. 210, pp. 60–65. Springer, Cham (2015). https://doi.org/10.1007/978-3-319-19593-3_5

Manikas, K., Hansen, K.M.: Software ecosystems—A systematic literature review. J. Syst. Softw. **86**(5), 1294–1306 (2013a)

Manikas, K., Hansen, K.M.: Reviewing the health of software ecosystems—a conceptual framework proposal. In: Proceedings of the 5th International Workshop on Software Ecosystems, vol. 987 of CEUR Workshop Proceedings, Potsdam, Germany, pp. 33–44 (2013b)

Moore, J.F.: Predators and prey: a new ecology of competition. Harv. Bus. Rev. **71**(3), 75–86 (1993)

Moore, J.F.: The Death of Competition: Leadership and Strategy in the Age of Business Ecosystems. Harper Business, New York (1996)

Mäntymäki, M., Salmela, H.: In search for the core of the business ecosystem concept: a conceptual comparison of business ecosystem, industry, cluster, and inter organizational network. In: Proceedings of the 9th International Workshop on Software Ecosystems, CEUR-WS, pp. 103–113 (2017)

Oh, D.-S., Phillips, F., Park, S., Lee, E.: Innovation ecosystems: a critical examination. Technovation **54**, 1–6 (2016)

Odum, E.P.: The strategy of ecosystem development. Sci. **164**, 262–270 (1966)

Peltoniemi, M., Vuori, E.: Business ecosystem as the new approach to complex adaptive business environments. In: Proceedings of e-Business Research Forum, pp. 267–281 (2004)

Plakidas, K., Stevanetic, S., Schall, D., Ionescu, T.B., Zdun, U.: How do software ecosystems evolve? a quantitative assessment of the R ecosystem. In Proceedings of the 20th International Systems and Software Product Line Conference (SPLC 2016), pp. 89–98. ACM (2016)

Seppänen, M., Hyrynsalmi, S., Manikas, K., Suominen, A.: Yet another ecosystem literature review: 10 + 1 research communities. In: 2017 IEEE European Technology and Engineering Management Summit (E-TEMS), pp. 1–8 (2017)

Suominen, A., Hyrynsalmi, S., Knuutila, T.: Young mobile phone users: radical and individual—not. Telemat. Inform. **31**(2), 266–281 (2014)

Teixeira, J., Hyrynsalmi, S.: How do software ecosystems co-evolve? In: Ojala, A., Holmström Olsson, H., Werder, K. (eds.) ICSOB 2017. LNBIP, vol. 304, pp. 115–130. Springer, Cham (2017). https://doi.org/10.1007/978-3-319-69191-6_8

Vargo, S.L., Lusch, R.F.: It's all B2b… and beyond: toward a systems perspective of the market. Ind. Mark. Manage. **40**(2), 181–187 (2011)

West, J., Wood, D.: Evolving an open ecosystem: the rise and fall of the Symbian platform. In: Collaboration and Competition in Business Ecosystems, vol. 30 of Advances in Strategic Management, pp. 27–67. Emerald Group Publishing Limited (2013)

Wnuk, K., Manikas, K., Runeson, P., Lantz, M., Weijden, O., Munir, H.: Evaluating the governance model of hardware-dependent software ecosystems – a case study of the axis ecosystem. In: Lassenius, C., Smolander, K. (eds.) ICSOB 2014. LNBIP, vol. 182, pp. 212–226. Springer, Cham (2014). https://doi.org/10.1007/978-3-319-08738-2_15

Implementation of Information Security in the EU Information Systems

An Estonian Case Study

Maris Järvsoo, Alexander Norta, Valentyna Tsap, Ingrid Pappel,
and Dirk Draheim[✉]

Large-Scale Systems Group, Tallinn University of Technology,
Akadeemia tee 15a, 12618 Tallinn, Estonia
{maris.jarvsoo,alexander.norta,valentyna.tsap,
ingrid.pappel,dirk.draheim}@ttu.ee

Abstract. In this paper we present the findings of a case-study on IT system security in the area of EU internal security and justice. We have analyzed the implementation of information security for the EU information systems EURODAC, SIS II and VIS in case of Estonia. The analysis comes in a situation, where there are multiple regulations, directives, guidelines; but it lacks a unified standard for the implementation of the member states subsystems. The main finding is that a separate standard is not necessary; however, there is a need for setting minimum requirements, ensuring security of the information systems, that come with appropriate guidelines that help the member states to achieve the minimum requirements. The second finding is that there is a need for greater cooperation and an increased knowledge exchange of the methods used in the member states. Following defined guidelines and exchanging knowledge would help to strengthen the level of security for the entire system.

Keywords: Schengen · GDPR · EU-LISA · EURODAC · SIS II
VIS · IT security · ISO 27001

1 Introduction

In this paper we analyze the implementation of information security in the largescale information systems operated by EU-LISA (European Agency for the Operational Management of large-scale IT Systems in the Area of Freedom, Security and Justice), that help to manage the border crossings and asylum requests to secure the Schengen Area. Since the formation of the European Union, its main goal has been a free market, freedom of movement and residence. In 1985, the Schengen Area was established and borders between the EU member states exist only on the map. Citizens from member states of the Schengen Area can move freely; border control exists only on the external border of the Schengen Area.

Freedom always comes with responsibilities – the member states have to make sure that travelers from third countries, who are entering the Schengen Area are people with good intentions and without criminal background. This is extremely important, because

S. A. Al-Sharhan et al. (Eds.): I3E 2018, LNCS 11195, pp. 150–163, 2018.
https://doi.org/10.1007/978-3-030-02131-3_15

the entering point to the area might not be the same as the travel destination. Take the Berlin terror attack on 19th of December 2016 as an example – the attacker who was driving the lorry into the crowd in Berlin, Germany, was later found in Milan, Italy. This illustrates how easy it is to travel to another country – even in a situation of heightened security risks. Cooperation is the crucial part in the context of free movement. Therefore, the European Commission has requested the development of information systems that share and control the information of travelers. The main information systems are SIS II (Schengen Information System II) [15], VIS/(Visa Information System) [16] and EURODAC (European Asylum Dactyloscopy Database) [12]. These systems share information between the member states, allowing authorized personnel to process personal data and see if a person is flagged for some reason.

The security of the persons crossing the borders or checked in other circumstances is also of highest priority. Therefore, the information security of the EU information systems is a very important topic. A good learning point are the cases of Danish and Swedish authorities in 2013, where information leaked from their national interfaces. The same hacker was involved in both cases and about 1.2 million records of personal data from the SIS information system were found from the hackers' devices. Hacking took place in the summer of 2012 and was discovered by the Swedes. None of the Danish systems alerted Danish stakeholders about the problems; they learned about it from Swedish officials.

Research Questions We analyze the implementation of information security of the systems SIS II, VIS and EURODAC from the perspective of the Estonian member state systems provider. The questions that we deal with are the following:

(i)   What is the exact policy making and management process of the EU information systems? In particular, how are system requirements managed?

(ii) How effective are the current regulations, how many of those are mandatoryand how is the implementation monitored by member states?

(iii) Does the EU need a unified standard on ensuring information security oflarge-scale information systems?

Methodology and Data In service of (i)–(iii) we have conducted an *in-depth review of the relevant EU regulations* (directives, implementing decisions, regulations). We present the outcome of this analysis. Furthermore, we have conducted a systematic expert interview with *the security officer of EU-LISA*. Furthermore, we have conducted systematic expert interviews with the *two key IT stakeholders* that have been responsible for the Estonian EU information systems for at least three years at the time of the research. We have systematically analyzed[1] the interviews. We present the outcome of this analysis.

Paper Outline We start with a detailed explanation of important backgrounds fact about the EU information systems and their implementation issues in Sect. 2. Section 3

---

[1] tool-based, standard thematic analysis with NVIVO.

presents our findings with respect to question (i). Section 4 presents our findings with respect to question (ii). Section 5 presents our findings with respect to question (iii). We discuss relevant related work throughout the paper and delve into some selected related in Sect. 6. We finish the paper with a conclusion including some concrete suggestions in Sect. 7.

2 Operations of the EU-LISA Information Systems

2.1 The EU-LISA Information Systems

The EU-LISA authority has been established in 2011 [21]. The authorities' responsibility is the preparation, development and operational management of the information systems SIS, VIS and EURODAC. The systems must be operational 24/7. Furthermore, EU-LISA is responsible for ensuring data and systems continuity, security, integrity, availability, compliance with EU data protection regulations [11, 18–20] and training of the national authorities. To serve these tasks EU-LISA needs to collaborate with national systems providers, data protection supervisors and the security officers network.

The *Schengen Information System* (SIS) [15] core function is exchange of information between national border control, police and customs officials. The exchanged information contains alerts about persons, e.g., missing persons and children; also, information about stolen and lost documents and property – money, vehicles, firearms. The EURODAC [12, 14] system is an instrument to fulfill the Dublin regulation [8] [2], which helps to compare fingerprints, to find out whether a person has already applied for asylum in another member state or whether a person stays illegally in a state. Thus, it helps to avoid outwitting the European law by "asylum shopping" (attempt to get asylum in more than one member state). The purpose of VIS [16] is to improve the visa policy and cooperation between member states; in particular, it facilitates the checks at the external borders of the Schengen Area. It serves the following tasks: proceeding visa applications, controlling persons and their visa against the system, managing asylum requests, identification and checking whether conditions for an entry, stay or residence are fulfilled.

The main parts of the information systems are central databases and uniform national interfaces. Every member state develops, operates, maintains its national systems, which hold copies of the central systems. The national copies are for conducting automated searches on member states' territory. Data is entered to the central system. It is not possible to search data from another member states' national interfaces. A communication infrastructure between central systems and national interfaces enables searches and information transfer. The communication infrastructure provides an encrypted network for the data exchange. Every Member State has the authority and responsibility for operating the national interfaces, assuring security and compliance with the regulations.

---

[2] formerly known as Dublin Convention.

2.2   Data Exchange and Protection in the Field of Police and Justice

By its nature, the field of police and justice that requires processing of sensitive personal data –data leakage or other illegitimate use of data might result in violation of privacy or personal harm. The field covers the areas of police and border control, asylum and immigration, judicial cooperation in civil as well as in criminal matters and police cooperation. Therefore, this field needs a tailormade protection method for data protection [4]. The data protection directive 95/46 makes no difference between fields of data usage, therefore data protection in a field of police and justice is not regulated specifically. The directive is not applying outside of the boundaries of community law. Despite of that, the member states have widened the scope of the directive by engagement of the directive to the national law [1, 26]. The need for a specific regulation for field was acknowledged already in 1987, by the council of Europe. Since then the provisions have been adopted and in 2005 the Krakow declaration was adopted [13]. Before the Krakow declaration Europol adopted an Eurojust decision in which the detailed framework regarding data protection and operation in police authorities was brought out [1].

Since the 9/11 terror attack in the USA, transmission of information from one field to another has increased so that information collected for specific purposes might be transmitted to another field and used for other purposes. This is a risk in terms of data protection and is not in accordance to the principles of integrity and human rights. The more officials and authorities have access to the information, the higher is the risk of entering the incorrect data that might affect the person in other situations; for example, the visa application process might be more difficult if the SIS II contains a note about the person or the police might use expired information during the discretion process. These problems can be solved by applying strict access management processes, e.g., task-oriented access [28].

With the new EU data protection regulation GDPR (General Data Protection Regulation) [20], the focus lays on the minimization of collected data. Therefore, data protection should be implemented by design, e.g., by measures such as "data protection by default". The GDPR contains a directive regarding data processing for prevention, investigation, detection and prosecution of criminal offences as a tailor-made tool for the police authorities [20].

2.3   Data Exchange and Protection Requirements

Exchange of the supplementary information of SIS II and VIS, between Member States and Central units goes according to the SIRENE (Supplementary Information Request at the National Entries) manual [9]. EURODAC data was transferred between the central unit and the member states by using the TESTA II (Trans-European Services for Telematics between Administrations) infrastructure [7], which is, basically, a virtual private network for public administrations. TESTA II was upgraded to a sTESTA. In 2006 and in 2013, the fourth generation was brought into live with TESTA-ng. TESTA can be used to exchange both classified and unclassified information. In case that the communication infrastructure cannot be used, the member states can use other sufficiently secured channels. To make sure that information can be transmitted to the authority, a security plan must contain the communication control protocol, where the requirements of the accepted authorities are listed [15].

According to the EU-LISA IS regulations [12, 15, 16], it is prohibited to make data available to the third parties such as international organisations or third countries. Member states shall have the independent supervisory authority that assures the lawfulness of the data processing procedures and helps to solve requests regarding personal information held in the information system. The national supervisory authority conducts an audit once in every four years. Similarly, the EU data protection supervisor conducts an audit once in every four years with respect to the central systems. To ensure a coordinated supervision, the national supervisory authorities and the EU data protection supervisor meet every half year to discuss problems, exchange information and unify the regulation.

3   Policy and Management

In this section, we analyse the policy making and management process of the EU information systems.

3.1   Document Analysis

Management of the Information Systems The overall security measures of the EU are covered by the EU regulation 2017/46/EC [11]. The regulation sets areas of responsibilities for different groups and authorities of the EU. Altogether, the it brings out nine different authorities and groups with their areas of responsibilities. The authorities are listed hierarchically, which means, that lower authorities and group reports to higher and some of the responsibilities are fulfilled together. Every authority monitors the execution of some areas of the strategies or policies and creates the frameworks within the service providers or national authorities must work in. Access to cryptology measures is given by the directorate of general human resources and security; and the access is asked by the system owners. Five of the nine authorities are creating strategies, frameworks and policies; three groups, i.e., system owners, data owners and LISOs (Local informatics security officers), provide input for the guiding documents. The last group, i.e., the users, is obligated to follow the rules and recommendations.

The NIS (Network and Information Systems) directive [18] came into force in May 2018. The NIS directive requires the usage of information security standards, however, leaves open the choice of the standard. The aim of the NIS directive is to gain a commonly high level of security of network and information systems across the EU. Therefore, the directive focuses on public-private cooperation and sets the requirement for the member states to establish an information security strategy. The main concerns are security incidents and their surveillance. Every member state must have a CERT (Computer Emergency Response Team) managing information security incidents. To equalize the level of security, the NIS directive sets reporting obligations to the member states. The commission evaluates the execution of the directive after every two years. In addition to the CERTs, each member state has to name an authority as contact point for the EU Commission. The contact point is also responsible for evaluation and application of the directive. The reporting obligation expands on every service provider – public or private – who operates with the critical infrastructure and internationally vital services. The NIS directive points out that it needs a common ground and understanding of the systems' security.

Cooperation The NIS directive [18] recommends a higher level of cooperation between the relevant authorities in the member states and EU authorities such as ENISA (The European Union Agency for Network and Information Security). It also suggest to consult with the interest groups in policy making and improving. Regarding SIS II, which is the largest information system in EU, the SIRENE manual [10] was created; in order to set the boundaries to the operations by the member states. SIRENE bureaus are the main contact points to every official operating with information entered to SIS II. Through the SIRENE bureau the cooperation with EUROPOL, EUROJUST and INTERPOL is organized. All SIRENE bureaus are cooperating with each other, in particular, to solve the issues on why information has been entered [10].

3.2 Interview Analysis

Management of the Information systems The EU-LISA security officer finds that despite the requirement of compiling security plans and setting the specific rules inside the State, there are member states that are not able to conduct the specific security plan. Some of the states are able, but not willing; therefore. the quality of the security plans is lacking behind; and based on them it is difficult to make management decisions. To help member states to raise the level of security knowledge and ability to develop the measures themselves, EU-LISA is working on a security and continuity management system, together with the business continuity plans and security incident management procedure; in order to make them more acceptable to the member states. That would grow their knowledge about preventing incidents and avoiding them to happen. The templates are being renewed together with the EU Commission, to ensure that their requirements are still satisfied. The requirement from the NIS directive is that all of the member states would use a standard to help them prepare the security of the systems and therefore those templates are being renewed to be compliant with relevant ISO requirements. The member states are aware of the need for the security plan, but the need for them is taken more as a requirement, that shall be done, but not as a strategic planning paper, that could help them to increase the level of security. The member states are rather following the internal state requirements and standards, as, e.g., the ISKE [23] standard in Estonia.

From the member state perspective, the management of the systems is bureaucratic, but they also see that large-scale information systems need some level of written bureaucracy to ensure continuity. There could be less paperwork, which would help to work faster with the developments. Every aspect shall be discussed to ensure a joint understanding, but the accepting rounds could be shorter. Each larger change needs to go through a change management group for final agreement, but before that discussions occur in working groups, after that in advisory groups, from which the first is focusing on the business side of the system and another is a technical group. The process through each group is long and takes a lot of time.

Cooperation The cooperation between member states and the central coordination organization is not as good as it should be. The cooperation is based on the required meetings and paperwork, that shall be done, but there is no open discussion, to help the whole EU system to improve. To start an open discussion the security officers network (SON) was created, where every member state could share the experience and therefore help out the others that are falling behind or could gain the knowledge needed to improve their own systems. The attitude is hard to brake; therefore, the SON is still working as a mandatory meeting, not as the open discussion round. Required security plans are presented, but some member states are trying to write the paper as superficial as possible or as they assume the EU-LISA would like to see it, to prevent further questions and discussions. The reality might not be compliant with the information presented on the paper. According to the EU-LISA experience, some of the member states are working hard to be independent and not give any information out to the EU, which makes ensuring the security of the central system much harder, because of the lack of knowledge on what is going on in the member state systems.

The cooperation between member states has been getting better over the time. Unofficial meetings have started occurring, where the developments are discussed. Usually, the highlights are brought up in there, but there is a chance to ask for help if needed. There are also working e-mailing lists. Despite that the communication could be better. The knowledge exchange is not working in daily bases, but the meetings initiated by the member states could be a starting point for that. The cooperation between some of the member states is better than the whole picture. The example in here is the Estonian-Finnish collaboration in testing the systems.

The inhibitors for the active cooperation are the official meetings, where the officials of the EU Commission are also present including to the member state representatives and EU-LISA. Those meetings are controlled and participants are holding back their thoughts. The presence of the EU Commission official is restraining the member states, which was the reason of starting the unofficial meetings. The cooperation between the EU-LISA and member States are mostly good and the necessity is understood, but there have been problems over the time regarding the communication – where one party is not understanding the responsibilities or the central control has trouble in understanding the situation of member states; and therefore the advice they are giving is not suitable. Therefore, the member state specialists are hoping that the inner process will be better soon.

3.3   Summary of Findings

The document analysis and interviews show that there are multiple levels of decision makers, which makes the decision process time consuming. Forms are created for the tasks, procedures of usage are set, but the importance and usage are still unclear. Documents such as the security plan (that should be helpful for member states in planning their security strategy; that should be helpful for the central decision makers for seeing the continuity process and give a hand if necessary) are not fulfilling their purpose, because they are seen as a bureaucratic procedure. On the other hand, some level of bureaucracy for managing the systems with the capacity as those is necessary. The level shall be looked over and updated.

The cooperation between member states is still weak, but it has started to develop. The specialists see that the cooperation between the member states will increase organically and that cannot be pushed, because by pushing it might lose its focus. Cooperation between the member states is evaluated as quite good and the need for an organization as EU-LISA is seen, but it has its problems. The main problems are communication problems, whenever one party is not able to understand the needs of the other. The biggest problem is with the EU Commission, which is seen as a biggest inhibitor of cooperation. In the official meetings where the EU Commission is present, the member states are holding back their thoughts and are not willing to open discussions.

EU-LISA also sees the problems and on their side the main problem is lack of communication. The regulated reports are given, but the knowledge exchange and unofficial communication is not working. EU-LISA tries to change the attitude and by creating SONs to induce the cooperation.

4   Ensuring Security in Data Exchange and Operation

This section deals with the question of how effective the current regulations are, how many of those are mandatory and how the implementation by member states is monitored.

4.1   Document Analysis

Data Exchange and Measures The aim of the GDPR regulation is to unify the requirements of the data regulations across the EU. According to the GDPR information can be processed only by the competent authorities and according to the rules set by the EU. The work of the authorities is controlled by the independent data protection officers, whose role is ensure that personal information is used only within the frames of the regulations and the rights of the data subject are not affected. GDPR is particularly relevant from the IS development perspective, because it encourages the privacy by design approach [19, 20]. All the information systems and their management shall be compliant with the principles of data protection set in those regulations. Regarding the information systems, used in the case, the personal data protection is vital, because of the nature of the systems. The collection of the data, storing and management has to be in correlation with the regulations. Data leakages shall be recorded, fixed and reported to the data protection authorities and their recommendations shall be considered. On the other hand, the data protection officers are the help for the data subject, whenever data subject needs the consultation, the authorities shall give it and regarding the deletion and correction of the data authorities shall observe the rights of the data subject are fulfilled [10, 12, 15–17, 19, 20].

The information exchange in case of the systems used in the field of internal security and justice is according to the system regulations through the information exchange interface, which allows the secure communication with other authorities. The information exchange goes through the TESTA network, which enables also the exchange of the classified information due to the encryption possibilities. The supplementary information exchange in SIS II is organised through SIRENE bureaus, where the information exchanged shall be on the specific forms. In all cases the other channels may be used only in extremely urgent cases or if the information systems are not operational.

Information Security and Measures The NIS directives' aim is to achieve an equally high level of the information security all over the EU. To achieve that goal, it is important for all member states to follow similar approaches regarding information system security. The NIS directive brings out the need for standardized minimum requirements and guidelines to achieve the outcome. The other important steps to gain the equally high level of security is the cooperation, information exchange and similar requirements for the public and private authorities who operate with the information systems regarding vital services. The NIS directive proposes that every member state shall have a national strategy for information security and policies to exploit. In addition to the national paperwork, the incidents shall be handled through the CIRT (Cyber Incident Respons Team) or CERT. In addition, the CIRT and CERT are reporting to the EU, therefore there is a shared incident knowledge allover the EU. The NIS recommends that the member states take into use some of the internationally accepted information security standards, to be able to equalize the level of security [18].

The system regulations bring up the need to put the managerial requirements and polices in place. The polices shall include access management policies (which must be implemented for the physical locations where the information is held or where the systems are located) and digital security measures, which include the access to the systems and logging process. Another measure that helps to prevent the manipulation of the information across the state borders is that the owner of the information entered to the system is the member state that enters the information at the first place; and the other member states shall transmit the information that should be implemented to the owner of the information [15–18].

4.2   Interview Analysis

Data Exchange and Measures The specialists see the existing information exchange network as secure in general. The information is moved through defined channels according to the defined protocol in the interface control document. The protocol itself arises more concerns. Despite the existing interface control document, the member states implement the sending of the forms differently and that can cause problems. Those problems are raised in the working group meetings and implementation details of the forms are being discussed. Solving those problems can be a slow process. The physical environment security is in accordance to the regulations, which is controlled by the local data protection authorities.

Information Security and Measures The security plans are mandatory, but the quality of the papers is low. This has many reasons: some of the states do not have enough knowledge to develop the complex security plans and systems, whereas some of the states are not willing to share the information to avoid questions and suggestions for improvement from the side of the EU. The variety in the quality is making the evaluation of the overall systems' security difficult. The member states do not have an overview about the others' security measures and do not know, whether and what international standards are used. The security measures required by the EU are comprehensive.

The specialists from the member state see the security rules as strict, in particular, the process described in the interface control document. Responses to some of the questions must pass multiple levels of contacts, because of the right to access rules. Every level of contact has the information they are allowed to process and therefore it is not possible to get the answers from just one level for some questions.

Specialists view some aspects as over-regulation. For example: whenever the report of data usage and handling has to be done, the member states must create their own reports, which will be combined by EU-LISA later, to present it to the EU Commission, despite they have access to all the information stored by member states and they could to it themselves. This situation has been brought up at the working groups for many times, but the obstacle are regulations which are not allowing EU-LISA to operate with the information that is held by member states. Member states have all proposed that they would give the mandate to EU-LISA to manage the information for creating the reports, to lower their own administrative burden, but until now, that has not been changed.

4.3   Summary of Findings

On the one hand security requirements by the EU are comprehensive, but grant enough freedom for the member State to choose the measures suitable for their inner legislation. This leads to a situation where it lacks overview about the used security measures, despite the evaluations conducted. The evaluations are member state specific and are not compared to see their compatibility to each other. Request brought out in NIS directive should give a clearer overview, if all member states would use the internationally accepted standards. On the other hand, some aspects are over-regulated, which leads to the administrative burden.

5   Usage of Standards

This section approaches main question of paper, i.e., whether the EU needs a unified standard on ensuring information security of large-scale information systems in case of the EU information systems.

5.1 Document Analysis

The first time that the need for the usage of internationally accepted information security standard is pointed out in the NIS directive is in its article 19, where it recommends to adopt standards to reduce the amount of the different approaches; but the directive does not detail out, which standard should be used [18]. The information systems' regulations use similar requirements for the systems security, but those requirements are high level and are not setting guidelines how to fulfill the requirements. The term "standard" is used in SIRENE manual [10], where the basic requirements as acceptability, continuity, confidentiality and access are described.

International standards such as ISO27001 [24], guidelines as ISO27002 [25] and baseline standards as the German IT-Grundschutz [6] and the Estonian ISKE [23] are used. The ISO standards are rather applied to the information management systems and their requirements, the polices that shall be implemented in the organization and less to the security of the systems itself; whereas the baseline standards are applied to both. The ISO requirements are in accordance to the requirements set by the EU regulations – requiring risk assessment, policies for access and operation of the systems. The base line standards evaluate the information systems based on the information stored in the systems, the users and the field of usage in addition to the managerial policy requirements.

5.2 Interview Analysis

The variety of standards, that could be used at state level is not the question. A problem is when a member state is not using any; then it is not possible to say whether it is moving in a right direction or whether its security work is consistent.

Specialists brought out the Estonian ISKE standard. The official audits are still in progress, but as the specialists see, ISKE measures are suitable for assuring the minimum-security requirements. The audit is completed for the EURODAC system and the results showed that ISKE is suitable and covers all the requirements set for the systems' security. On the other hand, it is hard to see, what other member states are using and if those standards or other security methods are suitable; and this is hindering cooperation. In addition to the cooperation there cannot be a certainty of the security of the other member states' systems if the security measures are not clearly stated. The specialists see the similar grounds in securing the systems as a good solution to increase the level of overall security. The problem, the specialists brought out for creating a standardized approach to systems security is the over-regulation. There are many regulations already in place, creating a new one might cause problems with existing internal state regulations and the capability of developing the systems according to the new regulations. The new regulation setting the specific requirements would be micromanaging by the EU Commission and therefore the member states are not able to develop according to their insights. Overall, requirements shall be acceptable and feasible for all the member states. The EU Commission cannot require high level security if some member states are not able to comply with them; on the other hand, some member states are capable for more, and because of the requirement they cannot develop higher level security for the information system.

5.3   Summary of Findings

The NIS directives' request for using the internationally accepted security standards would help to make the security evaluation clearer; but none of the interviewees brought out specific preference and need for all the member states to follow the same standard.

The interviewees would like to have a best practice example which shall be followed; but it should not become an official standard, to avoid the growing bureaucracy. They see the example as guideline and minimum requirements, but it should not be a standard that shall be followed line by line. The guideline should be flexible and mandatory only for the less capable parties. More capable member states can design their methods that are more than set on the minimum level.

6   Related Work

A similar research has been conducted by RAND corporation [27]. The analysis includes the same regulations as in this paper. The authors come up with similar results: even though there are many regulations, policies, and directives – they might not improve the overall security of the systems and instead can slow down the progress in IT. Change is needed in the form of less regulations, updated standards and more open communication and information sharing among states' specialists. The societal expectations have grown and the technologies have evolved; therefore, the existing systems and their regulations are getting outdated.

An analysis of the connection between European migration policies and digital technologies is provided by [22]. The analysis encompasses the EU information systems SIS II, VIS, EURODAC. The case of Italy and Spain is treated, two countries that are perceived as EU 'gatekeepers' in the last years. The research delves into compliance/non-compliance with surveillance systems in the southern European member states. Furhermore, it carves out differences between the two countries regarding their overall migration policies.

Discussion of compliance strategy of Schengen border states with respect to Eurodac regulations are treated independently by several authors [2, 3, 5, 29]. The research delves into the political and legal dimension of the compliance, whereas we treat the information security perspective in this paper.

7   Conclusion

There is a great amount of bureaucracy in the management of the EU information systems, which in some amount is necessary to operate such large-scale systems. The decision making goes through multiple levels of authorities and therefore the process is slow. The cooperation is mostly based on necessity or covered with the requirements of the regulations, but the knowledge exchange is still weak. The security requirements are comprehensive and give some amount of freedom to choose exact methods; but on the other hand they are bureaucratic and cause the administrative burden to the member states. The data exchange process is detailed and well regulated by an interface control document. Accepting already existing internationally accepted standards is preferable and gives a better overview of the security measures used. A unified standard is not necessary, but guidelines and examples should exist to gain a mandatory/minimum acceptable level. Through cooperation and knowledge sharing, the overall level of security can be raised by implementing those measures and thus the NIS directive expectations can be reached.

References

1. Alonso Blas, D.: Ensuring effective data protection in the field of police and judicialactivities: some considerations to achieve security, justice and freedom. ERA Forum **11**(2), 233–250 (2010)
2. Aus, J.: Supranational governance in an area of freedom, security and justice –eurodac and the politics of biometric control. Technical Report DEI Working Paper, no. 72, Sussex University Institute (2003)
3. Aus, J.: Eurodac – a solution looking for a problem? Eur. Integr. OnlinePapers **10**(6), 1–26 (2006)
4. Boehm, F.: Information Sharing and Data Protection in the Area of Freedom, Security and Justice – Towards Harmonised Data Protection Principles for Information Exchange at EU-level. Springer (2012)
5. Brouwer, E.: Eurodac: Its limitations and temptations. Eur. J. Migr. Law **4**(2), 231–247 (2002)
6. Bundesamt für Sicherheit in der Informationstechnik (BSI): IT Security Guidelines– IT-Grundschutz in brief. BSI, Bonn (2007)
7. Commission Staff Working Paper: First annual report to the Council and the European Parliament on the activities of the EURODAC Central Unit. Commission of the European Communities, Brussels (2004)
8. Conventions signed between Member States: CONVENTION determining theState responsible for examining applications for asylum lodged in one of the Member States of the European Communities. Offi. J. Eur. Union (L 254), 1–12 (1997)
9. Council of the European Union: SIRENE Manual. Off. J. Eur. Union (L 38), 1–24 (2003)
10. European Commission: COMMISSION IMPLEMENTING DECISION (EU) 2015/219 of 29 January 2015 replacing the Annex to Implementing Decision 2013/115/EU on the Sirene Manual and other implementing measures for the second generation Schengen Information System (SIS II). Off. J. Eur. Union (L 44), 75–116 (2015)
11. European Commission: COMMISSION DECISION (EU, Euratom) 2017/46 of 10 January 2017 on the security of communication and information systems in the European Commission. Off. J. Eur. Union (L 6), 40–51 (2017)
12. European Council: COUNCIL REGULATION (EC) No 2725/2000 of 11 December2000 concerning the establishment of 'Eurodac' for the comparison of fingerprints for the effective application of the Dublin Convention. Off. J. Eur. Union (L 316), 1–10 (2000)
13. European Data Protection Supervisor: DECLARATION. In: Spring Conference of European Data Protection Authorities, pp. 1–2. Krakow (2005)
14. European Data Protection Supervisor: Eurodac Supervision Coordination Group Second Inspection Report. Secretariat of the Eurodac Supervision Coordination Group, Brussels (2009)

15. European Parliament and Council: REGULATION (EC) No 1987/2006 of 20 December 2006 on the establishment, operation and use of the second generation Schengen Information System (SIS II). Off. J. Eur. Union (L 381), 4–23 (2006)
16. European Parliament and Council: REGULATION (EC) No 767/2008 of 9 July2008 concerning the Visa Information System (VIS) and the exchange of data between Member States on short-stay visas (VIS Regulation). Off. J. Eur. Union (L 218), 60–81 (2008)
17. European Parliament and Council: REGULATION (EU) No 603/2013 of 26 June2013 on the establishment of 'Eurodac' for the comparison of fingerprints for the effective application of Regulation (EU) No 604/2013. Off. J. Eur. Union (L 180), 1–30 (2013)
18. European Parliament and Council: DIRECTIVE (EU) 2016/1148 of 6 July 2016 concerning measures for a high common level of security of network and information systems across the Union. Off. J. Eur. Union (L 194), 1–30 (2016)
19. European Parliament and Council: DIRECTIVE (EU) 2016/680 of 27 April 2016 on the protection of natural persons with regard to the processing of personal data by competent authorities for the purposes of the prevention, investigation, detection or prosecution of criminal offences or the execution of criminal penalties, and on the free movement of such data, and repealing Council Framework Decision 2008/977/JHA. Off. J. Eur. Union (L 119), 89–131 (2016)
20. European Parliament and Council: REGULATION (EU) 2016/679 of 27 April 2016 on the protection of natural persons with regard to the processing of personal data and on the free movement of such data, and repealing Directive 95/46/EC (General Data Protection Regulation). Off. J. Eur. Union (L 119), 1–88 (2016)
21. European Parliament, Council of the European Union: REGULATION (EU) No1077/2011 of 25 October 2011 establishing a European Agency for the operational management of large-scale IT systems in the area of freedom, security and justice. Off. J. Eur. Union (L 286), 1–17 (2011)
22. Fragapane, S., Minaldi, G.: Migration policies and digital technologies in Europe: a comparison between italy and spain. J. Eur. Integr. **0**(0), 1–17 (2018)
23. Government of the Republic of Estonia: Infosüsteemide turvameetmete süsteem.Riigi Teataja (252) (2009)
24. ISO/IEC 27001:2013: Information technology – Security techniques – Informationsecurity management systems – Requirements. In: International Standardization Organization (2013)
25. ISO/IEC 27002:2013: Information technology – Security techniques – Code of practice for information security controls. In: International Standardization Organization (2013)
26. Marquenie, T.: The police and criminal justice authorities directive – data protection standards and impact on the legal framework. Comput. Law Secur. Rev. **33**(3), 324–340 (2017)
27. Robinson, N., Gaspers, J.: Information security and data protection legal and policy frameworks applicable to european union institutions and agencies. Technical report, RAND Corporation (2014)
28. Rull, A., Täks, E., Norta, A.: Towards Software-Agent Enhanced Privacy Protection, pp. 73–94. Springer (2014)
29. Trauner, F.: Asylum policy – the EU's 'crises' and the looming policy regimefailure. J. Eur. Integr. **38**(3), 311–325 (2016)

Bridging the Knowledge Divide in GCC Countries: The Role of Digital Technologies

Amer Al-Roubaie[✉]

College of Business and Finance, Ahlia University, Manama, Bahrain
aalroubaie@ahlia.edu.bh

Abstract. In recent years, emphasis in development studies has shifted toward knowledge creation and innovation that fosters economic growth and sustain development. Globalization is offering new opportunities, especially for developing countries, to acquire knowledge, information and skills for building capacity for development. Modern information and communication technologies (ICTs) are empowering countries to diversify the economic structure and enhance sectoral productivity through access to global markets. In this age of information, individuals, organizations and institutions are able to enhance communication and increase collaboration through social networking aimed at promoting innovation and improving global competitiveness. Digital technologies can be used to bridge the digital divide between rich and poor countries as a mechanism designed not only to increase connectivity and improve services, but also to facilitate innovation and capacity building for development. The aim of this paper is to examine the role that digital technologies plays in economic diversification in GCC countries. Digital technologies encourage investment in manufacturing production and knowledge creation, which stimulates linkages and support diversification. To this end, building capacity for digital economy could have a profound impact on the ability of these countries to speed up the process of socioeconomic transformation involving reduction of dependency on oil production.

Keywords: Globalization · Digital technologies · E-services · Knowledge creation · GCC countries

1 Introduction

In this age of information, digital services play an important role in societal transformation reflecting the contribution of modern technologies to building capacity for development. Recent advancement in information and communication technologies (ICTs), including high-speed internet, the smart phone and a wide array of applications accessible through android and the iPhone operating system (IOS), in addition to social media platforms, have empowered people to communicate across national boundaries making geographical locations no longer barriers to human interaction and business contact. Widening the scope of global connectivity has improved human understanding and increased information sharing aimed at bridging the digital divide and sustaining economic growth. Digital technologies are offering new opportunities, especially for

S. A. Al-Sharhan et al. (Eds.): I3E 2018, LNCS 11195, pp. 164–180, 2018.
https://doi.org/10.1007/978-3-030-02131-3_16

developing countries, to deepen integration into the global markets and gain access to technology, knowledge, skills and information. Building capacity for ICTs could help countries speed up the process of development and strengthen the fundamentals for building digital society driven by linkage creation and knowledge acquisition.

The knowledge economy entails knowledge sharing and information dissemination through networking and inclusive access to all. Individuals, organizations and institutions will be able to communicate, collaborate and cooperate in sharing information and exchanging knowledge to enhance productivity and support innovation. Today, the world digital population exceeds more than 4 billion people reflecting the rapid advancement in ICTs within and across nations. Thus future sustainability will be influenced by investment in digital technologies that enhance connectivity worldwide. Building capacity for a digital society will require investment in digital literacy to empower people to gain entry global markets, access to which would facilitate knowledge acquisition, technology transfer and innovation diffusion. Bridging the development gap underscores the importance of digital literacy as a key means to increase national ability taking advantage of the new opportunities offered by the information age.

Making use of external knowledge not only reduces the cost of economic growth, but also helps developing countries to leapfrog several stages in development. In GCC countries, governments have responded to the structural decline in oil prices with urgency to diversify the economy and reduce dependence on the energy sector. A high degree of dependence on rents obtained from production and export of a limited number of commodities increases economic vulnerability by making the economy more sensitive to changes in global cyclical fluctuations. Digital technologies facilitate economic diversification by providing economies with multiple opportunities to enhance productivity and promote development. Building digital capacity strengthens the country's ability to acquire skills, create knowledge and share information – all of which are necessary for diversification the productive structure and reduction in dependency on the vicissitudes of global commodities markets.

The failure of the export-led growth model, driven by oil rents, has renewed the call for development alternatives to reduce the risk of high degree of export concentration and sustain economic growth. In the GCC countries, governments have responded by adopting long-term strategies aimed at diversifying productivity through knowledge creation and innovation. Investment in human capital, building ICT infrastructure, institutional reforms and deepening access in the global markets are among the core components of the new strategy. The aim of this paper is to examine the role that digital services play in knowledge sharing and innovation dissemination to speed up the process of development and foster economic growth. Building capacity for digital technologies fosters creation of linkages and strengthens the fundamentals for knowledge creation, technology transfer and innovation diffusion. This paper focuses on the challenges and opportunities facing socio-economic development in GCC countries.

2 The Digital Economy

The term digital economy arises from the use of modern computers referring specifically to the use of the internet as a powerful device in communication and access to knowledge and information. The digital economy is a product of the information age in which networking and internet connectivity increased communications among people across national boundaries. The digital economy is defined by Oxford dictionary as an "economy which functions primarily by means of digital technology, especially electronic transactions made using the internet." "The transition to a digital economy can provide a boost to competitiveness across all sectors, new opportunities for business and entrepreneurial activity, and new avenues for assessing overseas markets. It also provides new tools for tackling persistent development and social problems." [1] Today, e-services are having profound impact on our daily activities by increasing global interconnections and changing human understanding. Digital technologies are expected to shape the path of future trends by allowing individuals, organizations and institutions to share knowledge and information essential in effective decision-making and policy construction. The digital economy is also called the internet economy in reference to the extensive use of the internet in connecting people worldwide. Few would gainsay that the internet is a powerful tool for communication serving to link providers with consumers of digitally-driven information irrespective of national boundaries.

The 2016 World Development Report by the World Bank focuses on digital dividends outlining the importance of digital technologies in fostering economic growth, improved service delivery and expanding opportunities for people worldwide. Digital technologies have the power to foster growth and promote innovation across various sectors of the economy. It is estimated that the digital economy accounts for 8% of the GDP in OECD countries. In China digital economy reached $3.4 trillion or 30.3% of the national GDP in 2016. This has been facilitated by the number of internet users in China accounting for 751 million out of the 3.89 billion internet users around the world in 2017 [2]. Entrepreneurs in the South, including GCC countries, can benefit from the digital economy as a mechanism to communicate, acquire and absorb knowledge with the effect of diversifying the productive structure and bridging the development gap. In addition, the digital economy underpins e-government through facilitation of transactions with the public involving improvement in government delivery in a range of eservices contributing to a reduction in transaction costs serving, through public sector efficiencies, to promote sustainable economic growth. In the digital economies, individuals, business and institutions are expected to benefit not only from lower transaction costs but from greater access to new markets. Increasing connectivity enables firms to acquire technical and managerial skills essentials for running firms effectively and meeting international standards. Changes in the global economy are increasingly driven by digital technologies as mechanisms facilitating information exchange and data provision for use in market transactions, knowledge creation and innovation diffusion.

The growing interconnectedness of people, organizations and institutions represent the foundation of the digital economy. The globalization of economic activities in recent decades is a product of advancement in ICTs. Mercantile transactions generate value and create new business opportunities derived from the services provided by the internet. In this regard, the digital economy should be defined to represent broader meaning than just an internet economy. The digital economy increases the speed of making decisions and dissemination of information allowing organizations to execute tasks faster and keep pace with technological development and market changes. Such digital services are also useful for building long term business strategies to ensure competiveness in the future. New technologies, including mobile and cloud computing, as well as artificial intelligence, are bridging the gap between producers and consumers by providing information and facilitating marketing of products in various locations across the globe. All GCC countries are adopting new economic strategies aimed at restructuring the productive system and reducing dependency on energy production and export which represents the main driver of development.

The digital economy could have a positive impact on human development by improving the lives of people, especially in developing countries where basic needs remain inadequate to meet the challenges facing these populations. Providing access to people through digital technologies allow sharing knowledge and information among and within regions, Such shared knowledge and information can be used to improve decision-making and increase an individual's capabilities to participate in development as, for example, as entrepreneur. Digital technologies also increase government interaction with citizens to provide services and contribute to people needs across national boundaries. Digital technologies provide not only services using local resources, but also access to the rest of the world. Such connectivity provides new opportunities for developing countries to increase exports and gain access to international markets.

The new economy, also known knowledge-based economy, uses knowledge and innovation as an alternative to labor and capital in the traditional economy. The private sector assumes a more proactive role in market activates by giving young entrepreneurs the opportunity to participate in transforming the economy into a knowledge-based economy. These new generations of entrepreneurs can utilize digital technologies to enhance connectivity and create new business models based on knowledge sharing, collaboration and joint ventures with foreign firms. In this age of the internet, collaboration is particularly important to gain access to knowledge, skills and information for development. Private enterprises can be connected to multiple companies across different countries to participate in knowledge sharing, research and development, data gathering and in a number of highly complex market activities. The digitization of the economy not only is transforming businesses and societies, but also is promoting innovation and sustainable development.

The digital model is changing the workings of all aspects of society, including human interaction, policy construction, decision-making and demand for skills and job requirements.

"Increased digitization and automation is leading to new types of jobs and employment, changing the nature and conditions of work and altering skills requirements, as well as affecting the functioning of the labor markets and the international division labour." [3] In the digital economy, scientific research and knowledge dissemination will increase due to rapid economic transformations fueling business opportunities expected to create digital revolutions shaping the future during the course of the 21st century. Economies will require increasing investment in building ICT infrastructure and strengthening connectivity in order to gain access to global markets. For developing countries in general and GCC in particular, innovation is linked to digital services making digital technologies important for obtaining social and economic benefit from ICTs.

During the last two decades China used the digital economy effectively to promote its etrade across the world. It is estimated that today China alones accounts for about 42% of the global e-commerce compared to less than one percent ten years ago. This is compared with the United States e-commerce at about 24%, down from 35% in 2005. Such rapid growth in China e-commerce reflects the importance of digital technologies in global integration and enhancing the country's capabilities to increase its share of trade worldwide. This made China a force to be reckoned with in digital technologies abroad and around the world. Payments through the internet by Chinese users increased from about 25% in 2013 to 68% in 2016 accounting for $790 billion, 11 times more than that of the United States. China's billiondollar-valued startups account for 43% of the global value of "unicorn" companies worldwide reflecting the rapid progress that China was able to achieve in digital technologies. Such rapid growth in digital business is attributed to the commercialization of digital business as well as to governmental supports and incentives for investment in digital technologies [4].

3   Innovation and Knowledge Creation in the Digital Economy

The knowledge economy is driven by knowledge and innovation aimed at increasing productivity through sharing of information and creating new knowledge to support linkage creation and promote economic diversification. As an input in production, knowledge appreciates in value over time making investment in research and development essential to create new knowledge and linkages. However, restructuring the productive system to increase the knowledge content in production will require investment in education to increase the stock of human capital, to stimulate building ICT infrastructure, to spur development of a national innovation system and to foster institutional reform to support the transformation of the economy into a knowledge-based economy. Although some GCC countries, including Bahrain and the UAE, have been able to achieve high scores in global competiveness, ICT infrastructure, innovation and other knowledge-related indicators, very little progress has been realized so far to support rapid transformation to a knowledge economy. Education remains among the important challenges facing these countries to mint high quality graduates capable of making effective decisions, conducting research and development and providing managerial and technical leadership.

Information represents an important input for promoting innovation and development of new products. Digital technologies facilitates access to information worldwide which provides entrepreneurs, running small- and medium-size enterprises, access to new methods and new ideas that enhance creativity in a process of innovation resulting in the development of new products. Having information strengthens the ability of the individuals and organizations not only to improve production techniques, but also to create new knowledge. Digital technologies connect people across disparate geographies enabling them to share knowledge and collaborate in new projects of common interest.

Connectivity is improving the business environment through social connections among scientists, policy makers, academicians and businesses resulting in the sharing of ideas and provision of solutions to existing problems. Educational institutions, including universities, in the GCC countries should facilitate such social connectivity to increase cooperation and collaboration to share information and conduct joint research to find solutions to the challenges facing the region. Digital technologies provide connection and easy access to knowledge and information by digitally connecting people across the region to work together and support innovation. In this regard, digital literacy and digital skills is essential to strengthen the fundamentals for knowledge creation and innovation diffusion.

Knowledge can be created through the process of knowledge use in different forms. Engagement in organizational socialization, involving sharing information to convert tacit knowledge into explicit, can be undertaken to create commercial value and to improve competitiveness. Similarly, the process of externalization converts explicit knowledge into another form of codified knowledge ready for use by users. To this end, individuals and organizations create knowledge through sharing ideas, exchanging opinions and circulating information and knowledge among groups or employees to stimulate creativity and engage people in critical thinking for solving problems and development of new methods foster productivity. Knowledge occurs when information is reformulated and converted into knowledge.

In the knowledge economy, it is the human mind rather than physical assets that drive economic growth and increase productivity. In other words, development is largely influenced by the mental capital measured by the stock of human capital and the quality of higher education institutions. Produced capital and natural capital are important for building productive capacity for development; however, knowledge creation is a product of human intellectual activities. In this regard, knowledge-based development requires investment in people aimed at increasing the country's intellectual capabilities to create knowledge and promote innovation. Digital technologies provide the foundation for knowledge sharing and knowledge transfer. Using digital technologies enable individuals and organization to increase interactions and collaboration which promote the sharing of knowledge and help to produce new knowledge.

Building capacity for digital infrastructure to enhance digital literacy and increase communication is essential for knowledge creation. Educational institutions including universities need to restructure curricula and put more emphasis on learning instead of teaching to improve communication skills, working as a team, inculcate entrepreneurial skills, engender flexibility and hone computing skills. Lifelong learning is essential to ensure adaptability to technological changes and market conditions. It is estimated that human capital contributes 65% to the wealth in high-income countries compared only to 40% in poor countries. In the Middle East, the contribution of human capital to the total wealth accounted for 35% in 2014 compared to 70% in OECD countries and 88% in United Kingdom. This makes investment in people the most valuable investment that a county can achieve to foster economic growth and support future sustainability [5].

The production of new knowledge also facilitates the development of new innovation which results in converting ideas or tacit knowledge into value. In the age of digital technologies, organizations are able to strengthen socialization not only through networking but also through the "internet of things" allowing communication and dissemination of new ideas and the discovery of new knowledge absent human-to-human or human-to-computer interaction. In this respect, innovation and knowledge are interrelated and investment in knowledge creation could facilitate innovation diffusion across the economy.

4   Digital Readiness in Arab States

Advancement in building Information and telecommunication Technologies (ICTs) infrastructure is measured by the ICT Development Index (IDI) illustrating a country's efforts to bridge the digital gap and deepen integration into the information age. The index measures the digital divide among nations in terms of capacity building for technological readiness and connectivity within and across nations. It reflects the level of connectivity infrastructure and the intensity use of ICT in society. IDI comprises three levels of ICT including ICT access, ICT use and ICT skills. (ITU, 2017, P. 26) With respect to the use of the internet, the percentage of individuals online in the total population varies from 91% in UAE to 57% in Morocco and 38% in Egypt.

With the exception to the GCC countries, connectivity in most countries in the Middle East remains inadequate to stimulate development and close the digital divide. Among world's regions, Africa is far behind the rest of the world in terms of the use of the internet serving as an obstacle to its catching up with the rest of the world. Africa needs to build ICT infrastructure capable of connecting individuals, institutions and businesses across the continent in order to stimulate market activities and provide inclusive e-services to all.

Wide digital gaps extant among Arab countries underlie different levels of readiness in digital technologies among and within countries in the region. The term digital divide is used to measure the "differences in ICT development within and between countries, regions, socioeconomic groupings." (ITU, 2017, P. 50) ICTs empower societies to create knowledge, increase productivity and to bridge the digital divide that narrows the gap between rich countries and poor countries. The developing countries, including the Arab world, need to invest in ICT infrastructure if they have to speed up the process of catching up with the industrialized countries.

Table 1 illustrates the gap in technological readiness as measured by IDI ranging from 7.60 in Bahrain, 2.55 in Sudan, 1.58 in Djibouti and 1.64 in Comoros in 2017. On average IDI readiness in the Arab world measures 4.84 compared with 5.11 worldwide and 7.52 in developed countries. In 2017, the Arab world experienced the lowest average improvement in IDI among all world regions reflecting the inability of the region to narrow down the digital gap and benefit from the information revolution. In the global ranking, 13 out of the 19 Arab countries experienced drop by one or two places in 2017. With the exception of the GCC countries scoring above average in global rankings, the rest of the countries in the Arab region remained far below the world average [6].

Table 1. Global and Regioals ICT indicators 2017

Country	IDI	Technological readiness	Individuals using the internet as % of population	Mobile phone subscription per 100 people
Iceland	8.98	6.17	98	103.7
S. Korea	8.85	5.54	90	118.5
Oman	6.43	4.40	74	159.9
UAE	7.21	5.82	91	187.3
Bahrain	7.60	5.15	93	185.3
S. Arabia	6.67	5.01	70	176.6
Kuwait	5.98	4.33	82	231.8
Egypt	4.63	3.26	38	111.0
Morocco	4.77	3.69	57	126.9
Malaysia	6.38	4.81	71	143.9
Qatar	7.21	5.35	93	153.6
Jordan	6.00	390	53	179.4
Nigeria	2.60	3.15	47	82.2
Chad	1.74	1.93	3	40.2
Africa	2.64	–	22	76.4
Arab States	4.84	–	44	111.0
Europe	7.50	–	71	114.9
Asia & Pacific	4.83	–	50	101.5
The Americas	5.21	–	76	–
World	5.11	–	44	98.5

Source: International Communication Union (ITU, 2017) Measuring the Information Society Report 2017, Vol. 1 (ITU: Geneva), World Bank, World Development Indicators 2017, World Economic Forum. The Global Competitiveness Report 2016/2017

Among the countries in the Arab region, Bahrain scored the highest IDI of 7.60 reflecting the government support for ICT development. The efforts by the government of Bahrain to transform its economy to a digital economy have borne fruit over the past 15 years. Today Bahrain is among the most connected countries in the world providing internet services to all residents in the country. Building digital infrastructure will help the country to close the digital divide and speed up the process of economic diversification. Currently, the digital economy accounts for 8% of the economy of Bahrain compared to 5.1% in Kuwait, 4.3% in the UAE and less than 1% in both Oman and Qatar. (McKenzie p. 25) To be inclusive, digital technologies must include everyone in order to ensure equal access to all members of the society. Participation in the digital economy requires access to the internet as well as digital literacy to encourage people using e-services and benefit form digitization. In relation to the status of digital readiness in the Middle East the Gulf News point out:

"Despite the burgeoning dependence on internet, the Middle East is marred by high illiteracy rates that widen the digital divide. Across the Arab world, an estimated 57 million adults are illiterate. Another major problem is that many Arabs do not have access to proper infrastructure. Without solving these issues, any effort to minimize the digital divide may prove to be futile" [7].

In the Arab world, as elsewhere, governments serve as a major supplier of public services to citizens. To enhance public sector capability to deliver services to the public will require improved digital literary on the part of the general public. In turn, improving digital literacy will require governments to provide internet access to empower users with the skills needed to search and obtain information online. Digital literacy denoted ability of the general public to use digital tools in their daily activities. In the information society, digital inclusion is essential to ensure that all society members, including rural population, women and students, as well as businesses, will be able to have access to digital services. In the Middle East, only 6% of the population lives under smart governance [8].

In the Middle East, digital technologies allow these countries to build new industries and expand productivity in the non-oil sector. In recent years, improvement in data processing and storage facilities have facilitated the emergence of what has come to be known as cloud computing. (UNCTAD: Information Economy Report 2013) By 2025, it is expected that most web services and ICT applications would be cloud delivered which require countries and organizations to enhance digital readiness to facilitate services through the cloud. Across the Arab world, digitization varies among countries which measure the digital gap among and within countries in the region. Countries such as Bahrain and UAE have invested heavily in digital technologies and, as a consequence, have been able to take advantage of the digital revolution and transform their societies into digital-based economies.

In a new society driven by smart technologies, which involve building digital infrastructure to improve the economy readiness ability to adopt and integrate into the information age, digitization requires new skills and training. Countries in the region must develop digital curricula to equip students with skills that match the demand for digital workforce. It requires rethinking education so as to ensure that students are able to operate technology and acquire the skills needed to use the web and search for information. Using the internet empowers individuals, institutions and organizations to make effective decisions and construct sound strategies aimed at improving efficiency and promoting innovation. Economic development entails an efficient allocation of resources designed to create a balance between and among sectors. To this end, collaboration, sharing knowledge and exchanging information through the internet accelerate the process of development and strengthen the country drive towards a knowledge-driven society.

Digital skills contribute to growth of SMEs by providing access to local, regional and global knowledge and information. In the knowledge economy, SMEs play critical role in productivity growth and knowledge creation through the use of digital services and internet connectivity. Thus curricula must address to need of the labor market by enhancing student capabilities to acquire such skills as critical thinking, technical and managerial skills, and problem solving. Familiarity with smart technologies underscores the importance of ICT literacy to empower users making use of digital services and strengthen global linkages.

In the Arab world, partnership and cooperation between the public and private sectors is essential to build capacity for digital economy. The role of the private sector in the digital economy is critical and, therefore, that both public and private institutions work together to build ICT capacity and narrow down the digital divide at both local and global levels. In a recent study by McKinsey and Company it is revealed that the Middle East region has realized 8% augmentation in its digital potential. "Digital includes the foundations and underlying technologies and capabilities such as network and connectivity, computing, and storage, all of which enable the digitization of back-end processes as well as B2B and B2C interactions" [9].

Countries of the GCC are making substantial efforts, investing heavily in ICT technologies, to increase the digitalization of their economies in order to catch up with the industrialized countries. "While the Middle East public sector entities are likely to spend over US15 billion in digital transformation enabling technologies in 2018, the GCC overall lags behind many developed countries in digital government. Countries in the region are not all at a similar stage of development with regard to government digitization levels" [10].

5   Closing the Digital Divide

The digital divide is a measure of the scale of the gap in the intensity use of ICT among "have" and "have-not" populations across or within countries. A digital divide is defined as an: "economic and social inequality with regard to access, use of, or impact of information and communication technologies." [11] The digital divide refers to the access of individuals and organizations to modern technologies, mainly ICT. It represents the socio-economic gap between and among countries in the use of the internet and digital technologies.

Recent literature on development studies focus on the importance of digital technologies in knowledge creation, and innovation dissemination. Most developing countries are lacking to adequate knowledge to support development. Digital technologies facilitate access to global knowledge which can be used to stimulate linkages and increase productivity. In this age of the internet, access to knowledge and information has become easy with little or no cost. This could save developing countries substantial amount of resources both financial and technical. In recent decades, the Arab world, particularly the GCC countries, has made good progress in building capacity for ICT to improve connectivity and bridge the digital divide.

To ensure connectivity across and within social classes, development must be inclusive. Governments should ensure access by building ICT infrastructure capable of connecting all people at all locations within the state. Connecting people and regions via the internet allows policy-makers, on the one hand, and business managers and entrepreneurs, on the other, to formulate policies and/or plans and to make sound decisions aimed at meeting public and corporate objectives, respectively.

Rapid changes in technology entail continuous training and lifelong learning to improve technological learning and upgrade technical skills. In a connected world, people should be able to adapt to changing circumstances as well as to operate in different geographical locations. Acquiring skills in linguistics, critical thinking, problem solving, creativity and people management are critical for meeting 21st century challenges. Investment in education and training enhances the national ICT readiness capabilities as well as increases the flexibility of the future work-force to adapt to technologically-induced changes in labor market demands.

Gender inequality among nations remains a matter of concern for many countries.

Connectivity should be inclusive for narrowing the digital divide by providing equal opportunity to all without discrimination against social groups because of gender, color, disability and religion. Exclusion of women, for example, would weaken development initiatives designed to close the digital divide. Women account for half of the population and, therefore, excluding them reduces labor force participation and lowers growth. In developing countries, internet access is estimated to represent 41% or just about half of the access attained in developed countries. In the new economy, work is being done online out of home; such represents an opportunity for women to participate in the economy, especially in conservative societies, where women are restricted from working with men. Under such circumstances, providing digital skills for women will speed up the process of development and increase growth.

The digital economy provides new opportunities for developing countries to increase productivity, promote innovation and engage in global trade. Small- and medium-sized enterprises and young entrepreneurs benefit from the digital economy by getting easy access to global markets and, in turn, contribute to local development. Digital technologies allow small enterprise to cut cost and sell their products competitively in world markets. ICTs empower entrepreneurs, especially women, to engage in market activities which enhance productivity, create jobs and improve competiveness. However, developing countries need to enhance ICT readiness if they are to obtain full benefit from the digital technologies. Inadequate ICT infrastructure, which weakens connectivity to global markets, not only hinders development and broadens the digital divide, but also increases global inequalities. "The ability of countries and enterprises to exploit new digital resources will become a key determinant of competitiveness." [12] In this regard, the educational system needs to contribute to the digitization of the economy by adapting curricula that facilitates labor market flexibility and provides students with the skills needed for participating in the information age.

Connectivity, driven by modern ICTs, could have positive impact on development helping developing countries to foster economic growth and accelerate the process of socioeconomic transformation. Challenges facing these countries such as poverty alleviation, population growth, urbanization, pollution and lack of adequate public services can be met with the use of digital services. ICTs usually empower society to build capacity for development by providing opportunities for people to share information and work more effectively towards finding solutions to the problems facing them. Studies have showed that per capita income is positively related to IDI reflecting the importance of ICT technologies in promoting human development. Improvement in income per capita represents aggregate measure involving structural transformation within the productive system of the society. In this regard, building ICT infrastructure increases the ability of both public and private sectors not only to strengthen partnership and participate in joint projects, but also expand the country choices through access to regional and global markets [13].

Digital technologies require special skills that workers need to acquire in order to be employed in the digital industry. Governments and educational institutions must ensure that the curricula used in teaching meet the need of labor markets and help workers adapt to the new technologies. The important challenges facing governments in developing counties is to close the skills gap by providing training for women to improve employability. Automation is replacing traditional jobs including bookkeepers, bank tellers, clerks and others. Empowering workers with new skills will be beneficial for both workers and the economy.

To make utilization of digital services effective, investment in digital literacy is prerequisite. Literacy in digital technologies facilitates connectivity among and within nations providing people and regions, particularly in isolated areas new opportunities, to gain access to external knowledge and information. Workers need to know how to use ICTs if bridging the gap to be closed. Poor areas lacking technical and financial resources to build ICT infrastructure, require governmental intervention in the form of investment in ICT infrastructure to provide access for all users within national boundaries.

In 2017, global sales online amounted to 2.3 trillion US$ and it is estimated that the total sales will reach 4.88 trillion US$ by the year 2021. In China alone an estimated 19% of all retail sales occurred via the internet. Revenues of Amazon.com from online sales amounted to $178 billion in 2017 compared to US136 billion in 2016. In the Middle East, sales as a percentage of the total global e-commerce were 1.8% in 2016 – the lowest among all world regions [14].

The digital economy in GCC countries encourages economic diversification by providing SMEs with new opportunities to participate in market activities and obtain technical and managerial skills for improving their operations and meeting global standards. In recent years, globalization has increased outsourcing providing new opportunities, especially for SMEs in developing countries, to be linked to global value chains (GVCs) and participate in the global economy producing goods and services for multinational corporations. Digital technologies can also help SMEs expanding choices to acquire financing from external sources. Foreign firms will be willing to finance local enterprises to produce goods and services for exports. MNCs benefit from digital services by linking operations involving manufacturing of parts of final products efficiently in different countries as a function of factor costs.

6   Knowledge Intensity and Digital Services

Digital technologies enhances the ability of an economy to produce high-tech products not only by improving the business environment to create knowledge and diffuse innovation, but also by providing global access, especially to local enterprises, to acquire skills, information and technology. Digitization facilitates cooperation and collaboration of productive enterprises both within and without the national boundary of an economy through sharing information and exchanging ideas. In developing countries, where knowledge is inadequate to stimulate linkages, acquiring knowledge from external sources could accelerate the process of knowledge creation. Technological learning through digital services enhances local firms' understanding and skills enabling them to produce high quality products at home. Digital technologies are important enablers offering new approach for local firms to collaborate with foreign firms and gain managerial and technical experiences which can be used to support local operations at home. As a consequence, local firms will be able to enhance technological learning not only to create knowledge in their organizations, but also to solve problems that local firms cannot accomplish on their own. Similarly, access to global knowledge is important for helping firms becoming innovative and capable of producing competitive products. Digital technologies facilitate continuous interaction between local firms and foreign markets searching for appropriate knowledge and suitable technologies to be utilized by domestic firms in production of goods and services. Internet connectivity is changing the way business and employees work and via sharing and communicating knowledge and ideas organizations are becoming innovative, creative and productive. To this end, organizations should integrate digital technologies into their strategies to ensure knowledge creation and global competitiveness.

The Economic Complexity Index (ECI) is a measure of the relative knowledge intensity in the economy. It explains the international variations in the content of knowledge in products exported by different countries as well as the inequality in incomes among nations. Knowledge intensity in products reflects the ability of the country to produce unique products very few countries can produce. Such uniqueness reflects a country's capabilities to create knowledge and promote innovation that strengthen the economy fundamentals to produce highly specialized products for exports. On the other hand, with respect to products with a low degree of sophistication, nearly all countries can easily produce. These are called ubiquitous products requiring very little knowledge such that many countries can produce them. However, countries that produce unique products are innovative and creative capable of producing and exporting goods even when the global economy flounders.

Table 2 lists countries ranked in accordance to the economic complexity index, product concentration index and diversification index for the year 2016. Switzerland, Japan and Singapore top the list of countries producing high degree of sophisticated products. In contrast, most countries in the Arab world fall in the category of ubiquity producing products with low levels of sophistication. The table also illustrates that the share of high-tech exports in total manufactured exports in all GCC countries is low compared to that of Japan, Singapore and Switzerland. This represents another important indicator that the economies of these countries remain producers of primary products with little or no knowledge is required in the production of goods and services.

7   E-Government and Digital Services

In countries where the public sector is heavily involved in the economy and society, digital technologies could play an important role in transforming government services into productive activities aimed at improving educational and health services, increasing sectoral productivity, alleviating poverty, distributing income and promoting

Table 2. Economic complexity index (ECI), 2016 for selected countries

Country	ECI	Concentration index	Diversification index	High-tech exports % total of exports
Switzerland	2.59625	0.288	0.645	26.4
Japan	2.4687	0.141	0.400	16.7
Singapore	2.12695	0.240	0.645	47.2
United States	1.55257	0.100	0.244	18.2
Malaysia	1.03133	0.174	0.442	43.9
Saudi Arabia	−0.355486	0.593	0.780	0.7
UAE	0.241859	0.227	0.543	–
Oman	−0.52902	0.506	0.753	4.3
Kuwait	−0.789111	0.627	0.823	0.1
Bahrain		0.32	0.678	1.5
Qatar	−0.525304	0.400	0.834	0.0
Egypt	−0.410868	0.154	0.581	1.3
Morocco	−1.09205	0.175	0.677	5.3
Jordan	−0.0100069	0.164	0.651	1.6
Algeria	−0.781585	0.489	0.816	0.2

Source: https://atlas.media.mit.edu/en/rankings/country/neci/ United Nations, Human Development Report 2016, United Nations-
http://unctadstat.unctad.org/wds/TableViewer/tableView.aspx

innovation. In the meantime, digital technologies represent new opportunities for the government to increase engagement in economic and social activities which are essential for fostering change and sustaining growth. People in isolated regions can access government services to stimulate market activities and create new job opportunities. Providing services through modern technologies could reduce costs of government delivery and improve efficiency. ICT can be used to empower SMEs by providing information on potential markets, commodity prices, online training and marketing. In doing so, the government will be able to cut back on costs of services provided for SMEs across sectors and regions. In peripheries where large rural populations live, e-services have the potential to increase productivity and improve living standards of millions of people outside of urban areas.

Countries in the Arab world, especially in GCC region, are making efforts to diversify their economies and reduce dependency on oil production and exports. Digital technologies facilitate diversification through knowledge sharing, information dissemination and access to global markets. ICTs enhance government effectiveness to expand services and allocate productive resources in a productive manner. Having citizens able to interact and communicate with all levels of government facilitate knowledge sharing and stimulate linkages which encourage local enterprises to participate in market activities and diversify productivity.

Digital government is defined as the "employment of the internet and world-wide-web for delivering government information and services to the citizens." [15] In countries where financial resources are inadequate to pay for government expenditures, the use of the internet could enhance the effectiveness of public services at affordable costs. E-government services offer new opportunities for people to acquire information and knowledge which encourage investment and create jobs. "Digital transformation will play a key role in modernizing public services, increasing service productivity and reducing labor intensity, increasing the level of satisfaction with and effectiveness of services, and increasing the openness of, trust in and engagement with government." [16].

Online education has become a popular means for teaching and learning especially among those who live in isolated areas, the poor, women, and disadvantaged groups in society. Online educational services provide new opportunities for people to collaborate, cooperate and share ideas and knowledge aimed at enhancing capabilities and allowing greater connectivity with external markets. Collaborations among universities in research and development increase national capabilities to promote innovation and create new knowledge. Global collaboration not only facilities knowledge acquisition and transfer of new ideas, but also enhances the quality of teaching and learning. Communication among teachers and students makes teaching and learning more effective by providing students with opportunity to communicate with teachers outside school time.

Human development improves engagement in economic activities and contribution to economy. Digital technologies can increase choices and reduce costs of doing business which provides incentives for MSEs and young entrepreneurs to participate in market activities and create new employment opportunities. In other words, connectivity empowers people, including women and young entrepreneurs, to utilize, manage, share and create information aimed at increasing productivity, promoting innovation and sustaining development. Using digital technologies, SMEs have greater opportunities to expand operations and take advantages of new businesses in different markets. Some markets in GCC, including Bahrain, are small to stimulate linkages creation and encourage investment. Opening up regional markets will make it attractive for SMEs to expand operations through joint venture or production for exports. In this regard, regional integration among GCC whereby countries cooperate to reduce trade barriers will make it easier for SMEs to increase cross border trade and investment.

8 Conclusion

In recent decades, the emergence of the internet has had a profound impact on human society by bringing people closer together despite geographical distance and cultural differences. Today almost half of the world population uses the internet not only for sharing information and exchanging ideas, but also for promoting global understanding and creating linkages among and within nations. Building capacity for ICTs help the developing countries, in particular, to surpass several stages in their development. The digital divide has been identified with inadequate ICTs infrastructure to increase access to technology, information and skills. The challenge facing many developing countries is to close the digital divide by investing in ICTs. Connectivity is used to measure the availability of connections to the existing infrastructure of ICTs.

Digital technologies have become key driver of socio-economic transformation in the 21st century underscoring the importance of investment in digital literacy and improving e-services to meet the challenges of economic diversification in the Arab region. Social networking and computer literacy are critical for knowledge sharing and technological learning aimed at empowering the region capabilities to close the digital divide and diversify the economic structure. The complex nature of economic development requires strengthening connectivity to enhance communications among various players and bridge the knowledge divide among and within countries of the region.

There are more than 90 countries offering on line services toady reflecting the role that digital technologies can play in promoting socio-economic progress. E-governments provide more inclusive and effective services that reach people in different locations. Public e-services not only improve public welfare and foster change, but also support democracy, by enabling more citizens to participate in decision making.

Digital technologies empower SMEs to increase participation in both local markets and the global economy. Accesses to global markets allow SMEs to acquire managerial and technical resources, which can be used to increase productivity and enhance competiveness. In other words, connectivity will enable SMEs to improve production processes and meet international standards.

References

1. UNCTAD: World Investment Report 2017, Investment and the Digital Economy, United Nations, Geneva, 156 (2017)
2. Financial Tribunes. https://financialtribune.com/articles/world-economy/77352/chinas-digital-economy-reaches-30-of-2016-gdp. Accessed 7 May 2018
3. UNCTAD: Information Economy Report 2017, United Nations, New York, XIV (2017)
4. The McKinsey Global Institute, Digital China: Powering the Economy to global competitiveness. https://www.mckinsey.com/global-themes/china/digital-china-powering-the-economyto-global-competitiveness. Accessed Dec 2017
5. World Bank: The Wealth of Nations. The World Bank, Washington (2018)
6. International Telecommunication Union: (ITU) Measuring the Information Society Report, vol. 1. International Telecommunication Union, Geneva (2017)
7. Gulf News Thinkers, Need to Bridge the Digital Divide. http://gulfnews.com/opinion/thinkers/need-to-bridge-the-digital-divide-1.1523204. Accessed 27 May 2015
8. Deloitte, National Transformation in the Middle East: A Digital Journey, 17. Accessed from https://www2.deloitte.com/content/dam/Deloitte/xe/Documents/technology-mediatelecommunications/dtme_tmt_national-transformation-in-the-middleeast/National%20Transformation%20in%20the%20Middle%20East%20%20A%20Digital%20Journey.pdf
9. The McKinsey Global Institute. *Op. Cit.*, 4
10. Deloitte, *Op. Cit.*, 67
11. Wikipedia. https://en.wikipedia.org/wiki/Digital_divide
12. UNCTAD, Op. Cit., XIV

13. International Communication Union (ITU), *Op. Cit.*, 50
14. https://www.statista.com/statistics/239300/number-of-online-buyers-in-selected-countries/
15. Wikipedia. https://en.wikipedia.org/wiki/E-government
16. OECD, Digital Government Strategies for Transforming Public Services in the Welfare Areas. http://www.oecd.org/gov/digital-government/Digital-Government-Strategies-Welfare Service.pdf. Accessed 9 (2016)

Design of an Algebraic Concept Operator for Adaptive Feedback in Physics

Andrew Thomas Bimba[1][(✉)], Norisma Idris[1],
Ahmed A. Al-Hunaiyyan[2], Rohana Binti Mahmud[1],
and Nor Liyana Bt Mohd Shuib[3]

[1] Department of Artificial Intelligence, University of Malaya,
Kuala Lumpur, Malaysia
bimba@siswa.um.edu.my
[2] Computer & Information Systems Department, College of Business Studies,
The Public Authority for Applied Education & Training (PAAET),
Kuwait City, Kuwait
[3] Department of Information Systems, University of Malaya,
Kuala Lumpur, Malaysia

Abstract. In an adaptive learning environment, the feedback provided during problem-solving requires a means, target, goal, and strategy. One of the challenges of representing feedback to meet these criteria, is the representation of the effect of multiple concepts on a single concept. Currently, most of the methods (linguistic knowledge base, expert knowledge base, and ontology) used in representing knowledge in an adaptive learning environment only provide relationships between a pair of concept. However, a cognitive knowledge base which represents a concept as an object, attribute, and relations (OAR) model, provides a means to determine the effect of multiple concepts on a single concept. Using the OAR model, the relationships between multiple pedagogical, domain, and student attributes are represented for providing adaptive feedback. Most researchers have proposed adaptive feedback methods that are not fully grounded in pedagogical principles. In addition, the three knowledge components of the learning environment (pedagogical, domain and student models) are mostly treated in isolation. A reason for this could be the complex nature of representing multiple adaptive feedback characteristics across the main components of a learning environment. Thus, there is a need to design a concept operator that can relate the three facets of knowledge in an adaptive learning environment. Using the algebraic concept operator R_i^{in}, the effect of multiple attributes of the three knowledge components on the student's performance is represented. The algebraic concept operator introduced in this article will allow teachers and pedagogy experts to understand and utilize a variety of effective feedback approaches.

Keywords: OAR model · Knowledge base · Pedagogy
Learning environment · Student · Problem solving

Supported by University of Malaya Research Grant [RP040B-15AET, 2015].

S. A. Al-Sharhan et al. (Eds.): I3E 2018, LNCS 11195, pp. 181–190, 2018.
https://doi.org/10.1007/978-3-030-02131-3_17

1   Introduction

In an adaptive learning environment, the feedback provided during problem solving requires a means, target, goal, and strategy [1]. One of the challenges of representing feedback to meet these criteria, is the representation of the effect of multiple concepts on a single concept. Currently, most of the methods (linguistic knowledge base, expert knowledge base, and ontology) used in representing knowledge in an adaptive learning environment only provide relationships between a pair of concept [2]. However, a cognitive knowledge base which represents a concept as an object, attribute, and relations (OAR) model, provides a means to determine the effect of multiple concepts on a single concept. Using the OAR model, the relationships between multiple adaptive feedback means, target, goal, and strategy are represented for providing adaptive feedback by showing the effect of these characteristics on the performance of the student. The proposed concept operator is initialized using randomly pre-configured relationships between the characteristics of the pedagogical, domain and student model. During the process of learning, these relationships are automatically updated to suggest the appropriate combination of adaptive feedback means, target, goal, and strategy which can lead to optimal performance for different students.

Knowledge in a adaptive learning environment can be represented in the form models. The three most important models are the pedagogical model, domain model, and the student model. The pedagogical model represents the knowledge and technique of teaching. Specific knowledge represented in the pedagogical model is based on a pedagogical principle or learning theory. This principle or theory determines the effective teaching methods, instructional methods, sequence of activities, feedback types, and assessments modeled by the learning environment. On the other hand, the domain model, is a facet of the pedagogical model, which represents the knowledge of the subject been learned. The domain model represents concepts, learning materials, facts, problems, solutions, feedback, rules, equations etc. Finally, the student model represents information about the student's knowledge of the domain, learning style, interactions with the system, response to feedback, emotional state, performance etc. These information determines the characteristics of the student during problem-solving.

Goldstein [10] defines a problem as *an obstacle between a present state and a goal and it is not immediately obvious how to get around the obstacle (p. 365)*. Two types of problems identified by Psychologists are well-structured and ill-structured problems. The well-structured, are problems that by applying certain procedures will lead to a correct answer, while ill-defined problems do not usually have a single correct answer and have an unclear process to arriving at a solution [16, 17]. Depending on the type of problem considered, the *Novice* tends to be more accurate when the problem at hand is well-structured, but in cases where the problems are ill-structured, the *Novice* tends to perform poorly [3, 8, 10, 12, 17–19]. This could be related to the fact that the *Novice* has little knowledge of the deep structure of the problem, thereby not understanding the under-lining principles and concepts related to such problems. Physics instructions are designed to help students improve their problem solving expertise [19]. This is why some physics problems are ill-structured, similar to most real-life and professional problems.

Physics is more closely associated to everyday experiences. Thus, having proficiency in physics is a relevant skill, which can be extended to solving everyday problems. Physics is generally regarded as a difficult subject. Factors contributing to this difficulty include: (1) the presence of misconceptions; (2) degree of logical precision and reasoning required; (3) mathematical skills required; (4) misinterpretation of question posed; (5) concept gaps; and (6) knowledge gaps [5, 19]. During physics problem-solving in an adaptive learning environment, feedback is provided to assist the student in achieving a set objective.

Most researchers have proposed adaptive feedback methods that are not fully grounded in pedagogical principles [9, 15]. In addition, the three main knowledge components of the learning environment (pedagogical, domain and student model) are mostly treated in isolation. A reason for this could be the complex nature of representing multiple adaptive feedback characteristics across the main components of a learning environment. Thus, there is a need to design a concept operator that can relate the three facets of knowledge in an adaptive learning environment.

The article is structured into 5 sections. First, feedback in an adaptive learning environment is introduced in Sect. 1 and a brief background on pedagogy and student modeling is presented in Sect. 2. In Sect. 3, we explain the design of an algebraic concept operator for adaptive feedback. Preliminary results, on the implementation of the algebraic concept operator is presented in Sect. 4. And finally, in Sect. 5 we conclude the article and highlight the future works.

2   Background

Educational institutions are relatively successful in arranging and conveying large forms of knowledge and standard pedagogical practices [6, 13]. However, little attention is paid to the strategies experts use to acquire knowledge in solving complex task. The emphasis, in educational institutions is mostly on formulaic methods for solving textbook problems. While few resources are devoted to high-order problem-solving which requires students to actively integrate and apply conceptual knowledge. In order to make a positive impact on student's skill acquisition, there is a need to understand how experts acquire skills and to formulate different methods that are appropriate to learning these skills [6]. Therefore, more effort should be made on recognizing cognitive and metacognitive strategies rather than low-level sub-skills and factual knowledge. To support student learning, teachers and educationists regularly use a wide range of educational theories and teaching strategies [20]. Over the past decades, researchers have developed various learning theories in an attempt to explain how knowledge is acquired. These include theories such as behaviorism, cognitivism, and constructivism. The cognitive approach places the learner and the internal mental processes at the center of teaching. Because cognitivism focuses on revealing the various processes involved in knowledge acquisition, thereby providing strategies that support students learning, tutors can utilize this in their effort to aid students in attaining their goals. The cognitive apprenticeship (CA) instructional approach utilizes cognitive and meta-cognitive skills and processes to guide learning [7]. The CA concept is defined by [6] as learning through guided experience, cognitive and meta-cognitive skills rather than physical skills and processes as in traditional apprenticeship. In CA learning environment, students cannot engage in the apprenticeship process alone, rather it involves modeling (demonstration by expert) and coaching in the initial stage of learning [7]. The CA model for designing learning environments has four dimensions: (i) content or domain (the type of knowledge required for expertise), (ii) method (teaching method to promote student development), (iii) sequencing (ordering learning activities), and (iv) sociology (social characteristics of the learning environment) [6, 14].

The selection of appropriate student's characteristics is significant in the early stages of developing a student model. It is important to consider what aspect of the student characteristics is to be modeled according to the type of system developed [11]. In order to implement adaptation in a learning environment it is necessary to model the flexibly stable, dynamic and domain dependent characteristics of the student [4]. The flexibly stable characteristics of the student includes cognitive styles, student's demographics, learning objectives and goals. The dynamic parameters are concerned with the students interactions and experience with the learning environment. These characteristics include the student's errors and mis-conceptions, motivations, attitude, collaboration, learning actions and behaviors. The domain dependent characteristics of the student involves the student's knowledge level and interest in a specific topic.

The development of an adaptive feedback environment requires the combination of pedagogical principles, domain attributes and various student's characteristics. This research emphasizes on the cognitive apprenticeship principle. The attributes of the students considered for adaptive feedback are the cognitive learning style, student's performance, and knowledge level. The cognitive apprenticeship approach to learning involves the guidance of a student to achieve cognitive and meta-cognitive skills with the help of an expert. This principle was selected for this research because it clearly supports feedback, thus providing an avenue to demonstrate the use of a dynamic knowledge base approach to adaptive feedback.

3 Algebraic Concept Relations for Adaptive Feedback in Physics

In this article, we focus on the cognitive apprenticeship (CA) pedagogical principle and the physics domain. In a CA principle, the main aim of designing teaching methods is to help students acquire and use cognitive and meta-cognitive strategies for discovering, utilizing and managing knowledge [6]. The acquisition and use of these strategies solely depends on the interaction between the student's current knowledge, the social and physical environment of the problem-solving and the intricacies of the problem-solving. The challenge is to represent the attributes of the CA principle that affect the type, timing, goal, and sequence of feedback, relating it to the characteristics of the domain and student models. The representation of the characteristics of all 3 models relating to adaptive feedback is shown in Fig. 1. The knowledge in the proposed pedagogy, domain, learner - cognitive knowledge base (PDL-CKB) model is based on the OAR model. The nodes of the concept network in Fig. 1, represents concepts in the pedagogy, domain and student model in an adaptive learning environment. The arcs represent the relationship between concepts and their attributes.

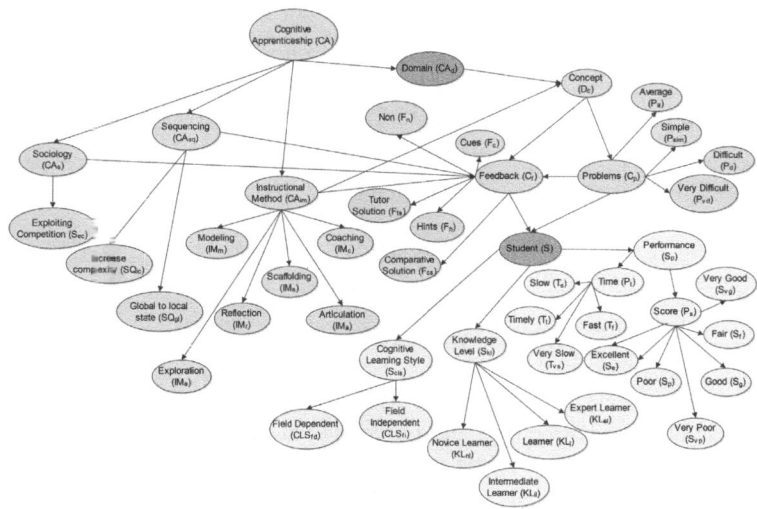

Fig. 1. PDL-CKB model for adaptive feedback in physics

An algebraic concept relation which provides adaptive feedback in physics is proposed. The main objective is to observe the relationship between the performance of a student based on the adaptive feedback provided. However, the adaptive feedback provided depends on the adaptive feedback means, goal, target, and strategy. These involves the 3 facet of the adaptive learning environment of pedagogy, domain, and student models. The effect of multiple concepts on a single concept is defined in Eq. 1.

$$R_i^{in} \subseteq \bigcup_{i=1}^{|R_i|} R_i^c \qquad (1)$$

The effect of a concept is represented as the union between all its related external concepts as shown in Eq. 1. where

- R_i^c is the internal relationships that exist between multiple concept that have a relation or effect on the current concept concerned.

For example, in an adaptive learning environment as shown in Fig. 1 the effect of the attributes of concepts within the pedagogy, domain, and student models on the performance of the student is represented in Eq. 2.

$$R_p^{in} \subseteq (R_{CA}^c \cup R_{CA_d}^c \cup R_S^c) \qquad (2)$$

where

- $R_{CA}^c \subseteq (CA_s \cup CA_{sq} \cup CA_{im})$ is the union of active sets of attributes within the pedagogical model which are related to the performance of a student at a given time.

- $R_{CA_d}^c \subseteq (D_c \cup C_f \cup C_p)$ is the union of active sets of attributes within the domain model which are related to the performance of a student at a given time.
- $R_S^c \subseteq (S_{cls} \cup S_{kl})$ is the union of active sets of attributes within the student model which are related to the performance of a student at a given time.

By expanding Eq. 2, all possible relationships between the performance of a student and the attributes of pedagogical, domain, and student model is presented in Eq. 3.

$$
\begin{aligned}
R_{s_p}^{in} \subseteq & \{\{S_{ec}\}\} \cup \{\{SQ_{ic}, SQ_{gl}\} \cup \{IM_m, IM_c, IM_s, IM_r, IM_a, IM_e\}\} \\
& \cup \{\{F_{ts}, F_h, F_c, F_n\} \cup \{D_c\} \cup \{P_{sim}, P_a, P_d, P_{vd}\}\} \\
& \cup \{\{CLS_{fd}, CLS_{fi}\} \cup \{KL_{nl}, KL_{il}, KL_l, KL_e\}\}\}
\end{aligned} \tag{3}
$$

During the learning process, not all attributes are activated at the same time. For example, a student cannot be a FI and FD learner at the same time. Therefore, at any given time (t), the effect of multiple concepts on the performance of a student can be represented as shown in Eq. 4.

$$
R_{s_p}^{in} \subseteq \{\{SQ_{ic}, IM_m\} \cup \{F_{ts}, D_c, P_{sim}\} \cup \{CLS_{fd}, KL_{nl}, KL_{il}, KL_l, KL_e\}\} \tag{4}
$$

$$
R_{s_p}^{in} \subseteq \{SQ_{ic}, IM_m, F_{ts}, D_c, P_{sim}, CLS_{fd}, KL_{nl}\} \tag{5}
$$

Using Eq. 5, the performance of a novice student KL_{nl} with a field Dependant cognitive learning style CLS_{fd}, solving a simple problem P_{sim} within a domain concept D_c, provided with an increasing complexity of feedback SQ_{ic} in a modeling stage IM_m can be easily represented. Thus, the system can automatically analyze the right combination of characteristics of the pedagogy, domain, and student models which provides the best performance for different type of students at different knowledge levels. In an adaptive feedback perspective, this implies an automatic update of the knowledge base, based on the best performance of different students solving different problems and receiving different feedbacks according to their individual characteristics and knowledge level on a specific concept. The proposed adaptive feedback model allows the knowledge base to make an automatic decision on the function, time, schedule, and type of feedback provided. At an initial state of building the knowledge base the knowledge bonding process selects random combinations of the required attributes needed to provide adaptive feedback to the student. As more students use the system, the knowledge base learns and updates its optimum combination of concepts to achieve an effective feedback to the student.

4 Preliminary Results

The provision of feedback based on the cognitive apprenticeship principle involves the instructional method, sequencing, sociology, and domain. When providing feedback in this context, a decision has to be made on what instructional method to be applied, the sequencing, and the application of a sociological component. In Table 1, a summary of the different forms of feedback provided based on the CA principle is presented. Certain interventions can be provided to the student before and during problem solving in a specific sequence. As seen in Table 1, there are 17 possible forms of feedbacks to be provided based on the feedback model presented in Fig. 1. The feedback attributes as shown in Table 1 are the characteristics of the CA pedagogical principle that determine the type of feedback that will be provided before and during problem-solving.

Table 1. Type of feedback based on the cognitive apprenticeship principle.

S/N feedback	ID	Feedback attributes	Before problem-solving	During problem-solving	Timing
1	FT1	Exploiting competition, global to local state, modelling	Student's worked-example	Student's solution	Immediate, after first error
2	FT2	Exploiting competition, modelling, increase complexity	Student's worked-example	Hints, clues, student's explanation	Immediate, after each error
3	FT3	Modelling, global to local state	Tutor's solution	Tutor's worked-example	Immediate, after first error
4	FT4	Increase complexity, modeling	Tutor's solution	Hints, cues, tutor's explanation	Immediate, after each error
5	FT5	Global to local state, scaffolding non	Non	Tutor's partial worked-example	Immediate, after more than one error. Provide feedback not more than twice.
6	FT6	Increase complexity, scaffolding	Non	Hints, cues, tutor partial explanation	Immediate, after each error. Provide feedback not more than twice.
7	FT7	Exploiting competition, global to local state, scaffolding	Non	Student's partial worked-example	Immediate, after first error. Provide feedback not more than twice.
8	FT8	Exploiting competition, increase complexity, scaffolding	Non	Hints, cues, student's partial explanation	Immediate, after each error. Provide feedback not more than twice.
9	FT9	Exploiting competition, global to local state, coaching	non	Student's worked-example	Immediate, after first error
10	FT10	Exploiting competition, increase complexity, coaching	Non	Hints, cues, student's explanation	Immediate, after each error
11	FT11	Global to local state, coaching	Non	Tutor's worked-example	Immediate, after first error
12	FT12	Increase complexity, coaching	Non	Hints, cues, tutor's explanation	Immediate, after first error
13	FT13	increase complexity, exploiting competition, articulation	non	student's explanation	at the end of problem-solving
14	FT14	Increase complexity, articulation	Non	Tutor's explanation	At the end of problem-solving
15	FT15	Global to local state, reflection	Non	Tutor's worked-solution	At the end of problem-solving
16	FT16	Global to local state, exploiting competition, reflection	Non	Student's worked-solution	At the end of problem-solving
17	FT17	Exploration	Non	Non	Result at the end of problem-solving

In the process of solving a problem there are different scenarios based on the domain attributes such as topic and problem and also the characteristics of the students which includes cognitive learning style and knowledge level. Based on these characteristics a total of 408 problem solving states are possible. In Table 2, a summary of these problem solving states are presented. As students solve problems, they receive feedback based on the pedagogical principles and their performance is feedback to the knowledge base according to the current problem solving state. These allow the knowledge base to be dynamic and the choice of feedback is based on the algebraic concept operation R_p^{in} defined.

Table 2. Relationship between students performance and pedagogy, domain, and student attributes

S/N	Problem solving state	Pedagogical model (PM)			Domain model (PM)			Student model (SM)		Effect of PM, DM, & SM on student's performance (R_p^{in})
1	pss1	Global to local state	Modelling	Exploiting competition	FT1	Average	Linear motion	Field independent	Novice	0.5
		0.5	0.5	NA	0.5	0.5	0.5	0.5	0.5	
2	pss2	Global to local state	Coaching	Exploiting competition	FT9	Difficult	Rotational motion	Field independent	Intermediate	0.32
		0.32	0.32	0.32	0.32	0.32	0.32	0.32	0.32	
3	pss3	Global to local state	Coaching	Exploiting competition	FT9	Simple	Rotational motion	Field independent	Expert	0.43
		0.43	0.43	NA	0.43	0.43	gravitation	0.43	0.43	
4	pss4	Global to local state	Coaching	Exploiting competition	FT9	Average	Static	Field independent	Intermediate	0.5
		0.5	0.5	NA	0.5	NA	0.5	0.5	0.5	
5	pss5	Global to local state	Coaching	Exploiting competition	FT9	Average	Linear motion	Field independent	Novice	0.27
		0.27	0.27	0.27	0.27	0.27	0.27	0.27	0.27	
6	pss6	Global to local state	Coaching	Exploiting competition	FT9	Average	Static	Field dependent	Expert	0.18
		0.18	0.18	0.18	0.18	0.18	Linear motion	Field dependent	0.18	

5   Conclusion

The aim of this article is to present the design of an algebraic concept operator which represents the relationship between student's performance and multiple attributes in the pedagogy, domain and student models. Figure 1, represents the relationship between the 3 facets (pedagogy, domain, and student models) of an adaptive learning environment. The model shows how full adaptive feedback characteristics can be modeled in the physics domain. It shows how concept algebra is applied to designing a concept association operator which defines the effect of multiple concepts on a single concept. Based on the preliminary results, about 17 adaptive feedback scenarios based on the cognitive apprenticeship principle are defined. Using the algebraic concept operator

R_p^{in}, the effect of multiple attributes of the pedagogy, domain, and student models on the student's performance is represented. These allows a selection of a effective adaptive feedback to be provided to the student during problem-solving. The algebraic concept operator introduced in this article will provide developers of adaptive learning environments with a means capturing effective relationships between multiple attributes in the pedagogy, domain, and student models. In addition it allows teachers and pedagogy experts to understand and utilize a variety of effective feedback approaches. In the future, a learning algorithm will be included to allow adjustments in the weights between the related concepts in the pedagogy, domain, and student models.

References

1. Bimba, A.T., Idris, N., Al-Hunaiyyan, A., Mahmud, R.B., Shuib, N.L.B.M.: Adaptive feedback in computer-based learning environments: a review. Adap. Beh. **25**(5), 217–234 (2017). https://doi.org/10.1177/1059712317727590
2. Bimba, A.T., Idris, N., Mahmud, R.B., Al-Hunaiyyan, A.: A cognitive knowledge-based framework for adaptive feedback. In: Phon-Amnuaisuk, S., Au, T.-W., Omar, S. (eds.) CIIS 2016. AISC, vol. 532, pp. 245–255. Springer, Cham (2017). https://doi.org/10.1007/978-3-319-48517-1_22
3. Chi, M.T.H., Feltovich, P.J., Glaser, R.: Categorization and representation of physics problems by experts and novices. Cogn. Sci. **5**(2), 121–152 (1981)
4. Chrysafiadi, K., Virvou, M.: Student modeling approaches: a literature review for the last decade. Expert Syst. Appl. **40**(11), 4715–4729 (2013)
5. Clement, J.: StudentsâĂŹ preconceptions in introductory mechanics. Am. J. Phys. **50**(1), 66–71 (1982)
6. Collins, A., Brown, J.S., Newman, S.E.: Cognitive apprenticeship: teaching the crafts of reading, writing, and mathematics. Knowing, Learn., Instr. Essays Honor. Robert Glas. **18**, 32–42 (1989)
7. Dennen, V.P., Burner, K.J.: The cognitive apprenticeship model in educationalpractice. Handb. Res. Educ. Commun. Technol. **3**, 425–439 (2008)
8. Docktor, J.L., Mestre, J.P., Ross, B.H.: Impact of a short intervention onnovicesâĂŹ categorization criteria. Phys. Rev. Spec. Top.-Phys. Educ. Res. **8**(2), 020102 (2012)
9. Gerdes, A., Jeuring, J., Heeren, B.: An interactive functional programming tutor. In: Proceedings of the 17th ACM Annual Conference on Innovation and Technology in Computer Science Education, pp. 250–255. ACM (2012)
10. Goldstein, E.B.: Cognitive psychology: Connecting mind, research and everyday experience. Nelson Educ. (2014)
11. GonzÃąlez, C., Burguillo, J.C., Llamas, M.: A qualitative comparison of techniques for student modeling in intelligent tutoring systems. In: Frontiers in Education Conference, 36th Annual, pp. 13–18. IEEE (2006)
12. Hardiman, P.T., Dufresne, R., Mestre, J.P.: The relation between problem categorization and problem solving among experts and novices. Mem. Cogn. **17**(5), 627–638 (1989)
13. Paul, B.: Helping students to become capable learners. Eur. J. Educ. **53**(2), 144–159 (2018). https://doi.org/10.1111/ejed.12273, https://onlinelibrary.wiley.com/doi/abs/
14. Polo, F.G.: Using the cognitive apprenticeship model to develop educational learning modules: An example from statics. In: 122nd American Society for Engineering Education Conference and Exposition, Seattle, WA (2015)

15. Rivers, K., Koedinger, K.R.: Data-driven hint generation in vast solution spaces: a self-improving python programming tutor. Int. J. Artif. Intell. Educ. **27**(1), 37–64 (2017)
16. Shekoyan, V., Etkina, E.: Introducing ill-structured problems in introductory physics recitations. In: AIP Conference Proceedings. AIP, vol. 951, pp. 192–195 (2007)
17. Shin, N., Jonassen, D.H., McGee, S.: Predictors of well-structured and ill-structured problem solving in an astronomy simulation. J. Res. Sci. Teach. **40**(1), 6–33 (2003)
18. Singh, C.: Categorization of problems to assess and improve proficiency as teachers and learners. Am. J. Phys. **77**(1), 73–80 (2009)
19. Soong, B., Mercer, N., Er, S.S.: Students' difficulties when solving physics problems: Results from an ict-infused revision intervention. In: Proceedings of the 17th International Conference on Computers in Education (ICCE), pp. 361–365 (2009)
20. Tompkins, E.K.: Application of cognitive apprenticeship model (ca) to library instruction. Coll. E Undergrad. Libr. **23**(1), 1–15 (2016)

Smart City and Green Development

A. Polzonetti[1(✉)] and M. Sagratella[2]

[1] University of Camerino, Camerino, Italy
alberto.polzonetti@unicam.it
[2] E-LIOS srl Spin off Unicam, Camerino, Italy
matteo.sagratella@e-lios.eu

Abstract. Smart city is a strategy that aims at employing technology to improve life quality in urban areas. Among its main objectives, the environment quality is the top one. The EU vision on smart cities is strongly focused on energy efficiency, on nearly-zero energy buildings, on the reduction of CO_2 emissions and so on. Therefore, some aspects of the smart city overlap with the idea of green city. Green city is an older but always updated vision, that aims at creating cities with a lower environmental impact, able to reduce the consumption of natural resources and to improve the quality of air and water.

This study is designed to understand if smart city and green city have similarities, to what extent they do overlap and how many synergies it is possible to create pursuing these two urban strategies at the same time. After a deep analysis of the international literature about these two subjects, we examined the portfolio of the initiatives that are usually employed, and we compared it with the international indicators related to the green city performances. We outlined overlapping areas and reached conclusions on the convergence of smart and green urban policies.

1 Introduction

Currently, the topics of green economy and sustainable growth are highly relevant, since the customers/consumers/citizens' sensitivity towards the environmental quality has increased. Economy and respect for the environment cannot and shouldn't be considered as opposing topics but rather as 'two sides of the same coin', as objectives to be both pursued in synergy and harmony [8].

This theme is more keenly felt by cities: in fact, the continuous and strong dimensional growth of urban centres produces an exponential increase of the pollution and the consumption of energy and natural resources such as water.

Besides, cities are the place where people, students and enterprises are concentrated: cities have always been the place selected for the production of goods and services, for related marketing and consumption. They are also the place where the tourist flows are more and more directed: their demand increases the consumption of resources and can make unsustainable the unresolved concerns related to, for example, mobility and pollution [15].

Cities are meeting the new needs and requirements by means of strategies that can be defined digital, green, smart and sustainable. These four strategy fields do not coincide with each other but show strong overlapping areas.

S. A. Al-Sharhan et al. (Eds.): I3E 2018, LNCS 11195, pp. 191–204, 2018.
https://doi.org/10.1007/978-3-030-02131-3_18

- The digital city is a city that largely employs ICT to convey data and information and to create bidirectional communication channels between citizens, institutions and enterprises.
- The green city is a city that aims at developing infrastructures, spaces, facilities and urban activities with a low or even with no environmental impact.
- The sustainable city is a city that aims at developing a socio-economical urban context able to balance economic development with respect for the environment and social equity.
- The smart city is a city focusing on the use of technologies to improve life quality in urban areas.

Overlaps and differences can be easily seen among these strategic policies for the city development. A local public transport system using advanced technology and ICT to reduce CO_2 emissions and to provide a better service to all citizens, with a special attention to the most disadvantaged groups of people such as disabled, older people, mums with strollers, is at the same time digital, smart, green and sustainable. On the contrary, the increasing of urban parks is a green project only, the General Register Office digitisation is a digital project only, the efficiency raising in energy production in smart grid is (almost) exclusively smart, and so on.

The concept of smart city that has spread in recent years tends to take in high consideration the smart, green and digital aspects simultaneously [10]. This city development line is emerging thanks mainly to the European Union guidelines that combine the guidance with funds and financing for the research and the implementation of smart projects, and it ends up prevail vs. other interpretations of smart city [1, 13].

Actually, the concept of smart city, both in academic definitions and practical implementations, takes on much wider and more heterogeneous meanings and contents and, drawing its perimeter seems quite difficult. Nevertheless, in the smart programs of the cities, the concern for the environment constantly appears as a core element.

Therefore, the research question is the following: which is the relation between green city and smart city? Are there common dimensions (and then indicators related to each dimension)? Is it possible to design policies that concur to the achievement of such common objectives?

2   Smart, Digital, Green E Sustainable

2.1   The Origin of the Concept of Smart City

The branch of research and government named smart city is today among the main strategies not only of cities but also of global member states and organizations such as UN, OECD, European Union. Cities have started many smart initiatives, and just as many are the European programs financing such initiatives and the reports, studies and researches of national and supranational bodies on this subject. However, the definition of smart city is not yet univocal or consolidated [14].

The main reason of this indeterminacy lays in the process that led to the success of the so-called smart initiatives. Often a bottom-up driven process, namely driven by isolated initiatives of citizens and enterprises; a process that started in territories, in the urban areas of some pilot cities and then has spread worldwide [5] 2011). To understand what a smart city is, it is first of all necessary to carry out three types of analysis:

- The historical analysis, studying how the topic has started and developed and in which time frame;
- The territorial analysis, exploring the coming up of smart experiences, researches or policies in urban areas and in the regions of the world, examining also how the phenomenon started and progressively spread itself;
- The terminology and content analysis that compares the different terms used to identify the cities that started a path for the improvement of the living conditions in their territories, thanks to the more or less intense use of advanced technologies such as – but not only – the ICT and the minimisation of environmental impact of the cities.

The historical analysis highlights how the smart city has far-off roots and how it constantly intertwines with the concept of digital city [9].

The historical analysis is a first distinctive element between digital city and smart city, that underlines the different development that the two experiences had in the past twenty years. Other relevant differences emerge from the analysis of territorial and content elements of these two smart city metaphors. The review of existing literature allows us to draw the most quoted definitions of digital city and smart city. By reading and interpreting them, some aspects become immediately clear, some of them can be deducted from the digital or smart name of the city.

The digital city is strictly related to the use of information technology and especially to some of its implementations such as Internet, broadband and fast Internet connections at urban areas level, the use of mobile access devices, not only the traditional PC, but especially, the so called smart devices (and here it is the first source of terminology confusion) such as smart-phones and tablets.

Among related key topics we find broadband and connectivity, that make the digital city also a wired city or a network city [7], the use of open data structures, thanks to which public information is accessible and available to everyone and this make the digital city also an information city [3]; the creation of digital services offered to citizens both by public bodies and by private enterprises and organizations [6]; the virtualization of spaces, behaviours and relationships that lead to the creation of a sort of virtual city overlapping the real one, with its own rules, behaviours, relationships etc. This makes a digital city also a virtual city or an ubiquitous city [2, 19].

The definitions of digital city do not talk of quality of life explicitly, but they show that the process of transformation of the city generated by digitisation policies is fully oriented towards the citizen and his needs. And indeed, one of the main obstacles to the full realization of the digital city is mainly the digital divide, which separates those who have the skills to access digital information and services from those who haven't, creating a form of virtual exclusion [16]. Exclusion not only in terms of fruition, but also in terms of offer, with some enterprises and public bodies that are able to offer digital information and services and others that do not have the knowledge and the skills to do so and remain excluded from the implementation of the digital city and from related appropriation of returns.

The analysis of the main definitions of smart city, highlights the primary characteristics of what a smart city should be. A first reading of the definitions suggests, in the first place, that the concept of smart city is much more indefinite than the digital city one. As a matter of fact, some definitions are impalpable and identify the smart city just as a city able to create good living conditions for its citizens, regardless of how it manages to do that and of what tools or technology are used [11]. Some definitions recall the digital city, recognising in those previous and more mature experiences a basis or a part of the smart city [5]. Other definitions are more concrete and refer to smart initiatives, infrastructures and activities mainly connected to some key elements of living in the city such as public transport, energy production and consumption, pollution and environmental impact of buildings and human or productive activities [10].

Actually, the main academic definitions of smart city are not able to represent what the smart city really is in the mind of those who – in municipal Governments, enterprises and University Departments – are involved in its design and realization. A more practical vision can be extrapolated from the reports of the major technological players, IBM, Oracle or Microsoft for example, or of the big research centres such as Gartner and the Stanford University, or even more from visiting the websites of the several Italian, European or global cities that have taken the path of smartness. The analysis carried out enabled us to understand that there are some common themes that can be found both in academic studies and in the empirical implementations of the smart city.

The main topic, shared by all the sources we analysed, regards the negative environmental impact of cities and the need of containing or reducing it, especially through the reduction of CO_2 but also through waste treatment, water quality etc. As a function of the relationship between city and environment, the smart city focuses on the enormous amount of energy used by the city, due to its residential and productive settlements and to the premises of enterprises, places of study and work, public bodies and, therefore, the need, on the one hand, of reducing the energy requirements and, on the other hand, of producing energy from clean and renewable sources. A smart city is not such if it does not make a wide use of the most innovative technology. Central is the key role of technology in the pursuit of all the smart city objectives and of the technology-based orientation of smart strategies, as well as the technologic, economic and social innovation that envisages in the smart city also a place of economic development with high added value and with a high content of technology and knowledge [21].

A theme partly included in the smart city concerns the so-called smart community; in fact, it is an evolution of the digital city that aims at connecting citizens, at making available open access to online information and at the fruition of digital services also with mobile devices. The topic of smart community draws the attention on the role of citizens and on their active involvement in city smartness projects. Finally, even the macro-objectives of the smart city (at a general level) are homogeneous: the smart city aims at the citizens' well-being; a tangible well-being, based on ease of access to services and infrastructures, on economical well-being, on participation and social inclusion. A well-being built on the contrast to the typical inconveniences deriving from living in a city, such as traffic, pollution, congestion of public or private transport, and on the study of innovative solutions to limit such inconveniences. According to this last and wider meaning, the smart city becomes a city able to carry out a positive role for its residents and visitors, regardless of the devices used to achieve the smartness objectives.

2.2   From Smart to Green

The study and analysis of the materials collected and described in the previous paragraph allows us to highlight two concepts of smart city. The first one could be defined as wide: according to it the smart city is an intelligent city creating excellent living conditions for all its citizens. The purpose of this concept is to emphasize how nowadays the quality of life strongly passes through cities, urban areas, through the activities taking place there and the ability of local policies to achieve good living conditions, that are often hindered by the excessive dimensions of cities and by their complexity.

The second concept, the more interesting one for our study, just defines the smart city as a subset of the successful city, that includes some issues such as infrastructures, energy, environmental impact, use of ICT; and where technology and innovation have a key role; all this is aimed at improving the quality of life in urban spaces and to attracting smart, innovative and fully developed persons and enterprises there.

According to this better focused meaning, the smart city actually takes on its own features, where technology, respect for the environment, use of ICT, applied to the physical elements of life in the city such as buildings and public transport, but also the virtual elements of urban life such as the need of receiving digital services or to accessing online information, are key elements to define a development path that is both sustainable and inclusive. According to this meaning, the smart city becomes partly green city, namely green city respectful of the environment, partly sustainable city, a city that defines paths of socio-economical development able to guarantee economic well-being, social inclusion and environmental quality to those living within its boundaries, not necessarily administrative ones but within the city area of influence.

Beyond definitions, the main difference between green city and sustainable city is not only the time frame: in the green city it is based on the present, in the sustainable city it is inter-temporal and through present and future generations. The main difference is that the sustainable city aims to reconcile environment, economy and social inclusion, stating that the respect for the environment and the sustainable use of natural resources are not in contrast with the economic wellbeing and the creation of value by enterprises and that the sustainable development has to aim at creating a balanced wealth also with regard to its distribution, avoiding the concentration of wealth in the hands of a few to the detriment of the economic and social inclusion of many. A sustainable city is also a fair city that aims at guaranteeing the internal well-being for everyone, no one excluded.

From the comparison between sustainable and smart city, we notice some overlapping elements between the two concepts. The main ones are the environment impact and the use of natural resources: they are present both in the sustainable city and in the smart city. Both these two ideas of city consider the economic development as a key element of urban life that, for the sustainable city, should be reconciled with the natural environment, whilst in the smart city; the smartness is even a source of sustainable economic growth. Citizens play a central role but is intended in two different ways: in the sustainable city it primarily pursues the aims of equity among people and generations in the distribution of economic and natural resources, whilst the smart city directs its efforts towards the quality of life in urban areas. The social inclusion is a topic that has been added only in recent times and, however, in a marginal and indefinite way.

What certainly distinguishes the smart city from the sustainable one is the key role played by technology and, in particular, by ICT and by the most innovative ad advanced technologies in the realization of smart, quality and attractive cities, where people can live well, and where it is possible to achieve a widespread well-being and to combat social exclusion.

When they started to talk about sustainable economy and cities, the information technologies were still in a pre-Internet phase and confined in large enterprises and organisations; the pervasiveness of ICT in daily life of SME and citizens was still far away. Also the dimensions of cities were more contained, megalopolis could be countend on the fingers of one hand and the psychological threshold of the 50% of the world population that goes to live in cities was not overcome yet. These elements modified the metaphor of city, but they did not reduce the awareness of how urgent it is to answer to the needs of life in urban areas, to environmental decay, to the use of energy sources, mainly in cities, that from the Middle Ages to the present days, have been, and increasingly will be, the focus of economic and social life.

3   Green and Smart City: A Comparison of Dimensions and Indicators

3.1   Dimensions and Indicators of the Green City

Within the framework of general policies aimed at pursuing a green vision for urban agglomerations, first we can refer to OECD contributions. In particular, the topic of the green growth of the OECD Declaration on Green Growth, of June 2009, was subsequently taken up and contextualised in the Green Cities Programme. This program aims at evaluating how much the urban green growth and the policies for sustainability can contribute to improving both the economic context and the environmental quality of metropolitan areas and, consequently, to increase the contribution of such areas to the national growth, to life quality and to competitiveness. In particular, the Green Growth Strategy identifies and promotes the activities necessary to reduce the environmental impact as potential sources of growth and refers to the need of internalise the negative environmental externalities. In these contributions, the green growth is intended to harmonise economic growth and environmental sustainability. As such, it only partially coincide with the concept of sustainable development since it focuses on economic efficiency and environmental protection that are only two of the three pillars of the sustainable development (that, as is known, includes also social equity and justice). The effort and the wish is that the social interests be integrated in the commitment for green growth [12].

Urban green growth especially focuses on economic growth and on development through urban activities able to limit the negative environmental externalities and the impact of natural resources and environmental services [17]. In fact, it is evident that the urban agglomeration significantly affects, mainly in new fast-growing metropolises (i.e. in the Far East), traffic congestion, pollution and the impact on the ecosystem and, hence, on the natural resources. The dimensions of the green city can be expressed in a series of indicators, many of which have given rise to the need of synthesize the different suggested variables in a single code.

Concluding this first part focused on dimensions and indicators of the green city, we can state the following:

- The suggested dimensions cover the traditional areas of environmental protection: water, air, earth (more in general, non-renewable resources), waste management and energy, as well as human activities strongly affecting these resources: urban mobility, waste and buildings management. However it is evident that, for example, urban mobility is strictly connected to the quality of air and can generate separate assessments of the interconnected and interdependent indicators;
- The suggested indicators are sometimes already operationalized, i.e. expressed as variables. The schemes propose then mixed (and therefore inconsistent) sets of indicators and variables;
- No indexes are built with the suggested variables: the task of synthetizing the multiplicity of variables and identifying a form of synthetic evaluation is left to the researcher who adopts the scheme.

It follows that the above is an interesting contribution to a more accurate and articulated knowledge of the green dimensions of a city, but it is not yet a valid tool for the measurement of the urban realities performance: the conceptual framework seems in fact to leave aside the definition of the strategic objectives of each specific city to which evaluations and measurements should necessarily and strictly be connected.

According to this framework and to the purposes of this study, it is evident the need of having at least one set of dimensions to be able to evaluate how smart initiatives can be qualified also as initiatives pursuing the green objectives of a city. Based on our findings, we suggest the following dimensions of a green city:

- Air quality
- Land use and consumption
- Energy consumption (efficiency raising, alternative and renewable energies)
- Waste production and management
- Mobility, transport and logistics.

3.2 Dimensions and Indicators of the Smart City

As we have seen, the relevant definitions are not univocal. In the first place because the city smartness is a process and, as such, continuously changing and evolving. Besides, the main object on which the process takes place, i.e. the city, shows some typical characters as well as a multiplicity of different connotations (dimension, localisation, resources, socioeconomic and political context, etc.) that make difficult and especially, in our opinion, not very useful, any attempt of referring to "a unit". It is certainly more functional to our purposes to identify which are the city dimensions that come into play in the context of a smart approach. We therefore intend to focus on two scientific contributions identifying those that should be the main characteristics of smart cities, the significant dimensions of their development that, consequently, identify the indicators pertinent to each dimension.

With this regard, we refer to Giffinger et al. [11] who stated that the smart city is "a city well performing in a forward-looking way in economy, people, governance, mobility, environment, and living, built on the smart combination of activities of self-decisive, independent and aware citizens". This approach not only considers the technology and digitalisation of structures and services (digital city) essential, but contemplates them in a project of improvement of life quality and in a wise management of resources, mainly natural ones (green city), through a participative governance (smart city). For this vision of city, the study identifies six areas of intervention whose design and management should be carried out in an intelligent perspective, built according to available resources and knowledge and with the active participation of independent and aware citizens. Every city can be defined as smart to the extent it is commited in the realization of:

- smart economy: competitiveness
- smart environment: natural resources
- smart governance: participation
- smart living: quality of life
- smart mobility: transport and ICT
- smart people: social and human capital.

Such dimensions are declined in 31 factors that make up the framework for the identification of indicators and the consequent evaluation of the performances of a smart city. In particular, this means to assess and measure aspects such as: entrepreneurial spirit, economic image, productivity, flexibility of labour market (that fall within the smart economy), environmental protection, pollution, sustainable management of resources (smart environment), participation in decision-making processes, public and social services, transparent governance (smart governance), individual safety, cultural and educational structures, touristic attractiveness, social cohesion (smart living), accessibility, availability of ICT infrastructures, sustainable, innovative and safe transport systems (smart mobility), continuous professional training, flexibility and creativity, mind and cultural openness (smart people).

The results provided by the adoption of such framework are undoubtedly interesting since they allow to highlight the best city performances, also with respect to specific issues.

It is interesting to remember the ranking of the Smart City Index carried out by the consulting company Between on 116 Italian chief municipalities on the basis of thematic areas. This index is not aimed at measuring the absolute level of smart innovation but the distance between the best city (score = 100) and the others [4]. The analyzed dimensions are the following:

- broad band
- smart mobility
- smart health
- smart education
- smart government
- alternative mobility
- renewable energies
- energy efficiency
- natural resources.

On this basis, were identified 19 sub-areas and 153 indicators representing a particularly innovative contribution for the identified areas and for the adopted measurements. Besides, it is interesting to notice that the adopted meaning of smart city first of all requires that it may be possible to observe a substantial difference between a "before" and a "after", that such changes derive from a path pursued and contextualizable in a clear vision but, above all, that such changes have a strong connotation of innovation, "tangible" and "widespread" within the city.

The contributions of Giffinger et al. [11] and Between [4] however point out the typical limits of rankings: they are a "photograph" of the situation of a group of cities providing a synthetic vision of a complex phenomenon but they do not satisfy the need of an articulated and specific knowledge. In fact, many characteristics of the smart city are analysed in cychotomous key only or otherwise different weights are assumed (discretional) or, again, are adopted wide or limited visions of a same dimension characterizing a smart city. The reason of these limits is clearly, because the definition of smart city is not univocal and the measurement of the performances of the cities that have started integrated projects are still scarce. The dimensions and indicators suggested by such contributions can however be a valid support for the evaluation of the policies to be included in order to identify if and to what extent they are consistent with the dimensions a smart city should have.

A significantly different approach is offered by the Siemens' Efficient Cities study carried out by Cittalia that aims at analyzing a macro group of 54 mediumlarge cities based on their infrastructural allocations [20]. The examined areas were urban environment quality, real estate assets, sustainable mobility and logistics, renewable energy, healthcare. The final result is the identification of six homogeneous groups of similar cities in which the different areas combine themselves bringing out one or more components: the cities of the environment, of the well-being, ideal cities, cities of the good living and of mobility, cities under development, of the energy.

Our interest for this study is based on its attempt to provide a richer and deeper, and then complete, knowledge of the city, through a multi-level classification: an initial level, based on factor analysis in main components (PCA) and a final one based on cluster analysis.

On the basis of a careful analysys of the doctrin' different contributions about the dimensions that should characterise green and smart cities, it emerges that the environment and energy topics are always present, though with different extent and importance, within the smart city concept and dimensions. As concerns the concept of green city examined in the first part, the illustrated contributions highlight in fact how the smartness of a city may not disregard a vision that considers essential the safeguard of natural resources, above all the non-renewable ones, the reduction of the environment impacts caused by human activities and enterprises processes, energy efficiency, and safety. This vision seems to include, or at least to overlap significantly, the green city concept with the smart city one.

4   Italian Smart City

Some Italian cities are an interesting, often mentioned, case of city planning and transformation according to a smart vision that began in 2010. The underlying vision, shared with stakeholders, is based on the way the term smart city is intended: "The Smart City improves the living quality through a sustainable economic development, based on research, innovation, technology and driven by the local leadership in a process of integrated planning".

The annual report examined was carried out by FPA in order to photograph the situation of Italian cities on their path to become "smart", that is to say nearer to citizens' need, more inclusive, more livable. FPA identified and analysed 15 urban dimensions that, in the national and international context, set out the objectives for the cities (poverty, education, air and water, energy, economic development, occupation, tourism and culture, research and innovation, digital transformation and transparency, sustainable mobility, waste, public green, soil and territory, legality and security, governance) (ICITY RATE 2017).

The set of these initiatives shows the participation of a large number of players: public subjects, private companies and citizens. The analysis, based on the description of the action and of the estimated result, provided a classification of the initiatives according to 5 dimensions among the ones suggested above: air quality, land use and consumption, energy consumption (efficiency raising, alternative and renewable energies), waste production and management, mobility, transport and logistics. As shown in Table 69 initiatives currently developed as smart (equal to the 68% of the total) show aspects that define them as green initiatives. Compared to the dimensions identified, the actions connected to the energy topic (containment of energy consumption, reconversion to alternative or renewable energies, etc.) show a higher frequency. Several are the initiatives connected to mobility, transport and logistics, too: many of which are classified also in the topic area "air quality and reduction in CO_2 emissions".

	Number of smart actions
Air quality	7
Soil use and consumption	6
Energy consumption	18
Waste production and management	2
Mobility, transport and logistics	14
Green impact	47

In the examined case, it is clear that the characteristics and factors of the smart city show areas of evident overlapping with those of the green city as well as areas that are only partially common.

5 Conclusions

The smart city topic is gaining a position of great interest and newness for public administrations but also for the research community and for enterprises. The literature analysis highlights how the smart city concept does not have an accredited and fully shared definition yet. This is mainly due to a process of bottom-up type implementation of the smart city: local administrations, enterprises and associations moved independently to carry out smart small actions or large projects, often without a direction or planning able to define vision, strategies, goals and contents of the smart city. The definitions are based on the collection of experiences under a unifying hat, trying to keep together a multiplicity of aspects sometimes very different one from the other.

On the contrary, the green city has older origins and a better-defined perimeter. Provided that the city is a huge agglomerate - larger and larger from the geographical and population points of view – that consumes natural resources and produces pollution, the green city is a urban planning strategy that tries to make the city greener thanks to public actions and single citizens behaviours aimed at the respect of the environment, that, at the same time, allows to its residents and visitors to enjoy healthier urban spaces.

The purpose of the Research questions of the study was to understand if there are relationships between smart city and green city, which are these relationships and how these two urban strategies can be directed towards this goal taking advantage of positive synergies. The analysis of the scientific literature, of national, international and local experiences on the smart city topic highlights that, among the several themes falling in the smart city perimeter, the environmental policies have a key role. This generates a partial overlapping between smart city and green city this does not mean that the two urban strategies fully coincide, nor that the green city can be considered as a subset of the smart city, because several are the differences that we can find in literature and in the analysis of empirical cases.

The key element that characterizes the smart city is technology, be it Information Technology or other engineering technologies applied to typical infrastructures of the urban fabric, such as roads, buildings, public lighting, transport, etc. On the contrary, the green city key element is the environment and its protection in every possible meaning of the word. The protection of the environment is also the clear objective of the green city, whilst the smart city has a much wider, ambitious but vague objective, that is to say, to improve the quality of life in the urban context. By intertwining above key elements and objectives, we can identify the overlappings between smart city and digital city. If we want to define such overlapping, we could say that smart city and digital city coincide where technology is employed to reduce the city impact on the use of natural resources, on energy consumption and soil, on air and water pollution.

In the above overlapping, it is possible to identify common dimensions, shared indicators and synergic policies to go towards a city that is both smart and green. In fact, the common dimensions are exactly those on which technology can intervene on taking positive actions on these green topics: air quality, soil use and consumption, energy consumption, waste management, logistic mobility and urban transport. The common indicators are those that aim at measuring the green impact obtained by smart actions, namely activities for the environment protection that employ innovative technologies. Let us think about the use of ICT to offer remote services and to avoid unnecessary travels the use of technologies for the production of energy from clean and renewable energy sources, the increase of energy efficiency of buildings, and so on.

We should keep in mind that not all the smart actions are also green and the other way round: it is therefore up to each city to determine what are its smart objectives, its green objectives and to identify overlappings and synergies to be supported with appropriate political, administrative and design measures. The specificity of the choices of every single city, though included in a smart/green overall vision common to other cities, clearly stands out from the empirical analysis of the report.

In the report, it is evident that the smart actions and projects were born in the absence of a well-outlined strategic framework and of definite objectives: this does not allow either to apply prioritization criteria among the actions to be carried out, or to measure and evaluate the achieved results. It follows that in the smart perimeter is included a really too wide and heterogeneous range of actions very different one from the other and lacking shared objectives.

Besides, the detailed analysis of all smart actions and projects of the report highlights how, mainly as regards European projects, the overlapping of smart and green strategies is very high. We should consider the following: the European projects are guided by strategic guidelines of the European Union, that tends to attribute to the smart city concept a much greener content than that emerging from the literature.

Overall, regarding the smart projects highlighted in the report, it also emerges that the energy component is predominant. Here we have to make another consideration: smart cities, thanks to the technological component, are a topic that strongly involves also the hi-tech sector companies that are particularly interested in the smart city as a potential market for their technological products. From the analysis of Genoa case, it comes into light that, lacking the city its own strategic vision, the choices of priority areas were heavily influenced by two forces: the areas where the European Union placed funds and the interest of partner companies of the Smart Cities.

In conclusion, both the literature analysis and the study of an empiric case allowed highlighting that a large shared area (Research question 1) exists between smart city and green city, whose dimension is influenced by the choices and priorities of each city with respect to the green objectives that can be achieved by using smart technologies. The dimensions of this overlapping regard the use of natural resources, energy consumption and polluting emissions (Research question 2). The smartness and greenness indicators of the city have to be applied considering that not all the smart activities have green impacts, and not all green actions are also smart, so that an indicator such as the reduction of CO_2 emissions should be interpreted in relation with the actions that generated it (Research question 3). Lastly, as regards the policies common to the smart city and green city strategies (Research question 4), relevant synergies are depending on the choices and on the vision of each city. It is up to each city to choose if and to what extent to be smart or green and if to pursue the green objectives through technology, citizens' virtuous behaviour or both.

References

1. Ahvenniemi, H., Huovila, A., Pinto-Seppä, I., Airaksinen, M.: What are the differences between sustainable and smart cities? Cities **60**, 234–245 (2017)
2. Anthopoulos, L., Fitsilis, P.: From digital to ubiquitous cities: defining a common architecture for urban development. In: 2010 Sixth International Conference on Intelligent Environments (IE). IEEE (2010)
3. Anthopoulos, L.: Smart utopia VS smart reality: learning by experience from 10 smart city cases. Cities **63**, 128–148 (2017)
4. Between, S.P.A.: Smart City Index-Confrontarsi per diventare smart, Report 2013 (2013)
5. Caragliu, A., Del Bo, C., Nijkamp, P.: Smart cities in Europe. J. Urban Technol. **18**(2), 6582 (2011)
6. Cleland, B., Wallace, J., Black, M.: The 'engage' system: using real-time digital technologies to support citizen-centred design in government. In: Saeed, S., Ramayah, T., Mahmood, Z. (eds.) User Centric E-Government. ISIS, pp. 183–201. Springer, Cham (2018). https://doi.org/10.1007/978-3-319-59442-2_11
7. Cocchia, A.: Smart and digital city: a systematic literature review. In: Dameri, R.P., Rosenthal-Sabroux, C. (eds.) Smart City. PI, pp. 13–43. Springer, Cham (2014). https://doi.org/10.1007/978-3-319-06160-3_2
8. Cutaia, L., Morabito, R.: Sostenibilità dei sistemi produttivi: strumenti e tecnologie verso la green economy. ENEA (2012)
9. Dameri, R.P.: Defining an evaluation framework for digital cities implementation. In: 2012 International Conference on Information Society (iSociety). IEEE (2012)
10. Dameri, R.P.: Searching for smart city definition: a comprehensive proposal. Int. J. Comput. Technol. **11**(5), 2544–2551 (2013)
11. Giffinger, R., Fertner, C., Kramar, H., Meijers, E., Plichler-Milhanovic, N.: Smart Cities: Ranking of European Medium-Sized Cities. Centre of Regional Science, Vienna (2007)
12. Hammer, S., Kamal-Chaoui, L., Robert, A., Plouin, M.: Cities and green growth: a conceptual framework. In: OECD Regional Development Working Papers 2011/08. OECD Publishing (2011). https://doi.org/10.1787/5kg0tflmzx34-en
13. Lamboglia, R., Cardoni, A., Dameri, R. P., Mancini, D. (eds.) Network, Smart and Open: Three Keywords for Information Systems Innovation , vol. 24. Springer (2018)
14. Nam, T., Pardo, T.: Conceptualizing smart city with dimensions of technology, people, and institutions. In: Proceedings of the 12th Annual International Digital Government Research Conference: Digital Government (2011)
15. OECD: Cities and Climate Change (2010a)
16. OECD: Good Governance far Digital Policies: How to Get the Most Out of ICT: The Case of Spain's Pian Avanza. OECD, Nov (2010b)
17. OECD: Green Growth in Cities, OECD Green Growth Studies. OECD Publishing (2013). http://dx.doi.org/10.1787/9789264195325-en
18. Pardo, T., Taewoo, N.: Conceptualizing smart city with dimensions of technology, people, and institutions. In: Proceedings of the 12th Annual International Conference on Digital Government Research, pp. 282–291. ACM New York (2011)

19. Schuler, D.: Digital cities and digital citizens. In: Tanabe, M., van den Besselaar, P., Ishida, T. (eds.) Digital Cities 2001. LNCS, vol. 2362, pp. 71–85. Springer, Heidelberg (2002). https://doi.org/10.1007/3-540-45636-8_6
20. Siemens: EfficienCITIES.Città-modello per lo sviluppo del Paese, Cittalia. Siemens-Economist Intelligence Unit (2009). European Green City Index (2012)
21. Zhuhadar, L., Thrasher, E., Marklin, S., de Pablos, P.O.: The next wave of innovation—review of smart cities intelligent operation systems. Comput. Hum. Behav. **66**, 273–281 (2017)

The Role of Data Analytics in Startup Companies: Exploring Challenges and Barriers

Vebjørn Berg$^{(\boxtimes)}$ ⓘ, Jørgen Birkeland ⓘ, Ilias O. Pappas ⓘ,
and Letizia Jaccheri ⓘ

Department of Computer Science, Norwegian University of Science and
Technology, Sem Sælandsvei 9, 7491 Trondheim, Norway
{vebjorbe,jorgebi}@stud.ntnu.no,
{ilpappas,letizia.jaccheri}@ntnu.no

Abstract. The advancement in technology is transforming societies into digital arenas and paves the way towards the achievement of digital transformation. With every transaction in the digital world leading to the generation of data, big data and their analytics have received major attention in various fields and different contexts, examining how they may benefit the different actors in the society. The present study aims to identify how startups that develop products with both software and hardware parts can generate value from data analytics and what challenges they face towards this direction. To this end, we performed a multiple-case study with early-stage startups and employed qualitative analysis on a dataset from 13 startups. Through semi-structured interviews, we examine how these companies use data analytics. The findings show that although the benefits from data analytics are clear, multiple barriers and challenges exist for the startups to be able to create value from them. The major ones are about their resources, including human skills, economical resources, as well as time management and privacy issues.

Keywords: Startups · Big data · Data analytics · Empirical research

1 Introduction

In the digital era of the 21st century information and knowledge becomes readily available to more and more people every day. Societies generate vast amounts of data every moment from multiple sources, transforming them into landscapes mediated by different digital media platforms, digital services, and technologies, leading to the creation of big data and business analytics ecosystems [1, 34]. The different actors of the society (i.e., industry, public and private organizations, entrepreneurs, academia, civil society) are increasingly realizing the potential of the generated data which can lead to value creation, business change, and social change. To this end, many entrepreneurs and startups are actively trying to harness the power of big data and create software and hardware with the potential to increase value, gain a competitive advantage, and improve various aspects of human life [2, 34].

S. A. Al-Sharhan et al. (Eds.): I3E 2018, LNCS 11195, pp. 205–216, 2018.
https://doi.org/10.1007/978-3-030-02131-3_19

Startups are newly created companies producing cutting-edge technology, having a major impact on the global economy [9]. In a context of extreme uncertainty and restricted economical, human, and physical resources, startups have unique challenges related to product development and innovation methods [10]. This results in a high number of failures, primarily due to self-destruction rather than competition [10, 11]. Operating in fast-changing, competitive high-risk environments, continuous experimentation is essential for learning and bringing products fast-to-market [12].

There is increasing literature on how big data analytics can generate value towards business or societal transformation [3, 4], however further work is needed in order to identify and overcome existing barriers that will allow practitioners to generate value from big data and analytics [5]. Digitization and big data analytics have disrupted business models and can be essential tools to reduce increasing failure rates of established companies [6]. Innovative startups profit on reduced barriers for entering markets with technologies disrupting current distribution channels, customer demands, and customer relationships [7]. Big data analytics plays a crucial role in complementing and even substituting labor for machines, especially in the context of value-creating managerial decisions [8]. Even if the barriers to entry are lowered, startups operate in a context of restricted resources and a lack of technical and managerial skills [13]. However, startups have some characteristics (e.g., ability to quickly change and scale business model) enabling them to compete with mature companies. The role and widespread of data analytics in startups is yet to be explored, even if utilization of such can be a major success factor in the ever-increasing competitive business landscapes [4].

This study focuses on how hardware startups can benefit from big data and seeks to identify the challenges they face which will allow them to make datadriven decisions and generate value from big data analytics. To this end, this paper will offer insight into software and hardware startup companies by answering the following research questions:

RQ1 How can startups create value from (big) data and analytics?
RQ2 What are the barriers for working with (big) data analytics in hardware startups?

To address these questions, this study performs a multiple-case study investigating early-stage European hardware startups, developing products of both hardware and software parts [33]. Even if the potential of (big) data analytics is huge, findings indicate that startups developing both hardware and software do not take advantage of such. To this end, there are identified several challenges and barriers for working with data analytics in such startups, including limited data variety and difficulty of performing business experimentation.

The rest of this paper is organized as follows: Sect. 2 presents background literature. Section 3 explains our research method, including case selections and data analysis procedure. Section 4 presents the findings from the interviews. Section 5 discusses the results, and highlights directions for future research.

2   Background

2.1   Product Development in Startups

The primary objective of startups is to speed up the product development in the early-stages, streamlining the learning process [12]. Startups must respond to fast-changing customer needs and requests [14], both by speeding up the decision and design processes [15]. Startups typically do so by utilizing an evolutionary prototyping approach, meaning that they iteratively refine an initial prototype aiming at quickly validating the product/market fit. Customer feedback highlights new functionality and improvements. As long-term planning is infeasible in the chaotic environment of startups, flexibility and reactiveness are necessary [18].

Instead of utilizing repeatable and controlled processes, startups take advantage of reactive, low-precision engineering practices with focus on the productivity and freedom of their teams [18]. Startups prefer ad-hoc development approaches customized to their own needs, limiting the administrative overhead. In an experimental environment constantly compromising between speed and quality, certain agile practices might not be beneficial (e.g., regular refactoring and test-first), as excessive administrative overhead can inhibit business experimentation [15]. To bring innovative products fast forward, startups depend on team members and resources dedicated to all aspects of the development process, and to be change-oriented and self-initiated. Startups capability to enter new markets and disrupt current business models is largely associated with the uniqueness of human capital and the different approaches they employ.

2.2   The Importance of Data Analytics

In the ever-increasing digital world, businesses need to develop and evolve their (big) data analytics capabilities and competencies which are key to achieving successful digital business [4, 19]. The evolution of the digital economy and its combination with (big) data analytics is challenging current business models with many startups disrupting well-established companies [20]. Big data refers to expansive collections of data (large volumes) that are updated quickly and frequently (high velocity) and that exhibit a huge range of different formats and content (wide variety) [21]. Yet, there is limited understanding of how entrepreneurs and startups need to change to embrace such technological innovations and generate value in the digital economy. Indeed, they need to build upon their main resources that include people, processes, and technology [22]. This is very important, as it allows businesses and decision-makers to respond almost instantaneously to market needs, thus increasing their operational agility. An iterative and incremental approach combined with frequent releases is essential for startups ability to quickly accommodate frequent change, and adapt prototyping to business strategy [16].

Startups and the individuals working there have the opportunity to take advantage of the available data and create new products transforming a market or an industry [3], and big data analytics may be viewed as resources in this process that enable value creation and digital transformation. Many software startups are using existing ecosystems (e.g., Apache Hadoop) to build value-added software and solutions [23].

Nonetheless, since various challenges exist in improving the value creation process, significant research is targeted on addressing these challenges taking into account engineering issues related to specifications, design, or requirements in software development [24]. However, a similar approach is not that easy to be followed by startups that develop both hardware and software. Availability of resources, as well as external and development dependencies, pose restrictions to the implementation of hardware [17], thus influencing the ability of these startups to utilize big data and analytics.

3   Research Method

To explore the research questions we performed semi-structured interviews on 13 early-stage European hardware startups. Semi-structured interviews are considered suitable for qualitative data analysis, and allowed for a discoverable approach as interviewees could express themselves more freely and provide their own perspectives on personal experiences related to the research topics [25]. The rest of this chapter presents our research process, including case selections and the collection and analysis of data.

3.1   Case and Subjects Selection

The units of analysis are people involved in product development in startup companies that deliver products with mixed hardware and software parts. We defined selection criteria as suggested by Runeson and Höst [26]. Table 1 presents basic information about each case. The *current stage* in the table is adopted from [27], however the first stage *startup* is replaced by *concept* to avoid misunderstandings.

Startups were relevant for inclusion in the study if they met the following criteria: (1) The startup develops both hardware and software parts. (2) The startup has been active for at least six months. (3) The startup has a first running prototype. (4) The startup's ambition is to scale its business. People from the relevant startups were eligible for participation if they had experience and/or knowledge about software and/or hardware development. If the candidate met the criteria, he/she was regarded as qualified for contributing to the research study.

We used five different channels to find relevant startups: (1) Innovation Center Gløshaugen, (2) NTNU Accel and FAKTRY, (3) our professional networks, (4) OsloTech and StartupLab, and (5) The Hub. Figure 1 presents examples of the products developed by the startups of this study.

3.2   Data Collection and Analysis Procedure

Data was collected using a semi-structured interview guideline between February and April 2018. Author one and two attended all interviews to avoid one single interpretation of the respondents' perspectives and insights on topics. This firstdegree data collection approach allowed us to control what data was collected, ensuring that all predefined interview questions were answered sufficiently, and exploring new directions

Table 1. Case descriptions

Case	Product	Current stage	Founded	Location	# of employees
Startup 1 (S1)	Smart gloves	Concept	2016	Norway	18
Startup 2 (S2)	Medtech biosensor	Concept	2017	Norway	5
Startup 3 (S3)	Physical exercise game	Stabilization	2016	Norway	5
Startup 4 (S4)	Unmanned aircraft system	Concept	2016	Norway	7
Startup 5 (S5)	Advanced noise cancellation	Concept	2017	Norway	5
Startup 6 (S6)	Medtech hydration monitoring	Concept	2016	Norway	10
Startup 7 (S7)	LPG management system	Stabilization	2016	Norway	8
Startup 8 (S8)	Cable cam system	Stabilization	2016	Norway	10
Startup 9 (S9)	Digital piggy bank	Concept	2017	Norway	4
Startup 10 (S10)	Collaborative camera	Growth	2014	Norway	50
Startup 11 (S11)	Interactive children's toy	Concept	2015	Netherlands	8
Startup 12 (S12)	3D-printer control board	Growth	2009	Norway	1
Startup 13 (S13)	Sensors for IoT	Growth	2007	Italy	25

Fig. 1. Product illustration from the investigated startups

by asking follow-up questions [26]. All interviews were recorded and transcribed shortly afterward. Before each interview, we looked into the cases' business background, either through their company websites or other relevant incubator or accelerator websites. Additionally, participants were encouraged to answer a simple questionnaire prior to interviews filling out basic information about themselves and the company. The following list presents the main topics and interview questions of the interview guideline:

- Business background
- Describe your product and team.
- Name the three largest challenges you have encountered.
- Product development
- What development process do you use?
- How are internal/external factors influencing product development?
- Data analytics
- How do you collect customer data?
- Have you used data analytics for requirements elicitation?
- What are challenges related to data analytics?

The interviews were undertaken in the language preferred by the interviewee (English or Norwegian). Several of the interviews were therefore undertaken in Norwegian as this made the interviewees more comfortable. This allowed them to express themselves more freely, and give more in-depth explanations. Because of this, it was necessary to translate some of the interviews when transcribing. As there often doesn't exist a one-to-one relationship between language and meaning [28], the translation of the transcribed interviews was ensured to "express all aspects of the meaning in a manner that is understandable" [29]. This implies that not all parts of the interviews were directly translated word-for-word.

A total of 68 pages of interview transcripts were analyzed using thematic coding analysis [30]. The transcripts were coded and analyzed using NVivo. Firstly, all authors read through the transcribed interviews to generate initial ideas. Secondly, descriptive coding was applied through an inductive coding approach to systematically identify concepts and topics of interest [31]. Related codes were combined into themes to create patterns and a meaningful whole of the unstructured codes [30]. Section 4 presents the findings from the analysis process.

3.3   Validity Procedure

The validity must be addressed for all phases of the case study to enable replication of research [26] and to ensure findings are trustworthy [30]. To ensure validity, we followed guidelines used in controlled empirical experiments in software engineering [32].

Interviewees were either CEOs or engineers with insight into business- and technical-related aspects. As the startups were mostly located in the same area, mainly consisting of young, inexperienced entrepreneurs, generalization is limited to cases with similar characteristics (i.e., early-stage European startups). To decrease the risk of biased interpretations, author one and two attended all interviews. Some interviews were in Norwegian, hence transcripts were not always verbatim to preserve the actual meaning of respondents. Recordings were transcribed shortly after each interview to mitigate bias. Since it is difficult to understand a startup and its dimensions within a time-span of 30 min, we collected data about the startups through incubator and company websites prior to interviews.

4 Results

4.1 Utilization of Data Analytics

Among the investigated startups, the usage of data analytics methods was generally limited. Operating in early stages, they were often determined to rapidly develop new features and perform customer validation. The startups in this study mostly relied on qualitative measures (e.g., interviews and observations) to obtain customer feedback. *"We have not used data analytics, and do not collect customer data."* When focusing on the short-term business goals, they minimized any effort spent on data analytics, rather focusing on the core-delivered values of their products to quickly release a minimum viable product to customers. Improving data collection measures was considered as a rather time-consuming activity. *"Data analytics is not something we currently spend time on."*

Although the startups commonly spent little time on gathering or learning from data analytics efforts some had a clear perception of the possible business opportunities and benefits from utilization of such. Even if so, data analytics was usually outside their business scope. *"We have looked at some future possibilities of data analytics, but it is not something we currently focus on."* A brake-pad in introducing greater focus towards data analytics was that the startups in this study did not have large amounts of data at their disposal. The restricted access to useful data inhibited potential value-adding activities from data analytics. *"It's too early for us to get something valuable from data analytics."*

The capabilities of team members greatly influence the associated success of startups. From the investigations, we saw an increased focus on data analytics in startups with team members having experience or expertise within the field. Despite for the general limited use of data analytics, possessing the required knowledge and skills of such can have a positive impact on its widespread adoption within a startup organization. *"We work with data analytics and do most of it ourselves [...] It requires that your company is able to get that expertise."*

Although some of the investigated startups were aware of opportunities and benefits associated with utilizing data analytics for decision-making and requirements elicitation, they mainly focused on the core-delivered functionalities of their products to speed-up development. The findings show, that value-adding activities related to data analytics were considered as less important compared to product development activities.

4.2 Barriers for Obtaining Deeper Customer Insight

Experimentation testing, and assessment can be a challenge to startups developing products including both software and hardware components. Physical prototypes are more resource-intensive to develop, in contrast to pure software products, thus limiting startups' ability to test products with a larger customer base. The testing ability of these startups will largely depend on their capacity (i.e., third-party dependency, financial and human resources) to produce prototypes: *"There is a great number of people who want to test our product, however, we do not have the capacity to produce enough prototypes. The main reason for this is hardware production, which happens in China, and the manual assembly we do ourselves."*

Findings from the investigated startups indicate that the amount of collected data in early stages is limited in terms of volume, velocity, and variety, as the data are generated mainly from one prototype used by a couple of users, thus restricting data capture along with their ability to generate value from them. This relates strongly to the early stages of a startup characterized by the existence of only a few customers, as well as to startups developing evolutionary independent systems. Startups may be reluctant to invest in data analytics due to the perceived limitations of the available data: *"The data amount is still a little too small to do any proper analysis of it, and we do not collect enough personal info yet to perform the analysis."*

Acquiring people with the necessary knowledge and skills in data analytics is one of the major challenges in generating value from (big) data. With startups looking for team members with knowledge in a wide area of fields (boundary spanning knowledge), it is not easy to put a significant focus on data analytics skills and knowledge. The investigated startups had limited expertise in performing data analytics, and knowledge about available tools suited to address startups' concerns or requirements. The findings show that attracting knowledgeable people is quite hard and with resources being severely restricted, hiring specialized people only to work with data analytics is rarely an opportunity, not to mention a priority of startups: *"Finding talented people is hard. Since we are a startup we cannot give very good salary [...] If we had more money we would employ someone to analyze product and customer data [...] I see the value of it, but for the time being, it is not a priority."*

The highly competitive environment of startups and severely limited resources imply startups strict priorities. Data analytics efforts may exhaust the already constrained financial and time resources. In addition, collecting the necessary data may present an additional cost of components (e.g., sensors and IoT technology) and human investments. This may be a priority startups are not willing to take: *"At the time this [data analytics] is not something we prioritize."*

Startups work with innovative technology and products for a wide area of markets. Certain markets may pose specific restrictions and regulations for data collection. This makes the customer testing an intricate process, involving a significant amount of paperwork. Storing customer data for later analyses may be illegal or too entangled, preventing the use of data analytics. Startups need guidelines for handling privacy (e.g., General Data Protection Regulation - GDPR) and security issues to fully take advantage of the benefits of data analytics: *"When working with hospitals, data becomes more complicated due to privacy."*

The uncertain conditions and fast-changing environment of startups mean long-term planning is not part of their business model, as this is not the way they operate. Some of the investigated startups' business managers lacked the required knowledge to implement data analytics and the potential value in their business plan: *"I see data analyses as the next step for our business [...] Currently we do not even know what our data can be used for."*

5   Discussion and Conclusions

This study examines how startups can generate value by employing data analytics methods. With the majority of the literature focusing on startups that create software, here, we choose to investigate startups that develop both hardware and software. This specific category of startups presents great interest due to specific challenges that differentiate them from typical software startups. Indeed these startups are more likely to face challenges such as limited availability of resources or to be dependant on external factors linked with hardware development [17]. Such challenges are expected to affect their ability to use big data and analytics in order to generate value.

The findings show that some of the startups are aware of the potential benefits from using (big) data analytics, however, they face various barriers and challenges which limit them from utilizing them in their business models and business process. Table 2 presents the main barriers to working with (big) data analytics as identified in this study. In detail, the startups face challenges related with their prototyping capacity, as they are able to develop only limited amount of hardware prototypes, thus limiting the number of users that can use them at the same time. This is directly linked with the limited financial resources that young startups have, as well as with the time-shortage that characterizes startups, since they are forced to work on short deadlines and intensive processes.

The challenge with the limited prototyping capacity can indirectly affect data availability. In detail, limited hardware and users lead to an impact to generated data. However, such limitations could be overcome by better planning and more focused testing of their products with their end-users. Furthermore, some of the startups mention that they face specific security and privacy issues related with the use of personal data, due to the nature of their business (e.g., medical technology tested at hospitals). Nonetheless, such barriers can be overcome with the collaboration of the different actors in the society (i.e., industry, government, academia), and the recently directive from EU on data protection (i.e., GDPR) is a step towards that direction. Finally, the startups indicate that generating knowledge from data analytics is not a primary objective for them, thus it is not included in their overall business strategies. This is also linked with the other barriers, regarding prototyping capacity and resource availability, since they believe that they are not able to achieve their short-term goals using data analytics.

Some business managers mention that they possess limited knowledge on what additional value data analytics could provide to their decision-making and design process. Increasing business managers' awareness around the potential knowledge and presenting them with practical information and knowledge will increase the potential of including data analytics in their business models. This can be achieved by offering to startups validated learning, through the use of cohort metrics (e.g., actionable, accessible, and auditable metrics) and analysis. As startups are characterized by short-term planning and frequent releases, utilizing big data analytics will allow startups to make data-driven decisions, which can be faster and with increased quality, thus being consistent with the agile environment that most startups operate.

Table 2. Barriers for working with (big) data analytics

Barrier	Description
Prototyping capacity	Physical prototypes are associated with individual development costs and time (e.g., third-party dependency)
Limitations of data	Data in early startup stages are characterized by low volume, velocity, and variety
Team capabilities	Startups have high demands for skillful teams with entrepreneurial capabilities. Experience using data analytics will positively impact its widespread organizational adoption
Financial resources	Hardware development includes production, manufacturing, and logistics, which require more initial human and financial investments
Time-shortage	The uncertain high-risk environment forces startups to release their products fast and to work under constant pressure
Security & privacy issues	Collecting customer and usage data for (big) data analytics have associated privacy and security issues
Integration with business strategy	Data analytics activities are usually outside the short-term business goals of startups

As with all empirical studies, this study has some limitations. Qualitative data collection measures imply that results and implications are subject to bias. To mitigate the risk of wrong interpretations, author one and two attended all interviews, preferably face-to-face on-site. Recordings were transcribed shortly afterward to preserve respondents' actual meanings. Furthermore, the study would profit from a wider collection of data, both to discover more challenges and to ensure credible conclusions. Also, employing quantitative methods would allow for data triangulation.

This study provides initial knowledge on data analytics in startups, however, future work should investigate more startups both to identify other challenges and barriers, and for generalization of results to a larger startup population (e.g., operating in different markets and lifecycle stages, and various geographical locations). Seeing that the widespread of data analytics is limited, startups need specific methods for utilizing analysis tools in early startup stages. Startup managers need guidance to understand how their data can generate revenues, and what knowledge is required for their organization to thrive from data analytics. Startups need directions for how to implement a data analytics strategy to benefit the company in the long run.

Acknowledgments. We would like to thank the startups that participated in this study. This project has received funding from the European Unions Horizon 2020 research and innovation programme under the Marie Sklodowska-Curie grant agreement No 751550.

References

1. Pappas, I.O., Jaccheri, L., Mikalef, P., Giannakos, M.N.: Social innovation and social entrepreneurship through big data: developing a reseach agenda. In: Presented at the 11th Mediterranean Conference on Information Systems (MCIS), Genoa, Italy (2017)
2. Otero, C.E., Peter, A.: Research directions for engineering big data analytics software. IEEE Intell. Syst. **30**, 13–19 (2015)
3. George, G., Haas, M.R., Pentland, A.: Big data and management. Acad. Manag. J. **57**, 321–326 (2014)
4. Mikalef, P., Pappas, I.O., Krogstie, J., Giannakos, M.: Big data analytics capabilities: a systematic literature review and research agenda. Inf. Syst. e-Bus. Manag., 1–32 (2017)
5. Vidgen, R., Shaw, S., Grant, D.B.: Management challenges in creating value from business analytics. Eur. J. Oper. Res. **261**, 626–639 (2017)
6. Weill, P., Woerner, S.L.: Thriving in an increasingly digital ecosystem. MIT Sloan Manag. Rev. **56**, 27 (2015)
7. Lucas Jr, H.C., Agarwal, R., Clemons, E.K., El Sawy, O.A., Weber, B.: Impactful research on transformational information technology: an opportunity to inform new audiences. Mis Q. **37** (2013)
8. Loebbecke, C., Picot, A.: Reflections on societal and business model transformation arising from digitization and big data analytics: a research agenda. J. Strat. Inf. Syst. **24**, 149–157 (2015)
9. Unterkalmsteiner, M., et al.: Software startups - a research agenda. E-Inf. Softw. Eng. J. **10**, 89–123 (2016)
10. Giardino, C., Bajwa, S.S., Wang, X., Abrahamsson, P.: Key challenges in early-stage software startups. In: Lassenius, C., Dingsøyr, T., Paasivaara, M. (eds.) XP 2015. LNBIP, vol. 212, pp. 52–63. Springer, Cham (2015). https://doi.org/10.1007/978-3-319-18612-2_5
11. Marmer, M., Herrmann, B.L., Dogrultan, E., Berman, R., Eesley, C., Blank, S.: Startup genome report extra: premature scaling. Startup Genome **10**, 1–56 (2011)
12. Nguyen-Duc, A., Wang, X., Abrahamsson, P.: What Influences the speed of prototyping? An empirical investigation of twenty software startups. In: Baumeister, H., Lichter, H., Riebisch, M. (eds.) XP 2017. LNBIP, vol. 283, pp. 20–36. Springer, Cham (2017). https://doi.org/10.1007/978-3-319-57633-6_2
13. Paternoster, N., Giardino, C., Unterkalmsteiner, M., Gorschek, T., Abrahamsson, P.: Software development in startup companies: a systematic mapping study. Inf. Softw. Technol. **56**, 1200–1218 (2014)
14. Bosch, J.: Speed, data, and ecosystems: the future of software engineering. IEEE Softw. **33**, 82–88 (2016)
15. Pantiuchina, J., Mondini, M., Khanna, D., Wang, X., Abrahamsson, P.: Are software startups applying agile practices? The state of the practice from a large survey. In: Baumeister, H., Lichter, H., Riebisch, M. (eds.) XP 2017. LNBIP, vol. 283, pp. 167–183. Springer, Cham (2017). https://doi.org/10.1007/978-3-319-57633-6_11
16. Coleman, G., O'Connor, R.V.: An investigation into software development process formation in software start-ups. J. Enterp. Inf. Manag. **21**, 633–648 (2008)
17. Ronkainen, J., Abrahamsson, P.: Software development under stringent hardware constraints: do agile methods have a chance? In: Marchesi, M., Succi, G. (eds.) XP 2003. LNCS, vol. 2675, pp. 73–79. Springer, Heidelberg (2003). https://doi.org/10.1007/3-540-44870-5_10

18. Berg, V., Birkeland, J., Nguyen-Duc, A., Pappas, I., Jaccheri, L.: Software startup engineering: a systematic mapping study. J. Syst. Softw. (2018). https://doi.org/10.1016/j.jss.2018.06.043

19. Pappas, I.O., Mikalef, P., Giannakos, M.N., Krogstie, J., Lekakos, G.: Social media and analytics for competitive performance: a conceptual research framework. In: Abramowicz, W., Alt, R., Franczyk, B. (eds.) BIS 2016. LNBIP, vol. 263, pp. 209–218. Springer, Cham (2017). https://doi.org/10.1007/978-3-319-52464-1_19

20. Chen, H., Chiang, R.H.L., Storey, V.C.: Business intelligence and analytics: from big data to big impact. MIS Q., 1165–1188 (2012). JSTOR

21. Davis, C.K.: Beyond data and analysis. Commun. ACM **57**, 39–41 (2014)

22. Carlsson, C.: Decision analytics - key to digitalisation. Inf. Sci. (2017)

23. Tan, W., Blake, M.B., Saleh, I., Dustdar, S.: Social-network-sourced big data analytics. IEEE Internet Comput. **17**, 62–69 (2013)

24. Otero, C.E., Peter, A.: Research directions for engineering big data analytics software. IEEE Intell. Syst. **30**, 13–19 (2015)

25. Oates, B.J.: Researching Information Systems and Computing. Sage, London (2005). ISBN 1446235440

26. Runeson, P., Höst, M.: Guidelines for conducting and reporting case study research in software engineering. Empir. Softw. Eng. **14**, 131 (2009)

27. Crowne, M.: Why software product startups fail and what to do about it. Evolution of software product development in startup companies. In: Engineering Management Conference, IEMC 2002, pp. 338–343. IEEE (2002)

28. Temple, B., Young, A.: Qualitative research and translation dilemmas. Qual. Res. **4**, 161–178 (2004)

29. Larson, M.: Translation: Theory and Practice, Tension and Interdependence. John Benjamins Publishing, Amsterdam (1991)

30. Cruzes, D.S., Dyba, T.: Recommended steps for thematic synthesis in software engineering. In: 2011 International Symposium on Empirical Software Engineering and Measurement (ESEM), pp. 275–284. IEEE (2011)

31. Saldaña, J.: The Coding Manual for Qualitative Researchers. Sage, London (2015)

32. Stanfill, R., Astleford, T.: Improving entrepreneurship team performance through market feasibility analysis, early identification of technical requirements, and intellectual property support. In: Proceedings of the American Society for Engineering Education Annual Conference & Exposition (2007)

33. DiResta, R., Forrest, B., Vinyard, R.: The Hardware Startup: Building Your Product, Business, and Brand. O'Reilly Media, Inc., USA (2015)

34. Pappas, I.O., Mikalef, P., Giannakos, M.N., Krogstie, J., Lekakos, G.: Big data and business analytics ecosystems: paving the way towards digital transformation and sustainable societies. Inf. Syst. e-Bus. Manage. (2018). https://doi.org/10.1007/s10257-018-0377-z

What is a Minimum Viable (Video) Game?

Towards a Research Agenda

Sami Hyrynsalmi[1]([⊠]), Eriks Klotins[2], Michael Unterkalmsteiner[2],
Tony Gorschek[2], Nirnaya Tripathi[3], Leandro Bento Pompermaier[4],
and Rafael Prikladnicki[4]

[1] Tampere University of Technology, Pori, Finland
sami.hyrynsalmi@tut.fi
[2] Software Engineering Research Lab, Blekinge Institute of Technology,
Karlskrona, Sweden
{eriks.klotins,mun,tgo}@bth.se
[3] University of Oulu, Oulu, Finland
nirnaya.tripathi@oulu.fi
[4] PUCRS—Pontifical Catholic University of Rio Grande do Sul,
Porto Alegre, Brazil
{leandro.pompermaier,rafael.prikladnicki}@pucrs.br

Abstract. The concept of 'Minimum Viable Product' (MVP) is largely adapted in the software industry as well as in academia. Minimum viable products are used to test hypotheses regarding the target audience, save resources from unnecessary development work and guide a company towards a stable business model. As the game industry is becoming an important business domain, it is not surprise that the concept has been adopted also in the game development. This study surveys how a Minimum Viable Game (MVG) is defined, what is reported in extant literature as well as present results from a small case study survey done to nine game development companies. The study shows that despite popularity of minimum viable games in the industrial fora, the presented views on the concept are diverged and there is lack of practical guidelines and research supporting game companies. This study points out research gaps in the area as well as calls for actions to further develop the concept and to define guidelines.

Keywords: Minimum viable product · Minimum viable game
Game business

1 Introduction

A key characteristic of the modern business world is *speed* [10]. An often repeated argument claims that the pace of business is going to even increase in the future [7,20]. The requirement for speeding up is visible also for start-ups, which

This work is partially funded by FAPERGS (17/2551-0001/205-4) and CNPq

S. A. Al-Sharhan et al. (Eds.): I3E 2018, LNCS 11195, pp. 217–231, 2018.
https://doi.org/10.1007/978-3-030-02131-3_20

aim to quickly find a repeatable and scalable business model [4]. As it is frequently stated, start-ups are lacking time and resources [12], and therefore, it is crucial for them to find quickly whether their product or service is suitable for markets.

In the beginning of the 2010s, the so-called *Lean Startup* methodology (LSU, hereafter), by Ries [35], started to gain popularity. The methodology aims, through continuous hypothesis testing, at validating whether there is business potential in the product or service. One of the methodology's cornerstones is the concept of *Minimum Viable Product* (MVP, hereafter). The concept was first defined already in 2001 by Frank Robinson (c.f. [28]), yet it became widely known with the raising popularity of the LSU [5]. According to Ries[1], *"the minimum viable product is that version of a new product which allows a team to collect the **maximum amount of validated learning** about customers with the **least effort.**"*[2]

The MVP concept can be seen as continuum of Blank's [3] *Customer development* methodology. In this methodology, Blank's key advice, for new entrepreneurs, is to face potential customers early upon—informally referred as the *'Get out of the building'* principle [4,15]—to collect valuable information on what customers want and are willing to pay for. As the objective of the LSU is to avoid of building a complete product before learning that it is not valuable for the customers [35], the concept of a minimum viable product fits well to test the suitability of product before it has been finished. In addition, it allows a company to redirect its product and strategy to areas that are the most fruitfull for the company.

As the global video game industry is estimated to reach a total revenue of over USD 80 billion[3] by the year of 2018, it is not surprising that also game development companies and game business advocates have been interested towards the MVP. For example, a senior manager[4] of Zynga Inc. revealed in an interview that *FarmVille*, a hugely popular Facebook game, was initially launched as a 'minimum viable product'. In addition, the popular *Pokémon Go* mobile game, by Niantic Inc., is in the grey literature often claimed[5] to be an example of a successful MVP usage in the video game industry.

---

[1] Eric Ries (August 3, 2009) Lessons Learned: Minimum Viable Product: a guide. http://www.startuplessonslearned.com/2009/08/minimum-viable-product-guide.html Last accessed September 23, 2018.

[2] Emphasises added by the authors of this paper.

[3] Statista (2018) Value of the global video games market from 2011 to 2020. https://www.statista.com/statistics/246888/value-of-the-global-video-game-market/ Last accessed September 23, 2018.

[4] Matt Purslow (February 28, 2011) FarmVille launched as a "minimum viable product". Took 32.5 million users in one day. https://www.pcgamer.com/farmville-launched-as-a-minimum-viable-product-took-32-5-million-users-in-one-day/. Last accessed September 23, 2018.

[5] E.g., Paul Frazier (August 12, 2016) Pokémon Go is a Minimal Viable Product. https://www.itx.com/ITX-Blog/Article/408/Pokemon-GO-is-a-Minimal-Viable-Product. Last accessed September 23, 2018.

However, there are a few remarkable differences between utility software and video games that should be acknowledged when the concept of MVP is adapted to new domains. First, while utility software solutions can be used for several years or even decades without major changes, the expected life-cycle of a computer game is much shorter. For example, the average length to complete the ten most popular games in the HowLongToBeat[6] service range from around 20 h to a bit over 100 h. While there are of course games which core game play can be repeated *ad infinitum*, games are, on average, disposable products that have to impress gamers quickly.

Second, whereas the utility software—such as a spreadsheet programme or a fitness tracker—should aim to help users in all possible ways, the games, instead, should aim to *challenge* the users [43]. Yet, too challenging as well as too helpful games create frustration [40]. Thus, the games' aim is to reach a *flow* experience [9]. However, this should be done with little or no delay as a gamer might get annoyed and switch game to another. Thirdly, the user experience and playability—i.e. overall quality of gameplay—is everything [32]. Whereas small irritating mistakes in a utility software can be tolerated for years, these can be fatal in a video game.

These contradictions between video games and utility software turn our focus towards the use of the minimum viable product concept in the game industry. The MVP was initially promoted for utility software solutions where adding a new feature or pivoting product's strategy would be more feasible approach than in the game industry. While MVPs in the software industry have been previously addressed (e.g. [15,28,33]), to the best of authors' knowledge, only a little of using MVPs—or *Minimum Viable Games* (MVGs, hereafter)—in the game industry is discussed in the extant literature (e.g. [19,36]).

The objective of this paper is to study how computer game start-ups perceive and use MVPs in their businesses. The study's approach is explorative, aiming to shed light on the current practices and extant knowledge. We use a recent structured review as a starting point and present an unstructured literature review on the area. As empirical data, we use a large global survey done with software start-ups (c.f. [25]). In total, the survey received 86 start-up stories and more than 23 000 data-points. In this study, we focus on the subset of the start-up companies identified to be video game companies. To the best of authors' knowledge, this study presents first empirical observations from using MVPs in the game industry. Based on the problems arisen from the empirical material as well as from the extant literature, we discuss needed future research actions and lay some building blocks for further inquires.

The remaining of this paper is organised as follows. Section 2 presents a review of literature as well as positions our view of a MVP. It is followed by a description of empirical research process used as well as an overview of the result in Sect. 3. Discussion is presented in Sect. 4 and finally, Sect. 5 concludes the study.

---

[6] How long does it take to beat your favorite games? https://www.howlongtobeat.com Last accessed September 23, 2018.

2   Review of Literature

According to the recent systematic mapping study on the evolution of the minimum viable product concept by Lenarduzzi and Taibi [28], the concept was first discussed by Frank Robinson as early as 2001 and then brought forth and popularised by Eric Ries and Steve Blank. In addition, the term has been discussed, with similar meaning, as early as 1999 by Goodwin and Ball [13] and in 2000 by Junk [21]. Altogether, Lenarduzzi and Taibi [28] found 22 different definitions for a MVP which were mostly published between 2012 and 2015. However, they also pointed out that most of those definitions were not referred or used by other than by the authors themselves.

In this study, we follow the market-oriented line of definitions, e.g., those given by Ries as a part of the LSU methodology. For instance, in his book, Ries [35, p. 93] elaborated MVP's concept more by stating that it *"[i]s not necessarily the smallest product imaginable; it is simply the fastest way to get through the Build-Measure-Learn feedback loop with the minimum amount of effort."* Also, Moogk [29] emphasise the value of a MVP to a new venture for engaging new customers and testing the product's value proposition.

In addition, it is worth to note that we draw a distinction between a *prototype* and a MVP. In our use, the former refers a product version that is used to test the product inside the organisation. The latter refers to a product version that is used to collect validated learning from potential customers and users. That is, in our use, an MVP aims to maximise learning from real customers—and therefore, from the market—with the minimum amount of effort needed. However, in the extant literature, differences and similarities between a prototype and a MVP are not always clearly defined (c.f. [28]).

In the extant literature, several studies have focused on different aspects of minimum viable products. For instance, Hokkanen [15] studied interweaving user experience design with the development of a MVP. Hokkanen, Kuusinen and Väänänen [16] presented a framework for start-up companies for design Minimum Viable User Experience (MVUX). In addition, Münch et al. [30] studied the creation of MVPs in industry-academia collaboration and Bosch et al. [8] as well as Björk et al. [1] have discussed on the usage of MVP as a part of software development model in early-stage start-ups. Furthermore, in a large survey with more than 4,000 companies, Wang et al. [42] found that early-stage start-ups list MVP as one of the key challenges.

However, the number of empirical studies reporting the use of MVPs in the industry is small. For example, Ngueyn-Duc and Abrahamsson [33] studied the usage of MVPs in five software start-ups and showed that the concept seems to be useful as a design artefact, a boundary spanning artefact as well as a reusable artefact. Khanna, Ngueyn-Duc and Wang [22] reported a case study on how two start-ups selected hypotheses they wished to test with their MVPs. The study showed that the relationships between business goals and hypotheses tested in MVPs are complex in their cases.

When the focus is narrowed down to the game industry and in the domain of computer games, the research in new companies and product launches is remarkable scarcer. This is surprising, given that most installed and used mobile applications are games [6,17]. Furthermore, there is lack of academic research about using MVPs in the game development. However, there is a series of work in grey literature devoted to characterise and guide on using MVPs.

For example, Tyler York[7] discusses on applicability of LSU methodology and MVPs in the game industry. In addition, some companies have reported their company's approach on using a MVP[8,9]. However, also alternative views and critique have been presented – the director of developer relations of Chillingo[10], the publisher of mobile games such as *Angry Birds* and *Cut the Rope*, stated that it is disrespectful from game developers to publish unfinished products and force gamers to wait for major features. In addition, while *Pokémon Go* has been praised as an example of publishing a MVP game in the grey literature, it has also been labelled to be a launch failure due to technical problems and lack of content early on[11].

In the extant literature, only Järvi et al. [19] and Rosenfield Boeira [36] have discussed the use of MVPs in the game development. Järvi et al. [19] present a conceptual design for a video game start-up accelerator and discuss on central concepts related to the accelerator program. They define a minimum viable game as a product version *"that implements the core game mechanics leaving out everything else.* In addition, they state that *"games are holistic products and it is not trivial to know what contributes to the players' experience and what can be left out of the game".* Finally, they also emphasise the difference between the MVG and MVP concepts as adding and removing new features in the latter is easier than in the former. In the case of MVG, the authors underline the importance of keeping the gameplay in balance with every changes made.

Rosenfield Boeira [36] discusses how MVPs can be used in the gaming industry and gives advice for the practitioners. The study notes the concepts of MVP and MVG, yet it presents a minimum viable game as a synonym for a MVP

---

[7] Tyler York (April 17, 2012) Making Lean Startup Tactics Work for Games. https://www.gamasutra.com/view/feature/168647/making_lean_startup_tactics_work_.php. Last accessed September 23, 2018.

[8] Juha Vainio (March 15, 2015) Starting up a game business: Working with Minimum Viable Products. https://gamasutra.com/blogs/JuhaVainio/20150903/252860/Starting_up_a_game_business_Working_with_Minimum_Viable_Products.php. Last accessed September 23, 2018.

[9] Alew Wavro (October 30, 2015) Astroneer's ex-AAA devs explore a strange new world of indie life. https://www.gamasutra.com/view/news/257267/Astroneers_exAAA_devs_explore_a_strange_new_world_of_indie_life.php. Last accessed September 23, 2018.

[10] Brendan Sinclair (November 19, 2015) "Minimum viable products are dinosaurs" https://www.gamesindustry.biz/articles/2015-11-19-minimum-viable-products-are-dinosaurs Last accessed September 23, 2018.

[11] Derek Anderson. 5 Steps for Creating a Minimum Viable Product (and the case of the Pokémon GO app). https://sphereinc.com/5-steps-for-creating-a-minimum-viable-product-and-the-case-of-the-pokemon-go-app/. Last accessed September 23, 2018.

in the video game industry. Furthermore, Rosenfield Boeira [36] draws a line between a MVG and a prototype, stating that MVG aims to deliver value to the client whereas a prototype delivers to the development company. That is, the prototype focuses on technical and the MVG to the commercial viability. For the sake of simplicity, we follow this divisions in the remaining of this study.

A classic example, often seen in the grey literature, is to consider the most minimum viable game of *Super Mario Bros.* Its minimum viable version, according to e.g. [36], would include only abilities for walking and jumping over the holes. While the basic game mechanism can be tried with this kind of a version, the question remains what kind of validated learning a game company would be able collect. The skeleton, left after stripping off everything extra, would be a yet another side-scrolling platform video game and we argue that testing it with customers would not bring much new information. To depart from the existing side-scrollers, the minimum viable version of a new game should contain enough content to validate whether the 'core fun' is exciting and enticing. Similarly for a totally new kind of a game, there should be enough content to test whether the hypothesis on the core gameplay mechanism holds.

To summarise our review of extant literature, it can be stated that an important question remains mainly unanswered. That is, what would be a *minimum viable game* for gathering the maximum amount of validated learning with minimum amount of extra effort? For example, music and audio are an important part of any game experience, yet they might not be an essential part for validating the core mechanisms and fun factors of a game. As our review of extant literature shows, not much has been done regarding this area. Therefore, the remaining of this article will first focus an empirical survey on whether video game start-ups are utilising MVGs in their work. Finally, we identify and present research gaps regarding the concept of MVG in the game industry.

3 Empirical Research

3.1 Research Process

This study uses a case survey method as a tool for data collection [27]. The case survey method combines case study with a survey [23,34], thus allowing an in-depth analysis of a larger number of cases. For this study, we used a large questionnaire designed to survey development practices in start-up companies. During the design phase, the survey was externally reviewed by 10 researchers and it was tested with four software start-ups [24]. The final questionnaire contains 85 questions in 10 sections[12].

The questionnaire was globally marketed to former and current software start-ups in social media, industrial events and by personal contacts. In addition, respondents were recruited with the help of, e.g., Software Start-up Research Network[13]. The data was collected from December 2016 to June 2017. In total,

---

[12] http://startupcontextmap.org/exp-survey/woifenw2.
[13] https://www.softwarestartups.org/.

the questionnaire received 86 usable responses from Europe, North- and South-America as well as from Asia. Some initial results of the survey on the technical debt's impact on software start-ups have been reported by Klotins et al. [24].

For this study, all responses of the survey were went through by the first two authors of this study independently. From the set, they selected game companies for further analysis. A game company is defined as an organisation which main product or service is a digital game. The game can be for, e.g., educational or purely a leisure purpose.

Finally, the selected case companies and their approaches to minimum viable product were analysed. In the analysis, we use the companies responses to multiple choice and open-ended questions. For this study, we selected a subset of 27 questions on which we focus on.

3.2 Companies

Out of the 86 response cases, nine were categorised to work in the field of game development. In Table 1, a short description of each company is given. In the following, each company's development approach is briefly described.

Company A produces animations and related educational games for preschool aged children. They have been able to stabilise their product and market size. Their products were mainly based on own ideas as well as analysis of similar educational games. The company followed a Waterfall-like development process and acquired most of the software development work from subcontractors. The company does not report of using prototypes or any kind of MVGs.

Also *Company B* works in the educational game sector; however, their focus is on school-aged children. They have not published their product yet to the market. Requirements ideas are based on market research, literature review and user studies. Customer interviews were video recorded and used for requirements validation. The company uses user-testing for its prototypes and an agile development model, but they did not have formal plans or actions for any kinds of minimum viable versions.

Company C develops mobile games for modern smart phone platforms. Ideas for their own games are gathered by following market trends and recent developments. In addition, the company does work-for-hire game development for other companies. Feedback is gathered with face-to-face interviews with players. The company uses 'MVPs' for collecting feedback from related partners such as publishers and partners. *Company C* acknowledges the need for using 'MVPs' to test fun and core game mechanisms of the game.

Company D works also with casual mobile games. Their main product has already reached a stable market position. Also they gather ideas for their own games by following market trends and development. The company uses prototypes but does not actively utilise customers in requirements validation; however, they use a selection of modern mobile game metrics to measure the game.

Also *Company E* develops mobile games and they, similarly, report of using market trends and previous experience as a source for the requirements ideas. The company uses 'MVP' approach in its development, yet the scope of the

Table 1. Companies included into the analysis and their overall characteristics.

Company	Domain	Development model	Idea sources	Requirements elicitation	Perceived successful
A	Animations and a group of educational Flash-based games targeted for pre-school children.	Waterfall -like	Internal sources, analysis of similar products.	N/A	N/A
B	An augmented reality educational games for school-aged children.	Agile	Internal sources, literature reviews, market research, potential customers.	Observations, customer interviews, analysis of similar products, brainstorming, prototyping.	N/A
C	Mobile games for adults and young adults.	Iterative	Internal sources, analysis of similar products, market trends, potential customers.	Customer interviews, observing, (internal) prototyping.	Fairly successful
D	Casual mobile games for all ages.	Iterative	Internal sources, analysis of similar products, market trends, potential customers.	Observing, analysing similar products, prototyping.	"Good enough"
E	Arcade mobile games.	Ad-hoc	Internal sources, analysis of similar products, market trends, potential customers.	Customer feedback, observing (monetization), similar products.	Successful
F	Gambling game.	N/A	Internal sources, standards.	Customer interviews, observing, MVGs.	N/A
G	Mobile games for "midcore" gamers.	Agile	Internal sources, analysis of similar products, potential customers.	Customer interviews, observing, prototyping.	Very low
H	Educational games for school-aged children.	Agile	Internal sources, analysis of similar products, customer tests.	Customer surveys, observing, analysis of similar products, MVGs.	N/A
I	Video games for all kinds of players.	Agile	Internal sources, analysis of similar products, market trends, potential customers.	Customer interviews, observing, analysis of similar products, prototyping.	Successful

In the table, N/A stands for information not being available, not wanted to disclose or not known by the respondent.

'MVP' is based on a gut feeling. The company uses A/B testing for fine-tuning KPIs while the product is measured based on profit metrics (such as average revenue per users).

Company F develops a game for easy and fast gambling. On the contrary to the other cases, they did not report of using similar products as a starting point for requirements engineering. However, the company extracted requirements from brainstorming sessions as well as observations, crafted a MVG and tested the game. In addition, the company reports of using customer interviews for feature prioritisation.

Company G develops games for a smart phone platform, focusing on people, who want games that require ability to succeed, but who do not have time. They have already published two titles. The company also uses similar products as a baseline for requirements gathering. They also report of using Lean start-up and Agile methods. However, while the company demonstrate prototypes to customers, they do not report of using actively any kinds of MVGs.

Company H builds an educational game, for a mobile platform, targeted at children aged from 7 to 12. They have not yet published the product. The company uses benchmarking against published solutions and brainstorming for creating requirements. The idea is tested with a MVG and target audience. The company reports prioritising game-play features and using MVGs to verify that core of the game has been captured successfully.

Company I focuses on development of video game to casual and hardcore players. The company uses a wide range of techniques to gather ideas and document requirements. In addition, they are verified with internal prototyping and using A/B testing when features can be verified with customers.

3.3   Analysis

There are some observations that should be noted from the case companies. Firstly, all of the companies reported that they had at least adequate experience working with similar kinds of products. For example, *Company C* reported that all members had worked earlier in different game development projects. Thus the case selection can be considered consisting of experienced developers and possible deviations due to inexperienced developers should not be present.

Secondly, only two companies (*F* and *H*) reported explicitly that they had used minimum viable products to test the game mechanisms and flow with the target audience. In addition, *Company E* and *Company I* are using A/B testing to fine-tune different aspects of a mature product, such as e.g. monetisation. While A/B testing can be used as part of a MVG, in these cases the testing seems to be used in a mature product; thus, it seems not be used to guide the development of the product.

However, several companies reported that they had created prototypes as a part of their development process, yet those prototypes where used mainly for in-house testing and testing with *"a small group of friends from the industry"* as reported by *Company C*. Nevertheless, MVGs, as vehicles of gathering validated information from the target audience, are infrequently utilised by the sample companies.

Furthermore, *Company C* and *Company E* reported that they had developed an 'MVP', but only for in-house use. Thus, this is more closely related to a in-house prototype than a product version used to gather validated information from the target audience. Nevertheless, this emphasises the confounded views on the concept in the field.

Thirdly, the few companies, that used metrics to measure their products, reported that they measured the success by revenue and number of downloads. This is in line with findings by Koskenvoima and Mäntymäki [26] who found that game start-ups do not use analytics as a source of competitive advantage but rather a risk management tool. However, it also shows that the case game companies do not heavily rely on the LSU methodology, as the use of using analytic tools together with MVP are listed as the corner stones of the methodology. In addition, to fully utilise the potential of MVGs, the companies should measure and analyse different aspects of customer behaviour.

4   Discussion

4.1   Key Observations

We recapitulate our key observations from the study in the following:

- Review of literature shows that there is a disputed view on the concept of 'minimum viable product'. On one hand, MVP is used in the literature to refer to any kind of a prototype. On the other hand, the concept has been used to refer to a product version used by the target audience in order to gather validated learning.
- Similarly, in the context of game industry, grey literature often emphasise a MVP—or a MVG—as the most simplistic version of the game. That is, this reflects more a technical prototype used in-house to test the game mechanism than a version offered to the target audience.
- There seems to be lack of discussion of minimum viable games and their development in the computer game field. However, there is a series of work devoted to game design [37–39]; yet, the focus is on designer's perspective and often omits, e.g., financial aspects.
- There is a lack of work addressing what are the benefits and drawbacks of using minimum viable games. A majority of the existing work has adapted a positive approach and the concept as well as implications should also be critically analysed.
- Developing a minimum viable product to gauge market interest in the product has been successfully adopted by two out of the nine case companies; however, a large majority did not use a MVP. We would be interested to explore further how a concept of MVP could be applied in the gaming domain.

To summarise the observations, there is surprisingly little done for the defining and guiding of designing MVGs in the game industry. Furthermore, the empirical inquiry shows that case companies are not fully utilising MVGs in their game development.

4.2 Towards a Formation of a Research Agenda

Our key argument is that game development companies and the game industry might benefit from the usage of MVGs for gaining validated learning with minimum amount of effort. This would allow saving resources from unnecessary development tasks. Yet, there is little scientific work done; thus, this area offers clear research gaps and fruitful questions for the researchers. In addition, while there is a growing interest towards software development practices in software development companies (c.f. [11,41]), there is hardly any work done on investing software development practices in start-up game companies.

The game industry's special characteristics make the field challenging. For example, video game development can be seen as a cooperation of three different viewpoints [14]: *design* or humanistic perspective, *business* perspective, and *constructive* or software engineering perspective. Therefore, it differs remarkably from regular software engineering projects and, for example, favours 'cowboy coders' more than traditional software engineering projects [31]. It is also worth to note that a 'minimum viable game' needs to intertwine all these three perspectives together.

First, there are existing literature of game design patterns and best practices [2], yet testing the game mechanisms with the target audience is an important step [39]. As discussed above, the game cannot be too challenging or too easy, and it should aim to reach the flow experience. In addition, the core game mechanism should lure players. While the basic game mechanisms can be tested with, e.g., pen and paper, defining what is needed for a minimum viable game is much more complex task. For example, should music and audio be included for evaluating the flow of a MVG?

Second, the game should also be financially viable; it should be able to earn enough profit to cover its development costs and provide a stable revenue stream to the development company. During the last years, different kinds of freemium models have gained popularity among the mobile game developers [18]. In addition of testing playability, a MVG should also help to address different financial aspects of the game. For example, is there a market for this kind of a game?

Third, construction perspective involves questions from the software engineering field and research of software start-ups (c.f. [41]). For example, how to build a MVG efficiently with existing components? However, as discussed in Sect. 2, even the concept of MVP is still a infrequently addressed theme in the extant literature and further work is needed for understanding how a MVG should be efficiently created. Finally, this study calls for the formulation of a research agenda to address the different facts of minimum viable games as well as briefly discusses on a few starting point for this work.

Naturally, this study has some limitations that are worth to note. First, the overall number of the case study game companies in our sample remained small. Thus, generalising the empirical results should be done only with a care. However, the sample includes a wide variety of different kinds of game companies Second, we used an unstructured literature review to collect existing studies. Whereas a systematic approach might have produced a larger number of studies, the used approach already revealed that the number of studies addressing this domain is small. Therefore, it is not likely that a systematic approach would remarkably improve the results.

5   Conclusion

This study surveyed extant academic and grey literature on the concept of a minimum viable product in the game industry, that is minimum viable games. The results show that the concept is used in various ways from a synonym to a in-house prototype to a vehicle to test customer hypotheses. In addition, the results of a case study survey on nine start-ups were used to show that also new game companies are infrequently using MVGs in their work development work. Yet, a few companies were successfully utilising MVGs, indicating that the concept could be useful also for a larger number of companies. Thus, this study request a research agenda to be formed to further advance this research area.

References

1. Björk, J., Ljungblad, J., Bosch, J.: Lean product development in early stage star-tups. In: Hyrynsalmi, S., Wnuk, K., Daneva, M., Mäkilä, T., Herrmann, A. (eds.) Proceedings of From Start-Ups to SaaS Conglomerate: Life Cycles of Software Products Workshop (IW-LCSP 2013), vol. 1095, pp. 19–32. CEUR-WS.org (2013). CEUR Workshop Proceedings ISSN 1613–0073
2. Bjork, S., Holopainen, J.: Patterns in Game Design. Charles River Media Game Development Series. Charles River Media, Newton (2005)
3. Blank, S.: The Four Steps to the Epiphany: Successful Strategies for Products that Win. Cafepress.com, Louisville (2005)
4. Blank, S., Dorf, B.: The Startup Owner's Manual: The Step-By-Step Guide for Building a Great Company. K&S Ranch, Seattle (2012)
5. Blank, S.: Why the lean start-up changes everything. Harvard Bus. Rev. **91**(5), 63–72 (2013)
6. Böhmer, M., Hecht, B., Schöning, J., Krüger, A., Bauer, G.: Falling asleep with angry birds, facebook and kindle: a large scale study on mobile application usage. In: Proceedings of the 13th International Conference on Human Computer Inter-action with Mobile Devices and Services, MobileHCI 2011, pp. 47–56. ACM, New York (2011). https://doi.org/10.1145/2037373.2037383
7. Bosch, J.: Speed, Data, and Ecosystems: Excelling in a Software-Driven World. CRC Press Inc., Boca Raton (2016)

8. Bosch, J., Holmström Olsson, H., Björk, J., Ljungblad, J.: The early stage software startup development model: a framework for operationalizing lean principles in software startups. In: Fitzgerald, B., Conboy, K., Power, K., Valerdi, R., Morgan, L., Stol, K.-J. (eds.) LESS 2013. LNBIP, vol. 167, pp. 1–15. Springer, Heidelberg (2013). https://doi.org/10.1007/978-3-642-44930-7_1

9. Csikszentmihalyi, M.: Flow: The Psychology of Optimal Experience. Harper Perennial, New York (1991)

10. Davis, S., Meyer, C.: Blur: The Speed of Change in the Connected Economy. Addison-Wesley, Reading (1999)

11. Giardino, C., Paternoster, N., Unterkalmsteiner, M., Gorschek, T., Abrahamsson, P.: Software development in startup companies: the greenfield startup model. IEEE Trans. Softw. Eng. **42**(6), 585–604 (2016). https://doi.org/10.1109/TSE.2015.2509970

12. Giardino, C., Unterkalmsteiner, M., Paternoster, N., Gorschek, T., Abrahamsson, P.: What do we know about software development in startups? IEEE Softw. **31**(5), 28–32 (2014). https://doi.org/10.1109/MS.2014.129

13. Goodwin, R., Ball, B.: Closing the loop on loyalty. Mark. Manag. **8**(1), 24–34 (1999)

14. Hakonen, H., Mäkilä, T., Smed, J., Best, A.: Learning to make computer games: an academic approach. Technical report 899, Turku Centre for Computer Science (2008)

15. Hokkanen, L.: From minimum viable to maximum lovable: developing a user experience strategy model for software startups. Doctoral dissertation, Tampere University of Technology, vol. 1483. TUT Publication, Tampere, Finland (2017)

16. Hokkanen, L., Kuusinen, K., Väänänen, K.: Minimum viable user experience: a framework for supporting product design in startups. In: Sharp, H., Hall, T. (eds.) XP 2016. LNBIP, vol. 251, pp. 66–78. Springer, Cham (2016). https://doi.org/10.1007/978-3-319-33515-5_6

17. Hyrynsalmi, S.: Letters from the war of ecosystems – an analysis of independent software vendors in mobile application marketplaces. Doctoral dissertation, University of Turku, Turku, Finland, December 2014. https://doi.org/10.13140/2.1.4076.4484. TUCS Dissertations no. 188

18. Hyrynsalmi, S., Suominen, A., Mäkilä, T., Järvi, A., Knuutila, T.: Revenue models of application developers in android market ecosystem. In: Cusumano, M.A., Iyer, B., Venkatraman, N. (eds.) ICSOB 2012. LNBIP, vol. 114, pp. 209–222. Springer, Heidelberg (2012). https://doi.org/10.1007/978-3-642-30746-1_17

19. Järvi, A., Mäkilä, T., Hyrynsalmi, S.: Game development accelerator – initial design and research approach. In: Hyrynsalmi, S., Wnuk, K., Daneva, M., Mäkilä, T., Herrmann, A. (eds.) Proceedings of From Start-Ups to SaaS Conglomerate: Life Cycles of Software Products, Ceur Workshop Proceedings, vol. 1095, pp. 47–58. CEUR-WS (2013). https://doi.org/10.13140/2.1.1354.0167

20. Järvinen, J., Huomo, T., Mikkonen, T., Tyrväinen, P.: From agile software development to mercury business. In: Lassenius, C., Smolander, K. (eds.) ICSOB 2014. LNBIP, vol. 182, pp. 58–71. Springer, Cham (2014). https://doi.org/10.1007/978-3-319-08738-2_5

21. Junk, W.S.: The dynamic balance between cost, schedule, features, and quality in software development projects. Technical report ID 83844–1010, University of Idao (2000)

22. Khanna, D., Nguyen-Duc, A., Wang, X.: From MVPs to pivots: a hypothesis-driven journey of two software startups. In: Proceedings of the 1st International Workshop on Software Engineering for Startups. ICSOB 2018, Springer, Heidelberg (2018)

23. Klotins, E.: Using the case survey method to explore engineering practices in software start-ups. In: Proceedings of the 1st International Workshop on Software Engineering for Startups, SoftStart 2017, pp. 24–26. IEEE Press, Piscataway (2017). https://doi.org/10.1109/SoftStart.2017...4

24. Klotins, E., et al.: Exploration of technical debt in start-ups. In: Proceedings of the 40th International Conference on Software Engineering: Software Engineering in Practice, ICSE-SEIP 2018, pp. 75–84. ACM, New York (2018). https://doi.org/10.1145/3183519.3183539

25. Klotins, E., Unterkalmsteiner, M., Gorschek, T.: Software engineering in start-up companies: an analysis of 88 experience reports. Empirical Softw. Eng. (2018). https://doi.org/10.1007/s10664-018-9620-y

26. Koskenvoima, A., Mäntymäki, M.: Why do small and medium-size freemium game developers use game analytics? In: Janssen, M., et al. (eds.) I3E 2015. LNCS, vol. 9373, pp. 326–337. Springer, Cham (2015). https://doi.org/10.1007/978-3-319-25013-7_26

27. Larsson, R.: Case survey methodology: quantitative analysis of patterns across case studies. Acad. Manag. J. **36**(6), 1515–1546 (1993)

28. Lenarduzzi, V., Taibi, D.: MVP explained: a systematic mapping study on the definitions of minimal viable product. In: 2016 42th Euromicro Conference on Software Engineering and Advanced Applications (SEAA), pp. 112–119, August 2016. https://doi.org/10.1109/SEAA.2016.56

29. Moogk, D.R.: Minimum viable product and the importance of experimentation in technology startups. Technol. Innov. Manag. Rev. **2**(3), 23–26 (2012)

30. Münch, J., Fagerholm, F., Johnson, P., Pirttilahti, J., Torkkel, J., Jäarvinen, J.: Creating minimum viable products in industry-academia collaborations. In: Fitzgerald, B., Conboy, K., Power, K., Valerdi, R., Morgan, L., Stol, K.-J. (eds.) LESS 2013. LNBIP, vol. 167, pp. 137–151. Springer, Heidelberg (2013). https://doi.org/10.1007/978-3-642-44930-7_9

31. Murphy-Hill, E., Zimmermann, T., Nagappan, N.: Cowboys, ankle sprains, and keepers of quality: how is video game development different from software development? In: Proceedings of the 36th International Conference on Software Engineering, ICSE 2014, pp. 1–11. ACM, New York (2014). https://doi.org/10.1145/2568225.2568226

32. Nacke, L.E., et al.: Playability and player experience research. In: Proceedings of the 2009 DiGRA International Conference: Breaking New Ground: Innovation in Games, Play, Practice and Theory, DiGRA 2009. Brunel University (2009)

33. Duc, A.N., Abrahamsson, P.: Minimum viable product or multiple facet product? The role of MVP in software startups. In: Sharp, H., Hall, T. (eds.) XP 2016. LNBIP, vol. 251, pp. 118–130. Springer, Cham (2016). https://doi.org/10.1007/978-3-319-33515-5_10

34. Petersen, K., et al.: Choosing component origins for software intensive systems: in-house, cots, OSS or outsourcing? - A case survey. IEEE Trans. Softw. Eng. **44**(3), 237–261 (2018). https://doi.org/10.1109/TSE.2017.2677909

35. Ries, E.: The Lean Startup : How Constant Innovation Creates Radically Successful Businesses. Portfolio Penguin, London (2011)

36. Rosenfield Boeira, J.N.: Mvps: Do we really need them? In: Lean Game Development: Apply Lean Frameworks to the Process of Game Development, pp. 33–48. Apress, Berkeley (2017). https://doi.org/10.1007/978-1-4842-3216-3_4

37. Rouse, R.: Game Design Theory and Practice, 2nd edn. Wordware Publishing Inc., Plano (2000)

38. Salen, K., Tekinbaş, K., Zimmerman, E.: Rules of Play: Game Design Fundamentals. Books 24 × 7 IT PRO. MIT Press (2004)
39. Schell, J.: The Art of Game Design: A book of lenses, 2nd edn. AK Peters/CRC Press, New York (2015)
40. Smed, J., Hakonen, H., Centre, T., Science, C.: Towards a definition of a computer game. Technical report 53, Turku Centre for Computer Science (2003)
41. Unterkalmsteiner, M., et al.: Software startups - a research agenda. e-Informatica Softw. Eng. J. **10**(1), 89–124 (2016). https://doi.org/10.5277/e-Inf160105
42. Wang, X., Edison, H., Bajwa, S.S., Giardino, C., Abrahamsson, P.: Key challenges in software startups across life cycle stages. In: Sharp, H., Hall, T. (eds.) XP 2016. LNBIP, vo . 251, pp. 169–182. Springer, Cham (2016). https://doi.org/10.1007/978-3-319-33515-5_14
43. Weinschenk, S., Barker, D.: Designing Effective Speech Interfaces. Wiley, New York (2000)

How to Avoid Financial Crises

Eleftherios Thalassinos[1,2](✉) and Yannis Thalassinos[3]

[1] University of Piraeus, Piraeus, Greece
thalassinos@ersj.eu
[2] University of Malta, Msida, Malta
[3] M.A. Kharafi & Sons, Kuwait City, Kuwait
jthalassinos@gmail.com

Abstract. The recent financial crisis unveiled the major deficiencies and weaknesses of the Eurozone structure. However, almost 10 years after the beginning of the crisis, the Eurozone is still dealing with its effects.

The article discusses some of the reasons of the global crises since the 1980s and focuses on the role of the Credit Rating Agencies ("CRAs") during the recent financial crisis. It presents the methodologies that are used in order to assess country risk, the relevant variables used in their evaluations, the problems they face and suggests possible ways to improve the process at a European level.

The article is organized in five sections as follows: the concept of country risk, platforms for assessing country risk, the determinants of country risk, the reasons behind the recent financial crises and the role of CRAs in the latest financial crisis.

Keywords: Financial crisis · Country risk · Internationalization

JEL Codes: F2 · F32

1 Introduction

The recent financial crisis was a good lesson on the economic disturbances that a global crisis can cause, especially for the countries of Eurozone and candidate countries. Member - states in Eurozone have given away their right to define their monetary policy and the available options to control their balances are very limited. On the other hand, they have accumulated experience on how to deal with future financial imbalances, if evaluated correctly and on a timely manner. Debates, discussions and extensive research have been conducted in an attempt to convince people about the benefit of an optimum monetary union. However, there is still a long way to shaping a solid and effective union. The European Monetary Union is by definition an incomplete optimum area with big loop holes and missing parts. A few countries, especially the PIIGS (Portugal, Ireland, Italy, Greece, Spain), have paid a heavy penalty for being members of the European Union, because they failed to comply with the prerequisites and policies imposed by the corresponding bodies during the membership period or before (Thalassinos and Stamatopoulos 2015; Thalassinos *et al.* 2014, 2015). This study presents views regarding the causes of the recent global financial crises and suggests initiatives on how to avoid them.

S. A. Al-Sharhan et al. (Eds.): I3E 2018, LNCS 11195, pp. 232–243, 2018.
https://doi.org/10.1007/978-3-030-02131-3_21

According to literature, Foreign Direct Investments (FDI) are closely related to country risk evaluation. Rating companies, namely Standard and Poor's, Fitch, Moody's, as well as specific departments of multinational corporations, are analysing subjectively the evolution of a country's risk. Rating grades appear to be important support-tools in decision-making; however, the provided ratings are used by decision makers as such, without any critical attitude.

The phenomenon of globalization has improved the understanding of country risk, and unpredicted recurring crises stress the fact that the assessment processes have significant shortcomings. Countries like Greece, Portugal, Spain, Cyprus, Ireland, Italy, which still face economic and social problems, are in a delicate situation for reasons presented in this article (Allegret *et al.* 2016; Grima and Caruana 2017).

In this context, this article aims to provide answers to the following questions: Are the rating organizations really accurate and objective in their ratings? What are the relevant variables in the analysis of a financial crisis because of a high-country risk? What are the problem areas and how can they be treated? What is the most appropriate approach for assessing country risk? The article is organized in four sections as follows.

2   The Concept of Country Risk

According to OECD, country risk encompasses transfer and convertibility risk (i.e. the risk a government imposes capital or exchange controls that prevent an entity from converting local currency into foreign currency and/or transferring funds to creditors located outside the country) and cases of force majeure (e.g. war, expropriation, revolution, civil disturbance, floods, earthquakes).

The country risk classifications are not sovereign risk classifications and should not, therefore, be compared with the sovereign risk classifications of private credit rating agencies (CRAs). Conceptually, they are more similar to the "country ceilings" that are produced by some of the major CRAs.

The concept of country risk is closely related to economic globalization as a process creating advantages and disadvantages, with the latter generating country risk according to IMF (2005) and for many years, it was considered an opaque, unpleasant fact of life better left in the hands of the IMF and the export credit agencies (Bouchet et al. 2003).

The realisation of "political risk" appeared for the first time in literature in the 1960s. Usher (1965) and Root (1968) were among the first authors to use the term. Researchers tried to estimate the risk of investing abroad, using the term "investment climate" (Gabriel 1966; Stobaugh 1969). Notwithstanding, as the next decades displayed, the concept of "political stability" in the respective country and how to measure the phenomenon and what the causal forces are, was shown to be more elaborate than was first expected and there is a long way to go before a solution is found. Different approaches on the concept of country risk are shown in Table 1.

There is a dispute between academics and practitioners with regard to the range of this research domain. In the relevant literature, the terms that are most commonly used are "country risk" and "political risk", when it comes to the concept of doing business abroad. The terms "cross border risk" or "sovereign risk" are used less. The oldest and

Table 1. Various approaches of literature on country risk

Terminologies	Definition of risk	Sources of risk	Nature of the investment	Historical perspective	Methodology
Political risk	Performance variance	Sovereign interference	Foreign direct investment	1960s–1970s	Qualitative
Country risk	Negative outcome	Environmental instability	Banking commercial loans	1980s	Qualitative
Sovereign risk Cross-border risk			Portfolio investment	1990s	

Source Boucher *et al.* (2003)

most frequently encountered term in literature is "political risk". The term "country risk" appeared in literature later in the 1970s. The new term is primarily a better description of the state of the economy, focusing on real factors and emphasising the entire picture. It was used primarily to describe the business environment, and then the banking sector before it became a general term, especially after the consequences of the international debt crisis in the 1980s. Desta (1985) commented that financial experts in international lending institutions choose to use the term "country risk" or "sovereign risk" instead of "political risk". The important aspect of this development is the fact that the political environment is now considered among the factors determining "sovereign risk".

What should be taken into consideration in the relevant literature is the fact that there is a differentiation between risk and uncertainty. When it comes to risk, the result is improbable, but the likelihood of the results is known or can be estimated. On the other hand, the term "uncertainty" refers to a status where the odds are unknown. Investors' target, by way of this concept, is to decrease uncertainty by becoming informed about the risk concerning the profits of the value of the firm, whilst always bearing in mind the variability of the future state of the economy. Consequently, the concept of country risk indicates the support of the investor, by diminishing the incertitude and discovering the changeability potential of profits and the worth of the foreign investment accordingly (Domowitz and Glen 1998).

Country risk has been divided, in the relevant literature, into six main categories. As defined by Coplin and O'Leavy (1994), country risk is a result of a mixture of risks oriented from several sources. The sources are economic, financial, transactional, institutional or political. Accepting that the correlation between the local economy, together with its political system, the social nature of the economy and the economic structure of the country and the international community is quite important, significant conclusions can be drawn regarding the magnitude of country risk. Although the six types of country risk may not be universally accepted, these notions are inclined to appear in the risk ratings of most companies. To facilitate this study, a short survey of these types of risks focusing on the sovereign risk, are presented below.

Economic Risk: This type of risk emerges from the possibility of harmful changes in basic economic policy targets, such as monetary and fiscal, or a change in competitive advantage of a country, such as decreased resources.

Economic risk tends to coincide with other types of risks, mostly with political risk, since they both have trade-offs with policy (Coplin and O'Leavy 1994; Caouette *et al.* 1998 and Saunders and Allen 2002).

Transfer Risk: This type of risk emerges when a foreign government decides to confine different types of capital investments. Normally, transfer risk is considered as a characteristic of a country's potential to gain foreign currency, mentioning that in order to earn foreign currency it is required to follow certain policies, whilst it is a very difficult task for most of the weak economies in the Eurozone (Coplin and O'Leavy 1994).

Exchange Risk: This type of risk contains an unanticipated alteration in the currency regime. Numerous quantitative measures are used to recognise transfer risk and also recognise exchange rate risk, especially when some of the imbalances could be reduced by the devaluation of the currency. This could lead to increasing transfer risk. Moreover, an isolated exchange risk could be assisted by a country's rate of exchange policy. As soon as the policy makers in the respective country try to control the currency system regime in a narrow trading range, it is inclined to realise a higher risk than fixed by the currency board systems regime. In case of a flexible exchange rate regime in a currency's value, it is allowed to fluctuate according to foreign exchange market conditions, whilst they generally support the lowest risk of generating an unexpected opposite exchange rate movement (Coplin and O'Leavy 1994 and Borio and Parker 2004).

Location or Neighbourhood Risk: This type of risk issue, in a geographic area, in a country's ally or in countries with common traits, causes spill-over effects.

Each country's geographic position is strategic and offers the simplest way to measure the location risk. Location could be specified by a country's international partners, global trading alliances (NAFTA, EU, etc.), the size of the economy, and the boundaries, as well as the interval by financially or politically significant countries or regions (Coplin and O'Leavy 1994 and Saunders and Allen 2002).

Political Risk: The origin of the concept of political risk is noteworthy. Significant changes in political institutions stem either from deviations in government controls, social structures or other non-economic factors. The capacity for conflicts, either internal or external, expropriation risk and original political analysis could be included. As far as risk estimation is concerned, many factors should be co-calculated, such as the relationships of various groups in a country, the method for drawing conclusions, the decision-making procedure by government agents as well as the credit-default history of the country (Coplin and O'Leavy 1994).

Sovereign Risk: Over the past few years, there have been quite a few cases of governments preparing to meet their loan obligations or back down on loans they vouched for. Sovereign risk could be related to transfer risk since a government may lack foreign exchange, as a result of unfortunate developments in its current account balances. The sovereign risk is so well-related to political risk that a government may decide not to fulfil its commitments, mainly for political reasons. In the relevant literature, the concept of sovereign risk is described as a separate type, as long as a private lender is confronted with a unique risk in dealing, such as the current financial crisis, and cannot claim a reimbursement from the foreign government unless they have its authorisation (see: Coplin and O'Leavy 1994; Caouette *et al.* 1998; Saunders and Allen 2002; Borio and Parker 2004 and Scholtens *et al.* 2004).

A country risk approach depends on the type of state considered or on the nature of the considered agent (Kold 2011). It should be noted that there is difference between sovereign and country risk. In general, the rating assigned by the analysts to the sovereign risk coincides with the maximum score of state (sovereign ceiling); no local agent does receive a rating higher than that of the sovereign risk. According to some researchers this is not always the right approach. As Meunier and Sollogoub (2005) highlight, during the Russian crisis, Gazprom continued to credit its own debt while the Russian Federation has suspended the payments.

Recent papers have presented new approaches to the country risk concept, and the number of entities that deal with its analysis has increased significantly. Other studies in the last decade (Arteta 2008; Reihart 2009; Giordano 2009) have developed new perspectives according to which risk can be contemplated as the perspective of the economic participants reached by risk creditors. banks, investors (financial or industrial risk), exporters (commercial risk).

3 Assessing Country Risk

Institutions that carry out country risk assessment except for the aforementioned CRAs are insurance companies (e.g. COFACE – Compagnie Française d'Assurance pour le Commerce Extérieur); consulting firms (North South Export in France, Business Environment Risk Intelligence); financial publications (Institutional Investor, Euro money Publications) and Banks.

CRAs are well known worldwide and monitor more than 95% of the government securities market. Their evaluations rank the states in terms of loans and bonds issued. Four major classes of risk are defined (A, B, C, D), for Standard & Poor's and Moody's, in descending order (from the lowest level of risk, when the country can repay both debt and interest, to the most unfortunate situation). Each class has two more sub-classes (AA, AAA) and two nuance indicators are used, " + " and "−". They point perspectives, the possible development of a note and are the first to change.

The weighting of the different determinants and the evaluation methodology are unknown to the public. Criteria and factors are divided into two categories; quantitative factors (objective criteria) and qualitative factors (subjective criteria).

The assessment of country risk could be used as a tool in decision making regarding FDI, commercial bank loans for the private and the public sector, portfolio investments and exporting.

However, a strategic investment decision should not be based only the assessment of country risk, but should be linked to the international situation, risk aversion, the perception of uncertainty, the host state characteristics (social and economic situation, labour costs and its qualification), market attractiveness, and the institutional framework.

The determinants of country risk can vary in terms of intensity and duration and it is almost impossible to control within the micro and macro environment (Thalassinos *et al.* 2015; Duguleana and Duguleana 2016; Boldeanu and Tache 2016). A number developed countries are constantly monitoring specific benchmarks and financial performance metrics in an effort to identify warnings in cases of unforeseen negative developments.

4 The Determinants of Country Risk

Currently there are several models of analysis of risk country; the most known are those proposed by BERI (Business Environmental Risk Intelligence), by the U.S. rating agencies (Standard & Poor's, Moody's, Fitch IBCA, Duff & Phelps) and by The Economist and Euromoney magazine.

The most common determinants included in these models are the following: `

Political environment: form of government, democratic participation, quality of succession power, the consensus of economic policy objectives, degree of integration in international economic exchanges, security and defense capacity of the country

Level of public debt: public financial assets, indebtedness of the State, State commitment regarding pension

Pricing: Inflation level, average economic interest rate, exchange policy, level of independence of central bank

Economic structure of incomes: standard of living, income levels and access to health services, existence of market economy, access to resources and their diversity

Flexibility balance of payments: impact of monetary/fiscal policy on national accounts, structure of current account, structure of capital flows

Prospects for economic growth: savings/investment project, rate/structure of economic growth

Fiscal flexibility: main budgetary constraints, fiscal policy discretion, pressure on public spending

External debt/liquidity level: currency composition of external debt, importance of banking system. history and payment incidents of extern service

In many cases, country risk problems begin with the deterioration of the fundamental economic and political structure of a state. Warning signals such as excessive debt or declining reserves should be regarded as symptoms of an increased risk. We consider that the analysis of fundamentals is very useful in activities such: identifying the vulnerabilities, finding the origins of problems, assessing difficulties (short-term ones or long-term ones), etc.

5   Recent Crises

It is almost impossible nowadays, to shield a national economy that operates as part of a globalized world. Any protection mechanism should be designed based on the specific characteristics of each country, however this is not possible due to constraints and obligations associated with supra-international authorities, institutions and orga-nizations regulating the world economy through rules, directives and frameworks that although they were established in a different era are of great importance today.

Several crises of different magnitude have affected the world economy one way or the other over the last few decades. Most of these crises had spread around hitting the weak economies harder than the strong ones. Crises due to nationalization, political reasons, financial failures, sovereign crises, oil or real estate shocks just to mention few of them.

During the Latin American debt crisis of the 1980s - a period often referred to as the "lost decade" - many Latin American countries became unable to service their foreign debt. The Federal Reserve and other international institutions responded to the crisis with a number of actions that ultimately helped alleviate the situation, albeit with some unintended consequences.

Unlike the debt crisis in Latin America, the debt crisis in East Asia in 1997, stemmed from inappropriate borrowing by the private sector. Due to high rates of economic growth and a booming economy, private firms and corporations looked to finance speculative investment projects. However, firms overstretched themselves and a combination of factors caused a depreciation in the exchange rate as they struggled to meet the payments.

The Russian Crisis of 1998 was really an extension of the Asian Crisis. The combination of declining economic output, falling oil prices, enormous budget deficits, and a currency pegged to the rising US dollar overwhelmed the fledgling Russian government. To maintain its peg to the dollar, Russia used its foreign exchange reserves to buy rubles. But as the country gradually depleted its foreign exchange reserves, it became clear that Russia would soon run out of reserves. At that point, the Russian government would no longer be able to maintain the ruble's peg to the US dollar. Upon exhausting its reserves, Russia defaulted on its debt and revalued the ruble on foreign exchange markets.

Some examples of more recent crises are the cases of Greece - a public debt crisis, Venezuela - a political crisis, Turkey - a nationalization crisis and Bulgaria - a cor-ruption crisis and more.

The multiplication and diversification process concern not only the country risk, but the economic risks. The liquidity crisis recorded in the financial markets led to easy propagation and to the sovereign debt crisis in 2010. Globalization and economic liberalization or too much regulation versus regional integration had led to economic inter-dependence.

The openness of the modern countries, where the national dimension is not the main component of the country risk anymore, has made countries more vulnerable to spill over effects of financial crises from other countries. Substantial financial liberalization and deregulation, financial innovation, multiplication and expansion of flows and financial products can lead to speculation.

In addition to the above other concerns are:

✓ Extended supply chains – increased vulnerability ("domino effect")
✓ Rising and volatile prices (oil, gas)/sovereign debt problem
✓ Asset prices collapse/geopolitical risks (Iran, Iraq)
✓ Environmental risks/terrorism/new risks/IT risks.
✓ Loss of autonomy and increased competition between states result to increased pressure from multinational corporations
✓ Attempt to give to supranational institutions greater importance than usual
✓ Existence of multiple agreements between international institutions
✓ Importance of regional trade blocks (over 65% of world trade)
✓ Network operating enterprises in addition to cultural homogenization vs nationalism

6   The Impact of Financial Crises on E-Commerce

As it is pointed out in the work of Ghadami et al. (2010) the recent financial crisis has affected online banking retail business (or B2C e-Commerce) in a negative way. The effect of the crisis can be observed within three different areas of the economy. More specifically, there is less credit available within the economy, which reduces the e-commerce spending and people prefer to save and reduce their expenditures. This behavior leads to falling consumer confidence and sentiment.

Less credit available: Financial crises are characterized by a shortage in capital funds due to rising uncertainties regarding loans, risks and inbalances in the banking sector. Low credit ratings by CRAs direct capital away from credits including the e-commerce. Therefore, the conclusion by Ghadami et al. (2010) regarding credit is valid.

Increase in saving rates: Limited credit creates conditions for an increase in saving rate since capital is going to save settlements during a financial crisis

Decline in consumption and falling consumer confidence and sentiment: The above affects negatively consumer confidence and spending

In the work by Heng (2001) the new banking environment is described as an alternative to transform banking and financial systems. E-Commerce provides a business opportunity for banks to offer innovative products however their attitude to proceed in such activities is positively related to their financial health. During financial crises these opportunities are eliminated and in some cases evaporated because of limited confidence among traders.

7   The Role of Cras in the Recent Crisis

Despite readability, rapidity, a recognized degree of simplicity and other advantages, a rating system is not free of a number of subjective elements. However, rating agencies do not provide insights regarding the methodology followed in order to reach to their conclusions. Rating models are not sufficiently explained and scoring systems do not always converge.

The rating agencies have never been far from controversy: at the turn of the millennium they came under fire for giving Enron a clean bill of health right up until the company collapsed in 2001. More recently, they have been subject to criticism in the wake of large losses, beginning in 2007 in the collateralized debt obligation market, that occurred despite products being assigned top ratings. In the US, a Senate report said the agencies deserve some of the blame for the recent financial meltdown. According to the report, the agencies helped banks disguise the risks of the investments they marketed, selling high risk securities with low risk labels

The October 2016 the European Parliament issued a briefing on role of CRAs in the recent crisis. It identifies a marked difference between the recent crises in the USA and the EU. Whilst in the USA the main focus was on the financial crisis, the EU faced both a financial crisis and a sovereign debt crisis, which were interlinked. The sovereign debt crisis was not confined to the euro area, as none of the first three EU countries affected were using the euro. There is evidence that agencies tend to be lax before a bubble is about to burst, only to become very severe once markets head down. Many say that the ratings of a number of private and public financial products were too high before the crises, and that the CRAs did not sense any crisis coming. Furthermore, with respect to the European sovereign debt crisis, it has been noted that the agencies did not see or take into account the imbalances in public finances as well as problems with the lack of sustainability of growth models. However, most analysts outside the agencies did not sense the problems either. In the USA, privatesector mortgage-backed securities had been rated in a very favorable manner, contributing to the real-estate bubble and fueling the securitization process. This is one specific area where over-optimistic ratings were a contributory factor to the financial crisis, and where inevitable downgrades accelerated the crisis.

With regard to the European sovereign debt crisis, for many years prior to the crisis the rating agencies did not sufficiently discriminate between sovereigns with divergent levels of accumulated debt. Once that crisis hit, there was a very fast adaptation, with a quick and brutal lowering of ratings. This could be observed very clearly in the peripheral euro- area economies, which enjoyed a rating privilege prior to the financial crisis, which then turned into a penalty as the crisis unfolded. There is controversy about how appropriate the ratings of sovereigns were after that adaptation. Some say that the ratings ended up being too low, thus magnifying the impact of the crises, whilst others estimate that, even after the adaptation, they were still more favorable than they should have been. Over-optimistic rates would have been the consequence of the ex-post bias, as well as prevalent conflicts of interest, whereby CRAs would still have been incentivized to over-rate financial products which, de facto, already were junk bonds, or in the process of becoming precisely that. The successive downgrading of

Greece's rates was a factor in the rise of the spreads of long-term government bond yields relative to the German Bund, and contagion to other Member States with less than solid fiscal fundamentals ensued. Euro-area countries like EPRS.

In the case of Greece, although the existence of a set of macroeconomic negative issues should not be denied, it should be pointed out that rating agencies reacted slowly at the beginning, and then brutally and abruptly downgraded the economy to junk status. The same did not happen during the crisis in Asia in 1997; then, the lack of well-drawn warnings (such as evolution of budget deficit, elevated foreign debt, slow capital formation, etc.), allowed the local economies to maintain high ratings. In addition, another parameter that should be considered is whether a country is market friendly or not. Greece has proved over the years that it is a "market friendly" country, whose good faith to international creditors cannot be put in doubt.

Regarding the activity of the rating agencies, some critical remarks can be made based on recent experience:

✓ they did not take into full account the fundamentals of the Greek economy and the measures taken by the EU (the consistent rescue package);

✓ they are too critical with countries, which can often negatively influence markets, and less critical with some dangerous financial products;

✓ there is maximum concurrence in their market (3 agencies represent more than 97% of the business);

✓ the opacity of the rating process and the level of objectivity sometimes is questionable;

✓ the ratings can have a pro-cyclical effect (late and too strong reactions from the agencies) – which can encourage speculation. The pro-cyclical effect is due to the chain of events of this type: downgrade – speculative pressure – deterioration of loan terms – higher interest rates - lower investment interest;

✓ The threat of imitation and use, without a critical analysis of the assessments made by rating agencies. Often, economic participants use the informational content of the rating and integrate its results, which are considered extremely reliable, in operations and decisions on various global markets. Sometimes, their bad influence may itself lead to pricing dislocations and can affect the behaviour of economic participants.

8 Conclusions

It became clear during the recent crisis that an over-reliance on external ratings – especially those from the CRAs – had the effect of pushing market participants to use mainly external ratings, and similarly to reduce investors' incentives to create their own assessment capacity. Together, these factors resulted in a mechanistic use of external ratings. In the recent crisis, market participants all reacted in a synchronized manner to downgrades, precipitating pro-cyclical effects.

As it was discussed above, following the subprime crisis and the sovereign debt crisis, rating agencies lag behind markets in their judgment. Their business model is flawed as they face major conflicts of interest and are very opaque in their methodologies. Also, the oligopolistic structure of the ratings market provides the three large CRAs with a very strong position in affecting investment decisions and market sentiment.

Several policy options to change the ratings industry have been put forward, including a network of small agencies, a European Rating Agency, or even the delegation of sovereign rating to the ECB. The first option is least preferred, because of the entry costs, coordination problems and the lack of economies of scale. The delegation of sovereign rating to the ECB would in principle be possible, but not preferable as it leads to a conflict of interest within the ECB. That leaves only the option of a European Rating Agency as a way to improve rating quality and transparency. However, it also requires high investment costs and time for reputation building

To avoid future financial crises, it is important to take measures to stabilize the economy by implementing sustainable macro-economic policies, to reform the supply side of the economy by improving its structure, to make extra imports due to borrowing only with productive uses (borrowing should simply generate eventually more money), to prevent any form of waste, to reduce the oversized state apparatus, to avoid important policy changes threatening domestic demand, to support consumption expenditures, to improve the effectiveness of the economy to reduce the size of the public sector tax system and to establish a stable political system.

References

Allegret, J.P., Raymond, H., Rharrabti, H.: The impact of the Eurozone crisis on European banks stocks, contagion or interdependence. Eur. Res. Stud. J. **19**(1), 129–147 (2016)

Boldeanu, T.F., Tache, I.: The financial system of the EU and the capital markets union. Eur. Res. Stud. J. **19**(1), 60–70 (2016)

Borio, C., Packer, F.: Assessing New Perspectives on Country Risk, BIS Quarterly Review, pp. 47–65 (December 2004)

Caouette, J.B., Altman, E.I., Narayanan, P.: Managing Credit Risk. Wiley, New York (1998)

Calverley, J.: Country Risk Analysis, 2nd edn. Butterworths, London (1990)

Coplin, W.D., O'Leary, M.K.: The Handbook of Country and Political Risk Analysis. Political Risk Services, International Business Communications, New York (1994)

Desta, A.: Assessing political risk in less developed countries. J. Bus. Strat. **5**(4), 40–53 (1985)

Domowitz, I., Glen, J., Madhavan, A.: Country and currency risk premia in an emerging market. J. Financ. Quant. Anal. **33**(2), 189–216 (1998)

Duguleana, L., Duguleana, C.: Structural aspects of the European Union Economy. Eur. Res. Stud. J. **19**(1), 93–128 (2016)

Gabriel, P.P.: The investment in the LDC: asset with a fixed maturity. C. J. World Bus. **1**(3), 109–119 (1966)

Ghadami, F., Aghaie, A., Mohammadkhan, M.: The impact of financial crisis on B2C e-commerce. I.Busoiness **2**(2), 193–200 (2010)

Grima, S., Caruana, L.: The effect of the financial crisis on emerging markets: a comparative analysis of the stock market situation before and after. Eur. Res. Stud. J. **20**(4B), 727–753 (2017)

Heng M.S.H.: Implications of e-commerce for banking and finance. In: Schmid, B., Stanoevska-Slabeva, K., Tschammer, V. (eds) Towards the E-Society. IFIP International Federation for Information Processing, vol 74. Springer, Boston, MA (2001)

Root, F.R.: The expropriation experience of American companies. Bus. Horiz. **11**(2), 69–74 (1968)

Saunders, A., Allen, L.: Credit Risk Measurement. Wiley, New York (2002)

Scholtens, B., Frenkel, M., Karmann, A.: Country Risk Analysis: Principles Practices and Policies. Springer, Berlin (2004)

Stobaugh, R.B.: How to analyze foreign investment climates. Harv. Bus. Rev. **47**(5), 100–108 (1969)

Thalassinos, E., Thalassinos, P.: Stock markets' integration analysis. Eur. Res. Stud. J. **9**(3–4), 3–14 (2006)

Thalassinos, I.E., Liapis, K., Thalassinos, E.J.: The role of the rating companies in the recent financial crisis in the Balkan and black sea area. Chapter book in Economic Crisis in Europe and the Balkans, Contributions to Economics, pp. 79–115. Springer International Publishing (2014). https://doi.org/10.1007/978-3-319-00494-5-6

Thalassinos, I.E., Stamatopoulos, D.T., Thalassinos, E.P.: The European Sovereign Debt crisis and the role of credit swaps. In: Ziemba, W.T., Malliaris, A.G. (eds) Chapter book in The WSPC Handbook of Futures Markets in memory of Late Milton Miller (Nobel 1990) World Scientific Handbook in Financial Economic Series, Chapter 20, vol. 5, pp. 605–639 (2015). ISBN: 978-981-4566-91-9. https://doi.org/10.1142/9789814566926_0020

Thalassinos, I.E., Stamatopoulos, Th: The Trilemma and the Eurozone: a pre-announced tragedy of the hellenic debt crisis. Eur. Res. Stud. J. **3**(3), 27–40 (2015)

Usher, D.: Political risk. Econ. Dev. Cult. Change **13**(4), 453–462 (1965)

Zaman, C., Meunier, B.: A decade of EU membership: evolution of competitiveness in Romania. Eur. Res. Stud. J. **20**(2A), 224–236 (2017)

Modeling the Role of C2C Information Quality on Purchase Decision in Facebook

Rafita Haque[1,2(✉)], Imran Mahmud[2], Md. Hasan Sharif[2],
S. Rayhan Kabir[2], Arpita Chowdhury[1], Farzana Akter[3],
and Amatul Bushra Akhi[3]

[1] Department of Computer Science and Engineering,
Asian University of Bangladesh, Dhaka, Bangladesh
rafitahaque93@gmail.com, arpitachy10@yahoo.com
[2] Department of Software Engineering, Daffodil International University,
Dhaka, Bangladesh
imranmahmud@daffodilvarsity.edu.bd,
{rafita.swe, sharif.swe, rayhan561}@diu.edu.bd
[3] Department of Computer Science and Engineering,
Daffodil International University, Dhaka, Bangladesh
{farzana.cse, akhi.cse}@diu.edu.bd

Abstract. A market which provides an innovative way to allow customers to interact with each other called Customer-to-customer (C2C) market. In C2C communications, online communities play an important role in decision making to buy a product. This investigation develops a research model for online communities of Facebook commerce (F-Commerce) in Bangladesh region, which is based on Information Adoption Model (IAM). This study exhibits a model to influences of C2C communication on Bangladeshi consumers' purchase decision in the online communities of F-Commerce. The proposed model used the Partial Least Squares (PLS) technique to test 120 effective survey data. This survey data has been taken from the Bangladesh Facebook users and strongly involved in product buy-sell at F-Commerce. The analyzed results show that Argument Quality (AQ), Source Credibility (SC) and Tie Strength (TS) positively influence Purchase Decision (PD) through Product Usefulness Evaluation (PUE). In addition, Tie Strength exhibits difference effect on Product Usefulness Evaluation between the contexts of consumers communicating with virtual consumers relationships. Theoretical and executive implications are discussed for constructing our proposed model.

Keywords: Social media · Facebook commerce
Consumer to consumer (C2C)

1 Introduction

At present people are getting easier to communicate with each other by the computer-mediated communication (CMC) technologies called social media [1]. Due to the growing amount web traffic, the social network sites (SNS) such as Facebook, Friendster, CyWorld and MySpace are the crucial web applications to access the

© IFIP International Federation for Information Processing 2018
Published by Springer Nature Switzerland AG 2018. All Rights Reserved
S. A. Al-Sharhan et al. (Eds.): I3E 2018, LNCS 11195, pp. 244–254, 2018.
https://doi.org/10.1007/978-3-030-02131-3_22

various visitors in rapid time now a day. Under the statistics collected by Alexa, which is a web traffic data analytics company, Facebook obtained the third rank of the most viewed websites in 2018 after Google and YouTube [2]. With the benefit of friend recommendations, widespread sharing and dynamic responses, Facebook become one of the most powerful tools for today's' social networking based e-commerce. Facebook commerce (F-commerce) prescribes to the purchase and selling of products through Facebook [3]. Furthermore, Facebook announced unique features within the site. To illustrate, the famous "like" button, rapid "share", easy "tag", dynamic "comment" and "friend" relationships. These features could positively affect the customers' purchase intention by obtaining more confident after friend recommendation. Social Networking Services (SNSs) consent the people and online sellers to engage in consumer-to-consumer social commerce (C2C s-commerce) [4–6]. Nowadays, Facebook users are cumulatively using the Facebook website to conduct the trade operations, by posting advertisements and buying or selling products from each other. This type of conception is called a Facebook C2C social commerce [7].

In Bangladesh the popularities of F-commerce are increasing, almost two thousands of Facebook pages are available [8–10]. These survey flourished manuscript has developed based on 5attributes (See Table 1). There are Argument Quality (AQ) [11], Tie Strength (TS) [12], Source Credibility (SC) [13], Product Usefulness Evaluation (PUE) [14] and Purchase Decision (PD) [15]. We have utilized these attributes because these attributes are very helpful and mostly used for finding the information quality in e-commerce. The literature review section has been demonstrated the importance of these five attributes. Our exploration develops a research model to investigate the influence of Facebook C2C communication on consumers' purchase decision. It also compares the differences between real and virtual relationship environments to better understand consumers' purchase decision in Facebook. This model has revealed which is based on the Information Adoption Model (IAM). IAM is a relatively new, effective and practical approach [16, 17]. Our findings can provide the better understanding of the role of C2C communication in Facebook communities for consumer behavior research in Bangladeshi domain.

Table 1. Five utilized attributes and their abbreviations.

Attributes	Abbreviation
Argument quality	**AQ**
Tie strength	**TS**
Source credibility	**SC**
Product usefulness evaluation	**PUE**
Purchase decision	**PD**

2 Literature Review

A recent study proposed a model which based on the Information Adoption Model (IAM) [18]. The results of this research have shown that AQ, SC, and TS positively influence the purchase decision, where used Partial Least Squares (PLS) technique [19, 20]. We applied this research model in Bangladeshi domain and shown more specific consumers behavior analysis in F-commerce.

Another study analyzed 297 effective data for understanding the influences of system quality, information quality, and service quality for a website to satisfy their consumers [21]. The results of the conception to evaluate the trustworthiness of online sellers showed that people are the key factors that make consumers trust towards online sellers [22]. The social media survey of consumer has shown that trust is more usefulness to make the intention of consumers to purchase through social networking sites [23].

An investigation managed to the effects of F-commerce browsing and usage intensity in predicting urge to purchase and impulse purchase behavior among the consumers [24]. An approach used 180 data that directly investigate and evaluate the success of e-commerce for any small and medium-sized companies [25]. E-commerce service based another research have measured the requirements feasibility for B2C environment [26].

A social learning theory has developed to examine customers' learning behaviors [27]. A decision support model which has exhibited to manage the buyer risk and improves the quality of supplier development [28]. A theory evaluates using 307 effective data and reveals that cognitive and relational capital positively affects buyers' loyalty [29]. One team researchers established a casual model to investigate review quality effect on product and purchase intention [30]. In this study, using 349 experimental data that proved demographically similar reviewers enhanced the effect of review quality.

In the above literature review, we observe that most of the research work focused on information quality which makes an intention for the consumer to purchase a product. We have divided the C2C information quality [31] of F-commerce into AQ, TS, SC, PUE and PD sections.

3 Research Model and Hypothesis Development

The intention of a consumer to purchase a product depends on information quality shown by the information adoption model [32, 33]. C2C communication refers to the transfer of the variety of information from one customer to another customer in a way that has the potential to change their preferences, actual purchase behavior, or the way they further interact with others [34]. In line with the information adoption model, the present study proposes that PUE (Product Usefulness Evaluation) has a positive influence on the PD (Purchase Decision) of consumers. Hypothesis 1 is shown as follows:

H1: PUE is positively associated with PD in F-commerce for Bangladesh domain.

According to the dual action models user decision making depends on persuasive information [35]. In accordance with information adoption model, the AQ (Argument Quality) data [11] is a momentous middle sign which exerts an essential influence on information. The Bangladeshi consumers are always eager to know about the product which is suitable for their personal usage [36]. So that, in the online marking, the information quality and consultation of related products is highly appreciated. In the context of AQ information is very meaningful because this makes a clear consciousness about the selected product. Hypothesis 2 is shown as follows:

H2: AQ is positively related to PUE in the Bangladesh region.

Another models user decision making depends on persuasive information [37]. The most common feature of C2C communication is the consumers easily get the advice from other consumers. Based on this shared knowledge the consumer can easily make a judgment which helps those to make the future prediction about consumer's behaviors [38]. The judgment provides a cue that SC (Source Credibility) is very important to judge product usefulness evaluation (PUE). According to information adoption model, the SC of informational data is a potential peripheral cue which exerts a significant impact on information usefulness. Hypothesis 3 is shown as follows:

H3: SC is positively related to PUE.

Hence, in line with the information adoption model, the present study proposes that SC has a positive impact on the PUE. Members can communicate with others without time and space limitation in online communities [39]. Product messages come from stronger ties may more effective for consumers with a shopping demand to judge the usefulness of a product involved in C2C communications. The TS (Tie Strength) exerts an impact on the effectiveness of word-of-mouth communications in the online context [40]. The individual-level tie strength is an important antecedent of PD in online peer communications [41]. The present study proposes that TS has a positive impact on the PUE at Facebook communications in Bangladesh. Hypothesis 4 is shown as follows:

H4: TS is positively related to PUE.

In the online community contexts, consumers can choose to mainly communicate with real or virtual relationships by participating in different communities [42]. A study pointed out social ties play a different role in consumer decision making in different communication contexts [43]. The strong ties information are more influential in consumer decision making than that from weak ties in the context of offline word of mouth (WOM) communications or C2C interaction [44].

Hypothesis process and proposed research model has been displayed in Fig. 1. H2, H2, H3 hypothesis are connected with H1 where Product Usefulness Evaluation (PUE) is connected with PD for purchasing product in Facebook market place.

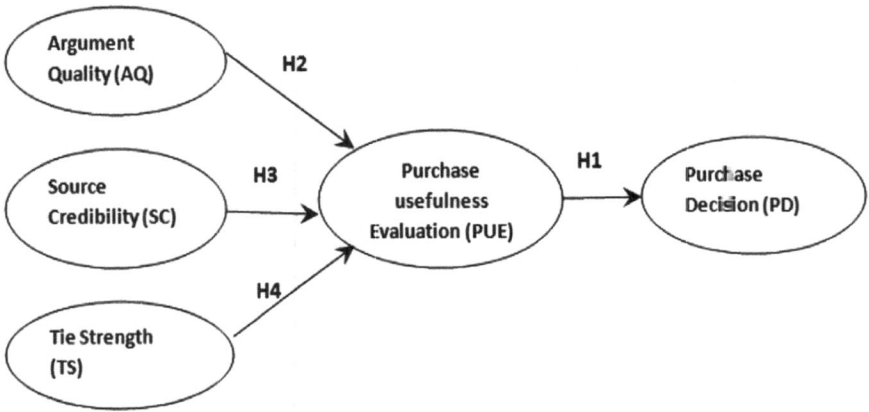

Fig. 1. Our research model.

4   Methods

4.1   Data Collection and Measurement

A survey was utilized to examine the impact of C2C communication on customer purchase choice. In this research, we did 120 surveys among the Bangladeshi Facebook users who are university students [45]. These survey data has been taken from the Bangladesh Facebook users and strongly involved in product buy-sell at F-Commerce. The analysis of surveys is based on PLS (Partial least squares), where we have used SmartPLS3.0 software [46]. The questionnaire survey consists of five attributes, which are AQ, TS, SC, PUE and PD (See Table 1.). These attributes are focused on purchase decision making to measure the constructs of our research model. Liket scale approach [47] have used for ranging from "1 = strongly disagree" to "7 = strongly agree", that presented with the set of attributes to measure the theoretical concepts. Following the recommended two-stage analytical procedures [48], we tested the measurement model (validity and reliability of the measures) followed by an examination of the structural model (testing the hypothesized relationship). To test the significance of the path coefficients (p) and the loadings a bootstrapping method was used [49].

5   Sample Profile

The demographic information of the respondents tabulated in Table 2, where derived from the descriptive analysis [50]. The majority of the age group (43.3%) was in the category of 22–25 years old. Most of the respondents were Male which is 76.7% and the frequency of the females is 23.3%. Most of the people are directly or indirectly connected to the internet as well as Facebook. In Table 1, we have analyzed our survey based on gender. Moreover, we separate the males and females and found that the male percentage is 23.3% and the female percentage is 76.7% (Table 3).

Table 2. Demographic information of different genders.

Gender	Frequency	Percent	Valid percent	Cumulative percent
Female	28	23.3	23.3	23.3
Male	92	76.7	76.7	100.0
Total	120	100.0	100.0	123.3

Table 3. Demographic information of several ages.

Age	Frequency	Percent	Valid percent	Cumulative percent
18–21	44	36.7	37.0	37.0
22–25	52	43.3	43.7	80.7
26–30	16	13.3	13.4	94.1
30+	7	5.8	5.9	100.0
Total	119	99.2	100.0	
Missing system	1	0.8		
Total	120	100.0		

6   Result and Data Analysis

6.1   Model Measurement

To assess the measurement model, two types of validity will be examined, first the convergent validity and then the discriminant validity [51]. The convergent validity of the measurement is usually ascertained by examining the loadings, average variance extracted and also the composite reliability [52]. The composite reliabilities were all higher than 0.7 and the AVE (Average Variance Extracted) was also higher than 0.5 as suggested in the literature (see Table 4). The discriminant validity of the measures (the degree to which items differentiate among constructs or measure distinct concepts) was examined by following criterion of comparing the correlations between constructs and the square root of the average variance extracted for that construct (see Table 5). All the values on the diagonals were greater than the corresponding row and column values indicating the measures were discriminant.

Table 4. Convergent validity

Attributes	Composite reliability	Average variance extracted (AVE)
AQ	0.737	0.584
PD	0.801	0.674
PUE	0.826	0.543
SC	0.857	0.749
TS	0.762	0.517

Table 5. Discriminant validity

Attributes	AQ	PD	PU	SC	TS
AQ	**0.764**				
PD	0.299	**0.821**			
PUE	0.294	0.436	**0.737**		
SC	0.299	0.193	0.528	**0.866**	
TS	0.326	0.324	0.518	0.503	**0.719**

6.2   Structural Model

To assess the structural model (Structural equation modeling) [53] suggested looking at the path coefficients(p), effect sizes (f^2), beta (β) and the corresponding t-statistic [54] via a bootstrapping procedure with a resample of various data or information. They also suggested that in addition to these basic measures researchers should also report the effect sizes (f^2) [55].

The outcomes of structural model test display that the path coefficients (p) are statistically significant ($p < 0.01$), barring for the coefficients of control attributes to PD. The f^2 of PD is 0.215, and the f^2 of PUE is 0.235 (Table 6).

Table 6. Structural model result

Hypothesis	Attributes	Original sample (O)	Sample mean (M)	Standard deviation (STDEV)	T-statistics (|O/STDEV|)	F values	Status
H1	AQ > PUE	0.087	0.100	0.077	1.141	0.254	Not supported
H2	PUE> PD	0.436	0.446	0.080	5.440	0.000	Supported
H3	SC > PUE	0.342	0.348	0.093	3.661	0.000	Supported
H4	TS > PUE	0.318	0.327	0.086	3.698	0.000	Supported

Our investigation shows that PUE ($\beta = 0.201$, $p < 0.01$) is a potential predictor of PD. As we hypothesized that PUE would positively effect on PD, hypothesis H1 is susceptible. The AQ ($\beta = -0.152$, $p < 0.01$), SC ($\beta = 0.319$, $p < 0.01$), and TS ($\beta = 0.307$, $p < 0.01$) are predictors of PUE. As we hypothesized that AQ, SC, and TS would positively affect PUE; hypotheses H2, H3, and H4 are adopted (Table 7).

Table 7. Effect size of calculation result

Attributes	Effect size	Remark
AQ	0.011	No
PUE	0.235	Large
SC	0.135	Small
TS	0.115	Small
PD	0.215	Large

7 Discussion

The research goal of this study was to investigate the role of information quality in increasing purchase intention in F-commerce for Bangladesh aspects. The significant impact of perceived reciprocal benefit on knowledge share indicates consumer will share knowledge based on their expectation of future benefit. If the consumer feels that sharing their knowledge in Facebook will be acknowledged by the consumers who sell their product, then the consumers might have a good impression on that their expected consumers. Hence PUE has a positive effect on the PD of consumers. Our second hypothesis H2 implies that if consumers enjoy being on the social network or if they enjoy helping other consumers then they are motivated to post knowledge related data on Facebook. We identified the objectives that increase the PD of F-commerce. AQ, TS, SC, PUE has a positive impact on consumers' actions.

8 Conclusion and Future Work

With the integrated model of our own concept for the role of information quality in F-commerce for Bangladesh region, we proposed a theory for making a prediction on F-commerce purchase decision-making approach. First, we tested the relationship between product usefulness evaluation and purchase decision making. After that, we tested the relationships of AQ, SC, TS and PUE with the dependent variable purchase decision (PD). Overall, these three arguments are found strong predictors of consumer purchase decision making. Although the findings provide meaningful implications, future studies should address several limitations. First, AQ, SC, and TS may not fully reflect the overall central and peripheral cues. Further study could add other cues. Second, the present study found that age and gender are not significant control variables of the purchase decision. The future study will be conducted on more features for better understanding by integrating the predictors of techno stress [56], perceived enjoyment of purchasing online [57] and security issues [58].

Acknowledgments. The research investigation was organized by the assist of the Software Engineering department, Daffodil International University. This examination has been guided based on thesis dissertation [59] under the supervision of Dr. Imran Mahmud. We have developed our proposed models at Cyber Security Center (CSC) laboratory. Cyber Security Center (CSC) is a one of the potential research labs of Daffodil International University.

References

1. Obar, J.A., Wildman, S.: Social media definition and the governance challenge: an introduction to the special issue. Telecommun. Policy **39**(9), 745–750 (2015)
2. Alexa Internet Inc., facebook.com Traffic Statistics. https://www.alexa.com/siteinfo/facebook.com. Accessed 10 May 2018
3. Leong, L.Y., Jaafar, N.I., Ainin, S.: Understanding Facebook commerce (f-commerce) actual purchase from an artificial neural network perspective. J. Electron. Commer. Res. **19**(1), 75–103 (2018)

4. Molinillo, S., Cabanillas, F.L., Sánchez, R.A.: A social commerce intention model for traditional e-commerce sites. J. Theor. Appl. Electron. Commer. Res. **13**(2), 80–93 (2018)
5. Sukrat, S., Mahatanankoon, P., Papasratorn, B.: The driving forces of C2C social commerce in Thailand: a developing framework. In: 9th International Conference on Advances in Information Technology, pp. 108–118. KnE Social Sciences, Bangkok (2017)
6. Wu, Y.L., Li, E.: Marketing mix, customer value, and customer loyalty in social commerce. Internet Res. **28**(1), 74–104 (2018)
7. Chen, J.V., Su, B., Widjaja, A.E.: Facebook C2C social commerce: a study of online impulse buying. Decis. Support Syst. **83**, 57–69 (2016)
8. Mahmud, F.: Daily Bangladesh Post, f-commerce on rise in Bangladesh (2017). http://www.thebangladeshpost.com/supplement/13991/pdf. Accessed 5 Jan 2018
9. Zabeen, M., Ara, H., Sarwar, N.: F-commerce in Bangladesh: "Venit, Vidit, Vicit". IOSR J. Hum. Soc. Sci. **17**(5), 1–08 (2013)
10. Ahmed, Z.: Effectiveness of Facebook marketing in startup business. A perspective on Harriken.com Limited. Internship report (BUS 400), BRAC University (2013)
11. Xu, X., Yao, Z.: Understanding the role of argument quality in the adoption of online reviews: an empirical study integrating value-based decision and needs theory. Online Inf. Rev. **39**(7), 885–902 (2015)
12. McGuire, G.M., Bielby, W.T.: The variable effects of tie strength and social resources. Work. Occup. **43**(1), 38–74 (2016)
13. Todd, P.R., Melancon, J.: Gender and live-streaming: source credibility and motivation. J. Res. Interact. Mark. **12**(1), 79–89 (2018)
14. Hügi, J., Schneider, R.: Building an online environment for usefulness evaluation. In: Aalberg, T., Papatheodorou, C., Dobreva, M., Tsakonas, G., Farrugia, Charles J. (eds.) TPDL 2013. LNCS, vol. 8092, pp. 366–369. Springer, Heidelberg (2013). https://doi.org/10.1007/978-3-642-40501-3_38
15. Hanaysha, J.R.: An examination of the factors affecting consumer's purchase decision in the Malaysian retail market. PSU Res. Rev. **2**(1), 7–29 (2018)
16. Wang, Y.: Information adoption model, a review of the literature. J. Econ. Bus. Manag. **4**(1), 618–622 (2016)
17. Taherdoost, H.: A review of technology acceptance and adoption models and theories. J. Econ. Bus. Manag. **22**, 960–967 (2018)
18. Zhu, D.H., Chang, Y.P., Luo, J.J.: Understanding the influence of C2C communication on purchase decision in online communities from a perspective of information adoption model. Telematics Inform. **33**(1), 8–16 (2016)
19. Avkiran, N.K.: Rise of the partial least squares structural equation modeling: an application in banking. In: Avkiran, N., Ringle, C. (eds.) Partial Least Squares Structural Equation Modeling. International Series in Operations Research & Management Science, vol. 267, pp. 1–29. Springer, Cham (2018). https://doi.org/10.1007/978-3-319-71691-6_1
20. Sarstedt, M., Mitchell, R., Gudergan, S. P.: Partial least squares structural equation modeling in HRM research. Int. J. Hum. Resour. Manag. (2018)
21. Lin, H.F.: The impact of website quality dimensions on customer satisfaction in the B2C E-commerce context. Total. Qual. Manag. Bus. Excel. **18**(4), 363–378 (2007)
22. Ramli, R., Bakar, A.A., Ismail, R., Aziz, N.: The trust effect towards online seller in social commerce. In: 6th International Conference on Computing and Informatics (ICOCI), Kuala Lumpur, Paper No. 030, pp. 317–322 (2017)
23. Hajli, M.N.: A study of the impact of social media on consumers. Int. J. Mark. Res. **56**(3), 387–404 (2014)
24. Leong, L.Y., Jaafar, N.I., Ainin, S.: The effects of Facebook browsing and usage intensity on impulse purchase in f-commerce. Comput. Hum. Behav. **78**, 160–173 (2018)

25. Choshin, M., Ghaffari, A.: An investigation of the impact of effective factors on the success of e-commerce in small-and medium-sized companies. Comput. Hum. Behav. **66**, 67–74 (2017)
26. Zuo, W., Huang, Q., Fan, C., Zhang, Z.: Quality management of B2C ecommerce service based on human factors engineering. Electron. Commer. Res. Appl. **12**(5), 309–320 (2013)
27. Chen, A., Lu, Y., Wang, B.: Customers' purchase decision-making process in social commerce: a social learning perspective. Int. J. Inf. Manag. **37**(6), 627–638 (2017)
28. Quigley, J., Walls, L., Demirel, G., MacCarthy, B., Parsa, M.: Supplier quality improvement: the value of information under uncertainty. Eur. J. Oper. Res. **264**(3), 932–947 (2017)
29. Chen, X., Huang, Q., Davison, R.M.: The role of website quality and social capital in building buyers' loyalty. Int. J. Inf. Manag. **37**(1), 1563–1574 (2017)
30. Shin, S.Y., Van Der Heide, B., Beyea, D., Dai, Y.N., Prchal, B.: Investigating moderating roles of goals, reviewer similarity, and self-disclosure on the effect of argument quality of online consumer reviews on attitude formation. Comput. Hum. Behav. **76**, 218–226 (2017)
31. Ge, M., Helfert, M.: A review of information quality research - develop a research agenda. In: 12th International Conference on Information Quality, pp. 76–91. MIT, Cambridge (2007)
32. Sussman, S.W., Siegal, W.S.: Informational influence in organizations: an integrated approach to knowledge adoption. Inf. Syst. Res. **14**(1), 47–65 (2003)
33. Tang, J., Sun, Y., Yang, S., Sun, Y.: Revisit the information adoption model by exploring the moderating role of tie strength: a perspective from construal level theory. In: Pacific Asia Conference on Information Systems (PACIS), paper no. 352. Semantic Scholar, Taiwan (2016)
34. Libai, B., et al.: Customer-to-customer interactions: broadening the scope of word of mouth research. J. Serv. Res. **13**(3), 267–282 (2010)
35. Yoon, C., et al.: Cognition, persuasion and decision making in older consumers. Telemat. Inform. **16**(3–4), 429–441 (2005)
36. Lautiainen, T.: Factors affecting consumers' buying decision in the selection of a coffee brand. Bachelor's thesis, Faculty of Business Administration, Saimaa University of Applied Sciences (2015)
37. Petty, R.E., Cacioppo, J.T.: The elaboration likelihood model of persuasion. Adv. Exp. Soc. Psychol. **19**, 123–205 (1986)
38. Afolabi, I.T., Oladipupo, O.O., Worlu, R.E.K., Akinyemi, I.O.: A systematic review of consumer behaviour prediction studies. Covenant. J. Bus. Soc. Sci. **7**(1), 41–60 (2016)
39. Dholakia, U.M., Bagozzi, R.P., Pearo, L.K.: A social influence model of consumer participation in network-and small-group-based virtual communities. Int. J. Res. Mark. **21**(3), 241–263 (2004)
40. Andreassen, T.W., Streukens, S.: Service innovation and electronic word-of-mouth: is it worth listening to? Manag. Serv. Qual. **19**(3), 249–265 (2009)
41. Wang, Y.: Information adoption model, a review of the literature. J. Econ. Bus. Manag. **4**(11), 618–622 (2016)
42. Zou, Y.: Social media review: the impact of social on brand-consumer relationships. In: Kubacki, K. (ed.) Ideas in Marketing: Finding the New and Polishing the Old. DMSPAMS, p. 624. Springer, Cham (2015). https://doi.org/10.1007/978-3-319-10951-0_230
43. Brown, J.J., Reingen, P.H.: Social ties and word-of-mouth referral behavior. J. Consum. Res. **14**(3), 350–362 (1987)
44. Kundu, S., Rajan, S.C.R.: Word of mouth: a literature review. Int. J. Econ. Manag. Sci. **6**(6), 1–9 (2017)

45. Doloto, U., Chen-Burger, Y.H.: A survey of business models in e-Commerce. In: Jezic, G., Howlett, R., Jain, L. (eds.) Agent and Multi-Agent Systems: Technologies and Applications. Smart Innovation, Systems and Technologies, vol. 38, pp. 249–259. Springer, Cham (2015). https://doi.org/10.1007/978-3-319-19728-9_21

46. Hair, J.F., Sarstedt, M., Ringle, C.M., Gudergan, S.P.: Advanced Issues in Partial Least Squares Structural Equation Modeling (PLS-SEM). Sage, Thousand Oaks (2018)

47. Ivanova, O.A., Ivanovab, V.V., Saltanb, A.A.: Likert-scale questionnaires as an educational tool in teaching discrete mathematics. J. Int. J. Math. Educ. Sci. Techno. (2018)

48. Anderson, J.C., Gerbing, D.W.: Structural equation modeling in practice: a review and recommended two-step approach. Psychol. Bull. 103(3), 411–423 (1988)

49. Wood, M.: Bootstrapping Confidence Levels for Hypotheses About Regression Models. University of Portsmouth Business School, Portland Street (2012)

50. Person, K.: A descriptive analysis of demographic characteristics and their influence on student attendance at programming board events. Educational Administration: Theses, dissertations, and Student Research 69 (2011)

51. Cheung, G.W., Wang, C.: Current approaches for assessing convergent and discriminant validity with SEM: issues and solutions. In: Academy of Management Proceedings, vol. 2017, no. (1), p. 12706 (2017)

52. Bacon, D.R., Sauer, P.L., Young, M.: Composite reliability in structural equations modeling. Educ. Psychol. Meas. 55(3), 394–406 (1995)

53. Sharma, P., Sharma, P., Nage, P., Bafna, D., Salvi, V.: Analyzing effect of structural equation modeling (SEM) approach in e-Commerce. IOSR J. Eng. (IOSRJEN) 7, 05–08 (2018)

54. Lakens, D.: Equivalence tests: a practical primer for t tests, correlations, and meta-analyses. Soc. Psychol. Pers. Sci. 8(4), 355–362 (2017)

55. Selya, A.S., Rose, J.S., Dierker, L.C., Hedeker, D., Mermelstein, R.J.: A practical guide to calculating Cohen's f^2, a measure of local effect size, from PROC MIXED. Front. Psychol. 3, Article 111 (2012)

56. Mahmud, I., Ramayah, T., Kurnia, S.: To use or not to use: Modelling end user grumbling as user resistance in pre-implementation stage of enterprise resource planning system. Inf. Syst. 69, 164–179 (2017)

57. Alzahrani, A.I., Mahmud, I., Ramayah, T., Alfarraj, O., Alalwan, N.: Extending the theory of planned behavior (TPB) to explain online game playing among Malaysian undergraduate students. Telemat. Inform. 34(4), 239–251 (2017)

58. Mahmud, I., Ramayah, T., Nayeem, M.M.H., Islam, S.M., Gan, P.L.: Modelling cyber-crime protection behaviour among computer users in the context of Bangladesh. In: Design Solutions for User-Centric Information Systems, pp. 253–273. IGI Global. (2017)

59. Haque, R.: The role of information quality in f-Commerce. Master's thesis, Department of Software Engineering, Daffodil International University (2017)

What Should I Wear Today? An IoT–Based Dress Assistant for the e–Society

Javier Gomez[1,2(✉)]

[1] Norwegian University of Science and Technology, Trondheim, Norway
javier.escribano@ntnu.no
[2] Universidad Autónoma de Madrid, Madrid, Spain
jg.escribano@uam.es

Abstract. Technology is turning into an augmentation of our memory and an invisible assistant in our daily lives. These issues arise many challenges but also opportunities for researchers, developers and even, final users. In this paper we present an example of this revolution, through an example of an Internet of Things (IoT) based smart shoe cabinet. Besides the assistance provided for different collectives with special needs, this prototype represent the new opportunities on data management and consumer profiling that these technologies already provide.

Keywords: IoT · Recommender system · Ubiquitous Computing
Assistive technologies · Human–computer interaction

1 Introduction

The Ubiquitous Computing term was coined by Mark Weiser in 1991 [25]. From that moment on, many problems and opportunities have arisen from that vision of a world rich in information and interaction. Ambient intelligence environments (also called smart environments) are one of the fields where Ubiquitous Computing can be naturally applied. We can define an active environment as a space limited by physical barriers, which is capable to sense and interact with its inhabitants.

These environments range from smart rooms to smart cities [3] and are equipped with different technologies. In the recent years, the society has experience an immersion on these technologies, under the umbrella term of Internet Of the Things (IoT) [13]. The arise of IoT came together with the corresponding use of massive data and analysis for different purposes, such as health [14], education [11], urban design [22] or business [10].

In parallel to the emerge of IoT, data–driven business models [7] arose as a result of the increasing number of data sources, such as social networks or mobile and wearable devices. New services, and their success, relies on deep data analysis of consumers' preferences and habits. Many of the most popular online commerce portals record user interaction, ask the user directly and rely on users' comments and valuations to improve their marketing campaigns, product recommendations and cross selling [9].

These examples suggest a direct relation and trend on distributed sensing and customised services (for example, in health or business opportunities). The more

© IFIP International Federation for Information Processing 2018
Published by Springer Nature Switzerland AG 2018. All Rights Reserved
S. A. Al-Sharhan et al. (Eds.): I3E 2018, LNCS 11195, pp. 255–263, 2018.
https://doi.org/10.1007/978-3-030-02131-3_23

information and more accurate data we have from the users, the more customised services and products we can offer to them.

In this paper we present an example of IoT device to address these different objectives. Particularly, we designed and developed a prototype of an IoT–based shoe cabinet that provides a smart service to help users choose the most appropriate shoes in order to: first, help users in their daily lives basic activities. Second, track users health by means of direct monitoring of their selection and use of different shoes and finally, provide an example of a service for brands to understand and measure users habits, preferences and narrow their targets.

Moreover, these systems, such as smart assistants, are conceived as assistive technologies for people with disabilities in many occasions. For example, dress selection relies on social conventions but, for some collectives, these conventions are not clear and then need support to choose appropriate clothes regarding the occasion. Although it may seem as a trivial task, they are usually trained on them at home but also in education centres, due to the relation of social skills and inclusion. Particularly, this is very important for job training. Being active in the job market and economically independent are key for autonomy [23].

Therefore, there seems to be a fruitful niche in which different collectives may benefit: people with or without disabilities, but also clothing companies, through the study of the data collected. As an example, in this paper we present a smart shoe cabinet that recommend (and register) the most appropriate pair of shoes to the user, regarding different variables.

This paper is organised as follows: in Sect. 2 we review the current state of the art and the related technologies. After that, in Sect. 3 we present the design and development process of the system. Finally, in Sect. 4 we discuss the possibilities that this type of system offer and future implications.

2   Related Work

Do-It-Yourself (DIY) approaches and IoT solutions are becoming popular. Probe of that is the market that arose among these technologies [18]. However, there is still a limited number of studies addressing the challenges and opportunities from different perspectives and for different collectives.

If we focus on smart dress systems, many of the solutions in the market are limited in terms of the technologies involved but also the target population addressed. For example, there are multiple applications for smartphones, such as "I style my self" [1], which allows the user to register her clothes and tag them (colour, occasion, preference). Based on this information, the system provides different outfits to inspire the user. Or "Whatoweather" [2], which provides outfit inspiration based on the weather at the user's location and current trends. However, it does not take into consideration the available clothes of the user. In contrast, "Stylebook" [4] allows users to register their clothes, but the recommendations are based on previous selections and trends. It also includes a calendar to plan the outfit. Another example was presented in [17]. This system uses advanced computer vision techniques to detect colours and Analytic Hierarchy Process (AHP) to provide intelligent recommendations. Finally,

"MyDressRecommender" [19] is a smartphone application that registers user's clothes and provides recommendations based on them, the weather and the agenda of the user. It was initially designed to help people with cognitive disabilities.

Although the number of smart wardrobes reported in the literature is limited, we can find interesting projects, such as HBar [24], a combination of smart garments and hangers that aim to make the management and maintenance of a smart wardrobe easier. The work provides a great view of the challenges around the topic, such as costs and reliability. These two factors seem to be the most decisive issues to address when developing IoT systems.

Finally, one recent contribution is an assistive technology solution to help people with dementia, presented in [6]. This system helps the user to pick the clothes and guides her to put them on properly. To do that, a special cabinet equipped with different sensors, a Kinect camera and an iPad was designed and developed. Besides, thanks to the use of visual marks, the system can check and help in the dressing process, as it is able to track the user and the clothes.

3   An IoT–Based Smart Shoe Cabinet

Shoe selection is influenced by different factors, such as the weather, the activities that will take place during the day (and the social conventions around it) and personal preferences. In order to facilitate users to make the decision, we designed and developed a prototype of a smart shoe cabinet. Following the idea of the "Ambient Umbrella" [20], that provides visual–light feedback in case of rain, we augmented a regular shoe cabinet by including sensors and actuators, as well as a recommender system. The experience is based on subtle interaction [12] and DIY technologies.

3.1   System Architecture

The system is modular and easily expandable. It is based on a client–server architecture and communication with third party services. A sketch of the architecture is included in Fig. 1. The server is unique in the system, while clients can be a varied number of shoe boxes that are organised in show cabinets.

All the modules communicate over a regular WiFi network, so no extra infrastructure nor wiring is needed, rather than the power cord.

1. **Server**: it is the main component of the system. It has different modules in order to address the different tasks, including the management tool, the recommendation engine, connection to third party services and communication with the shoe boxes.
2. **Shoe cabinet**: understood as a piece of furniture to store shoes. It is composed of one or more shoe boxes. This logic level in the architecture allows the server to arrange the shoe boxes for different users or locations.
3. **Shoe box**: it is the unit of the system, either from the logic point of view and also from the physical. Each box is autonomous, this is, contains all the hardware to sensor the user interaction, provide the feedback and communicate with the server.

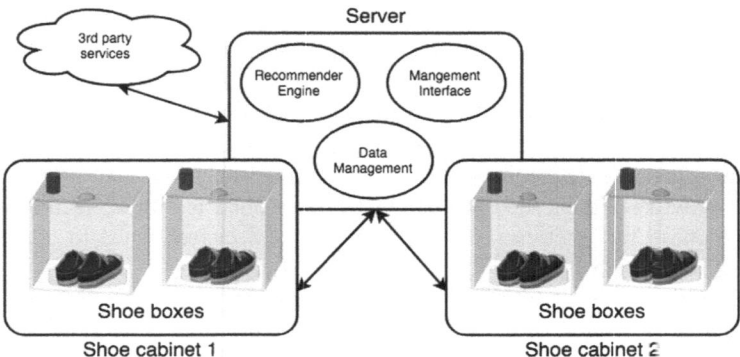

Fig. 1. System architecture schema.

4. **Third party services**: the weather forecast and calendar events are outsourced to popular external services.

3.2 Hardware Components

One of the main problems related to the acceptance of new technologies is the price. In order to address this possible limitation, we opted to use open and low cost components, such as Arduino and Raspberry Pi.

Therefore, we developed the server using a Raspberry Pi Model 3. This small computer has enough computational capabilities to execute all the modules and store the data. Its reduced price, but its varied possibilities and ports, turned it into a popular computer for different purposes. It is widely used in different contexts such as education [15], making [8] and even assistive technologies [5].

On the other hand, shoe boxes are based on commercial systems to storage shoes, augmented with technology. Every one contains the minimal hardware to operate. A picture of the prototype and the different technology pieces added to it can be found in Fig. 2. As can be seen in the Figure, all the hardware and wiring has been hidden as much as possible and installed so shoe boxes can be piled.

Fig. 2. Front and back view of the augmented shoe box

- **NFC reader**: shoes are identified by a NFC tag stuck on them. These stickers are cheap, can be stuck inside the shoe, under the insole without disturbing the user and allows the system to identify which shoe ID is stored in the box. This way, users can put any pair of shoes on any empty box, without registering additional information or keeping an order. The NFC reader is hidden on the bottom part of the box, so there is no risk of breaking it when putting the shoes inside.
- **Distance sensor**: a distance sensor installed on the top of the box allows the system to detect user interacting with the box. This is, when the user is getting a pair of shoes or putting them inside, and trigger the recommender system if necessary.
- **RGB LED–strip**: the recommendation is provided by means of a subtle and straightforward notification system, based on light colours. Red is to notify the user that the shoes she is taking are not recommended. Yellow, when the pair of shoes are not the best according to the context and green to notify her about the most appropriate ones. To provide these different notification colours, and RGB LED–strip is installed on the top of the box.
- **Switch sensor**: one of the boxes of the cabinet is equipped with an additional sensor (switch type) to detect user intention of interaction. It can be a light sensor or a magnetic switch that detects when the door of the wardrobe is opened. It is used as the trigger of the system.
- **Microcontroller**: every shoe box is autonomous thanks to the microcontroller with network capabilities installed on each one. It is in charge of all the tasks related to the box, this is, detecting using interaction and informing the server, turn on and off the LED strip according to the server's instructions and reading the shoes ID through the NFC reader and tag.

3.3   Data Model

In order to provide a functional and extendable example of system, both users and shoes were modelled in the system as related entities. Moreover, data registries, past recommendations and user actions are also modelled and stored in the database, so future analysis may be possible, in order to extract user preferences and patterns of usage.

The most important feature of users is the location. With that information the system can query weather services to provide an accurate recommendation. Besides, users configuration is also stored. Apart from user name and password, the system stores a "proactivity" flag for each user. This is, if the flag is active, the system will show the recommendation as soon as the user triggers the system (for example, by opening the door of the wardrobe where the shoe boxes are stored). In contrast, if the flag is not active, the system will wait for the user to interact (put the hand into one of the boxes to take a pair of shoes) to provide the feedback with the recommendation.

Shoes are modelled including the features that the recommender system needs to make the suggestion: the appropriate weather conditions to wear the shoes such as temperature (a range) and the weather (rainy/snowy/sunny, etc.) and the type of events in which the shoes can be worn, such as sports, formal events, work, etc. In this case, this attribute is a 3–tuplet, as there can be stored up to three different type of events (a list of priorities) for which the shoes are appropriate. Besides, the shoes' model also include a short description (for example, to provide the brand and the model or the colour), the NFC ID saved on the sticker and the availability.

To make the management task easier, a web–based interface is provided to users. Through this tool, they can add, remove or edit the shoes registered in the system, as well as analyse the system's logs.

3.4 Recommender System

The recommender system provides feedback to the user regarding the most appropriate pair of shoes for the day, considering the weather and the events on the user's agenda. Besides, every recommendation include, when possible, two pairs of shoes that fit the requirements, so we provide an extra variable to take part in the recommendation: user's preferences.

The engine is based on a decision tree and penalties. In this scenario, only shoes with active available flags are computed, and they are assigned a starting value of 0. After that, and according to the criteria, they receive different penalties. Once the criteria is applied, the shoes are sorted and the ones with lower values are selected. This schema is extracted and adapted from [19].

The first characteristic to evaluate is the event tag. With this computation we evaluate to what extend does the shoes fit the social conventions for the event, if the user has any on the day's agenda. The following penalties are applied in this case:

+0 if the type of the agenda event matches the 1st on the shoe's events list.
+4 if the type of the agenda event matches the 2nd on the shoe's events list.
+10 if the type of the agenda event matches the 3rd on the shoe's events list.
+25 if the type of the agenda event is not listed on the shoe's events list.

The second characteristic included in the computation is the temperature. In this case, the penalty depends on the difference between the suitable temperature range for the shoe and the expected temperature during the day:

+0 if the temperature is in the range of the shoes.
+5 if the temperature is in the range of the shoes ± 1 °C.
+7 if the temperature is in the range of the shoes ± 2 °C.
+11 if the temperature is in the range of the shoes ± 3 °C.
+25 if the temperature is in the range of the shoes ± 4 °C.

The third criteria is the weather. In this case we try to penalty wrong decisions, such as wearing summer shoes in a snowy day. Therefore, the scoring system is:

+0 if the weather is the weather of the shoes.
+2 if the weather is "rainy" and the shoes are for "snowy" weather.
+2 if the weather is "snowy" and the shoes are for "rainy" weather.
+4 in other case.

4   Challenges and Opportunities

As mentioned before, DIY technologies are opening a market to new customers and services. Besides, they usually offer customisation options, as users are the end point of the fabrication process. This may arise interest on users who need some adaptation or customisation, but they can not afford ad–hoc developments.

In this sense, a system like the smart shoe cabinet presented in this paper would help people with special needs, by providing them cues to dress appropriately for the weather and the social conventions related to their events. This additional level of independence may impact on their daily lives and contribute to self–realisation, as it is usually trained in the family and labour training centres. This distributed assistance, in combination with registries and analysis may increase the autonomy of the user to levels that were difficult to reach previously, due to the need of continuous supervision of the caregiver.

On the other hand, this system can also impact on the health of the user. It is widely known and reported the need of wearing the appropriate shoes and change them often. Wearing the same shoes every day may produce inflammation, injuries, feet pain, shoe deformation and shoe–life decrease. Therefore, a proactive system that include historical usage on their recommendations may lead to a healthier use of the shoes.

Finally, accurate user profiling and usage patterns discovery are two of the most important topics in marketing nowadays. Therefore, a sensor that would provide precise user preferences and habits may be also interesting for companies in order to target an specific population and run market studies.

Regarding the challenges, one of the most important issues that may arise is the privacy of the user. As long as technologies evolve, users are more aware of their privacy and, thus, Governments try to protect them with new laws and standards. In this sense, data has to be anonymised from the core of the system and shared information should be restricted. Moreover, users rights to read, edit or erase their information have to be granted. However, this collecting data on shoe preferences and usage is not a new issue. Mobile apps such as Nike+ [16] or Runtastic [21] already offer the option to record this information and they use it also as an input for rewards.

5   Conclusions and Future Work

In this paper we have presented the opportunities that IoT developments present to the e–Society, by means of an example of a smart shoe cabinet system. These approaches, based on open and reduced price technologies, as well as being conceived as Do-It-Yourself projects, illustrate the opportunities that may arise to help, know and improve people lives. Additionally, the collection of massive data may produce a valuable source of information for brands to study and know users' preferences and habits, opening another window to provide personalised market strategies (marketing, offers, etc.).

However, the paper only include the conception and development of a first prototype. For further iterations, a participatory design process and evaluation will take place, addressing the open questions that arose in this work.

Acknowledgements. This project has been carried out during the ternure of an ERCIM "Alain Bensoussan" fellow and partially funded by the project "eMadrid-CM: Investigación y Desarrollo de Tecnologías Educativas en la Comunidad de Madrid" (S2013/ICE-2715). The authors would like to acknowledge the support provided by the student Miguel A. Serrando during the design and development process.

References

1. I style myself (2018). http://www.istylemyself.com/. Accessed 18 June 2018
2. 4gotas & ZIBLEC: Whatoweather (2018). https://play.google.com/store/apps/details?id=com.ziblec.wtw. Accessed 18 June 2018
3. Augusto, J.C., Nakashima, H., Aghajan, H.: Ambient intelligence and smart environments: a state of the art. In: Nakashima, H., Aghajan, H., Augusto J.C. (eds.) Handbook of Ambient Intelligence and Smart Environments, pp. 3–31. Springer, Boston, MA (2010)
4. Left brain/Right brain: Stylebook (2018). http://www.stylebookapp.com/. Accessed 18 June 2018
5. Brennan, C.P., McCullagh, P.J., Galway, L., Lightbody, G.: Promoting autonomy in a smart home environment with a smarter interface. In: 2015 37th Annual International Conference of the IEEE Engineering in Medicine and Biology Society (EMBC), pp. 5032–5035. IEEE (2015)
6. Burleson, W., Lozano, C., Ravishankar, V., Lee, J., Mahoney, D.: An assistive technology system that provides personalized dressing support for people living with dementia: capability study. JMIR Med. Inform. 6(2), e21 (2018). https://doi.org/10.2196/medinform. 5587. Parra-Calderón, C.L. (ed.)
7. Chen, H., Chiang, R., Storey, V.: Business intelligence and analytics: from big data to big impact. MIS Q. 36(4), 1165–1188 (2012). http://www.jstor.org/stable/41703503
8. Cohen, J.: Maker principles and technologies in teacher education: a national survey. J. Technol. Teacher Educ. 25(1), 5–30 (2017)
9. Danescu-Niculescu-Mizil, C., Kossinets, G., Kleinberg, J., Lee, L.: How opinions are received by online communities: a case study on amazon. com helpfulness votes. In: Proceedings of the 18th International Conference on World Wide Web, pp. 141–150. ACM (2009)
10. Dijkman, R.M., Sprenkels, B., Peeters, T., Janssen, A.: Business models for the internet of things. Int. J. Inf. Manage. 35(6), 672–678 (2015)
11. Divitini, M., Giannakos, M.N., Mora, S., Papavlasopoulou, S., Iversen, O.S.: Make2learn with IoT: engaging children into joyful design and making of interactive connected objects. In: Proceedings of the 2017 Conference on Interaction Design and Children, pp. 757–760. ACM (2017)
12. García-Herranz, M., Olivera, F., Haya, P., Alamán, X.: Harnessing the interaction continuum for subtle assisted living. Sensors 12(7), 9829–9846 (2012)
13. Gubbi, J., Buyya, R., Marusic, S., Palaniswami, M.: Internet of things (IoT): A vision, architectural elements, and future directions. Fut. Gener. Comput. Syst. 29(7), 1645–1660 (2013)
14. Islam, S.R., Kwak, D., Kabir, M.H., Hossain, M., Kwak, K.S.: The internet of things for health care: a comprehensive survey. IEEE Access 3, 678–708 (2015)
15. Jamieson, P., Herdtner, J.: More missing the boatarduino, raspberry pi, and small prototyping boards and engineering education needs them. In: Frontiers in Education Conference (FIE), 2015 IEEE, pp. 1–6. IEEE (2015)

16. Nike: Nike+ Run Club (2018). https://itunes.apple.com/us/app/nike-runclub/id387771637? mt=8. Accessed 18 June 2018
17. Peifeng, H., Yuzhe, C., Jingping, S., Zhaomu, H.: Smart wardrobe system based on android platform. In 2016 IEEE International Conference on Cloud Computing and Big Data Analysis (ICCCBDA), pp. 279–285. IEEE (2016)
18. Perera, C., Liu, C.H., Jayawardena, S., Chen, M.: A survey on internet of things from industrial market perspective. IEEE Access **2**, 1660–1679 (2014)
19. Rojo Carracedo, J.A.: MyDressRecommender: un asistente de vestimenta Android para personas con limitaciones cognitivas. Master's thesis (2013)
20. Rose, D.: Enchanted Objects: Design, Human Desire, and the Internet of Things. Simon and Schuster (2014)
21. Runtastic: Runtastic pro (2018). https://www.runtastic.com/. Accessed 18 June 2018
22. Sanchez, L., et al.: Smartsantander: IoT experimentation over a smart city testbed. Comput. Netw. **61**, 217–238 (2014)
23. Taylor, J.L., Hodapp, R.M.: Doing nothing: adults with disabilities with no daily activities and their siblings. Am. J. Intellect. Dev. Disabil. **117**(1), 67–79 (2012)
24. Toney, A.P., Thomas, B.H., Marais, W.: Managing smart garments. In: 2006 10th IEEE International Symposium on Wearable Computers, pp. 91–94. IEEE (2006)
25. Weiser, M.: The computer for the 21st century. Mob. Comput. Commun. Rev. **3**(3), 3–11 (1999)

Generic Business Process Model for SMEs in M-Commerce Based on Talabat's Case Study

Fadi Safieddine[1]([⊠]) and Imad Nakhoul[2]

[1] School of Business and Management, Queen Mary, University of London,
Mile End Campus, Mile End Road, London E1 4NS, UK
F.Safieddine@qmul.ac.uk
[2] Nakhoul Corporation sarl Zouk Mikael, Boustany Center 182, Zouk, Lebanon
imad.nakhoul@nakhoulcorp.com

Abstract. SMEs face a variety of challenges in their attempts to keep up with the cyber revolution, even though SMEs are a major part of the world economy. In a previous publication, the authors established that 'B2C' model does not accurately represent or support SMEs in M-Commerce. Instead, the authors reviewed SMEs and SME supporting apps from mobile app marketplaces and suggested a model called 'B2i2C'. In this model, the 'i', in the form of intermediary business entity are playing a vital role in SMEs breakthrough into M-Commerce. Following on, this paper reviews business processes to generate a generic model adaptable to a variety of SME related products and services. This paper presents the case study of Talabat, one of the most successful GCC e-business models that supports SMEs to have come out from Kuwait. The information collected from online resources, student placements and feedback from operation managers attempt to emulate the business process model for a variety of 'B2i2C' business models. The generic model is then tested against three different scenarios to identify the level of similarity. The results demonstrate a high degree of adaptability of the model and a major opportunity to explore in the area of SME supporting app in M-Commerce.

Keywords: M-Commerce · SME · E-commerce · Disruptive business model BPMN · Business model · B2i2C

1 Introduction

M-Commerce is a method of trading online using wireless mobile devices [1] that has witnessed a revolution in recent years. However, mobile technology has its characteristics, challenges, and restrictions [2]. Businesses interested in having an Internet presence, have several choices. They can have informative websites which provide information related to their products and services with no direct selling or buying involved. Informative websites option remains fairly inexpensive. It is only when a business is making that switch to M-Commerce that we see a substantial increase in costs and challenges. Despite that, there are significant opportunities that exist in Mcommerce for a variety of businesses mainly focused on sales growth. With that, new

S. A. Al-Sharhan et al. (Eds.): I3E 2018, LNCS 11195, pp. 264–278, 2018.
https://doi.org/10.1007/978-3-030-02131-3_24

and disruptive business models [3] continue to outstrip other areas of E-commerce [4]. In moving on towards the M-Commerce business model, companies have the option to adapt their existing website to mobiles or to create an app that they can market through one of the key market app stores. Unlike the traditional approach of downloading applications by searching online, mobile application stores provided assurances and trust in the content that resulted in a boom in mobile downloads and M-Commerce [5]. The same cannot be said about Web-based M-Commerce which has had some limited success [6] as mainly informative. From a consumer point of view, individual Small-to-Medium Enterprise (SME) apps are hard to find, they come with an added cost associated with limited device space, and time spent comparing products/services. Therefore, consumers are reluctant to download individual SME apps for the purpose of comparison or otherwise. So, the real business prospect for SMEs in M-Commerce has come from the opportunities to be involved in new business models resulting in some cases in major successes [7]. A new business model involving intermediaries [8, 9] as well as Mass Customizations [10]. Together, these two models are considered to have a strong bearing in encouraging SME businesses to adopt an M-Commerce initiative. Evidently, there are opportunities for improvements and expansion to new SME related product and services. However, there has been little or no academic documentation to conceptualise the business process model for a successful SMEs supporting app in M-Commerce. This paper examines the case study of Talabat, one of the most successful SME supporting apps in the Middle East to develop a generic business process model for B2i2C that can be tested.

2   Literature Review

SMEs can have several different definitions depending on the region. Most popular definition suggests that an SME is a business that employs 250 or fewer people [11]. In the EU alone, SME represents more than 99% of businesses [12]. With a study by the World Bank Group suggesting that almost 90% of SMEs employ less than ten individuals [13]. While many SMEs have developed some online presence, a study in 2017 of the UK and Kuwait app market shows very few independent SMEs have been successful in promoting their mobile apps [9]. This comes from the fact that M-Commerce users' needs and expectations vary significantly from E-commerce users resulting in mobile applications being designed differently to E-commerce applications [14]; therefore, presenting real challenges for SMEs. To overcome these challenges, disruptive business models were being experimented to allow SMEs to break into the M-Commerce market.

2.1   M-Commerce Models for SMEs

A review of the literature shows no specific business models for SMEs or SMEs supporting apps bridging brick-and-mortar operations with a successful M-Commerce operation. On the other hand, M-Commerce is a derivative of E-commerce, and thus inherits the seven main types of informational added values [15]. However, M-Commerce has distinctiveness in what is called the Mobile Added Values (MAV) [16]. MAV helps rationalise the challenges we discussed and present a platform for evaluating the adding value and success of M-Commerce for SMEs.

2.2 SMEs and Mass Customisation

Before the advent of app marketplace stores, M-Commerce had some limited success mainly in areas of informational web pages or sales promotion rather than trading. The real potential of M-Commerce was the enabling of individualisation of the application, also called soft customisation, one of the main categories of mass customisation [16]. This specificity allows the apps to adapt to their corresponding devices. It also allowed the user to change the settings of the interface and customise it to their own needs. What is more, the individualisation of the apps allowed better targeting of users with specific content and promotions. On the other hand, Mass Customization goes beyond the experience of the app to the customisation of the product, service, or both. Collectively, SMEs are perfectly fitted to support Mass Customization [17]. According to [18, 19], Mass Customization allows clients' involvement in making individual adjustments to products thus producing altered mass quantities that could be offered to the masses.

Some of the first examples of Mass Customization E-commerce business models were service based comparison websites, such as hotel bookings, holiday sales, and insurance services. These E-commerce models went beyond just sales of packages by allowing users to customise packages based on their individual needs. What distinguished them from M-Commerce SMEs is that they are not geocentric local SME product or service. Mass Customization of products and services presents a competitive advantage in the lucrative online market [20]. Mass Customization business models allowed the reduction of cost and lead time of Mass Production yet tailor output to meet the individual needs of the customer [21, 22]. Technological advancements in Internet communication and M-Commerce has facilitated the transition from Mass Production to Mass Customization [21, 23] and ushered in a new generation of disruptive business models [24]. Despite this distinctive characteristic, SMEs faced a major hurdle in reaching their local M-Commerce audience.

2.3 Disruptive Business Models

The traditional business models of B2C, B2B, C2B, etc. are facing an onslaught of disruptive business models that are changing the landscape of business operations. In the case of mass customisation, these new models are allowing collaborative development between competing businesses to promote customised products and services [25]. An example of such collaborative work is that of the F2b2C model [26]. F2b2C involves businesses (b) acting as intermediaries for factories (F) as they send customised products directly to consumers (C) [27] as shown in Fig. 1. F2b2C represents what some tried to explain as B2B (factory to warehouse), followed by another B2B (intermediary warehouse to business), and finally B2C (business to consumer) [28].

These three models cannot be seen in isolation from each other but rather in an interrelated system since the products are never handled by the intermediary. Instead, these products an services are sent from factory to customer directly [27]. Another model with a specific successful record for SMEs in M-Commerce is B2i2C [9]. In this model, SME are small to medium size businesses (B) who tend to have a niche local exposure at marketing their products or services, (i) are intermediary businesses who provide a platform for comparing products or services with added value, and finally (C) the consumer who is able to compare, customise, and order with assurance of quality and reliability presented by the intermediary source. The role of the intermediary business is specific enough to be given the letter 'i' as it plays a significant role in developing trust through the independent reviews, the reliability of service, and convenience of not having to overload users' devices with apps or depending to some degree on unreliable online searches. Examples of B2i2C include Uber, an international intermediary taxi service app, Seamless, a US intermediary food delivery app, JustEat, a UK intermediary food delivery app, Trivago, international intermediary hotel booking app, Airbnb, an international private holiday home letting, and Talabat, a Kuwaiti startup that quickly became the GCC most successful food ordering app.

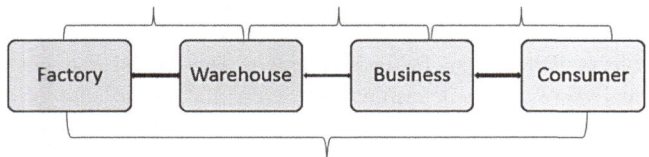

Fig. 1. F2b2C model [27].

2.4 Reflection on the Literature

Given the economic impact of SMEs and the ever-evolving landscape of mobile technologies and wearable technologies, understanding SMEs' supporting apps process model is significantly important. The business models presented in the literature do not provide a complete picture or understanding of the actual processes. These models do not explain the business processes involved in SME supporting apps and how they have helped provide new opportunities for SMEs in M-Commerce. Understanding the business processes will allow a better overview of how SME collaborations work, the importance of a reliable and trusted intermediary, and opportunities to develop these models in other areas where SMEs have struggled to keep up with the mobile commerce revolution. It is evident that B2i2C model is being replicated for a variety of products and services and there remain opportunities for new disruptive business models to be developed for the next generation of entrepreneurs.

3   Research Methodology

To better understand and evaluate the processes involved in B2i2C and specifically the business processes around SMEs supporting apps, the paper aims to use Business Process Modeling (BPMN) tool followed by a cognitive walkthrough of these processes. There are a variety of business process modeling tools in the market; for example Business Process Model and Notation (BPMN), Business Process Flowchart, UML Use case diagram and Activity Diagram, UML EDOC Business Processes, deployment flowchart, IDEF process mapping, Activity-Decision Flow (ADF) Diagram, and EventProcess Chains (EPCs). After the introduction of BPMN in 2004, the model evolved and improved allowing it to achieve standardisation status [29]. According to [30], BPMN has become the most widespread modelling tool to model business processes. Crucial to BPMN success is that the notations are easy to read. Therefore, the model allows easier visualisation of the processes and facilitates discussions among all stakeholders including analysts, developers, and management, while still being able to model intricate processes [31]. According to [32], BPMN success is a testimony to its ability to bridge the gap between business needs for visualising processes and IT needs for representing complex processes. Also, BPMN's many extensions allow a great level of details in areas of security [33], business rules [34], business events [35], and costs analysis [36]. However, it should be noted that in large-scale projects BPMN can be less effective. The model can get complex and difficult to read [37]. We can determine, however, that in the case of modelling the interactions for Talabat, as a generic B2i2C business process, BPMN is a suitable modelling tool to communicate these processes.

To ensure that BPMN is representative of the process, a methodology was devised to collect and cross-reference the information from three sources using a four-step process. First, the team reviewed the information provided online about the process of ordering at Talabat [38, 39]. In addition, Talabat online sources provided key details regarding how SMEs can join and other processes associated with their ordering system. In the second stage, the team reviewed the Business Process Flowchart (BPF) from a graduate student placement. The model, while not perfect, does connect some of the facts associated with internal processes. In the third step, the BPM is cross-referenced and checked with two of Talabat's operation managers. The Talabat managers contacted via LinkedIn verified existing processes to be valid and identified two missing processes. Finally, given all online sources and the improved BPM, the team developed a generic BPMN for B2i2C, and a cognitive walkthrough [40] is done for three examples of SME's business or services. For this paper, the team selected three unique test cases to perform the cognitive walkthroughs: Taxi ordering service, private holiday apartment rentals, and to stress test the diagram, the team selected a random SME service.

4 Outcome

4.1 Talabat's Online Sources

The Talabat website provides some details on how the process of registering SMEs and customers. For SMEs, the join us page explains that the company is the biggest online food ordering service in the GCC, with millions of registered users, and they invest in marketing that benefits the SMEs allowing them to increase their sales. There is also brief information on how the ordering process works [38]:

1. Customers order from Talabat.com using their computers, tablets and smartphones.
2. Customers select their area to find a restaurant that delivers to their area.
3. Customers order from our graphically rich online menus.
4. Customers pay by card or cash on delivery.
5. The restaurant receives orders on Talabat.com Web Linked Application or other seamless communication terminals.

After that, the SME is encouraged to fill a form to get the process of registering their business started.

For customers, the instructions include creating an account, which they can use social media login if they wish, or order without an account using their mobile number and something called 'express checkout' number. They would then select their geographic area and optionally select the cuisine they prefer and then search. For each restaurant, they can view the menu and add items to the cart. For each item, the customer can customise their order by editing the ingredients or the way it is cooked. Then they can enter their address or use the address that is already saved on the app. The customer can then either pay via the app using their credit or debit card or choose to pay cash on delivery. If it is a new phone number that is making the order, Talabat will ring to confirm it is legitimate [38]. The information on the website also includes a variety of tips on how to use Talabat services and cases where the customer may not be satisfied with the service or product. The website, however, does not explain how the data is handled after the order is collected other than indicating that as soon as the order is placed, the restaurant is instantly informed. This suggests that the communication is done electronically and consistent with the information presented to the SMEs that they will be informed "Web Linked Application or other seamless communication terminals."

4.2 Generating the Business Process Flowchart

Figures 2 and 3 represent the BPF process collected from online research and student's placement at Talabat. The model represents an example of an intermediary business entity. To keep the process generic, we will refer to Talabat as the intermediary and the business interested in joining as the SME.

While Figs. 2 and 3. explains a significant part of the process, these remains based on secondary sources. To verify these details, the team received feedback from two of Talabat's operational managers who indicated that the process is missing the registration, delivery information process, and the routing methods to the vendors. By

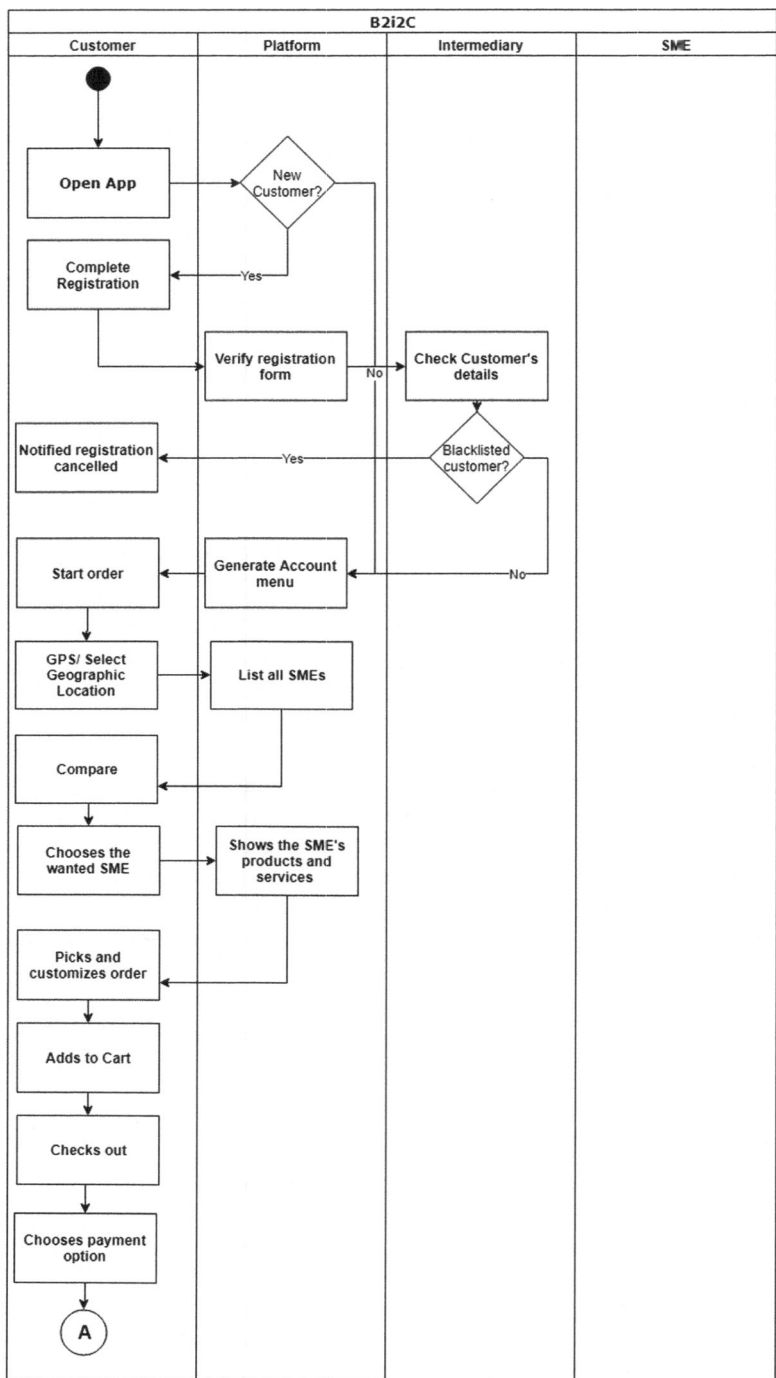

Fig. 2. Phase 1: business process Flowchart for Talabat.

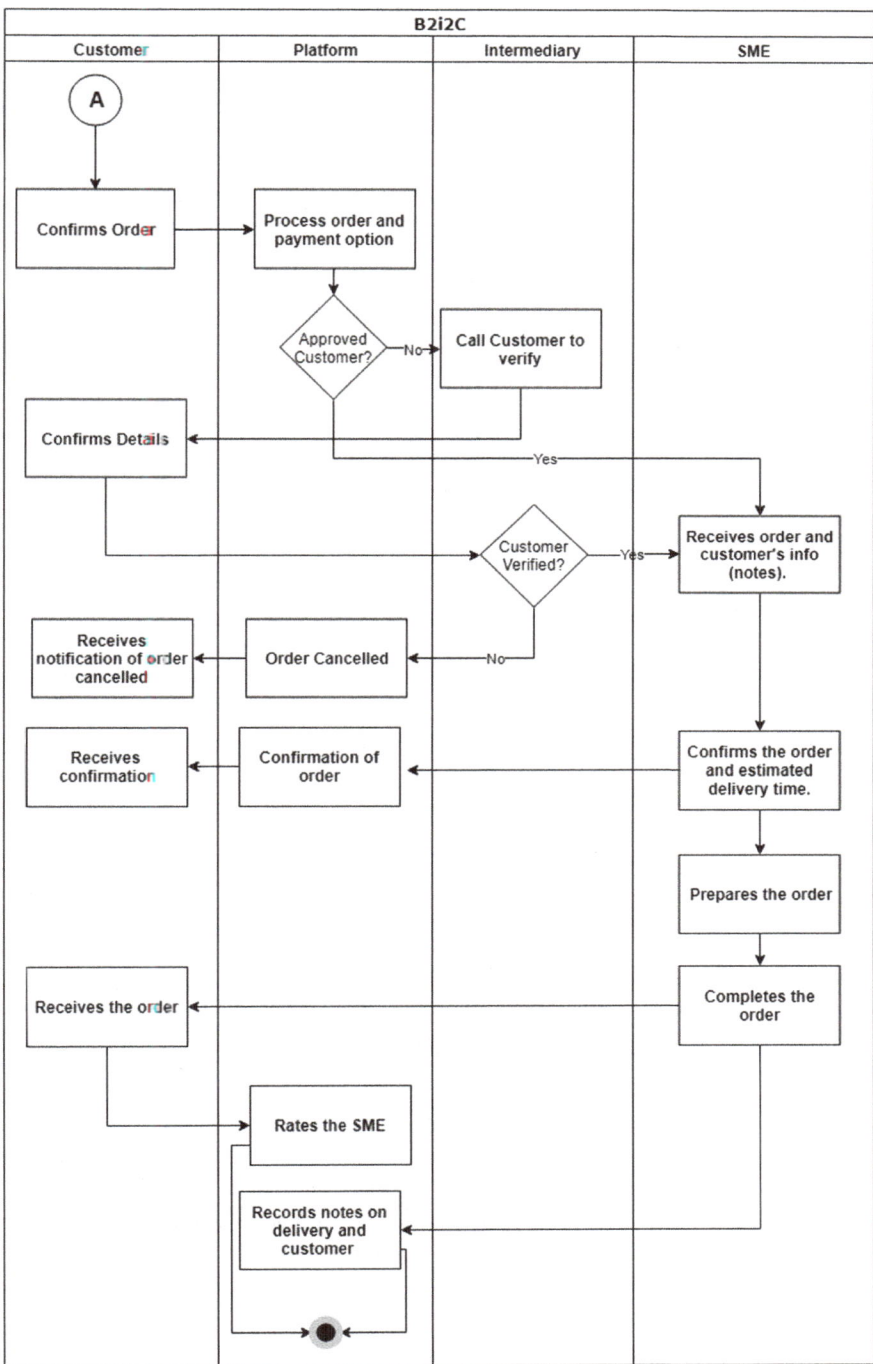

Fig. 3. Phase 2: business process Flowchart for Talabat.

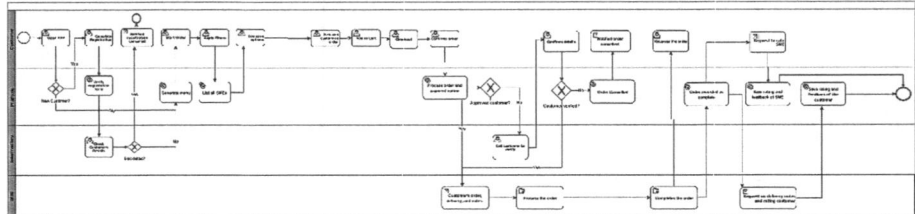

Fig. 4. Overview of the model.

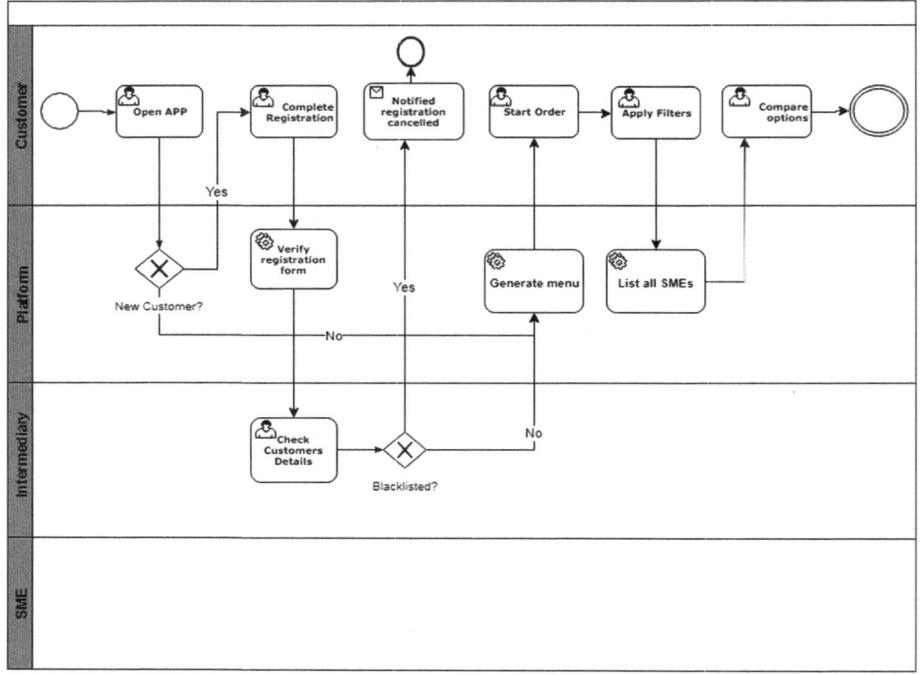

Fig. 5. Generic BPMN Phase 1: registration and start of the order process.

routing methods, the operation manager indicated that Talabat sends instruction on how to reach customers address. This could be information provided by the customer making the order, by customers who have ordered from that same address, or drivers who have attempted to deliver to that address. This information sharing is very valuable in many countries where addresses are less structured and GPS locations less reliable. Thus, ensuring the delivery arrives on time.

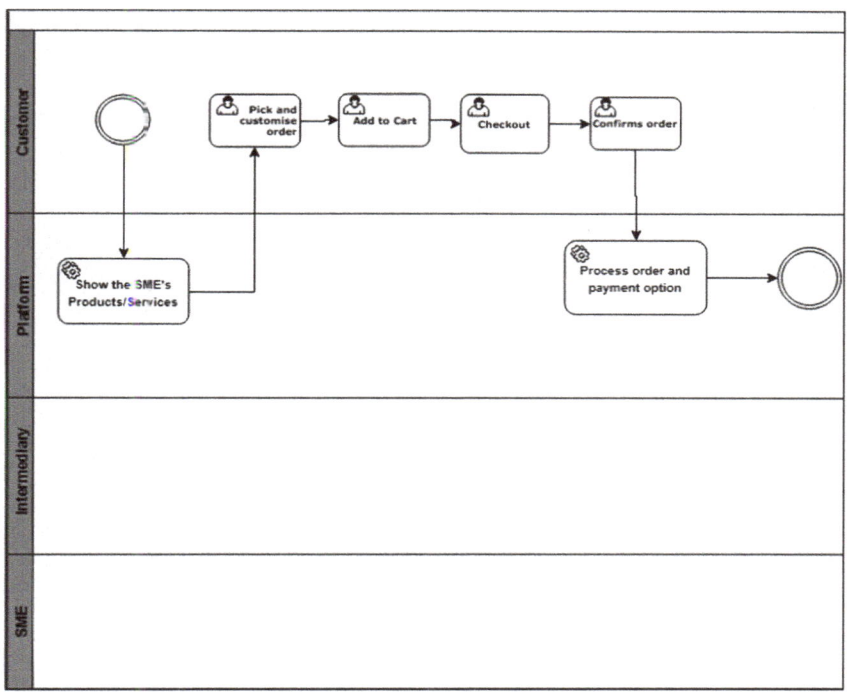

Fig. 6. Generic BPMN Phase 2: order process.

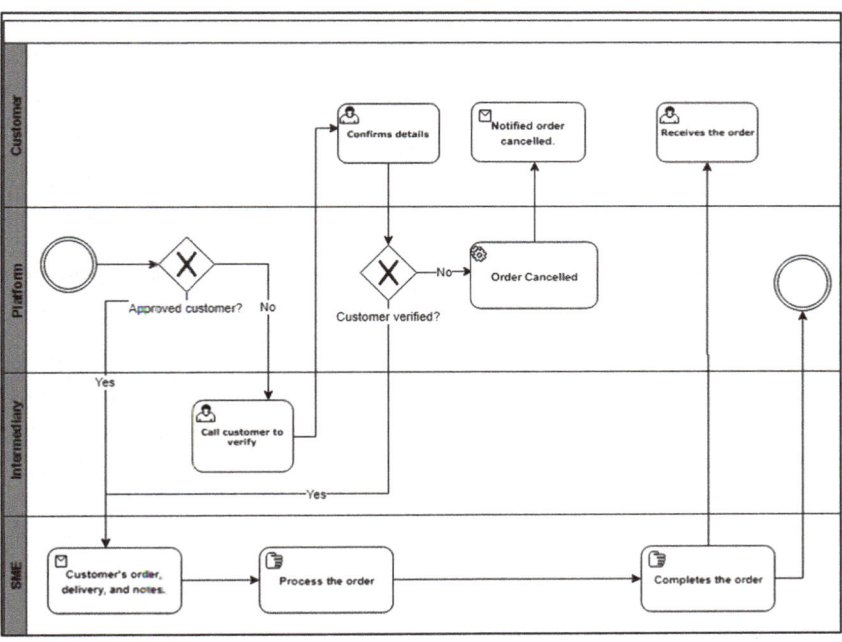

Fig. 7. Generic BPMN Phase 3: delivery of order.

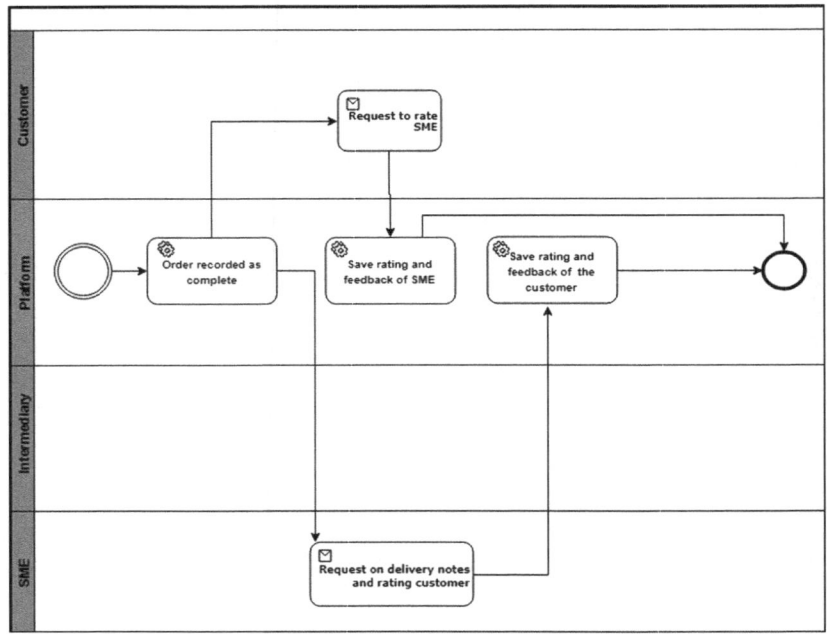

Fig. 8. Generic BPMN Phase 4: completing order and feedback.

4.3 Generic BPMN for B2i2C

Using Figs. 2 and 3 the team constructed a generic BPMN model for order taking for SME participation in M-Commerce model for B2i2C as presented in Fig. 4 with a breakdown in Figs. 5, 6, 7 and 8.

To test the model for its flexibility and generic applications in another context, the team ran cognitive walkthroughs for taxi ordering service, private holiday apartment rentals, and to truly test the diagram a random SME service in the form of laundry shops in Table 1.

Table 1 demonstrates that in all three scenarios, the generic model closely matched the expected processes. Where there are discrepancies, in three processes associated with taxi ordering, the processes of comparing SMEs and choosing SME is done by the platform rather than the customer. The third process, processing payment, happens after the service is completed and not before delivery. This walkthrough proved that the model is sufficiently generic and where differences are to be applied, these are minor and are associated with handling or sequence.

Table 1. BPMN walkthrough testing.

Role	Process	Case 1: Taxi	Case 2: Aprt	Case 3: Laundry
Customer	Open App	✓	✓	✓
Platform	New customers?	✓	✓	✓
Customer	Complete registation	✓	✓	✓
Platform	Verify registration form	✓	✓	✓
Intermediary	Check customers details	✓	✓	✓
Intermediary	Check if the customer is blacklisted?	✓	✓	✓
Customer	Notified registration is cancelled	✓	✓	✓
Platform	Generate menu	✓	✓	✓
Customer	Start order	✓	✓	✓
Customer	Apply filter	✓	✓	✓
Platform	List all SMEs	✓	✓	✓
Customer	Compare options	✗	✓	✓
Customer	Choose SME	✗	✓	✓
Platform	Show the SME's products/Services	✓	✓	✓
Customer	Pick and customise the order	✓	✓	✓
Customer	Add to cart	✓	✓	✓
Customer	Checkout	✓	✓	✓
Customer	Confirms order	✓	✓	✓
Platform	Process order and payment option	✗	✓	✓
Platform	Is customer approved?	✓	✓	✓
Intermediary	Call customer to verify	✓	✓	✓
Customer	Confirms details	✓	✓	✓
Platform	Customer verified?	✓	✓	✓
Platform	Order cancelled	✓	✓	✓
Customer	Notified order cancelled	✓	✓	✓
SME	Receives order, delivery, and notes	✓	✓	✓
SME	Process the order	✓	✓	✓
SME	Complete the order	✓	✓	✓
Customer	Receives the order	✓	✓	✓
Platform	Order recorded as complete	✓	✓	✓
Customer	Receives request to rate SME	✓	✓	✓
Platform	Save rating and feedback of SME	✓	✓	✓
SME	Receives request for delivery notes and rating customer	✓	✓	✓
Platform	Saves rating and feedback of the customer	✓	✓	✓

5   Conclusion

The paper set out to develop and prove a generic BPMN model for SME supporting apps based on a successful business model known as Talabat. The team were successful in demonstrating the applicability of the model in at least three case studies. Thus, this paper has helped formulate a model that could be adapted to new and emerging B2i2C models. The team acknowledges research limitation in the fact the model is based on only one case study and one type of product and service. The team also acknowledges that the three case studies used in the applicability test are conducted as a walkthrough rather than a field investigation. Further research is recommended to identify areas of improvements, missed details and exceptions. The model could also be expanded to explore new applications in areas not exploited thus opening new opportunities for SMEs in competing in an ever-changing digital market. In addition, ethical considerations need to be explored including regulations to ensure processes monopolised by major intermediaries are fair and allow ethical practices in how they support SMEs and consumers. Failure to do so will be detrimental to competition, diversity of SMEs, and consumers.

At the time of writing this paper, competition between intermediaries was found to be limited.

References

1. Veijalainen, J., Terziyan, V., Tirri, H.: Transaction management for M-Commerce at a mobile terminal. Electron. Comm. Res. Appl. 5(3), 229–245 (2006)
2. Felt, A.P., Finifter. M., Chin, E., Hanna, S., Wagner, D.: A survey of mobile malware in the wild. In: Proceedings of the 1st ACM Workshop on Security and Privacy in Smartphones and Mobile Devices, pp. 3–14. ACM, 17 Oct 2011
3. Johnson, M.W., Christensen, C.M., Kagermann, H.: Reinventing your business model. Harv. Bus. Rev. 86(12), 57–68 (2008)
4. Wakabayashi D.: Apple's app store sales hit $20 billion, signs of slower growth emerge. Wall Street J. (2018)
5. Sanz, B., Santos, I., Laorden, C., Ugarte-Pedrero, X., Bringas, P.G., Álvarez, G.: Puma: Permission usage to detect malware in android. In: Herrero, Á. et al. (eds.) International Joint Conference CISIS 2012-ICEUTE 12-SOCO 12 Special Sessions, pp. 289–298. Springer, Berlin, Heidelberg (2013)
6. The state of Mobile Applications for Retailers. Forrester Consulting (2015)
7. Safieddine, F.: M-Commerce. In: Kadry, S., El-Hami, A. (ed.) Innovations in E-Systems for Business and Commerce. CRC Routledge Publishing, London, UK (2016)
8. Anderson, P., Anderson, E.: The new e-commerce intermediaries. MIT Sloan Manag. Rev. 43(4), 53 (2002)
9. Nakhoul, I., Safieddine, F., Ismail, R.: Introducing B2i2C: an M-Commerce model for SMEs. In: 2017 International Conference on IEEE Engineering & MIS (ICEMIS), May 8, pp. 1–5. IEEE (2017)
10. Kaplan, A.M., Haenlein, M.: Toward a parsimonious definition of traditional and electronic mass customization. J. Product Innov. Manag. 23(2), 168–182 (2006)

11. Hauser, M.: A qualitative definition of SME. In: SBS Expert Meeting–Towards better Structural Business and SME statistics, OECD, Paris (2005)
12. Verheugen, G.: The new sme definition: user guide and model declaration. Enterprise and Industry Publications, European Commission (2005)
13. Kushnir, K., Mirmulstein, M.L., Ramalho, R.: Micro, Small, and Medium Enterprises Around the World: How Many are there, and What Affects the Count, pp. 1–9. World Bank/IFC MSME Country Indicators Analysis Note, Washington (2010)
14. Gonzalez, J.D.: A Roadmap to Wireless: The State of the Technology. Air2Web, Inc., Atlanta, GA (2002)
15. Bazijanec, B., Pousttchi, K., Turowski, K.: An approach for assessment of electronic offers. In: Núñez, M., Maamar, Z., Pelayo, Fernando L., Pousttchi, K., Rubio, F. (eds.) FORTE 2004. LNCS, vol. 3236, pp. 44–57. Springer, Heidelberg (2004). https://doi.org/10.1007/978-3-540-30233-9_4
16. Pousttchi, K., Selk, B., Turowski, K.: Enabling mobile commerce through mass customization. In: Workshop on Information Systems for Mass Customization, pp. 1–6 (2002)
17. Svensson, C., Barfod, A.: Limits and opportunities in mass customization for "build to order" SMEs. Comput. Ind. **49**(1), 77–89 (2002)
18. Pine, B.J.: Mass Customization: The New Frontier in Business Competition. Harvard Business Press (1993)
19. Tseng, M.M., Hu, S.J.: Mass customization. In: CIRP Encyclopedia of Production Engineering, pp. 836–843. Springer, Berlin, Heidelberg (2014)
20. Piller, F., Reichwald, R., Möslein, K.: Mass customization based e-business strategies. In: Proceedings of the SMS 20th International Conference, 15 Oct 2000
21. Helms, M.M., Ahmadi, M., Jih, W.J., Ettkin, L.P.: Technologies in support of mass customization strategy: Exploring the linkages between e-commerce and knowledge management. Comput. Ind. **59**(4), 351–363 (2008)
22. Piller, F.T., Moeslein, K., Stotko, C.M.: Does mass customization pay? An economic approach to evaluate customer integration. Prod. Plann. Control. **15**(4), 435–444 (2004)
23. Kamali, N., Loker, S.: Mass customization: on-line consumer involvement in product design. J. Comput. Med. Commun. **7**(4) JCMC741 (2002)
24. Wind, J., Rangaswamy, A.: Customerization: The next revolution in mass customization. J. Interact. Market. **15**(1), 13–32 (2001)
25. Helander, M., Zhang, L.: Web-based configure-to-order platform for collaborative development of customized products. In: International Conference on 2005 Cyberworlds, p. 8. IEEE, Nov 23 2005
26. Lu, S.C.: F2B2C – the Last Ten Miles of a complete e-commerce model. In: A Keynote Speech at 2001 Cybermediaries Conference, San Francisco, CA
27. Haag, S., Cummings, M., Dawkins, J.: Management information systems. Multimed. Syst., 280–97 (2013)
28. Tseng, M.M., Kjellberg, T., Lu, S.C.: Design in the new e-commerce era. CIRP Ann. Manuf. Technol. **52**(2), 509–519 (2003)
29. White, S.A.: BPMN Modeling and Reference Guide: Understanding and Using BPMN. Future Strategies Inc. (2008)
30. Aagesen, G., Krogstie, J.: Analysis and design of business processes using BPMN. In: Brocke, J., Rosemann, M. (eds.) Handbook on Business Process Management 1 2010. pp. 213–235. Springer, Berlin, Heidelberg

31. Birkmeier, D., Overhage, S.: Is BPMN really first choice in joint architecture development? an empirical study on the usability of BPMN and UML activity diagrams for business users. In: International Conference on the Quality of Software Architectures 2010 Jun 23, pp. 119–134. Springer, Berlin, Heidelberg

32. Rodríguez, A., Fernández-Medina, E., Piattini, M.: A BPMN extension for the modeling of security requirements in business processes. IEICE Trans. Inf. Syst. **90**(4), 745–752 (2007)

33. Milanovic, M., Gaševic, D., Wagner, G.: Combining rules and activities for modeling service-based business processes. In: Enterprise Distributed Object Computing Conference Workshops, 2008, pp. 11–22. IEEE. 12 Sep 2008

34. Milanovic, M., Gaševic, D., Wagner, G.: Combining rules and activities for modeling service-based business processes. In: Enterprise Distributed Object Computing Conference Workshops, pp. 11–22, IEEE, September 2008

35. Decker, G., Grosskopf, A., Barros, A.: A graphical notation for modeling complex events in business processes. In: 11th IEEE International Enterprise Distributed Object Computing Conference, EDOC 2007. 2007 Oct 15, pp. 27–27. IEEE (2007)

36. Magnani, Matteo, Montesi, Danilo: BPMN: how much does it cost? an incremental approach. In: Alonso, Gustavo, Dadam, Peter, Rosemann, Michael (eds.) BPM 2007. LNCS, vol. 4714, pp. 80–87. Springer, Heidelberg (2007). https://doi.org/10.1007/978-3-540-75183-0_6

37. Zur Muehlen, M., Recker, J., Indulska, M.: Sometimes less is more: are process modeling languages overly complex?. In: Eleventh International IEEE EDOC Conference Workshop, EDOC'07, pp. 197–204. IEEE, 2007 Oct 15

38. Talabat Frequently Asked Questions Page. https://www.talabat.com/uae/faq. Accessed 21 Apr 201804/21

39. Talabat Contact Us Page (join us tab). https://www.talabat.com/uae/contact-us. Accessed 21 Apr 2018

40. Blackmon, M.H., Polson, P.G., Kitajima, M., Lewis, C.: Cognitive walkthrough for the web. In: Proceedings of the SIGCHI Conference on Human Factors in Computing Systems, pp. 463–470. ACM, 2002 Apr 20

Electronic Financial Disclosure: Islamic Banking vs Conventional Banking in GCC

Adel M. Sarea[1(✉)], Abdalmuttaleb M. A. Musleh Al-Sartawi[1], and Azam Abdelhakeem Khalid[2]

[1] Department of Accounting and Economics, College of Business and Finance, Ahlia University, Manama, Kingdom of Bahrain
adelsarea@yahoo.com, amasartawi@hotmail.com,
asarea@ahlia.edu.bh
[2] Department of Accounting and Finance Faculty of Management and Economics, Universiti Pendidikan Sultan Idris, Tanjung Malim, Perak, Malaysia
azamabdelhakeem@gmail.com

Abstract. This paper examines electronic financial disclosure in Islamic banking vs conventional banking in Gulf cooperation council (GCC). A checklist was adopted to measure the level of electronic financial disclosure in Islamic banking vs conventional banking in GCC. The sample size consisted of total 90 banks in GCC (44 Islamic and 46 conventional) for the year 2017. The statistical analysis indicated that the overall level of of electronic financial disclosure (EFD) was 73%, and 78.6% by Islamic banks and conventional banks respectively. The results also report a significant and positive relationship with firm size, and an insignificant relationship with profitability, and age. This paper should be particularly relevant to central banking authorities considering in banking sector in GCC for strategizing policies in the future of EFD as well as to serve as a guide for academic EFD in banking sector in GCC.

Keywords: Financial accounting · Islamic banking vs conventional banking Electronic financial disclosure · GCC

1 Introduction and Literature Review: Need for the Study

This study seeks to contribute significantly to all aspects of banking sector through the electronic financial disclosure (EFD) for both Islamic banking and conventional banking sector by determining the levels of disclosure of EFD. The need of disclosing more information through EFD are increasingly raised in the previous studies connected by different scholar from different countries including GCC countries, some of the most important of these incentives are: firstly, the need for the development of the appropriate institutional and regulatory framework. This is necessary to address the peculiar factors contributing to financial instability, while provide support and guide regarding the increasing globalization and liberalization with their potential crossborder effects. Secondly, it would enhance and facilitate timely, accurate and reliable information for investors (Al-Sartawi 2017).

S. A. Al-Sharhan et al. (Eds.): I3E 2018, LNCS 11195, pp. 279–291, 2018.
https://doi.org/10.1007/978-3-030-02131-3_25

Despite the numerous challenges currently facing Islamic financial system, there is no doubt that the Islamic financial institutions (IFIs) comprising mainly of Islamic banking has steadfastly lay a formidable foundation in term of Internationally recognized Islamic financial transactions. In this regard, the impacts on the levels of EFD for both Islamic banking and conventional banking sector in term of external and internal influence on Islamic banking such as, foreign investment, globalization, international capital markets, international accounting firms and multinational organizations are due to the internal influences such as socio-cultural, national economic development levels, local capital markets and accounting professional body.

Islamic banking plays a major and important role in the Islamic economy system. The significance of this study emerges from the need of full information through EFD for both Islamic banking and conventional banking sector. Therefore, financial disclosure in Islamic banking is required to be prepared fairly and carefully. This will further enhance and improve the efficient operation of Islamic banks as an important player in the economies and an unambiguous source of a comprehensive development.

In this regard, this study attempts to evaluate the extent of the levels for both Islamic banking and conventional banking sector by determining the levels of disclosure of EFD. Furthermore, this study contributes to the accounting literature in terms of the impact of the changes in EFD on investors, regulators, accountants, and the media as well as on several other dimensions with expectation of assisting in the establishment of checklist for banking system in its operation.

The findings obtained from the current study are therefore expected to fill the gap in the literature review and contribute towards a better understanding and acceptability of the electronic financial disclosure for both Islamic banking and conventional banking sector. Therefore, as a result of the rapid increase in number of investors and shareholders in the financial markets, the need of disseminating financial statements has increased to fulfill the satisfaction of shareholders. Moreover, the disclosing of earning information by large firms requires being fair, it should be disseminated widely and simultaneously to the investors by internet (Jorgensen and Wingender 2004). Adopting EFD by companies has several benefits. Firstly, adopting internet financial disclosure enhances the companies' efficiency and attracts investors from all over the world. Secondly, EFD serves people who need to collect information about companies via internet. The users can easily access internet at any time, from anywhere and obtain efficient information inexpensively.

In addition, the adoption of EFD by the companies can enhance performance of these companies through the cooperating and exchanging of ideas, experiences and information between these companies. However, there are some factors that prevent companies from adopting EFD including: the necessity for a continuous updating of the information to benefit the users as much as possible, the illegality of requirements and the unwanted transparency in disclosing financial information. "Bin Au Khan and bin Ismail" (2012) summarize the advantages of the internet financial disclosure as: the globalism, investors' communication and timelines, whereas the disadvantages of exposing financial information electronic include the problems of privacy and security, cost and experiences. Based on the above discussion, it is clear that the investigation of the extant of adoption EFD by the listed banks in GCC is important in this study.

Recently, there have been too many researchers investigating the extent of disclosing financial reports electronic among firms all over the world. Researchers were interested in examining the effect of some selected characteristics (e.g. size, profitability, liquidity, leverage… etc.) on EFD companies. In related study, Khadaroo (2005) conducted a comparative study that compares the internet disclosure practices of Malaysian listed companies with those in Singapore. The study also examines the implications of web technology for business disclosure and the challenge it poses for standard-setting bodies. The results show that the companies listed in Singapore has more countenance than those in Malaysia. Moreover, the Singapore companies characterized more potential to use the Internet than those in Malaysia.

2 Electronic Financial Disclosure: A GCC Perspective

Several studies conducted in GCC discussing a number of issues related the EFD for both Islamic banking and conventional banking sector. For instance, the adoption of EFD to spread companies' information is a recent phenomenon and some studies consider its future implication. "Al-Motrafi" (2008) noted that the use of electronic financial disclosure in Saudi Arabia may involve rising the concerns of the accounting information disclosing, and this may lead users (such as auditors and regulators) to contribute in financial disclosure to extract regulations and moderate the use of EFD to fulfill statutory. Moreover, the researcher noted that firms may concentrate on innovation of EFD which may help companies induct a disclosure strategy to fulfill users satisfactory level (such as getting benefits by disseminating better information, and extant the companies communication). According to Al-Motrafi (2008) he examined the extent of using of EFD by Saudi public companies (113 companies); the researcher tested the influence of eight specific characteristics on disclosing financial disclosure attitudes. The study has found out that 95(84%) of the companies' own websites while only 51 companies (45%) are adopting EFD. Moreover, the findings of the study have noted that none of these companies possess comprehensive financial information. In addition, the study has also stated that firm's size and stock market are the main variables that affect the mount of corporate information posed.

Another study conducted by Oyelere and Mohamed (2007) in Oman stock market, study showed that of the 142 firms, 59% (84 companies) had an accessible Web site, and of these 84 companies only 31(36.9%) provided financial information on their home page. In related study, Al-Moghaiwli (2009) conducted a study to investigate the extent of internet disclosure practices of Qatar listed companies on the Doha Securities Market (DSM). The results indicated that 90.6% (39 companies) had websites and a total of 28 (71.8%) of these companies provided complete form for financial disclosure via internet. the ownership, firm size, and profit ratio structure are the main factors influencing EFD adoption. Another study conducted in Kuwait by "Alanezi" (2009) A total number of 179 companies listed on Kuwaiti joint-stock (KSX) were investigated. The variables of company size, type of auditors, profitability, liquidity, and leverage were examined. The study reported that 56% of the listed companies disclose financial information.

Momany and Pillai (2013) conducted an empirical study in the United Arab Emirates to investigate the extent of volunteer (EFD) among (UAE) firms listed on the Abu Dhabi finance market (ADX). 65 companies were examined, and the researchers used UAE electronic search engines to collect data. The researchers tested eight (8) characteristics including the effect of profit ratios, firm's volume, firm's age, the type of ownership and its concentration, debt ratios, corporate governance, and asset ratios. The logistic regression analysis used as well as several statistical tests were done like correlation variance. The main results showed that 89% of the listed companies had special sites on the Internet whereas the other 11% did not have any sites. The study also found out that 60% of the firms on Abu Dhabi possessed web-sites provided financial information electronic while 40% of the firms did not provide corporate finance information online. In addition, the results showed that 91% of the companies provided comprehensive financial statements whereas 9% provided partial financial statements. In addition to that, the findings showed that profitability and corporate governance were the significant factors that affect the adoption of EFD.

A similar study conducted by Miniaoui & Oyelere in UAE (2013) to investigate the determinants of disclosing corporate financial information online. The study stated that the firm size, industry sector, the leverage, and profitability were the most important variables of volunteer EFD. The study results showed, "larger companies with greater leverage are more likely to set up a website and use it for EFD than smaller less leveraged ones". The logistic regression analysis used to examine the significant factors of EFD by the firms. The study noted that the banking sectors, investment and finance sectors and insurance sector had the major portion (62%) of EFD companies.

In addition to that, Joshi & Al-Modhahki (2003) conducted study in Bahrain and Kuwait to determine the extent of disclosing corporate financing information. A sample of 75 companies (Kuwait 42 and Bahrain 33) was selected. Six (6) characteristics were tested; company size, profitability, debt ratio, industry type, auditor size, and country effect. The researchers analyzed the collected data about these companies and deduced that 47.6% of Kuwait companies owned website, while 48.5% of Bahrain companies did. They also concluded that the size and industry were the most significant variables that affect adopting EFD. Another study was carried out by (Mohamad & Oyelere 2008) to examine the practices of disclosing corporate information via internet in Bahrain. The study was preparatory and limited since it didn't investigate an in-depth view of the potential practices. The researchers collected data available about all the 49 listed companies in Bahrain Stock Exchange (BSE). They used Google and Yahoo engines and telephone calls to investigate whether the listed companies own websites or not. The study reported that 40 (81.6%) of the companies possess websites while only 27 (67.5%) of these companies were adopting EFD. Moreover, the findings showed that 34 companies provided historical information about themselves and 34 provided information about their services and products, whereas 31 companies provided financial information. In addition, the researchers stated that only 25 companies posed both annual reports and financial highlights.

3 Theory of Voluntary Disclosure: The Agency Theory

The agency theory interprets why organizations voluntarily disclose information primarily for stakeholders and public in general. The organizations believe that contact with agents is a good means for monitoring actions and this contact can be best achieved by disclosure of proper information. According to agency theory, there are conflicts of interest between two parties; outsiders and insiders. These conflicts are more likely to occur in larger organizations (Mohammad and Monirul 2012). This indicates that the advantage of disclosing information is correspondingly greater. The managers (insiders) usually need to be trustworthy to the shareholders (outsiders) through the reduction of agency cost by disclosing more information about the organization (Sweiti, and Attayah 2013).

"Francis et al." (2004) has argued that less outsider ownership results in less information asymmetry between the insider and outsider shareholders; therefore, ownership concentration reduces the need for strong corporate governance and transparency. According to "Zimbwa" (2005) companies with a greater concentration of shareholding are likely to have lower levels of transparency and thus not disclosing information whereas companies with higher leverage ratios are more likely to have higher levels of transparency and disclose more information as a result. This leads to the assumption that there is a relation between the firm's size, leverage and cost and benefits on the one hand and the disclosure of information on the other.

4   Research Design and Methodology

4.1   Sample Selection

The empirical study of the current research depends on a population which consists of all the listed banks in the GCC bourses for the year 2017. However, the required data were gathered from 90 banks (44 Islamic, and 46 conventional) out of 110 banks listed in the GCC bourses. Some of the banks were excluded from the study because they are suspended and closed, some of them their website was not functioning and some of them did not have an investor relations section on their websites. Moreover, the researchers used the banks' websites and the GCC Bourses websites to gather the data required for this study.

4.2   Measuring the Level of Electronic Financial Disclosure

For the current study the researchers have adopted a checklist used by Al-Sartawi (2016) Alrawahi and Sarea (2016) & Al jawder and Sarea (2016) consisting of 90 items (71 items for content and 19 items for presentation) to measure the EFD. Therefore, the EFD index is based on binary, that is, if a bank reported an item which was included in the checklist it received a score of 1 and if the bank did not report an item, a score of 0 was allocated. Accordingly, the Index for each bank was calculated by dividing the total earned scores of the bank by the total maximum possible score appropriate for the bank. Below formula shows the way of calculating the EFD index.

$$EFD = \sum_{i=1} \frac{di}{n}$$

Where: di: *disclosed item* equals One if the bank meets the checklist item and Zero otherwise. **n:** equals maximum score each bank can obtain.

5   Research Design and Methodology

5.1   Dependent Variable

Several research studies have addressed the issue of electronic disclosure in the GCC countries (Al-Sartawi 2016, and 2018). These studies have investigated the effect of several variables on EFD like corporate governance, and institutional investor. Yet there are negligible studies that actually investigate the association of firm characteristics with EFD Accordingly, this study would be an important contribution in filling the gap in the current literature by determining whether there is a relationship between the level of EFD and the type of banks that are listed in the GCC Bourses.

5.2   Independent Variables

5.2.1   Type of Bank

Previous studies conducted in several countries are used "type of bank" as independent variable, for instance, Heffernan and Fue (2008) they used dummy for type of bank: whether national joint stocks, city commercials and rural commercials. This bank dummy variable will provide a measure of the relative performance of the selected banks. This study could help in filling the gap in the literature by determining whether there is a positive relationship between the level of EFD and the type of banks in GCC.

5.3   Control Variables

5.3.1   Profitability (ROA)

However, based on Singhvi and Desai (1971) companies disclose more information when its profitability is above industry average in order to signal to the owners about its strong position to survive. Many studies have examined the relationship between profitability and the level of EFD (Oyelere et al. 2003; Agboola and Salawu 2012; Agyei-Mensah 2012; Adebimpe and Ikenna 2013. Meanwhile, Ashbaugh et al. (1999), Ettredge et al. (2002), Xiao et al. (2004) found contradictory results that do not support this relationship.

5.3.2   Firm Size

With regards to firm size, empirical evidence by Ashbaugh et al. (1999), Debreceny et al. (2002), Ferguson et al. (2002), and Omran and Ramdhony (2016) suggest firm size as a determinant to explain EFD. According to Agboola and Salawu (2012), larger companies are more perceptible, and as a result, may be more likely to disclose more information. Similarly, Adebimpe and Ikenna (2013) argue that large companies usually operate over wide geographical areas and undertake many products along with several divisional units. Hence, it is assumed that they have wellbuilt information systems that enable them to trace both financial and non-financial information for operational, tactical and strategic purposes. Moreover, Agboola and Salawu claim that the arguments in the literature lend support to higher disclosure by larger firms.

5.3.3 Age

Finally, with regards to age, previous studies reveal that there is a positive relationship with the level of EFD: Akhtaruddin (2005), Al-Shammari (2007). Older companies may be more motivated to disclose such information, as the disclosure is less likely to hurt their competitive position (Agboola and Salawu 2012) Therefore, older companies might have better and established reporting systems than newer companies. Therefore, based on the signaling theory, and theoretical and empirical literature, this paper establishes the following hypothesis as:

H1: There is a positive relationship between the type of the banks (Islamic or conventional) listed in the GCC Bourse and the level of EFD.

5.4 Model

The following regression model was used to test the hypothesis. The regression model was developed using the EFD as dependent variable, the type of banking as independent variable, and the firm characteristics as control variables.

$$EFD_i = \beta_0 + \beta_1 B\_Type_i + \beta_2 ROA_i + \beta_3 LFSZ_i + \beta_4 AGE_i + \varepsilon_i$$

Where:

Code	Variable Name	Operationalization
Dependent variable –:		
EFD	Electronic Financial Disclosure %	Total scored items by the company/Total maximum scores
Independent Variables-:		
B_Type	Bank Type	This is a binary Wherein 1 means that the bank is Islamic and 0 conventional
Control Variables-:		
ROA	Returned on assets	Net income/Total assets
LFSZ	Firm size	Natural logarithm of Total Assets
AGE	Firm Age	The difference between the establishing date of the firm and the report date
ε_i	Error	

6 Research Findings

6.1 Descriptive Analysis

As mentioned earlier, the level of EFD is measured by dividing the total score of every bank by the maximum probable scores. In 2000, the Financial accounting standards board (FASB) identified the two dimensions of financial reporting as both the content and presentation of information disclosed by companies' websites. Consequently, based on the adopted index, the maximum score of the EFD was 90 items constituting content dimensions of reporting and presentation dimensions. Where the content dimension included 71 items, the presentation dimension included 19 items.

The results shown in Table 1 suggest that the level of EFD was differed between Islamic and Conventional Banks. The conventional banks level was 78.6% and the Islamic banks level was 73%. This could be due to the characteristics and the regulation of conventional banks comparing to the Islamic banks, both types are working in GCC countries, but the Islamic banks still did not have its separate standers for disclosures. Overall, the results show that the level of electronic financial disclosure by the two types of banks can be considered as a fairly good level of reporting since the differences between them were not significant at the level of 5%.

Table 1. Level of electronic financial disclosure

Bank type	N.	EFD		Independent samples test	
		Mean	S. D	t-value	Sig
Islamic	44	7308	19341		
Conventional	46	7857	19341		
Total	**90**	**7588**	**18130**	**−1.444**	**0.076**[a]

[a]Difference is significant at the 0.10 level.

Additionally, the descriptive statistics for control variables, i.e. the firm characteristics, in Table 2 show that the mean of ROA is 0.10. As for the mean of firm size, i.e. Total Assets, it was 1.49 million, with a minimum of 367246 million and a maximum 1719741907. The normality distributions of total assets were skewed. Hence, natural logarithm was used in the regression analysis to reduce skewness and bring the distribution of the variables nearer to normality. Finally, the bank age ranges from 4 to 62 with a mean of 19, indicating fairly young banks.

Table 2. Descriptive statistics for dependent and control variables

Variable	Min.	Max	Mean	S. D
ROA	−0.05	85	0997	12438
Size	367246	1719741907	1.49E8	2.669E8
Age	4	62	19.14	14.471

6.2   Validity

To test the validity, the model of the study was checked for multicollinearity which involved conducting the Variance Inflation Factor (VIF). The VIF should be lower than 10 and tolerance should not be below 0.2. The VIF scores for each variable are reported in Table 3. The results indicate that since no VIF score exceeded 10 for any variable in the model, while no Tolerance score was below 0.2. So, it was concluded that there is no threat of multicollinearity.

Table 3. Collinearity statistics test

Variable	Tolerance	VIF
Type	.933	1.072
ROA	.739	1.354
Size	.992	1.008
Age	.771	1.297

Additionally, the researchers conducted the Pearson correlation test to measure the correlation between the dependent and independent variables. The results of the pairwise correlation presented in Table 4 below demonstrate a weak correlation between the variables where the correlation does not exceed 0.449.

Table 4. Correlations matrix

Variables	EFD	Type	ROA	Size	Age
EFD	1				
Type	−.152(.152) [a]	1			
ROA	.154(.148)	.257(.950)	1		
Size	.317(.432)	−.258(.588)	.163(.556)	1	
Age	−.274(.490)	.163(.124)	−.449(.236)	−.333(.756)	1

[a]Sig. between brackets.
[b]Correlation is significant at the 0.01 level (2-tailed).

6.3 Testing the Hypotheses

Table 5 reports the findings of the regression analysis of the model. These findings show that the value of calculated F- Statistic for the model is 2.799 at a confidence level 95%, where the p-value for the model is less than 5% at 0.022. This finding supports the significance of the regression model statistically.

Table 5. Regression analysis

	Type	ROA	Size	Age	
Beta	−.126	.169	.303	.027	
t-statistics	−1.810	1.440	2.983	.233	
Sig.	.030	.154	.004	.817	
R	R^2	AR2	S. E	F-statistics	Prob. (F)
0.378a	.243	.192	.17278	2.799	.022

The results as shown in the above table indicate a negative relationship between the level of EFD and the type of bank (Islamic or conventional), which could be due to Islamic banks disclosing less electronic financial information when compared to conventional banks as indicated by the overall levels of EFD. Reasons for this could be due to the high experience and age associated with conventional banks. Moreover, there is no clear regulation for disclosure in Islamic banks, and at the same time the Islamic banks follow double regulations which include both the Islamic standards and the central banks standards.

The firm characteristics such as profitability indicate that there is a positive but insignificant association with EFD, as the significance levels of the Return on Assets (ROA) variable is 0.154. This result is in line with the results reported by Ashbaugh et al. (1999) and Xiao et al. (2004). Thus, could be due to the profit and loss sharing (PLS) principle in Islamic banking when compared to conventional banks, where Islamic banks are protected and have more stable profits. Another reason could be related to the Islamic principle of trusteeship (Amanah) i.e. due to the trust between managers and investors, managers might not have the need to signal their justification for their compensation packages.

Regarding size, the study found a significant and positive relationship with EFD, i.e. significant at 0.004 as larger firms tend to have more resources than smaller firms, and therefore it is expected that they have efficient information systems that enable them to easily trace information for operational, tactical, and strategic purposes. This result is similar to Agboola and Salawu (2012), and Omran and Ramdhony (2016).

This study also failed to find an association between age and EFD at a significance level of 0.817. This is in line with the results of Adebimpe & Ikenna (2013), and Yusuf (2013) who also found an insignificant relationship with age. The insignificance of age shows that experience with investor relations does not necessarily encourage banks to undertake more advanced means of financial reporting such as EFD. One reason for this could be that when compared to conventional banks, Islamic banks in the GCC are relatively young.

Consequently, we can summarize that the level of EFD by the GCC banks has a positive relationship with size and a negative relationship with bank type. Moreover, it has a positive yet insignificant relationship with profitability and age.

7 Conclusion and Recommendations

This research study set out to examine and report on the extent and firm characteristics that determine the practices of EFD by Islamic banks vs conventional banks in the GCC countries. This paper is an important contribution to filling the gap in the literature, as there are a limited number of studies which deal with EFD from such a perspective. The paper creates awareness regarding EFD that might prove beneficial to the various stakeholders including investors, regulators and preparers of financial statements. Data was collected using the websites of 90 banks listed on the stock markets in the GCC countries for 2017. A checklist was adopted from Al-Sartawi (2016), Alrawahi and Sarea (2016) and Al jawder and Sarea (2016) to compute the total level of EFD.

The index measured both the content and presentation dimensions of the websites and online reports. This study found that the overall level of EFD in the GCC by

Islamic banks is 73%, while the level of EFD by conventional banks was 78.6%. The results report a significant negative relationship with bank type, and a positive relationship with firm size. On the other hand, the results show an insignificant relationship with profitability (ROA), and age. It can be concluded that that larger banks disclosed more financial information on their websites due to the availability of resources where they can benefit from the resulting lower costs. This is consistent with the agency theory that large firms attempt to reduce the high agency costs associated with information asymmetry between the management and investors by disclosing a large amount of information.

This study recommends that Islamic banks use the internet to improve their exposure and the availability of financial information when compared to conventional banks. For example, based on Agoobala and Salawu (2012) many of the processes that occur in remote places can be automated and fed into a firm-wide information system or intranet. Moreover, to promote the uniformity in disclosure by Islamic banks, both regulatory and professional bodies should jointly provide a template for EFD.

References

Adebimpe, O.U., Ikenna, E.A.: Internet financial reporting and company characteristics: a case of quoted companies in Nigeria. Res. J. Financ. Account. **4**(12), 72–80 (2013)

Agboola, A.A., Salawu M.K.: The determinants of internet financial disclosure: empirical evidence from Nigeria. Res. J. Financ. Account. **3**(11) (2012)

Agyei-Mensah, B.K.: Corporate financial reporting: Firm characteristics and the use of internet as a medium of communication by listed firms in Ghana. Afr. J. Bus. Manage. **6**(6), 2299–2309 (2012)

Akhtaruddin, M.: Corporate mandatory disclosure practices in Bangladesh. Int. J. Account. **40**, 399–422 (2005)

Al Jawder, N., Sarea, A.: Determinations of internet financial reporting: evidence form Bahrain bourse. Jordan J. Bus. Adm. **12**(4), 935–960 (2016)

Al-Anezi, F.S.: Factors Influencing Kuwaiti Companies' internet financial disclosure. J. Econ. Adm. Sci. **25**(2), 1–23 (2009). http://www.emeraldinsight.com.libweb.uob.edu.bh/journals. htm?issn=1026–116&volume=25&issue=2&articleid=17014762&show=html

Al-Moghaiwli, M.H.: A survey of internet financial disclosure in Qatar. J. Econ. Adm. Sci. **25**(1), 1–20 (2009). http://www.emeraldinsight.com.libweb.uob.edu.bh/journals.htm?issn=1026–4116&volume=25&issue=1&articleid=17014756&show=html#sthash.7wl9rBH1.dpuf   by http://libwebserver.uob.edu.bh/en/

Al-Motrafi, K.A.: Internet Financial Disclosure in Saudi Arabia: Users Perceptions and Disclosures Aston University (2008). http://eprints.aston.ac.uk/15266/1/AlMotrafi%2C_Khalid_A_2008.pdf

Alrawahi, F., Sarea, A.: An investigation of the level of compliance with international accounting standards (IAS 1) by listed firms in Bahrain Bourse. Int. J. Islam. Middle East. Financ. Manag. **9**(2), 254–276 (2016)

Al-Sartawi, Abdalmuttaleb: Online financial disclosure and firms' performance: evidence from the gulf cooperation council countries. World J. Entrep., Manag. Sustain. Dev. **14**(2), 178–190 (2018)

Al-Sartawi, Abdalmuttaleb: Measuring the level of online financial disclosure in the Gulf cooperation council countries. Corp. Own. Control. **14**(1), 547–558 (2016)

Al-Sartawi, A.: The effect of the electronic financial reporting on the market value added of the islamic banks in gulf cooperation council countries. In: 8th Global Islamic Marketing Conference, Istanbul 4–6 May. International Islamic Marketing Association, Turkey (2017)

Al-Shammari, B.: Determinants of internet financial disclosure by listed companies on the Kuwait Stock Exchange. J. Int. Bus. Economics. **7**(1), 162–178 (2007)

Ashbaugh, H., Johnstone, K., Warfield, T.: Corporate reporting on the internet. Account. Horiz. **13**(3), 241–257 (1999)

Bin Au Khan, M., bin Ismail, N. (2012). Various aspects of internet financial disclosure: evidence from malaysian academician. J. Glob. Bus. Econ. **4**(1), 1–15. http://libwebserver. uob.edu.bh/en/

Debreceny, R., Gray, G.L., Rahman, A.: The determinants of internet financial reporting. J. Account. Public Policy **21**(5), 371–395 (2002)

Ettredge, M., Richardson, V.J., Scolz, S.: Dissemination of information for investors at corporate web site. J. Account. Public Policy **21**(4–5), 357–369 (2002)

FASB (Financial Accounting Standard Board): Electronic Distribution of Business Reporting Information, Business Reporting Research Project (2000). http://accounting.rutgers.edu/raw/ fasb/brrp1.pdf

Ferguson, M.J., Lam, K.C.K., Lee, G.M.: Voluntary disclosure by state owned enterprises listed on the stock exchange of Hong Kong. J. Int. Financ. Manag. Account. **13**(2), 125152 (2002)

Francis, J., LaFond, R., Olsson, P., Schipper, K.: Costs of equity and earnings attributes. Acc. Rev. **79**(4), 967–1010 (2004)

Heffernan, S., Fu, M.: The determinants of bank performance in China (22 Aug 2008). Available at SSRN: https://ssrn.com/abstract=1247713 or http://dx.doi.org/10.2139/ssrn.1247713

Jorgensen, R.D., Wingender Jr., J.R.: A survey on the dissemination of earnings information by large firms. J. Appl. Financ. **14**(1), 77–84 (2004). http://libwebserver.uob.edu.bh/en/

Joshi, P.L., Al-Modhahki, J.: Financial disclosure on the internet: empirical evidence from Bahrain and Kuwait. Asia Rev. Account. **11**(1), 88–101 (2003)

Khadaroo, M.I.: Business disclosure on the internet in Malaysia and Singapore: a comparative study. Corp. Commun.: Int. J. **10**(1) (2005). www.emeraldinsight.com/1356-3289.htm (ABI/INFORM Global p. 58 2005)

Khan, M.N.A., Ismail, N.A.: Various aspects of internet financial disclosure: evidence from Malaysian academician. J. Glob. Bus. Econ. **4**(1), 1–15 (2012)

Miniaoui, H., Oyelere, P.: Determinants of internet financial disclosure practices: evidence from the UAE'. Rev. Pac. Basin Financ. Mark. Policies **16**(4), 1350026-1–1350026-25 (2013)

Mohammad, N., Monirul, A.H.: The voluntary disclosure of internet financial disclosure (EFD) in an emerging economy: a case of digital Bangladesh. J. Asia Bus. Stud. **6**(1), 17–42 (2012)

Mohamed, E., Oyelere, P.: A survey of internet financial reporting in Bahrain. Stud. Bus. Econ. **14**(1), 31–49 (2008)

Momany, M.T., Pillai, R.: Internet financial disclosure in UAE-analysis and implications. Glob. Rev. Account. Financ. **4**(2), 142–160 (2013). http://www.globalraf.com/static/documents/ September/2013/8.%20Munther.pdf

Omran, M., Ramdhony, D.: Determinants of internet financial reporting in African markets: the case of mauritius. J. Dev. Areas, Tenn. State Univ. Coll. Bus. **50**(4), 1–18 (2016)

Oyelere, P., Laswad, F., Fisher, R.: Determinants of internet financial disclosure by New Zealand companies. J. Int. Financ. Manag. Account. **14**(1), 26–63 (2003)

Oyelere, P., Mohamed, E.A.: Internet financial disclosure in Oman. J. Int. Financ. Manag. Account. (GJBR) **1**(2), 45–54 (2007). http://content.ebscohost.com.libweb.uob.edu.bh/pdf9/pdf/2007/61L9/01Jun07/32639783.pdf?T=P&P=AN&K=32639783&S=R&D=bth&EbscoContent=dGJyMNXb4kSeqLQ4y9fwOLCmr0yep65Ssqa4SraWxWXS&ContentCustomer=dGJyMPGts1C3qLdMuePfgeyx44Dt6fIA by http://libwebserver.uob.edu.bh/en/

Pendley, J.A., Rai, A.: Internet financial disclosure: an examination of current practice. Int. J. Discl. Gov. **6**(2), 89–105 (2009). https://doi.org/10.1057/jdg.2008.26. Retrieved from http://eds.a.ebscohost.com.libweb.uob.edu.bh/ehost/pdfviewer/pdfviewer?vid=5&sid=dfdbb460-4d95-4ecd-a6d8-3feec2394236%40sessionmgr4005&hid=4111 by http://libwebserver.uob.edu.bh/en/

Singhvi, S.S., Desai, H.B.: An empirical analysis of the quality of corporate financial disclosure. Account. Rev. **46**(1), 129–138 (1971)

Sweiti, I.M., Attayah, O.F.: Critical factors influencing voluntary disclosure: the palestine exchange "PEX". Glob. J. Manag. Bus. Res. Financ. **13**(6), 8–16 (2013)

Xiao, J.Z., Yang, H., Chow, C.W.: The determinants and characteristics of voluntary internet-based disclosures by listed Chinese companies. J. Account. Public Policy **23**(3), 191–225 (2004a)

Xiao, J.Z., Yang, H., Chow, C.W.: The determinants and characteristics of voluntary internet-based disclosures by listed Chinese companies. J. Account. Public Policy **23**(3), 191–225 (2004b)

Yusuf (2013). Internet corporate financial reporting: a study of quoted Nigerian companies. Afr. J. Account. Audit. Financ. **2**(3) 233–259

Zimbwa, C.: An empirical assessment of corporate transparency in Zimbabwe, Centre for Corporate Governance and Regulation Working Paper Series. Bournemouth University (2005). http://ibal.bmth.ac.uk/pdf_docs/424.pdf

Business Modeling and Flexibility in Software-Intensive Product Development - A Systematic Literature Review

Magnus Wilson[1,2(✉)] and Krzysztof Wnuk[2]

[1] Ericsson, Karlskona, Sweden
magnus.wilson@ericsson.com
[2] Department of Software Engineering, Blekinge Institute of Technology,
Karlskona, Sweden
krw@bth.se

Abstract. Continuously achieving and maintaining competitive advantage is the critical survival factor for software-intensive product development companies undergoing digitalization transformation. These companies remain uncertain if investments in business modeling is sufficient to cope with rapidly changing business models, technology, and customer demands. We conducted a Systematic Literature Review using the snowballing methodology to explore the effects of business modeling on business flexibility and variability in the realization. Our results confirm a research gap regarding translating desired strategic flexibility into business options that can efficiently and effectively be implemented using software-based variability in the realization. We conclude that more research is needed consolidating business model innovation, experimentation, and operationalization. Building on theories for learning and knowledge creation, we propose a framework for describing change and analyzing strategic, tactical and operational choices in business model experimentation.

1 Introduction

The inherently flexible nature of software fuels the ongoing digitalization transformation as it allows for rapid changes and adaptations in delivering value to the customers as a response to technology innovation and new business opportunities [1, 2]. A business model helps to manage and innovate the business toward value creation for all stakeholders [3], by supporting the choices and consequences of these choices in products, business processes, and organizations [4]. Optimizing value creation requires profound understanding of how the implemented business model interacts with products and stakeholders [5].

Software-intensive product development (SIPD) companies have a unique position for efficiently creating value appreciated by all stakeholders. Software is the main component in (1) the tools for implementing and supporting core business processes; (2) developing the software product itself, and; (3) integrating the product into the business ecosystem. SIPD companies adapt and integrate their software to the desired business model using business modeling [6].

S. A. Al-Sharhan et al. (Eds.): I3E 2018, LNCS 11195, pp. 292–304, 2018.
https://doi.org/10.1007/978-3-030-02131-3_26

Business modeling (BM) aims to analyze the business environment and drive change, by adapting and aligning the business strategy with the execution, to create value for all stakeholders [7, 8]. The literature suggests experimentation [9], collaboration [10], or trial-and-error learning [11] to deal with business model change. The speed of changes in the software business demands increased flexibility between strategy, implementation, and the business model execution [2].

Several prominent authors emphasized the lack of coherence and a clear focus in the business model research [8, 12–14]. In particular, there is a gap in understanding how business modeling interacts with the digital business strategy, and what effects business modeling have regarding selecting, developing, deploying, and monitoring the optimal set of business choices in software products.

This study investigates how flexibility is linked to business modeling for SIPD companies, and if business modeling can bridge the gap between managing business choices and developing variability in the business model realization. Based on the literature review results, we present a summary of the benefits and challenges associated with BM, including reported connections to the flexibility of the business. Next, we synthesize the findings, list trends for BM, and propose a framework to describe change based on changeability and contextual dimensions.

2 Background and Related Work

We base our work on the BM definition by Rohrbeck et al. as "*to be a creative and inventive activity that involves experimenting with content, structure, and governance of transactions that are designed to create and capture value*" [15]. Rohrbeck et al's definition supports our investigation of BM for SPID companies in two ways. Firstly, looking at a transaction that creates value as the unit of analysis for a business model [3], it allows for a value-driven business model analysis. Secondly, by introducing the word *experimenting*, it extends BM to a process of 'translating an idea into execution, test, and change until satisfied,' similar to the agile method of developing software products. However, experimentation requires fast feedback loops between business model planning and execution, so we complement the BM definition with the proposed capabilities needed for BM (Understand and share, Analyze, Manage, and Prospect) [6].

The term **flexibility** is introduced in different contexts, e.g., strategic flexibility, business flexibility, as a way to managed change. Manufacturing literature suggests that building flexibility entails identifying uncertainty, implementing the appropriate decisions, and monitoring the achieved flexibility [16]. Flexibility in software business models is extensively discussed in literature, e.g., covering pure software business models [17], open source/mixed source [18] and digital options [19], transitions from product-based business models to service-based models [20], or to industrial product-service systems and use models [21–23].

Strategic flexibility (flexible reallocation of resources, changing and adjusting plans and strategies, and maintaining options where needed) is an essential topic in business and management literature, e.g., [24, 25]. Business flexibility with the ambition to improve business performance is discussed by Mason and Mouzas [24].

They proposed a model where business model flexibility is a function of the network structure, relationship typology and business model focus.

Changeability increases speed and agility by introducing flexibility of strategic choices supported by variability in the realization [23]. Changeability applies to software-based products, their design, production and delivery. and production. We believe that BM will go through a similar evolution as how agile software development changed the ways of working for software development companies (with always working software). Such an evolution will force BM to new representations of information and flexibility, and demand automation tools for effective and efficient planning and execution of business models.

Variability in the realization is discussed under the term Software Product lines (SPL), with a focus on modular architectures and component structures. SPL emphasize creating a platform as a common code base, enabling product realization through variability and configuration management. Building a platform requires long-term investment and locks a company within a single solution for the commodity part of its products. A recent trend is to invest in software ecosystem participation, as a more efficient way of building and maintaining commodity parts of the products [26]. SPL literature mainly focuses on the technical aspects of product development and reuse, rather than business model flexibility.

3   Methodology

We considered software-intensive products as the unit of analysis and investigated the following research questions:

RQ1: *What benefits and challenges are associated with flexibility in business modeling?* We use RQ1 to investigate the contextual setting for business modeling and flexibility.

RQ2: *What effects of business modeling related to business flexibility and variability in the realization are reported in the literature?* RQ2 addresses how BM can support flexible business strategies and address the challenge of efficiently implementing the right flexibility in business options. This means deciding the right level of variability in realization.

3.1   The Snowball Methodology

The Systematic Literature Review (SLR) methodology is based on the guidelines for snowballing literature search proposed by Wohlin [27], outlined below[1].

STEP 1: Design of the Literature Review. We performed two open-ended interviews (60 min each) with an expert in Software Engineering (telecommunication industry with 25 years of experience) and Business management (professor in

---

[1] An Appendix with an illustration of the methodology process including all additional details on the study design are available at https://www.bth.se/wpcontent/uploads/2018/06/SLRBMFlexAppendix.pdf.

production management). We asked a question *"Does business modeling enable improvements in effectiveness and efficiency for a company?"*) to understand the terminology and support creating inclusion criteria (IC) and data extraction properties. We also created a study protocol.

STEP 2: Defining the Start Set. From the two interviews, we received recommendations about four relevant papers. Next, we searched Google Scholar to derive a collection of definitions and to develop the search strings (SS). We ended up with two search strings[2]. The search string is as follows:

SS1: (business modelling OR business model OR business ecosystem) AND value creation AND strategy SS2: ("business modelling" OR "business modeling" OR "business ecosystem") AND "business strategy" AND "value creation" AND ("effectiveness" OR "efficiency" OR "business flexibility" OR modularity OR "variability in realization" OR "governance" OR "multi-business")

Executing SS1 and SS2 (limited to title-abstract-keywords) resulted in 2948 papers. The first author applied the inclusion criteria on titles and abstracts, removing 2378 papers. The remaining 570 papers were put in an excel sheet and duplicates were discarded. The final 477 papers were screened more thoroughly (abstract, introduction, conclusion) by the first and the second authors. We also included one paper [8] recommended by the expert in business management, giving us 10 papers in the start set.

STEP 3: Execute Snowballing Iterations. Each snowballing iteration started with the first author collecting the references and the citations for each selected paper and applying the exclusion criteria followed by the inclusion criteria. Google Scholar (GS) was used for citations [27]. We used Cohens Kappa in the different iterations for quality assessment, see Sect. 3.2.

We screened 10414 citations and 2958 references in all snowballing iterations. Iteration 1 covered the start set and resulted in 35 selected studies (out of 612 references and 249 citations). Iteration 2 resulted in 2011 references and 10134 citations. Pre-screening (language, title, abbreviated abstract) gave us a remaining 1335 citations to screen. We selected 11 studies in iteration 2. Iteration 3 rendered 313 references and 30 citations, resulting in one new paper selected. Iteration 4 gave no further studies resulting in 57 studies selected for analysis[3].

STEP 4: Data Extraction, Analysis, and Synthesis. The data extraction properties (EP)[4] were designed and discussed before application. ATLAS Ti[5] and Excel were used to keep track of and analyze results, and to synthesize extracted information.

---

[2] SS1 uses stemming and SS2 doesn't. Also, "multi-business" was added upon recommendation of industry expert, since executing several business models in parallel is a significant challenge for large SIPD companies.

[3] See Appendix B available at https://www.bth.se/wp-content/uploads/2018/06/SLRBMFlexAppendix.pdf.

[4] See Appendix C, available at https://www.bth.se/wpcontent/uploads/2018/06/SLRBMFlexAppendix.pdf.

[5] Software for Qualitative Data Analysis, http://atlasti.com/.

Properties EP1–EP4 were used to analyze the relevance to industry for each papers contribution. Property EP3 (Rigor and Relevance) was also used for quality assessment. It helped us to evaluate how generalizable the different results were, see Sect. 3.2. Open coding [28] was used for properties EP5–EP9. The extracted data was thematically and narratively analyzed.

The results were iterated in two phases (a) RQ1 and (b) RQ2. For each phase, the first author prepared a summary of listed quotations from all studies. The list was then reviewed against the extracted result, and the first author had to explain a summary of each paper's findings to the reviewer. Both phases were reviewed by the second author.

3.2   Validity Threats

We adopted the validity guidelines suggested by Runeson [29]. We mitigated the industrial experience bias of the authors by conducting the two initial interviews and iterative refinement of the research questions and also by applying a grounded theory approach [28].

The selected ten papers in the start set are highly heterogeneous and therefore minimize the bias on specific author or terminology. Similarly, we mitigated the author's bias by calculating the Kappa coefficient when selecting the start set papers. The first and the second authors did the Kappa analysis, and the value was k = 0,566 and later k = 0,638. The Kappa analysis was also performed on 12% of the studies from the first snowballing iteration with a result of k = 0.763.

To mitigate author bias during extraction, six random studies were selected (of the 57 studies) and extracted by the first and second authors. The validation showed a discrepancy of one paper for extraction properties EP1–EP4 and after further discussion full agreement was reached. Also, the results to the RQs (EP5EP9) was iterated in two phases, and each phase was presented by first author before discussed and evaluated by the second author.

Rigor and relevance analysis was applied and adjusted to mitigate potential threats to conclusion validity [30]. The relevance parameter was coded using binary weights (0, 1, 2, and 4 instead of the recommended 0 and 1). We also decided to add property EP4 to specifically address the relevance of a papers content concerning our RQs (since the property EP3 and its relevance aspects only consider the research method and context of a paper). This provided higher resolution when discussing the relevance and comparing the papers.

We minimized potential internal validity threats by following the systematic mapping study guidelines, creating a review protocol and sharing the work associated with data extraction and analysis. Because of the interdisciplinary nature of this study, the risk remains that some aspects are underrepresented and other aspects are over-represented. In particular business model innovation or business process modeling seems to be heavily researched in the business management and the computer science community. However, we decided to focus on the interplay between the strategic intentions, the design of a business model, the realization of it, and the resulting effects on efficiency and effectiveness, rather than details on how individual steps are performed. We addressed this by our choice of a snowballing methodology. We also used grounded theory approach with open coding [28] to harmonize language between the different research fields.

4 Results

4.1 Benefits and Challenges Associated with Business Modeling (RQ1)

We extracted 263 quotes of purpose, benefits, and challenges of business modeling from the identified 57 papers[6]. Quotes of purpose (P) often sets the general context, while quotes of challenges (C) or benefits (B) often are a reflection of how well a solution to a specific problem works. We used open coding to thematically analyze these quotes into the following common areas: (1) Value creation/capture; (2) Assessment (decision control, clarity, visualization); (3) Mind-set and Knowledge; (4) Cost/Revenue; (5) Ends (Vision, goals, and objectives); and (6) Means (Mission, Strategy, Tactics, Directives), Resources)[7]. Also, we identified three primary contexts for BM: (1) Strategy & planning; (2) Daily operations (executing strategies and plans); and (3) Governance & communication.

The main purpose for BM is to stay competitive and improve business results. The quotes of purpose are often overlapping and cover a wide variety of more specific topics, like managing specific business aspects (e.g. offerings, market, cost, and revenue), capturing the business logic, over to a holistic nature like 'operationalize strategy', and 'appropriate value from technology'.

We analysed 90 quotes related to the 13 papers[8] explicitly discussing RQ2 (business flexibility and the variability in the realization). Comparing these 90 quotes with all 263 quotes, the strongest contextual coherence (Purpose, and Benefit or Challenge in the same primary context)[9] is still found in 'Governance & communication', but significantly higher (45% vs. 26%). It is also interesting to note the shift of quotes from 'Strategy & planning' towards 'Daily Operations', and from 'Mind-set and Knowledge' towards 'Means'. We believe this is a natural consequence, as the purpose of flexibility is promptly respond to change. This would also be a reasonable explanation for why there are significantly more challenges (36) than benefits (8) reported for these 13 papers, indicating that solutions to achieve flexibility are still immature[10].

The importance of contextual information is mentioned by seven studies [P8, P17, P18, P20, P25, P51, P59], but no author goes as far as to suggest how to describe the

---

[6] See Appendix D available at https://www.bth.se/wpcontent/uploads/2018/06/SLRBMFlexAppendix.pdf.

[7] We use the terms Assessment, Ends, and Means as defined by the Business Motivation Model Version 1.3 (BMM) by Object Management Group, http://www.omg.org/spec/BMM/.

[8] [P1] = [31],   [P3] = [32],   [P5] = [33],   [P8] = [10],   [P9] = [8],   [P24] = [34],   [P26] = [21], [P27] = [23], [P32] = [6], [P49] = [7], [P52] = [25], [P54] = [22], [P58] = [24].

[9] See Appendix E available at https://www.bth.se/wp-content/uploads/2018/06/SLRBMFlexAppendix.pdf.

[10] excluding the outlayer [P32] since it contains 25 claimed but unsubstantiated benefits and only 1 challenge.

contextual information or represent the information. The underlying purpose reported in the studies is contextually vague, e.g., 'Deal with uncertainty', 'Meeting customer's needs' [P2, P52, P54, P58].

Summarizing the most common challenge for papers explicitly discussing flexibility is how to deal with the dynamics of business models [P5, P9, P32, P49, P54, P58] and most of the quotes on challenges related to the non-existing solutions for governance (representation, simulation, assessment, decision-support, and feedback) of the proposed frameworks and methods. Since governance is not addressed, each individual method or framework may work in its specific context, but taken out of context or combined with other methods to form a solution for an enterprise, they fail to deliver the claimed benefits. The quotes of benefits are mostly unsubstantiated or claimed with limited empirical evidence.

4.2 Business Modeling, Business Flexibility, and Variability in Realization (RQ2)

Looking at the 90 quotes found in the 13 papers explicitly discussing flexibility, we conclude that business flexibility is one of the core aspects in BM [P1, P3, P27, P52, P58]. Succeeding in managing business flexibility increases competitive advantages and performance [P58, P1]. It is essential to understand (and quantify) the value (and cost) of flexibility to optimize the value creation and capture [P27]. Governance (intra-company as well as inter-company) becomes the critical component to facilitate the design of the business model, and link the strategy to the execution of the business model by controlling and aligning the design and invocation of options [P24, P27, P32, P54, P1].

Business flexibility as an option is discussed in the different contextual settings, and on several abstraction levels [P1, P3, P27, P32, P58]. Reim et al. divide options into business model options (chosen and decided during the business strategy development), and tactical options (comprise all the choices after the business model has been selected) [P3]. Many of these tactical options (contract, marketing, network, and product design) are related to investing in software products and business processes, e.g., integrating new IT systems like Product-Services Systems (PSS).

Mason and Mousas goes one abstraction level deeper and starts by categorizing options as downstream and upstream relationships, discussing flexibility on three abstraction levels, network (identify), company (develop), and individual (use) [P58]. Upstream has a network-focus with options related to the business model architecture (transactional relationship, network influence, and corporate ownership) and tied to the realization of the business by choosing resources, partners, and channels. Downstream has a market-driven focus with options related to the business model focus (customer focus, competitor focus, inter-functional co-ordination) and tied to understanding the customer needs. Woodard et al. discuss options for digital business strategy by introducing the concepts of Design Capital (cumulative stock of designs owned by the company) and Design moves (discrete strategic actions to optimize the Design capital) [P1].

Richter et al. also advocate a modular design and discuss options regarding a systems changeability (adaptability, agility, robustness, flexibility) by embedding flexibility early into system design [P27]. Flexibility must however not be an end in itself, but a conscious compromise between cost and benefit. Osterwalder et al. highlight the critical options managers make, when investing in IT for future strategic business agility, and speculate that business models play an essential role in facilitating such decisions [P32]. Neither of the studies proposes any details on how these concepts could be implemented in an industrial setting to facilitate flexibility with help of software.

Increasing flexibility is discussed in four papers [P3, P5, P8, P26]. Romero and Molina argue that collaborative networks and experience-centric networks can increase business flexibility and enable agility in dynamic and turbulent markets [P8]. By highlighting the value of co-creation and collaboration across multiple interactive channels, they illustrate how business flexibility can be addressed, but do not bring any further details as to how to manage the flexibility, nor how to measure it. Chew identifies service innovation, with a degree of service variability built into the services, as a way forward to exploit new technologies [P5]. Modularity, platforms, components, and interfaces are a foundation to meet the mass-customization requirements and become faster and more flexible. He concludes that service innovation and service architecture are not enough, but a corresponding modular organization and IT architecture is also required.

Papers [P3, P24, P26] argue that combining products and services into ProductService Systems (PSS) bridges business flexibility with the variability in the realization, and provides individualized, customer-oriented configurations and potential for mass-customization. However, PSS come with a new set of challenges (e.g., industrialization of service offerings) and are highly dependent on the continuous integration of large IT and software solutions into the life-cycle of the business model and organizations [P26].

Osterwalder et al. make propositions how the understanding of a business model, with all its business choices, facilitates and improves goals, the requirement engineering, and the choices of IS/IT infrastructure and applications will lead to more effective and efficient solutions [P32]. However, they do not discuss how the business flexibility is continuously transferred to flexibility in the realization and how these two are aligned.

Summary: Our identified studies offer only partial approaches and solutions (for BM) to manage the desired flexibility, and to facilitate pivoting in response to disruptive changes in the realization of the business model, e.g., products, organizations, processes, contracts, governance.

Choosing the right options and governance is discussed by seven papers [P1, P24, P27, P32, P49, P54, P58]. Kindstr̈om argues that understanding business flexibility is a critical aspect, during the service-based model transition. However, he provides no details and concludes that further research is needed how to industrialize service offering to a larger scale, and how to deal with variability in realization [P24]. Richter et al. discuss flexibility in the context of uncertainty, contracts in use-oriented business models, and IPSS [P27]. They perceive flexibility as the ability to react to changes, and suggest a method to determine the value of flexibility. They discuss (1) Real options for accessing flexibility and (2) Net options value of modularity in the design, and conclude with the need for future research on a combined view on the design of an IPSS and business models. They stress a focus on the IPSS design with the inter-company governance structure, since choosing the right flexibility, is crucial controlling parameter when optimizing value in an IPSS. Similarly, Woodard et al. recommend using a two-dimensional structure of real options and technical debt to facilitate decision-making on options [P1].

Eurich et al. propose a six-step approach to business model innovation based on network thinking [P49], to overcome the tendency of focusing on modelinternal consistency rather than the specific business situation. They argue that in a component-based structure, flexibility and explanatory power are lost, due to the abundant relationships, and often inexplicit dependencies between components and the dynamics of the environment. A vital part of the approach is to understand relevant choices, to make the options explicit, and to visualize relationships between these options. They do not detail how to manage flexibility from all these options and aspects but do recognize governance and early detection as shortcomings. Salgado et al. proposes a framework based on processes, goals, and rules to facilitate and visualize the desired flexibility on IT systems, but conclude their solution needs much research to become robust and scale to industrial settings [P56].

Meier and Boßlau argue that there is almost no attention in research to the dynamic aspects of business models (flexibility, validation, and implementation) [P54]. They propose a learning feedback system that integrates business model engineering and design, to transfer insights via a business model cockpit back into business model innovation or re-design. They suggest using System Dynamics and diagnostic simulations as a continuous design, validation and implementation of business models, but offer no empirical evidence on the effectiveness or efficiency of their solution.

5 Discussion

As Schneider and Spieth pointed out, the literature provides little evidence that business model innovation does improve dynamic capabilities and strategic flexibility [P52]. They also recommend future research to measure strategic flexibility.

Our review confirms their viewpoint regarding flexibility and we argue that efficient governance mechanisms focusing on continuously managing consistency and traceability of options, need to be built into both business and software architectures, to contentiously create and manage the required variability in realization. We also believe the concept of changeability as forwarded by Richter et al. [P27], implemented with a governance mechanism between business and software architecture, can play a pivotal role for the operationalization of flexible business models.

Supported by our results [P26, P27, P49, P54], we argue that variability in the realization is an important, but often overlooked aspect of business flexibility which must be an integrated part in the BM analysis and design phases. Business complexity and variability in realization should form a synergy and support conscious investments decision in technology and organization [32]. This puts SIPD companies in a unique position to invest in an optimal flexibility and software architecture for the business model realization. Constraining factors like speed, time-to-market, cost and automation levels, can be solved by software investments in any combination of the three aspects

(1) tools for core business processes, (2) the development of SW products itself, and (3) integration of the product into the ecosystem. From the results, we synthesized the following trends:

- experimentation and operationalization of flexible business models to manage the speed of change fueled by the digitalization of the value delivery [P1, P2, P9, P13, P15, P18, P49]
- changeability and modularity as ways to strategically address all new roles and values via choices to enable faster transitions from strategy to execution [P1, P3, P5, P6, P23, P25, P26, P27]
- need for multifaceted optimization of business models, as fueled by new roles and new values, complementing the more dominant single dimension of cost and revenue [P2, P7, P8, P9, P26, P53]

Our results also reveal an underlying issue of inhomogeneous, non-systematic, contextual descriptions. The importance of *"The parts are not the Whole"* is argued by Osterwalder et al. [P32] and conclude their paper with *"One of the shortcomings in business model literature is that the different authors rarely build on each other. Consequently, business model research as a whole advance more slowly than it could and often stays at a superficial level"*. Six years later Zott et al. still argue the same [P29], and after an additional three years, H¨oflinger reaches similar conclusions [P9]. He proposes the following further research directions: (1) further investigation of the business model concept itself, especially with regard to the coherence of the three underlying structures and their interdependencies; (2) considering the dynamics of business model change and innovation requires establishing governance mechanisms to facilitate feedback loops between planning and execution. The first step towards establishing such governance is to understand how change impacts existing business model realization, i.e., describe and document change, so all aspects related to this change can be addressed in the realization (organizations, rules, and IT systems). We illustrate this with an example of introducing a new feature in a product at a large organization to improve their agility and decrease time to market by 50%. The initial requirement engineering work by the R&D department resulted in the estimated effort of 2200 person hours. Later, this estimate exploded into a chain of business models and organizational changes affecting own staff, partners, processes, IT systems, changed policies in marketing and advertisement, as well as to change how the product is sold and who should sell it. The total change was estimated to 43 000 man-hours over a period of 7 months.

Since the full consequences of a change are greatly unknown until the change is fully implemented, the change often triggers several new changes. The change life-cycle is related to the realization life-cycle, and if new changes occur in already decided changes that are still not (fully) implemented, a rippling effect and propagation of new changes happen, rendering impacts and consequences hard to manage. Therefore, if the speed of changes is faster than the time to implement all changes, a gap grows. As a consequence, the initial business intent might not be fulfilled.

Inspired by the conversation theory by Pask et al. and the knowledge creation process in a business context [35], we speculate that this process of change, when integrated with the process of organizational learning, enables experimentation for a company (rapid and controlled transitions from idea to realization). The need for learning and knowledge transfer is also highlighted by Mason and Leek to handle dynamic business models [P46].

We, therefore, argue the necessity for having better contextual descriptions of a business model construct. Inspired by the aspects of changeability and ideas presented by Richter et al. on flexibility for use-oriented business models and value-based design [P27], we propose a framework describing and documenting change by four change-ability aspects (rows) and five contextual dimensions (columns), see Fig. 1. The white oval indicates a change that is introduced, e.g. a new product that requires new functions in marketing (=business function) to reduce time-to-market by 50% (=agility).

The key characteristic for this framework is to support experimentation and learning while maintaining a practical and efficient level of control (over change) [P9, P15, P18, P22, P36, P51]. That helps an organization to describe how a change propagates and influences the other aspects of changeability and contextual dimensions. Each element in the matrix contains one or several artifacts that are linked and related to real information used in companies. To remain consistent, each matrix element needs to be kept internally, vertically, and horizontally (IVH dimensions) consistent. For each change, the process of maintaining consistency needs to be repeated over the IVH dimensions. Hence axiomatization and efficient information representations are important.

To address the speed of changes challenge, we introduce the *Right-time binding* concept, defined as a flexibility management function optimized for multidimensional value. Right-time binding allows the invocation of specific options (i.e., choices related to particular change descriptions) to allow runtime decisions rather than during system design. Such flexibility does come at a price [P27], and Right-time binding becomes a vital part of the governance mechanisms to simulate and visualize consequences of choices (i.e., changes). It needs to be integrated into the governance mechanisms, the business architecture as well as the software architecture, acting as a bridge between the business model (strategy) and the operationalized business model (execution).

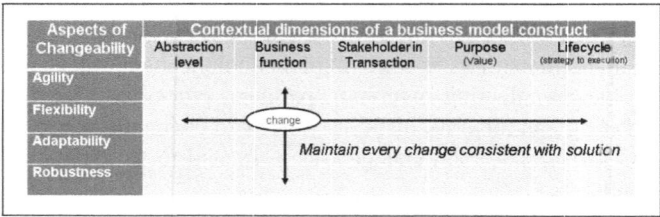

Fig. 1. Framework for describing and documenting change based on changeability aspects and contextual dimensions

6   Conclusions

This systematic literature review explores business modeling and flexibility within the lens of software-intensive product development. Digitalization of software business fuels the diversity of strategic, tactical, and operational choices [36] during efficient business model realizations. The literature provides little evidence that business model innovation utilizes changes to dynamic capabilities to improve strategic flexibility, and our review confirms this viewpoint regarding flexibility. We argue that efficient governance mechanisms focused on continuously managing consistency and traceability of options, need to be built into both the business architecture and the software architecture. Business modeling, supported by efficient information management tools, could become the bridge between the investments in software-enabled variability and the desired strategic flexibility. As the next step, we propose a framework for describing and analyzing change, based on changeability and contextual dimensions.

Acknowledgment. This work has been supported by the Professional Licentiate of Engineering (PLEng) Pilot Run 2014-2018 in cooperation with Ericsson AB. This work is also supported by the IKNOWDM project (20150033) from KKS in Sweden.

References

1. Matt, C., Hess, T., Benlian, A.: Digital transformation strategies. Bus. Inf. Syst. Eng. **57**, 339–343 (2015)
2. Bharadwaj, A., El Sawy, O.A., Pavlou, P.A., Venkatraman, V.: Digital businessstrategy: toward a next generation of insights. MIS Q. **37**(2), 471–482 (2013)
3. Zott, Christoph, Amit, Raphael: Business Model Design: an activity systemperspective. Long Range Plan. **43**(2–3), 216–226 (2010)
4. Casadesus-Masanell, R., Ricart, J.: From Strategy to Business Models and onto Tactics. Long Range Plan. **43**(2–3), 195–215 (2010)
5. Lepak, D., Smith, K., Taylor, S.: Introduction to special topic forum value creation and value capture: a multilevel perspective. Acad. Manag. Rev. **32**, 180–194 (2007)
6. Osterwalder, A., Pigneur, Y., Tucci, C.: Clarifying business models: origins, present, and future of the concept. Commun. Assoc. Inf. Syst. **15**(1), 1–25 (2005)
7. Eurich, M., Weiblen, T., Breitenmoser, P.: A six-step approach to business model innovation. Int. J. Entrep. Innov. Manag. **18**(4), 330–348 (2014)
8. Höflinger, N.: The business model concept and its antecedents and consequences towards a common understanding. In: Academy of Management Proceedings: Organization Development and Change, vol. 2014(1) (2014)
9. Chesbrough, H.: Business model innovation: opportunities and barriers. Long Range Plan. **43**(2–3), 354–363 (2010)
10. Romero, D., Molina, A.: Collaborative networked organisations and customer communities: value co-creation and co-innovation in the networking era. Prod. Plan. Control. **22**(5–6), 447–472 (2011)
11. Sosna, M., Trevinyo-Rodríguez, R., Velamuri, S.: Business model innovation through trial-and-error learning. Long Range Plan. **43**(2–3), 383–407 (2010)
12. Massa, L., Tucci, C.L., Afuah, A.: A critical assessment of business model research. Acad. Manag. Ann. **11**, 73–104 (2016)
13. Krumeich, J., Werth, D., Burkhart, T., Loos, P.: Towards a component-based description of business models: a state-of-the-art analysis. In: AMCIS 2012, vol. 1, pp. 266–277 (2012)
14. Zott, C., Amit, R., Massa, L.: The business model: recent developments and future research. J. Manag. **37**(4), 1019–1042 (2011)

15. Rohrbeck, R., Konnertz, L., Knab, S.: Collaborative business modelling for systemic and sustainability innovations. Int. J. Technol. Manage. **63**(1/2), 4 (2013)
16. Boyle, T.: Manufacturing flexibility: a strategic perspective. J. Manuf. Technol. Manag. **17**, 6–211 (2006)
17. Schief, M., Buxmann, P.: Business models in the software industry. In: 2012 45th HICSS Conference, pp. 3328–3337 (2012)
18. Casadesus-Masanell, R., Llanes, G.: Mixed source. Manage. Sci. **57**(7), 1212–1230 (2011)
19. Sambamurthy, V., Bharadwaj, A., Grover, V.: Shaping agility through digital options: reconceptualizing the role of information technology in contemporary firms. MIS Q. **27**(2), 237–264 (2003)
20. Zolnowski, A., Böhmann, T.: Business modeling for services: current state and research perspectives. In: AMCIS 2011 Proceedings - All Submissions. Paper 394, pp. 1–8 (2011)
21. Meier, H., Roy, R., Seliger, G.: Industrial Product-Service systems-IPS2. CIRP Annals - Manufacturing Technology **59**(2), 607–627 (2010)
22. Meier, H., Boßlau, M.: Design and engineering of dynamic business models for industrial product-service systems. In: Shimomura, Y., Kimita, K. (eds) The Philosopher's Stone for Sustainability. Springer, Heidelberg (2013). https://doi.org/10.1007/978-3-642-32847-3_30
23. Richter, A., Sadek, T., Steven, M.: Flexibility in industrial product-service systems and use-oriented business models. CIRP J. Manufact. Sci. Technol. **3**(2), 128–134 (2010)
24. Mason, K., Mouzas, S.: Flexible business models. Eur. J. Mark. **46**(10), 1340–1367 (2012)
25. Schneider, S., Spieth, P.A.: Business model innovation and strategic flexibility: insights from an experimental research design. Int. J. Innov. Manag. **18**(6), 1–22 (2014)
26. Bosch, J., Bosch-Sijtsema, P.: From integration to composition: on the impact of software product lines, global development and ecosystems. J. Syst. Softw. 83(1), 67–76 (2010)
27. Wohlin, C.: Guidelines for snowballing in systematic literature studies and a replication in software engineering. In: EASE 2014, pp. 1–10 (2014)
28. Corbin, J., Strauss, A.: Basics of Qualitative Research: Techniques and Procedures for Developing Grounded Theory. SAGE Publications, Thousand Oaks (2015)
29. Runeson, P., Höst, M.: Guidelines for conducting and reporting case study research in software engineering. Emp. Softw. Eng. **14**, 131–164 (2009)
30. Ivarsson, M., Gorschek, T.: A method for evaluating rigor and industrial relevance of technology evaluations. Empr. Softw. Eng. **16**, 365–395 (2011)
31. Woodard, C., Ramasubbu, N., Tschang, F., Sambamurthy, V.: Design capital and design moves: the logic of digital business strategy. MIS Q. Manag. Inf. Syst. **37**(2), 537–564 (2013)
32. Reim, W., Parida, V., Ortqvist, D.: Strategy, business models or tactics – what is product-service systems (PSS) literature talking about? In: ICED 2013, vol. 4 DS75-04, pp. 309–318 (2013)
33. Chew, K.: Linking a service innovation-based framework to business model design. In: IEEE 16th Conference on Business Informatics, pp. 191–198. IEEE (2014)
34. Kindström, D.: Towards a service-based business model - Key aspects for future competitive advantage. Eur. Manag. J. **28**(6), 479–490 (2010)
35. Silvander, J., Wilson, M., Wnuk, K., Svahnberg, M.: Supporting continuous changes to business intents. Int. J. Software Eng. Knowl. Eng. **27**, 1167–1198 (2017)
36. Anthony, R.: Planning and Control Systems; A Framework for Analysis. Graduate School of Business Administration. Harvard University, Boston (1965)

Conflicts of Interest, Information Quality and Management Decision

Saeed Askary$^{(\boxtimes)}$ and Shekar S. Shetty

Gulf University for Science and Technology (GUST), Hawally, Kuwait
{askary.s,shetty.s}@gust.edu.kw

Abstract. The existence of conflict of interests (COI) within different firms' level of management is often cited as the reason for the relationship for low information quality and ineffective decision making. We reveal how COI affects negatively decision making through low information quality longer time to produce information quality, shrinking optimal information quantity, and increasing in the information cost. Although, COI has been studied extensively by different organizational studies, there is no research showing how to measure the effect of COI on information quality from mathematical modeling perspective. Since effective and efficient management decisions closely depend on information quality, this paper provides the solutions to this problem.

Keywords: Conflict of interest · Cost · Information quality
Management decision · Timeliness

1 Introduction

Conflict of interests (COI) is one of the complicated organizational dilemma in current organizational enviornment in which analyzing, investigating, and yet suggesting an all-inclusive solution is demanding [4, 7, 9]. This paper shows that COI could affect adversely the quality, quantity and cost of good information. Managers, at different organizational level and to make critical decisions, need to access quality of information at a reasonable cost on-time. To show how COI affects the information quality and the negatively impact on business sustainability thorough increasing different business risks, this paper measure the COI damages and provides solutions to decrease or mitigate the effects.

Information and assets are two main resources almost all enterprises requiring to protect them are part of management responsibilities through designing and implementing an effective internal control system. By considering that information is an integral part of decision making process, the question that how COI can affect negatively on this process would be a significant research question. COI is one of multifaceted ethical problems within organization and measuring how and in what extent COI can affect management decision making gives a tool for manager to handle the problem. The purpose of this study is to measure what aspects of the information are more affected by COI and how the cost and time to produce the reliable information would be increased [14].

© IFIP International Federation for Information Processing 2018
Published by Springer Nature Switzerland AG 2018. All Rights Reserved
S. A. Al-Sharhan et al. (Eds.): I3E 2018, LNCS 11195, pp. 305–314, 2018.
https://doi.org/10.1007/978-3-030-02131-3_27

One argument in corporate governance is the impact of COI on ownership structure [3]. The importance of corporate governance practices to reduce the COI between managers and shareholders is to reduce earning management techniques. Regardless of considering frauds or illicit acts, earnings management would negatively affect the usefulness of annual reports presented by management to users, which later users apply the information as reliable way for the user decision-making process. Net income is one of the users' sensitive information lead to make judgments about managers in which can be manipulated through earning management techniques because of COI.

The issue of COI is not neglected by the US legislations. The Sarbanes–Oxley Act (SOX) of 2002 approached to the subject of COI in four sections: Section 206 (audit independence), Section 402 (financial disclosures), Section 406 (code of ethics for senior financial officers), and Section 501 (securities analysis). Section 206, 402, and 501 of the Act amended to Section 10A, 13, and 15C of the Securities Exchange Act of 1934. SOX (2002) highlighted the importance of COI in corporate governance, audit independence, financial disclosure, ethics and professional conducts in these sections. However, section 404 of the Act clearly says that management is responsible to design, implement, and maintained an effective and sound internal control system. The main purpose of the system is to protect assets and producing reliable and quality information. The cost of internal control system assumes to lower the cost of producing quality information. However, to produce more reliable and relevant information, firms pay for assurance services (e.g. audit of financial statements, review, etc.) and non-assurance services (e.g. consultancy, tax, etc.).

The rest of this paper organized as follow. First, this study reviews current literature about the effects of COI on information quality. From Sects. 2, 3, 4 and 5, our emphasis will be given to those COI aspects that affect greatly on enhancing information quality by looking at reducing information cost, cutting delay in delivering of the information (timeliness), and optimal quantity of the relevant and reliable information. Also the link between COI and corporate governance theories would be shown by analysis of some relevant cases and provide solutions to remove or mitigating the effect of COI on corporate governance mechanism. Discussion part will be presented at section seven and conclusion in the last section.

2   Information Quality

Management decisions, to have effective and efficient corporate results, vastly depend on information quality. Information quality should have those characteristics that is free from material misstatements, errors, frauds, but are also timely, complete, reliable, and relevance. Eventually, eliminating COI will cause manager to make great decision to bring valuable corporate results for the organizations. When information quality is integrated with professional management skills, then immense benefits should be normally great success the organizational goals. Information quality depend heavily on data quality. To be relevant and reliable information, the amount of information, timeliness and cost of the information supposed to be at the optimal points. That is, information quantity would be at the optimal points, producing the information cost is less than information benefits and the time of information availability to the decision makers is at the right time of management request.

Nelson detailed the different losses of COI within every organization. The following table shows three categories and effects of the losses: operation, legal and the public relations through direct, indirect and long-term effects [11] (Table 1).

Table 1. Organizational losses of COI

Loss categories	Direct	Indirect	Long-term
Operation	Staff time	Staff time	Staff burnout
	Ethic consultants time	Staff & consultants stress	Staff turnover
		Staff consultants	Additional staff needed
		Decreased staff moral	
Legal	Legal consultants	Staff time	Additional staff needed
	Legal fees	Staff stress	Budget adjustment
	Settlement fees	Reputation risk	Higher malpractice costs
	Court charges		
Public Relation	Public relationship time	Rebuilt public image	Negative public image
	Consultant time	Staff work diverted	Loss of market share
	Advertising costs	Staff morale and stress	Decreased philanthropic support

As the table implies, the COI deteriorates the information quality due to secrecy. The COI push the information producers have preference not to show all sufficient, relevance and reliable information as revealing the information will act against their benefits. Thus, hiding of that quality information protect their benefits and damage other interested group in the organization. One of theories in information quality emphasizing on COI and degree of information quality is the information asymmetric theory.

2.1   Theory of Information Asymmetry

Information asymmetry theory is based on the study of Akerlof (1970) in which the behavior of buyers and sellers of used goods is analyzed by abandoning the hypothesis of perfect information on the market and assuming the contrary, the uncertainty of regarding the quality of products purchased [1]. The arguments of Akerlof result by analyzing the market place of some product where the seller has more information about the quality of products than the buyer. Akerlof concluded that hypothetical information difficulties can lead either to the collapse of the entire market, or to its transformation by adverse selection, being chosen the poor quality products instead of the higher quality ones. Initially, the theory of asymmetry information marked the first research in the field of buyer behavior but then rapidly expanded in financial theory and considerably affected the classical theories of the firm [2].

The hypothesis concerning the informational asymmetry is closely related to the agency theory and to the existence of agency relationships. Dividend and other financing policies adopted by directors would create different interests between the directors and shareholders. In this context, the rational for dividends paid to shareholders is provided, although it is known that they will pay an additional tax for this additional income. An answer in the "signaling" theory area is that dividends can be a good sign for future investments, the investor pay more for a share because, on the market, a big level of dividend is interpreted as a good sign which will mean a higher price of the shares. Likewise, "signals" of a strong company can be emitted through debt policy because it is considered that a strong company is one which can afford a high rate of indebtedness in order to finance ambitious investment projects. In conclusion, effective corporate governance will determine the reduction of informational asymmetry effect and prevent the manifestation of unfair actions of the managers to gain prestige and reputation but affecting the company's growth.

2.2   Agency Theory

One of central corporate governance theories is agency theory, known as principal-agent problem. The fundamental theories related to agency theory that can be closely associated with corporate governance are steward theory, hazard theory, stakeholder theory, resource dependence theory, transaction cost theory, political theory, and ethical theories. Agency theory describes relationship between the owners of a company and its managers, the agent based on a contract which the first part (the principal) engages with the second part (the agent) to perform stewardship service on behalf of the principals [8].

Alleging the interests of managers and shareholders should be through corresponding interests of managers in their decision-making circumstances with shareholders' objective of maximizing the company value. The agency costs could be mitigated by, such mechanism as dividend payout, salary or remuneration package, regulatory mechanism, ethical and moral trainings etc. Third, Pérez. (2015) demonstrated that financial reporting depends heavily on presentation of valuable information in term of enough information quantity and quality that this will increase a firm's reputation [12]. COI between managers and owners of entities cause opportunistic behavior will end up with minimizing instead of maximizing the owners' benefits. Moral hazard would be in form of being secret actions and opportunistic behavior represented in asymmetric information. The COI eventually cause unfavorable result such as worse performance and even business failure.

3   Information Cost

First we show how much does producing quality information cost. Producing quality information has two components: basic cost and premium cost. Basic cost is the cost of producing quality information at basic level of reliability and quality. A reasonable cost contains fundamental part that without the information, decision cannot be made or useless at all. The cost of producing basic information supposed to be fixed cost; that is a certain amount of money to spend produce the information. However, the information to be useful for decision making, extra cost need to be spent to make the information to be at the primum level, very useful for making high quality decision(s). *The premium part is a variable cost, depend on the quality level.* Total actual information cost supposed to have two components of basic actual which is a fixed cost (BFC_a) and actual premium cost which is a variable cost (BVC_a), then:

$$TIC_a = BFC_a + PVC_a \tag{1}$$

To have high quality information, entities should pay extra cost of the information contain two important characteristics: relevance and reliability. TC_{rel} defines as total cost to produce relevance and TC_{reb} defines as total cost to produce reliable information. So, formula (1) expands to:

$$TIC_a = BFC_a + TC_{rel} + TC_{rev} \tag{2}$$

Each TC_{rel} and TC_{reb} are only variable parts. The δ and φ are the slopes of variable cost of producing relevance and reliable information. The formula can be expanded for total cost incurred due to reliability and relevance *as:*

$$TIC_a = BFC_a + (Q \cdot \delta) + (Q \cdot \varphi) \tag{3}$$

Formula 3 can be extending to formula (4):

$$TIC_a = BFC_a + Q(\delta + \varphi) \tag{4}$$

Proof. When there is COI, the slop of $\delta + \varphi$ is determent of costs depend on the Q which is the quantity of the information needed to remove the COI. Companies cannot reduce basic fixed information costs but the $Q(\delta + \varphi)$ would be depend on mitigating COI effects in the organizational culture. The lower the Q, the information costs would be reduced by lower ($\delta + \varphi$).

Transaction cost theory is relevant to our discussion and linked to information cost conception. Transaction cost theory is defined as operating costs of the economic system. By considering Arrow and Williamson discussion, information cost should be an vital part of transaction cost. In contrast to the agency theory, transaction cost theory concern about the efficiency of the corporate governance in maximizing the owners' wealth. This theory works as a mechanism to control information costs. If a company structure align with relatively efficient hierarchical shape, then the contractual relationships between the agent and principal should be at the lowest COI level. If the transactions incurred should be in ally with efficiency of governance structures, then information costs should be at the lowest level. Therefore, one effect mechanism to control information cost would be under the transaction costs justifications. An example of the transaction costs is the cost of designing an efficient and effective internal control systems by management in which will be controlled by the audit committee and external auditor annually.

In formula (4), if BFC_a is defined as the cost of designing and implementing internal control systems accompanied with supervision of the audit committee as required by SOX section 404, then $Q(\delta + \varphi)$ would be the variable part. The variable part is the cost of internal and external auditor and it is variable due to the size of information which is determined by the size of the company. Normally, big firms pay higher audit fee than the small to medium-size companies. In fact, the relevance and reliability of the financial information presented by manager to the users depend on the investigation of external auditors. Thus, the formula can be extended as follows:

$$TIC_a = ICS_T + Q(IAC_{p.u} + EAC_{p.u}) \tag{5}$$

Where:

ICS_T = Internal Control System at total costs
$IAC_{p.u}$ = Internal auditor cost per information unit
$EAC_{p.u}$ = External auditor cost per information unit
Q = the size of information depends on the number of transactions

COI causes information cost to be increased as results of cost of internal and external auditors. The complexity of determining information costs amplifies when the COI integrated with the core of the corporate accounting frauds and characterized with the corporate governance issues. Corporate board of directors uses monitoring mechanism through internal and external auditors as gatekeepers. Internal auditors and audit committees are internal corporate governance gatekeepers. The external influence through two groups: external auditor (i.e., CPAs), regulatory agencies such as government (e.g., the SEC through PCAOB) and nongovernment regulators (e.g., the New York Stock Exchange).

4   Optimal Information Quantity

The Optimal Information Quantity (OIQ) is defined as disclosure of the optimal amount of information to be available to make effective and efficient decision(s). First, the cost of producing OIQ should be at least equal to or less than the benefit of the OIQ for every firm. Second, determining the OIQ requires a professional judgement which require to be differentiated from industry to industry, size and nature of enterprises or businesses. Therefore, for most of the firms, having an indication or measure of the optimal amount of producing information would be helpful to make reasonable decisions.

Refer to the above discussion, to compensate of the extra information costs, TIC or total actual information costs should be equal to the total benefits of producing the information. TIB is total information benefits which is either risk-free or low level risk information. In fact, similar to produce any commercial goods or services, producing information has its own cost and therefore it should have the benefit more than its cost.

Therefore, TIC should be at least equal or more than TIB to be considered as cost-benefit effective action;

$$TIC_a = TIB_a \qquad (6)$$

The TIB_a is defined be equal to $Q \cdot \gamma$ in which γ is the slope or the benefit per unit of producing the information and Q is the quantity of the information or OIQ.

$$TIB_a = Q \times \gamma \qquad (7)$$

To make it abbreviate, we use Q. When formulas (4) and (7) are expanded then we have:

$$Q \cdot \gamma = BFC_a + Q(\delta + \varphi) \qquad (8)$$

$$BFC_a = Q \cdot \gamma + Q(\delta + \varphi) \qquad (9)$$

To determine how much quality information to be produced that equal total cost of producing to total benefit, mangers must use the formula:

$$Q = \frac{BFC_a}{\gamma - (\delta + \varphi)} \qquad (10)$$

We call $\gamma - (\delta + \varphi) = CM$ or contribution margin of producing useful information.

Proof. Regarding to applicability of the formula 10 and compliance risk for producing reliable financial statements for the users, is defined as the cost of design, implement and maintain a sound internal control system for a firm. Suppose the cost is $150,000 and the cost of external audit (BFC_a) for reducing the information risk and other non-assurance services (δ) for producing more relevant information quantitatively is $100,000 and $50,000, respectively. for making the reliable and relevant information. Both and j reduce the information risk. Information risk is the risk of information contained with wrong fact in which causes making wrong decision. If the quantity number of transactions proceeded by the system was 50,000 transactions last year, then $2 and φ is $1 per transaction prospectively. To find we assume a firm will be benefited of producing the optimal amount of the information of reducing the compliance risk. For example, for taxation penalization charges, if we assume the amount is, in average, $450,000, then would be $9 per each transaction. Putting all the information in the formula 8, then optimal number of transactions to be produced and cost effective for the year would be 25,000 transactions per annum. At least, a firm with the above information should produce the number of transactions to reduce the risk of compliance and information.

5 Timeliness

Under the efficient markets theory, transparency of information to the main stake-holders at the right time is a crucial element of an effective and efficient corporate governance. Transparency of information not only about quality and quantity of the information but also revealing of the information at the right time. Quality of the information combines the relevance and reliability characteristics of the information with the quantity for supporting understandability of the information [6]. However, any day delay causes the information to become less effective and injure effectiveness of decisions of the stakeholders [5].

Real time access to the information is a crucial factor influences on the information value. This issue highlighted by section 409 of SOX ACT 2002, which issuer to disclose to the public *on a rapid and current basis*. Right decision(s) should always be made at the right time. It is plausible that COI cause delay in providing the information at the right time to decision maker to prevent financial reporting failure [13]. Thus, it convinces to assume a negative relationship between delay in issuing the information at the right time and information value. If the current value of quality information lessen by passing time, then the question to answer is at what rate the information quality diminished. Suppose

I_r = *Information at the right time*
I_w = *Information at the wrong time*

The following figure shows that the value of information at the right time Ir = α · r⁻ᵗ. *By assuming that information value* is at the highest point of α, then as delay in issuing the information occurred, the information value would be decreased and eventually to become zero at ε point.

Thus, the difference between t_r and t_w is called *delay time* and the delay rate is −t. to be more accurate, the relationship assume to be non-linear. To measure how long will it take that the value of information, we developed the model. If

IV_r = information value at the right time
IV_w = information value at the wrong time
r_r = rate of negative return per day at the right time
t = delay time to make the information value at the right to zero

$$t = \frac{In(IV_r) - In(IV_w)}{In(1+r)} \tag{11}$$

If $\lim_{t \to d} IV_w = 0$ where t is the day when the information value would be zero, then the formula change to:

$$t = \frac{In(IV_r)}{In(1+r)} \tag{12}$$

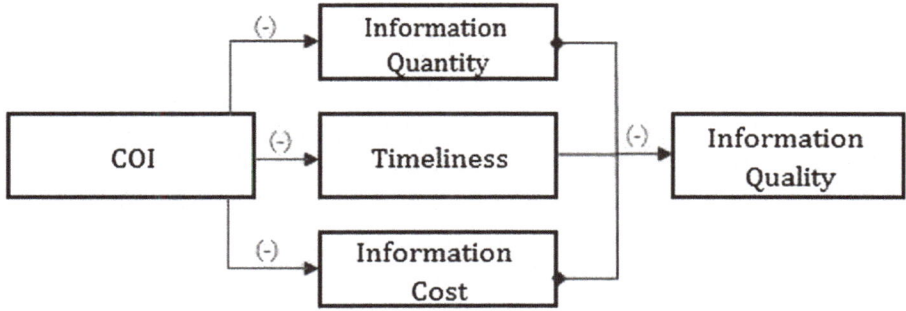

Fig. 1. Theoretical framework of COI effects on information quality

Figure 1 presumes, based on the paper, the negative effects of COI and information quality by looking at the three important characters: optimal quantity, time and cost.

6   COI Solutions

This section provides solutions to COI problem and answer the question of how to minimize the COI effect(s) on timeliness, cost and optimal quantity of information by refer to the equations developed in this study. Refer to formula 4, *if* Q considers to be constant, the information costs would be reduced by lower $(\delta + \varphi)$. Indeed, if $(\delta + \varphi)$ suppose to be constant, then Q should be lower to reduce COI. Regarding optimal quantity of information, if γ should be more than $(\delta + \varphi)$. By refer to Eq. 10, the bigger γ, then Q would be lower, therefore, this would be more economical for entities. By refer to Eq. 12, companies should elevate $In(1 + r)$, in which precisely this means that r should be higher.

7   Conclusion

This research mathematically showed how to measure COI and how it negatively impacts on management decision making by decreasing optimal information quantity, increasing information costs and make a longer period to produce quality information. While the interior effect of COI on management decision and entities performance has been examined extensively in management and other disciplines' literature, little is known about how to measure the harmful effect of COI on information quality. This study has provided evidence which suggest the ways of decreasing the negative effects of COI on information quality. The results therefore largely support many other empirical studies of the effect of COI on management decision in form of lowering information quality.

References

1. Akerlof, G.A.: The market for 'Lemons': quality uncertainty and the market mechanism. Q. J. Econ. The MIT Press. **84**(3), 488–500 (1970)
2. Boltona, P., Freixasb, X., Shapiro, J.: Conflicts of interest, information provision, and competition in the financial services industry. J. Financ. Econ. **85**, 297–330 (2007)
3. da Cunha, P.R., Piccoli, M.R.: Influence of board interlocking on earnings management *. Rev. Contab. Finanç. **28**(74), 179–196 (2017)
4. ECI: Conflicts of Interest. Ethics and Compliance Initiative, Ethics Research Center (ERC), USA (2016)
5. Ezat, A., El-Masry, A.: The impact of corporate governance on the timeliness of corporate internet reporting by Egyptian listed companies. Manag. Financ. **34**(12), 848–867 (2008)
6. Gullberg, C.: What makes accounting information timely? Qual. Res. Account. Manag. **13**(2), 189–215 (2016)
7. Lim, Y., Jung, K.: Conflict of interest or information sharing? evidence from affiliated analyst performance in Korea. Contemp. Account. Res. **29**(2), 505–537 (2012)
8. Makni, I., Kolsi, M.C., Affes, H.: The impact of corporate governance mechanisms on audit quality: evidence from Tunisia. IUP J. Corp. Gov. **11**(3), 48–70 (2012)
9. Mehrana, H., Stulz, R.M.: The economics of conflicts of interest in financial institutions. J. Financ. Econ. **58**, 267–296 (2007)
10. Mohd-sulaiman, A.: Financial reporting failures, board's competency and effectiveness. Int. J. Discl. Gov. **10**(2), 155–174 (2013)
11. Nelson, W.A., William B, Justin M., MacLeod, L.: The organizational costs of ethical conflicts. J. Healthc. Manag. **53**(1), 41–53 (2008)
12. Pérez, A.: Corporate reputation and CSR reporting to stakeholders. Corp. Commun. **20**(1), 11–29 (2015)
13. Pizzo, M.: Related party transactions under a contingency perspective. J. Manag. Gov. **17**(2), 309–330 (2013)
14. Xie, L.: Universal banking, conflicts of interest and firm growth. J. Financ. Serv. Res. **32**(3), 177–202 (2007)

Artificial Intelligence and Reliability of Accounting Information

Saeed Askary[(✉)], Nasser Abu-Ghazaleh, and Yasean A. Tahat

Gulf University for Science and Technology, Hawally, Kuwait
{askary.s, AbuGhazaleh.N, Tahat.Y}@gust.edu.kw

Abstract. Producing relevant and reliable accounting information is the main responsibility of accounting profession. Reliability and relevance of accounting information heavily depend on a sound internal control system as well as management and employees ethical and integrity characteristics. This paper shows how Artificial Intelligence innovatively works with the internal controls systems to help managers to produce high-quality accounting information by reducing information risk. Despite many types of research proposed using Artificial Intelligence in accounting and auditing, but none of them directly showed how to reduce information risk using Artificial Intelligence. The research benefits companies cut many costs and losses of failing to produce reliable accounting information, help managers to make a better decision and in overall improve entities performances. This paper proposes a general model to be applied by all type of business entities how practically use Artificial Intelligence to automate removing the weakness of internal control systems. This, in turn, reduces control risk, detection risk and increase audit quality by reducing accounting information risk.

Keywords: Artificial intelligence · Accounting information
Internal control systems · Reliability · Relevance

1 Introduction

The Institute of Chartered Accountants of England and Wales (ICAEW) issued "Artificial intelligence and the future of accountancy" article in 2017 and addressed applying and using this technique in accounting and auditing profession. ICAEW viewed from many successes in three perspectives: long-term visions, understand technology and application for accounting. Designing and developing knowledgeable organization using artificial intelligence technique is growing rapidly [21, 26]. All companies in the global business and economy deal with technology issues to survive in which Artificial Intelligence would be an appropriate solution for this problem [16]. Global Survey in Artificial Intelligence (2017) Forrester Research has predicted a "greater than 300% increase in investment in artificial intelligence in 2017", compared with 2016, a testament to the sector's rapid global growth. [25] banking and manufacturing would be more benefited from Artificial Intelligence. Artificial Intelligence application in accounting includes big data analysis, produce accurate, reliable, and on-time accounting information for the users. Brown *et al.* (1995) considered that Artificial

© IFIP International Federation for Information Processing 2018
Published by Springer Nature Switzerland AG 2018. All Rights Reserved
S. A. Al-Sharhan et al. (Eds.): I3E 2018, LNCS 11195, pp. 315–324, 2018.
https://doi.org/10.1007/978-3-030-02131-3_28

Intelligence impact significantly on accounting and auditing practices as well as internal control structure [5].

In long-term vision Artificial Intelligence helps accounting profession by focus on purpose of accounting profession for organization which is to use accounting information to make good decision by users of the information. In exploiting powerful technologies, think radically and being adaptable. In understanding technology, Artificial Intelligence helps human decision-making, strengths of machine learning, and to utilize the decision process of enterprises information management.

Accounting systems are moving very fast toward being more integrated with and intelligent logic through applying Artificial Intelligence [6]. Since the purpose of accounting profession is to provide relevant and reliable financial information for various users to make useful decisions, using Artificial Intelligence to produce such a reliable and relevant information would be more supportive. However, accounting systems are significantly depending on the internal control system to produce such a reliable information. For this reason, investigating how Artificial Intelligence help managers to remove weaknesses of internal control system to produce useful accounting information for the users would be questionable. This paper will show how Artificial Intelligence will enhance the efficiency and effectiveness of internal control system in producing highly reliable accounting information.

Artificial Intelligence is a mix of software and equipment as a substitute for human intelligence enable to solve complex business problems using reasoning, learning, elucidating, and recognizing patterns same as human expert. Artificial Intelligence uses expert system instead of expert human and apply machine intelligence instead of human intelligence. Artificial Intelligence has great impact on helping manager in making decision by reducing repetitive decisions, providing more precise information, simplifying complex decision factors, and fact processing data analysis [24].

The benefits of Artificial Intelligence in the future of accounting including reducing automotive tasks, increasing produced reliable financial information, simplifying complicated accounting and auditing cases, more accurate and precise information and timeliness for decision makers [5]. The gap in the literature shows that how Artificial Intelligence can reduce accounting information risk to increase confidence of the information users. This paper aims to address the gap of role of Artificial Intelligence in reducing accounting information risk.

The purpose of the study is to see how Artificial Intelligence help companies to remove internal control weaknesses to produce reliable accounting information. Although, there are many research about the importance of the Artificial Intelligence in business decision making but there is not any research show how Artificial Intelligence can improve the quality of accounting information by strengthens of the internal control systems. The rest of the paper is organized in this way. Frist, we review literature about the use of Artificial Intelligence in accounting and auditing profession. Then, we show how Artificial Intelligence can be applied in developing and designing internal control system to produce reliable accounting information. Finally, the paper shows how Artificial Intelligence can reduce the accounting information risk.

2   The Importance of Reliability of Accounting Information

According to Maines and Wahlen (2006) reliability is an essential characteristic for accounting information which is useful for decision making and it represents the extent to which the information is unbiased, free from error, and representationally faithful [22]. To achieve this, one of the crucial factor is to establish a strong internal control system. SEC defines internal control as 'a process, effected by an entity's board of directors, management and other personnel, designed to provide reasonable assurance regarding the reliability of financial reporting'. As stated by Elbannan (2009) the higher the quality of internal controls over financial reporting, and thus user better trust on the reports for making better decision [12].

One of the main problem in producing low quality accounting information is related to the weakness of internal control systems. The Sarbanes-Oxley Act of 2002 highlights the importance of information system controls by requiring management and auditors to report on the effectiveness of internal controls over the financial reporting component of the firm's management information systems [12]. One of the main reason for weakness of the internal control systems is related to poor corporate governance. Also, cost-benefit constrain may impact the developing, designing, implementing, and maintain an effective internal control systems [14].

To deal with removing weakness of the internal control system have been researched by many studies (e.g. see [6, 9, 12]). After initiating SOX 2002, the management of the companies, auditors, audit committee and SEC as well as PCAOB have paid more attention to the issue of removing weakness the internal control system [20]. Also, modern technology helped business enterprise to reduce the weakness of the internal control system. However, using effective innovate means such as Artificial Intelligence is more predictable then before.

There are a handful of research in accounting and auditing showing how Artificial Intelligence application to help to uncovered relationship between those variables affecting accounting information [18, 28]. Artificial Intelligence help better to cover all variables involved with a problem and not just cover a few of them in solving accounting and auditing dilemma. Artificial Intelligence would be one of the solution to remove weakness of internal control systems. Generally, Artificial Intelligence use the multitude of related technologies and then integrating those technologies into full solutions. Kahraman, et al. (2011) showed how intelligence techniques have been used in information management systems [16]. Artificial Intelligence use Intelligent decision support systems (IDSS) to automate performing and running activities. IDSS term describes decision support systems that heavily rely on using artificial intelligence techniques. The intelligence techniques used in enterprise information management (EIM) such as fuzzy set theory (FST), multi-agent systems (MAS), neural networks (NNs), genetic algorithms (GAs), ant colony optimization(ACO) and particle swarm optimization (PSO) (Ibid). For example, fuzzy logic and theory and neural network used for auditing research to predict fraud and improving audit quality (AlAli et al. [1], Beynon et al. [3]).

3 The Role of Internal Control Systems

The main purpose of almost every internal control system is to manage risks factor that prevent an enterprise to achieve their strategic goals. Every organization aims to achiever their strategic goals by designing, developing, implementing and maintaining an effective and efficient internal control systems. According to SOX (2002), management of publicly listed company is responsible to develop and maintain an effective and efficient internal control system. Figure 1 is an adjusted model of Ling's study that shows a dynamic internal control system.

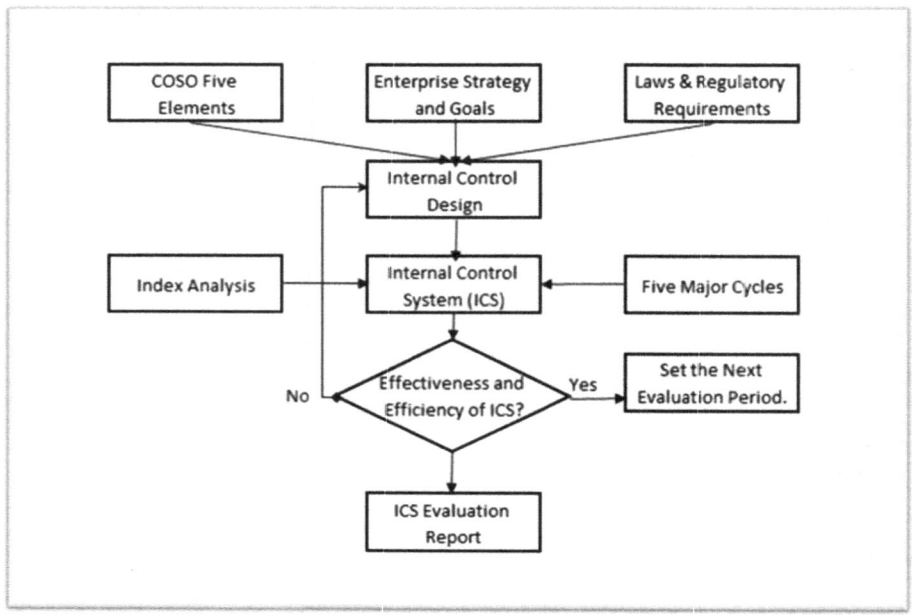

Fig. 1. Modified Ling [20] model

According to Ling [20] and as the Fig. 1 shows, internal control systems can be in optimal position by continuous internal control assessment and improvement. This could be achieved by applying COSO framework. According to Länsiluoto et al. [19] the COSO of the Treadway Commission has issued two globally recognized internal control frameworks. The first is *Internal Control – Integrated Framework*, and was published in 1992 and the second called *COSO Enterprise Risk Management*, issued in 2004. The frameworks of both are based on a conceptual framework compatible with COSO ERM (2004). COSO identifies that a central role of internal control is "…a means to identify and analyze risks, and to develop and manage appropriate responses to risks within acceptable levels and with a greater focus on anti-fraud measures…." Internal control has three types of objectives; operations, reporting, and compliance objectives [17].

CEO and CFO of public company's top management, has a responsibility to report through the management report on the effectiveness of internal control over financial reporting [13]. In internal control theory, the more stronger is the internal control system, the more reliable and high quality would be the accounting information and financial reporting. That is why external auditors should examine and report on the internal control effectiveness and efficiency along with audit report about the financial statements. Also, internal auditors, working under the audit committee, continuously monitor the issue and report to the committee on on-going basis.

The main weakness of internal control systems in every organization is related to the system disability to protect the assets and producing reliable and relevant accounting information. The system, at risk, allows fraudulent financial transaction being processed to the system in which produce unreliable accounting information. In this case, control risk would be high and auditor should be notified of detection risk. Thus, all those material misstatements that internal controls could not detect them, the auditor should find them by control test and in the worse case by increasing audit evidence in which will increase audit costs.

4   Internal Controls Systems and Information Reliability

In July, 2002, the United States government approved the Law Sarbanes-Oxley Act (SOX) in response to a wide range of financial scandals (e.g. Enron, WorldCom, etc.); one of the concern was about the internal control system strengthens and improving the accounting information quality. The general theory drawn from the law was based on the interaction between good corporate governance mechanism, strong internal control system, and high level of auditor's independence to produce reliable accounting information.

Canelas *et al.* (2013) raised the question about how information technologies through Artificial Intelligence can help and support decision making related to the SOX mandates [7]. There are two type of studies; one before the SOX Law and another one after the law introduced. The studies showed how companies concern about publishing truthful financial reports and suggesting some intelligent systems to support external auditors in their decision making processes to state if those reports were truthful or not. AI should help managers to produce the information in which would be more trustable for the users. This could be by removing and resolving complicated situations through Artificial Intelligence such as weakness of internal control system of cash, inventory, etc.

Doyle et al. (2005) studied the relationship between weak internal control and increased opportunities for intentional earnings management techniques and unintentional accounting estimation errors [11]. If Artificial Intelligence can strength the internal control systems, then the opportunities for intentional mistakes would be decreased. In turn, this will decrease control risk and higher the quality accounting information for the users.

Artificial Intelligence, in current high-powered technology, should help managers to remove weakness of internal controls through recognizing, analyzing and removing those weakness and then provide final solutions with more accurate and quick remedies before many damages incurred to the entity. Artificial Intelligence can reduce the accounting information risk by removing the weakness of internal control systems through the following solution. Artificial Intelligence can sense the weakness, comprehend the main problem, and do actions for removing the weakness through a programed expert decision making automatically [2].

4.1 Sense

Sense is similar to a border-control kiosk that uses computer vision technology such as facial recognition to uncover characteristics of weakness of internal controls. When this integrated with other technologies such as multispectral image analysis (e.g. video analytics, extensive information database and matching algorithms) it removes main weakness such as those related to inventory control systems.

4.2 Comprehend

Artificial Intelligence system also use technologies such as natural language processing, inference engine and expert systems to overcome the weakness of internal control system. Each of the technologies can be used through different applications. Date gathered from the sense section should be used by the technologies to be analyzed for the next section which is Act section.

4.3 Act

An Artificial Intelligence system acts in two ways; independently and in process. If Artificial Intelligence can work independently in regard to removing the weakness of internal controls, the Artificial Intelligence help to act this job without any human interfere to find, analysis and to decide how resolve the weakness without any human assistance. If the weakness suppose to be removed in process, then this kind of act would be applied for those internal control systems with discrete functions.

Artificial Intelligence, by reducing control risk, will be able to reduce auditor detection risk and acceptable audit risk. Detection risk is determined by dividing acceptable audit risk divided by inherent risk times control risk. Control risk is the risk related to weakness of internal control systems. Thus, Artificial Intelligence by reducing the control risk, this automatically reduce audit risk, increase audit quality, and therefore, reduce information risk for the users of the accounting information.

Moudud-Ul-Huq (2014) evidenced from Welch et al. (1998) study to introduce genetic algorithms as a potentially useful application by auditor for modeling fraud decisions [23]. Lensberg et al. (2006) applied genetic programming to bankruptcy prediction. This may also be useful in going-concern decisions when auditor form opinion on client with unpredictable business future. Neural networks have been proposed as a good application for a range of audit tasks. Due to their ability to model nonlinear relationships and handle incomplete data, neural networks may be particularly helpful for risk assessment tasks.

Koh et al. (2004) suggested the use of neural networks and data mining for going-concern predictions. They discovered that neural networks and decision trees are powerful tools in analyzing the complex, nonlinear and interactive relationships involved in going-concern analysis [18]. Fuzzy systems may be particularly useful for some audit tasks because of their inherent allowance of qualitative factors. For materiality decisions, this may be much better than typical quantitative rules of thumb (Comunale et al. 2005).

5 AI and Internal Control Systems

Moudud-Ul-Hug [23] listed ten subjects of accounting topics that can be integrated with Artificial Intelligence. Those subjects are credit authorizing and screening, mortgage risk analysis, financial and economic analysis, risk rating of exchange traded, detection of regularities in security price movement, prediction of default and bankruptcy, risk analysis of fixed income investment, detection of management fraud, machine learning techniques to automatically identify characteristics of fraud and artificial intelligence in marketing.

Using Bataller and Harris [2], we provide a practical model of using Artificial Intelligence to be applied for producing quality accounting information through mitigating weakness of internal controls in almost every industry. The following matrix shows managers to think and consider what type of internal control weakness can be automatically removed or augmented by Artificial Intelligence solutions.

The matrix in Fig. 2 shows two dimensions of data and work complexity. Both of the two dimensions should be considered from automation and improvement of internal control function perspectives. Automation of routine tasks can improve overall productivity in producing accounting information and effectiveness of internal controls.

Efficiency model characterizes with more toutine activities based on those rules, procedures and criteria that make internal controls to be stronger. The main goal is to design those controls that satisfy cost-benefit, quality performance and apply consistent in removing the weaknesses. In these Artificial Intelligence solution, humans involve with monitoring the accuracy and how the rules need to deal with the business conditions change. Machine learning capabilities should be applied for such rules. For example, with a minimal amounts of human intervention, internal controls monitor online data validity by applying codified knowledge and logic and make decision about accuracy and reliability of the data.

In expert model, Artificial Intelligence integrate judgmental tasks about how to remove the weakness of internal controls. Exactly like a financial advisor, the model provides the best solution based on the reality of the system condition and data, automated analysis and find the best solution robotically will be applied. Such system is able to search vast data sources, and making inferences and provide recommendations based on the knowledge. This model is similar to a medical diagnostic system which doctors find patient solution by testing different medical intricacy, the doctor judgement finally will be reported. Therefore, using natural language techniques and automated data analysis and searching, Artificial Intelligence will produce solution(s) for the weakness of the internal controls without need of human to intervene and judgement.

Effectiveness model suggests improvement in overall ability of the internal control systems to produce reliable and relevant accounting information. This require to design

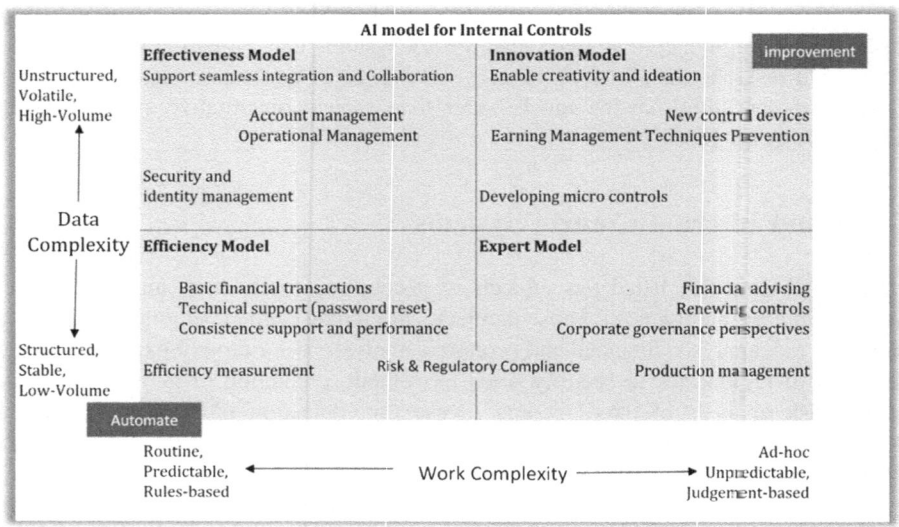

Fig. 2. AI model for internal control systems. **Source:** Modified from Bataler and Harris [2]

the model based on a considerable amount of knowledge about the business entity characteristics, the regulatory and legislative environment, and industry specification. In this model, the system should assure that all transactions and accounts are updated on ongoing base and automatically uses can access to the information through virtual agents. Users of the information are increasingly using agents such as Google now on their smartphones. Technologies such as natural language processing or speech recognition allow searching the internet and finding the answers in form of a formatted report.

At the innovative model, Artificial Intelligence solution allows to generate new control methods, objectives, and methodology by recommendation based on current control environment. An example of how Artificial Intelligence can augment creative controls is an intelligent software that it can analysis a control activity and then provide recommendations to increase the likelihood that the control will be at risk. Also, the model should prevent those earning management techniques by analyzing transactions and account balances. While humans make decision and act, technology helps identify alternatives and optimize recommendation [2].

Risk and regulatory compliance should be considered in two models; efficiency and expert. One of the major risk in today business is the risk of violating on not compliant with law and regulation. Artificial Intelligence techniques such machine learning could be used to automatically detect and identify the risk. Also, expert system could be used to find, analysis and generate solution using machine learning techniques.

6   Conclusion

To conclude, this research has contributed to knowledge in the following ways. First, the issue of using Artificial Intelligence in removing internal control systems weakness to produce quality accounting information initiative raised by this study. Second, to achieve this, a joint-working of accounting profession with Artificial Intelligence expertise to functionally developing software as well as applications for specific internal control systems are inevitable collaboration. Using Bataller and Harris [2], we provide a practical model of using Artificial Intelligence to be applied for producing quality accounting information through mitigating weakness of internal controls in almost every industry. Efficiency model characterizes with more toutine activities based on those rules, procedures and criteria that make internal controls to be stronger. In expert model, Artificial Intelligence integrate judgmental tasks about how to remove the weakness of internal controls. Exactly like a financial advisor, the model provides the best solution based on the reality of the system condition and data, automated analysis and find the best solution robotically will be applied. Effectiveness model suggests improvement in overall ability of the internal control systems to produce reliable and relevant accounting information. At the innovative model, Artificial Intelligence solution allows to generate new control methods, objectives, and methodology by recommendation based on current control environment.

References

1. AlAli, M., Almogren, A., Hassan, M.M., Rassan, A.B.: Improving risk assessment model of cyber security using fuzzy logic inference system. Comput. Secur. **74**, 323–339 (2018)
2. Bataller, C., Harris, J.: Turning Artificial Intelligence into Business Value. Today: Accenture Emerging Technology Group (2018)
3. Beynon, M.J., Peel, J.P., Tang, Y.-C.: The application of fuzzy decision tree analysis in an exposition of the antecedents of audit fees. Omega **32**(3), 231–244 (2004)
4. Bizarro, P.A., Dorian, M.: Artificial intelligence: the future of auditing. Intern. Audit. **32**(5), 21–26 (2017)
5. Brown, C.E., Coakley, J., Phllip, M.E.: Neural networks enter the world of management accounting. Manag. Account., 51–57, May 1995
6. Canada, J., Sutton, S.G., Kuhn, J.R.: The pervasive nature of IT controls. Int. J. Account. Inf. Manag. **17**(1), 106–119 (2009)
7. Canelas, J.Á.F., Martín, Q.M., Rodriguez, J.M.C.: Argumentative SOX compliant and quality decision support intelligent expert system over the purchase orders approval process. Appl. Math. Comput. Sci. **4**(4), 215–268 (2013)
8. Chang, S., Tsai, C.F., Shih, D.-H., Hwang, C.L.: The development of audit detection risk assessment system: using the fuzzy theory and audit risk model. Expert Syst. Appl. **35**(3), 1053–1067 (2008)
9. Cheh, J.J., Lee, J., Kim, I.: Determinants of internal control weaknesses. Contemp. Manag. Res. **6**(2), 159–176 (2010)
10. Dereli, T., Baykasoğlu, A., Sena Daş, G.: Fuzzy quality-team formation for value added auditing: a case study. J. Eng. Tech. Manage. **24**(4), 366–394 (2007)

11. Doyle, J., Ge, W., McVay, S.: Determinants of weaknesses in internal control over financial reporting and the implications for earnings quality. Working paper, University of Utah, University of Michigan, and New York University (2005)
12. Elbannan, M.A.: Quality of internal control over financial reporting, corporate governance and credit ratings. Int. J. Discl. Gov. **6**(2), 127–149 (2009)
13. Gramling, A., Schneider, A.: Effects of reporting relationship and type of internal control deficiency on internal auditors' internal control evaluations. Int. J. Discl. Gov. **33**(3), 318–335 (2018)
14. Gupta, P.P., Nayar, N.: Information content of control deficiency disclosures under the sarbanes-oxley act: an empirical investigation. Int. J. Discl. Gov. **4**(1), 3–23 (2007)
15. ICAEW: Artificial Intelligence and the Future of Accountancy. ICAEW IT Faculty, Chartered Accountant's Hall. Moorgate Place. London, UK (2017)
16. Kahraman, C., Kaya, I., Çevikcan, E.: Intelligence decision systems in enterprise information management. J. Enterp. Inf. Manag. **24**(4), 360–379 (2011)
17. Kinkela, K., Harris, P.: COSO updates practice framework. Intern. Audit. **28**(4), 35–40 (2013)
18. Koh, H.C., Low, C.K.: Going concern prediction using data mining techniques. Manag. Audit. J. **19**(3), 462–476 (2004)
19. Länsiluoto, A., Jokipii, A., Eklund, T.: Internal control effectiveness - a clustering approach. Manag. Audit. J. **31**(1), 5–34 (2016)
20. Ling, L.: Research on enterprise internal control financial assessment system based on artificial intelligence. Revista Ibérica De Sistemas e Tecnologias De Informação (16), 224–234 (2015)
21. Lu, H., Li, Y., Chen, M., Kim, H., Serikawa, S.: Brain intelligence: go beyond artificial intelligence. Mob. Netw. Appl. **23**(2), 368–375 (2018)
22. Maines, L.A., Wahlen, J.M.: The nature of accounting information reliability: inferences from archival and experimental research. Account. Horiz. **20**(4), 399–425 (2006)
23. Moudud-Ul-Huq, S.: The role of artificial intelligence in the development of accounting systems: a review. IUP J. Account. Res. Audit. Pract. **13**(2), 7–19 (2014)
24. Novac, C.: Artificial intelligence system for decision -making process. Civil Eng. **1**(2), 261–266 (2000). "Ovidius" University Annals Constantza
25. Segars, S.: AI Today, Ai tomorrow. In: N. R. P. Ltd (ed.) Global Artificial Intelligence Survey. ARM Northstar, UK (2017)
26. Todoroi, D.: How to create adaptable ROBO-intelligences? Acad. Econ. Studies Econ. Inform. **13**(1), 27–39 (2013)
27. US Securities and Exchange Commission: Management's Reports on Internal Control Over Financial Reporting and Certification of Disclosure in Exchange Act Periodic Reports - Frequently Asked Questions, Washington DC, 6 Oct 2004
28. Wang, Q.: Artificial neural network as cost engineering methods in a collaborative manufacturing environment. Int. J. Prod. Econ. **109**, 53–64 (2007)

Blockchain for Businesses: A Systematic Literature Review

Purva Grover[1]([✉]), Arpan Kumar Kar[1,2], and P. Vigneswara Ilavarasan[1]

[1] Indian Institute of Technology Delhi, New Delhi, India
groverdpurva@gmail.com
[2] Department of Marketing Management, University of Johannesburg, Johannesburg, South Africa

Abstract. This study tries to address the literature gap of what blockchain can offer to businesses in relation to consumers (B2C), businesses (B2B) and governments (B2G) through systematic literature review on blockchain. The review covers 40 articles from business, management and accounting peer review journals recognized by Scopus database. The review highlights how blockchain will facilitate instant payments, trusted interfaces and traceability of goods for the consumers. Businesses can use blockchain for snapshot sharing, machine-to-machine transactions, accounting, business process management and provenance traceability. Blockchain technology creating new business opportunities in government sector such as digital storage, authentication and maintenance of records; smart trust codification; new market for digital payment services and global commerce.

Keywords: Blockchain · Literature review · Technology usage Emerging technology

1 Introduction

Blockchain is a disruptive innovation [19, 26, 35] which can revolutionized organizations and offers various applications. Initially blockchain had emerged for the financial sector [22, 28]; but now researchers, academicians and industries are exploring blockchain for other applications in different sectors. Bitcoin was the first application built on blockchain which had facilitated money transfers and e-commerce activities [12].

Blockchain is a decentralized, permanent, transparent, immutable, trusted, peer-topeer transaction ledger systems [14, 18, 38] supported by algorithmic trust and distributed consensus mechanism which enables (a) secure information sharing; (b) long term preservation of digital records; and (c) verification and validation of digital transactions.

Blockchain projects had been initiated in multiple industries such as banking, insurance, supply chain, renewable energy, real estate, healthcare and many more [5]. Decentralization and disintermediation of blockchain is leading to ubiquitous commerce [38]. Blockchain is an attractive technological solutions for: (a) proof of

S. A. Al-Sharhan et al. (Eds.): I3E 2018, LNCS 11195, pp. 325–336, 2018.
https://doi.org/10.1007/978-3-030-02131-3_29

ownership; (b) trade ability; (c) trust among peers for real time transactions; (d) increased reliability; and (e) resilience to external threats [38].

Literature highlights technology features leading blockchain to technological commonwealth [19]: (a) disintermediation; (b) trustless exchange; (c) increased user control of information; (d) durable, secure decentralized networks; (e) transparency and immutability; and (f) maintenance of high-quality and accurate data; and also highlights technology features leading blockchain away from a technological commonwealth: (a) unresolved technical challenges; (b) unsettled regulatory environment; (c) cyber security and privacy concerns; (d) challenges to widespread adoption; (e) job loss due to automation; and (f) decreased corporate accountability. Literature indicates there is lot of complexity is involved in implementing and owning blockchain application [32] such as: (a) legal implications; (b) blockchain ownership; (c) operation of blockchain; (d) location of the ledger; and (e) control over the ledgers.

Rapid development of blockchain as an economic platform in different industries and huge demand of its characteristics and technological solutions had raised the need for the broad view of the use-case offered by the technology in context of the businesses. However this is missing in the existing literature. Therefore this study tries to address this literature gap and tries to investigate the answer for the question: What blockchain can offer to businesses in relation to consumers (B2C), businesses (B2B) and governments (B2G)?

The literature review helps us in identifying use-cases that had been offered by the blockchain in the past [10]. Through systematic literature review of the academic literature surrounding the blockchain in peer reviewed journal on subject area of business, management and accounting tries to highlight the various use-cases of the blockchain for B2C, B2B and B2G. The rest of the paper has been structured as follows: Sect. 2 discusses the methodology adopted for systematic literature review along with brief overview of the metadata of selected articles, Sect. 3 discusses use-cases of blockchain in B2C, B2B and B2G context. Section 4 discusses and concludes the study followed by discussing the limitation of the study along with future research directions.

2 Methodology for Systematic Literature Review

This section illustrates the procedure adopted for selecting the studies (Sect. 2.1) for systematic literature review for investigating blockchain offers to businesses in relation to consumers (B2C), businesses (B2B) and governments (B2G). The brief overview of metadata information of the studies is presented in Sect. 2.2.

2.1 Literature – Systematic Selection Protocol

For the current study, evidence based systematic literature review process suggested by Brereton and others (2007) [42] had been followed. The process model consists of the 10-stages, which can be grouped into three main phases outlined in Fig. 1. According to Elsevier, Scopus is the largest abstract database for journals, books and conference proceedings. Scopus provides rich interface to the user for selecting the studies on the basis of year, document type, subject area, keywords, source title, source type and language. Therefore to study what blockchain can offer to businesses in relation to consumers (B2C), businesses (B2B) and governments (B2G), Scopus was considered as the electronic database and subject area had been limited to "Business, Management and Accounting". For developing the review protocol previous studies in literature had been considered [39–42, 45]. The review protocol minimizes the bias in the study [42]. The review protocol had been formally reviewed by Prof. Arpan Kumar Kar and the results of it were considered by the review team as well.

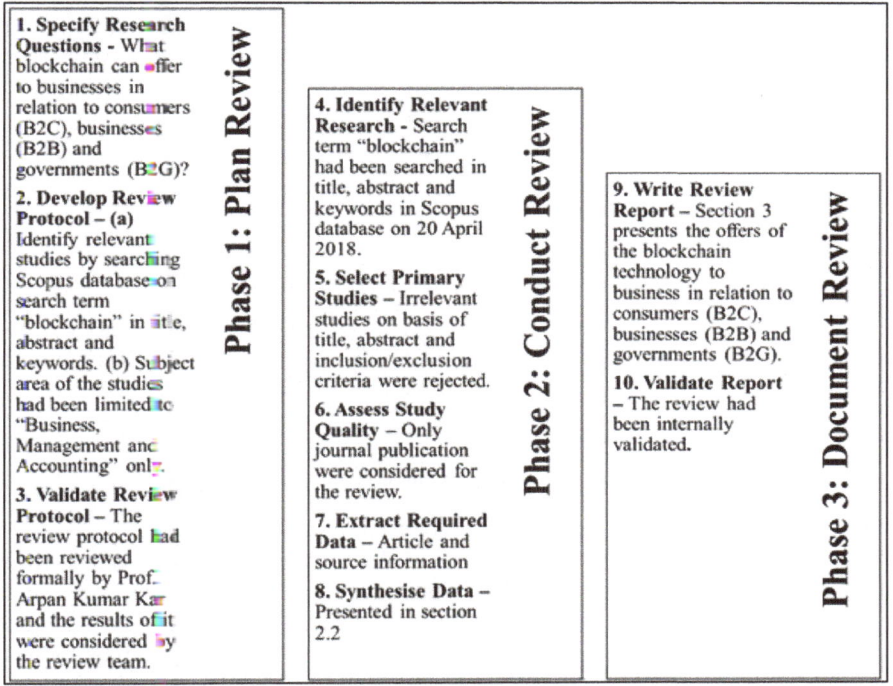

Fig. 1. Systematic literature review process followed

The search term "blockchain" in title, abstract and keywords field had been searched in Scopus database on 20th April 2018. The stage 5 (in Fig. 1), select primary studies is a two-step process. In first step irrelevant studies on basis of the title and abstract were rejected. In the second step inclusion/exclusion criteria was applied on the studies. The studies which provides the answers to the research questions were considered further in the review process. The studies not providing any information related to research question had been excluded. The studies selected for the current review had been restricted to journal publication only because of the following reasons [42]: (a) journals are well established and offers adequate indexing; (b) to make assure study had been written by expert; and (c) study had been reviewed by other experts in the field before publication. The metadata information for the selected studies had been extracted and analyzed. Results of it are presented in Sect. 2.2. Section 3 presents the offers of the blockchain technology to businesses in context to consumers (B2C), businesses (B2B) and governments (B2G). The review had been validated internally.

2.2 Brief Overview of Metadata of Selected Articles

This section tries to presents the brief overview of the metadata of the selected articles in terms of year of publication, journal, article titles and keywords. The Fig. 2 presents the journal and year wise count of the selected studies. In the selected studies two studies were published in 2016, 27 studies were published in 2017 and 11 studies were published in 2018. Journal wise highest number of the studies was published in journal "Strategic Change" in a Special Issue "The Future of Money and Further Applications of the Blockchain".

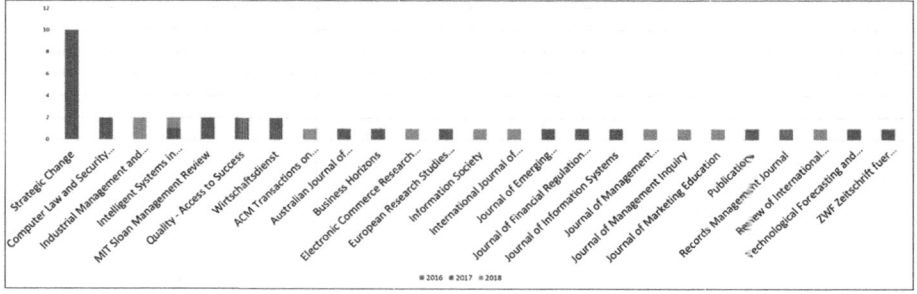

Fig. 2. Journal and year wise count of the selected studies

The Fig. 3a tries to give the overview of the keywords of the selected articles followed by the Fig. 3b tries to give the overview of the titles of the selected articles. Figure 3 depicts the blockchain had been associated with subject areas such as finance, accounting, fintech, corporations, management, manufacturing and marketing. Figure 3 illustrates blockchain had been associated with information and management in which processes, provenance and protection plays a role.

Fig. 3. (a) Word cloud on selected studies keywords; (b) Word cloud on selected studies article title

Figure 4 presents the association among keywords of the selected studies for the systematic literature review using paired words analysis. The paired word analysis had been applied over the keywords to better understand which keywords are being used together mostly. The analysis depicts the following words had been used often: (a) supply and traceability; (b) distributed ledger and entrepreneurship; (c) bitcoin and block; (d) provenance and smart; (e) distributed architectures; and many others. These all words highlighted above are strongly connected along with other words such as technology, disruptive, disintermediation, crowd, disruptor, managed, framework and contract. Thus these indicates the blockchain can be used for unbiased, trustworthy, distributed interface.

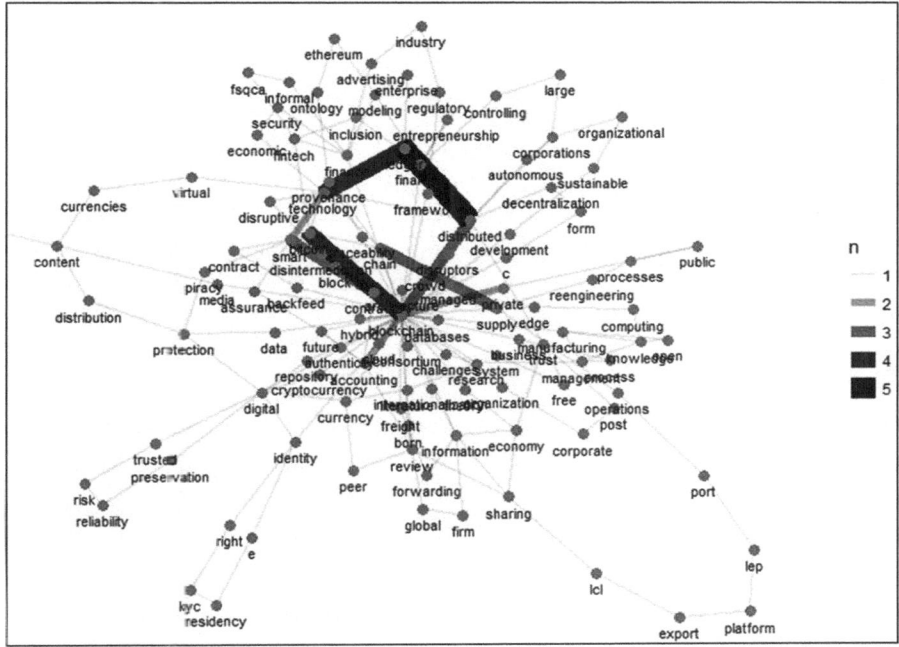

Fig. 4. Association among keywords of selected studies for systematic literature review

3 Blockchain for Businesses in Context to Consumers, Businesses and Governments

This sections had been divided into three section. The first section, highlights offers of blockchain for businesses to consumers. The second section list the blockchain offers for B2B followed by the third section which lists the blockchain offers in context of businesses to governments sector.

3.1   Business to Consumer Offers

Blockchain infrastructure has the ability to provide trusted user interfaces for consumers [34]. Literature indicates using blockchain infrastructure an individual can control their own personal data like identity proofs, citizenships, financial and educational records [14, 34]. Crypto currencies such as Bitcoins facilitates instant payment without a central bank or financial intermediaries [2, 12]. The instant payments provides consumers with the following benefits such as (a) low transaction cost; (b) faster transaction completion time; and (c) lessening coordination issues. Literature suggests blockchain can be used for giving incentives to researchers for doing peer review of scholarly papers [31]. The Table 1 lists the use-cases offered by blockchain for consumers along with the literature evidences and impacts. Popular offers that businesses can offer to their consumers are: (a) trusted user interfaces; (b) facility of instant payment for goods; (c) incentive receiving system; and (d) web interfaces for traceability of goods.

Table 1. Use-cases offered by blockchain for consumers

Applications	Literature evidences	Impacts
Trusted user interfaces	[7, 9, 14, 27, 43]	• Virtual direct one to one connections • Instant social sharing • Instant exchange of information • Protecting consumer privacy
Instant payments facilities (specially micro)	[2, 23, 29]	• Low transaction cost • Faster transaction completion time • Transferring money across the global without intermediaries, i.e. banks • Lessening coordinating issues
Incentive receiving system	[31]	• Receiving incentives virtually in secure way through blockchain infrastructure
Traceability of goods	[7, 15]	• Authenticity of luxury goods • Customer centricity • Improves informedness

3.2   Business to Business Offers

Literature indicates businesses is actively investigating in blockchain technology for commercial products and services [6]. Table 2 tries to list down the blockchain use-cases for businesses in selected articles along with literature evidences and their impacts. The company data can be warehouse on blockchain [34]. The blockchain will protect the data from security breaches. Using blockchain snapshot sharing can be done in one go which leads to transparency and removing layers of management within an organizations.

Kewell and other [13] had pointed out Everledger and Provenace are the companies working in supply chain operation. Blockchain streamlines the entire supply chain [38]

Table 2. Use-cases offered by blockchain for businesses

Applications	Literature Evidences	Impacts
Storing of the records	[3, 16, 22, 34]	• Data availability across the organization increases. • Reliability for the preservation of company record increases.
Snapshot sharing in one go	[13, 14, 33, 34, 38, 44]	• Sharing at the enterprise level • Horizon-scanning. • Improves transparency within organisations. • Flattens the hierarchy within firms.
Autonomous execution/Machine-to-Machine transactions	[30, 38]	• Autonomous economic agents, who send and receive money over IP. • Increased commercial efficiency
Accounting	[3, 4, 16, 24]	• Helps in verifying and auditing records • Brings transparency into the systems
Market disintermediation	[1, 22, 38]	• More efficient operations • Faster transactions • Direct linkages
Business process management	[21, 35]	• Builds mutual trust within a firm • Automation and monitoring
Provenance tracking	[8, 15, 27]	• Better supply chain operations • Authenticated ownership for digital assets • Increases transparency in the transactions • Sources of the products can be identified
Rapid internationalization	[37]	• Decentralized autonomous organization

and facilitates ownership, tracking and traceability of the assets [14]. Blockchain automates supply chain operations and makes it both responsive and cost-efficient [38]. Using blockchain machine-to-machine transactions is possible which can lead to market disintermediation [38] through autonomous economic agents, which send and receive money over IP. Autonomous economic agents may take the form of (a) autonomous vehicles; (b) independent certification agents for academic degrees or national identities; (c) for car parking ticket collection.

Literature suggests blockchain within and cross organizations can be used for (a) a real time, verifiable and transparent accounting system can be built [3, 16]; (b) container load optimization for international trading [33]; (c) legal and procedural standards for knowing your customer and suspicious transaction reporting requirements [32]. There is a need for business managers to understand potential benefit and threat of blockchain applications [35].

3.3   Business to Government Offers

Blockchain as a technology is creating new opportunities for business in government sector. Some of popular are listed in Table 3, these are: (a) digital storage, authentication and maintenance; (b) smart trust codification; (c) new market for digital payment services; and (d) global commerce. Government facilitates transaction and provides necessary institutional infrastructure [38]. There is a need in the government for keeping the trustworthy records [18] for the following use cases: (a) identity identification; (b) property titles; (c) election and voting [14]. Using blockchain these use cases can be recorded on immutable, transparent, and verifiably distributed ledger. Blockchain technology for these use cases can be divided into four transactional activities: (1) recording; (2) validating; (3) updating; and (4) authenticating [18]. Thus from these evidences it can be concluded blockchain is creating new opportunities for businesses in government sector.

Table 3. Use-cases offered on blockchain by businesses to governments

New businesses opportunities	Applications	Literature evidences	Impacts
Digital storage, authentication and maintenance	Land registries/Property rights	[11, 18]	• To stop illegal acquiring of properties
	Identity management and authentication	[14, 18, 19, 32]	• For country's immigration policies • For national security • For election and voting • Identification of identity frauds
Smart trust codification	Law and legal enforceability	[6, 11]	• Jurisprudence • Smart trusts through written code
New market for digital payment services	Financial inclusion	[14, 17, 38]	• For unbanked citizens at bottom of the pyramid leads to financial inclusion • Removes payment barriers
Global commerce	Cross border activities/Borderless commerce	[7, 28, 30, 32, 37, 38]	• A free global market • Commercial initiatives • Offers better services and products to the citizens. • Leads to global competitions among firms
	E-Residency	[32]	• Enables commercial activities

Estonian government is offering e-residency to every world citizen [32]. In this offer government issues digital identity to the citizens. These digital identities proof enables citizens to run an online company for commercial activities with both public and private sectors. E-residency is a commercial initiative of the Estonian government for borderless trade. E-residency leads to creation of new and false identities of the citizens which can be used for: (a) hiding real identity; (b) money laundering; and (c) organized crime [32].

Blockchain will eliminate fraud and corruption within government ecosystem [14]. Usage of blockchain in government ecosystem will offer speed, efficiency and trust to the people lying at the bottom of the pyramid. Kewell and other [14] had pointed out the government are working on blockchain initiatives along with startups. These countries are Ghana, Honduras, Sweden and Georgia. Under-socialized use cases of blockchain will foster the visions for the technology [13]. The Table 3 highlights some of the blockchain use-cases for government ecosystem.

4 Discussion and Conclusion

Internet took two decades for development and next decade for commercial purposes whereas blockchain is developing more rapidly as an economic platform [34], therefore there was a need for investigating the various use-cases offered by blockchain technology for businesses in relation to different stakeholders such as consumers and governments.

This study signifies blockchain will transform as well as revolutionized the way businesses are organized and managed in coming future which is in line with literature [34] and will affect daily operations of business activities and processes [30]. The Tables 1, 2 and 3 highlights the various blockchain use-cases for businesses in relation to consumers, businesses and governments along with their literature evidences and impacts. The summary of Tables 1, 2 and 3 had been presented in Table 4. The study points out using blockchain infrastructure, businesses can provide trusted user interfaces for consumers along with facilities of instant payments and better traceability of goods.

Table 4. Blockchain offers for businesses in context to B2C, B2B, B2G

Consumers	Businesses	Governments
• Trusted user interfaces • Instant payment facilities • New incentive receiving system • Traceability of goods	• Storing of the records, Snapshot sharing • Autonomous execution • Accounting • Market disintermediation • Business process management • Provenance tracking	• Digital storage, authentication and maintenance • Smart trust codification • New market of digital payment services • Global commerce

Blockchain technology can replace the supply chain labor intensive and time-consuming operations with a software, can automate and make it more responsive, consistence and real time reporting [22]. Blockchain infrastructure make feasible for businesses for snapshot sharing in one go along all the stakeholders leads to transparency within an organizations. The study points out blockchain can be used among organizations for various purposes such as accounting, international trading and knowledge sharing [3, 16, 32, 33]. Through blockchain government can offer a free global market [32]. Reduction in the cost of financial transactions through blockchain will result in widening financial inclusion [14]. Blockchain is more suited for multistakeholder governance model as it involves the participation of various participants [36]. Literature suggests the steps for organizations to understand and implement blockchain technology [34]. This study suggests researchers to pay attention to blockchain research opportunities for rapid internationalization of organizations.

5 Limitation and Future Work

For articles search for systematic literature review, only electronic database, Scopus had been considered for this study. Future studies can explore other databases as well. Only journal publication had been considered for high quality publication, future research can consider secondary resources as well for the literature review [42]. Only keyword "blockchain" had been used for searching the articles future studies can use other term such as "distributed ledger", "crypto currency", "smart contract" and many more terms which had been strongly related to blockchain in Fig. 4 This study had been restricted to subject area "Business, Management and Accounting" only, because of the research question had been explored in the study. Therefore future studies can explore the blockchain use-cases in the other subject area, by expanding the subject area to other areas such as decision sciences, computer science, social science and many more.

References

1. Adams, R., Parry, G., Godsiff, P., Ward, P.: The future of money and further applications of the blockchain. Strat. Chang. **26**(5), 417–422 (2017)
2. Brühl, V.: Bitcoins, blockchain and distributed ledgers. Econ. Serv. **97**(2), 135142 (2017)
3. Dai, J., Vasarhelyi, M.A.: Toward blockchain-based accounting and assurance. J. Inf. Syst. **31**(3), 5–21 (2017)
4. Dimbean-Creta, D.O.: Fintech–already new fashion in finance, but what about the future? Calitatea **18**(S3), 25–29 (2017)
5. Firica, O.: Blockchain technology: promises and realities of the year 2017. Calitatea **18**(S3), 51–58 (2017)
6. Giancaspro, M.: Is a 'smart contract' really a smart idea? Insights from a legal perspective. Comput. Law Secur. Rev. **33**(6), 825–835 (2017)
7. Gomber, P., Kauffman, R.J., Parker, C., Weber, B.W.: On the fintech revolution: interpreting the forces of innovation, disruption, and transformation in financial services. J. Manag. Inf. Syst. **35**(1), 220–265 (2018)
8. Grewal, D., Motyka, S., Levy, M.: The evolution and future of retailing and retailing education. J. Mark. Educ. **40**(1), 85–93 (2018)
9. Hanl, A., Michaelis, J.: Cryptocurrencies - a problem for monetary policy? Wirtschaftsdienst **97**(5), 363–370 (2017)

10. Hart, C.: Doing a literature review: releasing the social science research imagination. Sage, Thousand Oaks (1998)

11. Herian, R.: Blockchain and the (re) imagining of trusts jurisprudence. Strat. Chang. **26**(5), 453–460 (2017)

12. Holub, M., Johnson, J.: Bitcoin research across disciplines. Inf. Soc. **34**(2), 114–126 (2018)

13. Kewell, B., Michael Ward, P.: Blockchain futures: with or without Bitcoin?. Strat. Chang. **26** (5), 491–498 (2017)

14. Kewell, B., Adams, R., Parry, G.: Blockchain for good? Strat. Chang. **26**(5), 429437 (2017)

15. Kim, H.M., Laskowski, M.: Toward an ontology-driven blockchain design for supplychain provenance. Intell. Syst. Account. Financ. Manag. **25**(1), 1827 (2018)

16. Kokina, J., Mancha, R., Pachamanova, D.: Blockchain: emergent industry adoption and implications for accounting. J. Emerg. Technol. Account. **14**(2), 91100 (2017)

17. Larios-Hernández, G.J.: Blockchain entrepreneurship opportunity in the practices of the unbanked. Bus. Horiz. **60**(6), 865–874 (2017)

18. Lemieux, V.L.: Trusting records: is Blockchain technology the answer? Rec. Manag. J. **26** (2), 110–139 (2016)

19. Manski, S.: Building the blockchain world: technological commonwealth or just more of the same? Strat. Chang. **26**(5), 511–522 (2017)

20. McConaghy, M., McMullen, G., Parry, G., McConaghy, T., Holtzman, D.: Visibility and digital art: blockchain as an ownership layer on the Internet. Strat. Chang. **26**(5), 461470 (2017)

21. Mendling J. et al.: Blockchains for business process management-challenges and opportunities. ACM Trans. Manag. Inf. Syst. (TMIS) **9**(1), 4 (2018)

22. Michelman, P.: Seeing beyond the blockchain hype. MIT Sloan Manag. Rev. **58**(4), 17 (2017)

23. O'Dair, M., Beaven, Z.: The networked record industry: how blockchain technology could transform the record industry. Strat. Chang. **26**(5), 471–480 (2017)

24. O'Leary, D.E.: Configuring blockchain architectures for transaction information in blockchain consortiums: the case of accounting and supply chain systems. Intell. Syst. Account. Financ. Manag. **24**(4), 138–147 (2017)

25. Pazaitis, A., De Filippi, P., Kostakis, V.: Blockchain and value systems in the sharing economy: the illustrative case of Backfeed. Technol. Forecast. Soc. Chang. **125**, 105–115 (2017)

26. Petersen, M., Hackius, N., Kersten, W.: Blockchains for production and logistics. ZWF J. Econ. Fact. Oper. **111**(10), 626–629 (2016)

27. Plant, L.: Implications of open source blockchain for increasing efficiency and transparency of the digital content supply chain in the Australian telecommunications and media industry. Aust. J. Telecommun. Digit. Econ. **5**(3), 15 (2017)

28. Scott, B., Loonam, J., Kumar, V.: Exploring the rise of blockchain technology: towards distributed collaborative organizations. Strat. Chang. **26**(5), 423–428 (2017)

29. Seidel, M.D.L.: Questioning centralized organizations in a time of distributed trust. J. Manag. Inq. **27**(1), 40–44 (2018)

30. Shermin, V.: Disrupting governance with blockchains and smart contracts. Strat. Chang. **26** (5), 499–509 (2017)

31. Spearpoint, M.: A proposed currency system for academic peer review payments using the blockchain technology. Publications **5**(3), 19 (2017). https://doi.org/10.3390/publications5030019

32. Sullivan, C., Burger, E.: E-residency and blockchain. Comput. Law Secur. Rev. **33**(4), 470–481 (2017)

33. Tan, A.W.K., Zhao, Y., Halliday, T.: A blockchain model for less container load operations in China. Int. J. Inf. Syst. Supply Chain. Manag. (IJISSCM) **11**(2), 39–53 (2018)
34. Tapscott, D., Tapscott, A.: How blockchain will change organizations. MIT Sloan Manag. Rev. **58**(2), 10 (2017)
35. White, G.R.: Future applications of blockchain in business and management: a Delphi study. Strat. Chang. **26**(5), 439–451 (2017)
36. Yeoh, P.: Regulatory issues in blockchain technology. J. Financ. Regul. Compliance **25**(2), 196–208 (2017)
37. Zalan, T.: Born global on Blockchain. Rev. Int. Bus. Strat. **28**(1), 19–34 (2018)
38. Zamani, E.D., Giaglis, G.M.: With a little help from the miners: distributed ledger technology and market disintermediation. Ind. Manag. Data Syst. **118**(3), 637–652 (2018)
39. Chauhan, S., Agarwal, N., Kar, A.K.: Addressing big data challenges in smart cities: a systematic literature review. Info **18**(4), 73–90 (2016)
40. Chakraborty, A., Kar, A.K.: Swarm intelligence: a review of algorithms. In Nature-Inspired Computing and Optimization, vol. 10, pp. 475–494 (2017)
41. Grover, P., Kar, A.K.: Big data analytics: a review on theoretical contributions and tools used in literature. Glob. J. Flex. Syst. Manag. **18**(3), 203–229 (2017)
42. Brereton, P., Kitchenham, B.A., Budgen, D., Turner, M., Khalil, M.: Lessons from applying the systematic literature review process within the software engineering domain. J. Syst. Softw. **80**(4), 571–583 (2007)
43. Hawlitschek, F., Notheisen, B., Teubner, T.: The limits of trust-free systems: a literature review on blockchain technology and trust in the sharing economy. Electron. Commer. Res. Appl. **29**, 50–63 (2018)
44. Li, Z., Wang, W.M., Liu, G., Liu, L., He, J., Huang, G.Q.: Toward open manufacturing a cross-enterprises knowledge and services exchange framework based on blockchain and edge computing. Ind. Manag. Data Syst. **118**(1), 303–320 (2018)
45. Gupta, S., Kar, A.K., Baabdullah, A., Al-Khowaiter, W.A.: Big data with cognitive computing: a review for the future. Int. J. Inf. Manag. **42**, 78–89 (2018)

Transportation Management and Decision Support Systems within the Supply Chain Management Framework

Issam A. R. Moghrabi [(✉)] [iD] and Fatemah O. Ebrahim

College of Business Administration, Gulf University for Science
and Technology, Mubarak Al-Abdullah, Kuwait
moughrabi.i@gust.edu.kw

Abstract. With technology and globalization, supply chain expanded and therefore supporting software is required in order to ensure prompt decisions are appropriately made. The emphasis of this paper is on the transportation management system (TPS) that supports the decision making process within the supply chain management framework. Our hypothesis focuses on the routing and mapping module within TPS. To support the hypothesis, questionnaires were distributed to the managers of small scale businesses in Al-Shuwaikh commercial district in Kuwait and the results obtained helped rank the importance of four carefully selected modules embraced by transportation management systems. A methodical regression analysis approach was used to substantiate the findings as elucidated in the study presented here.

Keywords: Supply chain management · Transportation management system
Decision support systems

1 Introduction

Supply chain management is the management of the flow of goods and services, which include raw material supply, production and services, inventory management and goods delivery till it reach to the customers [1]. As per the definition, it is obvious that supply chain role is highly correlated to other roles and functions within the same organization and externally. Within the organization there should be strong integration with the production/operation module, information technology, marketing and procurement. External links will be with suppliers, customers and probably shipping companies if this is not part of the organization. Information technology can effectively support the globalization of the supply chain management process in many different ways where no manager's insight or a simple calculation process can be sufficient for making optimal or near-optimal business decisions. With globalization, there is an expansion of supply chains beyond any traditional boundaries and this incurs harder supply chain management decisions. In general, the supplier will focus on cost effectiveness, sufficient quantity of production, and sustaining quality during production. Also, while delivering to customers, committed time of delivery gains much significance due to its contribution to reaching the ultimate goal of the business in

© IFIP International Federation for Information Processing 2018
Published by Springer Nature Switzerland AG 2018. All Rights Reserved
S. A. Al-Sharhan et al. (Eds.): I3E 2018, LNCS 11195, pp. 337–343, 2018.
https://doi.org/10.1007/978-3-030-02131-3_30

terms of gaining revenue, customer satisfaction, loyalty and building brand and good reputation [1, 10].

During the supply chain management flow (Fig. 1), there should be a system to bring out the best outcome of each any every stage such that maximizing revenue, gaining customer satisfaction and optimizing the cost. Information systems help to achieve these outcomes effectively [2]. It would be even more effective if there is an integrated supply chain management system to gather all the stages and take decisions based on the biggest picture considering all inputs and external factors as well.

Fig. 1. Supply chain management flow [2].

In order to have effective supply chain management, it is essential to have integrated supply chain business processes [1]. Integration includes collaborative work between buyers and suppliers, product development, common systems, and shared information. This cannot be achieved without information systems. The intricate choice of supply chain management systems is dependent on many parameters, such as business size, business culture in term of willingness to adapt technology and the outcome required from this system [5]. Some systems focus on cost optimization, others on customer satisfaction and many of them help in finding the optimum decisions and solutions. In short, supply chain management systems aim to help in completing the business process effectively. Modules for supply chain management software include customer requirement processing, purchase order processing, sales and distribution, inventory management, goods receipt and warehouse management, supplier management/sourcing and transportation management. In this article, the focus will be on Transportation management system processes.

2 Transportation Management System

The emphasis of Transportation Management system (TMS) is on the transportation logistics that support the supply of products or services while minimizing both cost and time. TMS comprises several processes that interact to fulfill the overall functionality intended by the system (see Fig. 2). To emphasize the significance of the TMS, many authors [2, 6, 8, 17] pointed out that usually transportation cost consumes between 20 to 35% of the total production and logistics costs of a product. Therefore, any achievable savings in transportation cost will be likely to result in nontrivial savings on the overall production cost and related logistics.

The significance of transportation is mounting at a fast pace as the delivery channels are moving from national to international confines [6]. The dire need today is for good quality commodities at decreasing maintenance costs to ensure availability and robustness of items. Further, a powerful transportation module is essential for lessening costs through better path arranging, load enhancement, carrier, enhanced traceability across the transportation chain, offering options for improving in the transportation plan and supply chain execution Black [3]. Transport influences the production, logistical practices and delivery planning.

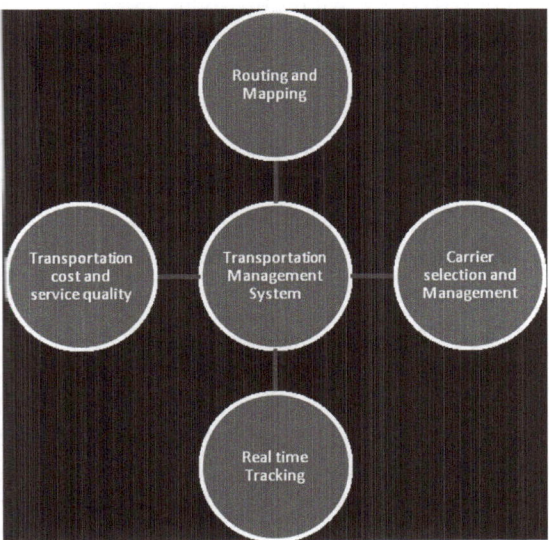

Fig. 2. Functions performed by transportation management system

This study aims to determine the rankings of the variables/processes of the transportation Management system in terms of importance. There are many processes embedded within TMS such as tracking, vehicle maintenance, fuel costing, warehousing communications, EDI implementations, accounting, traveler and cargo handling, inbound and outbound transportation mode, vehicle load, shipment batching of orders, scheme simulation, cost controls, optimizing terrestrial transport rounds, freight audit and payment, yard management, order visibility, carrier management, advanced shipping and many others. Yet this study will focus on only four processes since the firms considered in this study are small businesses in Kuwait and for which more functions are either not needed or do not have any added value for the business [9, 12–14]. The four processes are routing & mapping, transportation cost &service quality, carrier selection &management, and real time tracking. The results obtained are likely to vary for different firm sizes.

3   Research Hypothesis

Our hypothesis formulation assumes that Routing and Mapping is the most influential parameter of the TMS for small scale firms [9, 11]. The research instrument was a a questionnaire which embodies ranking questions and five -point Likert scale, where 1 indicates a strongly disagree and 5 denotes a strongly agree. Data was collected from different small scale firms in the Industrial area of Al-Shuwaikh in Kuwait in order to check the validity of the assumption in our hypothesis. The questionnaire was distributed to 57 managers in many business sectors such as car parts, supermarkets, meat preparation and packaging companies, plumbing supplies, restaurants. fast food, Varnish and Paint, furniture and others. All the questionnaires results were considered and regression analysis was applied and as a result is the hypothesis of Transportation management system ensures proper routing and mapping of the stock in small scale firms is acceptable. Thus, the following is the main hypothesis of the study:

Hypothesis: Transportation management system guarantees the optimal routing of products in small size businesses.

Objective: The objective is to study whether transportation management systems guarantees the optimal routing of products in small size businesses.

4   Data Analysis and Results Interpretation

To facilitate the analysis of the collected data and the interpretation of the results, a ranking table as well as linear regression are employed. The averages computed from the data collected from the study through the managers of the respective firms are tabulated in Table 1. The Table has in the first column the business categories to which the questionnaire was channeled. The numbers in the parentheses in that column indicate the count of the businesses participating in the study that fall under that specific business category. The last 4 columns to the right list the various processes a typical transportation management system performs. The numbers reported in the rows indicate the average score given to each process for each business category (5 indicates highest and 1 is for lowest). The roman letters in the four columns to the right denote the rank/importance of the function for a particular business category.

Table 1. Functions performed by transportation management system in small scale industries

Units/Factors	Transport cost and service quality	Routing and mapping	Carrier selection and management	Real time tracking
Meat preparation and packaging (7)	4(I)	3.3(II)	3(III)	1(IV)
Car parts (8)	3.2(I)	2(III)	1.8(I)	2.6(II)
Restaurants (10)	3(III)	4.3(I)	3.3(II)	4(IV)
Fast food (9)	4(II)	5(I)	3(III)	4(IV)
Varnish and Paint (6)	3(III)	4(I)	3.5(II)	1(IV)
Furniture (5)	3.8(II)	4(I)	3(III)	3(IV)
Marble (3)	2.6(II)	3(I)	2.2(III)	1(IV)
Coffee shops (7)	3(II)	3.8(I)	2.7(III)	2(IV)
Electronics	3.3(II)	3.4(I)	3.1(III)	2.1(IV)
Others (Miscellaneous) (2)	2.1(III)	3.6(I)	3(II)	2.3(IV)
Mean & Rank	3.2 (II)	3.64 (I)	2.86 (III)	2.2 (IV)

The results tabulated in Table 1 indicate that to the most of the businesses included in this study, Routing and Mapping is the most significant module in a typical TMS.

5   Regression Analysis Results

Regression analysis was used for testing our research hypothesis. The results of the analysis are reported in Table 2. The R value that came up indicates a 68% correlation between the independent variable, namely Transportation Management System, and the dependent one Routing and mapping. In addition, the R2 value denotes that the Transportation Management System can be used to justify a 63% variation in Routing and mapping. The adjusted 0.601 R2 value reported predicts an increase in the R2 value whenever another independent variable is also considered. The obtained value of β is a shows the strong kinship between the dependent and the independent variables. Significant changes in R square are found with F-values significant at 5% confidence level. Thus the hypothesis "Transportation management system guarantees the optimal routing of products in small size businesses." is acceptably good with a significance level of p < .06.

Table 2. Regression model summary

Model	R	R2	Adjusted R2	Std. Error of Estimate	F value ANOVA	Sig. Level	β	t	Sig. Level
1.	.688	.632	.601	.1791	32.266	.000	.658	8.8	.018

6   Study Limitations

Although this study went through methodical statistical analysis, the data sampled is taken from a specific industrial area. Thus, it can be argued that the results cannot be generalized to cover the whole of Kuwait. Despite the limitation of the sample, we strongly believe, based on our experience in Kuwait, that Al-Shwaikh Area is a typical commercial district that is replicated in different locations within the country. The results obtained from the study originate from the human input collected, a highly subjective source. However, this seems to be the sole source we rely on. We do not believe that this weakens the findings as similar consistent results were obtained in [16, 17]. Another limitation of the study is considering only small firms in Kuwait. However, this is the focus of the study presented here.

7   Conclusion

Supply chain management systems are usually offline tools can help improve the supply chain from many aspects, such as: supply calculation, demand forecasting, supply chain planning, supply chain scheduling, raw material distribution, supply chain optimization systems, such as transportation management, among others. The study presented here aims to highlight the significance of the Transportation Management Systems within the supply chain framework as one of the most important modules due to the cost factor involved. In specific, the study hypothesis and the results achieved confirm that the emphasis is to be placed on the Routing and Mapping module within TMS in small scale businesses. The output of our study divulges the average ranking of the processes performed by transportation management systems in small businesses in the Al-Shuwaikh Commercial Area in Kuwait. Among the numerous modules involved in TMS, the ranking presented in the study considers the most prominent and effective modules, namely "Transportation cost and service quality", "Routing and mapping", "Carrier selection and management", and "Real time Tracking". The variable "Routing and mapping" ranked first in terms of the determination of an optimal transportation and routing plan. In addition, regression analysis was utilized to confirm the research hypothesis "Transportation management system guarantees the optimal routing of products in small size businesses" with encouraging results.

References

1. Azadfallah, M.: A new aggregation rule for ranking suppliers in group decision making under multiple criteria. J. Supply Chain Manag. Syst.
2. Basheer, S., Srinivasan, K.K., Sivanandan, R.: Transp. Dev. Econ. 4. 8 (2018). V. **5**(4), 38–49 (2016). https://doi.org/10.1007/s40890-018-0061-5
3. Black, W.R.: An unpopular essay on transportation. J. Transp. Geogr. **9**, 1–11 (2001)
4. Caputo, A., Pelagagge, P., Scacchia, F.: Integrating transport systems in supply chain management software tools. Ind. Manag. Data Syst. **103**(7), 503–515 (2003). https://doi.org/10.1108/02635570310489205
5. Chalotra, V., Kumar, P.: Transportation management system functions and performance amplifying the span of small scale firms. J. Supply Chain Manag. Syst. **5**(4) (2016). Ebrahimnejad, A. Eng. **17**, 981 (2016). https://doi.org/10.1007/s11081-015-9277-y
6. Note on "A fuzzy approach to transport optimization problem", Optim
7. Kalakota, R., Whinston, A.B.: "Electronic Commerce" in A Manager's Guide. Addison Wesley, USA, pp. 285–316 (1997)
8. Karmaker, C.L.: A decision support system for warehouse location selection: a case study. J. Supply Chain Manag. Syst. **5**, 4 (2016)
9. Kumar, N.R.: Optimization of supply chain network modeling and performance measurement in flow of production. J. Supply Chain Manag. Syst. **3**(4), 1–6 (2014)
10. Luo, X., Jennings, N.R.: A spectrum of compromise aggregation operators for multiple attribute decision making. Artif. Intell. **171**(2007), 161–184 (2007)
11. Pedersen, E.L., Gray, R.: The transport selection criteria of Norwegian Exporters. Int. J. Phys. Distrib. Logist. Manag. **28**(2), 108 (1998)
12. Shahbandarzadeh, H., Haghighat, F.: Evaluation of the strategies of target market selection on the basis of IFE and EFE matrixes using LINMAP technique. Iranian J. Manag. Stud. (IJMS) **3**(3), 41–58 (2010)
13. Triantaphyllou, E.: Multi Criteria Decision Making Methods: A Comparative Study. Kluwer Academic Publishers (2000)
14. Wang, Y.M., Yang, J.B., Xu, D.L.: A preference aggregation method through the estimation of utility intervals. Comput. Oper. Res. **32**(2005), 2027–2049 (2005)
15. Wedley, W.C., Choo, E.U.: An Analysis of AHP Comparisons and Priorities. ASAC, Hlifax, Nova Scotia, pp. 16–28 (2008)
16. Zanakis, S.H., Solomon, A., Wishart, N., Dublish, S.: Multi attribute decision making: a simulation comparisons of select methods. Eur. J. Oper. Res. **107**(3), 507–529 (1998)
17. Yao, M.J., Hsu, H.: A new spanning tree-based genetic algorithm for the design of multistage supply chain networks with nonlinear transportation costs. Optim. Eng. **10**(219). https://doi.org/10.1007/s11081-008-9059-x

Identifying Social Media's Capability for Recognizing Entrepreneurial Opportunity: An Exploratory Study

Abdus-samad Temitope Olanrewaju[✉],
Mohammad Alamgir Hossain, Paul Mercieca, and Naomi Whiteside

RMIT University, Melbourne, Australia
abdus-samad.olanrewaju@rmit.edu.au

Abstract. Social media is believed to play an essential role in entrepreneurial opportunity recognition. However, little is known about the exact nature of the relationship between the capability of social media and entrepreneurial opportunity recognition. Addressing this gap in literature, we interviewed eleven Nigerian entrepreneurs to investigate how opportunity can be recognised via their engagement with social media platforms. It was found that, via Social Media, entrepreneurs recognise opportunities regarding introducing new products, entering new markets, better customer relations and participating in entrepreneurial events. We also identified that opportunity recognition is driven by five capabilities of social media: networking, searching, observation, experimenting, and social media data analytics. Implications of our findings and limitations are discussed.

Keywords: Social media · Opportunity recognition · Entrepreneur
Nigeria

1 Introduction

Social media (SM) is "a group of Internet-based applications that build on the ideological and technological foundations of Web 2.0 and allow the creation and exchange of user-generated content" [1]. It is becoming a norm in the daily activities of over three billion individuals using various platforms including Facebook, Instagram, LinkedIn, WhatsApp and Twitter [2]. Entrepreneurial use of SM has attracted attention from academic literature in recent times. Majority of the studies focus on the factors that influence SM adoption/use and its impact on firm performance. Although a number of advantages and benefits of SM have been reported in literature, the exact nature of the capabilities of SM for the entrepreneurs is yet to be established. Also, there is generally a lack of literature regarding how SM affects entrepreneur Opportunity Recognition (OR). Hence, the primary objective of this study is to explore the capabilities of SM and how they affect OR amongst entrepreneurs. This exploration was conducted via interviews with entrepreneurs in a developing country. The research has developed a framework that outlines how SM can support OR and most importantly in the context of a developing country.

S. A. Al-Sharhan et al. (Eds.): I3E 2018, LNCS 11195, pp. 344–354, 2018.
https://doi.org/10.1007/978-3-030-02131-3_31

Unlike developed countries, developing countries have relatively low governmental support and therefore the entrepreneurs are responsible for recognising opportunities and developing their businesses [3]. This leads to a high discontinuance rate amongst the entrepreneurs [4]. Moreover, earlier studies have highlighted the challenges faced in developing countries due to the dynamicity and complexity of their environment [5] which affects OR. Thus there is the need to further investigate the antecedents of OR on SM in from the context of a developing country to help them better recognise opportunities and enhance their business.

Nigeria is used as the case for this current study as it is enjoying an emerging adoption of SM by entrepreneurs. Nigeria is the most populous country in Africa with over 75% of its internet users on SM [6]. Unlike the developed countries, the government of Nigeria does not play a vital role in the establishment of new business and supporting them. Between March and May, Nigeria Small to Medium Enterprises (SMEs) recorded about 27% international trade that was aided by using digital tools [7]. The use of SM has allowed for entrepreneurs, mainly youths in Nigeria, to quickly start and operate their own business. Similar findings have been seen in previous studies in developing countries too [e.g. 8].

2 Background

Social media use by entrepreneurs has been increasing in recent years [9, 10]. Due to SM affordances [9, 11], it gives entrepreneurs the ability to perform several activities in an easier and quicker manner; this is a blessing particularly for the entrepreneurs in developing countries. SM also has been shown to be crucial in supporting entrepreneurial business process starting from idea exploration to business creation and growth [10, 12]; it also improves firm performance [11].

OR has been influenced by several factors that are well detailed in the traditional entrepreneur literature off SM. For example, the review paper of [13] developed an OR framework which has six vital factors that serve as its antecedents. These are social capital, systematic search, alertness, cognition/personality traits, environment, and prior knowledge. Similar factors have been identified by other studies too. However, [9] argued that entrepreneurial activities in digital platforms differ from offline platforms. This implies that OR drivers on SM may differ from what is seen in the offline literature. It is important to understand how the antecedents of OR behave.

Earlier studies identified that SM influences entrepreneurial OR [11, 12, 14, 15]. The opportunities recognized by entrepreneurs on SM may led to the creation of new businesses, especially in the developing countries where it aids social and economic development [8]. However, the dynamics of such influence remains to be understood. [16] reported that SM use positively influenced the relationship between entrepreneurial alertness and opportunity creation, and negatively impacted the relationship between prior knowledge and opportunity discovery and creation. However, they only discussed the moderating effect of SM and falls short in explaining how it influences OR.

3   Research Method

Studies on SM and OR are still few. Studies have identified that entrepreneur uses SM differently in mobilising resources and capital [9, 17]. Based on these findings, it is anticipated that entrepreneurs [9, 17] may recognise opportunity differently on SM. The existing theories do not cater the process. Therefore this study used qualitative approach that is "particularly well suited to new research areas or research areas for which existing theory seems inadequate" [18]. Specifically, this study carried out an explorative qualitative approach through interviews.

3.1   Selection of Interviewees

In selecting the respondents to be contacted for the interview, both purposive and snowball sampling was used. The researcher made sure that the entrepreneur had a presence on one or more SM platforms, had less than 20 employees, in either e-retail or service industry, business-to-consumer (B2C) oriented, and only the entrepreneur (founder0 was interviewed from each business. Similar criteria were used by earlier studies in entrepreneurship and SM [e.g. 9, 15, 17]. Based on the initial respondents, snowball sampling was then used to reach out to other potential participants. In total 11 entrepreneurs (14 businesses in total, where the entrepreneur had more than a business, it is signaled by the double year in the established column) were interviewed, which is sufficient to reach to a conclusion [19]. The interview was developed based on the literature. It was semi-structured and was conducted in English language. Table 1 summarizes the respondents' profile.

Table 1. Respondents profile.

Code	Business industry	Gender	Established	Platforms used
NGR1	E-tailing (Food)	Male	2016	Facebook, Instagram, Twitter
NGR2	Service (Editing)	Male	2009	Facebook, WhatsApp, Twitter, LinkedIn
NGR3	E-tailing (Fashion)	Male	2016	Instagram and Facebook
NGR4	Service (Technology)	Male	2012, 2016	Facebook, Instagram, Twitter
NGR5	Service (Technology)	Male	2012, 2016	Facebook, Instagram, Twitter
NGR6	Service/E-tailing (Marketing/Beauty)	Male	2011, 2016	Facebook, Twitter
NGR7	E-tailing (Fashion)	Female	2016	Instagram, WhatsApp
NGR8	E-tailing (Confectioneries)	Female	2015	Instagram, Facebook
NGR9	E-tailing (Fashion)	Female	2011	Instagram, Facebook
NGR10	Service (Beauty)	Female	2013	Instagram, Facebook
NGR11	Service (Photography)	Male	2015	Instagram

3.2   Data Analysis

Before analysing the data, the interviews were transcribed from the audio recording to text; then, the transcription was sent to the respondents for ensuring proper representation of their thoughts and validity of the transcribed data. The returned transcripts were then loaded into NVivo 11 for data analysis. The transcriptions were categorised by coding in detail using NVivo [20]. This allowed for classifying the codes under themes and dimensions that were only about OR and SM capabilities. Firstly, similar quotes were grouped from the interviews which formed the first-order concepts (e.g. "*interactivity*", "*scalability*"). The first-order concepts were then categorised under emerging themes (e.g. "*Networking capability*"). The emerging themes were arranged into dimensions (e.g. OR, SM capabilities). The findings were triangulated with the entrepreneurs SM platform usage for validity.

4   Findings

4.1   Opportunity Recognition

The respondents reported that they were able to identify several opportunities on SM platforms. The ways that 'opportunity' was operationalised in their businesses reflect what has been reported in previous literature. That is, as the variables of OR, the entrepreneurs discussed new products/services, new markets, and better customer relations. During the interview, the respondents stressed that the ability for them to participate in events such as competitions, training and seminars was an opportunity. They highlighted that they would not have been aware or attended the events if not for SM, which improved their business. The respondents unanimously agreed that SM had played a crucial role in their opportunity identification process. This is corroborated by them saying "*Yes... it helps*" NGR5, NGR7, NGR8, NGR9. "*SM has helped me to identify opportunities*" NGR3 & NGR10 "*...to expand and grow beyond our limited resources*" NGR4. For these respondents, it is clear that SM supports the discovery of new opportunities. The analysis of the respondents' interviews suggests that these new opportunities were regarding: introducing new products/services, entering new market, better customer relationships, and participating in new events which are discussed below.

Introducing New Products/Services. Social media allows entrepreneurs to recognise opportunities for introducing new products/services to the market, which was established in several responses. As said by NGR11, "*SM is where the ideas are...*", moreover, this was reflected by other respondents like NGR1 and NGR5. SM was found to play a vital role in recognising viable ideas which were later translated into business opportunities. NGR1, for example, explained how SM through birthday notification allows him to be aware of his friend's birthday. The notification enabled him to identify an opportunity and build a new service in his food delivery business around birthday parties which brought in more revenue.

SM also helps the entrepreneur in identifying opportunities to develop new products by allowing the customers to make them informed of new services that they can offer. For example, NGR5 explained that they were able to introduce new games on their gambling platform based on customer feedback such as female-oriented and traditional games that were not on their platform initially. He even stated that majority of the artists on their booking site were sourced based on their extensive customer network. To other respondents such as NGR7, NGR8, and NGR10, SM allows them to recognise opportunities of developing new products through its ability to make them aware of the latest trends and equally to guide them step-wisely on how to get it done.

Entering New Market. One of the most important ways that the respondents indicated that SM has helped them is in identifying and entering new market. The broad outreach capability of SM allows for the entrepreneurs to spot new markets which would have been impossible without it. For example, NGR11 was able to identify an international market (South Africa) for his digital products (pictures) which happened via a friend direct message (DM) on Instagram. In another scenario, NGR11 mentioned that SM brought him corporate clients such as Coca-Cola by giving his product extensive coverage that attracted their attention. For NGR1, SM allowed them to "*unveil*" a whole new market of clients due to the feedback gotten on SM platforms. In NGR4 case, the analytics of their SM data allowed them to study the market behaviour before deciding to expand. What is recurrent to all the interviewee is their admission that they will not have been able to recognise nor enter the new markets without the use of SM.

Better Customer Relations. Social media has allowed entrepreneurs to learn and discover better ways to serve their customers, which leads to improved customer relation and retention. However, the way it helps varies from respondent to respondent. In remembering how SM helps in better serving her customers, NGR10 recalled that it was via Instagram that she was able to have a business card which better allowed serving her customers through referrals and also to gain their trust. Equally, it helps the entrepreneur customers to grow confidence in their products which allows for the entrepreneur to build their brand reputation based on other customer reviews. As indicated by earlier research, a significant role played by SM in entrepreneur business is the feedback loop where it allows the entrepreneur to interact with their customer. This was further reported by NGR4 where SM serves as a virtual office that allows for improved efficiency through better response time, ability to act as a place to serve as information disseminator. This was also supported by NGR5 with him highlighting that SM platforms have helped in reducing client stress and costs by reducing phone calls or need of coming down to their office.

Participating in New Events. SM presented entrepreneurs the opportunities to better equip themselves with entrepreneurship skills as the SM network promoted new events such as competitions, training and seminars that could support their business development. NGR3 highlighted this:

> "*SM has helped me to identify opportunities. Because there is a lot of things that go on, Like SM help you to get invited to seminars, entrepreneurship development workshop. Those opportunities only arrive due to your presence on SM platforms*" NGR3.

Surprisingly, a good number of entrepreneurs experience participating in events as a form of opportunity, and they categorically stressed it as a distinct and unique opportunity afforded by SM. For example, NGR11 was opportune to partake in a competition in South Africa where he was able to meet other people. Other entrepreneurs repeated similar stories. NGR10 recalled that it was via SM that she was able to get an internship opportunity which helped in honing her skills which improved her business. NGR7 was able to know about a fashion trade-fair via SM that improved her product packaging and also meet topnotch designers. NGR8 was able to partake in a Google course on entrepreneurship via her SM account where she more about marketing. The effects of the events attended on their business were so significant that made them categorise it as an opportunity on its own.

4.2 Social Media Capabilities

Literature has stated that SM impacts entrepreneur OR, but it is silent on the SM capabilities that have direct impact on OR. The most significant driver of OR on SM is because it is open and public as mentioned by NGR6. Virtually all the respondents corroborated this stance with NGR5 stating that if there is any new thing that has people more than SM platforms, he will move there too. NGR6 summarises the several capabilities of SM on how it supports OR in the excerpt below.

> "It is because a lot of people are there, it is easy to watch people via SM, you know the best ideas come from seeing the problems that all these people have. So because Facebook has like 2 billion people, 17 million Nigerians on Facebook alone, so you know if it were the old ways, you would hire 20 people to watch people, how long will it take you to study 500 people in real life; but on SM, very easy, you watch them and find out their problems.... So I think the main characteristic is that there are a lot of people and it is good for surveying, and validating your idea... the ability to observe people, the ability to survey, the ability to search and the ability to network...." NGR6

In the course of the analysis, it was seen that SM supported entrepreneurs OR due to its capability for searching, networking, experimenting, observing and analyzing SM data (SM data analytic).

Networking Capability. The networking capability on SM platforms plays a crucial role for entrepreneurs in recognising opportunities. The ability to network and build social capital by meeting virtually with different people allows for entrepreneurs knowing about new opportunities, e.g. opening up new market can lead to the creation of new business interacting with other people that can potentially lead to new business creation; polishing their ideas to develop new products and services. Networking capability of SM was discussed based on [9].

The respondents identified opportunities through interacting with other people on SM. For example, NGR4 fine-tuned his idea for new service through interacting with people from other countries. NGR5 and NGR11 recognised new markets by pitching their business to higher ranked people they interacted with on SM. For NGR8, the scalability of SM allows for showcasing new products to clients which afforded the opportunity to serve her customers better. The interoperability affordance of SM allows the entrepreneur to recognise opportunities to better serve their clients through prompt dissemination of information across several SM platforms. [9] were able to view their network and equally be aware of other people network which helped in OR. The ability to associate with likeminded people on the SM platforms help them to be aware of new opportunities. Association on the platform is possible due to the availability of novel information that is useful to them, and they would not have been aware of except only via SM as said by NGR3. NGR6 further highlighted that this capability allowed for establishing network connections based on their current network circle. This allows them to conduct business based on the new network connections, ability to search or filter network connections based on their needs and belong to a community that renders them the required support.

Similarly, the transversability of SM allows for the "*ripple effect*" as termed by NGR1 and NGR6 which according to them is the most significant way that opportunities are recognised and resources mobilised via SM. This means that entrepreneurs through their ability to go through (transverse) their network and other people network tend to generate a string of connections that can be leveraged for their business use. For NGR6, the use of Facebook groups, and due to the transversability affordance of SM, he was able to navigate through the members, connect with them and from there build personal relationships that further enhance his OR. The visibility capability of SM according to the interview did not play a crucial role. The entrepreneurs stated that they were on SM due to its visibility in the first place, which makes them visible to others in the network. NGR5, for example, mentioned that the visibility opens up opportunities for new markets and customers by allowing celebrities fans to see them and know about their service.

Searching Capability. Searching capability in SM played paramount roles in recognising opportunities for the respondents. Most importantly regarding new products and equally serving their customers. This was achieved by searching for information in different locations and seeing other approaches regarding their business development. This capability is supported by the previous work of [9]. The findings were analysed under their dimensions of searchability and retrievability, persistence and reviewability, and asynchronicity. The respondents pointed that SM capability to search and retrieve goes together. It is fundamental in supporting their OR as they can get required information and see recent things that form the basis for new opportunities. NGR6 highlighted that the capability of SM search to be enhanced through the use of hashtags, locations, tweets, time duration which improves their OR; and as stressed by NGR10, it allows them to produce better and stay on top of their industry.

SM persistence and reviewability affordances allow the respondents to keep track of information. Respondents such as NGR7 and NGR11 stressed its importance with NGR7 even calling SM "*a library or an archive of information… take you down the memory lane*". They stated that the information can always be accessed when needed, either through searching on the SM platform or exporting it to their device using third-party applications which allows for OR. The asynchronicity of SM search allows for information to be extracted from one-way ties in the case of NGR6 through groups which allows him to come over the temporal limitations. By posting information on the group, NGR6 in the earlier part of the interview admitted to it giving him the chance to attend a seminar (webinar) that introduced new opportunities.

Observation Capability. Opportunities are recognised on SM primarily due to its openness and the massive number of people on it. This capability of SM makes it a fertile ground for observation. Observation was done by intentionally following some users or accounts for various purposes without actively contacting the person. In some scenarios, the respondents admitted having contacted those account owners for clarity. The underlying motive for observing as stated by NGR5 is to *"...learn from what they are doing... I said we get ideas from SM, from following other people and business and try to replicate it in our business."* This can take many forms as evidenced based on the interviews with the respondents. For example, NGR3 use SM to observe their competitors actions *" to stand out and add value to what we are doing"*. This allows them to identify opportunities, know what their competitors are doing and learn ways to beat the completion and stay ahead. While others identify opportunities regarding customer relations, better ways to produce and equally know what is in vogue to easily tap on the new wave. This was evidenced in discussions with NGR7, NGR8, and NGR10. For NGR10, she follows business in her niche and even goes a step ahead by putting on post notifications for her favourite accounts that she observes. This makes her aware of when they post, as she said, she *"...will be losing out"* if she does not do it.

Experimenting Capability. SM is making it easier for entrepreneurs to experiment with new products to check for their viability in the market before going large scale. This involves testing their products/ideas, validating them and equally streamline or targeting their products to specific markets. This was reported by NGR1, NGR5 and NGR6 where they discussed the strength of SM in allowing them to know which products to introduce to the market. For example, NGR6 said

> *"I easily test new products through SM, just put it out there with maybe $5 or less on Facebook ads and promote it just to see how people are going to engage with it....We use SM to validate products or services...you can also use social adverts to validate ideas to find out if people will are interested in what you want to do on that".*

The concept of targeting markets was expanded on by NGR5 when he explained that targeting allows them to reach the specific market faster, cheaper and more efficiently which would not have been attainable if not for SM

> *"SM helps us in targeting which is key; you can target so many demographics; you can decide that people you want to view your adverts should be men. It is simple and cost-effective.... Facebook helps us in target our markets and customers"* NGR5

Data Analytics Capability. SM platforms such as Facebook and Instagram allow entrepreneurs to analyze how people interact with their content. This was discussed by NGR4 where SM data analytics insights allow them to know the expectation of new markets. It also enables them to know how clients value the products, and thus how profit margin can be assured. Specifically, Instagram allows individual accounts to upgrade to a business account which comes along with an analysis-oriented platform that allows the entrepreneur to know how people engage with their content as seen in NGR10 and NGR11. This capability allows the entrepreneur to know which products of theirs are preferred by their clients, which allows for OR.

4.3   Summary of Findings

The data analysis suggests that SM supports several types of entrepreneur opportunities based on its capabilities. The capabilities identified by the respondents have their unique SM affordances that allow them to influence entrepreneur OR.

This study confirms that entrepreneurs can use SM as a means to identify new opportunity. This is influenced by various capabilities that have already been discussed in the preceding sections. The findings gotten from the Nigerian respondents were used in developing a framework (see Fig. 1) that aims at explaining how SM capabilities influences entrepreneur OR.

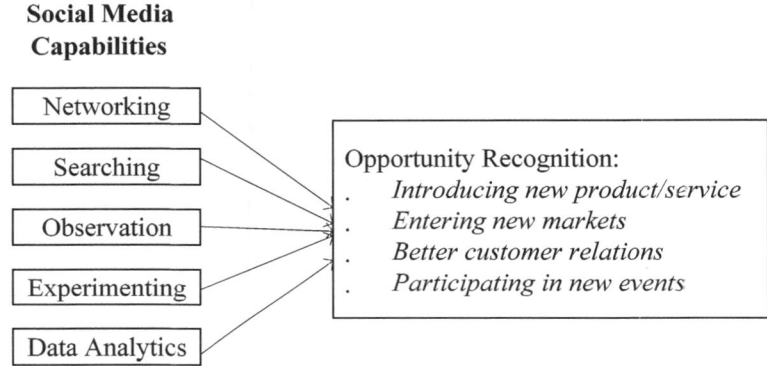

Fig. 1.   Opportunity recognition framework on social media

5   Conclusion

5.1   Implications of Findings

It is understood by prior studies that one of the primary benefits offered by SM is its ability to support entrepreneurs by identifying the relevant opportunities. It is more prominent in a developing country because of the unstructured governance of the respective government genies. Our study identified the several types of opportunities that entrepreneurs recognised on SM. It also details the various SM capabilities and affordances regarding how they help in OR on SM. Consequently, the study offers several implications for theory and practice.

The first implication for theory is that this study validates previous research propositions [e.g. 14] on the role of SM on entrepreneur OR. This is achieved by identifying several capabilities of SM that supports it. While previous research has highlighted similar factors such as observation and experimenting [see 21], it differs here because it is primarily based on SM capability; which allows it to be carried out by more entrepreneurs; instead of just the "innovative ones". This is due to it being more open, easier and faster in carrying out and does not necessarily require persistence and high creativity or associative thinking since it is an open field.

Secondly, as argued by [9], SM affordances allows for differences in entrepreneurs actions. This is illustrated in this study by seeing that SM supports OR via searching and networking differently from the offline media through its various affordances. Moreover, concerning the search, it was seen that SM due to its capabilities allows for search to be beneficial for those with prior experience and equally those searching systematically; and thus homogenise two stream of thought that emerges in the offline literature.

Thirdly, it highlights the role of SM data analytics that is readily available on the SM platforms as a capability of SM that supports OR. This is another theoretical contribution made by the study where it highlights its vital role for SMEs entrepreneurs in a developing country. Moreover, data analytics has mostly been attributed to big firms that have the resource base (human and technical), but due to the inclusion and simplification on SM platforms, the capability has allowed for the entrepreneurs to recognise new opportunities.

As the practical implication, this study highlights the opportunities that abound on SM platforms for entrepreneurs. This includes its ability to be a source for OR which helps in establishing new business, growing or expanding business and on the overall contributing to the economy. The findings indicate that entrepreneurs should make positive use of their SM platforms as it can further enhance their OR. Government stakeholders can sensitise on the benefit of SM in the creation and survival of businesses which will contribute positively to the economy.

5.2 Future Research

The study will be expanded beyond the exploring the role of SM to OR only, to an examination as to how it influences the resource mobilisation and opportunity exploitation of entrepreneurs from developing countries. Factors affecting SM use will be equally explored from developing country perspective thereby attempting to link SM use factors to how it influences their OR. In addition, the findings will be empirically tested and compared with entrepreneurs from developing countries to identify the difference between SM usage and OR amongst them.

References

1. Kaplan, A.M., Haenlein, M.: Users of the world, unite! The challenges and opportunities of social media. Bus. Horiz. **53**(1), 59–68 (2010)
2. Williams, B.: Social media reaches 3 billion users globally, says new report 2017 (cited 22 Mar 2018). Available from: https://mashable.com/2017/08/07/3-billionglobal-social-media-users/#KUVQS_kASaqp
3. Ojo, A.O., Oluwatayo, I.B.: Entrepreneurship as drivers of growth, wealth creation and sustainable development in Nigeria. Socioeconomica **4**(8), 325–332 (2016)
4. Olaposi, T.O., Akintelu, S.O., Oyebola, A.I.: The impact of socio-demographic characteristics on new product introductions. In: 2015 Portland International Conference on Management of Engineering and Technology (PICMET). IEEE, Oregon, USA (2015)

5. Stewart, W.H., May, R.C., Kalia, A.: Environmental perceptions and scanning in the United States and India: convergence in entrepreneurial information seeking? Entrep. Theory Pract. **32**(1), 83–106 (2008)
6. Amaefule, E.: 75% of Nigeria's online population use social media—Minister. 2017. Available from: http://punchng.com/75-of-nigerias-online-population-use-socialmedia-minister/
7. Adepetun, A.: Nigeria's small, medium enterprises record 27% international trade. The Guardian Nigeria 2017. Available from: https://guardian.ng/businessservices/nigerias-small-medium-enterprises-record-27-international-trade/
8. Alkhowaiter, W.: The power of Instagram in building small businesses. In: 15th IFIP WG 6.11 Conference on e-Business, e-Services, and e-Society. Springer International Publishing, Swansea, UK (2016)
9. Smith, C., Smith, J.B., Shaw, E.: Embracing digital networks: Entrepreneurs' social capital online. J. Bus. Ventur. **32**(1), 18–34 (2017)
10. Ahmad, S.Z., Ahmad, N., Bakar, A.R.A.: Reflections of entrepreneurs of small and medium-sized enterprises concerning the adoption of social media and its impact on performance outcomes: evidence from the UAE. Telemat. Inform. **35**, 6–17 (2018)
11. Wang, W., Pauleen, D.J., Zhang, T.: How social media applications affect B2B communication and improve business performance in SMEs. Ind. Mark. Manag. **54**, 4–14 (2016)
12. Mack, E.A., Marie-Pierre, L., Redican, K.: Entrepreneurs' use of internet and social media applications. Telecommun. Policy **41**(2), 120–139 (2017)
13. George, N.M., et al.: A systematic literature review of entrepreneurial opportunity recognition: insights on influencing factors. Int. Entrep. Manag. J. **12**(2), 309–350 (2016)
14. Nambisan, S., Zahra, S.A.: The role of demand-side narratives in opportunity formation and enactment. J. Bus. Ventur. Insights **5**, 70–75 (2016)
15. Fischer, E., Reuber, A.R.: Social interaction via new social media: (How) can interactions on Twitter affect effectual thinking and behavior? J. Bus. Ventur. **26**(1), 1–18 (2011)
16. Park, J.Y., Sung, C.S., Im, I.: Does social media use influence entrepreneurial opportunity? a review of its moderating role. Sustainability **9**(9), 1593 (2017)
17. Drummond, C., McGrath, H., O'Toole, T.: The impact of social media on resource mobilisation in entrepreneurial firms. Ind. Mark. Manag. **70**, 68–89 (2017)
18. Eisenhardt, K.M.: Building theories from case study research. Acad. Manag. Rev. **14**(4), 532–550 (1989)
19. Perry, C.: Processes of a case study methodology for postgraduate research in marketing. Eur. J. Mark. **32**(9/10), 785–802 (1998)
20. Bazeley, P., Jackson, K.: Qualitative data analysis with NVivo. Sage Publications Limited, New York (2013)
21. Dyer, J.H., Gregersen, H.B., Christensen, C.: Entrepreneur behaviors, opportunity recognition, and the origins of innovative ventures. Strateg. Entrep. J. **2**(4), 317–338 (2008)

The Influence of Social Media on Entrepreneur Motivation and Marketing Strategies in a Developing Country

Abdus-Samad Temitope Olanrewaju[(✉)], Naomi Whiteside,
Mohammad Alamgir Hossain, and Paul Mercieca

RMIT University, Melbourne, Australia
abdus-samad.olanrewaju@rmit.edu.au

Abstract. Entrepreneurs are increasingly using social media in running their businesses. This phenomenon is remarkable especially in developing countries where entrepreneurs now exploit business opportunities by using cheaper platforms. Prior studies claim that social media plays a crucial role in establishing a business and ensuring its survival through effective marketing. However, from the context of developing countries, limited research has sought to understand the role of social media in motivating entrepreneurs to start and market their businesses. This current study seeks to investigate this issue through a field study comprising interviews with Nigerian entrepreneurs. The research explores how social media shapes Nigerian entrepreneurs' motivation to start a business and how they market their businesses via social media. It was found that most of the entrepreneurs interviewed were opportunity-driven rather than necessity-driven due to opportunities afforded by SM. Furthermore, entrepreneurs devised several social media marketing approaches across different platforms to reach their audiences.

Keywords: Entrepreneur · Social media · SMEs · Necessity-driven
Opportunity-driven · Marketing · Developing country · Nigeria

1 Introduction

Social Media (SM) has grown by leaps and bounds in recent years. The use of SM is redefining business creation [1] and business marketing strategies [2]. Its use has made easier for entrepreneurs to advertise and sell their products [3]. Studies have explored the role of SM in marketing highlighting its use for customer relationship management, advertisement and building brand awareness [2, 4].

In developing countries, studies have identified that entrepreneurs start their business primarily out of necessity (necessity-driven) [5, 6]. The advent of SM has allowed for the creation of new businesses [3] by entrepreneurs in developing countries. However, the influence of SM and digital tools has been overlooked in research to date regarding its possible influence on entrepreneur motivation in starting their business. The importance of SM cannot be overemphasised. In Nigeria for example, digital platforms such as SM boosted Small to Medium Enterprises (SMEs) trade by around 27% between March and May 2017 due to recognition of new opportunities [7], and

S. A. Al-Sharhan et al. (Eds.): I3E 2018, LNCS 11195, pp. 355–364, 2018.
https://doi.org/10.1007/978-3-030-02131-3_32

can thus serve as an avenue for enhancing opportunity-driven entrepreneurship. In addition, SM can serve as an avenue where they can effectively market their products and reach out to their potential clients, therefore encouraging business creation and supporting business survival and growth.

Social media is actively researched in the academic literature with most studies examining its usage and its impact on firm performance e.g. [8]. Current research focuses on the role of SM role in establishing and marketing business in developed as opposed to developing countries [4]. This research seeks to extend the current literature through the provision of a case from a developing country. To achieve this, interviews were conducted with eleven Nigerian entrepreneurs. The research explored how SM influenced each entrepreneur's motivation for establishing a business and the SM marketing strategies they used.

The rest of this paper is structured as follows. A background of the literature is provided in the next section followed by the research method used. The results of the research are then presented. The implications of the findings and future work are then discussed.

2 Background

Earlier research has identified entrepreneur motivation for starting a business as either necessity-driven or opportunity-driven [5, 9]. *Opportunity-driven entrepreneurship* involves becoming an entrepreneur due to a "pull"; where a venture is started based on an unexploited or underexploited opportunity [6], or as a career option driven by choice [6, 9]. On the contrary, *necessity-driven entrepreneurship* involves been "pushed" into becoming an entrepreneur as a last resort. This may be due to the inexistence of a job or absence of a better alternative; both scenarios are more prevalent amongst developing countries [6, 10]. However, an emerging line of research has challenged this categorisation by identifying that the motives complement each other and may further evolve e.g. [11]. Recent research in developing countries especially in sub-Saharan Africa e.g. [10, 12] has identified that entrepreneurs cannot be strictly categorised as either necessity-driven or opportunity-driven. Moreover, with the advent of SM, entrepreneurs can identify opportunities [8, 13], which can lead to business creation that is not solely necessity-driven and thus further the understanding of business motivation regarding innovations like SM.

SM marketing has been actively studied recently culminating in several review papers and theoretical frameworks on the topic e.g. [2, 4, 14]. SM is playing a massive role in influencing the marketing landscape by enabling transition away from traditional media to focus on digital marketing. SM marketing can improve the visibility of the business. Increase in visibility has been a primary reason for social media use by entrepreneurs which leads to attracting new customers and an increase in sales [15, 16]. Moreover, it supports CRM where relationship with customers is improved [15, 17]. This is done via entrepreneur activities on SM platforms such as posting contents relating to customer endorsement, promotion and business activities [18, 19].

However, majority of the studies had been conducted in developed countries [4] and it will be vital in understanding how entrepreneurs in developing countries utilize SM for marketing.

In SM and entrepreneur research, majority of the studies have been geared towards understanding factors that drive SM adoption and its impact on firm performance. SM marketing has been studied by previous research where its impact on firm performance has been evaluated e.g. [19, 20] or as an outcome of SM use e.g. [8]. Recent review papers on SM marketing e.g. [2, 4] has aimed at exploring research on SM marketing, [4] identified on the need to explore the effectiveness of different platforms with respect to SM marketing which will be vital in theory building.

3 Research Method

Creswell [21] suggests that employing a qualitative approach is beneficial in exploring an area where little is known. In a bid to further understand how SM influences entrepreneur motivation and how they carry out their marketing activities on several SM platforms, an interview-based exploratory study was carried out.

A total of eleven interviews were carried out with Nigerian entrepreneurs which suffices to achieve deep insights to the research been investigated [22]. The respondents were identified by using a purposive and snowball sampling approach based on similar criteria used by [23, 24]. The criteria specified that the entrepreneurs should be present and active on at least one SM platform (Facebook, Twitter, Instagram, and LinkedIn), they have business-to-consumer oriented company, less than 20 employees and are either in the e-retail or service industry. The criteria were used to be sure that respondents are in the best position to talk about what is under study [25]. A semistructured interviewing approach was made use of where probes into the question were done when there is need to clarify information. The interview was done in English and transcribed by the researcher.

In analysing the data, the interview was transcribed and returned to the respondents to ensure that they were not misrepresented. This was followed by an initial reading of the interview transcripts to have an overall knowledge of the contents. The transcripts were then analysed in Nvivo11. The transcriptions were classified into emerging themes [26] that were related to business motivations, SM marketing strategies and the difference across several platforms. The findings from the interview were then supported by the observations of the respondents SM platforms usage for their business.

4 Findings

Eleven Nigerian entrepreneurs were interviewed in this current study. A profile of participants is provided in Table 1. Three of the interviewees had more than one business with varying establishment dates. The interviews explored how SM influenced the Nigerian entrepreneurs to establish a business and how they used these tools for marketing purposes. The results are presented in the following section. Overall, we

Table 1. Respondent profile.

Code	Business sector	Established	Platforms used
NGR1	E-tailing (Food)	2016	Facebook, Instagram, Twitter
NGR2	Service (Editing)	2009	Facebook, WhatsApp, Twitter, LinkedIn
NGR3	E-tailing (Fashion)	2016	Instagram and Facebook
NGR4	Service (Technology)	2012, 2016	Facebook, Instagram, Twitter
NGR5	Service (Technology)	2012, 2016	Facebook, Instagram, Twitter
NGR6	Service/E-tailing (Marketing/Beauty)	2011, 2016	Facebook, Twitter
NGR7	E-tailing (Fashion)	2016	Instagram, WhatsApp
NGR8	E-tailing (Confectioneries)	2015	Instagram, Facebook
NGR9	E-tailing (Fashion)	2011	Instagram, Facebook
NGR10	Service (Beauty)	2013	Instagram, Facebook
NGR11	Service (Photography)	2015	Instagram

identified how SM influences entrepreneur motivations and how they used it for marketing which will be discussed in subsequent subsections.

4.1 Motivation

The entrepreneurs felt that SM is a vital driving force for their businesses. SM play a crucial role in creating and running the business. Specifically, SM supports the entrepreneurs to discover and develop relationships and ideas for their businesses. Some respondents felt that without SM, they would not be in business. NGR5, for instance, stated that *"... without SM I do not think I will be able to run any of these businesses successfully .... SM is basically 90% of our business."*

The motivation to start a business of the respondents was found to be mostly opportunity-driven (9 of the respondents) with two being necessity-driven. The opportunities were borne out of personal hobbies or problem they tried to solve, and also based on challenges or opportunities posed by society. For example, NGR1 started his business around a challenge he faces which entails ordering food from restaurants at his convenience. SM motivated him starting the business by allowing him to validate the idea with others across several. NGR11 started his photography business based on passion which was driven by SM ability to allow him showcase his works; after which the money motivation factored in. NGR2 and NGR6 also founded their business around their passion where SM plays crucial roles for example for setting them up for customer acquisition and market exploration.

Other entrepreneurs founded their business based on societal opportunities and challenges. They used SM to solve societal problems that were pertinent to average citizens. For example, NGR4 developed a business leveraging SM crowd sourcing to tackle traffic congestion in the most populated state in Nigeria. A former governor of the state acknowledged their efforts. In addition, NGR3 aimed to promote the Nigerian economy and a green environment through manufacturing based on local raw materials. In the case of NGR5, his businesses were established around reducing online fraud in the entertainment industry and also improving the gambling sector. As stated earlier, two of the respondents motivation was necessity-driven. Necessity was highlighted by previous research as push factors such as the need to survive or earn more [6, 10]. For NGR9, it was the scarcity of white-collar jobs, while NGR7 established her business to earn more money. Based on the respondents, it is seen that majority of the entrepreneurs were opportunity-driven as SM affords them the ability validate, establish and run their business which would not have been possible in SM absence.

4.2 Marketing Strategies

From the interviews, several marketing strategies were uncovered through which their business was promoted, and customers were acquired. The majority of entrepreneurs advertise their products on SM platforms while some use offline platforms alongside. They use SM heavily use because of its ability to reach out to a large number of people and offers a level-playing ground for the entrepreneurs to compete with established brands despite their meagre resources. NGR5 made this argument when he said *"...the only way we can actually compete in the game is by focusing online and getting customers via online, and online is cheaper. .... But the thing for a small business, I think you will get more traction and customers on SM because it is cheap"* NGR5.

Online advertisement includes the use of SM platforms to promote a product to clients either through paid adverts or organically (i.e. without payment). All the respondents used an organic approach to reach their customers. This was achieved by posting their products on SM and by using SM hashtags to reach a broader audience. The shortcoming of the organic approach is its inability to reach a wider audience, beyond their current customer base. Consequently, five respondents made use of paid advertisements. For instance, NGR5 felt it was cheaper than the offline advertisement; while NGR8 uses paid advertisements occasionally based on need.

Influencer marketing involves entrepreneurs using influencers such as famous artists or people to advertise their brands on their respective SM handles. This practice was highlighted by NGR5 *"...influencer(s) are people with over 1million followers, those are the people we target... They are SM authorities and what they tell their fans is what the fans do. We use celebrity influencers too, we use celebrities to sell our product."* Other interviewees including NGR6 found influencers to be very useful. However, the shortcoming of this approach was highlighted by NGR8 and NGR9 who felt that it reduced the trust of clients in other businesses that did not use celebrities to advertise their products. Primarily, businesses that did not use influencers were placed at a disadvantage

Collaborative or cross-marketing can be described as a strategy where different entrepreneurs promote each other on their respective SM handles to reach out to a broader audience. This can be seen as a means of support for each other and enhance their outreach with little or no cost. In some instances, cross-promoted products may be complementary. Six respondents used this approach with NGR10 describing it as *"you rub my back I rub yours"* where both parties profit. NGR5 further explained by saying *"Sometimes we do cross-marketing, we tell them to post our logo on their page and tell their followers to follow us and we would equally do the same thing with our followers too."*

Some interviewees used offline advertisement to supplement their online presence and advertising. For most of the respondents, it was the first marketing strategy they used before moving on to SM. Most respondents relied on word of mouth marketing from family and friends, who referred their business to people in their social network. The role of SM in the referral procedure was interesting. For several respondents, SM served as a credibility checker; an entrepreneur portfolio that showcased them to the prospective clients amassed via referrals. The respondents were able to make optimal use of SM for their marketing activities and reaching out to their clients despite their limited resources.

4.3   Marketing Behaviours Exhibited on SM Platforms

The entrepreneurs used Instagram and Facebook more than Twitter. These platforms were selected based on criteria including age range of the target market, business type and purpose of use. Table 2 summarises the respondents perception about the various platforms.

Table 2. SM platform use and affordances.

	Facebook	Instagram	Twitter
Audience demography	All ages	Youth	Youth and adult
Perceived benefit	Brand awareness and fruitful engagement	Brand awareness and sales	Brand awareness and credibility
Frequency of sales and marketing posts	Medium	High	Low
Content posted	Text/images	Images	Text
Post source	Fed from Instagram	Primary	Fed from Instagram
Data consumption	Low	High	Low
Use for paid advertisement	High	High	Medium

The Respondents Used Several Platforms for Different Purposes as Characterised by NGR5:

We use them for different purposes basically. Facebook is just for awareness, is just for people to know that we have a particular show, that we are doing this and that. Twitter is just for credibility, so people can actually see that we are credible... Instagram is meant for marketing basically to get customers; of course we get customers from Twitter and Facebook but not as much as Instagram.

Virtually all of the respondents that made use of Instagram also used Facebook and vice-versa. This can primarily be traced back to the reason that both platforms are owned by same company, which allows for seamless integration and posting of content simultaneously on both platforms. Facebook was a preferred platform for advertising according to the respondents. This is because of the number of registered users on the platform. The growth of Instagram regarding the number of people on it is also making it an alternative platform for advertisement as mentioned by NGR11. This is because of the large amount of millennial on it who are perceived to be better financially as stated by NGR5. This meant that almost all the respondents generated more sales on Instagram.

Respondents when quizzed on why they felt Instagram had more impact on sales, the majority of the entrepreneurs could not give a definite answer with some saying that "*I really don't understand*" NGR8. A reason suggested by NGR10 is that Instagram offers more opportunity for entrepreneurs to sell themselves. Other suggestions ranged from the rich man syndrome as posited by NGR5, the visual component and attractiveness of Instagram as stated by NGR8 and NGR9. Several respondents (NGR8, NGR9, NGR10, NGR11) indicated that the outreach of Instagram was favourable, unlike Facebook where not everybody gets to see your post even if they are your friends.

Facebook, on the other hand, has its strength when it comes to brand awareness and engagement due to its leverage of large numbers of users (NGR5 and NGR6). NGR4 characterised Facebook as providing an '*official office*' where complaints may be posted and addressed. However, some respondents felt that Facebook was losing traction because it is mostly used to keep in touch with family and friends. For instance NGR8, NGR9 and NGR10 believed it was best used for personal purposes with little sales been derived from it. NGR10 noted that she could not remember anyone contacting her for business on Facebook. Even if she uploaded her work images on Facebook, it had few likes or comments, but on Instagram, the likes kept streaming in. The same sentiment was shared by NGR8. It was found that respondents whose business visual and retail-oriented make more use of Instagram than Facebook.

Twitter, due to its limitation regarding the number of characters per post and ability for retweets, was used more for brand marketing and less of advertisement. This is because according to NGR5 "*Twitter advert(s) are not as effective…*" Twitter was more used to increase brand awareness of their products to their clients, in the case of NGR1 and NGR3. It was also used for credibility enhancement by the entrepreneurs. This was described by NGR5 when he said that a celebrity following your account made it credible to followers. NGR4 also discussed the strength of Twitter in engaging with time-sensitive events, which might be difficult to achieve on other platforms. This was due to the nature of the NGR4's business that deals with traffic updates based on location. Moreover, the potential for Twitter to be misused or abused was identified by NGR3 and NGR4, which resulted in these entrepreneurs moving their audience and activities back to both Instagram and Facebook.

5   Implications

This study aimed at exploring how SM platforms influence entrepreneurial motivations and marketing strategies and thus offer both theoretical and practical implications. Firstly, although SM has been used by entrepreneurs for some years, understanding its role in developing countries is in its early stages. Entrepreneur characteristics and resources in developing countries lead to differences in entrepreneur motivation and marketing strategies. The research contributes to the literature by highlighting the role of SM in supporting opportunity-driven entrepreneurship in developing countries. SM also allows for the transition of entrepreneurs from being necessity-driven to been opportunity driven and thus it is consistent with previous studies [10, 12].

Secondly, the study advances understanding of SM marketing strategies adopted by entrepreneurs in a developing country. The study elicits the different ways that entrepreneurs market their products/services to their prospective clients. SM advertisement is well documented in developed countries [4]. However, this study further identifies other SM marketing strategies deployed by entrepreneurs to compete with established business and also promoting their products/services which might be unique to developing countries. The identified marketing strategies are feasible for entrepreneurs because it can be effective and less cost-intensive. Moreover, it furthers our understanding regarding the preference of entrepreneurs regarding the various SM platforms considered in this study.

6   Limitations

This study has a few limitations that should be addressed by future research studies. The study utilizes a small sample size where all of the respondents are highly educated (minimum of a university degree). Hence the findings may not be conclusive as educated people are more likely to identify opportunities on SM and thus develop marketing strategies better than the uneducated counterparts. Also, the study aimed at exploring entrepreneur motivation and marketing strategies regarding SM. In future studies, a theoretical model will be developed and empirically validated. Furthermore, the study can be extended in identifying and validating factors that influence entrepreneur SM use and (dis)continuous use, and empirically test them in a developing country.

7   Conclusion

Social media has been shown to afford opportunities more especially in supporting entrepreneurs in developing countries to establish and grow their business. In this study, SM allows for the entrepreneurs to establish opportunity-driven business; which as suggested leads to high performing ventures that benefit the economy. The marketing strategies equally uncovered shows how the entrepreneurs are using the little resources at their disposal to achieve the maximal advantage and compete with the established businesses.

References

1. Beninger, S., et al.: A road to empowerment: social media use by women entrepreneurs in Egypt. Int. J. Entrepreneurship Small Bus. **27**(2–3), 308–332 (2016)
2. Misirlis, N., Vlachopoulou, M.: Social media metrics and analytics in marketing– S3 M: a mapping literature review. Int. J. Inf. Manag. **38**(1), 270–276 (2018)
3. Alkhowaiter, W.: The power of Instagram in building small businesses. In: Dwivedi, Yogesh K., et al. (eds.) I3E 2016. LNCS, vol. 9844, pp. 59–64. Springer, Cham (2016). https://doi.org/10.1007/978-3-319-45234-0_6
4. Alalwan, A.A. et al.: Social media in marketing: a review and analysis of the existing literature. Telematics Inf. (2017)
5. Reynolds, P.D. et al.: Global Entrepreneurship Monitor: 2002 Executive Report. Babson College Babson Park, MA (2002)
6. Acs, Z.: How is entrepreneurship good for economic growth? Innovations **1**(1), 97–107 (2006)
7. Adepetun, A.: Nigeria's small, medium enterprises record 27% international trade. The Guardian Nigeria (2017). https://guardian.ng/businessservices/nigerias-small-medium-enterprises-record-27-international-trade/
8. Wang, W., Pauleen, D.J., Zhang, T.: How social media applications affect B2B communication and improve business performance in SMEs. Ind. Markt. Manag. **54**, 4–14 (2016)
9. Sternberg, R., Wennekers, S.: Determinants and effects of new business creation using global entrepreneurship monitor data. Small Bus. Econ. **24**(3), 193–203 (2005)
10. Langevang, T., Namatovu, R., Dawa, S.: Beyond necessity and opportunity entrepreneurship: motivations and aspirations of young entrepreneurs in Uganda. Int. Dev. Plan. Rev. **34**(4), 439–460 (2012)
11. Borozan, D., Pfeifer, S.: Exploring Entrepreneurs' motivation: comparison of croatia, european post-socialist and developed Countries. J. Entrepreneurship **23**(2), 263–287 (2014)
12. Adom, K.: Beyond the marginalization thesis: an examination of the motivations of informal entrepreneurs in sub-Saharan Africa: insights from Ghana. Int. J. Entrepreneurship Innov. **15**(2), 113–125 (2014)
13. Nambisan, S., Zahra, S.A.: The role of demand-side narratives in opportunity formation and enactment. J. Bus. Ventur. Insights **5**, 70–75 (2016)
14. Felix, R., Rauschnabel, P.A., Hinsch, C.: Elements of strategic social media marketing: a holistic framework. J. Bus. Res. **70**, 118–126 (2017)
15. Michaelidou, N., Siamagka, N.T., Christodoulides, G.: Usage, barriers and measurement of social media marketing: an exploratory investigation of small and medium B2B brands. Ind. Markt. Manag. **40**(7), 1153–1159 (2011)
16. Taiminen, H.M., Karjaluoto, H.: The usage of digital marketing channels in SMEs. J. Small Bus. Enterp. Dev. **22**(4), 633–651 (2015)
17. Nobre, H., Silva, D.: Social network marketing strategy and SME Strategy Benefits. J. Transnatl. Manag. **19**(2), 138–151 (2014)
18. Shih, C.-C., Lin, T.M.Y., Luarn, P.: Fan-centric social media: the Xiaomi phenomenon in China. Bus. Horizons **57**(3), 349–358 (2014)
19. Ha, S. et al.: Does Social Media Marketing Really Work for Online SMEs?: An Empirical Study (2016)
20. Parveen, F., Jaafar, N.I., Ainin, S.: Social media's impact on organizational performance and entrepreneurial orientation in organizations. Manag. Decis. **54**(9), 2208–2234 (2016)

21. Creswell, J.W.: Research Design: Qualitative, Quantitative, and Mixed Methods Approaches. Sage Publications, Thousand Oaks, California (2014)
22. Perry, C.: Processes of a case study methodology for postgraduate research in marketing. Eur. J. Markt. **32**(9/10), 785–802 (1998)
23. Smith, C., Smith, J.B., Shaw, E.: Embracing digital networks: Entrepreneurs' social capital online. J. Bus. Ventur. **32**(1), 18–34 (2017)
24. Fischer, E., Reuber, A.R.: Social interaction via new social media: (How) can interactions on Twitter affect effectual thinking and behavior? J. Bus. Ventur. **26**(1), 1–13 (2011)
25. Babbie, E.R.: The Practice of Social Research. Thirteenth ed. Nelson Education (2015)
26. Richards, L.: Handling Qualitative Data: A Practical Guide. Sage (2014)

Auditors' Usage of Computer-Assisted Audit Techniques (CAATs): Challenges and Opportunities

Raed Jameel Jaber[1] and Rami Mohammad Abu Wadi[2(✉)]

[1] Zarqa University, Zarqa, Jordan
raedjaber125@yahoo.com
[2] Ahlia University, Manama, Kingdom of Bahrain
rwadi@ahlia.edu.bh

Abstract. The objectives of this research is to give a clear view of the electronic auditing environment in companies, to determine the main benefits and challenges of Computer Assisted Audit Techniques (CAATs) and to review the opinions of researchers on Generalized Audit Software (GAS). The study also sheds the light on the reality of electronic auditing in Kingdom of Bahrain. The descriptive approach was used, where the previous studies were surveyed, discussed accurately, and then the results of the study were reached. The results showed the benefits and challenges of evolving from traditional audit techniques to CAATs. This research provides more detailed information about the use of GAS in the different sectors of companies. It also provides academic contribution not only in auditing area but also in information technology, especially in Bahrain. At the end of the study, there are suggestions for future research, which may help to get a qualitative achievement in the use of electronic audit and CAATs in Bahrain.

Keywords: Computer-Assisted audit techniques (CAATs)
Generalized audit software (GAS) · Auditor · Computer · Audit quality

1 Introduction

The endless shifts in the world of business are allegedly impacted by the current technology and information revolution. Computer-based tasks have successfully replaced paper-based tasks in the majority of today's business organizations. Auditing is one of the sectors that witnessed massive shifts. Paper-based auditing has also been replaced by computer-based auditing. However, it still exists and is used by some firms.

It is assured that to enable auditors issue high-quality accounting data as well as making simultaneous decisions, it is important to have and rely on quality data in addition to exist on-lin. Researchers in this domain assure that real-time data is essential for accuracy of outcomes in the auditing domain. When auditors obtain electronic data, they can handle it in a more flexible manner (Chang et al. 2008). This data is certainly accessible; transferable; is simply reserved, condensed, and organized in a manner better than the paper-based accounting data. Writers in the auditing domain suggested that Information technologies drive firms to do their transactions in an

© IFIP International Federation for Information Processing 2018
Published by Springer Nature Switzerland AG 2018. All Rights Reserved
S. A. Al-Sharhan et al. (Eds.): I3E 2018, LNCS 11195, pp. 365–375, 2018.
https://doi.org/10.1007/978-3-030-02131-3_33

electronica manner. They will be able to issue their financial statements electronically and on-line through realtime system. At the most recent times and under the umbrella of the real time accounting (RTA) systems, it is possible that financial data is processed electronically as well as having audit evidence available in an electronic form. This required from firms to replace their paper and traditional documents with electronic ones including orders for purchasing; invoices; and checks (Rezaee et al. 2001).

The change in business process that removes a traditional source of information requires the creation of new audit procedures to conduct financial audit. The primary objective of financial audit and generally accepted auditing standards (GAAS) does not change because all or a part of the client's records are in electronic form (Hanes et al. 2013).

Auditing Practice Regulation 1009 "Computer-Assisted Audit Techniques" (CAATs) is developed based on the International Auditing Practice Regulation IASP. "Computer Assisted Audit Techniques" was approved by the International Federation of Accountants (IFAC) in the 2001 edition (Ciprian-Costel 2014). Auditing firms and auditing specialists have actually introduced numerous CAATs. Such techniques have been improved to aid auditors in carrying out their auditing works depending on computerized accountancy information. The concept of computerized accounting information systems has found its way into the world of accounting as a result. It has been mentioned that one of the most significant and widely employed CAATs in electronic auditing is Generalized Audit Software which is abbreviated as (GAS) (Singleton 2006). GAS is used by auditors to analyze and audit either live or extracted data from a wide range of applications (Debreceny et al. 2005).

The modern computerized environment, in which any audited entity operates nowadays, creates new opportunities, but also new risks, additional rules regarding security accuracy and acceptable error rates, thus constantly influencing the auditors' work (Ciprian-Costel 2014). On the other hand, previous studies have shown many of the benefits of electronic auditing, especially with increasing of computerized accounting systems such as ERP (Enterprise Resource Planning) and the large volume of accounting transactions. Therefore, this research focuses on the use of Computerized Assisted Audit Techniques (CAATs) in the audit of companies.

This research assumes that the implementation of CAATs by the auditor will provide a positive influence on transparency, audit quality and accountability of financial statements of companies. Research about the use of CAATs and GAS is very limited. Therefore, to find a reference regarding factors related to the use of CAATs or GAS, this research reviews the literature of information system in auditing.

The following section will talk about the audit environment in the Kingdom of Bahrain and the extent of interest in using Computer – Assisted audit techniques in auditing process. The rest of the paper will discuss the key findings with reference to prior literature. The conclusion and suggestion for future research are discussed further.

1.1 Research Objectives

The main objective of this research is to give a clear picture of the electronic auditing environment in companies. The researchers aimed to determine the main benefits achieved by both internal and external auditors from the usage of CAATs. The researchers conducted a review of previous studies on GAS which is one of the most important of these audit techniques. Also, the researchers reviewed the practical reality of using the electronic tools of auditing in Bahrain

1.2   The Contributions of the Study

This research makes two contributions to the literature:

(1) This research contributes academically by providing comprehensive illustration of the utilization of CAATs and GAS by the auditor of the company in creating transparency, audit quality and accountability. Also, the study reviews the positive and negative opinions of researchers on the application of GAS in the company.
(2) This research gives a clear indication of the importance of electronic auditing in emerging economies such as Bahrain. The scarcity of previous studies on E-audit in Bahrain is might be due to the low number of audit failures. Since the establishment of the first shareholding companies until 2008, there were only three reported cases of audit failure (Al-Ajmi 2009). Consequently, this study investigates the use of electronic auditing techniques in Bahraini audit environment, while previous studies searched on other issues in auditing; such as corporate governance, independence and audit quality. Hence, this study provides additional insights to E-audit in Bahrain.

2   Literature Review

2.1   Audit and Information Technology in Bahrain

The audit in Bahrain is much respected profession like other parts of the world. Many audit firms are operating in Bahrain including all Big 4; The Big Four accounting firms refer to Deloitte & Touche (D&T), PricewaterhouseCoopers (PwC), KPMG, and Ernst & Young. The audit firms are specialized in a number of services, such as external audit, internal audit, taxation, consultancy services, fraud examinations and legal services. In Bahrain, the main services offered by the audit firms are external auditing and internal auditing. External auditing is focusing on providing a reasonable assurance on the financial statements free from material misstatements and according to International Financial Reporting Standards (IFRSs).

Audit services in Bahrain are provided by 24 accounting firms. Five of these are considered local; four are operating as foreign branches; and the remaining are linked to international firms. The Big 4; have a strong presence in Bahrain Kingdom (Joshi et al. 2009).

A survey in Bahrain of 300 financial and credit analysts shows that they considered auditors' opinion useful. Both groups assume that the characteristics of Big-Four firms allow them to produce better-quality reports than non-Big firms (Al-Ajmi 2009). Auditors in Bahrain indicated that the major process' problems are associated with the client's culture lack, access to information, evidence problems and poor accounting systems. All of these problems may ultimately lead to poor audit quality in Bahraini audit environment (Joshi et al. 2009).

Audit services in Bahrain are regulated by the Amiri Decree (No. 26 of 1996). To register at the Auditors Registrar at the Ministry of Industry and Commerce Applicants must satisfy the following conditions: (1) "must being a Bahraini citizen (with the exception of members of internationally recognized accounting/auditing societies and holders of CA, CPA, or ACCA qualifications recognized by the relevant authorities)". (2) "In accordance the law an auditing firm may be registered as a Partnership Company, a Branch of a Foreign Company or an Individual Establishment (sole proprietorship)" (http://www.moic.gov.bh).

The Central Bank of Bahrain (CBB) requires financial institutions to be audited by one of the big audit firms. It is also required from audit firms to get two licenses, the first to practice auditing and the second to offer auditing services to financial institutions. Auditors who are specialized licensees must be independent. Auditors who are resigned or removed from their tasks are required to inform the CBB of the reasons for the termination of their appointment. In Bahrain, it is not mandatory to switch audit firms, but experience has shown that switching of audit firms in many cases only after audit failure. The CBB requires auditors of financial institutions to switch auditing partners at least every five years (Said and Khasharmeh 2014).

On the other hand, the CBB requires commercial banks to appoint a specialized consulting firm for auditing on the electronic banking system, in order to expose the existing gaps and weaknesses in the system. If any such gaps found it can penetrate the data of customers, which may cause cases of fraud.The Central Bank is taking voluntary measures towards the violator banks. The bank should conduct the E-audit every six months, twice a year, and the auditor must be independent. We must clarify the meaning of the electronic auditing. It is the process of applying any sort of operating system by using information technology to assist the auditor in planning, control and documentation of the audit (Thomas and Henki 2009).

The Information Systems Audit and Control Association (ISACA), Bahrain branch, was established in Bahrain in October 2010; to enhance the role of information technology and security. Bahrain is a developed financial center in the Middle East region and relies heavily on IT in various financial transactions. The Bahraini branch of ISACA has a number of qualified human resources that will contribute to raising awareness of the importance of information systems in the Kingdom of Bahrain. It offers to its members some professional and specialized certificates in auditing, security of information systems and governance.

On the other hand, the internal auditing in Bahrain focuses on operations, internal controls, policies and procedures, corporate governance, risk management and compliance with laws, regulations and by-laws. Furthermore, the internal auditor is responsible to assess the internal controls of the audit and report to the client, whether there are effective internal controls to detect or prevent frauds and errors. The cost of these services may differ from one audit firm to another, depending on a number of factors, such as the size of the client, the number of transactions per year and the nature of the client business.

Banks use different ratings for the audit firms in Bahrain. This ranking influences on the amount that will be lending to a client. For example, KPMG Fakhro has "A" rating, and if a company provided the bank with an unqualified audit report from KPMG Fakhro, then the bank will lend the highest loan amount to the client. In contrary, if a client provided an audit report from an audit firm with a low rating, the client may even not get a loan or get lower amount of loan from the bank.

The audit market in Bahrain has special characteristics. It is characterized by dominance of few auditing firms; the Big Four, largely uncommon cases of switching audit firms, weak enforcement of regulation reverent to audit industry; with exception of those related to financial institutions (Al-Ajmi 2009).

Most of the companies in Bahrain are from Small and Medium Enterprises (SMEs). From April 2014, Bahrain and other Gulf Cooperation Council (GCC) countries are facing difficulties of budget deficiency due to the decrease in the prices of oil. The GCC economies are encouraging the market to save more rather than spending. GCC governments are trying to diversify their economic activities such as manufacturing, tourism, financial services and Information and Communication Technology (ICT) services and others. That's the reason, that companies in Bahrain and other GCC are more focusing on the external auditing, rather than any other services. The other reason of external auditing is its mandatory requirement as per the law. Further, this is because the audited financial statements are a requirement for many services, such as getting a loan from the bank, renewing the commercial registration, in addition to others. This fact can be reflected in the revenues of audit firms, as it generates the highest revenue from external audit among all the services provided.

Alqatanani and Hezabr (2015) surveyed a sample of 40 audit firms in Kingdom of Bahrain; to measure the extent of recognizing the auditing strategies in light of information technology. The most important findings of the study were: There is a Lack of sufficient level of awareness among auditors in Bahrain on auditing strategies and electronic audit, the level of using of information technology is low in various fields, the lack of financial resources and software needed to implement the electronic audits, the lack of appropriate level of scientific and practical training of staff to audit in the light of information technology, the lack of confidence in electronic procedures, fear of data loss and the inability to maintain data protection. In addition, there is a belief that the expansion through the use of information technology will lead to the downsizing of some employees.

2.2   Background of Electronic Audit

The auditing sector has always been perceived as a sector that exceeds being complicated. It is a sector that full of challenges. The auditing profession is one of the numerous domains that got impacted by the advances that took place in the entire world due to the technological and information revolution. Paper-based auditing became something of the past though there are auditing firms that still implement it. At the same time, paper-based auditing was quite replaced by electronic auditing. Electronic auditing has been referred to as "Computer assisted auditing, where electronic records are used to complete all or part of the audit" (Florida Department of Revenue 2002).

Technologies that do merely exist about twenty-five years ago have already gained power after being amended. These tools are now able to hide general mismanagement and fraudulent practices in an unbelievable that is completely different from the old-school auditors. Fortunately, technology managed to make use of some new trends in the auditor's quiver. Such trends have been found to be used in a particular manner. One of the most significant advantages for e-auditing is facilitating the processes of the confirmations that were considered by auditors as problematic and time-consuming issues. These issues are considered as more difficult, particularly; when there some kind of misuse which may leads to fraudulent practices. Unlike computer based auditing, paper-based editing has various disadvantages. Human intervention in the sequences of the activities is one of the most prominent disadvantages that has been given due attention by reviewers in this domain (Solieri and Hodowanitz 2016)

Literature shows that there are numerous computer-based auditing instruments and techniques that were introduced have been developed to aid auditors while doing their audits on computerized accountancy data. One of the most widely implemented software tools is known as generalized audit software (GAS) (Singleton 2006). This software which is referred to as "GAS" is implemented by auditors to analyze and audit the data they have; whether they are categorized as live data or extracted data from a wide array of applications (Debreceny et al. 2005). GAS has been referred to as that data extraction or data analysis software that was made up to carry out particular audit procedures and statistical analyses.

The functions of this software include browsing, analyzing, categorizing, summarizing, stratifying, sampling and implementing calculations. In spite of the fact that the majority of audits do currently apply electronic audit procedures on their audit work, the core processes of audit are not usually adopted without the automation offered by GAS. Nevertheless, auditors still tend to apply some of the most traditional auditing procedures while composing their own audit points of view depending on a sample of accounting transactions instead of investigating all the available data.

To illustrate the differences between CAATs and GAS, Braun and Davis defined CAATs as "any use of technology to assist in the completion of an audit". Based on this definition, there are various types of CAATs, ranging from word processing or electronic spreadsheets to expert system (Debreceny et al. 2005). Moreover, CAATs used by external and internal auditor can be grouped into electronic audit working paper, fraud detection, generalized audit software (GAS), and continuous monitoring (Mahzan and Lymer 2014). So that, we can say that GAS is one type of CAATs that helps auditor to do data extraction, data query, data summary, data analysis (Ahmi and Kent 2012). GAS is divided into two types which are commercially available software and internally developed software (Widuri et al. 2016).

2.3   Benefits of E-Auditing

It is nature of the records of the firms that makes auditors take the decision of whether or not; e-auditing is going to be applied instead of paper-based audit. There are numerous benefits that the firms harvest from the implementation of the e-audit. It is probable that electronic audits can minimize the overall endeavors exerted by the clients as well as the audit department to complete the audit. When the time required to fulfill the auditing processes is short, cost savings do directly exist. There are various examples in which, procedures that provide detailed audit are likely to be performed through electronic data in the same duration taken to audit a sample of paper documents.

Among the advantages of using the Computer-Assisted Audit Techniques (CAATs), we include:

(1) Testing the client's accounting software, as the auditor can verify whether it works correctly or not. Hence, the auditor can test the accounting program and its records directly at their origin, rather than testing paper documents that are supposed to be accurate replicas.

(2) Testing of large volumes of data in a short time and with good accuracy. When the auditor uses CAATs, he will be more confidence in his opinion.

(3) Cost effectiveness because, once an audit software is implemented, it can be used year after year to obtain audit evidence.

(4) CAATs can help in the transparency of financial reports within organizations because they are tools where fraudulent and misappropriated practices are easily detected (Olasanmi 2013).

The auditor should make comparisons between the results obtained using computer-assisted techniques and the results of traditional tests. If similar results are obtained, the auditor's general confidence will grow (Ciprian-Costel 2014).

3   Audit Quality and CAATs

Audit quality is a concept that has different definitions for different researches. DeAngelo (1981) hypothesizes a two-dimensional definition of audit quality: First, a material misstatement must be detected, and second, the material misstatement must be reported. Consequently, Titman and Trueman (1986) propose that a good auditor provides precise information regarding the firm's value. Audit quality is defined as the probability that financial statements contain no material misstatements (Palmrose 1988). While Davidson and Neu (1993) define audit quality as the ability of the auditor to detect and eliminate material misstatements and manipulations in the net income reported.

We can say that audit quality is the increasing function of the ability of an auditor to detect accounting misstatements and it is related to the degree of auditor independence. Here, the following question arises: Should the auditor use Computer-Assisted Audit Techniques (CAATs) to improve the audit quality?

Users of financial statements perceive audit reports to provide absolute assurance that company's financial statements have no material misstatements and do not perpetrate fraud (Epstein and Geiger 1994). However, auditors perceive audit reports to provide a reasonable assurance in terms of strict adherence to International Accounting Standards (IASs) requirements.

Previous studies show that auditor should utilize technology for audit process (DeAngelo 1981) because it can increase effectiveness and efficiency in making decision for audit (Janvrin et al. 2008). Moreover, the use of technology by auditor can increase the quality of audit procedure and the quality of audit result (Manson et al. 1998).

A study conducted by Ahmi and Kent (2012) was originally intended to explore the level of implementation of the external auditors in the UK for the GAS as an audit software on SMEs in the UK. Data statistical analysis showed that the implementation of GAS is not common in between UK auditors as seventy three auditors reported their rejection for implementing GAS as they find it is not that beneficial for their auditing clients. The benefits of the GAS implementation were confronted by its high cost.

Another study by Vasarhelyi and Romero (2014) found that integrating technology support teams with auditors is a process that leads to improving usability in addition to maximizing adoption of technologies in auditing. The main results of (Omonuk and Oni 2015) showed that there is a positive relationship between the use of CAATS and audit quality in Nigeria. Also, the study explained that local Nigerian firms are not effective in applying CAATs, and do not produce quality audit reports. The purpose of the study of Eni (2016) is to present and discuss the most recent concepts in auditing which is "the online collaborative audit system". Data analysis guided the researchers to introduce the online collaborative audit system which was defined by the researcher as "An inter-organizational system that employs the techniques of collaborative intelligence between the stakeholders of the audit process within a particular area that is dependent on the Internet". Though carrying out an assessment of the system design, the researchers were able to predict that an online collaborative system is likely to implement.

4   The Roles of Electronic Audit

As one of the most widely implemented audit software by audit firms GAS has been identified to enable auditors to find out the financial statements' misstatements whether or not, these misstatements are on purpose. This has been a great support for auditors to fulfill the overall audit objectives that include: verification of audit data, fulfillment, ownership, assessment, accuracy, categorization and disclosing the data produced via the accounting software (Debreceny et al. 2005). There are numerous packages of software included within GAS. These packages are: audit command language (ACL); IDEA; and ProAudit. Such packages of software are likely to permit auditors to interrogate various systems of accounting which guides auditors towards carrying out one hundred percent accurate, true, and fair data for their clients (Greenstein-Prosch et al. 2008).

Making use of electronic audit and its software packages has been identified to be extremely beneficial and significant. Implementation of the electronic audit has been given due care and support by the auditing standards. The benefits of the electronic audit and the implemented software such as GAS have been reviewed in various occasions and studies. This software investigated and was found to be compliant with a lot of functions of CAATTs that actually stem from auditing standards that were introduced by the American Institute of Certified Public Accountants (AICPA) (Janvrin et al. 2009).

In one of the most well-reputed countries for their auditing firms such as the UK, it has been found that implementing electronic audit and making use of the audit software as GAS overwhelms the audit profession. This is attributed to the fact that there is a wide recognition for the numerous functionalities and benefits provided by GAS to auditors and audit firms. There are assertions that audit software firms such as Sage which is a world class audit software provider has already provided their audit software to a number of seven hundred and sixty thousand SMEs all over the UK. This is an apparent evidence for the global tendency to employ electronic audit instruments and software. This can also be thought of as an evidence supporting auditors' usage of electronic audit and\or adopt software as GAS.

5   Conclusions and Suggestions for Future Studies

5.1   Conclusions

The following is the conclusion of this research:

- The main result of this paper is summarized by determining the benefits and challenges of evolving from traditional audit techniques to CAATs. In IT environments, the auditors would start using the tools of business intelligence, a key factor which contributes to making successful business decisions. CAATs enable auditors to test large amount of data quickly and accurately and therefore increase the confidence they have in their opinion. The findings of previous studies showed that CAATs have played a major role in fraud detection, transparency, audit quality and cost effectively. E-auditing is facilitating the processes of the confirmations that were considered by auditors as problematic and time-consuming issues.
- This research provides more detailed information about the use of GAS in the different sectors of companies. This research was conducted by reviewing many previous studies. Despite GAS is a wellknown program in extracting data, analyzing, browsing, classification, sampling and computation; auditors still tend to apply some of the most traditional audit procedures with their audit points. Some auditors found that GAS is not beneficial for their auditing clients. The benefits of the GAS implementation were confronted by its high cost.
- External auditors are recommended to use Computer Assisted Audit Techniques particularly when the majority of the available financial information would be in an electronic form.
- The features of the audit team individuals and integrating technology support teams with auditors; are improving usability in addition to maximizing adoption of technologies in auditing.
- It is required from auditors to make better understanding of the standards of IT audit and their guidelines on carrying out an IT audit. Here, the auditors must focus on audit standards related to IT, as published by AICPA and ISACA.
- The researchers predicted that an online collaborative system is likely to be implement, which achieves many benefits for auditors.
- I think that the study was able to shed light on a certain part of the practical reality of electronic auditing in Bahrain.

5.2   Suggestions for Future Studies

This research provides opportunities for future research, which are:

(1) Future research to measure the actual use of CAATs or GAS by the audit firms in Kingdom of Bahrain.
(2) Future research could examine quantitatively to what extent inhibiting factors affect the intention of the auditors in Bahrain to use CAATs or GAS.
(3) Future research could perform a model that links the quality of auditing as a dependent variable and the techniques of electronic auditing (CAATs) as an independent variable. This model can be tested quantitatively through an applied study of auditing companies in emerging economies as Bahrain.

References

Ahmi, A., Kent, S.: The utilisation of generalized audit software (GAS) by external auditors. Manag. Audit. J. **28**(2), 88–113 (2012)

Al-Ajmi, J.: Audit firm, corporate governance, and audit quality: evidence from Bahrain. Adv. Account. **25**(1), 64–74 (2009)

Alqatanani, K., Hezabr, A.: The effect of using accounting information systems to improve the value chain business organizations-empirical study. Eur. J. Account. Audit. Finance Res. **3**(6), 1–11 (2015)

Chang, S.-I., Wu, C.C., Chang, I.C.: The development of a computer auditing system sufficient for Sarbanes-Oxley section 404—a study on the purchasing and expenditure cycle of the ERP system. Inf. Syst. Manag. **25**(3), 211–229 (2008)

Ciprian-Costel, M.: Arguments on using computer-assisted audit techniques (Caat) and business intelligence to improve the work of the financial auditor. Manag. Strat. J. **26**(4), 212–220 (2014)

Davidson, R.A., Neu, D.: A note on the association between audit firm size and audit quality. Contemp. Account. Res. **9**(2), 479–488 (1993)

DeAngelo, L.E.: Auditor size and audit quality. J. Account. Econ. **3**(3), 183–199 (1981)

Debreceny, R., Lee, S.L., Neo, W., Shuling Toh, J.: Employing generalized audit software in the financial services sector: challenges and opportunities. Manag. Audit. J. **20**(6), 605–618 (2005)

Eni, L.C.: Considerations regarding the design of an online collaborative audit system. Manag. Audit. J. **31**(1), 64–86 (2016)

Epstein, M.J., Geiger, M.A.: Investor views of audit assurance: recent evidence of the expectation gap. J. Account. **177**(1), 60 (1994)

Greenstein-Prosch, M., McKee, T.E., Quick, R.: A comparison of the information technology knowledge of United States and German auditors. Int. J. Digit. Account. Res. **8**(July), 45–79 (2008)

Hanes, D.R., Porco, B.M., Thibodeau, J.C., Simply Soups Inc.: A teaching case designed to integrate the electronic cash confirmation process into the auditing curriculum. Issues Account. Educ. **29**(2), 349–369 (2013)

Janvrin, D., Bierstaker, J., Lowe, D.J.: An examination of audit information technology use and perceived importance. Account. Horiz. **22**(1), 1–21 (2009)

Janvrin, D., Lowe, D. J., Bierstaker, J.: Auditor acceptance of computer-assisted audit techniques. Iowa State University, Arizona State University and Villanova University, 4 (2008)

Joshi, P.L., Al Ajmi, J., Bremser, W.G.: A study of auditor–client relationships and problems in the Bahraini audit environment. Adv. Account. 25(2), 266–277 (2009)

Mahzan, N., Lymer, A.: Examining the adoption of computer-assisted audit tools and techniques: cases of generalized audit software use by internal auditors. Manag. Audit. J. 29(4), 327–349 (2014)

Manson, S., McCartney, S., Sherer, M., Wallace, W.A.: Audit automation in the UK and the US: a comparative study. Int. J. Audit. 2(3), 233–246 (1998)

Olasanmi, O.O.: Computer aided audit techniques and fraud detection. Res. J. Financ. Account. 4 (5), 67–80 (2013)

Omonuk, J.B., Oni, A.A.: Computer assisted audit techniques and audit quality in developing countries: evidence from Nigeria. J. Internet Bank. Commer. 20(3), 1 (2015)

Palmrose, Z.V.: Competitive manuscript co-winner: an analysis of auditor litigation and audit service quality. Account. Rev. 63, 55–73 (1988)

Rezaee, Z., Elam, R., Sharbatoghlie, A.: Continuous auditing: the audit of the future. Manag. Audit. J. 16(3), 150–158 (2001)

Said, K., Khasharmeh, H.: Auditors' perceptions on impact of mandatory audit firm rotation on auditor independence-evidence from Bahrain. J. Account. Tax. 6(1), 1 (2014)

Singleton, T.: IT audit basics: generalized audit software: effective and efficient tool for today's IT audits. Inf. Syst. Control J. 2, 11 (2006)

Solieri, S.A., Hodowanitz, J.: Electronic audit confirmations: leveraging technology to reduce the risk of fraud. J. Forensic Investig. Account. 8(1) (2016)

Thomas, W., Emerson, H.: Review of Theory and Practice, Translation and Localization by Ahmed Haggag and Kamal-uddin Saeed, pp. 436–438. Mars Publishing House, Saudi Arabia (2009)

Titman, S., Trueman, B.: Information quality and the valuation of new issues. J. Account. Econ. 8(2), 159–172 (1986)

Vasarhelyi, M.A., Romero, S.: Technology in audit engagements: a case study. Manag. Audit. J. 29(4), 350–365 (2014)

Widuri, R., O'Connell, B., Yapa, P.W.: Adopting generalized audit software: an Indonesian perspective. Manag. Audit. J. 31(8/9), 821–847 (2016)

The Use of Internet and Mobile Banking in the Czech Republic

Martina Hedvicakova[(✉)] and Libuse Svobodova

Faculty of Informatics and Management, University of Hradec Králové,
Rokitanskeho 62, 500 03 Hradec Kralove, Czech Republic
{Martina.hedvicakova,Libuse.svobodova}@uhk.cz

Abstract. Internet and mobile banking is becoming more important worldwide. New technologies have huge impact for the introduction of new functionalities in both internet and mobile banking. Growth of Internet users and smartphones also has an impact on this growth. The Czech Republic was using internet banking above the European Union average in 2017. In the European Union 51% of individuals used internet banking and 57% of individuals in the Czech Republic. The main aim of the article is to analyze the situation in the use of internet banking in the Czech Republic by the number and percentage of individuals and by age, gender and education. The second part of the article is focused on the analysis of ten banks with the largest number of clients in the Czech Republic, where they analyze the latest and most needed features of their mobile banking from the client and expert juries perspective. The article uses primary and secondary data.

Keywords: Internet banking · Mobile banking · Function · Bank

1 Introduction and Current Situation

With the sky rocking number of smartphone users and popularizing of internet worldwide, there with the phenomenal growth of e-banking transactions through mobile phones. According to a recent forecast (Internet world, 2015) [1].

Mobile and Internet Banking has a great contribute in online banking revolution, which is giving a competitive edge to the banks against their rivals. Especially "Transaction Alert/Confirmation" is most demanding service by users. Customers feel that after monetary transaction the SMS should be received, and they prefer the version of the IVR (Interactive Voice Response) banking service that provides (out-of-band) SMS confirmation over those one that does not [2]. Therefore, online banking helps banks to retain and enhance the loyalty of their existing customers, increase customer satisfaction, provide opportunity to the banks to increase market share, reduce administrative and operational cost and to improve banks' competitive positions against their rivals [3–5].

The popularity of Internet banking is growing worldwide. Internet banking is the only activity that students use to a lesser extent than the average population (of the monitored population).

S. A. Al-Sharhan et al. (Eds.): I3E 2018, LNCS 11195, pp. 376–386, 2018.
https://doi.org/10.1007/978-3-030-02131-3_34

2   The Literature Reviews

The market for banking services in the Czech Republic is characterised by high competition. The market was recently joined by four new 'low-cost' banks which opted for an offensive pricing strategy to enforce themselves. [6] One of the ways to keep the number of clients for existing banks is Internet and Mobile banking.

The Promotion of online banking technology enabled the banks to enhance its operations with cost cutting effectively and efficiently in order to handle daily banking affairs via online banking channel. Customers are being facilitated by reducing their visits in banks and they can carry out their transactions via internet or ATM Machines instead of personally visiting the branches [5].

With the growth of using e-banking transactions through mobile phones in China, it brings along with convenience of people's life as it enables people to have access to banking services anywhere and at any time as well as it conducts business more effectively [7].

When the consumer has a market overview then the optimal product can be chosen more or less easily. Soukal and Draessler [8] model more realistic situation where the consumer does not have a market overview and so the process of search has to be performed. The harder the search is the higher information asymmetry is. Currently, clients decide how according to the charges for current account and primarily by the level of Internet and Mobile Banking. Customers are particularly interested in the features to help control and manage their accounts.

In the last decade, Internet banking technology has made remarkable progress. However, there is a huge disparity across different nations all over the world in the diffusion of Internet banking services. This leads to the research question of Takieddine and Sun [9] study: why different countries exhibit different levels of Internet banking adoption? We will focus on the situation of Internet Banking in the Czech Republic. Regarding technological readiness the Czech Republic is doing better than the other Visegrad countries. Citizens are technological equipped, and they have competencies to use e-banking. [10] Černohorská et al. [11] examine the comparative performance of Banks for the Visegrad group (V4) of four Central European States for the period 2009–2013. Their results showed that average technical efficiency (for all banks) trended upward during the study period. This increase efficiency is not common for all banks in the Czech Republic, Poland, Hungary and Slovak. They found that efficiency for Czech, Polish and Slovak banks increase during research time. Development of efficiency Hungarian banks has on the contrary a downward trend from 0.882 in 2009 to 0.856 in 2013. We also founded that the Total Factor of Productivity (TFP) changes across all countries was relatively stable in 3 of the 4 observation periods.

Smaller firms, however, invested more in research and development (R&D) and Vokoun [12] was found no linear relationship for output characteristics.

3   The Goal of Article and Methodology

The article is based on primary and secondary sources. Secondary sources comprise information about Internet Banking in the Czech Republic and European Union, professional literature, information collected from professional press, discussions or previous participations in professional seminars and conferences relating to the chosen subject. Primary resources are based on information obtained from the web portals of individual banks in the Czech Republic. Then it was necessary to select, classify and up-date accessible relevant information from the numerous published materials that would provide the basic knowledge of the selected topic [13].

The goal of the article is to focus on the Internet Banking in the Czech Republic and its position within the European Union. The second part of the article analyzes new features in mobile applications at the top ten banks according to the number of clients in the Czech Republic. Mobile application data are used from competition Zlatá Koruna [19], where authors are jurors. Data on mobile applications are also obtained from the websites of individual banks.

The aim of the article is to verify the scientific question: At least 1/3 of the clients of the three largest banks (according to the number of clients) use mobile banking in the Czech Republic.

4   Internet Banking in European Union

By 2017, the share of EU-28 households with internet access had risen to 87%, some 32 percentage points higher than in 2007.

Broadband internet access was used by 85% of the households in the EU-28 in 2017, approximately double the share recorded in 2007 (42%) [14].

Figure 1 shows that on average 51% individuals aged 16–74 used Internet banking in in European Union in 2017. This share is constantly increasing and has doubled since 2007, when it stood at 25%.

Internet banking is particularly popular among 25 to 34 year old, with 68% using this facility. The use of internet banking tends to increase in line with the education level of the user. While only 24% of those with low education use e-banking, 77% of those with high education use this service.

Among EU Member States, internet banking is most common in Denmark (where 90% of people aged 16 to 74 said they were using it) and the Netherlands (89%), followed by the other Nordic countries - Finland (87%) and Sweden (86%).

The lowest shares were registered in Bulgaria (5%) and Romania (7%). Less than 30% of those between the ages of 16 and 74 use internet banking in Greece (25%) and Cyprus (28%) [15].

Internet Banking is second less popular among the youngest ones. Only 44% of younger internet users performed some kind of electronic transactions with a bank (for payment, transfers, etc. or for looking up account information) against 55% aged 55–74 and 65% aged 25–54 in 2016 [16].

More and more people use Internet banking in the Czech Republic. Internet Banking was used by 3.9 million individuals in 2015 and by 2017 4.5 million people.

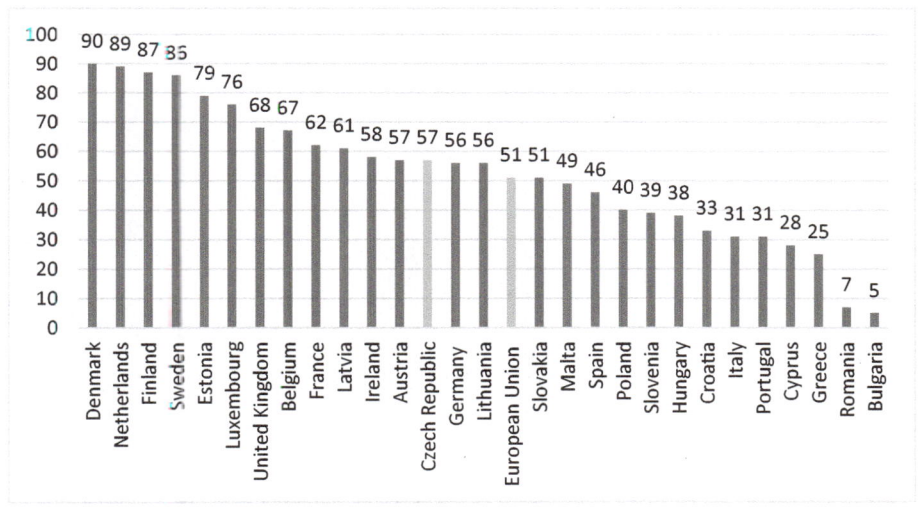

Fig. 1. People who used Internet banking in 2017 (% of individuals aged 16–74), Source: Eurostat [15], own processing

The Czech Republic has 10.6 million inhabitants. Figure 1 shows that the Czech Republic is above the EU average and 57% of individuals used Internet banking in 2017.

5 The Results of the Internet Banking in the Czech Republic

5.1 Internet Banking in the Czech Republic

Figure 2 shows individuals using Internet Banking in the Czech Republic. Only 0.9 million of Individuals used the Internet Banking in 2007. About 10 years later used the Internet Banking 4.5 millions of Individuals from 10.6 millions people in the Czech Republic.

11% of individuals used Internet Banking in the Czech Republic in 2007. In 2011, internet banking was used by 27% of individuals, by over 38% for two years. In 2015, growth slowed down, and Internet Banking was used by only 45% of individuals. 52% of individuals used Internet Banking in 2017.

In a deeper analysis and use of statistical functions, it was subsequently found that Internet Banking has increasing trend. The logarithmic trend explains 93% of the variance. The linear trend explains over 95% of the variance.

Overall, Internet Banking uses 52% of individuals in 2017. Of this, 55% of males and 49% of women use the internet banking in the Czech Republic (see Fig. 3).

66% of individuals using the Internet in 2017 and 52% of individuals using Internet Banking in the Czech Republic. Interestingly, in the 16-24 age group, all who use the Internet are also using Internet banking. This trend, with a slight decrease, can be observed for the age groups of 25–54 years. Since the age of 55, there has been a steep

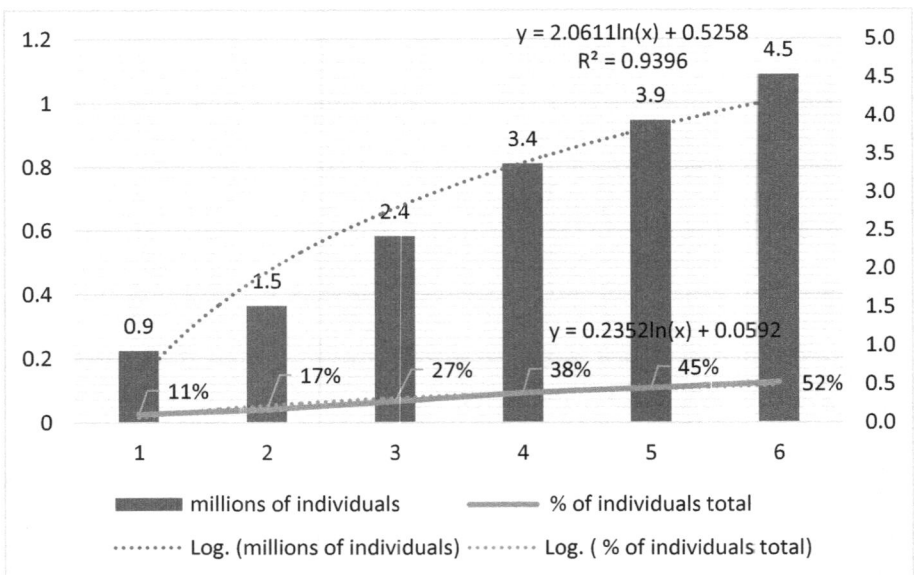

Fig. 2. Individuals using Internet banking in 2007, 2009, 2011, 2013, 2015 and 2017, Source: Czech statistical office, [17], own processing

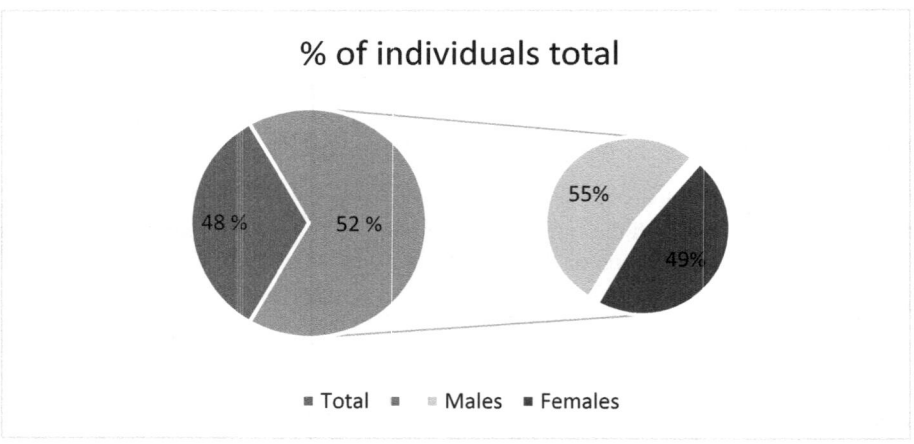

Fig. 3. Individuals using Internet banking by gender in 2017, Source: Czech statistical office, [17], own processing

decline in the use of Internet Banking. Only 12% of individuals from age 65 + use Internet Banking. The Internet uses 36% (see Fig. 4).

The increase in the share of the number of Internet banking users in the total population has been the highest in the Czech Republic over the last 10 years of all EU countries. High charges for mobile data defended a bigger use of Internet banking.

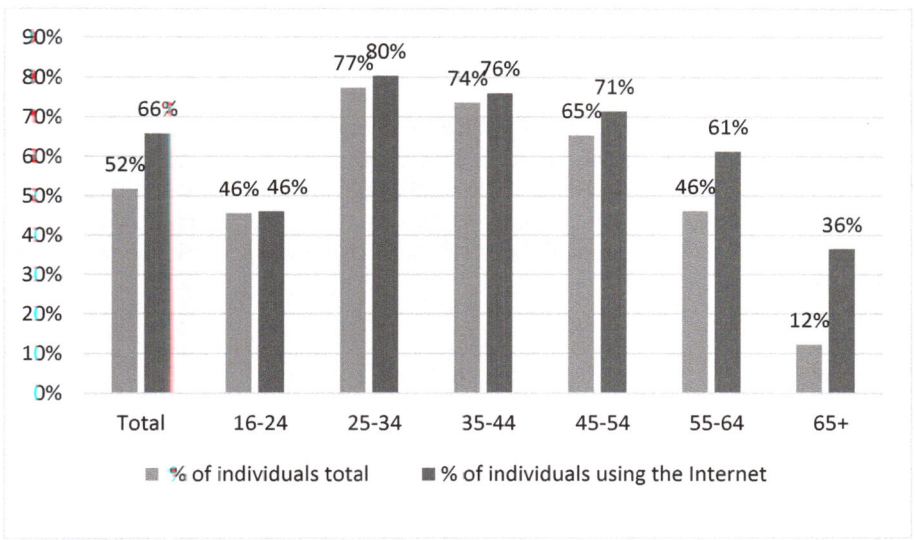

Fig. 4. Individuals using Internet banking by age in 2017, Source: Czech statistical office, [17], own processing

Every year a growing number of individuals using Internet Banking also by completed education. Internet Banking is used mostly with people with higher education. 80% of individuals with higher education uses Internet banking in 2017. For comparison, people with primary education use Internet banking only from 12.1% (See Fig. 5).

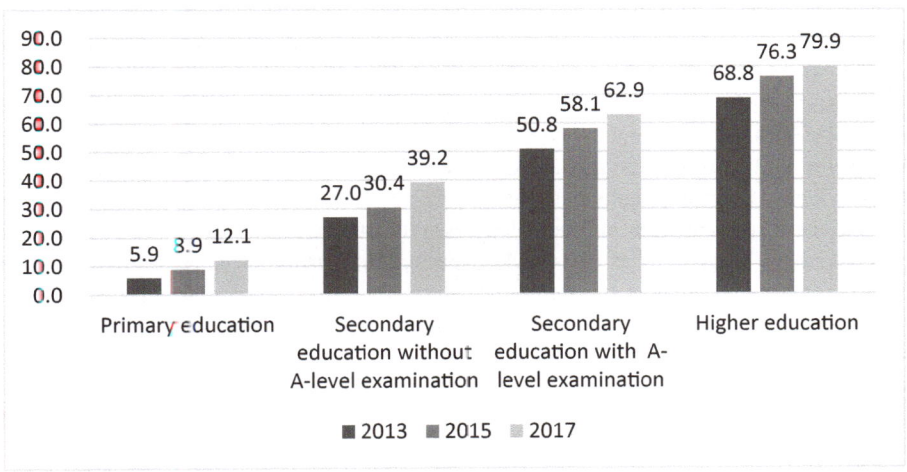

Fig. 5. Individuals using Internet banking by completed education (25+), Source: Czech statistical office, [17], own processing

5.2   Mobile Banking in the Czech Republic

In April 2018, forty-six banks and branches of foreign banks operated in the Czech banking market according to the Czech National Bank. The analysis of mobile banking functions will be performed at ten selected banks according to the number of clients. The banks examined include: Česká spořitelna, ČSOB, Komerční banka, MONETA Money Bank, Fio banka, mBank, Air Bank, Raiffeisenbank, UniCredit Bank and Equa bank.

These banks are currently the largest total assets of the Czech banking sector (excluding mBank, which would be 11th and vice versa, would be SberBank) (Table 1).

Table 1. Number of clients in 2016 and 2017, [18, 21, own processing]

Bank	Number of clients in 2016	Number of clients in 2017*	Use of mobile banking
Česká spořitelna	4 707 000	4 680 000	350 000
ČSOB	2 803 000	2 766 000	250 000
Komerční banka	1 654 000	1 654 000	500 000
Moneta money bank	970 000	1 000 000	200 000
FIO bank	670 000	770 000	
mBank	630 00	630 000	140 000
Air bank	515 000	596 966	300 000
Raiffeisen bank	500 000	does not state	
Unicredit bank	350 000	303 000	more than half
Equa bank	250 000	307 000	more than half

The research question has not been confirmed. The three largest banks by volume of clients: Česká spořitelna, ČSOB and Komerční banka have fewer than 1/3 of mobile banking users. This criterion was fulfilled only by Komerční banka. Much more is being used by Mobile Banking at smaller, low-cost banks. For example, Air Bank uses its mobile app 50% of clients. The two largest banks are conscious of a small number of mobile application users and are constantly developing new features and intuitive control. Česká spořitelna launched the George mobile application, where by the end of 2018 plans to increase the number of users over one million. Large banks are disadvantaged by a large number of branches, and clients are older age groups that prefer branch services rather than modern technologies.

FIO Bank was the first in the Czech Republic to launch Internet Banking in 1998. In 2011, FIO Bank launched its first mobile application. Although internet banking is used by 57% of users. Mobile banking is not as widespread. Users pay high fees for their data tariffs, which then hinder the increased use of Mobile Banking in the Czech Republic.

The authors of the article are the jury in the prestigious Zlatá Koruna (Golden Crown, competition [19]), which is oriented to the financial market in the Czech

Republic. They judge two areas: accounts and online applications. In total, ten areas are compared and one specifically for entrepreneurs.

The analysis confirms that currently eleven useful features are being promoted in mobile banking and new ones are still emerging [20, 19 and the websites of individual banks]. Important features include:

Open section:

- Fee calculator
- Exchange rates
- Branches
- Contacts
- Search for ATMs and branches

Secured section:

- Fingerprint, Touch ID (Reports, Overview of reports and details)
- Accounts (overview of balances on active accounts (current, savings and term) and their total by currency, Transaction history etc.)
- QR codes (Payment via QR codes)
- Reports (Overview of reports and details)
- Templates (Template overview, Template adding/editing/deleting)
- Payment orders (Placing orders between your accounts, Placing single CZK payment orders within the Czech Republic, Placing single EUR payment orders to Slovakia, Placing EUR payment orders in the Eurozone (TARGET2), Placing foreign payment orders, Overview of "pending" payments (with maturity in the future), Overview of incomplete payments) [21, 22]
- Mobile payment card management
- Arrangement of credit via mobile or via mobile application
- Opening a current account for a mobile phone or via mobile application
- Mobile cards for NFC mobile payments
- "Pay me" - a simple payment among people

Smart bank from **MONETA Money Bank** won the best mobile app. The main benefits of Smart bank v. 1.15 include: setting up a real online account via an application, sending money via iMessage (no account number, no login to Smart Bank), direct invoicing with QR code directly from the email, authorization of payments and sign in application via Face ID and Touch ID (no limit), virtual currency exchange FX Money.

The news that MONETA Money Bank introduced in 2017 were payment reporting and login to the application through Face ID and Touch ID, the ability to open a free account (no terms) and SmartBank directly from your mobile phone for a few clicks within 10 min, sending money over iMessage, invoice payments with QR code directly from email, virtual currency exchange FX Money, Apple Watch, Google Pay, widget as the first banking application in Central Europe I optimized the application for iPhone X and Face ID, loan, free and fully online from SmartBank on a few clicks.

In the first half of 2018 they planned iPad version, notification of change of balance through push notifications, OLED application mode, PDF statement from account, addition of other accounts from other banks (PSD2).

Overall rating Smart bank 1.15: Top rated mobile apps both by professional jury and by users themselves. Monthly updates are released with improvements and new features as per clients' requirements. The biggest advantage of this application is Google Pay, Face ID.

The second place was mBank with mobile application **mBank 3.0**. The main advantages of this Smart banking include: Net to minimalist design, introducing the application step by step, adapting apps to their needs (shortcuts to features the client prefers), linear navigation, end of the "hamburger menu" and one-handed control.

New features include: Maximum direct call to service mileage from a mobile application without the need for further verification at a telephone banker So just run the application, enter the 8-digit PIN, and then press the symbol green headphone and be connected directly with the banker to mLine. Establishing travel insurance in a mobile application.

Overall rating of mBank 3.0: The mobile application is modern and contains all the necessary security features that are currently required by clients. Some clients evaluated the minimalist design negatively. The biggest advantage of the application is that it is the first application with integrated Google Pay service, alerting for spending expenditures and integrated face recognition for the iOS.

Equa Bank ranked third with a new mobile application. This is a modern user design that takes into account trends in the most commonly used applications. Intuitive management.

All three applications are for Android and iOS smartphones.

6   Conclusion and Discussion

The aim of the first part of the article was to analyze the use of Internet banking in the European Union and especially in the Czech Republic. All the indicators surveyed had a growing trend and showed a growing trend in the use of Internet banking, although growth rates slowed down from 2015 onwards. Even so, the Czech Republic is above the EU average in using Internet Banking. Cheaper data tariffs from telephone operators contributes to faster growth of Internet and Mobile banking.

The second part analyzes the ten largest banks in the Czech Republic according to the number of clients. For these banks, it examines how the new features in its mobile banking and how it differs from the competition. The high competition in the banking market forces individual banks to offer constantly new features and services. All surveyed banks are trying to attract customers with its mobile applications. Banks monitor trends and customer requirements and strives to continually innovate their products. It is a question to discussion whether all functions for clients are needed and how long they will be offered by banks.

The three largest banks have less than 1/3 of mobile banking users. The scientific question was not confirmed. Smaller low-cost banks have up to half of mobile users. They have clients who are not afraid to change the bank and are willing to use a new technical solution. Their clients are in productive age, where the rate of Internet and mobile banking is the highest. Traditional conservative clients stay with large banks, but they offer all the service on a dense branch network.

It is a question of how the market will change because of "open banking" under the PSD2 (Revised Payment Service Directive) Directive, which aims to create a single payment market through bank and fintechs regulation.

Acknowledgement. The paper was written with the support of the specific project 6/2018 grant "DETERMINANTS OF COGNITIVE PROCESSES IMPACTING THE WORK PERFOR-MANCE" granted by the University of Hradec Králové, Czech Republic. We would like to thank student Eliška Čonková for cooperation in the processing of the article.

References

1. Criterio, Leadership of inquiry: building and sustaining capacity for school improvement. Educational Evaluation and Policy (2014)
2. Peevers, G., Douglas, G., Marshall, D., Jack, M.: On the role of SMS for transaction confirmation with IVR telephone banking. Int. J. Bank Mark. **29**(3), 206–223 (2011)
3. Khalfan, A., Yaqoub, S.Y., AlRefaei, Y., Al-Hajery, M.: Factors influencing the adoption of Internet banking in Oman: a descriptive case study analysis. Int. J. Financ. Serv. Manage. **1**(2), 155–172 (2006)
4. Almogbil, A.: Security, perceptions, and practices: challenges facing adoption of online banking in Saudi. Unpublished Ph.D. thesis, George Washington University, Washington
5. Omar, A.B., Sultan, N., Zaman, K., Bibi, N.: Customer perception towards online banking services: empirical evidence from Pakistan. J. Internet Bank. Commerce **16**(2) (2011)
6. Hedvicakova, M.: Key study of bank accounts for young people with using multi-criteria optimization and fuzzy analysis. Appl. Econ. **49**(36), 3599–3610 (2017)
7. Lin, L., Shiqian, W.: Factors influencing the behavior intention of E-banking transactions through mobile phones in China. J. Internet Bank. Commer. ISSN 1204-5357, http://www.icommercecentral.com/open-access/factors-influencing-the-behavior-intention-of-ebanking-transactions-through-mobile-phones-in-china.php?aid=86793. Accessed 10 2018
8. Soukal, I., Draessler, J.: Consumer desired price modeling – case study on the RCBS market. Proced. Soc. Behav. Sci. **62**, 916–920 (2012)
9. Takieddine, S., Sun, J.: Internet banking diffusion: a country-level analysis. Electr. Commer. Res. and Appl. **14**(5), 361–371. (2015) https://doi.org/10.1016/j.elerap.2015.06.001
10. Svobodova, L., Hedvicakova, M.: Technological readiness of the Czech Republic and the use of technology. In: Themistocleous, M., Morabito, V. (eds.) EMCIS 2017. LNBIP, vol. 299, pp. 670–678. Springer, Cham (2017). https://doi.org/10.1007/978-3-319-65930-5_53
11. Černohorská, L., Pilyavskyy, A., Aaronson, W.: Comparative performance of the visegrad group banks for the period 2009–2013. E a M: Ekonomie a Management, **20**(2), 175–187 (2017)
12. Vokoun, M.: Characteristics of the innovation activities of firms in Europe: a critical review of international differences. Rev. Econ. Perspect. **17**(3), 239–262 (2017)
13. Hedvičáková, M., Svobodová, L., Dittrichová, J., Král, M.: Financial literacy and money management of the pupils in the Czech education system. In: Proceedings of the 8th International Scientific Conference Finance and Performance of Firms in Science, Education and Practice, Tomas Bata University in Zlín, pp. 244–259 (2017). ISBN 978-80-7454-653-2
14. Eurostat: Digital economy and society statistics - households and individuals (2017). http://ec.europa.eu/eurostat/statistics-explained/index.php?title=Digital_economy_and_society_statistics_-_households_and_individuals. Accessed 14 June 2018

15. Eurostat: Internet banking on the rise (2018). http://ec.europa.eu/eurostat/web/products-eurostat-news/-/DDN-20180115-1. Accessed 17 June 2018
16. Eurostat: Archive: Internet access and use statistics - households and individuals (2016). http://ec.europa.eu/eurostat/statistics-explained/index.php?title=Archive:Internet_access_and_use_statistics_-_households_and_individuals. Accessed 17 June 2018
17. Czech Statistical Office: (2018) Informační společnost v číslech – (2018). https://www.czso.cz/csu/czso/informacni-spolecnost-v-cislech. Accessed 18 June 2018
18. DuoFinance, Banky podle velikosti? Počty klientů a aktiva v roce (2018). https://www.duofinance.cz/banky-cr-podle-poctu-klientu. Accessed 01 June 2018
19. Zlatá koruna. http://www.zlatakoruna.info/financni-produkty/on-line-aplikace. Accessed 20 June 2018
20. iDnes.cz, Analýza deseti bank: co už umí mobilní bankovnictví a co má úspěch. https://finance.idnes.cz/analyza-rijen-2017-co-umi-mobilni-bankovnictvi-smartbanking-10-bank-p8e-/sporeni.aspx?c=A171017_075039_sporeni_sov&strana=1#space-a. Accessed 08 June 2018
21. Fio bank, Smartbanking, https://www.fio.cz/bank-services/smartbanking#functions. Accessed 10 June 2018
22. Soukal, I., Draessler, J.: On the need for the next RCBS regulation. In: Soliman K.S. (ed.) Proceedings of the 25th International Business Information Management Association Conference - Innovation Vision 2020: From Regional Development Sustainability to Global Economic Growth, IBIMA 2015, pp. 679–687 (2015)

Solutions for Higher Competence in Financial Literacy of Pupils at Secondary School in the Czech Republic

Martina Hedvicakova[(✉)] and Libuse Svobodova

Faculty of Informatics and Management, University of Hradec Králové,
Rokitanskeho 62, 500 03 Hradec Kralove, Czech Republic
{Martina.hedvicakova,Libuse.svobodova}@uhk.cz

Abstract. Financial literacy now appears to be a key component of a successful national economy and successful personal finance and budgeting. Financial education, financial consumer protection and financial inclusion are the goal of top country policies. For this reason, it is necessary to assess the levels of financial literacy in each country. There are several solutions for education in this field. The aim of the article is to state selected solutions that will support financial literacy of pupils at secondary school in the Czech Republic. Paper is starting point to this issue for future analysis. Digital dementia is one of the issues solved in the article. Advanced technologies and their use are some presented solutions as are web portals, learning management systems, PC and Internet games, social networks, blogs or other possibilities. Three web portals that can be used for getting higher competencies in financial literacy will be presented and evaluated at the end of the article. Primary and secondary sources were used in the processing of the article.

Keywords: Financial literacy · Web portals · Education · Digital dementia
Competencies

1 Introduction

Financial literacy, its importance, measuring issues, implementation of financial education programms and related topics are frequently discussed in academic and public environment. High level of financial literacy makes a large contribution to the financial well-being of individuals, because financially literate individuals are more likely to plan for retirement Almenberg and Save-Soderbergh [1] more likely to participate in financial markets and perform better on their portfolio choice [2] and more likely to accumulate higher amounts of wealth (Lusardi and Mitchell [3]). In turn "lack of financial literacy was one of the factors contributing to ill-informed financial decisions and that these decisions could, in turn, have tremendous negative spillover" [4]. Ciemleja, Lace, Titko [5], Kantnerová [6] shows the level of financial literacy in different countries and find, if there is any, some methods, differences or connecting matters, what can be used for the improvement of the situation, if needed [7, 11, 12].

Digital media are omnipresent in our daily lives. This popularity is giving rise to fears about the possible negative consequences of computer and internet use [8].

S. A. Al-Sharhan et al. (Eds.): I3E 2018, LNCS 11195, pp. 387–396, 2018.
https://doi.org/10.1007/978-3-030-02131-3_35

2   The Literature Review

PISA [9], p. 36 defines the financial literacy as: "Financial literacy is knowledge and understanding of financial concepts and risks, and the skills, motivation and confidence to apply such knowledge and understanding in order to make effective decisions across a range of financial contexts, to improve the financial well-being of individuals and society, and to enable participation in economic life".

Understanding financial literacy among young people is essential for developing effective financial education programmes [10]. The financial education focuses on increasing the financial literacy. The financial literacy is defined by Atkinson and Messy [13] as "a combination of awareness, knowledge, skill, attitude and behaviour necessary to make sound financial decisions and ultimately achieve individual financial wellbeing" [14].

Financial education has a preventive and controlling role of debt, increasing savings and investment. As such, the teaching of financial education helps to leverage the knowledge of individuals regarding financial transactions, giving them useful tools for decision-making Potrich, Vieira and Mendes-da-Silva [15]. In this sense, financial education should cover the investment options, and convey the correct understanding of the concepts related to inflation, interest and taxation (Lusardi [16]), [17].

Marcolin and Abraham [18] identified the need for research focused specifically on measurement of financial literacy. Typically, financial literacy and/or financial knowledge indicators are used as inputs to model the need for financial education and explain variation in financial outcomes such as savings, investing and debt behavior. Far fewer studies specifically emphasize measurement of financial literacy as an objective. Huston [19] overview of the importance and measurement of financial literacy is presented to highlight current limitations and assist researchers in establishing standardized, commonly accepted, financial literacy tools.

Gajewski [20] presents lessons learned from almost 25 sears long experiences with different forms of E-learning. All experiences are definitely positive, but during the research, manpasses and traps have been recognized and observed. Widely used multimedia materials do not motivate poor students to learn. Instead of learning they prefer to watch the materials in a passive way. Mobile learning, in which all materials are available for smartphones, has increased this attitude towards learning. All quizzes and tests cannot be replaced by a real exam. Knowledge of the answers on hundreds of questions is not equal to the real knowledge of a certain field. Flipped classroom paradigm for learning at home was not accepted by students. Moreover, E-education creates chances for c-cheating. All these pitfalls and traps lead to the conclusion that F-education is not a straightforward remedy for all current education problems.

3   The Goal of Article and Methodology

The article is based on primary and secondary sources. Secondary sources comprise information about financial literacy and education in the Czech Republic and abroad, professional literature, information collected from professional press, discussions or previous participations in professional seminars and conferences relating to the chosen subject. Primary sources are based on the information gained from individual web portal and from the research done at four secondary schools in Liberec in the Czech Republic. Then it was necessary to select, classify and up-date accessible relevant information from the numerous published materials that would provide the basic knowledge of the selected topic [2, 7, 21].

The goal of the article is to focus on the financial literacy and the negative effects of education using only digital media. The aim of the paper is to state selected teaching materials that can be used to getting higher competencies in financial literacy of pupils at secondary school in the Czech Republic. Solutions are stated in more ways and also in the more and more popular electronic form. The sub-goal is to present and analyze web portals that can be used by teachers of pupils in the process of education. Web portals were selected according to Methodical portal (inspiration and teacher experience) that were prepared under the framework of Educational Programs in the National Institute for Education [22].

4 Digital Dementia

German psychiatrist Spitzer [23], in his book "Digital Dementia", demonstrates through a series of surveys that digital learning technology not only does not help but is even harmful. In simple terms, the basic thesis can be expressed as follows: By making computers, the Internet or GPS navigation easier for us, they take us away from "brain training." When we are certain that the information is stored somewhere and we can find it anytime, nothing When navigating in a car tells us where to go, we do not have to concentrate on the space in which we move, ourselves - without navigation - we are gradually losing our spatial orientation capability, and finally, when we become accustomed to the possibility to search for information and at the same time watch emails, chat, listen to music, etc., we lose our ability to concentrate, the ability to work intensively.

4.1 The Secondary Effects of Digital Media

- Because of working with digital media we use the most logical part of the head. Apart from logic, we neglect linguistic, verbal, musical, physical, visual, spatial, intrapersonal and interpersonal intelligence (emotional intelligence and empathy).
- The perception of the environment and of itself is largely suppressed by watching the display, as the glowing displays naturally attract attention without having to consciously take it. It can be observed that people working or playing on computers often ignore the needs of their body (hunger, thirst, need for movement, etc.) and do not perceive the outside world.
- Perception of time is difficult, for the same reason, especially if you are doing something to get enough of it.
- Definition of function and location. Considering the computer as a tool, it is difficult to define its purpose, as it is multipurpose. People are naturally used to adjusting their place and environment for their activity, which helps them keep their attention

and build up work habits. If you use one thing in bed, chairs, office, transport, for fun and for many kinds of work, it really costs a lot of energy to keep your goals in mind and build some work habits at all.

- Multitasking. People commonly perform a variety of activities or work in multiple applications at the same time. At the same time, they listen to music, play the game, watch chat, download files, read emails every 5 min, write a task or learn? The negative effect of switching attention has been confirmed by many studies.
- Physiological stress - work is particularly stressed on the eyes, spine and wrist (RMS syndrome), lack of movement.
- A test of will and purposefulness - the number of available applications, interactive and communication means, infinite amounts of information, videos and pictures, music, colorful advertisements and games prepared by psychologist teams, to engage as forever as possible, you do not see what you should do or what you want to do.
- Procrastination is a phenomenon today.
- There are risks of dependence that are known and demonstrable [24].

5   Solutions for Improving Financial Competencies

5.1   Financial Literacy Standard in the Czech Republic

The Ministry of Finance published the revised Financial Literacy Standard, which sets the target level of financial literacy for elementary and secondary school pupils on 20 July 2017. Compared to the financial literacy standards of 2007, these topics have been strengthened: cashless payments, protection of personal data, critical assessment of the supply of services and goods, budgeting and comparison of assets and liabilities, remuneration, financial product comparison, short and long term planning, age security, the emergence and risk of borrowings, the consequences of default and debt and over-indebtedness.

The revised standard of financial literacy will be implemented in the Framework Education Programs at their next revision. The National Institute of Education encourages primary and secondary schools to compare the revised standard of financial literacy with their school curriculum and, if necessary, their school education program in the field of financial education during a transitional period (i.e. until the revised standard of financial literacy is part of the framework educational programs) edited or completed. The current adaptation of school education programs is not an obligation at present, but only an option. In the case of adjusting the school education program according to the revised standard of financial literacy, this adjustment will also be in line with the current Framework Educational Program.

5.2   Possibilities for Improving Financial Literacy

It depends on the age of children, students or people that are in the productive age or pensioner what information do they need. Pupils will need basic information and knowledge in this field. Students will need deeper competencies in the financial world and citizens in the productive age or pensioners also. There are several possibilities, how to improve financial literacy and competences of pupils in the Czech Republic in this field. They are:

- Subject "Financial literacy" or more subjects focused on the financial competencies and discussion at school
- Project days at school
- Web portals
- PC and Internet games
- Social networks
- Blogs
- Desktop games
- Books
- Discussion with parents.

In 2016 was done in the cooperation with author of this article the research of financial literacy of pupils 8th and 9th grades of selected primary schools in the statutory city Liberec [25]. The aim of the research was to analyze the degree of financial literacy in selected primary schools in the statutory city Liberec and propose possible solutions for the improvement of this literacy. Research was done via questionnaire and discussion face to face was done in the classes. 237 pupils from 4 secondary schools participated in the research. After a short interviews done with pupils, it was founded, that the web portals were perceived to be one of the appropriate means of education. Portals are positively evaluated because they are in electronic form, which is currently trendy. Their use is an interesting part in education and it motive pupils to study. For pupils it is essential that the site is attractively crafted with an appropriate structure of knowledge related with its age.

5.3 Web Portal "Why Educate in Financial Literacy?"

In 2014, the Ministry of Finance of the Czech Republic launched a pilot version of the PSFV portal entitled "Why Financial Education?" which can be found at www.psfv.cz [26]. In particular, these sites:

- provide information on the functioning and risks in the world of finance,
- provide guidance and guidance in various areas of finance,
- help solve problems (over-indebtedness or financial market participants)
- highlight interesting websites with financial games, calculators and projects
- share PSFV members' information.

At first glance, the site is uninteresting, but after a done analysis it is really clear and fairly well developed. This is a glossary of the notions of the world of finance that every financially literate person should know and control. The headings are broken down into the nine basic training groups: Family finance, Description of the financial market, Consumer protection, Loans, Money and accounts, Investment, Insurance, Pensions, Conflict solving. Each section contains not only the basic concepts, but also other areas that undoubtedly belong to the given problem. Everything is well explained and the issue is supplemented with tutorials, calculators, links or a form.

In the other columns there are various tips and guides (such as How to Retire or Insurance, Information on Treaties, Payment Cards, etc.), Information for Professionals (where they are trained, Legislation, Financial literacy level measurement, etc.). There are also presented contacts in case of problems and need to seek help. Everything is accompanied by important and clear news and an overview of financial education projects.

The portal is an excellent electronic textbook not only for teachers, but also for children and parents who could help orient themselves in the complicated world of finance. All necessary and basic knowledge are provided, which is supplemented by up-to-date information, which is very advantageous because all information are presented in one web portal and it is not only a theoretical portal, see Fig. 1 – description of the financial market. Portal contains next parts: News, Family and Personal finance, Description of the financial market, Consumer protection, Loans, Money and accounts, Investment, Insurance, Pensions, Solving of conflicts, Tips & Guides, For professionals, Interesting links, Contacts, Dictionary of terms, They will help you and Test yourself.

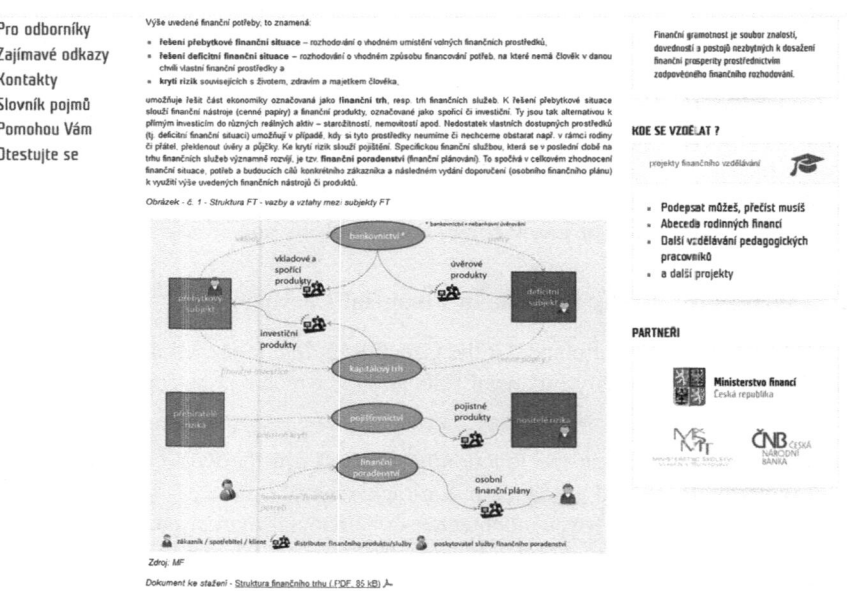

Fig. 1. Web portal "Why educate in financial literacy?" [26]

5.4   Web Portal "Money on the Run"

The Czech National Bank has launched and operates web portal focused on financial literacy. The site is designed for young people that are aged 18-35 and seeks to educate them in a comprehensible form. The pages are divided into 3 sections:

- budgeting
- financial services
- life events [27].

The site also includes quizzes, a glossary of terms and ten commandments about money. The portal can be used in school practice, but it is recommended especially for secondary school pupils than for elementary pupils (See Fig. 2).

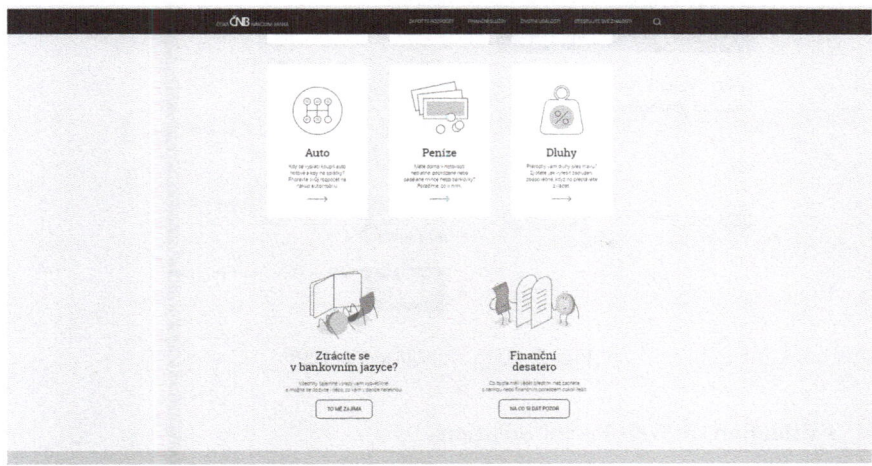

Fig. 2. Money on the run [27]

5.5   Web Portal "Life Without Debts"

Life without debts is the SEKO site, which implements the Fund for Further Education. It was the project of Integrated Portal of the Ministry of Labour and Social Affairs of the Czech Republic. [28] It is an animated series on financial literacy topics, which deals with the following 10 advices:

- The rich and the poor, everyone must calculate
- We save a lot of money when we save on little things
- Debt trap
- Debit or credit, that's a question!
- Do you have property? We'll borrow you!
- Just let him see that we have it!
- Civic Counseling - Do not be alone on it
- They borrow without rules …
- RPSN and contracts - More heads know more.
- About bread and water.

Although the materials are primarily intended for job seekers in socio-economic competencies, ten animated videos can be also used in school lessons. They are prepared in the easy form with the animated videos. All the spots are uploaded on the

YouTube Channel (see Fig. 3) [29]. Disadvantage of this site is only a few videos. There are no more materials presented for study.

Fig. 3. Life without debts [29]

5.6 Evaluation of Web Portal Solutions

After the analysis, it can be estimated that "Life without debts" is the simplest solution that contains only 10 videos without further study support. Therefore it can be only used as an illustration. "Money on the run" is a more complex solution. However, it does not cover all areas of financial literacy and it is intended for high school or older students. As the most appropriate study material to support the improvement of financial literacy was evaluated the "Why Educate in Financial Literacy" web portal, which contains all components of financial literacy outside of inflation. It also contains comprehensive study materials with clear pictures and quizzes on the selected topics.

6   Conclusion and Discussion

Appel, Schreiner [8] reviews the current empirical knowledge regarding the effects of computer and Internet use. The meta-analyses yield no evidence for a supposedly maladaptive influence of Internet use on social interactions, political and civic engagement, or loneliness. The relationships between Internet use and well-being or depression are small, but significant, as is the relationship between the use of digital media and obesity. On average, learning with the computer and Internet, including educational games, can have positive effects. However, there is substantial evidence for negative effects of violence in computer games on aggressive thoughts, feelings, and behavior.

Financial literacy, digital dementia and solutions for gaining higher competences in financial literacy of pupils in the Czech Republic were solved in the article. Main part of the article was focused on the specification of several solutions how to improve financial literacy. Solutions are based on the face to face communication, electronic form or printed form. Online materials are now trendy for pupils. This is also reason why the last part of the article is devoted to three chosen technical solutions that may be used in the process of education at schools but also as self-study. Short description and introduction of three Web portals recommended by the framework Educational Programs prepared in the National Institute for Education that are focused on the financial literacy in the Czech Republic, "How to educate in financial literacy", "Money on the run" and "Life without debts" are presented and analyzed. Web portal "Why Educate in Financial Literacy? was evaluated as the most comprehensive web portal solution that were analyzed in the article.

The current adaptation of school education programs is not an obligation at present, but only an option. The behavior of parents, neighborhoods and other components of the economy is another element that affects financial habits. It is recommended to speak and discuss about those issues and to ask in all times when we are not sure with our steps.

Acknowledgement. This study is supported by internal research project No. 2103 Investment evaluation within concept Industry 4.0 at Faculty of Informatics and Management, University of Hradec Kralove, Czech Republic. We would like to thank student Martin Král for cooperation in the processing of the article.

References

1. Almenberg, J., Save-Soderbergh, J.: Financial literacy and retirement planning in Sweden. Netspar Discussion Paper 01 2011–0218. http://arno.uvt.nl. Accessed 10 June 2018
2. van Rooij, M., Lusardi, A., Alessie, R.: Financial literacy and retirement planning in the Netherlands. J. Econ. Psychol. **32**, 593–608 (2011)
3. Lusardi, A., Mitchell, O.S.: Financial Literacy and Planning: Implications for Retirement Wellbeing. University Press, Oxford (2011)
4. OECD: PISA 2012 Financial literacy assessment framework. http://www.oecd.org/pisa/pisaproducts/45962580.pdf. Accessed 10 June 2018
5. Ciemleja, G., Lace, N., Titko, J.: Towards the practical evaluation of financial literacy: latvian survey. Proc. Soc. Behav. Sci. **156**(26), 13–17 (2014). https://doi.org/10.1016/j.sbspro.2014.11.111. 19th International Scientific Conference "Economics and Management 2014 (ICEM-2014)
6. Kantnerová, L.: The comparison of level of financial literacy in four countries. In: Proceedings of the 7th International Scientific Conference Finance and Performance of Firms in Science, Education and Practice, Tomas Bata University in Zlín, Zlín, pp. 559–570 (2015). ISBN 978-80-7454-482-8
7. Hedvicakova, M., Svobodova, L.: Web portals used in financial education as a support of financial literacy. Adv. Sci. Lett. **24**(4), 2948–2952 (2018)
8. Apple, M., Schreiner, C.: Digital dementia? Myths and scientific evidence concerning the effect of Internet use. Psychol. Rundsch. **65**(1), 1–10 (2014)
9. PISA/OECD: Financial Literacy Assessment Framework (2012). www.oecd.org. Accessed 10 June 2018

10. Astuti, P.H., Trinugroho, I.: Financial literacy and engagement in banking. J. Econ. Econ. Educ. Res. **17**(1), 1 (2016)
11. Lusardi, A., Tufano, P.: Debt Literacy, Financial Experiences, and Overindebtedness. NBER Working Paper no. 14808 (2009a)
12. Lusardi, A., Tufano, P.: Teach workers about the Perils of Debt. Harvard Bus. Rev. **87**, 22–24 (2009)
13. Atkinson, A., Messy, F.: Measuring financial literacy: results of the OECD. In: International Network on Financial Education (INFE) Pilot Study, OECD Working Papers on Finance, Insurance and Private Pensions, no. 15 (2012)
14. Soukal, I., Draessler, J.: Could financial literacy overcome price information asymmetry: empirical study. In: European Financial Systems 2015. Masarykova Univerzita, Brno, pp. 528–535 (2015)
15. Potrich, A.C.G., Vieira, K.M., Mendes-Da-Silva, W.: Development of a financial literacy model for university students. Manage. Res. Rev. **39**(3), 356–376 (2016)
16. Lusardi, A.: The importance of financial literacy. NBER Rep. **2**, 13–16 (2009)
17. da Silva, T.P., Dal Magro, B., Gorla, M.C., Nakamura, W.T.: Financial education level of high school students and its economic reflections. Revista de Administração **52**(3), 285–303 (2017)
18. Marcolin, S., Abraham, A.: Financial literacy research: current literature and future opportunities. http://ro.uow.edu.au/commpapers/223/. Accessed 10 June 2018
19. Huston, S.J.: Measuring financial literacy. J. Consum. Aff. **44**(2), 296–315 (2010)
20. Gajewski, R.R.: Pitfalls of E-education: from multimedia to digital dementia? In: Proceedings of the 2016 Federated Conference on Computer Science and Information Systems (FEDCSIS). Book Series: ACSIS-Annals of Computer Science and Information Systems, vol. 8, pp. 913–920 (2014)
21. Hedvičáková, M., Svobodová, L., Dittrichová, J., Král, M.: Financial literacy and money management of the pupils in the Czech education system. In: Proceedings of the 8th International Scientific Conference Finance and Performance of Firms in Science, Education and Practice, Tomas Bata University in Zlín, pp. 244–259
22. Financial literacy, Methodological portal. https://digifolio.rvp.cz/view/view.php?id=2939. Accessed 10 June 2018
23. Spitzel, M.: Digitální demence (Digital dementia), p. 343. Host, Brno (2014)
24. Komárek, M.: Hrozí našim dětem digitální demence? Druhý díl diskuse: Kdo o tablety vůbec stojí? (2014). http://literarky.cz/politika/domaci/17332-hrozi-naim-dtem-digitalni-demence-druhy-dil-diskuse-kdo-o-tablety-vbec-stoji. Accessed 10 June 2018
25. Vandírková, B.: Financial literacy of pupils 8th and 9th grade of selected primary schools in the statutory city Liberec. Bachelor thesis at University of Hradec Kralove (2016)
26. Web portal "Why Educate in Financial Literacy?" www.psfv.cz. Accessed 10 June 2018
27. Money on the run. https://www.penizenauteku.cz/. Accessed 10 June 2018
28. Training of jobseekers in socio-economic competencies (SEKO). https://portal.mpsv.cz/upcr/kp/pak/projekty_esf/ukoncene_projekty/narodni_individualni_projekty/vzdelavani_uchazecu_o_zamestnani_v_socioekonomicky. Accessed 18 July 2018
29. Life without debts. https://www.youtube.com/playlist?list=PLJBJQtzWUE6MhhEoUmjK8-Oav7J7vIJtg. Accessed 10 June 2018

A Fuzzy Multi-criteria Decision Making Approach for Analyzing the Risks and Benefits of Opening Data

Ahmad Luthfi[1,2(✉)] [iD], Zeenat Rehena[1,3] [iD], Marijn Janssen[1] [iD],
and Joep Crompvoets[4] [iD]

[1] Faculty of Technology, Policy and Management,
Delft University of Technology, Jaffalaan 5, 2628 BX Delft, The Netherlands
{a.luthfi, z.rehena, m.f.w.h.a.janssen}@tudelft.nl
[2] Universitas Islam Indonesia, Yogyakarta, Indonesia
ahmad.luthfi@uii.ac.id
[3] Aliah University, Kolkata, India
zeenatrehena@aliah.ac.in
[4] Katholieke Universiteit Leuven, Leuven, Belgium
joep.crompvoets@kuleuven.be

Abstract. Governments are releasing their data to the public to accomplish benefits like the creation of transparency, accountability, citizen engagement and to enable business innovation. At the same time, decision-makers are reluctant to open their data due to some potential risks like misuse, sensitivity, ownership, and inaccuracy of the data. The goal of the study presented in this paper is to develop a Fuzzy Multi-Criteria Decision Making (FMCDM) approach to analyze the risks and benefits to determine the decision to open a dataset. FMCDM is chosen due to its capability to measure and weight the relative importance of the criteria. FMCDM need the weighting of criteria as input. For this Fuzzy Analytical Hierarchy Process (FAHP) is utilized by collecting input from experts' knowledge and expertise. The scores for each criterion are summed up to rank the importance of the alternatives. Four main criteria are used, e.g. data sensitivity and data ownership representing risks criteria, and data availability and data trustworthy as benefits criteria. For each criterion, there were two sub-criteria identified. Four types of decisions to open data can be made: completely open, maintain suppression, provide limited access, and remain closed. A health patient record dataset is used to illustrate the approach. In further research, we recommend to develop automated approaches that take a dataset as an input and can provide an advice.

Keywords: Multi-criteria decision making · Fuzzy
Analytic Hierarchy process · Open data · Risks · Benefits

1 Introduction

The motivation to open data by governments and private organizations have increased extensively over the last few years. The creation of transparency and accountability, to sustain citizen engagement and to enable business innovation are the main drivers to

© IFIP International Federation for Information Processing 2018
Published by Springer Nature Switzerland AG 2018. All Rights Reserved
S. A. Al-Sharhan et al. (Eds.): I3E 2018, LNCS 11195, pp. 397–412, 2018.
https://doi.org/10.1007/978-3-030-02131-3_36

open more data [1–4]. The disclosure of data is expected to improve decisionmaking initiatives by both government and society [3, 5]. Furthermore, the opening of data by organizations can improve an organization's reputation by showing that they are an open institution [6].

However, although divers types of datasets have already been opened [7–9], in reality many datasets are still not opened [10]. There are several reasons why the data providers reluctance for opening datasets, including: (1) barriers of implementing the systems [11, 12]; (2) risks like inaccuracy, misuse, sensitivity, and inconsistency of the data [3, 10, 12–17]; and (3) inappropriate interpretation of the data resulting in an inadequate comprehend of the data [3]. Moreover, mistakes in interpreting data or misuse of data can jeopardize the reputation of data providers [11]. This result in many datasets to remain closed, whereas this might not be necessary.

The goal presented in this study is to develop a Fuzzy Multi-Criteria Decision Making (FMCDM) approach to analyze the risks and benefits and to determine the best alternative decision for a given dataset. The use of Fuzzy set theory in this research is to manage decision-making problem of alternative selection of a dataset status. These alternatives are developed by establishing and incorporating the FMCDM based on Fuzzy Analytic Hierarchy Process (FAHP) [18, 19]. The main function of the Fuzzy logic is to capture the expertise of open experts and to express it with computational approach [20–22]. A Fuzzy theory is based on the intuitive reasoning by considering the human subjectivity and incorrectness, which are common in the natural language [23]. The natural language is an intricate structure both in the human communication and the way how the human being thinks [23, 24].

Fuzzy theory is used in this paper to provide a mathematical strength for the emulation of the higher cognitive function from the human thought and perception associated with weights of the risks and benefit of opening data. The main function of the FMCDM is to assess the alternative selection with respect to predetermined criteria for a single decision making [25]. The appropriateness of the alternative compares to the criteria and the priority weights of each criterion can be analyzed and computed using linguistic matrix values reflected by the fuzzy [20, 26]. FAHP, furthermore, is used to determine the preference weightings of criteria by collecting expert's judgment [18, 27]. The scores for each criterion are summed up to rank the importance of the alternatives [28, 29].

This FAHP technique used in this study consists of the six following steps [18, 19, 27], namely: (1) select experts team; (2) determine the evaluation criteria and construct the hierarchy, including alternatives; (3) construct pairwise comparison matrix and evaluate the relative importance of the criteria; (4) transform the linguistic terms into triangular fuzzy number; (5) calculate the Fuzzy weights matrix, and check the consistency of the pairwise comparison matrix; and (6) select the best alternative. A dataset of health patient records is used in the illustration part to show how the risk and benefit multiple criteria can be analyzed by employing the FMCDM approach. The four possible decisions are completely open, maintain suppression, provide limited access, or remain closed. These are the alternatives for the FMCDM and decisions on these alternatives will be analyzed based on the four main criteria, namely data sensitivity and data ownership for the risk criteria, while data availability and data trustworthiness are the criteria for the benefit. Data sensitivity and ownership are selected as input because of these criteria can represent some privacy violation issues containing in health patient records dataset. For example, in the case of data sensitivity, by releasing the actual value of name, date of birth, place of birth, home address, or insurance provider of a patient, it might be potentially misused by the unauthorized users. In addition, data availability and data trustworthiness are chosen criteria due to they can reflect the benefit of transparency and accountability in opening data. Each of the criteria has sub-criteria to further refine the risks and benefits. In Sect. 3.3, we will explain the sub-criteria definition and relationship in more detail.

This paper is consists of six sections. In Sect. 1 the rationale of this research is presented, Sect. 2 contains the related work of decision-making to open data. In Sect. 3 the approaches are described, including proposed flow process, alternatives, and criteria selection for FMCDM which is based on FAHP method. Section 4 provides the illustration and results. Section 5 some findings of the study are provided. Finally, the paper will be concluded in Sect. 6.

2   Related Work

In order to present the current approaches of decision analysis in the domain of open data, we reviewed literature which is summarized in Table 1. We found three limited works about decision-making analysis for opening data. Existing work uses the following methods: (1) trade-offs method to weigh the values and risks of open data by conducting interview sections with exclusive groups like civil servants and archivists, (2) decision-support framework to develop a prototype based on the open data ecosystem for specific groups like business and private organization, and (3) an iterative method using Bayesian-belief Networks to weigh the risks and benefits of opening data.

Yet, none of these related works utilized an FMCDM approach in a sense to measure and determine the best alternative for deciding a single status of a dataset. Some possible advantages the use of the FMCDM approach compare to three other methods are: (1) the capability to consider the human subjectivity and incorrectness from the common natural language [32]; (2) provides assessment of the alternatives selection with respect to predetermined criteria for a single decision making [25]; and (3) its simplicity characteristic to evaluate multiple conflicting in decision-making as one of the most popular problems handled by researchers in the literature [25, 32].

3   Decision-Making Approach

In this section, we aim to describe the decision-making approach for analyzing risks and benefits of open data. Four subsections are described, namely flow process of the proposed method, alternatives, selection of criteria, and FAHP technique.

3.1   Flow Process of Proposed Method

To describe how the FMCDM approach works, we use a flow of decision-making process having three main phases, namely data source, evaluation, and decision. The

Table 1. The previous methods of decision support for opening data

	Name of approach	Research overview and boundary
1	Trade-offs method [10]	• A decision-making model offers respectfully capturing trade-offs, and in this method also providing guidance for weighing the potential values and risks of opening data. • No specific algorithm to weigh the risks and benefits of open data. • The trade-offs model can only be used for decision-making with Boolean expression (open or closed) decision.
2	Decision Support Framework [30]	• A developed prototype is based on the concept of open data ecosystems. • The proposed model is specifically for business and private organizations. • There was no evaluation and assessment model available
3	Iterative Model of Decision Support for opening data [31]	• An Iterative model decision support is based on the Bayesian-belief Network analysis. • The outcomes can be used to mitigate the risks and still gain benefits of opening data by taking action removing privacy-sensitive data from a dataset. • There are two alternative decisions available (Open or Closed).

entire process starts with the selection of the dataset from the data source to create the input for the evaluation phase. The input data are processed next in the evaluation phase. The output of the evaluation namely decision stage is a suggestion to make a decision. The latter is done by showing the rank of decision priority (decision), as shown in Fig. 1.

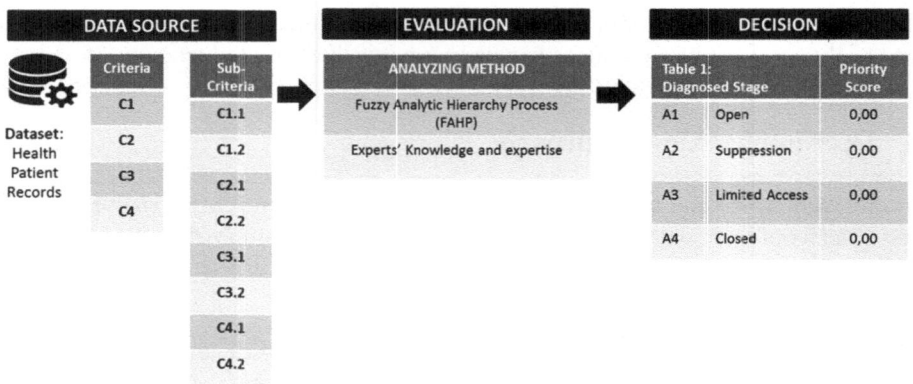

Fig. 1. The flow process of the approach

The flow process is based on the data source, evaluation of input data (data source) and decision. Figure 1 illustrates the staging of analyzing the risks and benefits of opening data, and it can be narrated as follows:

- **Data Source**: First, we need to select the type of a dataset. For example, in this study, we have chosen health patient records and Table 1: diagnosed stage (see Fig. 3) as the object to be analyzed. To define the criteria and sub-criteria, an extensive literature review related to the risks and benefits of opening data has done in Sect. 2. In this study, we designed four criteria and eight sub-criteria of the risks and benefits as the input data.
- **Evaluation**: In the second stage, we used FMCDM to assess the alternatives based on criteria defined in the data source elicitation phase and the criteria uses linguistic matrix values reflected by the Fuzzy. FMCDM works on Fuzzy AHP technique has an essential role to measure the relative importance of defined criteria for dealing with decision-making problem. To quantify the relative importance of the risks and benefits, we picked up the knowledge from the experts' judgment. There are two main steps to conduct an evaluation process by the experts in AHP, as follows [27, 33]: To begin with, experts should rank the criteria in a descending or ascending order of their significance. Then, determining the most important criteria and compare it with others. For example, an expert ranked that data sensitivity (C1) is higher or essentially important than data ownership (C2). Second, experts will determine the criteria weights by transforming pairwise comparison matrix into a triangular fuzzy number, as can be seen in Fig. 5.
- **Decision**: Finally, the outcome of this flow process is to get the final weights of the best alternative as the priority of a decision.

3.2 Alternatives

The following four alternatives of opening data in this paper are: opening the dataset (A1), maintaining a dataset suppression (A2), providing limited access (A3), or keeping the dataset closed (A4). First, the alternative "open the dataset" is defined as publishing the dataset presents a low risk to an individual or organization identity, and/or the potential benefits of the dataset substantially outweigh the potential risks. Second, the alternative "maintaining suppression" is specified as removing a data field and/or an individual record into particular groups or generate unique characteristics to avoid the personal identity. In this alternative, data that might create significant risks are not opened in the actual form, as the potential benefits do not outweigh the possibility of the risks. Third, the alternative "limited access" defines that only a certain group will be given access to the data. The level of openness is limited. Often those who will gain access have to sign a document that outlines the rules of access. The reason for this is releasing the dataset will create a moderate risk, or potential benefits of the dataset do not outweigh the potential privacy risks. Fourth, the alternative "keeping the dataset closed", it means that by publishing the dataset generates a very high risk to an individual or organization and significantly outweigh the potential benefits.

3.3   Selection of Criteria

Figure 2 represents the hierarchy of the four criteria, eight sub-criteria, and four alternatives. The four criteria C1, C2, C3 and C4 define data sensitivity, data ownership, data availability, and data trustworthy respectively. The data sensitivity (C1) composes of two sub-criteria: individual life-threatening (C1.1) and data identifiable (C1.2). Individual life-threatening (C1.1), can be defined as a potential risk to an individual or personal life because of the possibility to recognize the sensitive value of the dataset. Data identifiable (C1.2) is specified as the potential leak of the personal, organizational, business or even government data identifiable e.g. by combining some attributes of the field.

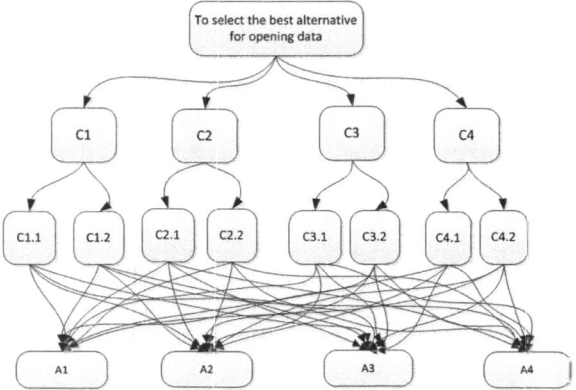

Fig. 2. The hierarchy of criteria and alternatives

The second criterion is data ownership (C2) which consists of two sub-criteria namely metadata scanning (C2.1) and fake or misleading (C2.2). Metadata scanning (C2.1) can be represented to figure out the property and structure of the dataset. Fake or misleading (C2.2) is defined by a user to potentially change and modify the dataset and affect an unreliable and wrong decision. Data availability (C3) is the third criterion and it has two sub-criteria namely data manageability (C3.1) and data recoverability (C3.2). Data manageability (C3.1) is specified as the chance to manage the availability and accessibility of the dataset. Data recoverability (C3.2) is indicated by delivering a dataset and it can have a highly positive impact on recovering the availability of the data. The fourth criterion is data trustworthiness (C4) which consists of two sub-criteria like data traceability (C4.1) and data authenticity (C4.2). Data traceability (C4.1) can make the possibility to trace the source of the dataset. Data authenticity (C4.2) is defined as the potentially affected to recognize the authentication of the data.

3.4   Fuzzy AHP Technique

The AHP process is a quantitative method that deals with the multi-attribute, multi-criteria, multi-period problem hierarchically [34]. Only with AHP, it is not possible to overcome the deficiency of the fuzziness during decision making [35]. Hence, in this study, the Fuzzy AHP which is the extension of the conventional AHP method by integrating fuzzy comparison ratios is used for multi-criteria analysis [18, 27, 34, 36]. It uses the triangular fuzzy number of fuzzy set theory directly into the pairwise comparison matrix of the AHP. The geometric mean method is used to generate fuzzy weights and performance scores [37]. The steps of the Fuzzy AHP can be summarized as follows:

- Step 1. Select experts. The quality of the evaluation process depends on experts' knowledge and experience. Hence the selection of experts is crucial.
- Step 2. Determine the evaluation criteria and construct the hierarchy including alternatives.
- Step 3: Construct pairwise comparison matrix and evaluate the relative importance of the criteria. The experts are expected to provide their judgment on the basis of their knowledge.
  For any expert the comparison matrix is given by Eq. (1) as:

(a)
$$\tilde{C}_k = \begin{bmatrix} 1 & \tilde{c}12\ldots & \tilde{c}1n \\ \vdots & \ddots & \vdots \\ \tilde{c}n1 & \tilde{c}n1\ldots & 1 \end{bmatrix} \tag{1}$$

where n is the number of criteria, $\tilde{C}_k$ is a pairwise comparison matrix belongs to kth expert for k = 1, 2.. k.

(b) Arithmetic mean is used to aggregate experts' opinion as given in Eq. (2).

$$\tilde{C} = \frac{1}{k}\left(\frac{1}{c} + \frac{2}{c} + \ldots + \frac{k}{c}\right) \tag{2}$$

- Step 4: Transform the linguistic terms into triangular fuzzy numbers. The following linguistic terms provided in Table 2 are utilized for the evaluation procedure.
- Step 5: Calculate the fuzzy weight matrix using Eqs. (3) and (4).

$$\tilde{r}_i = (\tilde{c}_{i1} \otimes \tilde{c}_{i2} \otimes \ldots \otimes \tilde{c}_{in})^{\frac{1}{n}} \tag{3}$$

$$\tilde{w}_i = \tilde{r}_i \otimes (\tilde{r}_1 + \tilde{r}_2 + \cdots \tilde{r}_n)^{-1} \tag{4}$$

where $\tilde{r}_i$ is the geometric mean of fuzzy comparison value and $\tilde{w}_i$ is the fuzzy weight of the ith criteria.

Table 2. The fuzzy linguistic scales (adapted from: [18])

Fuzzy number	Linguistic scales	Scale of fuzzy number
1	Equal Important (EI)	(1,1,3)
3	Weakly Important (WI)	(1,3,5)
5	Essentially Important (SI)	(3,5,7)
7	Very Strongly Important (VI)	(5,7,9)
9	Absolutely Important (AI)	(7,9,9)

- Step 6: Apply normalization procedure as Eq. (5)

$$w_i = \frac{\tilde{w}_i}{\sum_{j=1}^{n} \tilde{w}_j} \tag{5}$$

4   Illustration of FMCDM

In this section, we will illustrate the FMCDM using a health patient records dataset with the help of Fuzzy AHP technique. The reason for selecting this dataset is that it contains the typical both benefits and risks. The variety of benefits from the selected dataset, include the data availability of the hospital medical records by providing accurate, up-to-date, and enable quick access by the users to the patient records. However, from the side of the risks, by releasing the patient health records attributes, it might also encounter endangers like the name_of_patient, date_of_birth, and place_of_birth that result in the identification of individuals in a privacy violation.

4.1   Data Source: Health Patient Records Dataset

In the scenario of the illustration part, we designed that the government proposes a Department of Health to release a dataset of medical records of patient to the public that can enable individual or organization to access and see the current trend of a disease [38, 39]. By doing so, for instance, the government is able to generate a location map related to the disease landscape for some regions or specific attributes. However, if the government decides to open the dataset and actual values immediately, there are some potential privacy issues of the patients containing in the dataset that might be very harmful like misuse, inaccuracy, and identifiable of the data [39, 40, 41]. Figure 3 shows the dataset structure of the health patient records that will be analyzed using FMCDM in this study.

For the illustration of this work, we designed to analyze the Table 1 namely Diagnosed Stage which is containing six attributes/fields: Name_of_patient, Date_of_birth, Place_of_Birth, Gender, Race, Insurance, Stage, and TNM_staging.

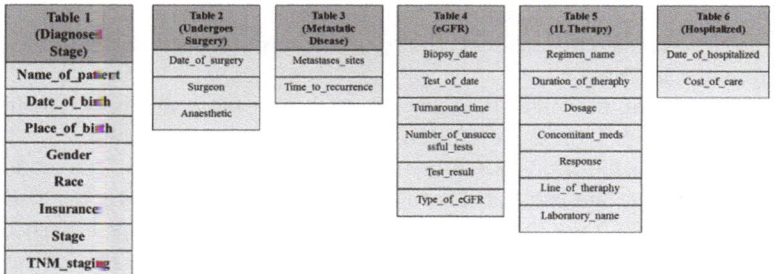

Fig. 3. Raw table of Health Patient Records (adapted from: [31, 43])

4.2   Evaluation: Analyzing the Dataset

The following steps are the scenarios of FMCDM. Figure 4 shows the hierarchy of criteria and alternatives are used in the illustration of FMCDM.

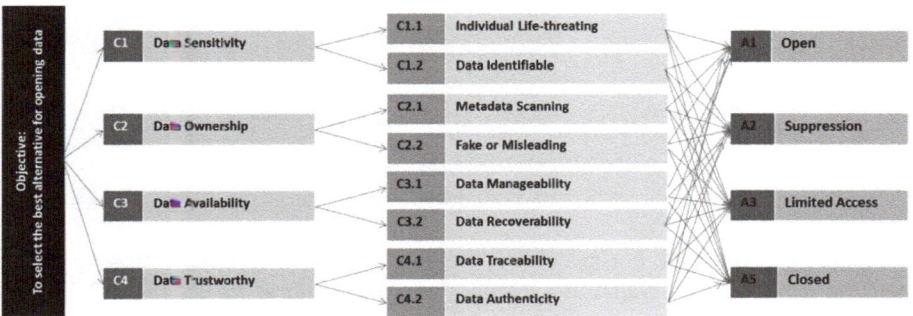

Fig. 4. Hierarchy of criteria and alternatives for the illustration

- Step 1. Establish an expert team. We picked up the knowledge as well as expertise from some experts. The selected experts were interviewed based on the three consideration rationales, namely: (1) Domain knowledge, where the importance of educational background of the experts in this field ought to accommodate various specializations with partial overlap to confirm completeness of the data and available information [42]; (2) Functional knowledge, where the experts chose are capable in the scope of the existing problems and the requirements of the process as well as solution proposed [42]; and (3) Best practice, where the interviewee's expertise and their own insight have to be outstanding to warrant the quality as well as the validity of information sources [43].
- Step 2. Determine the evaluation criteria and construct the hierarchy including alternatives.
- Step 3. Construct pairwise comparison matrix and evaluate the relative importance of criteria. The experts are asked to provide their consideration based on their knowledge and expertise. For simplicity, in this illustration a pairwise comparison

matrix for expert one is given in Fig. 5. Before the experts started to quantify the criteria, we expected to construct a Fuzzy evaluation linguistic scale for the weights as presented in Table 2.

- Step 4: Transform the linguistic terms into triangular fuzzy numbers. The linguistic terms provided in Table 2 are utilized for the evaluation procedure.
- Step 5: Calculate the fuzzy weight matrix using Eqs. (3) and (4). The final weights of the alternatives are calculated using Eqs. (3), (4), and (5). The linguistic terms provided in Table 2 are utilized for the evaluation and fuzzy operational laws are used for the calculation [18, 27]. Illustrative examples for weights of subcriteria C11 and C12 are given as follows:

Calculating sub-criteria: Linguistic terms for the pairwise comparison, we are getting from Fig. 5 and the corresponding fuzzy numbers are getting from the Table 2. For example, pairwise comparison of (C1.1 C1.2) is "Equal Important" and the fuzzy number of this linguistic term is (1, 1, 3).

$$\tilde{r}_{c11} = (\tilde{c}_{c11c11} \otimes \tilde{c}_{c11c11})^{\frac{1}{2}}$$
$$\tilde{r}_{c11} = ((1,1,1) \otimes (3,5,7))^{\frac{1}{2}}$$
$$\tilde{r}_{c11} = (1.73, 2.23, 2.64)$$
$$\tilde{r}_{c12} = (\tilde{c}_{c12c11} \otimes \tilde{c}_{c12c12})^{\frac{1}{2}}$$
$$\tilde{r}_{c12} = ((1/(3,5,7)) \otimes (1,1,1))^{\frac{1}{2}}$$
$$\tilde{r}_{c12} = (0.37, 0.44, 0.57)$$

Calculating weights: For calculating weights, we are using Eq. 4. In the previous step, we are getting the value of $\tilde{r}_{1.1}$ and $\tilde{r}_{1.2}$ and putting these values in the following equation.

$$\tilde{w}_{c1.1} = (0.36, 0.5, 1.10)$$
$$\tilde{w}_{c1.2} = \tilde{r}_{c1.2} \otimes (\tilde{r}_{c1.1} + \tilde{r}_{c1.2})^{-1}$$
$$\tilde{w}_{c1.2} = (0.57, 1.1) \otimes [(1,1,1.73) + (0.57, 1.1)]^{-1}$$
$$\tilde{w}_{c1.2} = (0.2, 0.5, 0.63)$$

- Step 6: Apply normalization procedure.

Normalized weight values: To find the normalized weights of C1.1 and C1.2 we used Eq. 5.

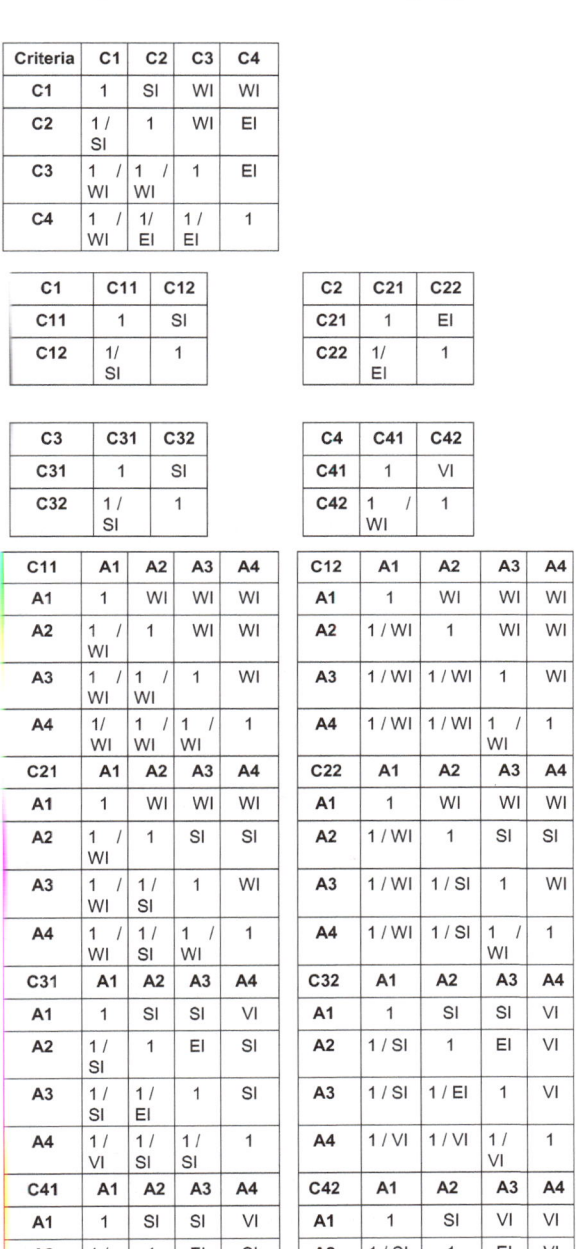

Fig. 5. The pairwise comparison matrices of criteria and alternatives

$$w_{c1.1} = \frac{\tilde{w}_{c1.1}}{\sum_{j=1}^{2} \tilde{w}_{1j}} = \frac{L_{c1.1} + M_{c1.1} + U_{c1.1}}{\tilde{w}_{c1.1} + \tilde{w}_{c1.2}}$$

$$w_{c1.1} = \frac{(0.36 + 0.5 + 1.10)}{(0.36 + 0.5 + 1.10 + 0.2 + 0.5 + 0.63)} = 0.59$$

$$w_{c1.2} = \frac{\tilde{w}_{c1.2}}{\sum_{j=1}^{2} \tilde{w}_{1j}} = \frac{L_{c1.2} + M_{c1.2} + U_{c1.2}}{\tilde{w}_{c1.1} + \tilde{w}_{c1.2}}$$

$$w_{c1.2} = \frac{(0.2 + 0.5 + 0.63)}{(0.36 + 0.5 + 1.10 + 0.2 + 0.5 + 0.63)} = 0.40$$

The similar calculation approach is applied for all pairwise comparisons. The final weights of the alternatives are provided in Table 3. An illustrative example for W_{A1} is given as follows:

Table 3. Final weights of the criteria and alternatives

	C1		C2		C3		C4		
	0.53		0.25		0.13		0.07		
	C1.1	C1.2	C2.1	C2.2	C.31	C3.2	C4.1	C4.2	
	0.59	0.40	0.82	0.17	0.59	0.40	0.59	0.40	Weight
A1	0.39	0.41	0.41	0.41	0.44	0.35	0.44	0.35	0.34
A2	0.40	0.39	0.82	0.83	0.23	0.44	0.23	0.44	0.43
A3	0.06	0.13	0.26	0.13	0.08	0.15	0.08	0.15	0.08
A4	0.05	0.05	0.10	0.05	0.22	0.05	0.22	0.05	0.06

$$W_{A1} = C1 \times C11 \times A1 + C1 \times C12 \times A1 + \cdots + C4 \times C41 \times A1 + C4 \times C42 \times A1$$
$$W_{A1} = 0.53 \times 0.59 \times 0.39 + 0.53 \times 0.40 \times 0.41 + \cdots + 0.07 \times 0.59 \times 044 + 0.07 \times 0.40 \times 0.35$$
$$W_{A1} = 0.34$$

4.3   Decision: Recommendations

According to the Table 3, the highest priority of the decision for the Table 1 (Diagnose Stage) of Health Patient Records is A2 (0.42), following by A1 (0.34), and A3 (0.08), while in the last ranking of decision recommendation is A4 (0.06). Based on the analyzing and computing process, in this case we recommended that the Table 1 (Diagnose Stage) should be maintaining suppression as the highest priority recommendation in this illustration.

5   Findings

In order to present the recommendations based on the final results of the analyzing process using FMCDM, we designed a graphical view to support the decision-makers to decide to release their dataset. Figure 6 shows how the Fuzzy AHP could help the decision-makers with the better understanding of the comparison score for each alternative.

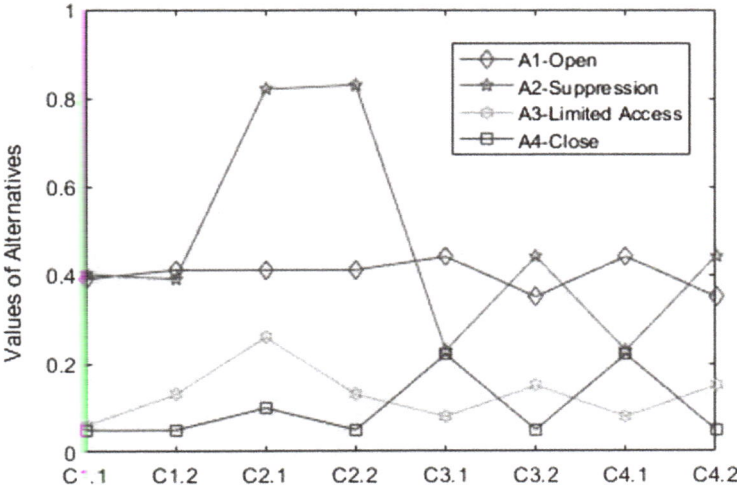

Fig. 6. Ranking of decision recommendations

Furthermore, to design the action plan of the maintaining suppression, some possible procedures could be taken into account as follows: (1) removing a data field or an individual attributes into particular group of the data and replace it into unique characteristics; (2) obscuring a data field by making substitution precise data values with ranges to minimize the provision of the personal identity; and (3) Aggregating a data field by summarizing the data across the amounts of the data and visualizing the data value into statistics form like graphics or charts.

6   Conclusion

In this paper, we presented the results of a study by utilizing Fuzzy AHP to analyze the risks and benefits of opening data for determining the best alternative in the health patient records dataset. A set of criteria and a variety of sub-criteria were designed and identified base on the literature review and experts' judgment. Some advantages the use of the FMCDM approach compare to other three methods as follows: (1) the capability to transform the human subjectivity and incorrectness from the common natural language to weights the complex problems, and (2) provides assessment method of the selected alternatives to rank a single decision making. However, a disadvantage found while using this approach is because the fuzzy is a ruled-based system, hence it needs to get enough rules to be accurate and expressively. The contribution resulted from this paper is to provide a decision-making model to analyze the potential risks and benefits of opening data. A given dataset is evaluated by taking action like measuring and weighing the relative importance of the multiple criteria.

Thus, the approach might contribute decision makers to decide to open a dataset. In the further research, we recommend refining this approach by adding more datasets in which and advice for (not) opening data can be generated without human involvement.

Acknowledgments. The Second author of this paper is very thankful to gLINK project (http://www.glink-edu.eu/) for funding part of this research work.

References

1. Ali-Eldin, A.M.T., Zuiderwijk, A., Janssen, M.: Opening more data: a new privacy scoring model of open data. In: Seventh International Symposium on Business Modelling and Software Design (BMSD 2017). SCITEPRESS - Science and Technology Publication, Lda, Barcelona, Spain (2017)
2. Lourenço, R.P.: An analysis of open government portals: a perspective of transparency for accountability. Gov. Inf. Q. **32**(3), 323–332 (2015)
3. Zuiderwijk, A., Janssen, M.: Open data policies, their implementation and impact: a framework for comparison. Gov. Inf. Q. **31**(1) (2013)
4. Luthfi, Ahmad, Janssen, Marijn, Crompvoets, Joep: A Causal Explanatory Model of Bayesian-belief Networks for Analysing the Risks of Opening Data. In: Shishkov, Boris (ed.) BMSD 2018. LNBIP, vol. 319, pp. 289–297. Springer, Cham (2018). https://doi.org/10.1007/978-3-319-94214-8_20
5. Ubaldi, B.: Open government data: towards empirical analysis of open government data initiatives. OECD Working Papers on Public Governance, vol 22, p. 60 (2013)
6. Janssen, M., Charalabidis, Y., Zuiderwijk, A.: Benefits, adoption barriers and myths of open data and open government. Inf. Syst. Manag. **29**(4), 258–268 (2012)
7. Grimmelikhujsen, S.G., Meijer, A.J.: Effects of transparency on the perceived trustworthiness of a government organization: evidence from an online experiment. J Public Adm. Res. Theor. **24**(1), 137–157 (2014)
8. Kulk, S., Loenen, B.V.: Brave new open data world? Int. J. Spatial Data Infrasruct. Res. **7**, 196–206 (2012)
9. Meijer, A., Thaens, M.: Public information strategies: making government information available to citizens. Inf. Polity **14**(1–2), 31–45 (2009)
10. Zuiderwijk, A., Janssen, M.: Towards decision support for disclosing data: closed or open data? Inf. Polity **20**(2–3), 103–107 (2015)
11. Barry, E., Bannister, F.: Barriers to open data release: a view from the top. Inf. Polity **19**(1–2), 129–152 (2014)
12. Martin, S., et al.: Risk analysis to overcome barriers to open data. Electron. J. e-Gov. **11**(1), 348–359 (2013)
13. Barnickel, N., et al.: Berlin open data strategy, in concept, pilot system and recommendations for action. In: 2012, Organisational, legal and technical aspects of Open Data in Berlin (2012)

14. Conradie, P., Choenni, S.: On the barriers for local government releasing open data. Gov. Inf. Q. S10–S17 (2014)
15. Uhlir, P.F.: The socioeconomic effects of public sector information on digital networks: toward a better understanding of different access and reuse policies. In: National Research Council. Washington DC (2009)
16. Walter, S.: Heterogeneous database integration in biomedicine. J. Biomed. Inf. **34**(4), 285–298 (2001)
17. Zuiderwijk, A., Janssen, M., David, C.: Innovation with open data: Essential elements of open data ecosystems. Inf. Polity **19**(2–3), 17–33 (2014)
18. Hsieh, T.-Y., Lu, S.-T., Tzeng, G.-H.: Fuzzy MCDM approach for planning and design tenders selection in public office buildings. Int. J. Proj. Manag. **22**, 573–584 (2004)
19. Rezaei, P., et al.: Application of Fuzzy Multi-Criteria Decision Making Analysis for Evaluating and Selecting the Best Location for Construction of Underground Dam. Acta Polytech. Hung. **10**(7), 187–205 (2013)
20. Zadeh, L.A.: The concept of linguistic variable and its application to approximate reasoning. Inf. Sci. **8**(3), 199–249 (1975)
21. Fuller, R.: Fuzzy logic and neural nets in intelligent systems, in information system day. In: Carlsson, C. (ed.) Turku Centre for Computer Science, p. 7494 (1999)
22. Gupta, M.M.: Fuzzy Logic and Neural Systems. International Series in Intelligent Technologies, p. 225–244 (1995)
23. Werro, N.: Fuzzy Classification of Online Customers. Fuzzy Management Methods. Springer, Cham (2015)
24. Novák, K.: An Introduction to Fuzzy Logic Applications in Intelligent System, pp. 185–200. Kluwer Academic, Dordrecht (1992)
25. Kahraman, C., Onar, S.C., Oztaysi, B.: Fuzzy multicriteria decision-making: a literature review. Int. J. Comput. Intell. Syst. **8**(4), 637–666 (2015)
26. Chen, S.-J., Hwang, C.-L.: Fuzzy Multiple Attribute Decision Making. Lecturer Notes in Economics and Mathematical Systems, vol. 375. Springer, Berlin (1992)
27. Hancerliogullari, G., Oymen, K.H., Koksalmis, E.: The use of multi-criteria decision making models in evaluating anesthesia method options in circumcision surgery. BMC Med. Inf. Decis. Mak. **17**(14) (2017)
28. Lin, C., Twu, C.H.: Fuzzy MCDM for evaluating fashion trend alternatives. Int. J. Cloth. Sci. Technol. **24**(2/3), 141–153 (2012)
29. Sloane, E., Liberatore, M., Nydick, R.: Medical decision support using the analytic hierarchy process. J. Health Inf. Manag. **16**(4), 38–43 (2011)
30. Buda, A., et al.: Decision Support Framework for Opening Business Data, in Department of Engineering Systems and Services. Delft University of Technology, Delft (2015)
31. Luthfi, A., Janssen, M.: A conceptual model of decision-making support for opening data. In 7th International Conference, E-Democracy 2017, CCIS 792, pp. 95–105. Springer, Athens, Greece (2017)
32. Mohsen, D., et al.: A combined fuzzy MCDM approach for identifiying the suitable lands for urban development: an example from Bandar ABBS, Iran. J. Urban Environ. Eng. **8**(1), 11–27 (2014)
33. Podvezko, V.: Application of AHP technique. J. Bus. Econ. Manag. **10**(2), 181–189 (2011)
34. Saaty, T.: The Analytic Hierarchy Process Planning, Priority Setting, Resource Allocation. McGraw, New York (1980)
35. Kuo, M.S., Liang, G.S., Huang, W.C.: Extension of the multicriteria analysis with pairwise comparison under a fuzzy environment. J. Sci. Direct **43**, 268–285 (2006)
36. Isselhardt, D.J., Cappuci, J.: The analytic hierarchy process in medical decision making a tutorial. Med. Decis. Mak. **1**, 40–50 (1989)

37. Sehra, S.K., Brar, Y.S., Kaur, N.: Multi criteria decision making approach for selecting effort estimation model. Int. J. Comput. Appl. **39**(1), 10–17 (2012)
38. Kostkova, P., et al.: Who owns the data? Open data for healthcare. Front. Public Health **4**(7), 1–6 (2016)
39. Bøttcher, S.G., Dethlefsen, C.: Learning Bayesian Networks with R. In: Department of Mathematical Science, Vienna University of Technology, Aalborg University Denmark (2003)
40. Ozair, F.F., et al.: Ethical issues in electronic health records: A general overview. Perspect. Clin. Res. **6**(2), 73–76 (2015)
41. Abernethy, A.: Real world evidence: opportunities and challenges, 2016, Flatiron Health
42. Teicher, M., Interviewing Subject Matter Experts, in International Cost Estimating and Analysis Association (ICEAA) (2015)
43. Herland, K., Hämmäinen, H., Kekolahti, P.: Information security risks assessment of smartphones using bayesian networks. J. Cyber Secur. **4**, 65–85 (2016)

Analysis of the Banking Sector in the Czech Republic

Martina Hedvicakova$^{(\boxtimes)}$ and Pavel Prazak

Faculty of Informatics and Management, University of Hradec Králové,
Rokitanskeho 62, 500 03 Hradec Kralove, Czech Republic
{martina.hedvicakova,pavel.prazak}@uhk.cz

Abstract. Forty-six banks and foreign bank branches were operating in the Czech Republic in May 2018. The banking market in the Czech Republic is characterized by high fees for account management and information asymmetries. For this reason, there are number of fees accounts comparators on the market. One of these is the Bank Charge Calculator, which allows clients to run their current account expenditures by their set criteria. The aim of the article is to analyze the current state of the banking sector for individuals. Based on data from the Bank Charge Calculator, a Client Index is calculated to allow responders to calculate the average monthly cost of running their current account according to defined criteria and service requirements. The value of this Client Index was used to propose a pay-off function in the game theory model. Client Index values serve to express the price level on the RCBS market.

Keywords: Game theory · Client Index · Bargaining · Pay-off matrix
Decision tree · Bank charges

1 Introduction

There is a high level of competition on the Czech banking market. Nevertheless, Retail core banking services (RCBS) are characterized by a high degree of asymmetry of information. Information asymmetry is a situation where one side of the market benefits from the information advantage at the expense of the second one. This situation does not necessarily mean the market disequilibrium. We can imply the F. A. Hayek's [1] thoughts and say that equilibrium can be achieved under the different levels of informedness. [2] The second problem is high fees for current account in the Czech Republic.

Stigler [3] is solving the situation where the consumer prefers the lowest price on homogenous product, but the prices are yet to be discovered in order to make choice. Soukal and Draesller [2] suggest calculating the optimal price to be searched for. By term optimal price it is meant price that is optimal by search costs to search revenue, in other words total savings, and by the quality and quantity demanded (regarding RCBS we mean range and frequency of the requested services). The optimal price on the market will probably be different from the optimal price computed by the model because of the optimal cost of the search and the probabilistic problem of search. For a

S. A. Al-Sharhan et al. (Eds.): I3E 2018, LNCS 11195, pp. 413–424, 2018.
https://doi.org/10.1007/978-3-030-02131-3_37

closer theoretical description of the rework of Stigler's model please see (Hedvicakova et al. [4]).

Trust is a crucial element of a viable banking industry. Dahlstrom et al. [5] present a structural equations model based on a prisoner's dilemma logic to analyze the unique effects of trust between corporate customers and their banks. The results based on 252 corporate bank customers reveal an intriguing mixed strategy between trust from one party and opportunism from the other. The implication is that mutual trust seems to reduce the perception of risk in the market while bank opportunism significantly escalates perceived risk. They analyses also show that when the corporate customer trusts the bank, perceived risk is significantly reduced.

2   Theoretical Bases

Customer satisfaction is an important factor in the performance and competitiveness of banks [6–9]. Compliance with the consumers' needs and requirements [10], comprehensive customer care and the bank customers' satisfaction is currently at the centre of attention of researchers and bankers (as it represents an important marketing variable for most of the companies [11–13].

Mosk [14] examines bargaining as a mechanism to resolve information problems. He develops a parsimonious model of a credit negotiation between a bank and firms with varying levels of impatience. In equilibrium, impatient firms accept the bank's offer immediately, while patient firms wait and negotiate price adjustments. Mosk [14] examines bargaining as a mechanism to resolve information problems.

The issue of increasing profit and reducing operational costs is the most important subject in banking management. One of the ways to solve this problem, is the cooperation (coalition) of banks together in order to reduce costs and simultaneously increase the operating profit. To solve this problem is Khanizad and Montazer [15] model for the participation of banks using game theory with which the banks can cooperate to achieve higher profits while providing their services.

On the other hand, given the current competitive environment among banks in the capital market, less attention has been paid to the cooperation of banks in providing services and attracting customers and investments and consequently studies of banks co-operation in providing services in the micro market (retail customers) were often on the limited inter-banking cooperation. For example, in some studies such as references [15–19].

We live in what might be called the imperial age of game theory, in whichgame heory has become influential in an ever-growing variety of other disciplines. Game theory is now a standard tool in political science but can be used in all sectors, including banking. For example, McCarty and Meirowitz (2007) provide a book-length overview of how game theory can be used to examine the relations between countries, the behavior of political parties, electoral behavior, the workings of legislatures, lobbying, and so on [20].

Game theory usually analyses decision-making processes in various fields. Kapliński [21]. Our research is oriented in the fields of game theory with application in banking sector.

According to most authors, the criterion for dividing bargaining is whether the bargaining defends the position or interests of clients. There is a contrast in the terminology between the individual types of bargaining. For example, Plamínek [22] distinguishes between competitive, cooperative, virtual and principled bargaining. As early as six years later, the same author [23] only sets forth competitive, cooperative and principled bargaining. Holá [24] sets forth positional (competitive) bargaining and constructive (principled) bargaining [13, 25].

3   The Aim and Methodology of the Paper

In the Czech Republic there is a high asymmetry of information on the RCBS (Retail core banking services) market. For this reason, clients are searching on the internet for a variety of comparison, according to which they would find the cheapest bank account according to their preferences and the services they use. For this reason, a Bank Charges Calculator was created, available at: http://www.bankovnipoplatky.com/kalkulator.html, which compares the average monthly cost of running a current account according to the criteria specified by the respondent. The frequency of the individual items of the fee schedules is monitored based on a questionnaire (e.g. how many times clients use the given service and how much is charged for the service, what turnover and balance they have in their accounts, etc.) The Client Index was calculated based on these data. Since 2013, the Client Index is calculated quarterly using the statistical software IBM PASW 18 and MS Excel 2013. Data on the amount of bank charges and commissions has been obtained from publicly available data by banks (fee schedules, annual reports, bank accounts and documents on the financial situation of the bank, etc.). The average costs of a specific account are established by the arithmetic average of clients who have chosen the monitored account computed by the Calculator. See Eqs. 1 and 2. Data collection took place from 2012 until first quarter 2018. The calculation is preceded by the verification validation part, in order not to distort the result e.g. respondents who should not use retail products (self-employed, small entrepreneurs with frequencies of banking services which the client can never achieve in the civil account) or respondents who only form clicked without key services. This methodology is more accurate, but it requires a greater number of clients. The number of accounts with a lack of respondents for calculation is much higher. On average, 2000 respondents filled in the Calculator per quarter. For a more detailed description of the methodology see e.g. [26–28] or [13]. The author of the article analyzes the data for this project.

$$AC_h = \frac{1}{n_h} \sum_{h=1}^{k} \sum_{i=1}^{n_h} C_{hi}, \tag{1}$$

where AC_h represents average costs of account number h, further i represents client serial number, c_{hi} is the cost of client i that uses account h monthly, k is the total number of monitored accounts and n_h is the number of clients that use accounts *h*. More details can be found in [27, 28]. For the rest of calculation can be used the following formulas

$$w_h = \frac{n_h}{n}$$

$$CI = \sum_{h=1}^{k} w_h \cdot AC_h \tag{2}$$

It means that the resulting value of the Client Index (2) is calculated as the weighted value of the average cost of each account. Scales are derived from relative frequencies, respectively: of the shares of respondents of individual accounts as a whole [27, 28].

The aim of the article is to analyze the current state of the RCBS market in the Czech Republic. Based on the Client Index calculations for each quarter, calculate the average value that clients pay on average for managing their current account monthly and quarterly. This amount includes, for example, fees for credit and debit cards or insurance, which is paid once a year. The calculated average value Client Index will be used in game theory chapter for negotiation between the client and the bank. Client Index values serve to express the price level on the RCBS market.

4 Actual Situation in the Banking Sector in the Czech Republic

In May 2018, 46 banks and foreign bank branches were operating in the Czech Republic (excluding the CNB). The number of banks is increasing, even though it currently holds a bank license for one bank less than in 2017. In 2009, 39 banks were in the market and 47 banks in 2017. The largest share of this increase was made by branches of foreign banks from the European Union, from 18 in 2009 to 23 in 2017.

Although the number of licenses granted by the bank grows, there is a gradual reduction in the number of branches. This trend is mainly due to the growing influence of digitization, which takes place worldwide, and of course in the Czech Republic. The reduction of branches in small towns takes place mainly at the three largest banks in the Czech Republic: Česká spořitelna, Komerční banka and ČSOB. These banks have the widest network of branches from all banks in the banking market in the Czech Republic. There is also a reduction of branches and staff reductions.

With the growth of digitization, there is increasing number individuals using Internet Banking. In 2017, 52% of individuals used Internet Banking in the Czech Republic. Internet banking is the most used age group of 25–44 years. See Fig. 1.

Using Internet Banking instead of bank branches brings savings to clients. Clients can pay lower costs for account management.

The Czech Republic is in the percentage of individuals using Internet banking above the European Union average. Around half (51%) of adult Europeans use internet banking. This share is constantly increasing and has doubled since 2007, when it stood at 25%. Internet banking is particularly popular among 25 to 34 years old, with 68%

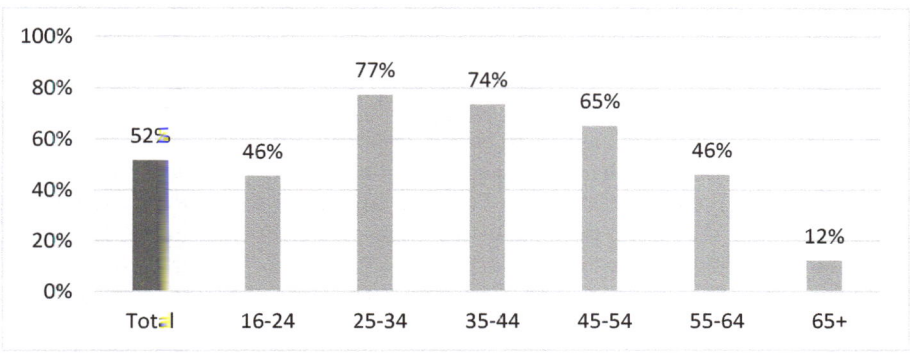

Fig. 1. Individuals using Internet Banking by age in 2017,   Source: Czech Statistical Office, [29], own processing

using this facility. The use of internet banking tends to increase in line with the education level of the user [30].

The total assets of the Czech banking sector stood at CZK 7,564 billion at the end of May 2018. Loans to residents are the predominant asset item. Their volume reached CZK 5,609 billion. Deposits of residents, which are the most important item among banking sector liabilities, totaled CZK 4,397 billion [31].

Among the three largest banks, according to the number of clients operating on the Czech banking market, are Česká spořitelna, ČSOB and Komerční banka. The fourth bank, which has over millions of clients, is Moneta. See Table 1.

Table 1. Number of clients in 2015 and 2018, [32, own processing], *2017

Bank	to 31. 3. 2018	to 31. 3. 2015
Česká spořitelna	4,68 million	5 million
ČSOB	3,671 million	2,9 million
Komerční banka	1,666 million	1,6 million
Moneta/GE Money Bank	1,034 million	1 million
Fio banka	815 million	480 000
mBank	650 000*	534 000
Raiffeisenbank	not published	not published estimated 500 000
Air Bank	618 342	343 000
UniCredit Bank	415 000	343 000
Hello bank	400 000 *	did not exist
Equa bank	323 000	140 000
Sberbank	115 000	86 000
Creditas	40 000	not published
Expobank	20 261	not published
Oberbank	16 000	not published

Most clients lost the largest bank: Česká Spořitelna. Still more clients get "low-cost" banks such as mBank, Air Bank or Fio Bank. More and more citizens of the Czech Republic have more than one bank account. This causes a high level of competition in the banking market. Bank clients also have chance for bargaining with the main bank. They can negotiate free of charge or premium services.

The second criterion for bank size is the size of the total assets. The Czech National Bank ranks among the big banks with financial institutions with a total asset of over CZK 400 billion. The largest three banks are ČSOB, which exceeded CZK 1.5 trillion, the second is Česká spořitelna and the third Komerční banka. The last bank that meets the criteria of the Czech National Bank is a bank Unicredit Bank. [32].

1 Euro is 25,92 CZK in July 2018.

The population of the Czech Republic was 10 613 350 at 31 March 2018 according to the Czech Statistical Office. Table 1 shows that most people have more than one current account in the Czech Republic. Clients are trying to reduce account costs by combining current accounts with different banks.

5   The Results of the Research of Bank Charges

In 2014, the Client Index level was in the range of 179–183 CZK per month (6,905-7,06 Eur /month). 1 Euro is CZK 25.92 in July 2018. Due to the low difference in index values, the Client index is expressed in CZK only.

The following year, the biggest fluctuations took place. The Client Index ranged from 180 to 188 CZK /month. See Fig. 2.

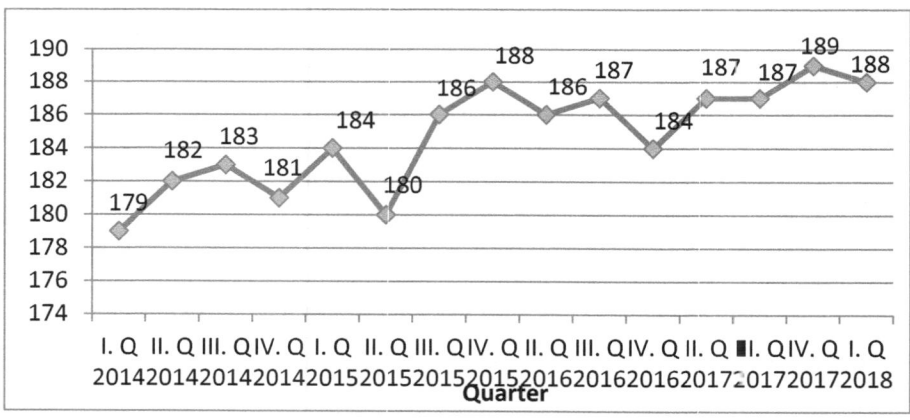

Fig. 2. Client Index – the average costs of bank account in CZK.   Source: www.bankovnipoplatky.com, The author's own arrangement

Since 2016, the average cost of the bank account has stabilized at 184 - 186 CZK / month. And this trend continued in the years to come. The highest value of the Client Index was in the fourth quarter of 2017, when clients paid an average of 189 CZK for maintaining their account. In the next quarter there was only a slight decrease of one crown. The increase in the value of the Client Index in the last quarters of the given years is due to the increased shopping activity of clients during Christmas and the increased use of debit and credit cards associated with the selection from foreign ATMs. Also, during summer holidays, bank account fees are increasing due to withdrawals from ATMs abroad, which are charged at higher rates in most banks.

Analysis of the survey data revealed that the average Client Index is 185 CZK between 2014 and the first quarter of 2018. This value was used in the game theory chapter and value modeling is built on this value. This value was calculated as the arithmetic mean of all valid values from the questionnaire survey in 2014–2018. It is important for setting the average amount for running a current account monthly and for negotiation.

It is very interesting that even though several low-budget banks have entered the market in the last seven years and many clients have set up an account with them. the value of the Client Index did not change significantly and recorded a sharp rise in the penultimate quarter of 2015. This is most likely due to the fact that clients still keep their current account even with a large bank that has not canceled and pays the fees. And low-cost banks have higher charges for their premium services.

6   Game Theory During the Bargaining Process Between the Bank and the Client

The relationship between the bank and its client regarding bank charges can be considered as a conflict of two players in game theory. Game theory deals with mathematical modelling of problems in which it is necessary to choose decision-making processes [13, 33–35].

In the game related to bank charges, which shall be labelled G, we will consider two players, the bank B and its client K, [13]. If the set of players is labelled by H, then $H = \{B, K\}$. The client K shall have two strategies available; he/she can be active or passive. In case of the active strategy A, he/she shall be interested in the amount of charges for the maintaining of his/her account with the bank, he/she shall demand a discount and in case the bank does not grant it, he/she will be ready to leave for another bank. In case of the passive strategy P, he/she shall not be actively interested in discounts for maintaining his/her bank account, however, he/she will not refuse them if they are offered and he/she will not be ready to change banks. Therefore, for the set of strategies X_K of the client, $X_K = \{A, P\}$. The bank B shall also have two strategies available; it can either offer cooperation or it remains firm. In case of the cooperative strategy that is denoted S, it shall offer its client a discount for maintaining the client's account or benefits. In case of firm strategy N, the bank shall not offer either any discount for maintaining the account or any benefits. Therefore, for the set of strategies of the bank X_B, $X_B = \{S, N\}$. Let's label the pay-off functions of the client C or bank B respectively, $f_K(x, y)$ or $f_B(x, y)$ respectively, where $x \in X_K$ a $y \in X_B$. These pay-off functions shall express the price for maintaining an account in CZK. The values of the pay-off function of the bank $f_B(x, y)$ can be summarized using the following Table 2. If we consider an antagonistic conflict, where one of the players wins what the other player loses, it holds that $f_K(x, y) + f_B(x, y) = 0$ and it is a zero-sum game. The values of the pay-off function of the client $f_K(x, y)$ have the opposite sign, so it is not necessary to state them explicitly. The interpretation of these pay-offs may be, for example, as follows: $f_B(A, N) = -188$ means that if the bank does not accede to the proposal of the active client, it loses an income of 188 CZK per month (this is the value of the Client index calculated in the previous chapter). Similarly, $f_B(P, N) = 188$ means, that if the bank does not offer any discount to the passive client, it keeps a monthly income of 188 CZK.

Table 2. Values of the pay-off matrix of the bank

Client K/bank B	S	N
A	50	-188
P	120	188

Source: The author's own arrangement

The optimum strategy of the players can be found using the Nash equilibrium [33]. This is a game configuration that has the following property for each of the players: if all the other players use strategies from the given equilibrium, then the individual player cannot increase his or her pay-off by choosing a different strategy.

We shall further assume that it is a game with complete information where the players know the sets of their strategies and the amounts of their pay-offs. We shall characterize the game using a sequence of decisions by the client and the bank that follow one after another. We shall therefore suppose it is a game in an extensive form that can be illustrated using the game tree at Fig. 3.

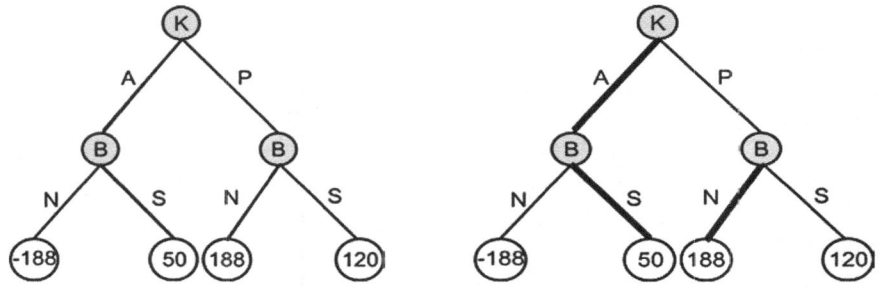

Fig. 3. On the left is the game tree with decision nodes K and B in which the client K, or the bank B make decisions and with final nodes that express the value of the game from the bank's point of view. On the right is the same game tree that demonstrates backward induction. Source: The author's own arrangement

The game in the extensive form can be solved using the method of backward induction, [34]. This method is also depicted at Fig. 3. Let's consider all the decision nodes whose edges lead to the final nodes of the game tree. In the present case, these are two nodes of player B. In each of these decision nodes, we choose the edge that leads to the best final node from the perspective of the player to whom the node belongs, and we highlight it. We note the determined edge. For each decision node, we assign the pay-offs that correspond to the found best final node. We leave out all the edges stemming from the decision node, including their final nodes. This way there arises a new decision tree with new final points and their pay-offs. The whole procedure can now be repeated until we get to the root of the game tree. In our case, we finish after two steps and the rational client K chooses the edge that leads to a lower monthly charge for maintaining the account, i.e., he/she chooses the strategy of an active client A, see Fig. 3. This is how we found the Nash equilibrium $(x^o, y^o) = (A, S)$, which means that the bank client should be active during the bargaining process about the monthly price for his or her bank account. The bank should offer its client a discount so as not to lose him or her. It needs to be stressed that this result was obtained under the assumption that the game participants have complete information available, when the players know all the possible scenarios of the game. The requirement of an informed and active bank client is essential to achieve the found result of the game. The result leads us to the type of bargaining known as WIN-WIN.

7   Conclusion and Discussion

The aim of the article was to analyze the current situation on the banking market in the Czech Republic. Using the Client Index, which measures the average cost for a current account per month were calculated quarterly average values (up to 2015 were calculated as monthly and quarterly value). The average client will pay CZK 188 per month (7,137 Eur /month) at the bank. This value was used in the last section dealing with banking theory.

The Czech banking market is changing and digitizing. Czech Republic in the number of users of Internet banking on the average of the European Union. Due to the high number of banks, there is a high level of competition in the banking market. Banks are forced by clients to constantly develop new technical innovations. One of them is the simplest and most intuitive control of Internet banking. At present, however, emphasis is placed on mobile banking. Banks are trying to attract clients with new solutions and security measures that are quick and easy to control. This is one of the reasons why clients stay with large traditional banks where they pay high fees for managing their account, even though the market is constantly growing with low-cost banks that offer free account maintenance's.

According to the Czech Statistical Office, the Czech Republic has 10 613 350 inhabitants. Table 1. Number of clients in 2015 and 2018 shows that the Czechs own more than one bank account. Czechs are a conservative nation and, despite the high cost of keeping an account, they do not interrupt their account with a large bank.

Solutions and opportunities for banks and clients is a novelty on the market - open banking.

The European directive known by the acronym PSD2 (Payment Services Directive 2) gave an open banking, aimed at creating a single market for payments through the regulation of banks and new payment service providers. The new Czech Payment System Act, which entered into force in January 2018, is also based on this directive.

As a result, clients are gradually being able to manage their payment accounts with different banks and carry out certain operations with them through just one mobile or Internet application. Open banking enabled Creditas first, followed Fio, Equa bank or Air Bank. By the end of the year wants to establish an open banking, other banks such Česká spořitelna and others, [37].

Through open banking, clients can better manage their money and better manage and monitor the amount of individual product and service charges. This can reduce the monthly cost of managing your bank accounts. This also gives them a better chance of negotiating with the bank.

In terms of bargaining and game theory, WIN-WIN has emerged as the best strategy. The WIN-WIN strategy is most often applied in practice because banks try not to lose their clients. If the client actively negotiates, they will in most cases comply with it. It is a question for discussion why the citizens of the Czech Republic do not negotiate more with the bank and prefer to create new accounts, even if they keep their old account.

Acknowledgement. The paper was written with the support of the specific project 6/2018 grant "DETERMINANTS OF COGNITIVE PROCESSES IMPACTING THE WORK PERFORMANCE" granted by the University of Hradec Králové, Czech Republic. We would like to thank student Eliška Čonková for cooperation in the processing of the article.

References

1. Hayek, F.A.: Individualism and Economic Order. University of Chicago Press, Chicago (1958)
2. Soukal, I., Draessler, J.: Consumer desired price modeling – case study on the RCBS market. Proced. Soc. Behav. Sci. **62**, 916–920 (2012). ISSN 1877-0428
3. Stigler, G.J.: The economics of information. J. Political Econ. 213–225 (1961)
4. Hedvicakova, M., Soukal, I., Draessler, J.: Probabilistic model of optimal price search on the retail core banking services market. Int. J. Math. Models Methods Appl. Sci., 386–393 (2012)
5. Dahlstrom, R., Nygaard, A., Kimasheva, M., lvnes, A.M.: How to recover trust in the banking industry? A game theory approach to empirical analyses of bank and corporate customer relationships. Int. J. Bank Markt. **32**(4), 268–278 (2014). https://doi.org/10.1108/ijbm-03-2014-0042
6. Keisidou, E., Lazaros, S., Maditions, D.I., Thalassinos, E.I.: Customer satisfaction, loyalty and fi nancial performance: a holistic approach of the Greek banking sector. Int. J. Bank Markt. **31**(4), 259–288 (2013). https://doi.org/10.1108/ijbm-11-2012-0114
7. Chavan, J., Ahmad, F.: Factors affecting on customer satisfaction in retail banking: an empirical study. Int. J. Bus. Manag. Invent. **2**(1), 55–62 (2013)
8. Hedvicakova, M.: Key study of bank accounts for young people with using multi-criteria optimization and fuzzy analysis. Appl. Econ. **49**(36), 3599–3610 (2017). https://doi.org/10.1080/00036846.2016.1265073

9. Belás, J., Chochoľáková, A., Gabčová., L.: Satisfaction and loyalty of banking customers: a gender approach. Econ. Sociol. **8**(1), 176–188 (2015). https://doi.org/10.14254/2071-789X.2015/8-1/14

10. Bilan, Y.: Sustainable development of a company: building of new level relationship with the consumers of XXI. Century. Amfi teatru Economic **15**(7), 687–701 (2013)

11. Munari, L., Lelasi, F., Bajetta, L.: Customer satisfaction management in italian banks. Qual. Res. Financ. Markt. **5**(2), 139–160 (2013). https://doi.org/10.1108/qrfm-11-2011-0028

12. Belás, j., Lenka Gabčová, L.: The relationship among customer satisfaction, loyalty and financial performance of commercial banks. E&M Ekonomie a Manag. **19**(1), 132–147 (2016). https://doi.org/10.15240/tul/001/2016-1-010

13. Hedvicakova, M., Prazak, P.: Bargaining between the client and the bank and game theory. In: European, Mediterranean and Middle Eastern Conference on Information Systems (EMCIS), Limasol, Cyprus, in press (2018)

14. Mosk, T. C.: Bargaining with a bank. SAFE Working Paper No. 211 (2018). Available at SSRN: https://ssrn.com/abstract=3186111 or http://dx.doi.org/10.2139/ssrn.3186111

15. Khanizad, R., Montazer, G.: Participation against competition in banking markets based on cooperative game theory. J. Financ. Data Sci. **4**(1), 16–28 (2018). https://doi.org/10.1016/j.jfds.2017.09.002

16. Faigle, U., Kern, W.: The Shapley value for cooperative games under Precedence constrains. Int. J. Game Theor. **21**(1992), 249–266 (1992)

17. Katsev, I., Yanovskaya, E.: The prenucleolus for games with restricted cooperationMath. Soc. Sci. **66**(2013), 56–65 (2013)

18. Naumova, N.: Generalized proportional solutions to games with restricted cooperation. In: Petrosyan, L.A., Zenkevich, N. (eds.), Contributions to Game Theory and Management, vol. 5, Graguate School of Management SPbU, Saint Petersburg, pp. 230–242 (2012)

19. Bjorndal, E., Hamers, H., Koster, M.: Cost allocation in a bank ATM network math methods. Oper. Res. **59**(2004), 405–418 (2014)

20. Samuelson, L.: Game theory in economics and beyond. J. Econ. Perspect. **30**(4), 107–130 (2016)

21. Kapliński, O, Tamošaitiene, J.: Game theory applications in construction engineering and management. Journal Ukio Technologinis ir Ekonominis Vystymas **16**(2), 348–363 (2010)

22. Plamínek, J.: Řešení konfliktů a umění rozhodovat. Vyd. 1. Praha: Argo, 198 s (1994). ISBN: 8085794144

23. Plamínek, J.: Synergický management: vedení, spolupráce a konflikty lidí ve firmách a týmech. Praha: Argo, 328 s (2000). ISBN 80-7203-258-5

24. Holá, L.: Mediace v teorii a praxi, Praha, Grada Publishing, 272 s. (2011). ISBN: 978-80-247-3134-6

25. Fisher, R., URY, W., Patton, B.: Dohoda jistá: zásady úspěšného vyjednávání. Vyd. 1. Přeložil Aleš Lisa. Management Press, Praha. 174 s (1994). ISBN 80-85603-48-9

26. Bankovní poplatky: Klientský index – metodika (2018). https://www.bankovnipoplatky.com/klientsky-index—metodika-12507.html. Accessed 15 May 2018

27. Draessler, J. Soukal, I., Hedvičáková, M.: Shluková analýza poptávkové strany trhu základních bankovních služeb. E + M Ekonomie a Management **14**(4), 102–114 (2011). ISSN: 1212-3609

28. Soukal, I., Hedvicakova, M.: Retail core banking services e-banking client cluster identification Procedia Comput. Sci. J., 1205–1210 (2010)

29. Czech Statistcal Office: Informační společnost v číslech – 2018 (2018). https://www.czso.cz/csu/czso/informacni-spolecnost-v-cislech. Accessed 10 May 2018

30. Eurostat: Internet banking on the rise (2018). http://ec.europa.eu/eurostat/web/products-eurostat-news/-/DDN-20180115-1. Accessed 10 June 2018

31. Czech National Bank (2018). https://www.cnb.cz/en/statistics/money_and_banking_stat/banking_statistics/bank_stat_komentar.html. Accessed 10 June 2018

32. Aktualne.cz. (2018). https://zpravy.aktualne.cz/finance/nejvetsi-banky-v-cesku-zebricek-bank-podle-velikosti-poradi/r ~ ba7b166e5a6a11e8bacfac1f6b220ee8/?redirected= 1532079954. Accessed 10 June 2018

33. Carmichel, F.: A Guide to Game Theory. Prentice Hall, Harlow (2005). ISBN 0-273- 68496-5

34. Gintis, H.: Game Theory Evolving, A Problem-Centered Introduction to Modeling Strategic Interaction. Princeton University Press, New Jersey (2009). ISBN 978-0-691-14050-6

35. Vega-Redondo, F.: Economics and the Theory of Games. Cambridge University Press, Cambridge (2003). 978-0-521-77590-8

36. Brualdi, R.A.: Introductory Combinatorics. Prentice Hall, New Jersey (2010). ISBN 0-13-602040-2

37. Novinky.cz. (2018). https://www.novinky.cz/finance/477529-otevrene-bankovnictvi-se-rozjizdi.html. Accessed 20 June 20 2018

Factors Determining Optimal Social Media Network Portfolio for Accounting Firms: The Case of the Czech Republic

Libuše Svobodová[(✉)] and Martina Hedvičáková

University of Hradec Králové,
Rokitanského 62, 500 03 Hradec Králové, Czech Republic
{libuse.svobodova,martina.hedvicakova}@uhk.cz

Abstract. Over the last few years, online social networks have experienced exponential growth in both profile registrations and social interactions. They are widely used in the personal life but also in the business. The goal of the article is to state the most often used accounting software and their producers in the connection with use of social networks by producers of accounting software in the Czech Republic. The sub-goal is to present records gained from Socialbakers focused on the evolution of fans on Facebook and how a company decides on the use of the optimal mix of platforms. Classification of social networks, social media and accounting software are solved and shortly described at the first theoretical part. Main producers of accounting software and analysis of social networks that are used by producers of accounting software are presented in the main part of the article. It is also analyzed whether producers of accounting software have direct links from web pages on the selected social networks. The last part is devoted to selected social networks and how to use it in the companies producing accounting software. Selected topic is up-to-date and it is not often solved in the literature. The topic is important to the professional public. It was founded that most often used social network by producers of accounting software are Facebook, YouTube and Twitter. The links from web pages are often used also in the connection with Google+. All companies do not put links on the used social networks.

Keywords: Accounting software · Communication · Information
Social network · Use

1 Introduction

Measuring and evaluation of company performance is carried out in companies through accountancy and other software. Producers of accounting software are trying to increase their efficiency and profitability and sell as many products and licenses as possible. This is related to communication not only with new customers but also with current ones. At present time, one of the major channels of communication is web sites and social networks. Their advantage over printed one is fast delivery, possible updates, or lower costs. Social networks are widely used not only in the personal life, but also in the commercial sphere. They have a lot of effects on the society. Increased

S. A. Al-Sharhan et al. (Eds.): I3E 2018, LNCS 11195, pp. 425–435, 2018.
https://doi.org/10.1007/978-3-030-02131-3_38

online communication and fastened communication are some of them. The question may be whether the companies that produce accounting software in the Czech Republic use selected social networks for communication with their customers, potential customers, students and next audience. Businesses that would like to implement new accounting software take into consideration lot of criteria. One of the key elements in the selection may be communication with producer of the accounting software via various channels. Selection of new accounting software was solved in the previous research done by Svobodová, Černá [1].

The organization of the paper is follows. Firstly theoretical background is described. The main part of the article is focused on the evaluation of use of social networks by producers of accounting systems. The paper contributes to the exploration of utilization of Web 2.0 phenomenon and social networks by companies and individuals in the field of accounting software. Topic of producers of accounting software and communication via social networks were connected because companies are searching how to save money in all areas of doing business, earn more money, have a larger share on the market and other goals. Social media are very often perceived as the possibility how to save money in the communication with customers and how to engage attention. Contrary people like to use social networks that are nowadays modern, popular and often used not only by one generation.

2   Literature Review

2.1   Web 2.0

Web 2.0 concept was defined by Tim O'Reilly in 2004 as a designation of the new generation of the Web. "Web 2.0 is the business revolution in the computer industry, which is caused by deflection in the understanding of the Web as a platform. Key among those rules is this: build applications that will be better and better due to the network effect with an increasing number of people" [2]. O'Reilly [2] defined the main differences between classical Web site and a new generation web. In terms of software development Web 2.0 is characterized as a shift from centralized processing and services to decentralization. Second generation web gave users the ability to handle their website and use social networks to converge with other users and attract potential customers. Web 2.0 is a term for applications where the user affects the content or communicates with other users. These applications then become social networks.

2.2   Social Networks

A sociologist Barnes [3] is considered to be the author of the definition of the social network. The term social network is associated with the Internet and directly with the social networks on the Internet. But this is not the only connection there is a need to deal with the concept of social network from the sociological point of view, therefore, the social network can be described as a "map of the area near and distant surroundings where relationships of involved people are defined" [3].

Černá, Svobodová [4] presented in previous research the most often used social networks Facebook, Instagram and Twitter or Svobodová [5] use of YouTube.

Social networks have global popularity. One of the most common online activities in the EU-28 in 2017 was participation in social networking. More than half (54%) of individuals aged 16 to 74 used the internet for social networking, for example using sites such as Facebook or Twitter in the EU [6]. According to Czech statistical office [7] 48.3% of individuals aged 16–74 use social networks in the Czech Republic.

2.3 Social Media

Social media are applications which become social networks via users' use.

Social media are a form of electronic communication (social networking and microblogging networks), through which users create online communities to share information, ideas, personal messages and other content (videos) [8]. Social media can be divided on the basis to marketing tactics as Social networks (Facebook, MySpace, LinkedIn); Blogs, video blogs, microblogs (Twitter); Discussion forums, Q & A portals (Yahoo Answers); Wikis (Wikipedia, Google Knol); Bookmarking systems (Digg, Delicious, Jagg); Shared multimedia (YouTube, Flickr); Virtual worlds (Second Life, The Sims) [9].

How Brand Actions and User Actions Influence Brand Value by use of social networks is solved in [10] and performance measurement system to quantify the contribution of social media is presented in [11]. Du and Jiang [12] find that company use of social media is associated with firm performance, measured by stock price and return on assets. When testing the individual association of the various platforms and firm performance, the authors find that only Facebook and Twitter has a statistically significant relationship. They observe that half of the firms use one or both of these platforms.

2.4 Accounting Software

The term refers to software accounting software that handles accounting and financial processes. The offer of accounting software focuses on the specific size of the company. According to company size amount of income, the number of transactions processed and the number of employees differs. There are special offers to the market according to company size small, medium and large businesses. Accounting software in each segment focuses on something else. At the level of small companies the offer covers standard accounting modules, such as purchase orders, payroll, billing, etc. Generally at this level the software runs on a separate system and supports multiple users who are incorporated into database software. The acquisition cost of such software is low and can be purchased as so called box software. Accounting software provides medium-sized organizations with complete components for processing of financial activity of the company which is usually specialized. The last segment of the large organizations is favouring the complex connections between companies using ERP systems. These systems are expensive. The development of the system itself is a tiny item in the final list. The largest expenses include consulting, training, workflow reengineering, organizational restructuring costs, installation and commissioning itself [13].

2.5 The Main Purposes of Selected Social Networks

The subchapter contains theoretical background of purposes of selected social networks

- Facebook - Facebook for marketing allows businesses, organizations and public figures to connect with customers, fans and constituents through the website. Businesses and other brands create pages where they can post content, provide organizational news, offer deals, introduce products and manage customer service relationships. They also can reach a large number of people with targeted advertising, creating ads specifically for Facebook that are tailored to appear on the pages of specific groups of people they hope to reach [27].
- YouTube - companies might gain a lot from short videos on YouTube showing the benefits of their products and also videos how to use products. YouTube is all about getting visitors to stay and consume video after video so that they can see ad after ad. According to one small study, conducted by Phil Nottingham of Distilled, only 0.72% of viewers of YouTube channels with URL's in the description clicked thru to the linked site. What that tells us is, if you are trying to get people to come to your website, YouTube might not be the tool to click thru to the linked site [28].
- Twitter - it is a social networking and microblog provider that allows users to send and read posts sent by other users, known as tweets. The main purpose of Twitter is to make profits for those running the business (founders, investors, employees and more). From a user's perspective, it may serve many purposes including but not limited to: Keep an eye on trending events/news, Connect with like-minded people, Marketing or promotion of business, Stalk and spam, Vent out emotions or anger, Business Support, Finding and connecting with influencers [29].
- Google+ - the purpose of Google plus is to provide a binder to the web experience of a user. It is one of the top components of Google ecosystem now solving a multitude of problems not only for Google but for the whole web. It also helps provide a web identity to users [30]. Glusman presented [31] 7 Reasons Why You Should Be Using Google+ For Your Business.
- LinkedIn - it is a professional social network where professionals meet and discuss their work interests and they are also looking for new employees. LinkedIn is a professional social media network, where users create profiles highlighting current and prior work experience. You can upload resumes, connect with colleagues and classmates and build a network that can help you advance in your career [32].
- Instagram - the app allows users to upload photos and videos to the service, which can be edited with various filters, and organized with tags and location information. An account's posts can be shared publicly or with pre-approved followers. Users can browse other users' content by tags and locations, and view trending content. Users can "like" photos, and follow other users to add their content to a feed [33].

3 Methodology and Goal

The goal of the article is to present the most often used accounting software, their producers in the connection with use of social networks by producers of accounting software and links with producer's web pages in the Czech Republic. The sub-goal is to present records gained from Socialbakers focused on the evolution of fans on Facebook and how a company decides on the use of the optimal mix of platforms.

The article was prepared on the basis of print and electronic resources. Specialized articles that deal with issue of financial accounting or social media can be found. By contrast, printed literature on accounting (economic) software doesn't nearly occurs on the Czech market. Available books on accounting are primarily concerned with the processing and are intended for teaching or as a handbook for accountants. Specialized materials in the field of information technology are in particular focused on the area of enterprise information technologies and their application. Publications on ERP systems are available in this field and in most cases they contain accounting (economic) software, but they do not aim deeper on it. In contrast to the situation on the Czech market there are a lot of foreign sources abroad. In case that we link accounting software and their producers and social networks together there are not a lot of articles focused on this issue. The existing literature focused separately on the accounting software and Facebook or social media or social network in the connection of promotion of the brand or product, communication with customers or training etc. There were not founded relevant articles in databases Web of Knowledge or Scopus focused on the interconnected topic. This topic is still in its infancy. The intention of the article is to stimulate a conversation and proposes ways in which to frame early and future research.

The main part of the article is based on the available resources of the most often used accounting SW and their producers in the Czech Republic. Selected accounting SW will be applicable for SME. The selection was done due the highest proportion on the market. In the next step was done analysis whether the producers of accounting SW use selected social networks or not and whether are web pages of the producers connected with their social networks. Next part of the article is devoted to statistics of fans from individual companies. Data was obtained from Socialbakers [14]. The last part is devoted to optimal use of platforms by companies producing accounting SW.

4 Results

The first part contains the results of selection from accounting software products and their producers. Data were selected from the SystemOnLine website [15] which deals with statistical data about accounting, economic and ERP systems and with their use, information about functions, prices etc. in the Czech Republic. Accounting software for SME in the Czech Republic will be included into next processing. The second part contains information about social network Facebook, YouTube, Twitter, Instagram, Google+, LinkedIn and their use by accounting software producers. Next topic is focused on the interconnection of social networks with web pages of companies.

4.1 Accounting Software and Producers

On the basis of gained results from the investigation a selection of the below discussed results have been made utilizing SystemOnLine website. Individual companies regularly update detailed information about accounting software products, including the number of installations, number of hot-line workers, number of consultants of the product, functions of the product, price, etc. In the filter it was firstly entered - 'find a product that has more than 10,000 installations'. The following products were displayed: Ekonom, Pohoda, Money S3 and "Účto" (Accounting). Due the larger sample of the companies was the selection repeated with the smaller number of installations that were reduced on 5,000 installations. Into research will be added Abra Gen, Helios Orange and Stereo Ježek Software (SW). In the next search specific data of all other products were found. Table 1 shows all the above mentioned accounting software and ERP systems. Pohoda with more than 200,000 licenses and Money S3 with more than 60,000 licenses are the most widely used box systems in the Czech Republic. Ekonom has representation in 35,000 licenses followed with other product Účto Tichý with 24,200 licenses on the second type of accounting in the Czech Republic that use most of the business entities. In Table 1 there are presented name of product, name of producers, number of installations, size of the biggest installation, workers on hot-line and number of consultants of the product. Some data were not filled in by the companies.

Table 1. Accounting software, more than 5,000 installations [15, own elaboration]

Name of product	Name of producer	Number of installations	Size of the biggest installation	Workers on hot-line	Number of consultants of the product
Pohoda	Stormware	200 000+	60	76	100
Money S3	Solitea CR	60 000	50	65	120
Ekonom	Elisoft	35 000	25	8	15
Účto Tichý	Tichý & spol.	24 200		4	A few tens
Abra Gen	Abra Software	9 400		20	64
Helios Orange	Asseco Solutions	6 088	250	101	203
Stereo Ježek SW	Ježek Software	5 000		8	44

Company Solitea Česká republika (Solitea CR) was till October 2017 known and named as Cígler Software. The biggest installation recorded product Helios Orange with 250 installations. Pohoda with 60 and Money S3 with 50 were on the next positions. Účto Tichý and Stereo Ježek Software is focused mostly on the small companies. From accessible sources it is possible to mention, that the biggest number of workers on hot-line is in company Asseco Solutions. It can be connected also with their other products that they offer to bigger companies. The smallest number of workers on hot-line recorded Účto Tichý with 4 employees and Ekonom and Stereo

Ježek Software with 8 workers. Asseco has also the biggest number of consultants. Less consultants recorded Ekonom. Účto Tichý and Stereo Ježek Software. Účto Tichý and Ježek Software closely cooperate. Účto Tichý has software for individuals (sole traders) that lead single-entry bookkeeping and Ježek Software for corporate bodies that lead double-entry bookkeeping. Pohoda, Money, Ekonom and also Abra offers both types of accounting used in the Czech Republic. Almost all companies actualize information about them. The newest one was done 11th of June 2018 by Abra Software and Ekonom 6th of June 2018. In 2018 15th of March actualize also Solitea CR. Tichý & spol. recorded the oldest data from 8th of November 2016. Stormware with the biggest number of licences updated more than year ago 16th of February and Ježek Software also 1st of June.

4.2 Accounting Software, Web Pages and Social Networks

In the next part of the research there were analysed social networks Facebook, Twitter, Instagram, YouTube, Google+ and LinkedIn in the connection with producers of accounting software in the Czech Republic. It was searched whether or not have the producers of accounting software account on the widely used social network Facebook or on others. Accounts of the individual brands were searched on the all mentioned social networks. Results are presented in Table 2.

Table 2. Use of social networks and direct links between companies www and social networks [16–19, own elaboration]

	Facebook		YouTube		Twitter		Google+		Linkedin	
	Use	Link	Use	Link	Use	Link	Use	Link	Use	Link
Pohoda	X	X	X	X	X	X	X	X	X	-
Money 33	X	X	X	-	X	-	X	X	X	X
Ekonom	X	X	X	-	X	-	X	-	X	X
Účto Tichý	X	-	X	-	-	-	-	-	-	-
Abra Ger.	X	X	X	X	X	X	X	X	X	X
Helios Orange	X	X	X	X	X	X	X	-	X	X
Stereo Ježek SW	X	X	X	-	X	X	X	X	X	-

It was founded that all producers use social networks Facebook and YouTube for communication with audience. Twitter and Google+ use all producers instead Tichý & spol. Table also presents interconnection between web pages and direct links on social networks where their accounts were founded. It was founded that all companies instead Účto Tichý have direct links of their Facebook profile. Even though all companies use YouTube, the direct link from the first page uses only two companies Abra Software and Asseco Solutions. Next link has also Stormware but it is necessary to click more times. Twitter has not links on the websites in all companies. Elisoft and Solitea CR is missing those information. Links on Google+ were not found for companies Asseco Solutions and Elisoft. Links on Linkeid in missing in company Stormware and Ježek

Software. Company Abra is the only one that have links on all social networks that they use. Other social networks are also used. Solitea CR has the link on their Skype. Asseco Solutions use also blog and Elisoft use Instagram.

All producers instead Tichý & spol. have produced and presented video courses for all free of charge. Abra Software have free training only for license owners [20–26].

4.3   Producers of Accounting Software + Facebook + Socialbakers

Producers of accounting software were put into analytics tools that offer Socialbakers [14]. The number of fans in the last year and their changes were indicated. The evaluation started on June 19, 2017 and ended on June 18, 2018. It was founded that the biggest group of fans on the social network Facebook has company Asseco Solutions. Number of their fans at the end of the monitored period was 11 556. 9 518 fans were local (Czech Republic) – 81.12%, 1 560 from Slovakia (13.3%) and 0.85% from United Kingdom, 0.73% from Germany and 0.42% from USA. Solitea CR has 2 868 fans at the end of the monitored period. Almost 93% were from the Czech Republic. Next countries were again Slovakia (5.04%), Belgium, Germany and United Kingdom.

Number of fans of next companies, % and distribution of fans:

- Abra SW – 719, 90.72%, Slovakia (4.99%), Germany, United Kingdom, Indonesia
- Ježek SW – 380, 94.7%, Germany, Slovakia, Canada, Nigeria
- Ekonom – 73, 92.86%, United States, Serbia, Slovakia, Malaysia
- Stormware – 187, 84.12%, Slovakia (13.53%), Poland, Canada and Italy
- Účto Tichý – 42, 97.3% and Austria with 1 fan is 2.7%.

Numbers of fans were changing in the monitored period. The difference between starting date for monitoring and ending day (19th of June 2017–18th of June 2018) is presented in Fig. 1.

The largest increase was recorded in Ježek SW by 126 fans. It was also the highest % growth. All companies monitored growth instead Helios and Solitea, but from the whole numbers they loss only 2.2% and 0.9% of fans in comparison with starting and ending period.

4.4   Optimal Use of Platforms by Companies Producing Accounting Software

Recommended optimal Social Media Network portfolio for accounting firms in the Czech Republic is use of selected social networks. They were selected due functions that they provide and also they are widely used by citizens and companies.

- Facebook – use for posting content, provide organizational news, offer deals, introduce products and manage customer service relationships. It can be used periodically but mostly when something is new in the area.
- YouTube – using video to show how to use accounting software. It is recommended to use when some changes in the software is done to show how to use it in the new way. There can be uploaded also videos that are connected with FAQ.

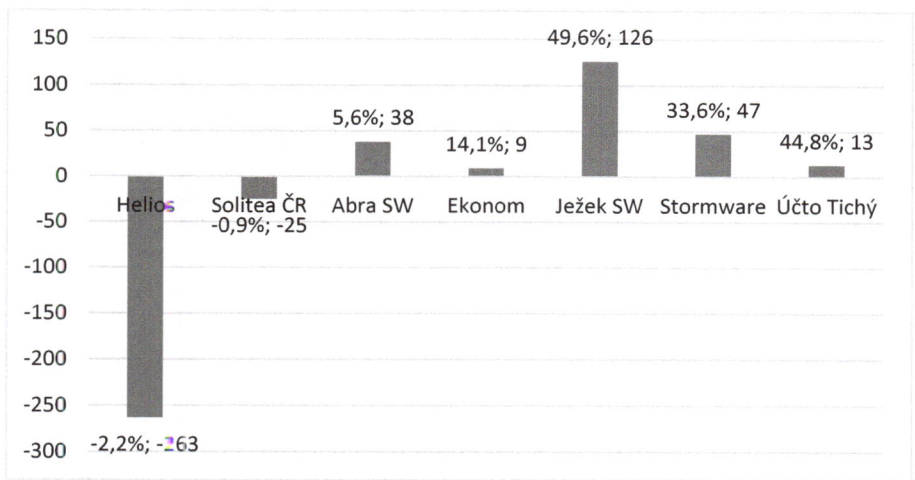

Fig. 1. Increases and decreases of number of fans on Facebook in the last year [14, own elaboration]

- Twitter – through short news reports about news and actualization of products.
- Google+ – it is the social network that offers the most tools and features. It is recommended to use user profile as a publicly visible account of a user that is connected to many Google properties. Circles enables users to organize people into groups or lists for sharing across various Google products and services. Companies can use also Stream, Identity service, +1 Button, Google+ pages, Communities, Events, Discover, Photography etc.
- LinkedIn – use to inform for seeking of new employee. Current employees can inform about situation in the company from employee point of view.
- Instagram – use for posting of actual photo or video from the business environment.

Companies may use also WhatsApp, Viber, Blogs and other social networks if necessary. Important is to connect social networks with the www pages of companies. The links should be placed clearly on the first page and then if necessary by the individual topics.

5   Conclusion and Discussion

Social networks fit knowledge management as they open the door to new ways of communication, enable development, editing, sharing and storing materials on the virtual platform. Social networks are nowadays one of the most popular and most often used channels to inform and communicate not only in the private sphere but also at business environment.

The goal of the article was to present the most often used accounting software, their producers in the connection with use of social networks by producers of accounting software and links with producer's web pages in the Czech Republic. The sub-goal was to present records gained from Socialbakers focused on the evolution of fans on Facebook and to state use of platforms by companies producing accounting software.

It has been founded that all producers use Facebook and YouTube. Twitter, Google+ and Linkedin use all companies instead Účto Tichý. Unfortunately not all used social networks and individual accounts have links on the websites of the companies. Elisoft has no 3 links, on YouTube, Twitter and Google+. Solitea CR missed two links, YouTube and Twitter. Stereo Ježek has not link on YouTube and Linkedin. Stormware has not presented link on Linkedin and Asseco Solution on Google+. Účto Tichý is the weakest in using social networks.

The largest share of the fans on Facebook has Asseco Solution followed by Solitea. After a big gap are Abra Software, Ježek Software, Ekonom and Stormware. Účto Tichý is in the last position with 42 fans. Most of the fans are from the Czech Republic. The second group were Slovakia. Reason can be also similar products that are sold in both countries. Asseco Solutions have the biggest share of users from abroad. Results show interesting fact. Pohoda, that is the most often used, has the third smallest record of fans, only 187. The largest increase of fans in the last year recorded Ježek Software and Stormware. On the contrary, the decrease recorded Asseco Solutions that has also the largest number of the fans and Solitea. In % decrease is only 2.2% and 0.9% according to first and last date of the monitored period.

Companies can be advised to manage all of the listed social networks (Facebook, YouTube, Twitter, Google+, LinkedIn and Instagram) and to get benefits from their use in order to retain existing customers and at the same time gain new customers. Even though social networking means additional costs for companies, they can inform professional audience and customers about new developments in the area of accounting and accounting products just now. It is less expensive than printed form or other types of marketing tools.

In future there is potential for an interesting research and area of exploration. It can be also investigated topics of posts, number of posts, like, focusing, tracking, tweets, use of mobile apps, their use, training and posts and use of YouTube.

Acknowledgement. This paper is supported by specific project No. 2103/2018 "Investment evaluation within concept Industry 4.0" at Faculty of Informatics and Management, University of Hradec Kralove, Czech Republic. We would like to thank student Jan Hruška for cooperation in the processing of the article.

References

1. Svobodová, L., Černá, M.: Accounting, economic and ERP systems on the Czech scene. Adv. Sci. Lett. **22**(5–6), 1170–1174 (2016)
2. O'Reilly, T.: What is Web 2.0: Design Patterns and Business Models for the next generation of software. http://www.oreillynet.com/pub/a/oreilly/tim/news/2005/09/30/what-is-web-20.html. Accessed 18 June 2018
3. Barnes, J.: Class and committees in a Norwegian Island Parish. Hum. Relat. **7**, 39–58 (1954)
4. Černá, M., Svobodová, L., Haviger, J.: Perception and utilization of Facebook by university students: case study. In: Proceedings of the 15th European Conference on e-Learning, ECEL, pp. 105–113 (2016)

5. Svobodová, L.: Utilization and benefits of YouTube for the educational purposes: a review study. In: Proceedings of the 15th European Conference on e-Learning, pp. 789–793 (2016)
6. Eurostat. Digital economy and society statistics - households and individuals (2017). http://ec.europa.eu/eurostat/statistics-explained/index.php?title=Digital_economy_and_society_statistics_-_households_and_individuals. Accessed 18 June 2018
7. Czech statistical office. https://www.czso.cz/csu/czso/information-society-in-figures. Accessed 18 June 2018
8. Social media – Definition and More from the Free Merriam. Webster Dictionary. http://www.merriam-webster.com/dictionary/social%20media. Accessed 18 June 2018
9. Janouch, V.: Internetový marketing Prosaďte se na webu a sociálních sítích, p. 216. Computer Press, Brno (2010)
10. Colicev, A., O'Connor, P., Vinzi, V.E.: Is investing in social media really worth it? How brand actions and user actions influence brand value. Serv. Sci. **8**(2), 152–168 (2016)
11. Agostino, D., Sidorova, Y.: A performance measurement system to quantify the contribution of social media: new requirements for metrics and methods. Meas. Bus. Excel. **20**(2), 38–51 (2016)
12. Du, H., Jiang, W.: Do social media matter? Initial empirical evidence. J. Inf. Syst. **29**(2), 51–70 (2015)
13. Dočkalová, P.: Criteria for selection of an economic system. IT Systems: With an overview of the world of information technology, November 2008. http://www.systemonline.cz/ekonomicke-systemy/kriteria-pick-economic-system-1.htm. Accessed 18 June 2018
14. Socialbakers. https://suite.socialbakers.com/234916/analytics/?c-d1=last-30&c-l=0. Accessed 18 June 2018
15. System online. http://www.systemonline.cz/prehled-informacnich-systemu/ekonomicke-systemy. Accessed 18 June 2018
16. Facebook. https://www.facebook.com/. Accessed 18 June 2018
17. Instagram. https://www.instagram.com/. Accessed 18 June 2018
18. Twitter. https://twitter.com/. Accessed 18 June 2018
19. YouTube. https://www.youtube.com/. Accessed 18 June 2018
20. Abra Software. https://www.abra.eu/. Accessed 18 June 2018
21. Asseco Solutions. http://www.helios.eu/. Accessed 18 June 2018
22. Elisoft, Ekonom. http://www.ekonom-system.cz/cz/home. Accessed 18 June 2018
23. Ježek Software. https://www.jezeksw.cz/. Accessed 18 June 2018
24. Solitea Česká republika. http://www.money.cz/. Accessed 18 June 2018
25. Stormware. https://www.stormware.cz/. Accessed 18 June 2018
26. Účto Tichý. https://www.ucto-tichy.cz/. Accessed 18 June 2018
27. The Purpose of Facebook. https://www.techwalla.com/articles/the-purpose-of-facebook. Accessed 22 July 2018
28. What is the purpose of YouTube? https://www.quora.com/What-is-the-purpose-of-YouTube. Accessed 22 July 2018
29. What is the main purpose of Twitter? https://www.quora.com/What-is-the-main-purpose-of-Twitter. Accessed 22 July 2018
30. What is the main purpose for Google+? https://www.quora.com/What-is-the-main-purpose-for-Google+. Accessed 22 July 2018
31. Glusman, A.: 7 Reasons Why You Should Be Using Google+ For Your Business. https://www.business2community.com/google-plus/7-reasons-using-google-business-01126869. Accessed 22 July 2018
32. Cornell, S.: Purpose of LinkedIn. https://smallbusiness.chron.com/purpose-linkedin-62179.html. Accessed 22 July 2018
33. Instagram. https://en.wikipedia.org/wiki/Instagram. Accessed 22 July 2018

How Can Technology Support Education in War – WarAware Education Platform for Syria

Nada Almasri, Luay Tahat[(✉)], and Laila Al Terkawai

Department of Management Information Systems,
Gulf University for Science and Technology, West Mishref, Kuwait
{Almasri.n, tahat.l, alterkawai}@gust.edu.kw

Abstract. The well-known Syria crisis has made it very challenging for thousands of Syrian children to have access to education. In this paper, we propose digital education platform to allow displaced Syrian kids as well as kids in the refugee camps in bordering countries, to have access to education. The proposed platform consists of four pillars: Hardware, Software, Curriculum, and Support services. We start by looking at the efforts performed in the field of education in war situations, and we extract from them the lessons learned and recommendations. We provide four main characteristics of war impacting kids' education: (1) insecurity, (2) instability, (3) lack of resources, and (4) lack of adults' supervision. We then use these four characteristics along with the extracted recommendations, as the grounds for drafting three design considerations for the implementation of a digital education platform. The three design considerations are supervised self-directed learning method, context-aware education, and kids-oriented design. Finally, we use these design considerations to provide design recommendations for the four pillars of the platform. We conclude our work by discussing the validity of the platform, its implementation feasibility, and challenges facing the implementation.

Keywords: Education in war · Education in emergencies
War characterization · Supervised self-directed learning
Digital learning platform for kids · Design considerations
Context-aware education · Kids-oriented design

1 Introduction

War impacts all aspects of the society. It impacts the economic, the social life, the psychosocial stability of the population, the educational system, and all other aspects. The interplay between all of these affected aspects drastically impact kids. The interplay between the impact of war on the educational system and the impact of war on kids play an important role in defining the educational challenges facing kids in war situations.

The impact of war on kids goes way beyond its impact on adults. While adults have reached the point where they already have shaped personalities, established judgment/moral inner-system, and some level of base-knowledge of life/career skills;

© IFIP International Federation for Information Processing 2018
Published by Springer Nature Switzerland AG 2018. All Rights Reserved
S. A. Al-Sharhan et al. (Eds.): I3E 2018, LNCS 11195, pp. 436–448, 2018.
https://doi.org/10.1007/978-3-030-02131-3_39

kids, who represent the future of the society in the post-conflict period, are yet to build all of these aspects of their lives. This developmental process is already complex, and war conditions make it even more challenging with the risk of long-term negative impacts on one's self, the society, as well as future generations. The impact of war on kids ranges from direct physical impact to indirect and long-term impact. As direct impact, kids may suffer from disabilities caused by war injuries, they may lose one or both of their parents; the primary caregivers for them, and they would live in distress caused by the sense of insecurity and instability encountered during war. Moreover, kids who lost their primary caregivers, are at higher risks of different kinds of exploitation such as child labour, sexual abuse, and recruitment in armed forces. A child growing up in such circumstances of war may suffer as an adult from long lasting psychological impacts such as post-traumatic stress disorder.

As for the impact of war on education, it is reported by the UNESCO that in war affected areas, the educational system is deliberately targeted [1]. UNESCO reports that over a period of three years (2007 to 2009), at least 31 countries had their educational system deliberately attacked by rebels, armies or repressive regimes. During war, the educational infrastructure is destroyed, teachers are either killed or displaced, and fewer funding for schools supplies is provided by authorities and by parents who prioritize funding survival related tasks such as safety, food, health, and shelter. Targeting the educational system during war results in decreased access to schools, the degradation of the quality of education, and the lower educational attainment [2, 3].

This combined impact of war on kids and on education makes it challenging for kids to pursue their education, which plays an important role in shaping their personalities and in determining their future success in life. Indeed, at the long term, studies in criminology found negative correlation between educational attainment and crime [4, 5]. Studies in education found that youth delinquent behaviour can be associated to early childhood factors which can be lessened with well-designed early childhood education [6]. Thus, the UNESCO emphasize the critical role of education in post-conflict stability of the community [7, 8]. Indeed, education is being considered as the fourth pillar when responding to humanitarian crisis following food, shelter, and healthcare [9]. With respect to Syria crisis, the UNICEF reports that the number of children affected by Syria Crisis is six-million children, among which almost 2,800,000 are displaced children, and two-million children are located in hard to reach areas, while 133,000 children under siege in eastern Aleppo area only. Over two-million children are out of school in Syria, and over 700,000 Syrian refugee children are out of any form of education in neighbouring countries [10].

While the war situation makes it challenging to offer conventional educational systems, the rapid advances in information and communication technology can greatly help. Indeed, technology is rapidly advancing in different fields: Hardware, software, and telecommunication. With these advances in technological aspects, we increasingly see all non-technical fields integrating technology to enhance their effectiveness. Medicine, Art, and Education are among these fields which are greatly benefiting from technology integration.

In war-affected areas, the United Nations (UN) agencies as well as several non-governmental organizations (NGOs) have initiated different projects and initiatives to use technology for the implementation of educational platforms [11]. Given the emergency nature of the implementation of these educational systems, little efforts were done to ground these projects on research-based concepts. Additionally, little was done to implement a mechanism to measure the impact of these projects, and ways to adapt them at a higher scale. The main critics received about these projects is that they focused on the technology itself, and they placed little emphasis on more critical educational components such as the curriculum, the learning environment, and the adaption of the technology to serve the particular needs of kids in war-affected areas.

In this paper, we start Sect. 2 by looking at the efforts performed in the field of education in war affected areas, and we extract from them the lessons learned and recommendations. In Sect. 3, we provide four main characteristics of war, and we look at their impact on children and their education. In Sect. 4, we use these four charac-teristics along with the extracted recommendations, as the grounds for drafting three design considerations for the implementation of context-aware digital education plat-form. Finally, Sect. 5 lays out the four pillars of the platform: Hardware, Software, Curriculum, and Supporting Services.

2 Efforts Performed in the Field of Education in Emergencies

In this section, we explore the work done in the field of education in war. We consider research papers and reports, as well as projects and initiatives. The work considered is focused on work which gives insights on educational challenges in war situation in general or in Syria crisis context in particular.

2.1 Machel Report

The Machel report is an expert report released by the secretary-general of the UN in 1996. It addressed the impact of armed conflict on children, and it presented an action plan to improve child protection in war zones [7]. The report which was prepared by Graca Machel, was later followed up by a book in 2001 to assess the actions taken in response to the recommendations of the 1996 report and to extend it with further insights and recommendations [9].

Among other issues, Machel addressed the psychological impact of war on kids, and she viewed education as means of survival. Her recommendations addressing these two areas focus on providing educational and psychosocial support for children as an integral part of all humanitarian efforts, and she emphasizes the importance of edu-cating the children in ware-related issues such as landmine and peace education. Finally, she encourages involving the community in curriculum planning to ensure that it is childrights based and locally relevant.

2.2 Learning for a Future

The UNHCR published a book compiling a collection of five literature review papers presented at 2001 workshop "Refugee Education in Developing Countries: Policy and Practice" [11]. The book addresses education in emergencies, quality and attainment in refugee schools, peace education for refugee youth, and vocational training for refugees. The book gives insights and general recommendations for efforts targeting refugee education.

The book formulates the basic principles of education in emergencies as: adopting community-based approach and capacity-building; training refugee teachers, youth leaders, and refugee schools administrators; meeting psychological need of the children; providing rapid response to educational needs; emphasizing durable solutions; encouraging regional approach to certification; integrating survival, peace-building, and citizenship messages, broadening the education to consider a verity of groups, and promoting interagency cooperation.

2.3   The Quantitative Impact of Conflict on Education

UNISCO institute for statistics released a commissioned report in 2011 evaluating the quantitative impact of conflict on education in 25 countries touched by armed conflicts. The study measured schooling and retention by looking at the share of the population without formal schooling and the average number of years of formal education. The study didn't include Syria as it was conducted in the same year of the Syrian uprising. In general, the study found significant negative impact of conflict on the proportion of the population with formal education, the average years of education attained, and the literacy rate. Additionally, the study found that "*cohorts that were of school-going age during a time of conflict have lower educational attainment that persists over time, indicating that these children generally do not resume their education after a conflict to attain levels of education similar to non-exposed cohorts*" [3].

2.4   Innovation Labs

"Innovation at UNHCR 2014" is a report presented by the UNHRCR innovation unit. It highlights the five pillars which form the framework around which the unit operates.

Innovation labs are one of these five pillars. They "apply principles of human-centred design and prototyping to address complex refuges challenges" [13]. The report highlights the five-step approach to developing projects by the unit. The five steps are defining the challenges, identify solutions, test solutions, refine solutions, and scale solutions. The project they address are around five themes: learn, home, link, and energy. The learn theme is focused on expanding education opportunities for refugees and displaced people. Under this themes, the report lists six projects in different conflict-affected countries (but they don't include Syria) without providing any further details about the projects. One of the most interesting sections of the report is the lessons learned section. The five key lesson they highlight are: Senior management engagement in the field prior to implementation, embedding new projects with ongoing education strategies instead of independent projects, engaging youth and the community in the design process, having dedicated staff, and securing multi-year funding.

2.5   Barriers to Education in Conflict-Affected Countries

Another paper commissioned by the UNESCO institute for statistics was released in 2014 to shed the light on educational challenges during war, and to "suggest policy interventions to break barriers to the implementation and effectiveness of education systems" [8].

The report distinguishes between supply-side barriers and demand-side barriers. Supply-side barriers are related to the destruction of infrastructure, social institutions and markets, while demand-side barriers are related to the changes in economic and social structures within families and communities along with the persistent insecurity. The report also discusses the importance of education in achieving stability in conflictaffected countries. It outlines two strategies to support stability through the educational system. The first strategy focuses on educating children and young people as agents of positive social change by involving them in several constructive social programs and activities. The second proposed strategy is to build the enabling environment for more effective education by reducing poverty and the need of child labour, reintegrating traumatized kids and kids who experienced interruption in the their education back into the educational system through inclusive educational system, and fostering aspirations by instilling their sense of confidence and by addressing the mental health and cognitive growths for kids who experienced war atrocities to give them the sense of normalcy.

2.6 Syria Education Sector Analysis

A recent UNICEF report released in 2016 asses the effects of the crisis on education in Syria between as well as in refugee camps in neighbouring countries in the period of 2011 and 2015 [14]. The study provides both quantitative and qualitative analysis. The quantitative analysis shows that 2.1 million children inside Syria are out of school. The enrolment rates inside Syria dropped by 44% between 2011 and 2015. As for refugees in neighbouring countries, while the enrolment rate has been decreasing between 2012 and 2015 from 73% to 53%, in terms of absolute numbers, 627,000 children out of 1.3 million are out of school. The qualitative analysis identifies four main reasons for this drop in enrolment: security and fear, earning money to support the family, education is not a priority (compared to survival), and learning costs. In addition, the qualitative analysis identify several educational challenges including: the decrease in the quality of education caused by the overcrowded classrooms, reduced school hours, and high rate of absenteeism for both students and teachers; the lack of school supplies such as textbooks, classroom boards, stationaries, and other teaching aids; the absence of proper teacher training to deal with emergencies and traumatized children; and the lack of recreational and extracurricular activities and psychosocial support to students.

The study concluded by making several recommendations including: encouraging the active involvement of the parents' community in the education process; increasing the coordination among educational partners in Syria, and sharing evidence-based data, and lessons learned in order to avoid duplicated effort and scale up what works well; promoting psychosocial support through recreational and extracurricular activities, and initiating support group sessions for students and staff; developing creative teaching strategies to deal with the lack of educational resources; supporting the development of selflearning materials for children who are unable to attend school; and extending school hours in safe days to make it up for missed days.

2.7 One Laptop Per Child (OLPC)

One laptop per child program was initiated by MIT media lab in 2005. The idea of the program was to provide elementary kids in developing countries with affordable "$100 laptops". A number of developing countries adopted the program either as a pilot project for a few schools, or for at a large scale. Currently only a few research work performed formal and informal evaluation of the effectiveness of the program and they show varied findings [15, 16].

The program was criticized as being "a laptop" initiative not an educational initiative. Indeed, the program didn't integrate pedagogy at its heart, and it didn't provide guidance on ways to integrate the use of computers into the learning process. Additionally, the program didn't consider the social and cultural context of the deployment environment [17, 18].

Bhatta [19] introduced a framework for implementing the OLPC model. The framework consists of planning and implementation of four key areas: digital contents, teachers' preparation, network and power infrastructure, and the development of the government's capacity in all of the previously mentioned three areas.

3 Characterizing War-Situation

When it comes to kids' education during war, war situations can be characterized by the following main traits: insecurity, instability, lack of resources, and lack of adult support and supervision. Each of these trait is described below.

3.1 Insecurity

In the absence of security, sending kids to schools becomes a real challenge to parents. Not only the schools are intentionally targeted during conflicts [1], but also the way to the school is not safe. Parents in war face the dilemma of taking the risk of sending their kids to school or keeping them presumably safe at home.

Whether planed or not, kids abduction in the presence of insecurity is very common. In Syria, kids are abducted for two main reasons. In the relatively more secure areas under the Syrian regime control, kids' abduction is performed mainly for financial gains obtained as ransoms from parents. Young adults' abduction, however, is believed to be done by the regime security services as a way to keep the people oppressed and under constant fear, and in many cases abducted people are found dead with signs of torture. In the areas under the control of armed rebels, kids are recruited in the armed conflict as child soldiers which are easily manipulated [23].

Syrians who fled the war in Syria and settled in neighbouring countries also suffer from a different type of insecurity caused by tensions between refugees and host communities, as well as the tension within the refugee camps community caused by the rough conditions of life in refugee camps [20].

3.2   Instability

In the insecure war situation, families are frequently displaced looking for a safer place. In many cases they are moving from one neighbourhood to another, from one city to another, and even from one country to another. This shelter instability issue, causes economic, emotional as well social instability for displaced people who had to leave all their belongings and homes behind and settle temporarily in a different shelter within a different society. Additionally, in war situation, the family status is also unstable. In many cases a member of the family is killed, kidnapped, disabled with a war injury, or separated from the rest of the family during an attempt to escape bombing or during a clandestine attempt to cross the borders to another country.

In such unstable environment, kids' education is constantly interrupted, and the continuity of the education becomes very challenging with different curricula and different instruction languages. Additionally, with the economic and social instability, older kids are either forced or choose to make survival choices (work, get married, or join militant groups) which don't include education.

3.3   Lack of Resources

While the lack of resources is usually one of the reasons behind interstate conflicts, in intrastate conflicts such as in Syria crisis, lack of resources is a consequence of the war. In Syria crisis, there is a clear lack of all resources: food, medical supplies, clothes, fuel, energy sources, educational supplies, and even qualified experts (doctors, engineers, teachers, etc.).

The lack of resources inside Syria is caused by the destruction of the agriculture sector (the major economic source in Syria), the difficulty in transporting products, and the regime's enforced siege on some opposition controlled areas. The educational sector is highly affected by this lack of resources. Schools are either destroyed or used as shelters, and school supplies are either limited or not available. Additionally, a number of teachers and administrative staff are either killed, joined the armed conflict, or fled the area. Parents, authorities, and humanitarian organizations are prioritizing spending funds on shelter, food, and medical supplies over school supplies. While resources are relatively available in areas under the Syrian regime control, the prices are usually very high for internally displaced families.

Whether in urban areas or in refugee camps, lack of resources is also an issue for Syrian refugees in neighbouring countries. Most refugee camps are supported by the UNHCR and charitable organizations, however the educational fund they receive is a lot less compared to the actual needs [10].

3.4   Lack of Adults' Support and Supervision

As it is always the case in war, it is common to have increased numbers of orphans, kids with single parents, or unaccompanied kids who were separated from their families. In these circumstances, child labour, abuse, and exploitation are common phenomena. Additionally, even when kids live with both parents, the high stress of war affects adults' ability to provide proper parenting [12, 21]. Parents are preoccupied by finding ways for survival. Their focus and priority goes to finding safe shelter, food, and medications. and to keeping their kids alive. Additionally, in many cases parents prioritize work for older kids compared to education.

In such circumstances, kids are either left with no responsible adult who can provide emotional support or educational/behavioural supervision, or with preoccupied stressed parents who are themselves in need of social and psychological support. In such circumstances, kids are vulnerable and are easy subjects of abuse and exploitation. This is why many researchers believe that education doesn't only help children in securing decent future, but it also plays a role in distracting kids from the stress of war and it allows them to have a sense of normalcy by following a daily normal life routine of going to school and meeting with other kids and consequently it plays a natural role in lessening the psychological impact of trauma and displacement [12]. Education also plays a role in enhancing the kids chances in getting the appropriate knowledge they need to protect themselves from abuse and to establish their moral code of distinguishing right from wrong.

4 Design Considerations in War

In this paper we propose a digital context-aware platform for education in emergencies. The platform emphasizes student' home-based self-learning method with frequent supervision and follow up by a teacher. The platform has four pillars: Hardware, Software, Curriculum, and Supporting Services. The specifications of these pillars are based on three design considerations which are derived from the context of war. The three design considerations are detailed below.

4.1 Supervised Self-directed Learning Method

Given the unique situation of children impacted by war, the system should enable kids to follow their course of study regardless to whether they are physically present at school or not. Due to instability, and insecurity issues, children as well as teachers have high rate of absenteeism. To deal with this on/off situation, the system should be designed so that it can be used independentely by the child at home, while at the same time being periodically supervised by a teacher within or outside the context of the school. This would allow children who are unable to attend school (e.g. under siege) to continue their education independently.

In this context, self-directed learning is well suited to allow kids to independently learn from home. While in the general sense, self-directed learning is a learning method followed by adults who have greater autonomy; organization; and motivation; when a pure self-directed learning method is applied with kids it could be problematic. Although the tough conditions of life during war increase the kids' autonomy, and might create fierce eagerness to learn as they view education as their way out of the poor life conditions, children don't have enough life experiences or organizational skills to organize their education within a formal curriculum which lead them to an accredited middle-school or high-school degrees. Accordingly, we suggest complementing the independent learning of kids by a formal periodical supervision performed by an adult educator, hence the term "supervised" is added to "self-directed" learning. In this context, the supervised self-directed learning focuses on allowing the children to independently and flexibly explorer learning materials and resources which are linked to a pre-defined curriculum, while at the same time periodically supervising the kids' learning, and redirecting them towards the curriculum when their learning greatly diverges from the curriculum.

This suggested learning method has two main implications. First, it suggests implementing a monitoring and follow up mechanism to keep the child on the right track. Consequently, it forms the basis of study continuity for the children, where the teachers can (remotely) follow up individual children progress. In addition, this aspect of supervision adds the formalism required to allow the children's re-integration at school when the situations are more stable. The second implication of supervised self-learning is the need for collaboration and sharing mechanisms to allow effective interaction between the students and the teachers.

This learning method is well suited during emergencies since it mainly focuses on empowering kids with the learning materials they need to perform their study independently, while it requires minimal support and supervision from educators, which means that a small number of teachers can follow up a larger number of students. It also means that children can still follow up their education at their own pace regardless of their conditions: children in hot-zone war, children under siege, young married girls, or working adolescents.

Finally, it is worth noting that the suggested supervised self-learning method with a digital platform focuses on empowering the student with digital self-learning material to be used independently at home, but it doesn't carry any assumptions about the use of the digital platform at school for learning.

4.2 Context-Aware Education

We introduce the term "Context-Aware Education" to refer to the education process which takes into consideration the context of the learning environment. In our proposed platform, the context that we want the education to focus on is the "the different possible situations in war context". We, thus, propose this type of education to take into consideration the context of war in two dimensions: the learning outcome dimension, and the learning tools and aids dimension.

In the first dimension, context-aware education expands the learning outcomes of a traditional curriculum to take into consideration the unique situation of the war and of refugee camps. In a traditional educational system, the curriculum is built around: Math, Science, Language Art, and Social Studies, while at the same time, behavioural, and social aspects of the curriculum are implicitly present through the context of the school community and under the supervision of qualified teachers, social workers, and administrators.

In the context of war, where the school society is compromised, behavioural, and social aspects as well as war related concerns should be explicitly integrated into the curriculum. These may include for example: health and safety education, peace and conflict resolution strategies, protection and defence practices, and psychosocial wellness. Indeed, in the long term, today's children's are tomorrow's society builders, and if they are well equipped with the appropriate peace education, the chances of future conflicts can be reduced. Additionally, in the post-conflict period, the community would need well equipped young adults to rebuild the society.

The second dimension of context-aware education deals with the lack of resources available in the learning environment such as school supplies, learning aids, teachers, and even learning-time can be viewed as one of the educational resources. Contextaware education deals with the lack of these resources by finding alternatives when these resources are not available. For example, how to teach a 5-yrs old child to hold a pen and write when pencils and papers are not available? How to teach an older child in vocational education how to sew a dress without textiles? How to teach a child a concept without a teacher? How to teach a child a concept in shorter time than originally planned? Based on the context, the 5-yr child can be offered as an alternative to use a stick to trace the letters on the sand or the snow, plastic/paper bags or tree leaves (or any other material available in the surrounding environment) can be offered as an alternative to fabrics, self-learning materials can help a child learn independently, and innovative teaching strategies can help a teacher cover more concepts in shorter time to a larger number of kids. In a digital context, hardcopies of textbooks can be replaced by softcopies, interactive digital forms can replace work-sheets, touch-screen/stylus/digital forms can replace the need for traditional school supplies, etc. Consequently, context-aware education requires creativity approaches in teaching and learning strategies, and it requires adapting the curriculum so that the same learning outcomes can be achieved using alternative learning aids and solutions.

4.3   Kids-Oriented Design

As opposed to adults, kids are still in the development process; their physical, cognitive, and emotional abilities keep changing until they become mature adults. Since the main targeted users of the educational system are kids and juniors under 18 years old, who may or may not be supported or supervised by adults, it is important to consider kids' needs, limitations, and challenges when designing the digital education platform. In this context, kids-oriented design goes beyond an appealing user interface for kids.

Kids-Oriented design would address kids' physical abilities, mental/cognitive abilities, and emotional/social abilities. In addition, given the expected lack of adults' support in war situation, the system should be designed to be used independently by the kids while taking into consideration the child's online safety, age-appropriateness of contents, ease of use, as well as automated maintenance and support.

Additionally, with kids-oriented design, the system should be built keeping in mind that "one system doesn't fit all", and it doesn't even fit one child who is developing over time. An appealing system for a 7 years old child will be a boring system for the same child at age 8, and what works for an 8 years old child will not work for a 15 years old child.

Finally, kids-oriented design would maximize the opportunities to exploit the inquisitive, impatient, adventurous, and creative nature of kids.

5   Four Pillars of the Education Platform

Taking into consideration the three design considerations presented in Sect. 4, the system can be designed based on four pillars: Hardware, Software, Curriculum, and Support.

The hardware should be portable with diverse ways for connectivity (Bluetooth, WiFi, 4G, Ethernet etc.). It should be rugged and energy efficient. The software should be supported by a monitoring and follow-up mechanisms, as well as collaboration and remote access assistance tools. Additionally, a pluggable architecture of the curriculum would allow large scale participation in the development of the curriculum by a large community of educators while keeping the material well-structured according to an approved standard. It is worth noting here that a curriculum in war context should be extended beyond math, language art, science, and foreign languages. For example, an extended curriculum could include health and safety education, peace and conflict resolution principles, child protection and self-defence practices, tolerance and positive citizenship in addition to other topics relevant to the specific context where the system is being used.

Since several curricula are adopted in different areas; inside Syria, in refugee camps, and in bordering countries outside refugee camps [22]; it is almost impossible to use one curriculum in all varying contexts. Consequently, the platform should allow for the flexible integration of different curricula. Regardless of the chosen curriculum, the learning materials should be designed for self-learning.

Finally, in addition to hardware, software, and curriculum, a very critical component to ensure the continuity of using the system is the support services. Support services should consider technical support, educational support, as well as psychosocial support. Such services should not be assumed available on the ground, consequently, the platform should be designed to integrate these services online.

6   Conclusion

The presented framework was derived from the body of work done to address education challenges during war. The platform was designed following four steps: (1) Understanding the context of war and extracting the main war characteristics relevant to kids and their education, (2) Extracting strength, weaknesses, and recommendations from the work done in the field of education in war in general and the use of technology as a solution in particular, (3) Adopting three major design considerations based on the extracted recommendations, (4) Specifying the main components of the platform based on the adopted design considerations.

Although the state of the art of all components of the platform shows that the implementation of the platform is feasible, given the extended scale of context-aware education, the implementation process requires massive scale and support to adapt exiting hardware, software, and curriculum to war context in general and to Arabic language and Syrian social community in particular. Consequently, adopting open source software, and keeping the implementation process open to community's as well as volunteers' participation is a key factor in the fast implementation and adoption of the educational system.

Additionally, the cost of the implementation of the platform is clearly another challenge. Assuming active participation of NGOs and volunteers in content development, the major cost attributed to the system would be the price of the hardware (laptops, tablets, solar chargers). The expectation is that for context-aware hardware, the minimum base-line price would be that of OLPC laptops which were engineered to work on poor communities of the developing countries, however OLPC failed to reach the promised $100 price.

Finally, despite the challenges, we believe that the benefits of the system outweigh the downsides. In addition, while the presented platform was designed mainly to address Syria crisis, it can be considered as a step toward a sustainable solution for education in emergencies that agencies like UNICEF and UNHCR are looking for.

References

1. O'Malley, B.: Education under attack–2010. UNESCO (2010)
2. Jones, A., Naylor, R.: The Quantitative Impact of Armed Conflict on Education: Counting the Human and Financial Cost. CfBT Education Trust (2014)
3. Unesco: The Hidden Crisis: Armed Conflict and Education. UNESCO (2011)
4. Lochner, L.: Education, work, and crime: A human capital approach. Int. Econ. Rev. **45**(3), 811–843 (2004)
5. Lochner, L.: Education and crime. Univ. West. Ont. **5**(8), 1–14 (2007)
6. Yoshikawa, H.: Long-term effects of early childhood programs on social outcomes and delinquency. Futur. Child., 51–75 (1995)
7. Machel, G.: Impact of Armed Conflict on Children. UN (1996)
8. Justino, P.: Barriers to education in conflict-affected countries: policy and opprtunities. Commissioned by UNESCO (2014). Retrieved from http://allinschool.org/wp-content/uploads/2015/01/OOSC-2014-Conflict-andeducation-final.pdf, 23 Nov 2016
9. Machel, G.: The Impact of War on Children: A Review of Progress Since the 1996 United Nations Report on the Impact of Armed Conflict on Children. United Nations Children's Fund, 3 UN Plaza, New York, NY 10017 (2001)
10. UNICEF: Syria crisis report, Sep 2016. Retrived from https://www.unicef.org/appeals/files/UNICEF_Syria_Crisis_Situation_Report_Sept_2016.pdf
11. Global Business Coalition for Education: Exploring the Potential of Technology to Deliver Education & Skills to Syrian Refugee Youth. GBCE (2016)
12. Crisp, J., Talbot, C., Cipollone, D.B.: Learning for a Future: Refugee Education in Developing Countries. United Nations Publications, Sales & Marketing Section, Room C-113, Palais des Nations, 1211 Geneva 10, Switzerland (2001)
13. UNHCR: Innovation at UNHCR – Anything But Business as Ususal. UNHCR (2014)
14. Whole of Syria Education Focal Point: Syria Education Sector Analysis. Whole of Syria Education Focal Point (2016)
15. Cristia, J., Ibarrarán, P., Cueto, S., Santiago, A., Severín, E.: Technology and child development evidence from the one laptop per child program (2012)
16. Nugroho, D., Lonsdale, M.: Evaluation of OLPC programs global: a literature review (2010)
17. Kraemer, K.L., Dedrick, J., Sharma, P.: One laptop per child: vision vs. reality. Commun. ACM **52**(6), 66–73 (2009)

18. Warschauer, M., Morgan, A.: Can One Laptop per Child save the world's poor? J. Int. Aff. **64**, 33–51 (2010)
19. Bhatta, S.D.: Tackling the problems of quality and disparity in Nepal's school education: the OLPC Model. Stud. Nepali Hist. Soc. **11**(1), 17–47 (2008)
20. UNHCR: Future of Syria. http://unhcr.org/FutureOfSyria/. Last accessed 23 Nov 2016
21. Tolfree, D.: Restoring playfulness: different approaches to assisting children who are psychologically affected by war or displacement. Rädda Barnen (1996)
22. UNICEF: Curriculum, Accreditation and Certification for Syrian Children in Syria, Turkey, Lebanon, Jordan, Iraq and Egypt. UNICEF, Mar 2015
23. Whole of Syria Education Focal Point: Self-learning for out-of-school children in Syria UNICEF and UNRWA joint education programme. http://wos-education.org/uploads/self-learning_materials/without_logo/Self_learning_brief_note_Spread_English.pdf. Last accessed 23 Nov 2016

Information Technology Governance and Electronic Financial Disclosure

Abdalmuttaleb M. A. Musleh Al-Sartawi[1(✉)],
Rami Mohammad Abu Wadi[1], and Azzam Hannoon[2]

[1] Department of Accounting, College of Business and Finance, Ahlia University,
P.O. Box 10878, Manama, Kingdom of Bahrain
amasartawi@hotmail.com, rwadi@ahlia.edu.bh
[2] College of Business Administration, American University in the Emirates,
Dubai, UAE
azzamhannon@hotmail.com

Abstract. This study set out to link two fundamental topics of corporate governance: Information technology governance (ITG) and the level of electronic financial disclosure (EFD). The paper aimed to examine the extent of ITG in the UAE listed firms, the level of EFD by UAE listed firms and the association between the two variables. The researchers collected data from a sample of 103 firms listed in the financial stock markets of the UAE for the years 2016–2017. A regression analysis was used to test the relationship between the dependent and independent variables. Consequently, the study found a positive and significant relationship between ITG and EFD. From a practical perspective, this paper is aimed at the board of directors and executive managers, as IT governance is their responsibility. Furthermore, from a theoretical perspective, this paper offers a unique point of view, which adds to the literature review discussing IT governance mechanisms, and EFD. The study would also be of interest to the international investment community, regulators, policy makers and governments in the UAE, the Middle East as well as the other GCC countries.

Keywords: Information technology governance
Electronic financial disclosure · UAE

1 Introduction

Disclosure is a term that frequently changes among researchers. Clinch and Verrecchia define voluntary disclosure as a firm's policy to disclose information that depends both on the characteristics of the economy and the ex-post realization of the information before its disclosure; therefore, possessing an endogenous disposition. Based on Yang et al. (2016), several studies have recognized that one of the key determinants of a firm's voluntary disclosure strategy is corporate governance (CG), and it is associated with the dissemination of management earnings forecasts, earnings press releases, and corporate restructuring disclosure to decision-makers.

Recently, electronic financial disclosure (EFD) has been perceived as one of the most important platforms used by firms in communicating information to stakeholders (Drake et al. 2017). A pioneering study by Lymer et al. (1999) describes EFD as the

S. A. Al-Sharhan et al. (Eds.): I3E 2018, LNCS 11195, pp. 449–458, 2018.
https://doi.org/10.1007/978-3-030-02131-3_40

public reporting of financial and operating data by a business enterprise through Internet-based communications media. Due to its low cost, managers are able to disclose accurate and relevant information more frequently through EFD. This helps firms to adhere to the principles of corporate governance by enhancing transparency and reducing information asymmetry and agency related costs.

Another significant corporate governance issue currently faced by the modern firm is related to Information Technology Governance (ITG). Previous research shows that information technology has a direct effect on corporate governance (Farhanghi et al. 2013). According to the website of the IT Governance Institute (ITGI) (2018), ITG is a subset of corporate governance which focuses on information technology systems, and how their performances are measured, and risks managed. McCollum (2006) claims that the Sarbanes-Oxley Act of 2002 has alerted the board of directors to their firm's need to prioritize Information technology governance. Therefore, due to the critical need of ITG, Huff et al. (2004) demands that an IT expert should be appointed to the board to provide diverse views based on practical experience or background they have in the field of information technology. Moreover, since information technology is a part of corporate governance, Damianides (2005) argues that the reliability and level of financial disclosure is greatly influenced by a strictly governed IT environment. Therefore, it would be interesting to examine the level of EFD from an IT governance perspective.

Consequently, this paper aims to link two fundamental topics of corporate governance: modern disclosure practices and IT Governance. The study was undertaken to address the following main research questions. First, what is the extent of Information Technology Governance (ITG) by UAE listed firms? What is the level of Electronic Financial Disclosure (EFD) by UAE listed firms? Finally, what is the relationship between ITG and the level of Electronic Financial Disclosure in the UAE?

1.1 Why UAE?

The United Arab Emirates is used as a context of this study for several reasons. Firstly, the UAE considers infrastructure and technology as a highly significant basis of social and economic development (Arafat et al. 2018) as it is moving from an undiversified oil dependent economy to a diversified non-oil dependent economy. The UAE is, therefore, viewed as the financial hub of the region with a perfect legal system and a good investment environment. In 2014, the UAE's Telecommunication and Regulatory Authority (TRA 2014) published their fifth sector annual review stating that 85% of the country's population regularly uses the Internet.

Hussainey and Alfiriji (2012) believe that the UAE, especially Dubai, is the destination of choice for international investors due to three main reasons: speed, culture and governance, as the UAE has initiated the application of international standards of corporate governance in 2010 in an attempt to merge with the global economy (Hasan 2012). Consequently, as a financial hub which attaches great importance to technology and foreign investments, the UAE provides a unique and interesting context to study the relationship between ITG and EFD.

This paper is written with the board of directors and executive managers in mind, because IT governance is in due course their responsibility. Moreover, to the best of the researcher's knowledge negligible studies have examined the level of EFD in the UAE; thus, contributing knowledge to the literature related to electronic disclosure, ITG, and the UAE. Despite the study having significance to the UAE business environment, it can provide contributions to the Middle Eastern countries, mainly the Cooperation Council for the Arab States of the Gulf (GCC countries), as they share comparable economic, political and social environments. Moreover, the paper offers implications for firms considering IT-experienced nominations to their boards.

2 Literature Review

2.1 Electronic Financial Disclosure

The fundamental theory that underlies the disclosure practices of firms in relation to corporate governance is the agency theory. The agency theory involves the conflicts of interest resulting from the differences between the interests of shareholders and that of managers. The relevant literature presents arguments stating that managers have incentives to make investment decisions that reduce the risk of losing their jobs or increase their compensation (Hussainey and Alfiriji 2012). In turn, this conflict between managers and shareholders gives rise to monitoring costs and other costs by the agent to assure the shareholders that there will be no harm to their interests (Al-Sartawi 2016).

Fama and Jensen (1983) argue that the responsibility of the board of directors in an agency framework is to solve agency issues between managers and shareholders by suggesting a fixed compensation, and replacing managers that do not create value for the shareholders (Carter et al. 2003). According to Healy and Palepu (2001), corporate governance plays a crucial role in reducing the information gap between the firm and investors who are less informed than the managers. So, to reduce this information gap (asymmetry) and the related agency costs, firms need to disclose accurate, transparent and timely information to the public. This could be achieved through electronic financial disclosure (EFD).

Poon and Yu (2012) defined EFD as the use of the firms' websites to disseminate both financial and non-financial information. The advancement in broadband technology has significantly increased accessibility to the Internet. It is now cheaper, easier, and much quicker for people to communicate globally. Thus, traditional financial reporting is becoming less effective compared to the usage of electronic financial disclosure. Almilia (2009) stated that electronic-based reporting removes the restrictions of paper-based reports. As a result, traditional paper-based corporate reporting has become less effective for decision makers. Similarly, Keliwon et al. (2018) differentiate between electronic financial disclosure and the traditional reporting in terms of the methods of reporting information. EFD considers all information that could boost the performance of firms through the internet, including financial and non-financial information, aside from the information contained in annual reports. While traditional reporting concentrates only on the information in annual reports.

Several studies have investigated the determinants and the level of electronic financial disclosure (Al-Sartawi 2017; Ekramy 2017), however no study has used IT governance as a determinant beforehand.

2.2   Information Technology Governance

Grais and Pellegrini (2006) claim that there is no particular recipe for the perfect corporate governance plan. However, there are basic principles that constitute what is considered as good corporate governance such as having defined duties and expectations for board members, disclosure and transparency requirements, welldefined shareholder rights, and mechanisms to ensure compliance and hold board members accountable. From this point of view, ITG is perceived as a significant issue faced by firms because the board of directors is used as an internal governance mechanism that reduces agency conflicts and costs.

Rau (2004) defines IT governance as the way senior management interacts and communicates with IT leaders to ensure that technology investments enable the achievement of business strategy in an effective and efficient manner. Likewise, Li et al. (2007) describe IT governance as leadership, organizational structures, and control processes which ensure that the IT of the firms is able support and expand the company and achieve its objectives. Nolan and McFarlan (2005) regard ITG as "a vital asset that requires intense board-security and assistance". Therefore, as ITG increases the firms' responsiveness to stakeholders, it can be applied to electronic financial disclosure.

Moreover, along with Nolan and McFarlan (2005), recommends that an ITG group of expert independent directors need to be appointed to the board, as in the case with the audit committee, due to economic and regulatory matters related to the Sarbanes-Oxley compliance and corporate governance. Thus, these directors are required to be experts in IT, and understand the dynamic potential of information technology in changing the business environment. This notion is supported by the resource dependence theory, which states the importance of the board of directors as resources for the firm to reach external resources (Ribeiro and Colauto 2016). Despite this need for an IT expert on the board, Valentine and Stewart (2013) found that board level willingness to reduce the gap between awareness and action is very low or non-existent. On the other hand, in the case of the UAE, Nicho and Khan (2017) found that the objectivity of ITG is well-defined and emphasized.

Additionally, Damianides (2005) found a positive relationship between ITG and the reliability and the level of financial disclosure. The need for upto-date, frequent and accurate information, therefore places IT security at the core of executives' and directors' concerns. Accordingly, this study hypothesizes that there is a relationship between Information Technology governance and the level of electronic financial disclosure.

3   Methodology

In order to address the research questions, mainly the relationship between ITG and the level of EFD in the UAE, the current study collected data from all the 103 firms listed in the financial stock markets of the UAE for the period 2016–2017. Consequently, the study measures the level of ITG in UAE firms by determining the percentage of the members of the board of directors who have an IT background or experience. Additionally, the study adopted a checklist used by Al-Sartawi (2016) to measure the level of EFD. So, if a firm disclosed any financial information by using any electronic platform it received a score of 1, and 0 if otherwise.

To test the hypothesis, the following regression model was developed using EFD as a dependent variable, and ITG as an independent variable. Additionally, the study used the board of directors' size, firm age, firm size and financial leverage as control variables.

Study Model:

$$EFD_i = \beta_0 + \beta_1 ITG_i + \beta_2 BD\_size_i + \beta_3 LF\_size_i + \beta_4 LVG_i + \beta_5 AGE_i + \varepsilon_i$$

Code	Variable Name	Operationalization
Dependent variable		
EFD	Electronic financial disclosure	This is a binary Wherein 1 means that the company discloses financial data and 0 otherwise
Independent Variables – Board compensation:		
ITG	Directors with IT background and experience %	The percentage of members who have IT background and experience to the total board size
Control Variables:		
BD_size	Board size	Natural logarithm of Total Assets
F_size	Firm size	Natural logarithm of Total Assets
LVG	Leverage	Total liabilities/ Total Assets
AGE	Firm Age	The difference between the establishing date of the firm and the report date
εi	Error	

4   Data Analysis

4.1   Descriptive Statistics

Table 1 reports the descriptive analysis of the independent, dependent and control variables. The maximum level of information technology governance (ITG) was 57% by UAE firms while the minimum was 0% with a mean of 6.2% indicating a low level of ITG. This result is in line with Valentine and Stewart (2013) who state that there is a gap between ITG need and reality. With regards to the level of EFD, UAE achieved a maximum level of 100%, with an overall mean of 78.3%., which is considered as a moderate level of EFD by UAE firms considering the high level of internet usage in the country.

Table 1. Descriptive statistics for continues variables

Variables	N	Minimum	Maximum	Mean	Std. Deviation
ITG	206	.00	.57	.0620	.11494
Assets	206	32.27	3412461.5	72425.9	3.15257E5
Lev	206	−.44	.98	.3510	.31587
AGE	206	1	49	25.56	14.094
EFD	206	.05	1.00	.7833	.16762
BS	206	5	12	7.59	1.284

Additionally, the descriptive statistics for control variables show that the mean of firm size, i.e. Total Assets, was 72,425.99, with a minimum of 32.27 and a maximum 3,412,461.54, which indicates fairly large firms. The normality distributions of the total assets were skewed, so natural logarithm was used in the regression analysis to reduce the skewness and bring the distribution of the variables nearer to normality. Moreover, the mean leverage of the firms was approximately 35% showing firms with somewhat medium debts. The average size of the UAE boards is 8 members, while, firm age ranges from 2 to 50 with a mean of 26.56.

4.2   Validity

Table 2 summarizes the Pearson's correlation matrix. This will support the study in testing the statistical relationship between the independent and the dependent variables, and whether multicollinearity exists among the data before assessing the model.

Table 2. Pearson correlation matrix

	ITG	Assets	Lev	AGE	EFD	BS
ITG	1					
Asset s	−.068	1				
	.335					
Lev	.004	−.045	1			
	.958	.522				
AGE	.116	−.069	−.049	1		
	.096	.326	.482			
EFD	.131	.063	−.061	.146[b]	1	
	.060	.371	.384	.036		
BS	−.066	−.115	.303[a]	.099	−.007	1
	.346	.100	.000	.158	.922	

[a]Correlation is significant at the 0.01 level (2-tailed).
[b]Correlation is significant at the 0.05 level (2-tailed).

Table 2 shows that leverage and board size had the highest correlation (0.303). This correlation is significant; correlation coefficients should not be considered damaging until they exceed 0.80.

A Variance Inflation Factor (VIF) test was used to check the data for multi-collinearity. This test was used as according to James et al. (2017), VIF calculates the severity of multicollinearity and measures how much the variance of an estimated regression coefficient is affected by collinearity. The VIF should be lower than 10 and the tolerance test should not be below 0.2. The VIF scores for all variables, both independent and dependent, are reported in Table 3. The results indicate that no VIF score exceeded 10 for any variable in the model, and no tolerance score was below 0.2. So, it was concluded that there is no threat of multicollinearity. The table also reports the normality test, where the skewness test and the kurtosis test suggest that all the predictive variables are normally distributed except for size which was doctored using natural logarithm.

Table 3. Collinearity statistics test

Model	Tolerance	VIF	Kurtosis	Skewness
ITG	.978	1.023	3.840	2.039
Assets	.967	1.034	75.132	8.149
Lev	.881	1.135	−.931	.235
AGE	.962	1.040	−1.514	−.076
BS	.888	1.126	3.053	1.442

Furthermore, to detect the presence of autocorrelation at lag 1 in the prediction errors or residuals from the regression analysis, the Durbin Watson test was used as reported in Table 4. The Durbin Watson (D-W) value of the model was (1.9). Thus, we can further conclude that there is no autocorrelation founded in the model because the (DW) value was approximately 2.

Table 4. Autocorrelation test

Model	R	R 2	Adj. R^2	Std. Error	Durbin-Watson
1	.194	.038	.014	.1665	1.9

4.3 Regression Results

Table 5 reports the findings of the regression analysis. The findings indicate that the model was reflecting the relationship between the variables in a statistically appropriate way. According to the table, the model has an adjusted R^2 of 0.38 which shows that the model explains approximately 38% of the variation in the EFD amongst the UAE listed firms. However, the probability of the F-statistic with a significance 1.71 means that the ITG was not significant in interpreting the EFD level.

Table 5. Regression analysis

Variables	Beta	T. test		Sig.
ITG	.117	1.666		.097[*]
Assets	.006	.087		.931
Lev	−.058	−.779		.437
AGE	.130	1.837		.068
BS	.005	.071		.944
R²			.308	
F			1.567	
Prob. (F)			1.71	

[*]pv < 1%; ** pv < 5%; ***pv < 10%.

The main hypothesis of the study states that there is a relationship between ITG and EFD by firms listed in the UAE markets. The result indicates that there is a significant and positive relationship between the dependent and independent variables, i.e., the higher the level of ITG on the board, the higher the level of disclosure. This could be due to the existence of IT experts on the board, which brings to light the importance of technology in disseminating financial information to interested parties, as they understand the dynamic potential of IT on the business environment. This result is comparable to the study by Li et al. (2012). Moreover, since the UAE invests highly in technology, this offers a potentially beneficial effect on corporate governance by providing a rich environment for cultivating disclosure.

With regards to the control variables (covariates), the study found a significant and positive relationship between the level of EFD and age. One reason for this could be that younger firms might be more hesitant to disclose certain information such as research expenditure and capital expenditure to the competition (Owusu-Ansah 1998). On the other hand, there was a negative yet insignificant relationship with leverage. This could be because firms with higher leverage tend to be more conservative and try not to disclose to stakeholders that they are indebted. Finally, the results show no relationship between firm size, board size and the level of electronic financial disclosure.

5   Summary and Conclusions

This study aimed to address several research questions: (1) the extent of ITG in the UAE listed firms, (2) the level of EFD by UAE listed firms and (3) the association between the two variables. To answer the research questions the researchers collected data from a sample of 103 firms listed in the financial stock markets of the UAE for the years 2016–2017.

The study reported an overall level of EFD in the UAE at 78.3% which is a somewhat moderate level compared to the percentage of users of Internet in the UAE, which is 85%. Secondly, with regards to ITG, the overall level of its implementation is 6.2% which is very low. The researchers tested the relationship between the dependent and independent variables, and found a positive and significant relationship between ITG and EFD. As for the control variables, the analysis reported a positive and significant relationship with age. While there was an insignificant and negative relationship with leverage, and no relationship with firm size and board size.

From a practical perspective, this paper is aimed at the board of directors and executive managers, as IT governance is their responsibility. As the level of ITG in the UAE firms is very low, this paper advises the board of directors to pay more attention to the percentage of independent members who are IT experts and understand the various technological advancements and how they can be utilized by the firm. These results can be used by the GCC countries as they share similar social, political and economic environments to the UAE. Furthermore, from a theoretical perspective, this paper offers a unique point of view which adds to the literature review discussing IT governance mechanisms, and EFD. The study would also be of interest to the international investment community, regulators, policy makers and governments in the UAE, the Middle East as well as the other GCC countries. This paper suggests having a study that further investigates the relationship between ITG and performance. Future studies could also test the relationship between ITG and social media disclosure which is a step beyond EFD, as social media is a two-way communication tool, unlike EFD which is a one-way communication tool.

References

Almilia, L.: determining factors of internet financial reporting in indonesia. Account. Tax. **1**(1), 87–99 (2009)

Al-Sartawi, A.: Measuring the level of online financial disclosure in the Gulf Cooperation Council Countries. Corp. Ownersh. Control **14**(1), 547–558 (2016)

Al-Sartawi, A.: The effect of the electronic financial reporting on the market value added of the islamic banks in gulf cooperation council countries. In: 8th Global Islamic Marketing Conference. 4–6 May. International Islamic Marketing Association, Turkey (2017)

Arafat, W., Bing, Z., Al-Mutawakel, O.: Infrastructure developing and economic growth in United Arab Emirates. Bus. Econ. Res. **8**(1), 95114 (2018)

Carter, D.A., Simkins, B.J, Simpson, G.W.: Corporate governance, board diversity, and firm value. Financ. Rev. **38**, 33–53 (2003)

Damianides, M.: Sarbanes-Oxley and IT governance: new guidance on IT control and compliance. Inf. Syst. Manag. **22**(1), 77–85 (2005)

Ekramy, S.M.: Internet financial reporting determinants: a meta-analytic review. J. Financ. Report. Account. **15**(1), 116–154 (2017)

Fama, E.F., Jensen, M.C.: Separation of ownership and control. J. Law Econ. **24**, 301–325 (1983)

Farhanghi, A.A., Abbaspour, A., Ghassemi, R.A.: The effect of information technology on organizational structure and firm performance: an analysis of Consultant Engineers Firms (CEF) in Iran. Procedia-Soc. Behav. Sci. **81**, 644–649 (2013)

Grais, W., Pellegrini, M.: Corporate governance in institutions offering islamic financial services: issues and options: world bank policy research. Working Paper No. 4052. SSRN: https://ssrn.com/abstract=940709 (2006)

Hasan Al-Tamimi, H.A.: The effects of corporate governance on performance and financial distress: the experience of UAE national banks. J. Financ. Regul. Compliance **20**(2), 169–181 (2012)

Healy, P.M., Palepu, K.G.: Information asymmetry, corporate disclosure, and the capital markets: a review of the empirical disclosure literature. J. Account. Econ. **31**(1), 405–440 (2001)

Huff, S., Maher, P.M., Munro, M.: The IT attention deficit: information technology and boards of directors. In: International Conference on IT Governance, Auckland (2004)

Hussainey, K., Aljifri, K.: Corporate governance mechanisms and capital structure in UAE. J. Appl. Account. Res. **13**(2), 145–160 (2012)

James, G., Witten, D., Hastie, T., Tibshirani, R.: An Introduction to Statistical Learning, 8th edn. Springer Science, Business Media New York (2017). ISBN 978-14614-7138-7

Keliwon, K.B., Shukor, Z.A., Hassan, M.S.: Internet financial reporting (IFR) disclosure position and firm value. Asian J. Account. Govance. **9** (2018)

Li, C., Lim, J.-H., Wang, Q.: Internal and external influences on IT control governance. Int. J. Account. Inf. Syst. **8**(4), 225–239 (2007)

Lymer, A.: Internet and the future of reporting in Europe. Eur. Account. Rev. **8**(2), 289–301 (1999)

McCollum, T.: On the road to good governance: internal auditors need to make sure they're moving in the right direction when reviewing corporate practices and behaviors. Intern. Audit. **63**(5), 40–47 (2006)

Nicho, M., Khan, S., Rahman, M.S.M.K.: Managing information security risk using integrated governance risk and compliance. In: 2017 International Conference on Computer and Applications (ICCA). IEEE (2017)

Nolan, R., McFarlan, F.W.: Information technology and the board of directors. Harv. Bus. Rev. **83**(10), 96 (2005)

Owusu-Ansah, S.: The impact of corporate attribites on the extent of mandatory disclosure and reporting by listed companies in Zimbabwe. Int. J. Account. **33**(5), 605–631 (1998)

Poon, P.L., Yu, Y.T.: Degree of internet corporate reporting: a research framework. Inf. Res. **17**(1), 509 (2012)

Rau, K.G.: Effective governance of IT: design objectives, roles, and relationships. Inf. Syst. Manage. **21**(4), 35–42 (2004)

Ribeiro, F., Colauto, R.D.: The relationship between board interlocking and income smoothing practices. Rev. Contab. Finanças **27**(70), 55–66 (2016)

Telecommunication Regulatory Authority: UAE Telecommunications Sector Developments and Indicators, 5th Annual Sector Review. https://www.tra.gov.ae/assets/q0Z5B3sI.pptx.aspx (2014)

TIAA-CREF. TIAA-CREF Policy Statement on Corporate Governance (New York) (1997)

Valentine, E.L.H., Stewart, G.: The emerging role of the board of directors in enterprise business technology governance. Int. J. Discl. Govance. **10**(4), 346–362 (2013)

Yang, J., Liu, S., Zhou, D.: Voluntary financial disclosure on social media: does corporate governance matter? (2016). SSRN: https://ssrn.com/abstract=2836570

Examining the Factors Affecting Behavioural Intention to Adopt Mobile Health in Jordan

Ali Alalwan[⊠], Abdullah M. Baabdullah, Nripendra P. Rana,
Yogesh K. Dwivedi, Fadia Hudaib, and Ahmad Shammout

Amman College of Banking and Financial Studies, Al-Balqa' Applied
University, Amman, Jordan
alwan.a.a.ali@gmail.com, ykdwivedi@gmail.com,
y.k.dwivedi@swansea.ac.uk,
ahmad.b.shammout@gmail.com, baabdullah@kau.edu.sa,
n.p.rana@swansea.ac.uk

Abstract. Health organizations worldwide express a considerable attention to utilize Mobile technology applications to provide a better health services to their people. One of the most emerging apps in this regard is Mobile health (M-health). Large amount of efforts, money, and time have been invested to provide such innovative technology. Yet, the adoption rate of these systems is still low. Additionally, such system has never been examined over the Jordanian context. Thus, this study aims to test the most important factors that could shape the intention of Jordanian people to use Mhealth. Four factors: perceived usefulness, social influence, awareness, and innovativeness were proposed as key predictor of behavioural intention. Data was collected using convenience sample size of 365 and was analyzed using structural equation modelling. The main statistical findings supported the role of perceived usefulness, social influence, and innovativeness. More discussion will also be provided regarding the current study practical and theoretical implications.

Keywords: M-heath · Jordan · Adoption

1 Introduction

Mobile technology has been growing dramatically over the recent years either in terms of number of users or the range of applications and technical products and services provided (i.e. Mobile learning, Mobile commerce, Mobile banking, and Mobile healthcare) (Shareef et al. 2018). For instance, the number of mobile subscribers worldwide reached 4.77 billion in 2017 as stated by Statista (2018a). This represents a lot of opportunities for organizations from different sectors (i.e. government, education, banking, healthcare) to utilize such vehicles to deliver their services in an advanced and innovative way to their customers (Shareef et al. 2016, 2018). In this regard, about 3.8 million apps that are presented in Android and about 2 million for Apple's App store (Statista 2018b).

Such applications have also been the focus of attention of health organizations to serve their patients and provide their services and information in an effective and

© IFIP International Federation for Information Processing 2018
Published by Springer Nature Switzerland AG 2018. All Rights Reserved
S. A. Al-Sharhan et al. (Eds.): I3E 2018, LNCS 11195, pp. 459–467, 2018.
https://doi.org/10.1007/978-3-030-02131-3_41

modern channel saving the time and efforts of both health organizations and recipients of health services (Shareef et al. 2012). Indeed, one of the man reasons that enhance the current prosperity of mobile usage and acceptance is the huge interest to invest in mobile technology by health and medical organizations (Statista 2018c). In this instance, according to the same report of Statista (2018c), the market size of Mhealth was about 21 billion dollars and this number is projected to increase to 60 billion dollars by (2020).

This prevalence of M-health could be returned firstly to the ability of such system to enhance the quality of medical services provided; having more interactive communicative channel with recipients of health services; cutting cost; hindering the impact of time and place restrictions (Shareef et al. 2016; Schnall et al. 2016). Additionally, people increasingly have more health conscious and therefore, are more interested in adopting M-health applications (Atallah et al. 2018; Brown III et al. 2013). Conceptually, M-health could be defined as a novel and new system empowered by using smart phones, personal digital assistants (PDAs), and any other mobile technology to attain a wide range of healthcare and preventive health services (Singh et al. 2017).

In Jordan, there is a recent interest in utilizing mobile facilities to provide and secure adequate level of healthcare services especially for residents of remote areas. For instance, a new project with cost of $1 million introduced by the Health Ministry of Jordan to serve about 10,000 people in the southern region is a "quantum leap (Jordan Times 2015). However, permanent challenge for any new system like M-health is to convince people about the benefits of such system and accordingly motivate them to adopt it (Alalwan et al. 2016; Lee and Han 2015). Therefore, there is a need to discover and examine the main aspects that could shape the Jordanian people intention toward M-health care applications. Nevertheless, as a new and very novel technology in Jordan, the related issues of mobile health have not yet received attention from researchers in Jordan. Accordingly, this study aims to identify and examines the main factors that could predict the Jordanian intention to adopt Mhealthcare.

2   Theoretical Foundation

As discussed above, the adoption of M-health is the corner stone of the success of implementing such systems. Thus, a good number of studies that have recently attempts to explore and examine the main factors predicting the customers' intention and adoption (i.e. Dwivedi et al. 2016; Hoque and Sorwar 2017; Lee and Han 2015). Such of that Lee and Han (2015) identified four factors: usefulness, monetary value, convenience value, illness experience as key determinants of Intention to adopt Mhealth. Their statistical results largely supported the impact of usefulness, convenience value, and monetary value while illness experience did not have any impact in this regard. Extending the Unified Theory of Acceptance and Use of Technology (UTAUT2) was also formulated Dwivedi et al. (2016) to predict the adoption of M-health. According to Dwivedi et al. (2016), excluding hedonic motivation, the rest factors of UTAUT2 (performance expectancy, effort expectancy, facilitating conditions, social influence, price value) have a direct influence on intention to adopt M-health. Likewise, Hoque and Sorwar (2017) propose their model base on UTAUT and technology anxiety and resistance to change. Their empirical findings supported the effect of effort expectancy, performance expectancy, social influence, technology anxiety, and resistance to change on the customers' intention to adopt M-health. Perceived value, perceived behavioural control, perceived physical condition, subjective norm, technology anxiety, and self-actualization need were tested by Deng et al. (2014). Deng et al. (2014) also considered the moderation impact of age on the relationship between these predictors and intention to adopt M-health.

Their practical results found out that the impact of these factors significantly different form older to middle-aged. Differently, Zhang et al. (2017) provided statistical evidences regarding the main obstacles (health habit, sunk cost, transition cost, and privacy concerns) that hinder the customer's willingness to adopt M-health. Even though, there is an international interest in testing the adoption of M-heath, in Jordan, there is not any study that has tested such issues. This, in turn, motivates this study to consider the Jordanian health sector as well as to identify the main factors that could shape the Jordanian individual intention to adopt M-health applications.

3   Conceptual Model and Research Hypotheses

As noticed in the previous studies, there are a number of factors such as performance expectancy, usefulness, and social influence. The importance of these factors have been repeated in different studies (Alalwan et al. 2017; Dwivedi et al. 2016, 2017a, b; Hoque and Sorwar 2017; Lee and Han 2015). Therefore, these factors namely: perceived usefulness and social influence were considered in the current study model. However, over the mobile technology literature, innovativeness and awareness have been largely validated as key predictors of customers intention to adopt Mobile technology (i.e. Kapoor et al. 2015; Lu et al. 2005; Slade et al. 2015; Lee and Son 2017; Velmurugan and Velmurugan 2014). Therefore, both innovativeness and awareness were considered in the current study model. It was also supposed that perceived usefulness could be predicted by both innovativeness and awareness. The proposed conceptual model and research hypothesises are presented below (Fig. 1):

H1: Perceived usefulness will positively influence people intention to adopt Mhealth in Jordan.
H2: Social influence will positively influence Jordanian people intention to adopt M-health.
H3: Innovativeness will positively influence Jordanian people intention to adopt Mhealth.
H4: Innovativeness will positively influence perceived usefulness of M-health.
H5: Awareness will positively influence Jordanian people intention to adopt Mhealth.
H6: Awareness will positively influence perceived usefulness of M-health.

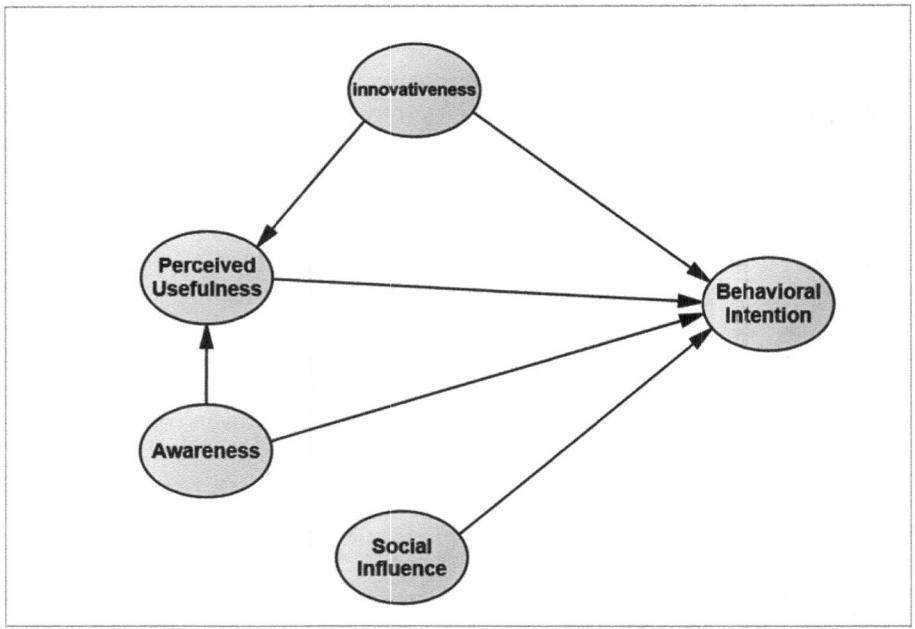

Fig. 1. Conceptual model   Adapted from Dwivedi et al. (2016), Lee and Son (2017), Velmurugan and Velmurugan (2014)

4   Research Methodology

A questionnaire survey was conducted to collect the required data from a convenience sample size of 600 Jordanian people. Those respondents were approached in several places at hospitals and medical centers in Jordan. Researchers firstly provided those respondents with a brief about the concept of M-health and their features and benefits. Then, the questionnaire was left with respondents to be completed. The main scale items of usefulness and behavioral intention was tested from scale proposed by Davis et al. (1989). Social influence was tested using measure items from Venkatesh et al. (2012). A scale used by Aldás-Manzano et al. (2009) was considered to test Innovativeness while Rogers (2003) scale was adopted to examine awareness. Seven point Likert scale was employed to test these items. The questionnaire was converted to Arabic using back translation method suggested by Brislin (1976). A pilot study was also applied to for more sureness regarding factors reliability and validity. The results in this regard largely support all factors validity as well as Cronbach's alpha not less than 0.70 was recorded for all factors (Nunnally 1978).

5   Results

5.1   Response Rate

Out of 600 questionnaires allocated, 365 that are returned and found to be valid for further analyses. The vast majority of respondents (41.6%) were noticed to be within age group of 25 to 35. About 52.6% of the current study participants were female where about 47.4% are male. Regarding the educational level, more than 70% of respondents hold a bachelor degree or above and have income level between 400 JOD and 800 JOD. Descriptive statistics also indicted that more than 93.2% have been using smart phones for more than 3 years.

5.2   Structural Equation Modeling Analyses (SEM)

Two stage method of SEM was applied using AMOS 21.0. Five factors (BI, USF, AW, SI, and INN) with their items are targeted in the first stage of SEM: measurement model. The revised version of the measurement model was noticed to be adequately fit the observed data as all fit indices were noticed within their acceptable level as follow: CMIN/DF was 2.874, GFI = 0.921, AGFI = 0.886, NFI = 0.932, CFI = 0.958 and RMSEA = 0.055 (Hair et al. 2010; Byrne 2010). Both average variance extracted (AVE) and composite reliability (CR) were also examined and their results as presented in Table 1 existing withier their cut-off value (higher than 0.70 for CR and 0.60 for AVE). As seen in Table 1, the squared root of AVE for each construct was larger than the corresponding inter-constructs-correlation estimates, which in turn, supports the discriminant validity of the current study constructs.

Table 1. Constructs reliability and validity

	CR	AVE	SI	USF	INN	AW	BI
SI	0.885	0.722	0.850				
USF	0.874	0.637	0.299	0.798			
INN	0.910	0.773	0.350	0.249	0.879		
AW	0.901	0.696	0.498	0.280	0.685	0.834	
BI	0.891	0.673	0.357	0.353	0.492	0.402	0.821

At the second stage of SEM, structural model was tested with six causal paths that are presented in the current study model. The fit indices of structural model were approved to have acceptable values as such CMIN/DF was 2.954, GFI = 0.913, AGFI = 0.854, NFI = 0.921, CFI = 0.95 and RMSEA = 0.058 (Hair et al. 2010; Byrne 2010). About 45% of variance was accounted in the behavioural intention to use Mobile health care applications and about 32% of variance in perceived usefulness (Table 2).

According to the path coefficient analyses, innovativeness ($\gamma = 0.39$, p < 0.000) was the most powerful factor affecting Jordanian customer's intention to adopt Mobile healthcare applications followed by perceived usefulness ($\gamma = 0.22$, p < 0.000); and

Table 2. Results of standardized estimates of structural model

	Hypothesized path	Estimate	S.E.	C.R.	P
H1	BI <—	USF	0.22	.072	3.843	***
H2	BI <—	SI	0.13	.042	3.129	.002
H3	BI <—	INN	0.39	.050	5.966	***
H4	USF <—	INN	0.15	.042	2.187	.029
H5	USF <—	AW	0.16	.042	2.325	.020
H6	BI <—	AW	0.03	.050	.042	.966

then social influence ($\gamma = 0.13$, $p < 0.002$). Yet, awareness does not reflect any variance in the behavioural intention ($\gamma = 0.03$, $p < 0.966$). Further, USF was found to be significantly predicted by the role of both innovativeness ($\gamma = 0.15$ $p < 0.029$); and awareness ($\gamma = 0.16 < 0.20$).

6 Discussion

As proposed in the current study introduction, this study attempts to provide further understanding regarding the main factors that could shape the Jordanian people perception and intention toward M-health. Thus, an empirical study was necessarily to be conducted. The main statistical results yielded largely supported the predictive validity of the current study model due to the fact that about 45% and 32% of variance was accounted in behavioural intention and perceived usefulness. This, in turn, supports the theoretical foundation proposed in the current study.

Statistical results also supported the impacting role of innovativeness in contributing both perceived usefulness and behavioural intention. This means that those respondents who have a high degree of innovativeness are more likely to positively value the benefits and utilities of M-health as well as they are more likely to be motivated to adopt such system soon. This could be attributed to the fact that Mhealth as any other mobile technologies is more novel and pioneer system, and accordingly, it is a manifestation of modern life. Different Mobile technology studies that have addressed the role of innovativeness such as Lu et al. (2005), Slade et al. (2015), Lee and Son (2017).

Perceived usefulness was the second strongest factor enhancing the behavioural intention to adopt M-health. As long as individuals perceived using M-health more efficient and productive than traditional way of attaining health services, they will be more motivated to adopt such services. In fact, Mobile technology and all related applications enjoy with high degree of Mobility, which in turns, empower individuals to access a wide range of services without time and place restrictions. As well as, Mhealth helps patients particularly to reduce waiting time of medical services and accordingly saving their time and efforts as well. Such results related to perceived usefulness are in the line with these studies that have supported the related area of Mhealth applications (i.e. Rana et al. 2017; Lee and Han 2015; Dwivedi et al. 2016). Statistical results have proved the role of social influence in predicting behavioral intention to adopt M-health. This means that people are more affected by the opinion and suggestions coming from their social system. Such results could be attributed to the fact that social system in Jordan positively look at the mobile applications overall and people would like to share and generalize their positive experience with such applications with their friends, colleagues, and relatives. From the other hand, Mhealth is very new and novel technology. Accordingly, individuals who do not have adequate experience and information to cope with such novel and new systems are more likely to be influenced by opinions and information coming from people surrounding them (Venkatesh et al. 2012). Such results are compatible to other studies that have assured the role of social influence (i.e. Dwivedi et al. 2016; Hoque and Sorwar 2017).

Finally, even though there was not any effect for awareness on the behavioural intention, awareness is still very important factor in the current study model by it impact on the perceived usefulness. People who fully aware the main features of Mhealth and its associated benefits are more likely to perceive using such system as more productive and saving their time and efforts. This could be returned to increase health awareness and the importance of health technology among people in Jordan and worldwide. There is good number of studies (i.e. Kapoor et al. 2013; Vishwanath and Goldhaber 2003; Ajili et al. 2012; Alsheikh and Bojei 2014) that have supported the role of awareness in shaping the people perception toward new systems.

6.1   Theoretical and Practical Implications

Even though there is a growing interest in studying the related issues of M-health applications, this area still require further examination and explanation. Therefore, this study represents a good theoretical contribution by focusing more on the main aspects of M-health. In details, this study was successfully able to propose a solid theoretical model comprising a group of the most important factors (i.e. perceived usefulness and social influence). As well as, innovativeness and awareness have not been considered by prior M-health studies. Therefore, this study introduces another considerable contribution by expanding the current understanding regarding these factors. Further, the data was collected from 365 respondents and are analysed using SEM. By doing so, this study was successfully able to provide solid statistical evidence regarding the main factors predicting behavioural intention to adopt Mhealth. There are a few studies that have tested the adoption of M-health in developing countries. This is in addition to the fact that there is no study that has tested such technology in Jordan yet. Accordingly, This study represents a real contribution by expanding the current awareness and understanding regarding this phenomena in Jordan and developing countries as well.

From practical perspectives, a number of issues related to the current study findings have to be the focus of attention of M-heath service providers. Firstly, the significant role of usefulness should be taken into account. For instance, health organizations have to convince their target market about the benefits and utilities comprised in using M-heath such as less waiting time, less efforts, more convenience of time and location than traditional tools to attain the medical services. Organizations have also focus more in the novelty and newness of M-health along with the fact that using M-heath is a part of current modern life. This, in turn, will largely enhance the level of innovativeness existing in using M-health.

7 Limitations and Future Research Directions

There is a number of limitations that have to be addressed in the current study. Such as, convenience sampling was used in comparison with probability sampling method. This, in turn, reflects on the generalizability of the current study results. Further, this study only considers the behavioural intention while the actual use of M-health was nt tested. Thus, future studies could provide more accurate view about this area by considering the actual use behaviour. This study does not take into account the impact of resources and facilities required to use M-health, which in turn, represents an important of direction should be tested by future studies. The moderation effect of age and gender was not tested in the current study. Accordingly, these aspects have been the focus of attention of future studies. Finally, this study was conducted in Jordan, and accordingly, testing the related issues of M-health in different developing and developed countries could provide further understanding in this respect.

References

Alalwan, A.A., Dwivedi, Y.K., Rana, N.P.: Factors influencing adoption of mobile banking by Jordanian bank customers: extending UTAUT2 with trust. Int. J. Inf. Manage. **37**(3), 99–110 (2017)

Alalwan, A.A., Dwivedi, Y.K., Rana, N.P., Williams, M.D.: Consumer adoption of mobile banking in Jordan: examining the role of usefulness, ease of use, perceived risk and self-efficacy. J. Enterp. Inf. Manag. **29**(1), 118–139 (2016)

Aldás-Manzano, J., Lassala-Navarré, C., Ruiz-Mafé, C., Sanz-Blas, S.: The role of consumer innovativeness and perceived risk in online banking usage. Int. J. Bank Mark. **27**(1), 53–75 (2009)

Atallah, N., Khalifa, M., Elmetwally, A., Househ, M.: The Prevalence and Usage of Mobile Health Applications among Mental Health Patients in Saudi Arabia. Comput. Methods Programs Biomed. **156**, 163–168 (2018)

Brislin, R.: Comparative research methodology: Cross-cultural studies. Int. J. Psychol. **11**(3), 215–229 (1976)

Brown III, W., Yen, P.Y., Rojas, M., Schnall, R.: Assessment of the Health IT Usability Evaluation Model (Health-ITUEM) for evaluating mobile health (mHealth) technology. J. Biomed. Inform. **46**(6), 1080–1087 (2013)

Byrne, B.: Structural Equation Modeling with AMOS: Basic Concepts, Applications and Programming, 6th edn. Taylor & Francis Group, New York, USA (2010)

Davis, F.D., Bagozzi, R.P., Warshaw, P.R.: User acceptance of computer technology: a comparison of two theoretical models. Manage. Sci. **35**(8), 982–1003 (1989)

Deng, Z., Mo, X., Liu, S.: Comparison of the middle-aged and older users' adoption of mobile health services in China. Int. J. Med. Inform. **83**(3), 210–224 (2014)

Dwivedi, Y.K., Rana, N.P., Janssen, M., Lal, B., Williams, M.D., Clement, M.: An empirical validation of a unified model of electronic government adoption (UMEGA). Gov. Inf. Q. **34**(2), 211–230 (2017a)

Dwivedi, Y.K., Rana, N.P., Jeyaraj, A., Clement, M., Williams, M.D. Re-examining the unified theory of acceptance and use of technology (UTAUT): towards a revised theoretical model. Inf. Syst. Front., 1–16 (2017b). https://doi.org/10.1007/s10796-017-9774-y

Dwivedi, Y.K., Shareef, M.A., Simintiras, A.C., Lal, B., Weerakkody, V.: A generalised adoption model for services: A cross-country comparison of mobile health (m-health). Gov. Inf. Q. **33**(1), 174187 (2016)

Hair Jr., J.F., Black, W.C., Babin, B.J., Anderson, R.E.: Multivariate Data Analysis: A Global Perspective, 7th edn. Pearson Education International, Upper Saddle River (2010)

Hoque, R., Sorwar, G.: Understanding factors influencing the adoption of mHealth by the elderly: an extension of the UTAUT model. Int. J. Med. Inform. **101**, 75–84 (2017)

Kapoor, K.K., Dwivedi, Y.K., Williams, M.D.: Empirical examination of the role of three sets of innovation attributes for determining adoption of IRCTC mobile ticketing service. Inf. Syst. Manag. **32**(2), 153–173 (2015)

Lee, E., Han, S.: Determinants of adoption of mobile health services. Online Inf. Rev. **39**(4), 556–573 (2015)

Lee, J., Son, J.: The effects of consumer innovativeness on mobile app download: focusing on comparison of innovators and noninnovators. Mob. Inf. Syst. (2017)

Lu, J., Yao, J.E., Yu, C.S.: Personal innovativeness, social influences and adoption of wireless internet services via mobile technology. J. Strateg. Inf. Syst. **14**(3), 245–268 (2005)

Nunnally, J.C.: Psychometric Theory. McGraw-Hill, New York, NY (1978)

Rana, N.P., Dwivedi, Y.K., Lal, B., Williams, M.D., Clement, M.: Citizens' adoption of an electronic government system: towards a unified view. Inf. Syst. Front. **19**(3), 549–568 (2017)

Rogers, E.M.: Diffusion of Innovations, 5th edn. Free Press, New York, NY (2003)

Schnall, R., et al.: A user-centered model for designing consumer mobile health (mHealth) applications (apps). J. Biomed. Inform. **60**, 243–251 (2016)

Shareef, M.A., Archer, N., Dwivedi, Y.K.: Examining adoption behavior of mobile government. J. Comput. Inf. Syst. **53**(2), 3949 (2012)

Shareef, M.A., Baabdullah, A., Dutta, S., Kumar, V., Dwivedi, Y.K.: Consumer adoption of mobile banking services: an empirical examination of factors according to adoption stages. J. Retail. Consum. Serv. **43**, 54–67 (2018)

Shareef, M.A., Dwivedi, Y.K., Kumar, V., Kumar, U.: Reformation of public service to meet citizens' needs as customers: evaluating SMS as an alternative service delivery channel. Comput. Hum. Behav. **61**, 255–270 (2016)

Singh, K., Landman, A., Bates, D.W.: Mobile health applications: the authors reply. Health Aff. **36**(2), 384–384 (2017)

Slade, E.L., Dwivedi, Y.K., Piercy, N.C., Williams, M.D.: Modeling consumers' adoption intentions of remote mobile payments in the United Kingdom: extending UTAUT with innovativeness, risk, and trust. Psychol. Mark. **32**(8), 860–873 (2015)

Statista (2018b). https://www.statista.com/statistics/276623/number-of-appsavailable-in-leading-app-stores/

Statista (2018c). https://www.statista.com/topics/2263/mhealth/

The Jordan Times (2015). http://www.jordantimes.com/news/local/mobile-clinicsouthern-region-boost-healthcare-services%E2%80%99

Velmurugan, M.S., Velmurugan, M.S.: Consumers' awareness, perceived ease of use toward information technology adoption in 3G mobile phones' usages in India. Asian J. Mark. **8**(1), 1–23 (2014)

Venkatesh, V., Morris, M., Davis, G., Davis, F.: User acceptance of information technology: toward a unified view. MIS Q. **27**(3), 425–478 (2003)

Venkatesh, V., Thong, J.Y.L., Xu, X.: Consumer acceptance and use of information technology: extending the unified theory of acceptance and use of technology. MIS Q. **36**(1), 157–178 (2012)

The Determinants of RFID Use and Its Benefits in Hospitals: An Empirical Study Examining Beyond Adoption

Mohammad Alamgir Hossain[1](✉) and Azizah Ahmad[2]

[1] School of Business IT and Logistics, RMIT University, Melbourne, Australia
mohammad.hossain@rmit.edu.au
[2] Institute for Advanced and Smart Digital Opportunities, School of Computing,
Universiti Utara Malaysia, Sintok, Malaysia
azie@uum.edu.my

Abstract. Going beyond traditional 'adoption', this study examines the determinants of the 'use' of radio frequency identification (RFID) technology and identifies the perceived benefits of such use. From extant literature, we developed a research model from organizational setting (i.e., hospitals), which we validated using survey data from 142 healthcare organizations. The collected data were analyzed by partial-least-squares (PLS) methods. The results show that a hospital's RFID use is influenced by the following technological organizational-environmental (TOE) factors: *information privacy* (technology), *absorptive capacity* and *resource readiness* (organization), and *coercive pressure* (environment). RFID use, in turn, impacts both economic and operational benefits. Additionally, *size of hospital* found to be an important control variable to RFID use. Therefore we further investigated the combined effect of *hospital size* and *RFID use* on *perceived benefits* (i.e., the moderation effect). The results showed that *hospital size* has moderating effect on the relationship between *RFID use* and *economic benefits*, but not between *RFID use* and *operational benefits*. The implications, particularly from the perspective of a healthcare setting, have been discussed.

Keywords: RFID · Adoption · Use · Hospital · TOE framework
Empirical

1 Introduction

In the field of information systems (IS), in order to examine the success (or failure) of an innovation, behavioral studies have traditionally and predominantly focused on the adoption perspective – by examining the process by which an innovation is accepted [1]. Nevertheless, some studies also examined the 'continuance' behavior in individual setting [2], which is slightly different in organizational setting where adoption is followed by routinization and extension [3]. The common aspect of both types of studies is they rely on 'intention' of users – both to adopt and continue the use of an innovation. However, scholars argue that 'intention' does not necessarily always confirm the actual success of a technology. They suggest to ascertain actual usage criteria believing 'usage' "as a surrogate measure for information systems success" [4, p. 144]. Also, Shih and Venkatesh [5] acknowledged that studying 'adoption' is important but we should investigate more on the 'use' behavior. They further suggested that, in order to claim the success (or failure) of an innovation, the relevant outcomes should be studied. Therefore, this research aims to examine the determinants of RFID use and the perceived benefits of such use.

Though RFID technology has been invented in 1940s, its industrial and commercial application was not discernible before the mandates imposed by Wal*Mart and the Department of Defense (DoD), USA to their suppliers in late 90 s. Since then, the application and use of RFID continues to grow. According to Mark Roberti, the Editor of RFID Journal, *"companies will have no choice but to use RFID, just as they have no choice but to use the Internet today"* [6, p. 16]. His prediction comes true as RFID technology now has been used in almost every industry including retail, manufacturing, service, and agriculture [7]. In the service industry itself, RFID has been used in libraries, museums, and hospitals [7].

A basic RFID system consists of three components: (a) each *tag* is comprised of a microchip and an antenna, (b) *reader* communicates with tags, and (c) *software/middleware* transfers data. The tags, which can be attached to virtually anything, receive signal with their antennas and 'backscatter' their stored data to the reader via low-power radio frequencies [8]. The reader decodes received data and transfers it to database(s) through middleware. RFID can identify an object uniquely and can store large amount of data ($\sim$ 30 times more than a traditional barcode) [8]. In fact, RFID is the only technology that permits simultaneous scanning. Hence, RFID has tremendous potential in hospitals because of its ability to identify the patients as well as medical devices uniquely and efficiently with no human interventions (e.g., as manual scanning is required with barcode technology) [8]. In recent times, many hospitals and healthcare facilities use RFID tags on patient wristbands (e.g., newborn infants) and valuable assets to provide accurate identification. Also RFID readers install at doors and other appropriate locations determine patients' and assets' locations. This mechanism additionally restricts unauthorized access to designated areas [9].

Looking at the literature related to RFID adoption-diffusion in hospitals, few attempts can be reported. For example, along with the literature review [7], Cao et al. [10] conducted a case study explaining adoption of RFID in hospitals. Similarly, Chen et al. [2] identified the key drivers for continued use of RFID in emergency rooms. However, a convincing growth is yet to observe in terms of RFID use in hospitals [11], although RFID is believed to provide the highest possible safety to a patient, and where hospitals can save enormously by increasing efficiencies in patient care as well as managing assets [12]. It is imperative that RFID should be seriously considered by related authorities. One potential solution is to develop confidence to the decision-makers with providing empirical evidence and successful cases from already-adopters. Our study examines the elements that may lead to RFID use in hospitals, it also incorporates the perceived benefits; and thus we reveal the perceptions of the actual players who already use RFID. Thus, this study offers implications to decision-makers to understand important factors and thereby to take informed decisions.

2 The Research Model

2.1 The Determinants of RFID Use in Hospitals

In order to examine the determinants of RFID use in hospitals, the technology organization-environment (TOE) framework, proposed by Tornatzky and Fleischer [13], has been considered as the theoretical underpinning. TOE is one of the popular theoretical frameworks used to study the organizational behavior towards accepting a technological innovation. TOE posits that the acceptance decision of a technology is dependent on technological, organizational, and environmental characteristics. Since its inception TOE has been tested in various domains and received a lot of empirical support; RFID field is no exception [e.g., 2, 10]. However, although a few attempts have been observed to identify TOE variables and to develop a conceptual/research model [2, 10], as far the authors' knowledge, no empirical work has been reported that validated a TOE model in hospitals' setting. Moreover, little is known if TOE framework holds right when is extended beyond the 'acceptance' phenomenon (i.e., to study 'use'). Based on the extant literature on RFID, we draw upon this framework to understand the use of RFID and the relevant benefits in an organizational setting.

Technological Dimensions. Tornatzky and Fleischer [13] evidenced that relative advantage (e.g., perceived usefulness), complexity, and compatibility are the main technological factors that impact technology implementation; their role has been well studied in RFID-literature [e.g., 14]. In addition, in the context of RFID use in hospitals, *information privacy* of the customers and *information accuracy* are critical [7] and therefore have been considered as the technological variables in our model.

Information Privacy. In healthcare setting, *informational privacy* is the right of a patient to control "over the collection, use, disclosure and retention of his or her personal information, including his or her personal health information" [15, p. 7]. In this definition the critical aspect is *personal health information*, which the Personal Health Information Protection Act (PHIPA) defines as identifying information about an individual that, among other things, relates to the physical or mental health of the individual, identifies a provider of health care to the individual, or identifies the substitute decision-maker of the individual [17]. Under PHIPA compliance, health service custodians (e.g., hospitals, health-care practitioners, pharmacies) are allowed to collect, use and disclose personal health information only with the consent of the individual to whom the personal health information relates. They are also required to comply with the wishes of an individual who withholds or withdraws consent, or who gives express instructions that the information must not be used or disclosed elsewhere [15].

RFID systems introduce a key ethical concern regarding information privacy because of its strength (e.g., unique identification of the objects, tracking and tracing of the movements of objects, etc.). It is understood that patients' confidentiality is extremely important and highly challenging in healthcare industry than in other industries (e.g., retail). In healthcare facilities, when an RFID tag is associated with a patient, a unique number is assigned to the patient. The number can associate with any type of personal information, such as patient name, gender, address, medical history, drug therapy program, and more. In our context, privacy concerns can include inappropriate collection, intentional misuse, or unauthorized disclosure of healthcare information resulting from RFID use. The higher provision of protecting patients' personal health information generated from an RFID system, the higher will be its use [7, 10]. Therefore:

H1: Information privacy is positively associated with RFID use in hospitals.

Data Accuracy. Accuracy of data generated by RFID systems is critical for hospitals and patients. However, RFID systems are not always reliable. The accuracy of RFID data is dependent on several factors including tagged object, tag placement, angle of rotation, read distance, and if the transmission is affected by electromagnetic waves generated by other systems. Besides, presence of local magnetic interference, metal objects, or liquid containing items can also affect read accuracy and thus data accuracy [7]. As RFID signals can be affected by interference of the other devices using low-frequencies and transmit signals, data may create 'noise' and produce dirty data [17]. In a hospital, RFID systems need to be able to locate the assets (e.g., patients, doctors, medical equipment) accurately [18]. Based on common organizational behavior, higher the possibility of reliable and accurate data generated by RFID systems, there will be higher use of RFID in hospitals [7]. Therefore:

H2: Accuracy of information obtained from RFID systems is positively associated with RFID use in hospitals.

Organizational Dimensions. Organizational factors explain why some organizations perform better than others, in terms of adopting and using a technology. TOE suggests that organizational characteristics are extremely relevant and must be considered in any organizational innovation research [13]. In the context of hospitals, *absorptive capacity* and *resource readiness* are critical [10].

Absorptive Capacity. Absorptive capacity can be defined as "a set of organizational routines and strategic processes by which firms acquire, assimilate, transform, and exploit knowledge for purpose of value creation" [19, p. 198]. IS studies, dealing with organizational adoption and use of technology- and knowledge-based innovation, consider *absorptive capacity* as an important organizational characteristic [e.g., 20]. RFID studies too understand that, both the knowledge that an organization hold and obtain from different sources help them to develop managerial absorptive capacity. To be successful, acquired knowledge needs to be applied to perform operational tasks. Generally it is accepted that the higher the capability of a hospital to assimilate and exploit RFID knowledge, the higher will be the use of RFID. Hence:

H3: Absorptive capacity of the management of a hospital is positively associated with RFID use in hospitals.

Resource Readiness. A complex and expensive technological innovation like RFID needs strong resource-base. Social cognitive theory emphasize "...*People will not adopt innovations even though they are favorable disposed toward them if they lack the money, the skills, or the resources that may be needed. The more resources innovations require, the lower their adoptability*" [21, p. 290]. RFID adoption and use comes with the availability of financial and human resources of an organization [3].

Financial resource is required to pay the associated costs including implementation, integration, and on-going costs. And, availability of technical resources, such as technical know-how and expertise, are critical for RFID use because RFID projects require technical expertise to address the implementation and maintenance challenges and to customize the software according to the business processes [3]. Currently, lack of skilled RFID professionals is a major challenge; around 80% of the companies do not have access to skilled RFID workers [22]. It is more likely that a hospital with sufficient resource readiness will be more in a position to use RFID than the others [23]. Thus:

H4: Resource readiness is positively associated with RFID use in hospitals.

Environmental Dimensions. Organizations do not operate in isolation; they do need to comply with the rules and regulations from external environment (e.g., industry standards) while fighting against competitors [13]. Recalling the impact of Wal*Mart and DoD, in general, environmental factors have been recognized as important drivers for the organizational adoption of RFID. In the context of RFID technology in healthcare industry, the environmental factors are *coercive pressure* to compliance with legislations and *environmental uncertainty* [3].

Coercive Pressure. Unlike retail supply chain where Wal*Mart and other retailers are driving RFID deployment, there are no entities requiring health care providers to implement RFID. However, the U.S. Food and Drug Administration (FDA) is planning to mandate RFID technology for device and patient identification in hospitals [8]. Also, FDA and the Healthcare Distribution Management Association (HDMA) issued an 'endorsement', however not a mandate, recommending tagging drugs at palletlevel (but encouraging item-level tagging for the drugs that are small but expensive and therefore are more likely to be counterfeited) [9, 23]. Thus the pressure to use RFID in healthcare outlets is becoming more apparent than before. The pressure is also coming from patients, insurance companies [24], and medical practitioners [8]. Altogether, the more the pressure a hospital experiences from the external entities, the more will be RFID use. Therefore, we postulate:

H5: Coercive pressure is positively associated with RFID use in hospitals.

Environmental Uncertainty. In an RFID-based business-environment, external uncertainty is related to the inability to predict the demand of RFID data should customers' need and preference are changed [25] and uncertainty of RFID standards [24]. Kimberly and Evanisko [26] found that environmental uncertainty would influence the organizational adoption of RFID in hospitals. Since RFID is still in its early stage of development and acceptance by hospitals, there are large numbers of questions that are unanswered with regard to its actual use. There are always unpleasant uncertainties about the return-on-investment and the size of the market of RFID, and with regard to the capabilities of the technology itself (see discussion on *data accuracy*). Also, to some extent, the effect of RFID on inter-organizational relationships is uncertain [25]. The cumulative impact of uncertainty is negatively associated with its use.

H6: Environmental uncertainty is negatively associated with RFID use in hospitals.

2.2 The Benefits of RFID Use in Hospitals

Economic Benefits. RFID-based systems can help prevent valuable assets and equipment from stealing [12]. It is estimated that, by implementing RFID, a 200-bed hospital can save $600,000 annually while a 500-bed could save $1 million from less shrinkage and improved staff productivity [17]. RFID systems increases hospitals' efficiencies (discussed in the next section), which also save costs through efficiency improvements [7] and improving inventory and asset tracking [24]. RFID reduces insurance premium too [7]. Consequently, an RFID system has substantial economic benefits to offer to a hospital. Therefore we propose:

H7: RFID use in hospitals is positively associated with higher economic benefits.

Operational Benefits. RFID systems increase patient care by quick retrieval of patient information [7]. RFID supports staff with immediate and accurate access to patient information, assisting quick and correct decisions. RFID systems also can identify patient's current location and traces back the prior locations and thus improve accuracy of patient information, especially for infants and old. An advanced setting also improves patient drug compliance (e.g., allergy) and alerts in case of errors (e.g., wrong medication, excessive dosage, and incompatibility with the patient). Furthermore, RFID-based asset management systems can find the required equipment with minimal delay and can save lives [2]. Besides, security can be improved by RFID enabled access control systems [1, 7]. Overall, RFID systems can improve operational efficiency significantly. Hence, we suggest:

H8: RFID use in hospitals is associated with higher operational benefits.

3 Research Method

This research adopted quantitative method. An online survey collected responses from mid-level and senior managers of hospitals from China where the hospitals have been using RFID for some time. Overall, 166 respondents were returned but 14 were unusable. Among them 62.3% are private and the rest are public hospitals. The respondents are from various positions: director and above 16.8%, departmental administrator/manager 21.6%, unit administrator/manager 32.7%, and the rest (28.9%) are executives. In terms of number of employees, 27.5% have over 500 employees, about 34.5% have between 100 and 500 employees, and the rest 38% have below 100 employees.

The constructs have been measured with items from prior literature. Specifically, *information privacy* was adopted from [29] and *data accuracy* from [18, 30]. *Absorptive capacity* was measured with items used in [19]. The measures of *resource readiness, coercive pressure, and external uncertainty* were adopted from [3]. *RFID use* was adopted from [31], *operational benefits* were from [32], and *economic benefits* from [30]. We considered the number of employees as a proxy of size of hospital [33]. Data were analyzed by partial least squares (PLS) methods [34].

4   Results

4.1   Evaluating the Measurement Model

Following standard PLS procedure, the validity of the constructs was established by examining their reliability, convergent validity, and discriminant validity. *First*, internal consistency of each construct was calculated with composite reliability (CR) value of >=0.7 [34]. *Second*, in order to evaluate convergent validity, outer loadings of the indicators and average variance extracted (AVE) were calculated; all items achieved the 0.7 threshold of loading (*see* Table 1) and the constructs with 0.5 AVE [34]. The values of CR and AVE are reported in Table 2. *Third*, discriminant validity was assessed based on two methods: cross-loading matrix (not reported in the paper because of the space constraint), and Fornell-Larcker criterion (*see* Table 2). The collective evidence suggests that the constructs demonstrate good measurement properties.

Table 1. The psychometric properties of the constructs

Items	Loading	Item	Loading
IP1. No serious privacy problem	0.912	CP1. Agencies push for RFID	0.936
IP2. Can handle personal info securely	0.937	CP2. Becoming a requirement	0.948
IP3. No concern with privacy	0.821	CP3. Without RFID will lose market	0.964
IP4. No threats to privacy	0.743	CP4. Difficult to run without RFID	0.915
DA1. Enhances data accuracy	0.942	EU1. Technology keeps changing	0.881
DA2. Enhances asset visibility	0.875	EU2. Not sure what data needed	0.933
DA3. Can capture most 'things'	0.934	EU3. Requirements vary	0.943
DA4. Locate equipment correctly	0.856	EB1. Loss prevention	0.930
AC1. Good at acquiring new knowledge	0.846	EB2. Inventory spoilage	0.900
AC2. Recognize market demand quickly	0.891	EB3. Quicken processes	0.921
AC3. Staff share (new) experience	0.882	OB1. Improves resource utilization	0.962
AC4. Clearly know how activities should be performed	0.716	OB2. Mainstreaming administrative processes	0.980
RR1. Financial resource	0.864	OB3. Improves communication	0.971
RR2. Expert human	0.932	USE1. Number of times use/day	0.901
RR3. Technical resources	0.890	USE2. Number of applications	0.910
		USE3. % of operations done by RFID	0.894

Table 2. Construct reliability and discriminant validity tests

	CR	AVE	IP	DA	AC	RR	CP	EU	EB	OP	USE
IP	0.946	0.815	**0.903**								
DA	0.916	0.734	0.412	**0.857**							
AC	0.903	0.700	0.278	0.517	**0.837**						
RR	0.913	0.723	0.506	0.634	0.263	**0.850**					
CP	0.969	0.886	0.283	0.653	0.498	0.621	**0.941**				
EU	0.943	0.846	0.398	0.806	0.272	0.737	0.658	**0.920**			
EB	0.940	0.840	0.549	0.756	0.518	0.546	0.525	0.578	**0.917**		
OB	0.980	0.943	0.821	0.192	0.204	0.440	0.050	0.154	0.419	**0.971**	
USE	0.936	0.785	0.417	0.592	0.691	0.619	0.821	0.514	0.612	0.317	**0.886**

4.2 Testing the Structural Model and Moderating Effects

The results of the structural model are summarized in Table 3. It is observed that among the eight hypotheses leading from the determinants, H1, H3, H4, and H6 were supported. Then, both hypotheses related to use and benefits (i.e., H7, H8) are accepted. The R^2 (0.831) value of *RFID use* is 'substantial'.

We also examined the effect of two control variables. It was found that *size of hospital* had significant effect on *RFID use* ($\beta = 0.110$, $t = 2.441$, $p = 0.015$), which implies that larger hospitals are more likely to be higher user of RFID. However, *type of hospital* (private *vs.* public) did not have an impact ($\beta = 0.003$, $t = 0.066$, $p = 0.947$). Since the *size of hospital* had an impact on *RFID use*, it is possible that *hospital size* also has an impact on *perceived benefits*. Therefore, we tested the moderating effect of *hospital size* on the relationship between *RFID use* and *perceived benefits*. The two stage moderation tests showed that *hospital size* moderates the relationship between *RFID use* ($\beta = 0.233$, $t = 2.832$, $p = 0.005$) and *economic benefit*, but not on the relationship between *RFID use* and *operation benefit* ($\beta = 0.058$, $t = 0.599$, $p = 0.550$).

Table 3. Hypotheses testing

	β value	t statistics	p value		β value	t statistics	p value
H1	0.093*	2.548	0.011	H5	0.541	6.319***	0.000
H2	−0.87ns	0.708	0.480	H6	−0.120	1.067ns	0.287
H3	0.381***	6.992	0.000	H7	0.762	9.422***	0.000
H4	0.245*	2.593	0.010	H8	0.371	2.874**	0.004

Significance level $*p < 0.05$, $**p < 0.01$, $***p < 0.001$; ns: not significant

5 Discussion and Implications

5.1 Technological Variables

The findings of this study showed statistical evidence to support a positive relationship between *information privacy* and *RFID use* in hospitals. Privacy, specifically to information, is a critical component of civilization. Everyone has the right not to disclose (and stop others to do so) his or her personal information. This right is more critical in Asian societies where people do not feel comfortable to share medical conditions with others, especially if it is related with sexual behavior (e.g., HIV, impotence), drug treatments, and mental disorder, among many. In a traditional healthcare facility in Asia, leaking information is a common phenomenon. As RFID systems secure access control (to rooms and even documents), only authorized people can access to the customer information. Top of that, RFID systems use privacy-enhancing technological measures (e.g., anonymization), which improves information security. In case of a privacy incident, by using tracking history, at least the people who accessed the information can be obtained. Therefore, although initially RFID was treated as a technology to hamper information privacy, the current safeguard mechanisms actually prove that RFID systems rather increase data/information privacy; consequently, healthcare facilitates and patients are welcoming this technology.

However, the influence of *data accuracy* is not significant. In recent times, technological developments overcome the limitations of RFID (e.g., working in liquid and metal environments). Therefore, it is plausible that the respondents are confident that RFID is well capable of producing quality data at any environment (e.g., having other devices emitting radio signals, from any angle, etc.). Still, management should revisit strategies periodically ensuring how data accuracy can be sustained and improved.

5.2   Organizational Variables

Regarding the organizational factors it is found that both *absorptive capacity* and *resource readiness* are important for RFID use in hospitals; the relative values suggest that the former variable is more important. It is important for the hospitals' strategic management to understand the value and capability of RFID technology and then apply it in operational applications. They need to plan how the organizational knowledge can be used to apply RFID in operational operations and get the most out of it. This research indicates that a hospital which has higher absorptive capacity is better in a position to use RFID systems; in other words, higher the absorptive capacity, higher will be the use of RFID. This result suggests that absorptive capacity is a necessary condition for a hospital to use RFID to its full potential. Therefore, hospitals need to develop the ability to transform and exploit external knowledge as well as process the internal knowledge, and then develop a knowledge management system that integrates the both.

Further, the results suggest that higher resource readiness is associated with higher use of RFID in hospitals. This implies that the management of a hospital needs to configure the required resource, acquire and apply them accordingly so that the use of RFID system is increased. Alongside, they need to develop strategies to address resource issues (e.g., financing, RFID experts) when all possible business processes will be integrated in the RFID system. Such proficiency is essential for successful implementing and maintenance of RFID systems (e.g., for customization, scalability).

5.3   Environmental Variables

This study emphasizes the importance of exercising pressure to influence hospitals to use RFID technology, where applicable. Until the major healthcare agencies mandate RFID in hospitals, pressure could be exercised by the customers, consumer protection advocates, lobbyists, and insurance companies. Meanwhile, the hospitals may experience mimetic and competitive pressure. Interestingly, Angeles [35] found that firms complying with RFID mandates have higher levels of absorptive capacity than their noncompliant counterparts. Therefore, lack of knowledge or expertise would not be an excuse anymore; rather, knowledge and experience can be developed once RFID is used in business operations. Hence, there should be consistent pressure for it.

However, the influence of *(external) environmental uncertainty* is not significant, which is consistent with current literature [e.g., 3]. Given the successful deployment of RFID systems in many hospitals, the respondents can be confident that the demand for RFID-based healthcare systems is the future. The market with stringent demand of RFID-based healthcare system is increasingly getting bigger. Moreover, the technological base of RFID is quite strong since it has been proven since 1940s. Therefore, the respondents of this research obliterate the presence of external uncertainty on RFID use in hospitals.

5.4   Perceived Benefits

Our study advocates that RFID use in hospitals is strongly and positively associated with both economic and operational benefits; this is an encouraging finding against some misperceptions and worries against the benefits reaped from RFID. The main economic benefits actually derive from cost saving. Managing the (expensive) medical assets and human assets with an RFID system will potentially reduce expenses, irregularities, and corruption in a hospital while increasing efficiency. The moderation test further found that bigger hospitals derive more economic benefits from RFID use than the smaller hospitals. It is plausible that the return on investment will be quicker and positive for bigger hospitals when the RFID infrastructure is enjoyed by many operations. Similarly, the economy of scale enables the larger hospitals to lower the costs.

RFID use increases operational benefits in hospitals. The benefits mostly derive from access control and traceability mechanism. Using RFID hospitals limit unwanted access of the visitors and/or staff to certain areas. Such mechanism reduces many irregularities of hospitals operations (e.g., infant misplacing/selling, misuse of blood, organ, medicines, and machineries). Moreover, by using RFID systems hospitals can create a lifetime record of each customer, which can be further used when the patient returns. The non-significant moderation effect of *hospital size* on *operation benefits* suggests that hospitals can derive operational benefits by using RFID systems, regardless of the size. In other words, RFID does offer operational benefits to all hospitals. This encourages hospitals to use RFID systems if the financial calculations support.

6 Limitations and Future Work

This study has some limitations that can be addressed by future research. This study examined the perceived determinants and benefits of RFID use in hospitals, assuming that the 'data analysis capability' of the hospitals is same for each hospital. Also, we suspect that the dependent variable i.e., *RFID use* is over-simplified, which can be better examined with at least two dimensions namely *variety of* use and *rate of use*. It is logical to posit that higher the absorptive capacity a hospital possesses higher will be the variety of use, for example. Therefore, future study can examine the effect of the determinants on these two dimensions. Furthermore, the current study analysed cross-sectional data obtained at a single point of time; further research with longitudinal data may verify the perceptions if they hold same in different point of time (of diffusion stages e.g., implementing, routinization). Finally, a multi-group analysis comparing the perceptions and their relative importance between the already-adopters and yet-to-adopting hospitals would be interesting to understand if the perceptions are consistent and equally important.

References

1. Chong, A.Y.-L., et al.: Predicting RFID adoption in healthcare supply chain from the perspectives of users. Int. J. Prod. Econ. **159**, 6675 (2015)
2. Chen, C.C., et al.: Key drivers for the continued use of RFID technology in the emergency room. Manag. Res. News **31**(4), 273–288 (2008)
3. Hossain, M.A., Quaddus, M., Islam, N.: Developing and validating a model explaining the assimilation process of RFID: an empirical study. Inf. Syst. Front. **18**(4), 645–663 (2016)
4. Taylor, S., Todd, P.A.: Understanding information technology usage: a test of competing models. Inf. Syst. Res. **6**(2), 144–176 (1995)
5. Shih, C.-F., Venkatesh, A.: Beyond adoption: development and application of a use-diffusion model. J. Mark. **68**(1), 59–72 (2004)
6. McGinity, M.: RFID: is this game of tag fair play? Commun. ACM **47**(1), 15–18 (2004)
7. Fosso Wamba, S., Anand, A., Carter, L.: A literature review of RFID-enabled healthcare applications and issues. Int. J. Inf. Manag. **33**(5), 875–891 (2013)
8. Corporation, A.D.: Unique device identification; Comments of Avery Dennison Corporation (2006)
9. Reiner, J., Sullivan, M.: RFID in healthcare: a panacea for the regulations and issues affecting the industry. Healthc. Purch. News **29**(6), 74–76 (2005)
10. Cao, Q., Jones, D.R., Sheng, H.: Contained nomadic information environments: technology, organization, and environment influences on adoption of hospital RFID patient tracking. Inf. Manag. **51**(2), 225–239 (2014)
11. Roberti, M.: Good and bad news about RFID in hospitals (2008). http://www.rfidjournal.com/articles/view?4198. Accessed 16 May 2018
12. Paaske, S., et al.: The benefits and barriers to RFID technology in healthcare. On-Line J. Nurs. Inform. **21**(2), 1–12 (2017)
13. Tornatzky, L.G, Fleischer, M.: Process of Technological Innovation. Lexington Books, Lexington, Mass (1990)
14. Zailani, S., et al.: Determinants of RFID adoption in Malaysia's healthcare industry: occupational level as a moderator. J. Med. Syst. **39**(1), 172 (2015)

15. IPC&HP: RFID and privacy: guidance for health-care providers. information and privacy commissioner of Ontario (IPC)
16. Hewlett-Packard (HP). Personal Health Information Protection Act (2004)
17. Wicks, A.M., Visich, J.K., Li, S.: Radio frequency identification applications in hospital environment. Hosp. Top. **84**(3), 3–9 (2006)
18. van der Togt R., Bakker, P.J., Jaspers, M.W.: A framework for performance and data quality assessment of Radio Frequency IDentification (RFID) systems in health care settings. J. Biomed. Inform. **44**(2), 372–383 (2011)
19. Zahra, S.A., George, G.: Absorptive capacity: a review, reconceptualization, and extension. Academ. Manag. Rev. **27**(2), 185–203 (2002)
20. Park, J.-H., Suh, H.-J., Yang, H.-D.: Perceived absorptive capacity of individual users in performance of Enterprise Resource Planning (ERP) usage: the case for Korean firms. Inf. Manag. **44**(3), 300–312 (2007)
21. Bandura, A.: Social cognitive theory of mass communication. Media Psycholog. **3**(3), 265–299 (2001)
22. Juels, A.: Help wanted. RFID J. (2005). Accessed 29 Aug 2017 https://www.rfidjournal.com/purchase-access?type=Article&id=1548&r=%2Farticles%2Fview%3F1548%2F2
23. Lee, C., Shim, J.: An exploratory study of radio frequency identification (RFID) adoption in the healthcare industry. Eur. J. Inf. Syst. **16**, 712–724 (2007)
24. Shah, S.: Pharmaceutical RFID: from mandates to endorsements and laws. n.d. http://www.pharmamanufacturing.com/assets/Media/MediaManager/ptt0602_abiresearch_rfid-in-pharma.pdf
25. Visich, J., Li, S., Reyes, P.: Radio frequency identification implementation in hospitals: insights for health care executives and managers. Prod. Inven. Manag. J. **48**(1), 50–61 (2012)
26. Lee, C., Shim, J.: An exploratory study of radio frequency identification (RFID) adoption in the healthcare industry. Eur. J. Inf. Syst. **16**(6), 712–724 (2007)
27. Kimberly, J.R., Evanisko, M.J.: Organizational innovation: the influence of individual, organizational, and contextual factors on hospital adoption of technological and administrative innovations. Acad. Manag. J. **24**(4), 689–713 (1981)
28. Cannon, A.F., et al.: RFID in the contemporary supply chain: multiple perspectives on its benefits and risks. Int. J. Oper. Prod. Manag. **28**(5), 433–454 (2008)
29. Malhotra, N.K., Kim, S.S., Agarwal, J.: Internet users' information privacy concerns (IUIPC): the construct, the scale, and a causal model. Inf. Syst. Res. **15**(4), 336–355 (2004)
30. Roberti, M.: The myth of perfect read accuracy (2009). http://www.rfidjournal.com/articles/pdf?4975. Accessed 16 May 2018
31. Bhattacherjee, A., Perlos, J., Sanford, C.: Information technology continuance: a theoretical extension and empirical test. J. Comput. Inf. Syst. **49**(1), 17–26 (2008)
32. Reyes, P.M, Li, S., Visich, J.K.: Determinants of RFID adoption stage and perceived benefits. Eur. J. Oper. Res. **254**(3), 801–812 (2016)
33. Ferrer, G., Dew, N., Apte, U.: When is RFID right for your service? Int. J. Prod. Econ. **124**(2), 414–425 (2010)
34. Hair Jr., J.F., et al.: A Primer on Partial Least Squares Structural Equation Modeling (PLSSEM), 2nd edn. Sage Publications, New York (2017)
35. Angeles, R.: RFID mandate compliance: absorptive capacity attributes as differentiating dynamic capabilities. Int. J. Value Chain Manag. **2**(3), 287–312 (2008)

Assimilation of Business Intelligence Systems: The Mediating Role of Organizational Knowledge Culture

Azizah Ahmad[1] and Mohammad Alamgir Hossain[2(✉)]

[1] Institute for Advanced and Smart Digital Opportunities, School of Computing, Universiti Utara Malaysia, Sintok, Malaysia
azie@uum.edu.my
[2] School of Business IT and Logistics, RMIT University, Melbourne, Australia
mohammad.hossain@rmit.edu.au

Abstract. This study examined the assimilation of business intelligence (BI) systems in firms. Based on the innovation assimilation concepts from information systems (IS) studies and considering the resource-based theory (RBT) as the theoretical underpinning, an initial research model was developed. The model was then validated with survey data that we collected from 153 managers and executives from Malaysia. The collected data were analyzed by partialleast-squares (PLS) methods. The results show that the assimilation stages (i.e., implementation and routinization) are not sequential (in other words, successful implementation does not ensure routinized use of BI systems); rather, implementation of BI systems enhances organizational knowledge culture, which in turn drives routinized use of BI systems. Data analyses also find that implementation of BI systems is dependent on three factors: quality of the BI system itself, quality of its users, and the governance of BI systems in firms. Our results offer new insights to theory and practice.

Keywords: Business Intelligence (BI) · Assimilation · Implementation
Routinization · Organizational knowledge culture
Resource-Based Theory (RBT)

1 Introduction

Business intelligence (BI) systems are considered as information technology (IT) based tools that assist firms to achieve competitive advantage through improved knowledge and decision-making. BI system can be defined as "an organized and systematic process by which organizations acquire, analyze, and disseminate information from both internal and external information sources significant for their business activities and for decision making" [1, p. 32]. Studies [e.g., 2] demonstrated that BI provide firms the ability to analyze business data and information; such ability supports and improves organizational decision making across various departments in a range of business activities. Organizations employ BI in various functions including marketing research, competitor analysis, and customer relationship management. A wide variety of industries including logistics, manufacturing, retail, financial institutions,

S. A. Al-Sharhan et al. (Eds.): I3E 2018, LNCS 11195, pp. 480–491, 2018.
https://doi.org/10.1007/978-3-030-02131-3_43

telecommunication, marketing, utilities have been using BI systems. The interest on BI systems has even been increasing with the progression of 'big data' [3, 4]. The deployment of BI applications in today's firms is increasing and the demand for BI is stronger than ever before. Gartner report predicts that the worldwide spending on BI system would reach US $18.3 billion in 2018. However, other recent reports [e.g., 5] 'terrify' companies by identifying that 70–80% BI system projects fail [6]. Tapadinhas [6] warns that, even if corporates achieve a successful implementation of a BI system, many users eventually disengage themselves from using it. But, in order to realize the most out of any BI system, it is essential that firms use it regularly in decision-making operations [4].

Numerous information systems (IS) studies agree that many innovations are initially accepted by firms, which really are not used to their full potential [e.g., 8]. IS studies also established that the migration from initial deployment to 'full utilization' is complex. Unlike general concept-based innovations, BI systems entail considerable set-up costs and their assimilation involves complex processes. Li and Hsieh [9, p. 659] demonstrate that "after gaining first-hand usage experience in the acceptance stage, employees develop a certain level of understanding about an implemented IS, which enables them to achieve work objectives in the post-acceptance stage" by using the system in routine applications. Therefore, understanding assimilation of BI systems is important. Although a number of studies discretely examine the adoption [8] and extended use of BI systems [4], however, to the best of the authors' knowledge, an integrated effort explaining the assimilation is missing in literature. Therefore, this current study aims to develop and validate a model that explains the assimilation of BI systems in firms.

In recent years Malaysia is experiencing tremendous changes both in government services as well as corporate businesses with the application of latest IT solutions [9]. It is one of the forerunners of using various IT systems including RFID technology [10]. BI system experience no exception; various industries in Malaysia including banking and financial, communications, education, government, healthcare, manufacturing, retail, and service have adopted BIS [13]. Still, the success of BI systems is minimal [14]. Aligning this issue with our research aim, we collected survey response from the decision-makers (i.e., managers and executives) from Malaysia. We used structural equation modeling (SEM) techniques to analyze the data. Overall, data analyses found that the successful deployment of BI systems leads to routinized use only when the organization's culture is improved. This research contributes to theory by considering 'assimilation' as a process than a construct and applying it in a new context. It also offers implications to organizational decision-makers to revisit their BI systems strategies.

The rest of the paper is structured as follows. First, we discuss the theoretical perspectives that underpin the conceptual model of the study and then develop hypotheses to be empirically tested. Next, we discuss the research method followed by presenting the results and discussing our findings. Finally, we briefly discuss the theoretical and practical implications of the study as well as the limitations.

2   Theoretical Background

A convincing effort has been observed in literature examining adoption behaviour of firms towards an innovation. Studies suggest that the nature and process of adoption of an innovation is important to understand its initial acceptance; they further suggest that post-adoption process is even more important and worthy to realize the ultimate success of the innovation [8, 9]. Among a few post-adoption stages, 'assimilation' is the most popular. However, prior studies argued that 'assimilation' is rather a process that involved certain stages. For example, Thompson [15] examined 'assimilation' as a three stage process involving initiation, adoption, and implementation. Similarly, Zhu, Kraemer [8] examined it as a three staged process: initiation, adoption, and routinization. Recently, Hossain et al. [12] explained 'assimilation' as a four-stage process consisting initiation, adoption, routinization, and extension.

There are a number of studies that considered 'assimilation' as a construct; however, this current study considers 'assimilation' as a process that covers several stage (i.e., stage approach) than considering it as variable. Also, while some studies [e.g., 8] consider that 'assimilation' combines both pre-adoption and post-adoption stages, our study considers that 'assimilation' covers only the post-adoption stages given that the innovation in question is already adopted, which is consistent with prior studies [e.g., 16]. Based on prior works, this study considers that 'assimilation' of BI system in firms consists of two stages namely implementation and routinization. *Implementation* occurs when a firm puts an innovation into use [17]. Then, *routinization* happens when the innovation is 'subsumed' into the organizational activities and is practiced in operational functions in such a manner that it is not treated as a noble or foreign technology. In other words, *routinization* "describes the state in which IS use is integrated as a normal part of the employees' work processes" [9, p. 661]. *Routinization* assures continued use [16].

Over the last decades organizations are becoming keener to use technologies in business operations. Such organizational-behavior relies on the resource-based theory (RBT) [18], which postulates that unique resources that a firm possesses would bring competitive advantage. RBT focuses on identifying the value of firm resources. More specifically, it explains how firms acquire, develop, maintain, and use resources in a manner that establishes and sustains their competitive advantage. In other words, (the identification and utilization of) firm's internal resources can be the tools to be competitive and successful.

In the current context, firm's unique resources could influence the implementation of BI system, which would be the basis for sustained competitive advantage [3]. Since BI systems are knowledge-creation mechanisms, we only consider the knowledge related resources that affect the systems. To the quest of important organizational resources for the successful implementation of BI system, studies suggest that quality of employees who will use the BI systems (i.e., the users) as the most critical. Studies also established that firm's internal governance related to BI systems that is important [19].

3   The Research Model

We propose a research model that is based on resource-based view (RBV) with the assistance from IS assimilation studies. Consistent with innovation diffusion theory [17] and IS success model [20], our model assumes that the success of a BI system can be realized if the users (i.e., employees of a firm) routinize its use in regular decision-making. In this process, based on RBV, the successful deployment of a BI system is dependent on the organizational resources including user quality and governance of BI systems (H1, H2. respectively). Also, inspired by the 'system quality' aspect from IS success model, quality of BI a system is considered as an antecedent of its successful implementation (H3). Moreover, a successful deployment of BI systems improves organization's culture, which in turn contributes to the routinized use of the system – a mediation effect (H4).

3.1   Antecedents of a Successful Deployment of BIS

User Quality. Regarding the human resource perspective on BI assets, skilled employees is highlighted as important factor. The recent literature review conducted by Trieu [3] suggested that humans are the primary resources for BI success. Grublješič and Jaklič [4] identified a number of important characteristics of BI system users. Quality users equipped with strong technical, business, and analytical skills are critical because values of BI system can only be tapped by the users who are capable of analyzing information and turn them into sound business decisions [21]. In addition, Strange and Hostmann [22] stated that utilization of BI tools is only part of the formula for BI success; more is related with integrating BI systems with company's requirements, priorities, and data management, which require people with unique skills. One of the reasons for the unsuccessful stories of the Malaysian firms can be the scarcity of people with the right skills in BI systems [21]. Thus, it can be inferred that that:

H1: Quality of the users of a BI system is associated with its successful implementation.

System Governance. Challenging previous studies that claimed business governance as a constraint to its success, Matney and Larson [19] argued that BI governance is the key for the success of BI systems. Also, governance is needed to glean intelligence from data generated by BI systems. The definition of BI governance is simple – "defining and implementing an infrastructure that supports enterprise goals" [19, p. 29]. BI governance basically deals with the business process side than the technological aspects. Watson and Wixom [23] emphasized that both people and processes must be in place to manage and support BI. Recent studies [e.g., 24] found that solid BI governance – which includes controlling, directing, establishing and enforcing related BI policies – promotes resourceful thinking within an organization, and has significant impact on the successful implementation of BI systems. Therefore:

H2: BI system governance is associated with its successful implementation.

BI System Quality. IS success model [20] considers *system quality* as an important determinant of the successful implementation of a system. A number of proponents of IS success model evidenced that this relationship in many contexts; BI systems domain has no exception. For example, Grublješič and Jaklič [4] found that BI system quality is a strong determinant of BI use. Generally, higher system quality is expected to lead to higher use of a system [20]. In fact, Yeoh and Popovic˘ [25] suggest that *system quality* is one of the success factors of BI system implementation. It is sensible that a reliable BI system with higher usability, consistent user interface, and easier to use and learn will be more-successfully implemented in a firm. Therefore, organizations that acquire a high quality BI system are more likely to be successful in implementing it.

H3: BI system quality is associated with its successful implementation.

3.2 Mediating Effect of Organizational Knowledge Culture

Extant literature on BI agrees that technology cannot increase employee productivity unless it is used effectively [3]. *Organizational culture* refers to a system of shared meaning held by the members of an organization that distinguishes the organization from others [26]. Organizational culture, in general, has been considered as an important driver for the success of knowledge-related initiatives. Creating a culture of 'learning organization' has become an important strategic objective for many firms that hinges on the acquisition of information. Prior studies [e.g., 27] evidenced that a large percentage of BI applications fail not because of technology but for a dysfunctional organizational knowledge culture where the knowledge generated from the knowledge-systems are not shared properly. A functional *organizational knowledge culture* encourages employees to create and share knowledge within a firm [28]. Studies indicate that, in order to realize their full potential, BI systems have to be integrated in organizations regular decision-making so that the BI systems are considered as an integral practice of business operations/activities and not as 'foreign' tools to the organizational operations [29]. Based on the prior works, our proposed model argues that:

H4: Organizational knowledge culture has a mediating effect between implementation and routinized use of a BI system.

4 Research Method

This research adopted quantitative method. A survey was administered to a sample of 1,000 executives through contact persons. To increase the response, the study administered follow-up phone calls and reminders. 166 questionnaires were eventually obtained but 13 were with missing values, resulted 153 usable responses. The demographics have been representative of the population (*see* Table 1). For example, around 37% of the respondents were female, where World Bank data (www.data.worldbank.org) says the contribution of female in Malaysian labour force was 38.1% in 2016.

The measurement items were based on previous works from BI literature. The instrument items were based on Likert scale, ranging from 'strongly disagree' to 'strongly agree'; a six-point Likert scale was employed in this study with the rationale

Table 1. The demographics of the respondents

Gender		Job position	
Male	63.2%	Director and above	9.9%
Female	36.8%	Dept. manager	14.4%
		Operation manager	24.2%
		Operation officer	51.6%
Age		Industry	
20–30 year	13.1%	Manufacturing	26.2%
31–40 year	39.2%	Retail	23.6%
41–50	35.3%	Logistics	15.2%
51 and over	12.4%	Financial institutions	11.1%
		Telecommunication	10.8%
		Marketing & others	13.1%

that most Asian respondents has the tendency of selecting the middle point [30]. All constructs were operationalized as reflective. Specifically, *user quality* was measured by using the instruments from [21]. BI *system quality* was measured using the items in [20] and *BI system governance* was measured by the scales in [19]. The instruments for *organization knowledge culture* and *system implementation* were adopted from [29], and *routinized use* was from [31]. The items for each construct are presented in Table 2. Data were analyzed by partial least squares (PLS)-based SEM.

5   Results

5.1   Evaluating the Measurement Model

The assessment of the measurement model was established by examining convergent validity, reliability, and discriminant validity. First, convergent validity was assessed with the outer loadings of the indicators and the average variance extracted (AVE) of the constructs. The bold values shown in Table 2 represent item loading of the respective construct; all item loadings were greater than the threshold of 0.70 [32]. Similarly, all construct's AVE was well above of 0.5 (see Table 3). Then, internal consistency was assessed with composite reliability (CR) values. As Table 3 shows, all CR values satisfied the 0.7 threshold [32]. Finally, we assessed discriminant validity with two measures. As the first approach to assess the discriminant validity of the indicators, we checked cross-loadings. Table 2 shows that the indicator's loading on the associated construct is greater than any of its cross-loadings (i.e., its correlation) on other constructs [32]. The second approach to assess discriminant validity was checking Fornell-Larcker criterion, which compares the square root of the AVE values with the latent variable correlations. Table 3 shows that the square root of each construct's AVE is greater than its highest correlation with any other construct. Thus, our indicators and constructs passed the discriminant tests.

Table 2 The cross-loading matrix

	Items	UQ	SG	SQ	OC	SI	SR
UQ1	Technical skill	**0.776**	0.365	0.394	0.342	0.368	0.354
UQ2	Analytical skill	**0.749**	0.421	0.496	0.316	0.307	0.405
UQ3	Competence	**0.790**	0.514	0.515	0.359	0.394	0.397
UQ4	Understand requirements	**0.775**	0.440	0.476	0.317	0.345	0.327
UQ5	Ability to use data	**0.835**	0.481	0.504	0.505	0.459	0.422
SG1	Management support	0.407	**0.712**	0.427	0.216	0.360	0.128
SG2	Necessary training provided	0.537	**0.772**	0.514	0.419	0.491	0.387
SG3	Policy in place	0.423	**0.844**	0.680	0.453	0.502	0.407
SG4	Manage implementation	0.475	**0.829**	0.533	0.418	0.504	0.356
SG5	Enforce top-down directive	0.420	**0.831**	0.611	0.368	0.463	0.29
SQ1	Usability	0.503	0.602	**0.865**	0.458	0.416	0.445
SQ2	Adaptability	0.432	0.581	**0.815**	0.341	0.380	0.324
SQ3	Reliability	0.500	0.611	**0.800**	0.428	0.448	0.370
SQ4	Response time	0.425	0.532	**0.829**	0.411	0.372	0.358
SQ5	Availability	0.597	0.548	**0.811**	0.587	0.525	0.512
OKC1	Knowledge is shared	0.364	0.398	0.464	**0.872**	0.509	0.523
OKC2	Knowledge sharing is encouraged	0.454	0.445	0.497	**0.860**	0.573	0.598
OKC3	Incentive to share knowledge	0.387	0.364	0.461	**0.837**	0.410	0.554
OKC4	Policy for knowledge sharing	0.391	0.323	0.403	**0.862**	0.410	0.550
OKC5	knowledge portals are available	0.383	0.469	0.471	**0.721**	0.462	0.397
SI1	System in use in all units	0.352	0.424	0.380	0.401	**0.753**	0.323
SI2	Data are integrated in BI system	0.296	0.401	0.319	0.381	**0.760**	0.236
SI3	Rely on it to take decision	0.480	0.522	0.468	0.576	**0.857**	0.410
SI4	Comprehensive business alignment	0.410	0.535	0.518	0.465	**0.866**	0.367
SR1	Incorporated into regular schedule	0.420	0.461	0.463	0.563	0.385	**0.827**
SR2	Part of normal work routine	0.400	0.295	0.434	0.557	0.368	**0.911**
SR3	BI is a normal part of my work	0.452	0.301	0.402	0.542	0.349	**0.879**

Note: UQ, User Quality; SG, (BI) System Governance; SQ, (BI) System Quality; OKC, Organ-izational Knowledge Culture; SI, (BI) System Implementation; SR, (BI) System Routinization

5.2 Testing the Structural Model and Hypotheses

The structural model deals with testing the hypothesized relationships. A bootstrapping procedure was used to establish the significance of the path coefficients; the values are summarized in Table 4. It is observed that the hypotheses leading to BI systems deployment (H1, H2, H3) were supported. Also, the R^2 value of SI (38.9%) and SR (40.2%) indicate that the model successfully explains the current phenomenon.

Table 3. Construct reliability and discriminant validity tests

	Alpha	CR	AVE	UQ	SG	SQ	OKC	SI	SR
					Fornell-Larcker discriminant criterion				
UQ	0.846	0.890	0.617	**0.786**					
SG	0.858	0.898	0.638	0.567	**0.799**				
SQ	0.883	0.914	0.680	0.606	0.698	**0.825**			
OKC	0.888	0.918	0.693	0.477	0.479	0.552	**0.832**		
SI	0.826	0.884	0.657	0.484	0.587	0.529	0.572	**0.811**	
SR	0.843	0.906	0.763	0.486	0.405	0.497	0.635	0.421	**0.873**

Note. Alpha, Cronbach's alpha; CR, Composite Reliability; AVE, Average Variance Extracted

To begin the mediation analysis, first we tested the indirect effect. The indirect effect (i.e., 0.334) from BI system implementation (SI) via organizational knowledge culture (OKC) to routinized use (SU) is the product of path coefficients from SI to OKC and from OKC to SU (i.e., 0.572 * 0.586). To test the significance of these path coefficients' products, we ran the bootstrapping routine with default values. We found that the indirect effect is significant since neither of the 95% confidence intervals includes zero. The empirical t value of the indirect effect (0.334) for the OKC to SR relationship is 4.869, yielding a p value of 0.000. Next, the direct relationship from SI to SR is weak (0.086) and statistically nonsignificant ($t = 0.978, p = 0.328$). Hence, we conclude that OKC does have a *full* mediation effect between (SI) and routinized use (SR); thus H4 is accepted.

Table 4. Structural properties of the model

	β value	SE	t value	p value
UQ to SI (H1)	0.172*	0.083	2.082	0.037
SG to SI (H2)	0.375**	0.087	4.303	0.000
SQ to SI (H3)	0.172*	0.078	2.095	0.036

SE, Standard error; Significance level *$p < 0.05$, **$p < 0.001$; ns: not significant

6 Discussion and Implications

This study managed to reiterate the reason for relatively low implementation success rate and the relatively low satisfaction from BI projects. The reasons identified from our study include user skill-related issues, BI system issues (e.g., technical complexity, inflexibility), and lack of governance. Our finding is consistent with current literature [e.g., 3] that suggests that sophisticated BI system and high quality human resources are favorable for 'BI assets' which are recognized as necessary conditions for the success of BI systems.

As hypothesized in this study, firm's internal resources are found to have an influence on the successful implementation of BI systems. Among the two resource variables, first, it is found that *user quality* is important. It is intuitive that the main actors of the BI system (i.e., the users) determine the success of BI. They need to possess certain skills (including technical, analytical) to use BI systems as well as to interpret and use the outputs of BI systems. Therefore, firms have to arrange regular training sessions, workshops and interactive sessions to upgrade the users. Next, the hypothesis related to the role of BI system governance in stimulating implementation of BI systems had significant statistical evidence. In fact, among the three antecedents of BI implementation, *BI governance* has come up as the strongest. Effective BI governance may include strong management support that provides sufficient funding, infrastructure, staffing, and appropriate policies regarding BI. Having good BI governance in place (in terms of providing supportive infrastructure including resource allocation and training) is a prerequisite for BI systems' success in firms. In order to ensure continuous support and sponsor the successful implementation of BI systems, it is prescribed by this study that BI steering committee should comprise of high-level executives. As a consequence, executives may want to look into their existing BI governance in their firms and focus on developing supportive BI governance.

Our results show that the higher quality of BI systems, higher the likelihood of their successful implementation. It is found that, in the past, many BI systems could not be successful because of the quality in terms of mainly usability [20]. Therefore, BI systems should possess critical technical features such as reliability, consistent user interface, quick response time, and quality of documentation. Also, a BI system should be customizable based on firm requirements, user ergonomics, and business processes. Also, the system should be easy to use and easy to learn. It should also mimic the way the users perform a business process and take decision so that the users do not consider it as an alien, which needs significant effort and involves learning curve.

The results of the mediation test suggest that a successful implantation of a BI system has positive influence on improving organizational knowledge culture. BI systems are knowledge-acquiring and knowledge-generating engine; upon their implementation, organizational knowledge culture – the way a firm generate and share knowledge – has to be changed. A supportive organizational culture is vital in encouraging staff to create and share knowledge within a firm. This finding suggests that BI systems should change organization culture than building the systems to fit firm's culture – McDermott and O'Dell [33] provided examples supporting our claim.

The mediation results also show that successful implementation of a BI system can develop good culture of knowledge sharing within a firm, which in turn decides the success of the system by routinizing its use in decision-making processes (e.g., to generating new products, improving business operations and customer service). Hence, managers should make endeavors to create a knowledge-intensive culture for staff to believe that knowledge sharing actively reward them as well as the firm. Also, firms need to be transformed into learning organizations which facilitates learning for all employees. If they successfully create a supportive knowledge culture, there will be good chance that the BI systems will be successfully routinized. Hence, organizations should put more emphasize on promoting and building appropriate knowledge culture.

7 Limitations and Future Works

Despite contributing new and valuable insights to BI systems literature, this study has been faced with some limitations that may inform future research. First, realizing the Cloud BI systems as essential in recent times, companies are moving towards Cloud BI systems (e.g., Amazon AWS, Microsoft Azure, Google Cloud, and IBM Bluemix). Forbes find that the adoption of Cloud BI systems in 2018 is almost doubled from 2016 [34]. Our study examined the traditional enterprise-wide BI systems; future studies could test the model in the Cloud context. Second, we used a self-reported survey that may have resulted in self-selection bias particularly to measure 'routinized use'. Although the CMV tests did not expose any concerns, it is still not possible to claim definitively that the data are free from self-reported bias. Future research could use actual (objective) usage data from BI system users. Third, we collected data from one country at a given point of time. Future studies could investigate this model in different cultures and use longitudinal data. Finally, we relied on Elbashir et al. [2] study which suggests that *firm size* does not affect organizational use of BI systems; still large organizations may exploit BI's potential better than smaller organizations. Therefore, the effect of firm size is worthy to investigate in a future study.

References

1. Lönnqvist, A. Pirttimäki, V.: The measurement of business intelligence. Inf. Syst. Manage. **23**(1), 32 (2006)
2. Elbashir, M.Z., Collier, P.A., Davern, M.J.: Measuring the effects of business intelligence systems: the relationship between business process and organizational performance. Int. J. Account. Inf. Syst. **9**(3), 135–153 (2008)
3. Trieu, V.-H.: Getting value from business intelligence systems: a review and research agenda. Decis. Support Syst. **93**, 111–124 (2017)
4. Grublješič, T. Jaklič, J.: Conceptualization of the business intelligence extended use model. J. Comput. Inf. Syst. **55**(3), 72–82 (2015)
5. Goodwin, B.: Poor communication to blame for business intelligence failure, says Gartner (2011). https://www.computerweekly.com/news/1280094776/Poor-communication-to-blamefor-business-intelligence-failure-says-Gartner. Accessed 4 May 2018
6. Phocas: Why do business intelligence projects fail? (2017). https://www.phocassoftware.com/business-intelligence-blog/whybusiness-intelligence-projects-fail. Accessed 4 May 2018
7. Tapadinhas, J.: Understanding why users disengage from the corporate BI initiative (2015). https://www.gartner.com/doc/3072718/understanding-users-disengage-corporate-bi. Accessed 4 May 2018
8. Zhu, K., Kraemer, K.L., Xu, S.: The process of innovation assimilation by firms in different countries: a technology diffusion perspective on E-business. Manage. Sci. **52**(10), 1157–1576 (2006)
9. Li, X., Hsieh, J.P.-A., Rai, A.: Motivational differences across post-acceptance information system usage behaviors: an investigation in the business intelligence systems context. Inf. Syst. Res. **24**(3), 659–682 (2013)

10. Puklavec, B., Oliveira, T., Popovic, A.: Unpacking business intelligence systems adoption determinants: an exploratory study of small and medium enterprises. Econ. Bus. Rev. Cent. South-East. Eur. **16**(2), 185 (2014)

11. PPC: MyKad is Malaysia ahead of the game? (2015). https://www.ppc.com.au/mykad-is-malaysia-ahead-of-the-game/. Accessed 25 May 2018

12. Hossain, M.A., Quaddus, M., Islam, N.: Developing and validating a model explaining the assimilation process of RFID: an empirical study. Inf. Syst. Front. **18**(4), 645–663 (2016)

13. Ong, I.L., Siew, P.H., Wong, S.F.: Understanding business intelligence adoption and its values: some examples from Malaysian companies (2011)

14. Qushem, U.B., Zeki, A.M., Abubakar. A.: Successful business intelligence system for SME: an analytical study in Malaysia. In: IOP Conference Series: Materials Science and Engineering. IOP Publishing (2017)

15. Thompson, V.A.: Bureaucracy and innovation. Adm. Sci. Q. **10**(1), 1–20 (1965)

16. Zmud, R.W., Apple, L.E.: Measuring technology incorporation/infusion. J. Prod. Innov. Manag. **9**(2), 148–155 (1992)

17. Rogers, E.M.: Diffusion of Innovation. Free Press, New York (2003)

18. Barney, J.: Firm resources and sustained competitive advantage. J. Manage. **17**(1), 99–120 (1991)

19. Matney, D., Larson, D.: The four components of BI governance. Bus. Intell. J. **9**(3), 29–36 (2004)

20. Delone, W.H., McLean, E.R.: The DeLone and McLean model of information systems success: a ten-year update. J. Manage. Inform. Syst. **19**(4), 9–30 (2003)

21. Avery, K.L., Watson, H.J.: Training data warehouse end users. Bus. Intell. J. **9**(4), 40–51 (2004)

22. Strange, K.H., Hostmann, B.: BI competency center is core to BI success. Gartner Res. **22** (2003)

23. Watson, H.J., Wixom, B.H.: The current state of business intelligence. Computer **40**(9) (2007)

24. Park, Y., El Sawy, O.A., Fiss, P.C.: The role of business intelligence and communication technologies in organizational agility: a configurational approach. J. Assoc. Inf. Syst. **18**(9), 648686 (2017)

25. Yeoh, W., Popovič, A.: Extending the understanding of critical success factors for implementing business intelligence systems. J. Assoc. Inf. Sci. Technol. **67**(1), 134–147 (2016)

26. O'Neill, J.W., Beauvais, L.L., Scholl, R.W.: The use of organizational culture and structure to guide strategic behavior: an information processing perspective. J. Behav. Appl. Manage. **2**(2), 816 (2016)

27. Chuah, M.-H., Wong, K.-L.: The implementation of enterprise business intelligence: case study approach. J. Southeast Asian Res. **2013**, 1 (2013)

28. Popovič, A.: If we implement it, will they come? User resistance in post-acceptance usage behaviour within a business intelligence systems context. Econ. Res. Ekonomska istraživanja **30**(1), 911–921 (2017)

29. Bach, M.P., Čeljo, A., Zoroja, J.: Technology acceptance model for business intelligence systems: preliminary research. Proc. Comput. Sci. **100**, 995–1001 (2016)

30. Nadler, J.T., Weston, R., Voyles, E.C.: Stuck in the middle: the use and interpretation of mid-points in items on questionnaires. J. Gen. Psychol. **142**(2), 71–89 (2015)

31. Sundaram, S., et al.: Technology use on the front line: how information technology enhances individual performance. J. Acad. Mark. Sci. **35**(1), 101–112 (2007)

32. Hair Jr., J.F., et al.: A Primer on Partial Least Squares Structural Equation Modeling (PLS-SE), 2nd edn. Sage Publications, Thousand Oaks (2017)
33. McDermott, R., O'Dell, C.: Overcoming cultural barriers to sharing knowledge. J. Knowl. Manage. **5**(1), 76–85 (2001)
34. Columbus, L.: The state of cloud business intelligence (2018). https://www.forbes.com/sites/louiscolumbus/2018/04/08/thestate-of-cloud-business-intelligence-2018/#2f1898b82180. Accessed 4 May 2018

The Relationship Between Audit Committee Characteristics and the Level of Sustainability Report Disclosure

Amina Mohammed Buallay[1(✉)] and Esra Saleh AlDhaen[2]

[1] Brunel University London, London, UK
ameena.buallay.87@gmail.com
[2] Ahlia University, Manama, Bahrain
esaldhaen@ahlia.edu.bh

Abstract. This study examined the relationship between Audit committee (AC) characteristics and the level of sustainability report disclosure in gulf countries (GCC). We examined 59 listed banks listed during the period from 2013 to 2017. The results showed that AC size, independency of AC members and AC meetings have significant and positive impact on sustainability report disclosure. However, AC member's financial expertise has negative and significant impact on the sustainability disclosure. The study provides insights about the level of sustainability reporting in GCC countries and how this kind of non-financial disclosure could improve through governance practices especially AC, which might be utilized by banks to explore how AC can and does play a role in contributing towards achievement of the sustainability disclosure.

Keywords: Audit Committee (AC) characteristics
Sustainability reporting (SR) · Gulf Cooperation Countries (GCC)

1 Introduction

Governance and disclosure act as the key success factor in business world. Several bankruptcies have occurred worldwide due to lack of governance and disclosures. This increases the significant of transparency and greater demands for accountability for financial and non-financial information.

Last few years, sustainability reporting (GRI) becomes a serious research line focus on the non-financial disclosures. The GRI covers environmental social and governance disclosure. Wilburn and Wilburn (2013) stated that sustainability performance indicators (environmental, social and governance) can help a firm creates sustainability strategies and stakeholders evaluates the firm's sustainability performance (Leung and Gray 2016; Rao and Tilt 2016).

GRI Sustainability Reporting Guidelines defines sustainability reporting as "re process that assists organizations in setting goals measuring performance and managing change towards a sustainable global economy one that combines long term profitability with social responsibility and environmental care" (GRI 2011, p. 85). Sustainability reporting communicating the firm's economic, environmental, social and governance

S. A. Al-Sharhan et al. (Eds.): I3E 2018, LNCS 11195, pp. 492–503, 2018.
https://doi.org/10.1007/978-3-030-02131-3_44

performance, so reflecting positive and negative impacts (Gray et al. 1995; Mistry et al. 2014; Sharma and Kelly 2014).

Since the implementation of sustainability reporting and adoption of corporate governance are still in its early stages in GCC countries and emerging market, significant empirical research is not yet adopted. Therefore, this study provides the earliest empirical research that discusses the relation between AC characterises and sustainability reporting of GCC banks.

This study investigates the capability of AC characterises to better support the disclosure of sustainability information.

Sustainability disclosure are assumed to be significant for all stakeholders; hence factors affecting the sustainability information disclosure need to be highlighted. This study contributes to literature in many ways. First, from academic level; it sheds the light on the rare prior studies that shows the effect of AC characteristics on sustainability disclosure considering sample from emerging economy (such as gulf countries). Second, from practical perspectives; this study provides insights about the relationship between AC characteristics and the disclosure of sustainability, which might be utilized by organizations to re-arrange the roles within them, reassign internal priorities, to escalate position in their environment. Third, from economy level, our findings should be of interest to regulators and policy makers in emerging markets, who have already adopted governance and considering sustainability reporting in their respective contexts.

The study is divided into the following sections: First section being introduction, further part of this study is divided into five sections. Section 2 discusses literature review and developing hypotheses. Section 3 presents the design and research methodology. Section 4 shows the descriptive statistics. Section 5 presents empirical analysis results. Section 6 presents the study's conclusion, recommendations and the scope for further research.

2   Literature Review and Hypothesis Development

Previous literature in the field argued that there is a lack of common sustainability reporting standards which allows of a level of inconsistency in some cases (Krivačić 2017) it was also argued a lack of understanding to the definitions of sustainability reports and standards allows for deficiency in reporting made by inexperience managers in particular for governmental sectors. From a practical point of view (KPMG 2013) declared that from 93% of world's largest cooperation's publishing their reports only 59% employs a level of assurance.

Krivačić (2017) highlighted that largest cooperation's lacks sustainability reporting assurance which may be related to various factors that is at organisational and governance level. Deloitte (2013) emphasised on the need of investigating Sustainability Report Assurance as such reports leads to a high level and strategic decision making. From the above arguments, it is visible that there is a need to investigate sustainability reporting to resolve the challenges faced by cooperation's and large organizations to resolve in terms of reliability.

Previous studies in the field has defined three types of assurance providers: (1) Internal Auditors, (2) Consultants and (3) Professional Accounting Firms. Despite various studies, the literature examining SRA provider choice remains relatively limited (e.g., Simnett et al. 2009a, b; Kolk and Perego 2010; Pflugrath et al. 2011; Perego and Kolk 2012; Casey and Grenier 2015).

Various studies investigated Audit Committee (AC) characteristics, the studies stated that the effectiveness of an AC depends on its characteristics (Akhtaruddin and Haron 2010; Dhaliwal et al. 2010; Li et al. 2012). In a similar context, it was highlighted that a reliable mixture of experience, expertise, and capabilities are crucial in supporting an AC's ability will efficiently carry out its responsibilities (Madi et al. 2014). It was also argued that the efficiency of an AC is enhanced by financial expertise of committee members; this is a key characteristic that ensures effective operation (Baxter and Cotter 2009). Lisic et al. (2011) also argued that it is not necessary when a financial expert on the AC effective monitoring will be conducted.

Arguments established to separate AC financial expertise from the AC which is expected to have an effective outcome, (Bedard and Gendron 2010) stated that financial expertise allows AC members to categorize and debate questions that challenge managers and external auditors to a bigger scope of financial reporting quality, this practice is expected to improve the clearness and reliability of corporate reporting. Baxter and Cotter (Baxter and Cotter 2009) stated that the level, activities, and responsibilities of an AC are crucial in terms of improving the reliability in enhancing earnings quality.

Kent et al. (2010) found a positive relation between an AC's financial expertise and the quality of financial reporting which is opposing with the above-mentioned arguments, which clearly indicates that there is a need to investigate this area further.

This paper aims to examine the relationship between Audit committee (AC) characteristics and the level of sustainability report disclosure focusing on the gulf cooperation countries (GCC), this paper intends to investigate the relationship between Audit Committee and highlights the characteristics of AC in terms of (1) AC members' financial expertise (2) AC size affect (3) AC board independence (4) AC frequency of meetings and below hypothesis constructed as follows:

H_{1a}: AC members' financial expertise affect the level of ESG disclosure of GCC listed Banks.

Also, the size of any given AC has positive effect on earnings quality. The bigger an AC is the more effective it is due to the fact that they comprise of members with diverse knowledge and expertise in order to perform more reliable monitoring of financial practices (Hamdan et al. 2013). Thoopsamut and Jaikengkit (2009) found that the audit firm size is not significantly related to earnings management. In their previous work, Allegrini and Greco (2013) stated the fact that the resource dependency theory argues that a large AC is more eager to dedicate resources and authority to effectively carry out responsibilities. The more directors there are on an AC, the more diversity and expertise and capabilities there are that would guarantee operative monitoring (Bedard and Gendron 2010). Therefore, a large number of AC members are more likely to aid a committee to expose and solve issues and dilemmas in corporate reporting processes (Li et al. 2012). This means that size is an integral factor for an AC to oversee corporate disclosure practices (Persons 2009). Persons found evidence that numerous directors on AC's tend to improve the level of voluntary disclosures. Therefore, the second alternative hypothesis constructed as follows:

H1b: AC size effect the level of ESG disclosure of GCC listed Banks.

Baxter and Cotter (2009) stated that an AC's independence is a key characteristic that influences a committee's competence and effectiveness in the process of managing financial statements. Also, AC's independence is greatly related to the measurement of earnings quality. Independent AC (AC) is expected to play a key role in financial reporting, auditing, and corporate governance; independent directors put an effort in enhancing the processes conducted by board members and even bring in specialists to make use of their expertise and knowledge, to provide continuity, and to assist in recognizing alliances and acquisitions; those directors help sustains a morally ethical climate within the organization (Kantudu and Samaila 2015). Therefore, the third alternative hypothesis constructed as follows:

H1c: AC board independence affect the level of ESG disclosure of GCC listed Banks.

DeZoort et al. (2002) define the frequency of meetings as an evaluation of an auditor committee's due diligence. The frequency of meetings is a core element in the reliability and efficiency of a company's activities and processes, although there were few studies that acknowledged the connection between the performance of the company and the number of meetings (Ioana 2014). The frequency of meetings is an important characteristic of auditor committees. Board members that regularly meet are more likely to accomplish their work and responsibilities attentively and successfully. Thorough boards would more effectively improve the level of oversight of the process of financial reporting both directly and indirectly through choices of external auditors and the AC (Yatim et al. 2006). Raghunandan and Rama (2007) and Sharma et al. (2009) found that the frequency of AC meetings is positively associated with growth and profitability. Also, Abbott et al. (2000) and Beasley et al. (2000) found that the increasing frequency of meetings is related to better quality of financial statements. Therefore, the fourth alternative hypothesis constructed as follows:

H1d: AC frequency of meetings affect the level of ESG disclosure of GCC listed Banks.

Hamdan and Mushtaha (2011) combine the four AC characteristics discussed above in one study; they aim towards evaluating the relationship between an organization having an audit reporting and the characteristics of AC's in Jordanian companies. Results of the study projected a positive impact in regard to the size of AC's in terms of the report of external auditors. Moreover, the independence of executive and non-executive AC members, or the number of meetings has no impact on views of external auditors.

3 Research Methodology

3.1 Study Population, Sample and Resources of Data

The study depends on the selected sample which is 295 observations for 59 listed banks in Gulf Cooperation Council stock exchange (Saudi, Bahrain, Kuwait, UAE, Qatar and Oman) for five years from 2013 to 2017 (see Table 1).

Table 1. Sample selection

Country	No. banks	No. observations
Bahrain	7	35
Kuwait	9	45
Oman	8	40
Qatar	9	45
Saudi	12	60
UAE	14	70
GCC	**59**	**295**

3.2 The Study Variables

The independent variable (AC characterises) has been measured using the AC members' financial expertise, AC size, Independency of AC and AC frequency of meetings (Al-Sartawi et al. 2013; Hamdan et al. 2013).

The dependent variable (ESG score) measured using index of three disclosure indicators (environmental disclosure, corporate social disclosure and corporate governance disclosure) (Buallay 2018).

Three control variables will be discussed for all estimated models of our study. They are: bank Size, bank age and Audit Quality (Buallay et al. 2017; Buallay 2017; Hamdan et al. 2017) (Table 2).

3.3 Study Model

In order to measure the relationship between audit committee characteristics and sustainability disclosure; the study estimates the linear regression model as follows:

$$ESG_{it} = \beta_0 + \beta_1 ACFE_{itg} + \beta_2 ACSZ_{itg} + \beta_3 ACIND_{itg} + \beta_4 ACM_{itg}$$
$$+ \beta_5 SZ_{itg} + \beta_6 AG_{itg} + \beta_7 AQ_{itg} + \varepsilon_{itg}$$

Where: ESG: is a continuous variable; the dependent variable is the ESG score. $\beta 0$: is the constant and $\beta 1-7$: is the slope of the controls and independent variables. The independent variable is audit committee characteristics. The control variables are (bank

Table 2. Variables measurement

Variables	Labels	Measurements
Dependent variables:		
ESG disclosure	ESG	Bloomberg index which combine the Environmental disclosure, corporate governance disclosure and corporate social responsibility disclosure
Independent variables:		
Audit Committee members' financial expertise	ACFE	No. of members has experience greater than 5 years as audit committee member
Audit Committee size	ACSZ	No. of audit committee members.
Audit Committee independence	ACIND	No. of independent audit committee members
Audit Committee meetings	ACM	No. of audit committee meetings per year
Control variables:		
Bank size	SZ	Total assets
Bank age	AG	The number of years since the Bank was established
Audit quality	AQ	Dummy variable; 1 if the bank's external auditor one of the big four audit firms and 0 otherwise

size, bank age and audit quality). (ε): random error. (i) Stands for the banks; (t) stands for the period and (g) represent the country.

3.4 Model Validity

To check the validity of the study model and data, several tests were performed like, normal distribution test, time series stationarity test, autocorrelation and Multicolinearity and models were checked for not having homoscedasticity. Errors were corrected and results are believed to be accurate.

4 Descriptive Analysis

In this section, we used the descriptive statistics in order to describe the study variables. As shown in Table (3), the mean of AC size is almost 3 and it ranges from 2 to 8, and according to the Code of Corporate Governance in gulf countries at least 3 members must be assigned in the AC, this means that the majority are following this rule. As for the frequency of meeting, there should be at least 4 meeting per year, the number of meetings range between 2–10 meetings and the mean is 4.38. This indicates that the majority are clearly following the code. Moving to the member's independence, the majority of the members of the committee including the chairman must be independent directors according to the corporate governance code. The mean is 0.557 which indicates that the board is increasing the independence of members that stimulates in attracting more investors and avoiding conflict of interest among the board. As for the financial expertise it appears that all members in gulf's listed banks have the right experience to acquire these positions.

Table 3. Descriptive analysis

Variables	Label	Descriptive			
		Mean	Max	Min	SD
Dependent variables:					
Sustainability disclosure	ESG	34.01	61.212	2.489	4.459
Independent variables:					
Audit Committee members' financial expertise	ACFE	4.2	8	8	0.471
Audit Committee size	ACSZ	3.8	7	2	1.251
Audit Committee independence	ACIND	5.77	3	0	0.084
Audit Committee meetings	ACM	4.38	10	1	2.68
Control variables:					
Bank size (LN)	SZ	24.001	56.331	4.665	2.551
Bank age	AG	20.738	54	4	1.004

ESG score mean is 34.01 which is between 61.212 and .2.489. This index is extracted from Bloomberg database. The mean level of the ESG specify that majority of the banks are using a reasonable amount of sustainability reporting. Moreover, Kingdome of Bahrain is developing their selves in order to adopt new features and trends to allow an accurate presentation of sustainability information and transparency.

5   Empirical Analysis and Discussions

We create the linear model in order to answer the question: Is there effect of audit committee characteristics on the level of sustainability disclosure?

The results reveal that ESG simple regression model have high statistical significance and high explanatory power as P-value of F-test is less than 5% (0.000). For the AC member's financial expertise, we found that sustainability disclosure has negative significant relationship with AC member's financial expertise. To clarify the results, when there is a financial expert on the AC then that does not mean that there is more effective sustainability disclosure. Rather, monitoring effectiveness of AC financial expertise depends on the authority of top management. Therefore, we accept the alternative hypothesis (H1); AC members' financial expertise affect the level of ESG disclosure of GCC listed Banks.

The findings of (H1) is in line with the previous study conducted by Lisic et al. (2011), therefore in Banking sector it is found that financial experts does not necessary have effective sustainability disclosure and recommended to have a senior level overseeing to the overall operations, this is also in support of various studies related to strategic decision making and the contribution of factors related to level of authority throughout the reporting process (Aldhaen 2017).

Additionally, we found that committee size has positive relationship with sustainability disclosure. Based on this result, it is believed that a smaller board is able to disclose sustainability information and make better decisions and that a larger committee size may lead to less information disclosure. The smaller AC size is able to direct and make better decisions regarding the disclosure whereas the bigger AC size may lead to a less performance regarding the disclosure. Therefore, we accept the alternative hypothesis (H2); AC size affect the level of ESG disclosure of GCC listed Banks.

The findings of (H2) is considered the novelty of this research, most of the previous studies concluded that the larger of the audit committee is the most effective outcome for the sustainability disclosure (Hamdan et al. 2013), some other studies argued that the level of the committee does not really any have any relationship on the sustainability disclosure Thoopsamut and Jaikengkit (2009), from the analysis it is found that in Banks in GCC countries the smaller audit committee is the more effective outcomes. The findings of H2 also raise a question for future research as it is only focused on Banks in GCC region and not other type of organizations.

Further, the results reveal that AC member's independency influenced positively the ESG model, which is significant at 1%. This indicates that AC independency GCC banks are powerful to realize the full potential of the governance, corporate social responsibility and environmental information. This means that independence AC members has influence over sustainability disclosure. Therefore, we accept the alternative hypothesis (H3); AC independency affect the level of ESG disclosure of GCC listed Banks.

The findings of (H3) is in conjunction with Baxter and Cotter (2009); it is clearly indicated that audit committee in banks in GCC region have a better potential of sustainability disclosure when they are independent, as the proposed outcomes usually have better rational decisions as they are supporting the governance rather than being part of its own operations. Therefore; it is recommended to have a separated audit committees in Banks in GCC region which will allow sustainability disclosure.

Last but not least, there is a significant positive relationship between AC frequency of meetings and ESG, which is significant at 5%. This is due to the fact that as these meetings increase, awareness and experience increases among members, and there will be more encouragement of non-financial information disclosure on the sustainability reports. Therefore, we accept the alternative hypothesis (H4); AC frequency of meetings affect the level of ESG disclosure of GCC listed Banks.

The findings on (H4) is in contradiction of the study conducted by Hamdan and Mushtaha (201_), however the previous study was conducted in Jordan and therefore other environmental and internal performance factors may be considered. The results indicate that the frequency of meeting does support an effective outcome of sustainability reports, this is maybe due to following up on operations, awareness and other aspects. The findings of H4 also raise a question for future research as it is only focused on Banks in GCC region and not other type of organizations.

For the control variables, bank size found to be significant with ESG. this is a great indication that the banks with greater total assets are that most banks disclosing sustainability information. Moreover, bank age is positively affects the ESG disclosure; old banks disclose more sustainable information. Finally, Audit quality is positively affects the ESG disclosure; the real reason why these banks acquire or hire these name brand auditors is to avoid conflict of interest in their structured ownership (Table 4).

Table 4. Simple regression results

Variables	Label	ESG model	
		β	t-Statistic
Independent variable			
Audit Committee members' financial expertise	ACFE	−0.347	−3.036***
			0.000
Audit Committee size	ACSZ	0.446	2.370***
			0.001
Audit Committee independence	ACIND	0.599	6.483**
			0.000
Audit Committee meetings	ACM	0.109	1.719**
			0.040
Control variables:			
Bank size	SZ	0.175	1.602**
			0.049
Bank age	AG	0.388	3.448***
			0.000
Audit quality	ADT	0.835	8.011***
			0.000
R2		0.425	
Adj. R2		0.317	
F-Statistic		22.668	
p-value		0.000	

Significance at: **5% and ***1% levels

6   Conclusion, Limitation and Recommended Future Research

The study investigated AC characteristics and sustainability in banks listed in GCC stock exchange and the relationship between AC characteristics and sustainability reporting. The data collected is a pooled data during the period 2013–2017. As an outcome of this study, the results indicated that AC size, independency of AC members and AC meetings have significant and has a positive impact on sustainability disclosure. However, AC member's financial expertise has negative and significant impact on the sustainability disclosure.

As an outcome of this study, it is recommended the banks in GCC to focus more on AC's characteristics to assure more sustainable transparency to their stakeholders. For instance; AC size should be considered taking into account the organizational size, which is expected to increase the effectiveness of the AC as well as Sustainability Report Disclosure

As a future research, it is recommended to explore the reasons of negative relationship between AC member's financial expertise and sustainability disclosure in particularly in Banking Sector in the GCC region and consider increasing number of countries may explore the extent to which our results generalize to these different and diverse countrie .

It is also recommended to investigate similar study in other sectors than banks and outside the GCC region, and consider AC characteristic affect other forms of reporting such as integrated reporting and intellectual capital reporting.

As a limitation of this research there has been limited studies investigated in this sector, the absence of literature offered the sustainability reporting in GCC region is still lacking. As well as the study considers only the banking sector and neglects other sectors, which may offer other useful results on the connection between AC characteristics and sustainability reporting.

References

Abbott, L.J., Park Y., Parker, S.: The effects of audit committee activity and independence on corporate fraud. Manag. Financ. **26**(11), 55–68 (2000)

Akhtaruddin, M., Haron, H.: Board ownership, audit committees' effectiveness and corporate voluntary disclosures. Asian Rev. Account. **18**(1), 68–82 (2010)

Aldhaen, E.S.: Study of the strategic decision making process in higher education institutions. Indep. J. Teach. Learn. **12**(2), 139 (2017)

Allegrini, M., Greco, G.: Corporate boards, audit committees and voluntary disclosure: evidence from Italian listed companies. J. Manag. Gov. **17**(1), 187–216 (2013)

Al-Sartawi, A., Hamdan, A., Subry, M., Imad, A.: The effect of audit committees on earnings management empirical study on manufacturing listed companies before the international financial crisis. An-Najah Univ. J. Res.-Hum. An-Najah Univ. **27**(4), 819–846 (2013)

Baxter, P., Cotter J.: Audit committees and earnings quality. Account. Financ. **49**(2), 267–290 (2009)

Beasley, M.S., Carcello, J.V., Hermanson, D.R., Lapides, P.D.: Fraudulent financial reporting: consideration of industry traits and corporate governance mechanisms. Account. Horiz. **14**(4), 441–454 (2000)

Bedard, J., Gendron, Y.: Strengthening the financial reporting system: can audit committees deliver? Int. J. Audit. **14**(2), 174–210 (2010)

Buallay, A.: Is sustainability reporting (ESG) associated with performance? Evidence from the European banking sector. Manag. Environ. Qual. Int. J. (2018)

Buallay, A.M.: The relationship between intellectual capital and firm performance. Corp. Gov. Organ. Behav. Rev. **1**(1), 32–41 (2017). http://doi.org/10.22495/cgobr_v1_i1_p4

Buallay, A., Hamdan, A., Zureigat, Q.: Corporate governance and firm performance: evidence from Saudi Arabia. Australas. Account. Bus. Financ. J. **11**(1), 78 (2017)

Casey, R.J., Grenier, J.H.: Understanding and contributing to the enigma of corporate social responsibility (CSR) assurance in the United States. Audit. J. Pract. Theory **34**(1), 97–130 (2015)

Deloitte 2013: Sustainability disclosure: considerations for audit committees. https://deloitte.wsj.com/cfo/2013/09/20/sustainability-disclosure-considerations-for-audit-committees/

DeZoort, F.T., Hermanson, D.R., Archambeault, D.S., Reed, S.A.: Audit committee effectiveness: a synthesis of the empirical audit committee literature. J. Account. Lit. **21** (2002)

Dhaliwal, D.A.N., Naiker, V.I.C., Navissi, F.: The association between accruals quality and the characteristics of accounting experts and mix of expertise on audit committees. Contemp. Account. Res. **27**(3), 787–827 (2010)

Global Reporting Initiative (GRI): Sustainability reporting guidelines: Version 3.1. GRI, Amsterdam (2011)

Gray, R., Kouhy, K., Lavers, S.: Corporate social and environmental reporting: a review of the literature and a longitudinal study of UK disclosures accounting. Audit. Account. J. **8**(2), 47–77 (1995)

Hamdan, A.M., Sarea, A.M., Reyad, S.M.R.: The impact of audit committee characteristics on the performance: evidence from Jordan. Int. Manag. Rev. **9**(1), 32 (2013)

Hamdan, A., Mushtaha, S.: The relationship between audit committee characteristics and type of auditor's report: an empirical study on the public shareholding industrial companies listed at Amman Bourse. Arab. J. Account. **14**(1), 109–163 (2011)

Hamdan, A.M., Buallay, A.M., Alareeni, B.A.: The moderating role of corporate governance on the relationship between intellectual capital efficiency and firm's performance: evidence from Saudi Arabia. Int. J. Learn. Intellect. Cap. **14**(4), 295–318 (2017)

Ioana, A. N. G. H. E. L.: Study regarding the impact of the audit committee characteristics on company performance. Stud. Bus. Econ. **9**(2) (2014)

Kantudu, A.S., Samaila, I.A.: Board characteristics, independent audit committee and financial reporting quality of oil marketing firms: evidence from Nigeria. J. Financ. Account. Manag. **6**(2), 34 (2015)

Kent, P., Routledge, J., Stewart, J.: Innate and discretionary accruals quality and corporate governance. Account. Financ. **50**(1), 171–195 (2010)

KPMG 2013: KPMG International: The KPMG survey of corporate responsibility reporting (2013). http://www.kpmg.com/global/en/issuesandinsights/articlespublications/corporate-responsibility/pages/corporate-responsibility-reporting-survey-2013.aspx

Kolk, A., Perego, P.: Determinants of the adoption of sustainability assurance statements: an international investigation. Bus. Strat. Environ. **19**(3), 182–198 (2010)

Krivačić, D.: Sustainability reporting quality: the analysis of companies in Croatia. J. Account. Manag. **7**(1), 1–14 (2017)

Leung, T.C.H., Gray, R.: Social responsibility disclosure in the international gambling industry: a research note. Meditari Account. Res. **24**(1), 73–90 (2016)

Li, J., Mangena, M., Pike, R.: The effect of audit committee characteristics on intellectual capital disclosure. Br. Account. Rev. **44**(2), 98–110 (2012)

Lisic, L., Neal, T., Zhang, Y.: Audit Committee Financial Expertise and Restatements: The Moderating Effect of CEO Power. School of Management, George Mason University, Fairfax (2011)

Madi, H.K., Ishak, Z., Manaf, N.A.A.: The impact of audit committee characteristics on corporate voluntary disclosure. Proc. Soc. Behav. Sci. **164**, 486–492 (2014)

Mistry, V., Sharma, U., Low, M.: Management accountants' perception of their role in accounting for sustainable development: an exploratory study. Pac. Account. Rev. **26**(1/2), 112–133 (2014)

Perego, P., Kolk, A.: Multinationals' accountability on sustainability: the evolution of third-party assurance of sustainability reports. J. Bus. Ethics **110**(2), 173–190 (2012)

Persons, O.S.: Audit committee characteristics and earlier voluntary ethics disclosure among fraud and no-fraud firms. Int. J. Discl. Gov. **6**(4), 284–297 (2009)

Pflugrath, G., Roebuck, P., Simnett, R.: Impact of assurance and assurer's professional affiliation on financial analysts' assessment of credibility of corporate social responsibility information. Audit. J. Pract. Theory **30**(3), 239–254 (2011)

Raghunandan, K., Rama, D.V.: Determinants of audit committee diligence. Account. Horiz. **21** (3), 265–279 (2007)

Rao, K., Tilt, C.: Board diversity and CSR reporting: an Australian study. Meditari Account. Res. **24**(2), 182–210 (2016)

Sharma, U., Kelly, M.: Students' perceptions of education for sustainable development in the accounting and business curriculum at a business school in New Zealand. Meditari Account. Res. **22**(2), 130–148 (2014)

Sharma, V., Naiker, V., Lee, B.: Determinants of audit committee meeting frequency: evidence from a voluntary governance system. Account. Horiz. **23**(3), 245–263 (2009)

Simnett, R.A., Vanstraelen, A., Fong, C.W.: Assurance on sustainability reports: an international comparison. Account. Rev. **84**(3), 937–967 (2009a)

Simnett, R.A., Nugent, M., Huggins, A.L.: Developing international assurance standards on greenhouse gas statements. Account. Horiz. **23**(4), 347–363 (2009b)

Thoopsamut, W., Jaikengkit, A.O.: The relationship between Audit committee characteristics, audit firm size and earnings management in quarterly financial reports of companies listed in the Stock Exchange of Thailand. In: Selected Contributions from the 8th Global Conference/Firenze University Press (2009)

Wilburn, K., Wilburn, R.: Using global reporting initiative indicators for CSR programs. J. Glob. Responsib. **4**(1), 62–75 (2013)

Yatim, P., Kent, P., Clarkson, P.: Governance structures, ethnicity, and audit fees of Malaysian listed firms. Manag. Audit. J. **21**(7), 757–782 (2006)

Relating Big Data and Data Quality in Financial Service Organizations

Agung Wahyudi[✉], Adiska Farhani[✉], and Marijn Janssen[✉]

Delft University of Technology, Jaffalaan 5, 2628 BX Delft, The Netherlands
{a.wahyudi, M.F.W.H.A.Janssen}@tudelft.nl,
A.F.Haryadi@student.tudelft.nl

Abstract. Today's financial service organizations have a data deluge. A number of V's are often used to characterize big data, whereas traditional data quality is characterized by a number of dimensions. Our objective is to investigate the complex relationship between big data and data quality. We do this by comparing the big data characteristics with data quality dimensions. Data quality has been researched for decades and there are well-defined dimensions which were adopted, whereas big data characteristics represented by eleven V's were used to characterize big data. Literature review and ten cases in financial service organizations were invested to analyze the relationship between data quality and big data. Whereas the big data characteristics and data quality have been viewed as separated domain ours findings show that these domains are intertwined and closely related. Findings from this study suggest that variety is the most dominant big data characteristic relating with most data quality dimensions, such as accuracy, objectivity, believability, understandability, interpretability, consistent representation, accessibility, ease of operations, relevance, completeness, timeliness, and value-added. Not surprisingly, the most dominant data quality dimension is value-added which relates with variety, validity, visibility, and vast resources. The most mentioned pair of big data characteristic and data quality dimension is Velocity-Timeliness. Our findings suggest that term 'big data' is misleading as that mostly volume ('big') was not an issue and variety, validity and veracity were found to be more important.

Keywords: Big data · 11 V · Data quality · Variety · Value
Finance service organization

1 Introduction

Todays' organizations are harvesting more and more data using technologies such as mobile computing, social networks, cloud computing, and internet of things (IoT) (Akerkar 2013). This data deluge can be used to create a competitive advantage over competitors and create significant benefits (LaValle et al. 2013) such as better understanding of customer's behavior, more effective and efficient marketing, more precise market forecasting, and more manageable asset risks (Beattie and Meara 2013; PricewaterhouseCoopers 2013). Manyika et al. (2011) argues that finance and insurance organizations have one of the highest potential to take advantage from big data.

© IFIP International Federation for Information Processing 2018
Published by Springer Nature Switzerland AG 2018. All Rights Reserved
S. A. Al-Sharhan et al. (Eds.): I3E 2018, LNCS 11195, pp. 504–519, 2018.
https://doi.org/10.1007/978-3-030-02131-3_45

However, creating value from big data is a daunting task. Reid's et al. (2015) study revealed that two thirds of businesses across Europe and North America failed to extract value from their data. A number of challenges impede the creation of value from data by the financial service organizations (The Economist Intelligence Unit 2012). Data quality is one of the challenges that are frequently mentioned in the literature impeding value creation from big data (Chen et al. 2014; Fan et al. 2014; Janssen et al. 2016; Leavitt 2013; Marx 2013; Zhou et al. 2014; Zicari 2014).

Data quality is a multi-dimensional construct (Eppler 2001; Fox et al. 1994; Miller 1996; Tayi and Ballou 1998; Wang and Strong 1996). In data quality the role of the data custodian is a key elements in the relationship between colleting and creating value from data. Data custodians process data from data producers/providers and generate information for data consumer. Wang and Strong's (1996) definition of data quality embraces the data custodian's perspective, "data quality is data that is fit for use by data custodian" (p. 6). To be fit for data custodian' task, the data should not only be intrinsically good, but also have proper representation, properly accessed and retrieved from the source, as well as appropriate for contextual use.

Insufficient data quality hinders the value creation from the data (Verhoef et al. 2015). Redman (1998) found that lack of data quality results in disadvantages a the operational, tactical and strategic level, including:

- Operational level: lower customer satisfaction, an increase in costs, and lower employee satisfaction;
- Tactical level: poorer decision making, longer time to make decision, more difficulties to implement data warehouse, more difficulties to reengineer, and increased organization mistrust;
- Strategy level: more difficulties to set strategy, more difficulties to execute strategy, contribution to issues of data ownership, compromise ability to align organizations, and diverting management attention.

Moreover, poor data quality is also associated with great amount of quality cost. According to Eckerson (2002) poor data quality costs US businesses $600 billion annually (3.5% of GDP).

Our objective is to understand the relationship between big data and data quality in financial service organizations. This research is among the first that studied the relationship between big data and data quality. For this purpose, we formulated a research approach which is presented in Sect. 2. We then discussed key concepts and theories on the basis of state-of-the-art literature in Sect. 3. Big data will be measured by looking at its defining characteristics (the V's) and data quality will be measured using the commonly found dimensions in the literature. Next case studies and the corresponding findings is presented in Sect. 4. This resulted in the relationship between the big data characteristics and data quality dimensions. Finally, conclusions will be drawn in Sect. 5.

2   Research Approach

To attain our objective, i.e. investigating correlation between big data and data quality, three main steps were taken

1. Literature review to further detail the big data and the data quality. This resulted in big data construct which is represented by its characteristics (V's) and data quality construct which is represented by its dimensions. The constructs are employed as the basis for investigating the case studies.
2. Online case studies from financial service organizations by content analysis to extract data quality issues and the corresponding big data characteristics. The result is list of data quality issues as a consequence of big data characteristics. These cases did not enable us to understand the causal relation;
3. In-depth case studies at financial service organizations to cross-reference and further refine the findings from online case studies. The refined list of data quality issues is mapped to the corresponding data quality dimensions.

First literature about big data characteristics and data quality dimensions were investigated. To review big data characteristics, we surveyed the literatures during 2011–2016 for any statements of 'big data' or 'data-intensive' in Scopus. 22,362 documents were found. After carefully checked the contents, we focused on nine papers that are strongly relevant with big data characteristics. The same approach was utilized to study the data quality concepts. Using the statements 'data quality' or 'information quality', we found 7,468 documents in Scopus. However, we concentrated to 13 articles that discussed comprehensively about data quality and its dimensions

The aim of the desk research was to find relevant cases. To explore the relationship between big data characteristics and data quality in financial industry a desk research to online articles and corresponding white papers was conducted with systematic approach. The search started with narrowing down 10 biggest banks Europe based on Banks Daily's ranking[1] and 10 biggest insurance companies in Europe based on Relbanks's ranking[2] to keep the focus of this research. The search is conducted through Google Search with keyword "big data" < institution name > (e.g. "big data" Barclays). From the 2000 search results (10 Google Search pages of 10 search result per page for each institution), 2 of the authors independently selected relevant articles which results in a list 32 articles that were relevant with big data quality and produced within 5-years' timeframe (2011–2016). After further analysis, seven online cases were selected providing sufficient details (e.g. mentioning data input, information output, and problematic big data quality issues) for being able to analyze them, as described in Table 1. The cases were analyzed for its big data characteristics and data quality dimension using content analysis of the case studies' documents and interview transcripts using NVivo software. Content analysis has been widely used in qualitative study to analyze and extract information from text, web pages, and various documents (Hsieh and Shannon 2005).

In addition, we conducted three in-depth case studies to confirm and refine our findings from the previous step. It is important to see how the findings implemented in real-life practices as well as to find out the possible missing challenges. The criteria of case study selection were defined as follows: (1) the organization must be an information-intensive financial service organization; (2) the organization should make

---

[1] See http://www.banksdaily.com/topbanks/Europe/market-cap-2015.html.

[2] See http://www.relbanks.com/top-insurance-companies/europe.

Table 1. Online cases that are used in this study

Case	Organization	Big data objective	Source
1	ING Bank	Customer retention	https://goo.gl/RTWLh9
2	Barclays	Customer retention	https://goo.gl/BEWqOI
3	UBS Bank	Risk identification	https://goo.gl/ZNwO6H
4	Allianz Insurance	Fraud detection	https://goo.gl/XPLwLo
5	ING Bank	Fraud detection	https://goo.gl/KaomAQ
6	Barclays, RBS Bank	Complaint monitoring	https://goo.gl/hQHxCe https://goo.gl/MS8c1Z
7	BBVA	New product proposition	https://goo.gl/KUtXn5

use of big data; (3) The organization is willing to cooperate and share information that are required to conduct this study. Three case studies were created by conducting interviews and investigating documents. The summary of offline case studies are presented in Table 2.

Table 2. In-depth cases that are used in the study

	Case 1	Case 2	Case 3
Organization	Retail banking	Retail banking	Insurance
Big data case	Balance Sheet Reduction (Risk Management)	Credit Risk Assessment (Risk Management)	Single Customer View (Customer Acquisition and Retention)
Project's goal	Ensuring mortgage data quality meets the buyer's expectation	– Assessing the most appropriate credit risk level of a company – Providing the most suitable loan	Obtaining a single view of a customer from multiple databases to improve customer service experience
Information output	Mortgage files (supporting data about mortgages)	– Credit risk level – Most suitable loan for the company	A single customer view/profile

3 Literature Background: Key Concepts

3.1 Big Data Concept

Big data is used in various ways and has no uniform definition (Chemitiganti 2016; Ward and Barker 2013). Big data is often described in through white papers, reports, and articles about emerging trends and technology. A lack of formal definition may lead to research into multiple and inconsistent paths. Nevertheless, there is consensus about what constitutes the characteristics of big data. The big data have changed over time. As the initial big data characteristic the three V's of Volume, Velocity, and Variety were introduced by Douglas (2001). Later, IBM added a new V called Veracity, which addresses the uncertainty and trustworthiness of data and data source (2012). The V's continues to evolve to 5 V's (Leboeuf 2016), 8 V's (m-Brain, n.d.), and 9 V's (Fernández et al. 2014). Our literature review that 11 different V's are mentioned in the literature and reports. As our objective is to take a comprehensive view we take all V's into account and define these V's to avoid any confusion about overlap between these characteristics. The characteristics and their definitions are presented in Table 3. These will be used to analyze the big data used in the case studies.

Table 3. Big data characteristics

No	Big data characteristics	Defined characteristic of the data
1	Volume	Huge size of the data (Douglas et al. 2001)
2	Velocity	Unprecedented speed of data creation and data must be must be processed in a timely manner (Douglas et al. 2001)
3	Variety	Various sources of the data and diverse format of the data (structured, semi-structured, unstructured data) (Douglas 2001)
4	Variability	Changing meanings and interpretations for the data based on its context (Owais and Hussein 2016)
5	Veracity	Questionable trustworthiness of the data (authenticity, origin/reputation, availability, accountability) (Tee 2013)
6	Validity	Questionable data generation with respect to regulations and procedures (compliance) (Hulstijn et al. 2011)
7	Volatility	Huge and up-to-date data needed for temporary and quick action (Owais and Hussein 2016)
8	Visibility	Many invisible relationship from the contents inside the data (Owais and Hussein 2016)
9	Viability	Too many contents inside the data, but only few are useful (Dini 2016)
10	Vast resources	The data need very high network bandwidth, huge computing power, large memory/storage for retrieving and processing (Dini 2016)
11	Value	Questionable benefit derived from the data (Owais and Hussein 2016)

3.2   Data Quality (DQ) Concept

Data is the lifeblood of financial industry and DQ is key to the success of any financial organization (Zahay et al. 2012). Financial players such as analysts, risk managers, and traders rely on data in their value chain. Poor DQ such an inaccurate or biased data may lead to misleading insights and even wrong conclusions. Financial industry was reported to loss $10 billion annually from poor DQ (Klaus 2011). In addition, as a highly regulated industry, finance service organizations must conform to several regulations which require high DQ (Glowalla and Sunyaev 2012).

Quality is rather a subjective term, i.e. the interpretation of 'high quality' may differ from person to person. Moreover, the notion may change based on the circumstances. Various definitions of DQ are found in the literature (Eppler 2001; Huang et al. 1998; Kahn and Strong 1998; Miller 1996; Mouzhi and Helfert 2007; Tayi and Ballou 1998; Wang 1998; Wang et al. 1993). Overall, the term DQ depends not only on its intrinsic quality (conformance to specification), but also the actual use of the data (conformance with customer's expectation) (Wang and Strong 1996). Knowing the customers and their business needs is a precursor to understand how DQ will be perceived (Fig. 1).

DQ is a multidimensional concept (Eppler 2001; Fox et al. 1994; Miller 1996; Tayi and Ballou 1998; Wang and Strong 1996). However, there is neither a consensus on what constitute the dimensions of DQ, nor the exact meaning of each dimension (Nelson et al. 2005). The dimensions of DQ vary among scholars (Bovee et al. 2001; Fox et al. 1994; Miller 1996; Naumann 2002; Wang and Strong 1996). However, the most cited DQ dimensions are the dimensions of Wang and Strong (1996), They list sixteen DQ dimensions categorized into four thematic, namely intrinsic, accessibility, contextual, and representational quality, as shown in Fig. 2.

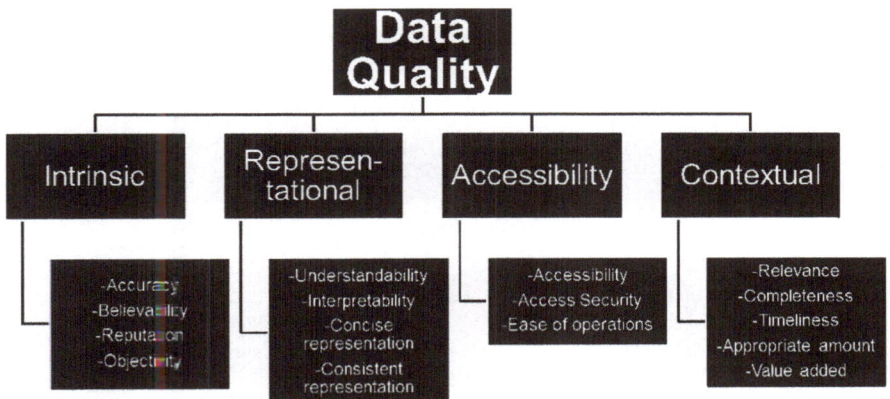

Fig. 1. DQ category and dimensions (adapted from Wang and Strong 1996)

Intrinsic quality is referring to internal properties of the data, e.g. accuracy, objectivity, believability, and reputation. *Accesibility* quality emphasizes the importance of computer systems that store and provide access to data. *Representational* quality consists of understandability, interpretability, concise representation, and consistent representation. *Contextual* quality, which highlights the requirement that DQ must be considered within the context of the task at hand, consists of value-added, relevance, timeliness, completeness, and appropriate amount.

4   Correlation Between Big Data and Data Quality in Financial Service Organizations

Our aim was to investigate the relationship between big data characteristics and DQ dimensions as depicted in Fig. 2. The big data characteristics and DQ dimensions are used to investigate the case studies. Using content analysis these are mapped and the relationship explored. There are eleven Vs that represent big data (their definition were given in Sect. 3) and four category of DQ that includes 16 dimensions (see Sect. 3 for their definition). We conducted seven cases that were carefully selected as explained in Sect. 2 to study the correlation. Three more in-depth case studies were performed to confirm and refine the findings and investigate the relationship in detail. DQ issues emerged from big data characteristics mentioned in case studies were explained as follow. Although big data characteristics and DQ dimensions are different, we found both 'value' refers to the same definition. Therefore we opted only one 'value' in the matrix, i.e. 'value' as a DQ dimension.

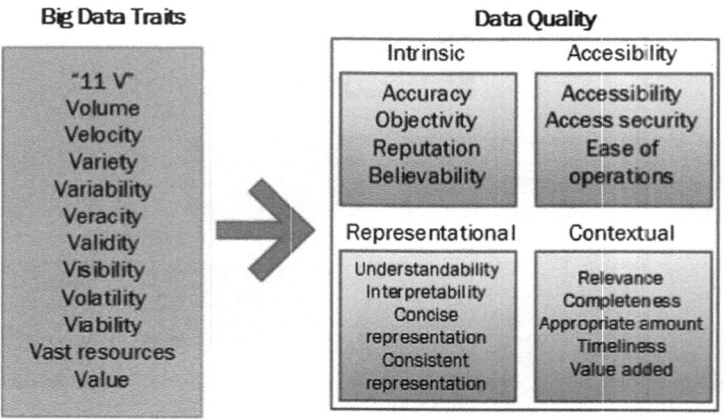

Fig. 2. Relating big data characteristics to DQ dimension

4.1   Volume

Volume was not frequently mentioned affecting DQ issue in the case. Huge size of data could increase chance to discover hidden patterns, such as finding a suspicious fraud. In addition, larger volume most likely leads to higher representativeness. However, bigger size could also bring troubles. In case 3 and 7, *information overload* was caused by volume of the data. It affected the level of amount of the data that is needed for the task in hand. For example, UBS Bank found in several situations that the transaction data for risk identification was too large for pre-processing.

4.2 Velocity

Many financial service organizations need real-time data for their activities such as fraud detection, complaint monitoring, and customer retention. Therefore, they were very concerned with the timeliness of the data. *Outdated data* is mentioned as an important issue by most cases (case 1, 2, 4, 5, 6, and 7). For example, data like credit card transactions is useful for the fraud detection and avoiding the fraud can have a huge impact, but becomes useless if it is not processed in real-time to predict and prevent the subsequent fraud.

4.3 Variety

Most cases mentioned the necessity to combine data from multiple sources in order to reveal more insightful value. However, incorporating many data sources results in a number of DQ issues, such as:

(1) *Different value was reported by same field from multiple data* (case 3 and 6). An example is having a different zip code for the same person in different data sources;

(2) *Inconsistent field's accuracy from multiple data* (case 3 and 6), e.g. which one is the accurate one from multiple zipcodes for the same person?;

(3) *Varied population representativeness from multiple data* (case 3 and 6), e.g. some data have true objectivity but others like social media data tend to be biased and the data represents only certain group of population (e.g. youth, people with good internet connection);

(4) *Inconsistent field's format from multiple data* (case 3 and 6, also confirmed in in-depth case 3). An simple example is that the content of field 'name' is varied in multiple data (e.g. John Clarke Doe, J. Doe, J. C. Doe);

(5) *Inconsistent field's content from multiple data* (case 3 and 6). An example is having 'male' and 'man' in the 'sex' field;

(6) *Different terminologies/semantics/definitions from multiple data* (case 2, 4, and 5). For example the term 'risk' in the data differs across data sources from various domains, especially data from non-specific finance domain;

(7) *Various requirements for access from multiple data producers/providers* (case 1, 5, and 7). Some data providers provide a secure API, whereas others may prefer insecure API or even refer plain data transfer to ensure a high speed;

(8) *Complex structure of the data* (case 1, 2, 4, 5, 6, and 7). An example is unstructured content from social media that contains lexical complexity;

(9) *Duplicate and redundant data sources* (case 1 and 6, confirmed in in-depth case 1, 2, and 3). In offline case 1, there are two legacy systems for mortgages for the private banking and for the company which keep different record of information, but refer to the same mortgage;

(10) *Incomplete content of the field in the data* (case 2 and 6, confirmed in in-depth case 1). In in-depth case 1, previously customers can use post bus as an address, but based on new regulation now they must use postal code. Because the postal code data was not required previously, the absence of this data would make the mortgage information considered as incomplete;

(11) *Timeliness from multiple data* (case 3, 4, and 7) causes difficulties to combine those data in the same timeframe, e.g. statistics data from Eurostat or World Bank was collected at different points in time and cannot be combined to infer at useful insights;

(12) *Complex relationship among data* (case 1, 2, 4, 5, 6, and 7). The more varied and numerous data fed into the system, the more complex the relationship resides in those data and the more complex it is to be combined In these cases we found that the data could not be combined as the data analysts were not able to unravel the complexity.

4.4 Variability

Variability of the data is rarely mentioned in the cases. The DQ issues originate from the use of social media data. In case 3, *different contextual meaning and sentiment for same content in the data* occurs, e.g. 'happy' and 'happy?☹'. Real sentiments are hard to express. It brings difficulties to operate the data if the organization uses a traditional way (e.g. static algorithm) to process the content. Moreover, *the meaning of the words changes dependent on the context and the time* which brings in the need to dynamically interpret the sentiment. The word could change from positive sentiment to neutral sentiment or even to negative sentiment after contextually use by communities along the time. For example, the word 'advertisement' which formerly gave a neutral sentiment currently shifts to a negative sentiment. It's because nowadays people are annoyed by too many digital ads in web pages. On the contrary, some words may shift from neutral or negative sentiment to positive sentiment, such as 'vegetarian' that before was neutral now becoming more positive due to people's conscience of nature reservation and personal health.

4.5 Veracity

Since many organizations involve many data sources into their data processing, they may face trustworthy issues on the authenticity, origin/reputation, availability, and accountability of the data, especially with the data is freely available in the Internet. The following DQ issues were found

(1) *Inaccurate content often found from self-reported data* like social media (case 2). For example complaint came from black campaigner or fake account;

(2) *Unclear reliability and credibility of data providers* (case 3, confirmed in indepth case 2), e.g. blogs or untrusted media;

(3) *Unclear ownership of the data* (case 2, confirmed in in-depth case 2) may discourage organizations to use the data because they might not able to access the data if there is dispute in the future regarding commercial use of the data;

(4) *Unclear responsibility to maintain content of the data* (case 2) might hinder use of the data for long term because the data could be complete and timely at the moment but useless in the future if the content and update of the data is not managed properly; the data from untrusted data source such as social media probably tends to have low objectivity, i.e. representing only portion of population (case 2, 3, 6, and 7).

4.6   Validity

Validity strongly represents the compliance of data generation with respect to procedures and regulations. Finance service organizations are among institutions that are mandated to strictly comply with external regulations such as privacy law and confidentiality agreement, as well as internal regulations and procedures, such as SOPs for data entry, service level agreements with partners and among internal units. Hence, the validity of the data should be carefully assessed beforehand because invalid data may bring trouble in the future.

Validity impacts the following DQ issues are the following

(1) *Inaccurate content of the field in the data due to manual entry* (raised from offline case 1 and 3) creates difficulties to understand the data, e.g. wrong address, wrong postal code or wrong spelling in mortgage data because of disobedience to DQ control procedures;
(2) Wrong coding or tagging in the data (case 3);
(3) *Uncertainty about the right to use the data.* For example no knowledge about licenses or the impact of the privacy regulation (case 1, 2, and 3, confirmed in in-depth case 1) might limit or even remove access of the organizations to personal data;
(4) *Difficult to extract value from anonymous data* (case 1, 2, and 3) as a consequence of privacy compliance because person-related field (e.g. name, phone number, email address) is the primary key of multiple data that are going to be combined;
(5) Anonymous field makes the data become incomplete for the task in hand (case 1, 2, and 3).

4.7   Visibility

Almost all the cases mentioned that it is difficult to discover the relationship among variables within the data. For example, it's difficult to reveal which group of ages that have increasing internet banking usage over time in certain country by only viewing the data. Moreover, the more sources combined in the process, the more variables are added and the more complex relationship among the variables. *Unless the organizations build capability to visualize big data, that relationship is difficult to discover* (case 1, 2, 3, 4, 5, 6, and 7).

4.8   Vast Resource

Some cases mentioned that *vast resources are essentially required in order to retrieve and process the data* (case 2 and 5). Retrieving huge size, very rapid generation, variety of the data needs, sufficient network bandwidth (especially if the organizations decided to put the data analytics platform in the cloud), computing power, and storage. Moreover, *data engineering skills* are required to retrieve and operate the data. Besides that, to discover the relationship among variables in the data and finally get the insight from the data organizations require *data scientist skills* (case 1, 2, 4, 5, 6, and 7).

4.9   Volatility, Viability, Value

No case mentioned volatility and viability characteristic of big data influence DQ. An explanation for this is that these factors are less essential for finance service organizations. Meanwhile, value is not coded from the investigated cases because it is conflicting with value-added dimension of DQ and 'value' is not big data specific.

5   Mapping Big Data and Data Quality

From the aforementioned DQ issues that were resulted by big data characteristics, each issue was then mapped into DQ dimension, as shown in Fig. 3. The corresponding case number either online or offline are put near the arrow.

The finding indicates there are no relationship between viability and volatility characteristic of big data with DQ in the investigated finance service organizations. The most dominant correlation is Velocity-Timeliness that were found in all online cases. The relationship reflects that finance service organizations perceive the rapid generation of the data and real-time use of data, such as credit card transaction data or insurance holder's claim, plays an important role to create timely value of data, such as for fraud detection. The next dominant correlation is Variety-Ease of operations, interpreted as inclusion of data from multiple sources that may come with inconsistent formats and conflicting contents makes organizations difficult to process the data. Variety-Value added follows behind, which indicate that value creation is strongly influenced by number of data sources and complexity level of content (unstructured) residing in the data. Another most dominant pair is Visibility-Value which reflect the need of visualization to quickly discover the relationship among variables in the data. Vast resources-Value added is the next, which indicates the need of vast resources (hardware, software, data engineers, and data scientists) to retrieve, exploit, visualize and analyze the data so the value from the data could be derived.

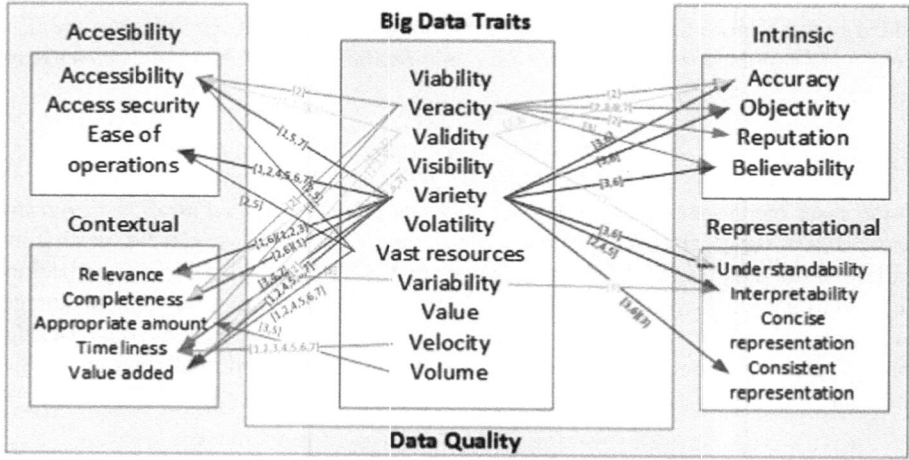

Fig. 3. Impact of big data characteristics on DQ dimensions ([x]: online case number, (x): offline case number)

The Table 4 was summarized from Fig. 3. It constructs a matrix that matches big data characteristics to DQ dimension. The number indicated in the pair represents the number of cases that mentioned the correlation.

Table 4. Number of cases from correlation pair between big data characteristics and DQ dimension

Data Quality	Volume	Velocity	Variety	Variability	Veracity	Validity	Volatility	Visibility	Viability	Vast Resources	Value	SUM
Intrinsic												17
Accuracy	0	0	2	0	1	2	0	0	0	0	0	5
Believability	0	0	2	0	2	0	0	0	0	0	0	4
Reputation	0	0	0	0	2	0	0	0	0	0	0	2
Objectivity	0	0	2	0	4	0	0	0	0	0	0	6
Representational												10
Concise representation	0	0	0	0	0	0	0	0	0	0	0	0
Consistent representation	0	0	3	0	0	0	0	0	0	0	0	3
Understandability	0	0	2	0	0	1	0	0	0	0	0	3
Interpretability	0	0	3	1	0	0	0	0	0	0	0	4
Accessibility												19
Accessibility	0	0	3	0	2	4	0	0	0	2	0	11
Access security	0	0	0	0	0	0	0	0	0	0	0	0
Ease of operations	0	0	6	0	0	0	0	0	0	2	0	8
Contextual												47
Relevance	0	0	5	1	0	0	0	0	0	0	0	6
Completeness	0	0	3	0	1	3	0	0	0	0	0	7
Timeliness	0	7	3	0	1	0	0	0	0	0	0	11
Appropriate amount	2	0	0	0	0	0	0	0	0	0	0	2
Value added	0	0	6	0	0	3	0	6	0	6	0	21
SUM	2	7	40	2	13	13	0	6	0	10	0	

From big data characteristics, variety is the most dominant one in our cases of the financial service organizations. It influences all categories of DQ, i.e. intrinsic, representational, accessibility, and contextual DQ. The reason for this is that nowadays organizations utilize multiple data sources, for example the ones that have formerly been ignored – namely "long tail" of big data, as well as new generated ones (Bean 2016). The next most influential big data characteristic is Validity which reflects organization's compliance to regulation and procedures, for example about use of personal data (e.g. privacy law, untraceable requests, and confidentiality agreements). Compliance to privacy is very vital for service organizations (Yu et al. 2015), especially bank and insurance companies (Breaux et al. 2006; Karagiannis et al. 2007). Moreover, validity affects the accessibility to customer's data in the long run, meaning that one day organization may loss its right to access the personal data if the customer or regulator requests to disclose or remove personal data. As a result, completeness of the data drops and value creation process (e.g. analyzing data) becomes more complex if anonymous data is the only way organization can use. Another dominant big data characteristic is veracity. Veracity or trustworthiness of the data is inevitable when multiple data sources are utilized to discover more insights (Leboeuf 2016). Since veracity includes authenticity, origin/reputation, availability, accountability of the data (Tee 2013), unsurprisingly intrinsic quality which embodied the issues is mostly influenced by this characteristic.

As depicted in Table 4, the most correlated category of DQ dimension is contextual quality. It is unsurprising because every organization tries their best for extracting contexts from big data. Two dimensions from contextual quality are dominant in the finding, i.e. value-added and timeliness. Since today's organizations struggle creating business value from the data (Reid et al. 2015), the value from use of the data needs ample research. Another dominant correlated DQ dimension is accessibility which sounds the awareness of the financial service organizations to compliance.

6 Conclusion

The objective of this paper is to investigate the relation between big data and data quality. This study is among the first that investigated the complex relationship. To attain the objective, we conducted literature review, online and offline case studies in financial service organizations. Seven online case studies were initially performed to reveal the correlation, followed by three offline studies for cross-referencing and refining the findings. DQ issues raised from the case studies are then coded and mapped into the corresponding pair of big data characteristic and DQ dimension using content analysis. This provided detailed insight into the relationships between the V's of big data and dimensions of DQ. The Vs' take a blackbox perspective on the data. It characterizes the data form the outside. Meanwhile, DQ is about the actual data and can only be determined when investigating the data and by opening the blackbox. The V's characteristics and DQ are similar in the sense that they provide insight about the data. They are complementary as the V's take a look from the outside and at the possible usage, whereas, DQ look at the actual datasets.

The most related pair is Velocity-Timeliness, which indicates the more rapid the data being generated and processed, the better timely the data to use. This is followed by Variety-Ease of operations (more data sources and more varied structure of the data, the more complexity to retrieve, exploit, analyze and visualize the data), Variety-Value (the more data sources and more varied structure of the data resulting in more difficult to create value from the data), Visibility-Value (the more hidden relationship within the data, the more difficult to create value from the data) and Vast resources-Value (the more resources needed to process the data, the more difficult to create value from the data). Except for Viability and Volatility all Vs of big data influence DQ. Concise representation and access security were not found to be DQ issues in the cases. Variety is the most dominant factor impacting all categories of DQ, followed by Validity and Veracity. This suggest that term 'big data' is misleading as in our research we found that most of the time volume ('big') was not an issue and variety, validity and veracity is much more important.

Our findings suggest that organizations should take care of managing the variety of data and also ensure the validity and veracity of big data. The most correlated category of DQ dimension is contextual quality, which includes value and timeliness as the most dominant correlated DQ dimensions, followed by accessibility. These findings suggest that more effort should be spent on improving contextual use of the data as well as ensuring long-term accessibility to the data.

Further research recommendation is to cross-reference the findings with big data implementation in other information-intensive domains, such as telecommunication, government, and retail for generalization. This findings also open avenue to develop tools to improve and manage big DQ.

Acknowledgement. Part of the research was funded and supported by PT. Telekomunikasi Indonesia, Tbk. in the context of the Global Education Program 2015.

References

Akerkar, R.: Big Data Computing. CRC Press (2013)

Bean, R.: Variety, not volume, is driving big data initiatives. MIT Sloan Manag. Rev., 1–5 (2016)

Beattie, C., Meara B.: How big is "big data" in healthcare? Oliver Wieman (2013). Accessed from http://blogs.sas.com/content/hls/2011/10/21/how-big-is-big-data-inhealthcare/

Bovee, M., Srivastava, R., Mak, B.: A conceptual framework and belief-function approach to assessing overall information quality. In: Paper Presented at the Proceedings of the 6th International Conference on Information Quality, vol. 18, pp. 51–74 (2001)

Breaux, T.D., Vail, M.W., Antón, A.I.: Towards regulatory compliance: extracting rights and obligations to align requirements with regulations. In: Proceedings of the IEEE International Conference on Requirements Engineering, pp. 46–55 (2006). https://doi.org/10.1109/RE.2006.68

Chemitiganti, V.: Big Data Use Cases Across Financial Services (2016). Accessed from http://www.wallstreetandtech.com/data-management/big-data-use-cases-acrossfinancial-services/d/d-id/1268649?

Chen, C.L.P., Zhang, C.-Y.: Data-intensive applications, challenges, techniques and technologies: a survey on Big Data. Inf. Sci. (2014). https://doi.org/10.1016/j.ins.2014.01.015

Dini, P.: Big Data : Processing Anatomy (2016)

Douglas, L.: 3D data management: controlling data volume, velocity and variety. Gartner (2001). Accessed 6 June 2001

Eckerson, W.W.: Data quality and the bottom line. TDWI Report, The Data Warehouse Institute (2002)

Eppler, M.J.: A generic framework for information quality in knowledge-intensive processes. In: Proceedings of the Sixth International Conference on Information Quality, pp. 329–346 (2001)

Fan, J.Q., Han, F., Liu, H.: Challenges of big data analysis. Natl. Sci. Rev. 1(2), 293–314 (2014). https://doi.org/10.1093/nsr/nwt032

Fernández, A. et al.: Big Data with Cloud Computing: an insight on the computing environment, MapReduce, and programming frameworks. Wiley Interdiscip. Rev. Data Min. Knowl. Discov. 4(5), 380–409 (2014). https://doi.org/10.1002/widm.1134

Fox, C., Levitin, A., Redman, T.: The notion of data and its quality dimensions. Inf. Process. Manag. 30(1), 9–19 (1994)

Glowalla, P., Sunyaev, A.: Process-driven data and information quality management in the financial service sector in the financial service sector (2012)

Hsieh, H.-F., Shannon, S.E.: Three approaches to qualitative content analysis. Qual. Health Res. 15(9), 1277–1288 (2005). https://doi.org/10.1177/1049732305276687

Huang, K.-T., Lee, Y.W., Wang, R.Y. Quality Information and Knowledge. Prentice Hall PTR (1998)

Hulstijn, J., van der Jagt, J., Heijboer, P.: Integrity of electronic patient records. In: Janssen, M., Scholl, Hans J., Wimmer, Maria A., Tan, Y.-h. (eds.) EGOV 2011. LNCS, vol. 6846, pp. 378–391. Springer, Heidelberg (2011). https://doi.org/10.1007/978-3-642-22878-0_32

IBM: Global Technology Outlook (2012). Accessed from http://www.research.ibm.com/careers/internships/index.shtml?lnk=intern-btn

Janssen, M., Van Der Voort, H., Wahyudi, A.: Factors influencing big data decisionmaking quality. J. Bus. Res. (2016). https://doi.org/10.1016/j.jbusres.2016.08.007

Kahn, B.K., Strong, D.M.: Product and service performance model for information quality: an update. In: Proceedings of the 1998 Conference on Information Quality (1998). Accessed from http://mitiq.mit.edu/ICIQ/Documents/IQConference1998/Papers/ProductServicePerformanceModelforIQ.pdf

Karagiannis, D., Mylopoulos, J., Schwab, M.: Business process-based regulation compliance: the case of the Sarbanes-Oxley Act. In: Proceedings - 15th IEEE International Requirements Engineering Conference, RE 2007, (October), pp. 315–321 (2007). https://doi.org/10.1109/RE.2007.11

Klaus, K.: On the importance of data quality in services: an application in the financial industry. In: 2011 International Conference on Emerging Intelligent Data and Web Technologies, pp. 148–152 (2011). https://doi.org/10.1109/EIDWT.2011.31

LaValle, S., Lesser, E., Shockley, R., Hopkins, M.S., Kruschwitz, N.: Big data, analytics and the path from insights to value. Mit Sloan Manag. Rev. 21 (2013)

Leavitt, N.: Storage challenge: where will all that big data go? Computer 46(9), 22–25 (2013)

Leboeuf, K.: The 5 vs of big data: predictions for 2016. Excelacom, Inc, (1), 3–5 (2016). Accessed from http://www.excelacom.com/resources/blog/the-5-vs-of-big-datapredictions-for-2016

m-Brain. (n.d.). Big data technology with 8 V's. Accessed from https://www.mbrain.com/home/technology/big-data-with-8-vs/

Manyika, J., Chui, M., Brown, B., Bughin, J., Dobbs, R., Roxburgh, C., Byers, A.H.: Big data: the next frontier for innovation, competition, and productivity (2011)

Marx, V.: The big challenges of big data. Nature 498(7453), 255–260 (2013)

Miller, H.: The multiple dimensions of information quality. Inf. Syst. Manag. 13(2), 79 (1996). https://doi.org/10.1080/10580539608906992

Mouzhi, G., Helfert, M.: A review of information quality research. Proc. Int. Conf. Inf. Q. (ICIQ) 2007, 1–16 (2007). https://doi.org/10.1049/cp:20070800

Naumann, F.: Quality-Driven Query Answering for Integrated Information Systems, vol. 43, pp. 1–175. Springer, Berlin (2002)

Nelson, R.R., Todd, P.A., Wixom, B.H. Antecedents of information and system quality: an empirical examination within the context of data warehousing. J. Manag. Inf. Syst. 21(4), 199–235 (2005). https://doi.org/10.1362/026725705774538390

Owais, S.S., Hussein, N.S.: Extract five categories CPIVW from the 9 V's characteristics of the big data. Int. J. Adv. Comput. Sci. Appl. 7(3), 254–258 (2016)

PricewaterhouseCoopers: Where have you been all my life? How the financial services industry can unlock the value in Big Data (2013)

Redman, T.C.: The impact of poor data quality on the typical enterprise. Commun. ACM 41(2), 79–82 (1998)

Reid, C., Petley, R., McClean, J., Jones, K., Ruck, P.: Seizing the information advantage. PWC Iron Mt. (2015)

Tayi, G.K., Ballou, D.P.: Examining data quality. Commun. ACM 41(2), 54–57 (1998)

Tee, J.: Handling the four 'V's of big data: volume, velocity, variety, and veracity (2013). Accessed from http://www.theserverside.com/feature/Handling-the-four-Vs-of-big-datavolume-velocity-variety-and-veracity

The Economist Intelligence Unit: The Deciding Factor: Big Data & Decision Making. Capgemini (2012). Accessed from http://www.capgemini.com/sites/default/files/resource/pdf/The_Deciding_Factor__Big_Data___Decision_Making.pdf

Verhoef, P.C., Kooge, E., Walk, N.: Creating value with big data analytics: making smarter marketing decisions. Routledge (2015)

Wang, R.Y.: A product perspective on total data quality management. Commun. ACM **41**(2), 58–65 (1998). https://doi.org/10.1145/269012.269022

Wang, R.Y., Kon, H.B., Madnick, S.E.: Data quality requirements analysis and modeling. In: Proceedings of IEEE 9th International Conference on Data Engineering, pp. 670–677 (April 1993). https://doi.org/10.1109/ICDE.1993.344012

Wang, R.Y., Strong, D.M.: Beyond accuracy: what data quality means to data consumers. Source J. Manag. Inf. Syst. 12(4), 5–33 (1996). https://doi.org/10.2307/40398176

Ward, J.S., Barker, A.: Undefined By Data: A Survey of Big Data Definitions (2013)

Yu, Y., Mu, Y., Ateniese, G.: Recent advances in security and privacy in big data J.UCS special issue. J. Univers. Comput. Sci. **21**(3), 365–368 (2015)

Zahay, D., Peltier, J., Krishen, A.S.: Building the foundation for customer data quality in CRM systems for financial services firms. J. Database Mark. Cust. Strateg. Manag. **19**(1), 5–16 (2012). https://doi.org/10.1057/dbm.2012.6

Zhou, Z.H., Chawla, N.V, Jin, Y.C., Williams, G.J.: Big data opportunities and challenges: discussions from data analytics perspectives. IEEE Comput. Intell. Mag. **9**(4), 62–74 (2014). https://doi.org/10.1109/mci.2014.2350953

Zicari, R.V.: Big data: challenges and opportunities. Big Data Comput. 103–128 (2014)

Representational Quality Challenges of Big Data: Insights from Comparative Case Studies

Agung Wahyudi[1(✉)], Samuli Pekkola[2], and Marijn Janssen[1]

[1] Delft University of Technology, Jaffalaan 5, 2628 BX Delft, The Netherlands
{a.wahyudi, M.F.W.H.A.Janssen}@tudelft.nl
[2] Tampere University of Technology, PO Box 541, 33101 Tampere, Finland
samuli.pekkola@tut.fi

Abstract. Big data is said to provide many benefits. However, as data originates from multiple sources with different quality, big data is not easy to use.
Representational quality refers to the concise and consistent representation of
data to allow ease of understanding of the data and interpretability. In this paper,
we investigate the challenges in creating representational quality of big data.
Two case studies are investigated to understand the challenges emerging from
big data. Our findings suggest that the veracity and velocity of big data makes
interpretation more difficult. Our findings also suggest that decisions are made
ad-hoc and decision-makers often are not able to understand the ins and outs.
Sense-making is one of the main challenges in big data. Taking a naturalistic
decision-making view can be used to understand the challenges of big data
processing, interpretation and use in decision-making better. We recommend
that big data research should focus more on easy interpretation of the data.

Keywords: Big data · Interpretation · Sense-making
Naturalistic decision making

1 Introduction

Big data can provide a number of benefits such as better understanding the customers,
effective and efficient the marketing effort and fraud prevention & detection, all aiming
for creating a competitive advantage (Beattie and Meara 2013; LaValle et al. 2013).
Gaining these advantages is not easy as big data often originates from multiple sources,
each having different and varying data quality (DQ). The diversity of formats and
difference in quality makes big data complex to manage (Wahyudi and Janssen 2016).

DQ is defined "as its scale of fitness for use by data consumers" (Wang and Strong
1996, p. 6) which implies broad characteristics, i.e. not only intrinsic properties of the
data but also other aspects, such as representation, accessibility and value-creation
context (Wang and Strong 1996; Wang et al. 2002). Representational Data Quality
(RDQ), a subset of DQ, emphasizes how the data is structured and comprehended by the
data consumers (Wang and Strong 1996, p. 21). It is represented by dimensions such as
understandability, interpretability, consistent representation, and concise representation.

RDQ varies due to veracity and variety of big data. Inclusion of multiple sources
brings varied levels of trustworthiness, interpretability, and representation. RDQ issues

S. A. Al-Sharhan et al. (Eds.): I3E 2018, LNCS 11195, pp. 520–538, 2018.
https://doi.org/10.1007/978-3-030-02131-3_46

such as lack of metadata, heterogenous sampling periods, different meaning of terminologies, unstructured or semi-structured representation, variety of data format, and lack of a primary key on data are reported in literature as challenges for extracting values from big data (Hilbert 2016; Zuiderwijk et al. 2012).

Such issues create a complex endeavor to any organization for interpreting big data for subsequent use like a decision making (Janssen et al. 2016). First interpretation problem is that stakeholders' interpretation often unfit to the senses so that it inhibits further action (Weick et al. 2005). Moreover, multiple interpretations on the same dataset are often occurred in a multiactor environment.

Many studies often take one viewpoint, such as focus on e data (Leavitt 2013; Qiu 2016; Yaqoob et al. 2016; Zhou et al. 2014), the process or solution (Geerdink 2013; Merelli et al. 2014; Scarf 2015; Wahyudi et al. 2018), or the action (Hofmann 2015; Osuszek et al. 2016; Power 2014; The Economist Intelligence Unit 2012). An perspective including all phases from raw data to the decision-making and including data, process and organizational aspects is missing. Such a perspective should help us to arrive at a broader, socio-tech view of big data challenges.

This paper locks at the process from big data to a decision making in an integrated manner. We start by providing the background of big data representational quality. Next, the literature is surveyed to identify the challenges of big data RDQ according to the big data usage cycle. In Sect. 4, we discuss our research approaches. Two cases regarding big data interpretation are presented in Sect. 5, i.e. a case in a telecom and a case in a manufacturing company. We elaborate the findings in more details in Sect. 6. Finally, the conclusions are drawn in Sect. 7.

2 Big Data Representational Quality

Turning big data into a decision is influenced by contractual governance, relational governance, big data analytics capability, knowledge exchange, collaboration, process integration and standardization, flexible infrastructure, staff, decision maker quality, and data quality of the big data sources (Janssen et al. 2016). Low quality big data provides little value, hinders people to interpret it, and results in questionable decisions.

DQ is defined "as its scale of fitness for use by data consumers" (Wang and Strong 1996, p. 6). This implies that DQ ranges from internal dimensions such as accuracy and completeness to wider properties such as relevance to the task in hand, how secured the method of data retrieval, and how easy the data to be operated.

Representational Data Quality (RDQ) emphasizes how the data is structured and comprehended by the data consumers. It includes "aspects related to the format of the data (i.e. concise representation and consistent representation) and the meaning of the data (understandability and interpretability)" (Wang and Strong 1996, p. 21). Concise and consistent representation describe how well and persistent is the content structure of the data. The extent of data consumers' acceptance of the data is specified by understandability and interpretability.

The RDQ dimensions are defined as follow. Understandability is the extent to which data are clear, unambiguity and easily comprehendible (Wang and Strong 1996). Interpretability is the extent to which language, units and data definitions are clear

(Wang and Strong 1996). Concise representation is the extent to which data are compactly represented without being overwhelming (i.e., brief in presentation, yet complete and to the point) (Wang and Strong 1996). Consistent representation is the extent to which data are always presented in the same format and are compatible with previous data (Lee 2002; Wand and Wang 1996).

RDQ covers many aspects and requires that data is structured and fully comprehended by the data consumers so that it is interpretable, easy to understand, and represented in a concise and consistent manner. Yet, big data is often not structured. Velocity and veracity often prevent this. RDQ can be decomposed of a number of dimensions, including understandability, interpretability, concise representation, and consistent representation.

3   RDQ Challenges in Literature

In this section, we discuss the big data usage lifecycle. In each step, the main challenges from the literature are discussed.

3.1   Big Data Usage Lifecycle: From Big Data to Decision

To analyze big data necessitates understanding of overall journey of big data value creation, i.e. from big data to action. literature shows several steps for the big data processes (Bizer et al. 2012; Chen et al. 2014). In this research we use four interactive and iterative steps as depicted in Fig. 1. We refer to these steps as the big data usage lifecycle, as the use of big data is a continuous learning process.

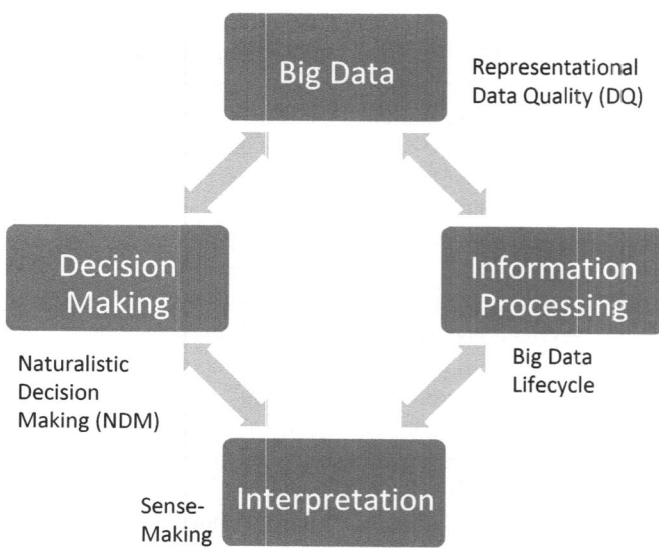

Fig. 1. Big data usage lifecycle

3.2   Challenges in Big Data Step

Big data is commonly described by its characteristics. Initial big data characteristics consist of three V's, i.e. Volume, Velocity, and Variety (Gartner 2001). Over time, the number of V's is expanding. Currently 11 V's are identified, including Variability, Veracity, Validity, Volatility, Visibility, Viability, Vast resources, Value (Fernández et al. 2014; Leboeuf 2016; m-Brain n.d.).

From all characteristics of big data, RDQ is strongly related with the veracity and variety (Katal et al. 2013). Veracity is the characteristic of big data that conveys questionable trustworthiness of the data (e.g. authenticity, origin/reputation, availability, accountability) (Tee 2013). Meanwhile, variety imposes the use of various data sources and diverse format (i.e. structured, semi-structured, unstructured data) (Douglas 2001).

Internal big data (i.e. data sourced internally) is owned and managed by the organization itself. As a consequence, the dataset usually has high RDQ, i.e. well-presented, in a standardized format, concise and structured. Meanwhile, other datasets, especially external large datasets (e.g. open data or social media), often have insufficient RDQ due to lack of proper description (e.g. unit) on observation records, unstructured content, lack of metadata, missing a primary key, among many others.

Variety of data sources introduces various levels of understandability and interpretability. Human-made image data, such as doctors' handwritings in medical records, is difficult for computers to interpret and analyze due to its unique style and the quality of personal handwriting (Strong et al. 1997). The doctors' coding system may also differ from one hospital to another. Another example is the low resolution document scans, which is also difficult to read and understand. Lack of metadata and the observational unit creates an interpretability problem. Although the variable name is usually known, the unit of measurement is not. This makes it difficult to interpret the value of the variable. Multiple interpretation could occur without metadata since terminologies may differ. Inclusion of unstructured contents is also problematic for interpretation. Ermolayev et al. (2013) mentions 42% of respondents find unstructured content e.g. social media and email, too difficult to interpret. Furthermore, 40% of respondents believe that they have too much unstructured data (Zicari 2012).

Due to variety of big data, some data may not comply with the organization's quality standards, such as conciseness. Data may have multiple variables merged together (e.g. variable income and population into variable per-capita) (Wickham 2012). Sawant (2013) mentions that 90% of data are noise and Gantz and Reinsel (2011b) that only 0.5% of all data are analyzable.

Consistency is inevitably met with a variety of data sources and heterogeneous systems. For example, currency in a U.S. database is mostly in dollar, whereas those in a Japanese database are in yen. The format of date may also become an issue.

3.3   Challenges in the Information Processing Step

The V's characterizing big data complicate information processing. Insights are mostly derived from multiple diverse datasets (Wahyudi et al. 2018). Interpretation may begin directly by looking at the content of observation on the raw dataset, such as rain precipitation in a dataset from a weather station. However, most interpretations are resulted from multiple datasets combination, e.g. combination of weather data and flight data to determine the impact of bad weather to the departure/arrival delay. Combining many datasets needs a big data lifecycle that compromises of a number of stages, such as discover, access, exploit, analyze, and manage (Wahyudi and Janssen 2016).

Discover involves activities for looking for the right datasets for the task at hand. In discover stage, activities like search, quality assessment, and making an agreement with data providers are important in matching relevant and required datasets.

Those data are retrieved in the *Access* stage. In the access stage, the stakeholders retrieve datasets from the providers and pool them in a central repository, e.g. a data lake. *Exploit* includes activities for data preparation and data transformation. In this stage, the datasets are prepared, cleansed, combined, transformed, and aggregated using different operations such as conditioning, filtering, manipulating, partitioning, reformatting, sorting, joining, merging, and grouping. In *Analyze* stage, the relationships within the data are investigated by using a model or a set of hypotheses. Various analytical methods are employed, e.g. predictive analytics, text mining, time series, trade-off analytics, machine/deep learning, and natural language processing. Once the data is processed, the result are disseminated and communicated to corresponding stakeholders. A number of media are introduced for such purpose, e.g. a dashboard, reports, alerts, or notifications (Matheus et al. 2018). This keeps the stakeholders informed about the situation under concern.

Manage stage is the stage where all activities are orchestrated and managed to ensure smooth data processing sequences. The functions include data catalogs, metadata, process integration, and security.

There are a number of RDQ challenges in this process. First, substantial efforts are made to overcome multiple levels of conciseness and consistency. To get the data tidy and homogenous, a number of activities, such as cleansing, normalizing, preparing, transforming, and aggregating the data, need to be done in the Exploit stage. Interpretability causes difficulties to analyze the data. The lack of primary key in the data need more efforts to query and combine. Second, data with low interpretability is difficult to analyze and integrate with other data. For example, combining multiple datasets with a different sampling period and incorporating a dataset without a (clearly explained) metadata is challenging in Analyze step.

3.4   Challenges in the Interpretation Step

Interpretation can be conducted on the raw dataset or on the processed information from a data lifecycle which is further disseminated using different media (Matheus et al. 2018; Wahyudi et al. 2018). Interpretation of the data or processed data (i.e. information) relies on sense-making. Sense or meaning is defined as "mental representation of possible relationships among things, events, and relationships" (Baumeister 1991, p. 15). Sense of data is made by using the sense-making process that relies on individual sense-making capacity, carved out through work, experiences, and training.

Making sense of the data or information is referred to as sense-making. "Sensemaking is a way station on the road to a consensually constructed, coordinated system of action" (Taylor and Van Every 1999, p. 275). Sense-making is a process that has the seven identifiable characteristics (Weick et al. 2005). First, it is grounded in identity construction, meaning that sense-making is a subjective process where individual change is derived from three fundamental needs: the need for self-enhancement, the selfefficacy motive, and the need for self-consistency. Second, sense-making is a retrospective process. People understand what they are doing only after the completion of the action. Sense-making is a backward process that the future action is determined by what the actor has learned in the past. Third, sense-making is enactive of sensible environments. Sense-making is shaped by the context of the environment in which people interact. Fourth, sense-making is a social process. People develop sensemaking in an organizational network of collectively shared meanings and agreed vocabularies. Fifth, sense-making is an ongoing process which neither starts nor stops. People chop certain moments out of continuous flows and extract cues for these moments. Sixth, sense-making is focused on and by extracted cues process. Seventh, sense-making is driven by plausibility rather than accuracy. For individual perspective, plausibility is more important than accuracy. People in any given situation are exposed to multiple cues, with multiple meanings, often intended for multiple audiences. They should make sense of it based on their capacity. The interpretation does not have to be accurate, merely plausible and acceptable.

Sense-making occurs along the data lifecycle (i.e. from discover to analyze). If the data fit in the stakeholder's sense, he proceeds to the subsequent actions, i.e. make a data-driven decision. However, it is not always the case. Misinterpretation or multi-interpretation phenomena are trivial in a multi-actor environment comprising stakeholders with different requirements and different levels of capacity such as knowledge, expertise, and skill. Different persons on the same job probably have different meanings on the same data. For example, an experienced sales manager may doubt information about top sales area that is out of his prediction and sense that has been carved through guidance, pattern, skill, and knowledge during his lifetime work. His initial prediction that is the area where most of his clients reside may not come up on the dashboard. As a result, he probably needs certain steps (e.g. validation of the information) prior to taking further actions. A competent engineer may recognize a cause of certain machine trouble just looking at few symptoms (i.e. fewer data). This is because he has trained his sense through guidance, pattern, skill, training and knowledge that have been encountered during his work. Meanwhile, others may need more datasets (e.g. environment's measures, machine logs) to understand the situation better. Their initial prediction may not align with the information on the dashboard or report. Consequently, validation of the information (e.g. more datasets that support the finding, other hypotheses' testing) prior to taking further actions.

Multi-interpretation occurs in a multiple-stakeholder situation when same information is interpreted differently. Front-end units (e.g. customer retention department) and back-end units may have a different interpretation of the same performance figure, e.g. customer handling time. The front-end unit may not be satisfied with the figure because the number of customers increases their dissatisfaction towards current service delivery. On the other hand, as long as the figure complies with the performance indicator or SLA targets, the back-end unit remains satisfied.

Sense-making relies on RDQ. Low interpretability data such as the absence or unclarity of metadata and the lack of convention of vocabularies or metrics within the organization may cause misinterpretations. Unavailability of metadata and unclear metadata descriptions create different interpretations among the data consumers. Multi-interpretation could be a result of the lack of definition of vocabularies or metrics. For example, throughput can be perceived differently by various stakeholders; some may consider it as the end-to-end transfer rate while others may refer it to the actual connection speed between the end user and the nearest point of the providers' equipment.

3.5   Challenges in the Decision Making Step

People take actions by their interpretations of the situation. The sense-making interpretation plays also an important role in the decision-making. Decision is primarily not driven by a set of choices but subjectively. This is the area of naturalistic decision making (NDM), which is "an attempt to understand how people make decisions in real-world contexts that are meaningful and familiar to them" (Lipshitz and Klein 2001, p. 332).

In a NDM four aspects are relevant. e.g. (1) process-oriented, (2) situation-action matching decision rules, (3) context-bound information modeling and (4) empirical based prescription. First, NDM views decision-making as a process-oriented activity that focuses on the cognitive process of proficient decision makers rather than predicting which options will be implemented (Lipshitz and Klein 2001). This view is complementary to big data which is often used to show various options and insights. To be valid, NDM has to describe what information decision makers actually seek, how they interpret it, and which decision rules they actually use. Second, NDM follows situation-action matching decision rules. Proficient decision makers make a decision on various forms of matching on the situation in hand and not by concurrent choices. Appropriateness is more important than outcome superiority. Third, NDM is context bound informal modeling. Proficient decision making is driven by experience-tied knowledge. Last, NDM offers empirical-based prescription, namely deriving prescriptions from descriptive models of expert performance.

There are a number of challenges in this step. First, very often the data or extracted information unfits to stakeholder's sense. Consequently, decision makers face a dilemmatic situation when the information is different with their sense.

Another challenge is that sense-making and naturalistic decision making are difficult to standardize since they are subjective. They may work perfectly in individual level but to code them as a standard in an organization and internalize the standard are impossible.

3.6   Overview of RDQ Challenges

We summarize the RDQ challenges in every step of big data usage lifecycle in Table 1.

Table 1. Summary of RDQ challenges

Big data usage lifecycle step	RDQ Challenges	Descriptions	References
Big data	• Lack of proper description (e.g. unit) on variables • Too much unstructured content • Lack of metadata • Missing a primary key • Unconcise variables (e.g. date and hour in a single variable) • Inconsistency sampling periods • Inconsistent format of observations due to use of heterogeneous systems • Understandability issue for machine (e.g. human-made image and low resolution document)	Variety and veracity of big data sources introduced various level of understandability, interpretability, conciseness, and consistency	(Ermolayev et al. 2013; Gantz and Reinsel 2011a; Sawant and Shah 2013; Wickham 2012; Zicari 2012; Zuiderwijk et al. 2012)
Information processing	• Need substantial efforts to overcome multiple levels of conciseness and consistency of big data • Data with low interpretability is difficult to analyze and join with other data	Most insights need to be extracted from multiple big datasets with different levels of RDQ which require a big data platform to process with in a big data lifecycle	(Ji et al. 2012; Matheus et al. 2018; Wahyudi et al. 2018)
Interpretation	• Low interpretability data causes misinterpretation • People with different levels of senses (due to experiences and capabilities) may have different interpretation on a data • Multi-interpretation occurs in a multiple-stakeholder situation	Wrong or multiple interpretations on the same data might occur among data consumers	(Baumeister 1991; Taylor and Van Every 1999; Weick et al. 2005)

(continued)

Table 1. (*continued*)

Big data usage lifecycle step	RDQ Challenges	Descriptions	References
Decision making	• Frequently the extracted information unfits to stakeholder's sense; Decision makers faced a dilemmatic situation when the information is different with their sense • Sense-making and naturalistic decision making is difficult to be standardized in an organization since they introduces subjectivity	Decision is hardly made naturalistically in case the information is out of sense	(Lipshitz and Klein 2001)

4 Research Approach

This study investigates the challenges of RDQ of big data. To understand the process of turning big data into the decision, we investigate real-life scenarios. This necessitates deep understanding of the context (Dale et al. 1992; Davenport et al. 2010). Then we can construct and decompose the decision-making process and divided it into notable steps and concepts, described earlier.

We conduct a qualitative and comparative case study (Yin 2013) to gain deep understanding about the process of big data decision making. Case study research is a widely used in information systems research, and is well suited for investigating organizational issues (Benbasat et al. 1987). We compared a telecommunication case and a manufacturing case. They were selected because of variety of challenges and aspects of representational quality.

The first case consists of six interviews with the people in charge of network performance management in the operation department. They included the network performance analyst/scientists, radio network specialists, big data platform engineer, and network performance manager. The interviews were conducted through a video call and lasted for 30–60 min. We also investigated various documents; service level agreements, quarter reports (i.e. InfoMemo), network performance reports, SOPs, manuals, and the network configuration document.

For the second case, twelve open-ended interviews were conducted. The interviewees include Vice president of product management; Global product manager, Condition monitoring engineer, Business development manager, PLM manager, Manager conceptual design & analysis, Chief mechanical engineer, Quality engineer, Unit manager, Finland; Sales manager, Northern Europe; Customer service engineer; Development engineer. The open-ended interviews focused on different themes related to service development and information usage. The themes included information needs, managerial practices, knowledge concepts, information technology and information systems, and knowledge and network dynamics. The interviews were conducted face-to-face in the company premises. They lasted for 30–90 min.

5   Case Studies

5.1   Case 1: From Network Performance Data to Network Optimization Decision (Telecom Case)

Background. A mobile telecom company in Indonesia is the first case. As of September 2017, 73% of the population of Indonesia are their subscribers. Around 152 thousand Base Transceiver Stations are serving the massive number of subscribers. In 2014, the company has been utilizing big data platform to support them in operation and maintenance. Operational effectiveness and cost efficiency are strived to achieve using the platform.

Findings. The telecom company utilizes big data for a multi-vendor scheme in their business, but usually clusters the same brand in one region. However, in a specific region, multi-vendor approach may occur as it supports faster service deployment and keeps competitiveness among vendors high, e.g. in terms of price, performance, or service. Inevitably, the company has to deal with the complexity raised by multi-vendor environment.

Due to large customer base, the company collects vast amounts of data related to connection activity, for example call detail records, connection records, cell handover logs, authentication, authorization, and accounting records, and network performance data. Every network device collects the data and pools it into a centralized operational system support (OSS).

The first case study focuses on the network performance data, specifically the dataset related to drop call rate (DCR). DCR is the fraction of the calls, which were cut off before the speaking parties had finished their conversation and hung up. This fraction is measured as a ratio to all calls, and usually denoted in percentage. The bigger the ratio, the worse performance the network indicates. The company internally aimed at DCR rate of less than 2%.

Each vendor has different terminologies and mechanisms to derive DCR. For example, some vendors report DCR value directly in their proprietary applications while the others did not directly report DCR but its components, i.e. the number of drop calls and the number of total calls.

Regarding accessibility, also there are different data collection methods. Some vendors allow data collection directly from their databases while some provide only a streaming text file or a certain port for streaming the data. The network data is usually at an aggregated level. Mostly the level of granularity is on base transceiver station level although some providers may grant access to raw data, i.e. the network performance counter record.

Representation quality of DCR-related data was good in the case. This is understandable as the variables have defined names (e.g. "dropped call rate", "drop call", "total call"), and their values are generated digitally. The data is easily interpretable since its metadata is explicitly articulated in the vendors' technical guidebook. Also, as the variables (i.e. the number of calls) has no unit, its interpretation is easy. The data is represented concisely as variables are not merged, and there is no consistent representation issue since the values are integers and unitless. The level of granularity of the data from every vendor is consistent.

The vendors have different naming conventions and data generation policies (such as sampling period and granularity), so the DCR-related data need to be prepared, tidied, filtered, and transformed before being aggregated on the level of base stations, clusters, regions, or national.

Data delivery is managed at the vendors' OSS from where the data is moved to the data analytics cloud. Batch and real-time processing are separated in the vendors' data processing platform (Marz and Warren 2015). The batch layer retrieves the dataset and stores it in the master copy. Then it pre-computes the batch views on updated master datasets. The data is also forwarded to speed layer for real-time operation. This ensures new data being represented in query functions quickly. Once new batch views are available, the serving layer automatically swaps those in so that the most up-todate results are available. The DCR figure is visualized in a Tableau dashboard. A number of reports are also built by using Tableau application (Fig. 2).

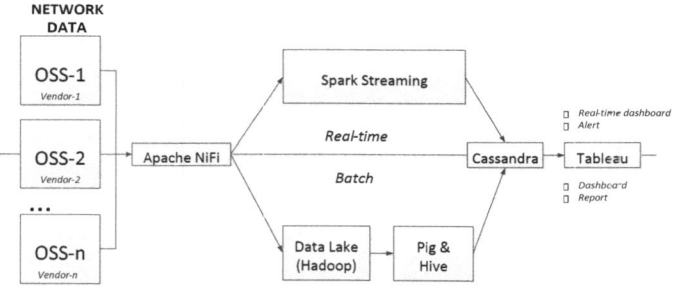

Fig. 2. Big data platform (for processing DCR-related datasets)

Interpreting DCR values is subjective, i.e. it varies between the analysts. The values may also contradict with the experienced field analysts' presumptions, carved out from everyday complaints (i.e. social and sensible to the environment). The analysts have tacit understanding about problematic sites (i.e. retrospective aspect), so they perceived it strange to have some clusters repeatedly harvesting complaints with a good DCR value. On the other hand, areas with fewer complaint sometimes have higher DCR than the more complaint areas (i.e. extracting specific cues aspect). Therefore, some areas are plausible with the corresponding DCR, but others are not (i.e. plausibility aspect).

The interpretation problems hinder the operation managers to make decisions on resource allocation for network optimization. He usually delegates the network performance review process to the analysts (i.e. process-orientation aspect). Based on his/her input, the manager may allocate resources to improve DCR of certain areas (i.e.

situation-matching decision rules aspect), and follow them up (i.e. appropriateness aspect). He may also have experiences from previous network optimizations (i.e. empirical-based prescription aspect) before deciding to proceed with allocating resources (i.e. context-informal modeling aspect). As a response to the situation, the manager postponed the network optimization. Instead he initiated an investigation on finding how drop call value is derived or generated in every vendor's OSS.

The investigation resulted that every vendor employs different definition for a drop call. Every flow in a call flow could end the call, resulting different classes of call terminations. Every vendor has their own interpretation of which termination classes could be categorized as drop calls. Some vendors only include radio frequency termination while others include terminations that occurred in their own premises and neglect drops in interconnected equipment, or even include all abnormal terminations.

Retrospectively, the findings indicate the interpretation quality of the DCR-related data varies from initially good to poor due to different references used to define a drop call. Standardization (i.e. which termination classes belong to a drop call) might restore the interpretation quality of the data.

5.2   Case 2: From Maintenance Data to Decision (Manufacturing Case)

Background. The second case is a globally operating Finnish manufacturing company of about 1000 employees and service partners, and operations in 15 countries. About 90% of their products are exported worldwide. Service business plays a minimal role as only 1/3 of the turnover (total 105M€ in 2016) origins from services. In 2015, the company wanted to increase this share by better utilizing internal and external data for product maintenance and for advanced telemonitoring services.

Findings. The service development began with mapping the needs and current maintenance processes and data available. In principle, the maintenance process was adequate and well defined, with a limited number of actors; engineers and repairmen. The products, when getting broken, are either fixed on-site (seldom) or disassembled from the larger machine and shipped to Finland for maintenance work. However, there is no standardized information system but the data was recorded on spreadsheets or text documents, or on a very primitive database. The copies of these records were sent to the customers, but not used for any other purpose or data analysis. There is evidently a lot of room for improvements, new services, and new businesses.

When analyzing the data and the process in details, the situation turned out to be worse than initially expected. Although the process was quite straightforward, it was not documented, defined in details, or unambiguously supported. This meant that when the engineers did their work, they did it in their own way, used the document template (spreadsheets, text documents), the tool (paper, computer) and the style (database entry, text entry, picture) they preferred, and documented the details as they found appropriate. All this made the latter use of data difficult.

Let us illustrate this with an example. One of the ideas for new services was the ability to predict the machine (product) breaks. It was assumed that certain weather conditions increase the failure likelihood. As every maintenance report included a timestamp, testing this assumption was considered easy. It turned out to be impossible.

The date information was ambiguous. It could indicate the time the machine breaks, the time the broken part is unmounted, the time the part is sent to Finland to the company's premises, the time it arrives there, the time maintenance work begins – or the time it is finished. The interpretation of the time stamp depended on the person filling in the report, making the merge of date and weather impossible.

Service development was thus problematic from several points of views. Representative data quality varies. Understandability was low as different data entries were named differently or placed in different cells in the spreadsheet. Data interpretations were impossible to make from the data and their consistency varied. On the other hand, no variables were merged which kept the concise representation high. The processes to record data, analyze it, and provide services were simple, but these problems prevented smooth information processing and the development of different systems. Data quality problems resulted that information needs and requirements for an information system could not be generated. Initial assumptions about what information could and should be used in the analysis and forthcoming services could not be tested.

The company had a hunch what could be interesting. They knew some variables would correlate, but not how. Our trials resulted in 54 issues that the engineers considered making sense. Thus, from the sense-making perspective already partially incomplete and poor quality data assisted in systems requirements specification, and generally, what is needed in building big data analytics capabilities and new services. This was the basis for decision-making in the development project, not for making decisions by the data.

6   Discussion

We identified a number of challenges in interpreting big data for a data-driven action from our cases. Those challenges are summarized in Table 1.

We summarize our findings from the two cases in Table 2. Different organizations perceive the representational quality of big data in a different way due to the inclusion of a variety of data sources. In Case 1, the telecom initially had a good representational data quality of the relevant data, i.e. easy to understand, interpretable, concise represented, and consistently represented. Later on, they found out that they had a multiple interpretation problem. In Case 2, the relevant data had low understandability, low interpretability, and varied consistency.

To deal with varying data quality and to serve the organizations with a ready-tocombine data that eventually leads to better user's interpretation, big data platform is required. As organizations may have the different legacy technology, business & IT strategy, data objectives, resources availability, and environmental landscape, they may have different requirements of the information system. The telecom in Case 1 had a clear list of functionalities that a big data platform should possess to attain all big data objectives within the organization. On the other hand, the requirements seem to be not straightforward in the manufacturing company in Case 2 that a number of follow-up actions need to be taken. The choice of big data solution, i.e. off-the-shelf commercial or open sourced, may differ across organizations. In Case 1, the organization preferred

Table 2. Summary of the challenges per step in the big data use cycle

Phase	Description	Case-1	Case-2
Data	Representational Data Quality Understandibility: *extent to understand the content* Interpretability: *extent of interpretation of the content* Concise representation: *how concise the data is represented* Consistent representation: *how consistent the representation*	Understandibility Having proper variable names, digitally generated (high) Interpretability Initial quality is high (i.e. the metadata was easy to understand); but after first cycle, it is found out that the data had low interpretability due the use of multiple definitions Concise representation No variables were merged (high) Consistent representation The variables had a consistent format, consistent granularity level (high)	Understandibility Different data entries were named differently or placed in different cells in the spreadsheet (low) Interpretability Multi-interpretation on the timestamp of the data (low) Concise representation No variables were merged (high) Consistent representation Consistency is varied depending on the reporting unit (low-high) **Problems with data integrity, conformity, and accuracy**
Information Processing	Big Data Lifecycle Includes cyclic stages of pro- cessing big data to better inter-pret the data, i.e. discover ➔ access ➔ exploit ➔ analyze ➔ manage	Deployed an architecture for big data platform: batch, serving, and speed layer using various applications	Due to low representation quality, it is difficult to define requirements for an information system. **Problems with technological support and undefined data collection practices**
Interpretation	Sense-making Interpretation of raw datasets or processed information using the individual sense that has properties: (1) subjective, (2) retrospective, (3) enactive of sensible environments, (4) social contextual, (5) always ongoing,	Some DCRs are appropriate, but some are out of sense, i.e. some cluster that harvests many complaints have a good DCR, but fewer complaint areas sometimes have higher DCR than the more complaint areas	The engineers' sense indicated correlations among some variables. **Problem with data quality prevented the testing of this assumption**

(continued)

Table 2. (*continued*)

Phase	Description	Case-1	Case-2
	(6) targeted cues focused, and (7) plausibility-oriented		
Decision	Naturalistic Decision Making Decision making occurred at individual level relying on sense, that is characterized by: (1) process-oriented, (2) situation-action matching, (3) appropriateness seeking, (4) context-bound informal modeling, (5) empirical-based	Decision made is whether to allocate resources (i.e. worker, cost, time) for network optimization project. An investigation was conducted on inappropriate DCRs, indicating the different definition of drop call among vendors. After standardization, the interpretation becomes the same	Decision made is in the development project, i.e. what is needed in building analytics capabilities and new services **Problems with the processes and understanding what the big data and say and is actually wanted or possible. This resulted in poor decision making**

to use open-sourced big data solution because they did not want to depend on certain providers and build their internal capabilities with customized solutions.

The processed information may be perceived in various ways by multiple stakeholders within the organization. In Case 1, more experienced analysts perceived that some DCRs did not make sense, while some juniors just took the data for granted. The out-of-sense DCR represented some clusters that often harvest major complaints and according to their sense should have bad network performance, unfortunately turn out to have a good DCR. Meanwhile in Case 2, although the data quality is insufficient for further interpretation, the engineers already had a sense of the data, e.g. some correlations might exist among variables in the data. The properties of sense-making are clearly indicated in the cases, such as subjectivity (e.g. multi-interpretation occurred), retrospectiveness (e.g. interpretation quality that seems initially good turns out to be problematic later on), enactiveness of sensible environments (e.g. customer perception about the services did not match with the network performance data), social context (e.g. dealing with perception of multiple actors and reaching multistakeholder consensus), always ongoing process (e.g. DCR consensus may change over time responding customer need and aligning organization's dynamic goal), targeted cues focus (e.g. only DCR-related information is relevant), and plausibility orientation (e.g. the evaluation on DCR is to validate the appropriateness).

Certainly every organization has different types of decision that should be made. For example, in Case 1 the operational manager had to decide on allocating resources (i.e. worker, cost, time) for network optimization project based on his or his subordinates' interpretation of DCR information. Meanwhile, in Case 2, the decision was made about what is needed in building analytics capabilities and new services in the development project.

The way how the decision was taken in both cases suggested naturalistic manner. It is indicated by a number of NDM properties such as process-oriented (e.g. operation manager decision was based on analysts' reviewing process and his interpretation), situation-action matching (e.g. allocating resources for network optimization if the DCR is low or giving good points in SLA for vendors if the DCR is high), appropriateness seeking (e.g. further investigation was required to validate the inappropriate DCR), context-bound informal modelling (e.g. the sense of analysts automatically mind modeled the DCR under concern), and empirical-based (e.g. determining which network to be improved was carved out by working experiences).

Some recursive or retrospective actions most probably occurred. For example, in Case 1, the multi-interpretation on the DCR further leads to a thorough investigation about the appropriateness of the DCR. The investigation then revealed multiinterpretation problem on each vendor's data, i.e. they used a different definition of drop call in an entire call flow. A countermeasure initiative such as employing a standardization could help the organization to have the same interpretation.

7   Conclusion

Representational quality aspects affects how the decision-makers interpret the data. Big data that are coming from multiple sources result in challenges representational data quality (RDQ), which comprises understandability, interpretability, concise representation, and consistent representation of the data. One of the underlying cause is the involvement of various stakeholders resulted in fragmentation as activities are conducted by different people not being aware of what is happening in the whole process. Studies focusing on this whole process are rare.

RDQ challenges in every phase of big data usage lifecycle. Variety and veracity of big data sources introduced various level of understandability, interpretability, conciseness, and consistency. Challenges like lack of proper description (e.g. unit) on variables, too much unstructured content, lack of metadata, and among others are encountered. Most insights need to be extracted from multiple big datasets with different levels of RDQ which require a big data platform to process with in a big data lifecycle. The big data processes in the platform spans from *discover* to *analyze*. Data consumers face a number of challenges to process big data such as requiring substantial efforts to overcome multiple levels of conciseness and consistency of big data and dealing with low interpretability data. The resulted information is subsequently interpreted by the data consumers by aligning the data with their sense. Different data consumers may have wrong or multiple interpretations on the same data due to low interpretability on the data, different levels of senses (due to experiences and capabilities), and multiple-stakeholder environment. Interpretation supports data consumers for performing a data-driven action such as decision making. A number of challenges need to tackled, e.g. out of sense data hinders decision making and sense-making & naturalistic decision making is difficult to be standardized in an organization since they introduces subjectivity. As suggested by the literature and confirmed by the case studies, the sense-making is identified by a number of properties, e.g. subjectivity, retrospective, enactive to sensible environments, social contextual, and plausibility driven. Sense-making can be challenged by the data quality. If the data quality is poor or poorly represented, its interpretations are consequently wrong. This may have significant impacts on the big data and big data projects since bad experiences and war stories get distributed.

The cases shows that RDQ challenges could occur in any stage of big data usage cycle. In case 1, the organization intially perceived that the data has good RDQ. However, their sense conflicted with the extracted information. Interpretability of the data was then found out to be problematic due to the use of different definitions of a certain terminology in a multi-vendor environment. On the other hand, in Case 2 were no terminology issues. There the challenges largely origin from poor quality data, which could not be intergrated. In both cases, there were RDQ challenges at the very beginning of the lifecycle. They just emerged differently, and for different reasons.

Acknowledgment. Part of the research was funded and supported by PT. Telekomunikasi Indonesia, Tbk. in the context of the Global Education Program 2015. This study was partly funded by the Academy of Finland, grant #306000.

References

Baumeister, R.F.: Meanings of Life. Guilford Press, New York (1991)

Beattie, C., Meara, B.: How big is "big data" in healthcare? Oliver Wieman (2013). Retrieved from http://blogs.sas.com/content/hls/2011/10/21/how-bigis-big-data-in-healthcare/

Benbasat, I., Goldstein, D.K., Mead, M.: The case research strategy in studies of information systems. MIS Q. **11**, 369–386 (1987)

Bizer, C., Boncz, P., Brodie, M.L., Erling, O.: The meaningful use of big data: four perspectives–four challenges. SIGMOD Rec. **40**(4), 56–60 (2012). https://doi.org/10.1145/2094114.2094129

Chen, M., Mao, S., Liu, Y.: Big data: a survey. Mobile Netw. Appl. **19**(2), 171–209 (2014)

Dale, L., et al.: The impact of data integration on the costs and benefits of the impact of data integration on the costs and benefits of information systems introduction. Mis Q. **16**(3), 293–311 (1992). https://doi.org/10.2307/249530

Davenport, T.H., Harris, J.G., Morison, R.: Analytics at Work: Smarter Decisions, Better Results. Harvard Business Press, Boston (2010)

Douglas, L.: 3D data management: controlling data volume, velocity and variety. Gartner (2001)

Ermolayev, V., Akerkar, R., Terziyan, V., Cochez, M.: Towards evolving knowledge ecosystems for big data understanding. In: Big Data Computing, 1st edn, pp. 3–55 (2013). https://www.taylorfrancis.com/books/e/9781466578388. ISBN 9781466578388

Fernández, A., et al.: Big Data with Cloud Computing: An insight on the computing environment, MapReduce, and programming frameworks. Wiley Interdiscip. Rev. Data Min. Knowl. Discov. **4**(5), 380–409 (2014). https://doi.org/10.1002/widm.1134

Gantz, J., Reinsel, D.: Extracting Value from chaos state of the universe: an executive summary. IDC IView (June), 1–12. (2011b). Retrieved from http://idcdocserv.com/1142

Gantz, J., Reinsel, D.: Extracting value from chaos. IDC Iview **1142**, 9–10 (2011)

Geerdink, B.: A reference architecture for big data solutions: introducing a model to perform predictive analytics using big data technology. In: 2013 8th International Conference for Internet Technology and Secured Transactions, ICITST, pp. 71–76 (2013). https://doi.org/10.1109/ICITST.2013.6750165

Hilbert, M.: Big data for development: a review of promises and challenges big data for development: a review of promises and challenges. Dev. Policy Rev. **34**(1), 135–174 (2016). Retrieved from http://escholarship.org/reader_feedback.html%5Cnhttp://escholarship.org/uc/item/4nq8z7dn%5Cnhttp://www.escholarship.org/help_copyright.html#reuse%5Cnhttp://doi.org/10.1111/dpr.12142

Hofmann, E. (2015). Big data and supply chain decisions: the impact of volume, variety and velocity properties on the bullwhip effect. Int. J. Prod. Res. **7543**, 1–19 (2015). https://doi.org/10.1080/00207543.2015.1061222

Janssen, M., Van Der Voort, H., Wahyudi, A.: Factors influencing big data decision-making quality. J. Bus. Res. (2016). https://doi.org/10.1016/j.jbusres.2016.08.007

Ji, C., Li, Y., Qiu, W. Jin, Y., Xu, Y., Awada, U., et al.: Big data processing: big challenges and opportunities. J. Interconnect. Netw. **13** (2012). https://doi.org/10.1142/S0219265912500090

Katal, A., Wazid, M., Goudar, R.H.: Big data: Issues, challenges, tools and Good practices. In: 2013 6th International Conference on Contemporary Computing, IC3, pp. 404–409 (2013). https://doi.org/10.1109/IC3.2013.6612229

LaValle, S., Lesser, E., Shockley, R., Hopkins, M. S., Kruschwitz, N.: Big data, analytics and the path from insights to value. Mit Sloan Manag. Rev. **52**, 21 (2013)

Leavitt, N.: Storage challenge: Where will all that big data go? Computer **46**(9), 22–25 (2013)

Leboeuf, K.: The 5 Vs of Big Data: Predictions for 2016. Excelacom, Inc, (1), 3–5 (2016). Retrieved from http://www.excelacom.com/resources/blog/the-5-vs-of-bigdata-predictions-for-2016

Lee, Y.W., Strong, D.M., Kahn, B.K., Wang, R.Y.: AIMQ: a methodology for information quality assessment. Inf. Manag. **40**(2), 133–146 (2002)

Lipshitz, R., Klein, G.: Taking stock of naturalistic decision making. Decis. Mak. (2001). Retrieved from http://onlinelibrary.wiley.com/doi/10.1002/bdm.381/full

Marz, N., Warren, J.: Big Data: Principles And Best Practices Of Scalable Real-Time Data Systems, (Vol. 37). Manning Publications Co. (2015). https://doi.org/10.1073/pnas.0703993104

Matheus, R., Janssen, M., Maheshwari, D.: Data science empowering the public: data-driven dashboards for transparent and accountable decision making in smart cities. Gov. Inf. Q. 0–1 (2018). https://doi.org/10.1016/j.giq.2018.01.006 (November 2016)

Merelli, I., Pérez-Sánchez, H., Gesing, S., D'Agostino, D.: Managing, analysing, and integrating big data in medical bioinformatics: open problems and future perspectives. BioMed Res. Int. (2014). https://doi.org/10.1155/2014/134023

Osuszek, L., Stanek, S., Twardowski, Z.: Leverage big data analytics for dynamic informed decisions with advanced case management. J. Decis. Syst. **25**(sup1), 436–449 (2016). https://doi.org/10.1080/12460125.2016.1187401

Power, D.J.: Using 'Big Data' for analytics and decision support. J. Decis. Syst. **23**(2), 222–228 (2014). https://doi.org/10.1080/12460125.2014.888848

Qiu, P.: Big data: More challenges! Technometrics **58**(3), 283–284 (2016). https://doi.org/10.1080/00401706.2016.1196946

Sawant, N., Shah, H.: Big Data Application Architecture Q&A: A Problem-Solution Approach. Apress, Berkely, CA (2013)

Scarf, A.: Modeling and Processing for Next-Generation Big-Data Technologies, vol. 4, pp. 283–317 (2015). https://doi.org/10.1007/978-3-319-09177-8

Strong, D.M., Lee, Y.W., Wang, R.Y.: Data quality in context. Commun. ACM **40**(5), 103–110 (1997)

Taylor, J.R., Van Every, E.J.: The Emergent Organization: Communication as Its Site and Surface. Routledge, London (1999)

Tee, J.: Handling the four 'V's of big data: volume, velocity, variety, and veracity (2013). Retrieved from http://www.theserverside.com/feature/Handling-thefour-Vs-of-big-data-volume-velocity-variety-and-veracity

The Economist Intelligence Unit: The Deciding Factor: Big Data & Decision Making. Capgemini (2012). Retrieved from http://www.capgemini.com/sites/default/files/resource/pdf/The_Deciding_Factor__Big_Data___Decision_Making.pdf

Wahyudi, A., Janssen, M.: Towards process patterns for processing data having various qualities. In: Conference on e-Business, e-Services and e-Society, vol. 9844, pp. 493–504 (2016). https://doi.org/10.1007/978-3-319-45234-0

Wahyudi, A., Kuk, G., Janssen, M.: A process pattern model for tackling and improving big data quality. Inf. Syst. Front. 1–13 (2018). https://doi.org/10.1007/s10796-017-9822-7

Wand, Y., Wang, R.Y.: Anchoring data quality dimensions in ontological foundations. Commun. ACM **39**(11), 86–95 (1996)

Wang, R.Y., Strong, D.M.: Beyond accuracy: What data quality means to data consumers. Source J. Manag. Inf. Syst. **12**(4), (1996). https://doi.org/10.2307/40398176

Wang, R.Y., Ziad, M., Lee, Y.W.: Data Quality. Advances in Database Systems, vol. 23. Kluwer Academic Publishers, New York (2002)

Weick, K.E., Sutcliffe, K.M., Obstfeld, D.: Organizing and the process of sensemaking. Organ. Sci. **16**(4), 409–421 (2005). https://doi.org/10.1287/orsc.1050.0133

Wickham, H. (2012). Tidy data. J. Stat. Soft. **46**(10). https://doi.org/10.18637/jss.v059.i10

Merelli, I., Pérez-Sánchez, H., Gesing, S., D'Agostino, D.: m-Brain. (n.d.). Big Data Technology with 8 V's. Retrieved from https://www.mbrain.com/home/technology/big-data-with-8-vs/

Yaqoob, I., et al.: Big data: from beginning to future. Int. J. Inf. Manag. **36**(6), 1231–1247 (2016). https://doi.org/10.1016/j.ijinfomgt.2016.07.009

Yin, R.K.: Case Study Research: Design and Methods. Sage Publications, Thousand Oaks (2013)

Zhou, Z.H., Chawla, N.V, Jin, Y.C., Williams, G. J.: Big data opportunities and challenges: discussions from data analytics perspectives. IEEE Comput. Intell. Mag. **9**(4), 62–74 (2014). https://doi.org/10.1109/mci.2014.2350953

Zicari, R.: Managing big data. an interview with David Gorbet (2012). Retrieved from http://www.odbms.org/blog/2012/07/managing-big-data-an-interviewwith-david-gorbet/

Zuiderwijk, A., Janssen, M., Choenni, S., Meijer, R., Alibaks, R.S.: Sociotechnical impediments of open data. Electron. J. E-Gov. **10**(2), 156–172 (2012)

ERP Adoption and Use in Production Research: An Archival Analysis and Future Research Directions

Samuel Fosso Wamba[1](✉), Jean Robert Kala Kamdjoug[2],
Shahriar Akter[3], and Kevin Carillo[1]

[1] Toulouse Business School, 1 Place Alphonse Jourdain,
31068 Toulouse, France
s.fosso-wamba@tbs-education.fr
[2] Catholic University of Central Africa, B.P. 11628 Yaoundé, Cameroon
[3] Sydney Business School, Faculty of Business, University of Wollongong,
Northfields Ave, Wollongong, NSW 2522, Australia

Abstract. The enterprise resource planning (ERP) adoption and use phenomenon has attracted much of the attention of production researchers over the last two to three decades. Through a systematic literature review, the purpose of this paper is to conduct a detailed examination of the investigation of ERP adoption and use in production research, more specifically. The paper provides a synthetic view of the various research approaches and designs having been used and presents an overview of the studied: vendors/systems, ERP deployment types, implementation outcomes, benefits, critical success factors, risk factors and effects based on identified 61 articles. Further research directions are proposed including the urgent need for researchers to examine ERP implementation with regards to IoT, big data analytics, machine learning and blockchain. The contribution of this study lies in the provided taxonomy, the detailed description of classifications, the adopted methodology, and the identification of research gaps.

Keywords: ERP · Adoption and use · Literature review · Research agenda

1 Introduction

Running a business today is more and more difficult, especially with the evolving environment, the constant search for efficiency, and the more and more complex integration of sophisticated technologies. To manage a company effectively, the implementation of an Enterprise Resource Planning (ERP) system seems to be a logical and straightforward solution, provided it is wisely used. However, despite the promise of a high operational and strategic impact (if a sound business process analysis is performed), it remains challenging to easily familiarize with the use of ERPs (in order to manage computerised data exchanges) and to integrate software packages within them. As a result, ERPs have gradually become an important focus for a number of academic and corporate investigations over the past two to three decades. The existing literature on this subject has attributed several qualifiers to ERPs: the 'most strategic and most valuable tool with which to develop and improve a firm's competitiveness'

S. A. Al-Sharhan et al. (Eds.): I3E 2018, LNCS 11195, pp. 539–556, 2018.
https://doi.org/10.1007/978-3-030-02131-3_47

(p. 94) [1]; the 'single biggest information technology (IT) investment an organisation can make' (p. 1037) [2]; a 'link through the entire supply chain aimed at best industry and management practices' (p. 537) [3]; the 'most widely accepted choices to obtain competitive advantage' (p. 397) [4]; and even the 'most difficult system development projects' (p. 1236) [5]. The rationale behind such statements is that ERPs have thoroughly transformed modern-day businesses. Not only have they improved coordination and task efficiency [6] while standardising the flow of management information [1], they also have been able to provide a total integrated solution for the organisation's information-processing requests [2] and to facilitate inter-firm relationships [7].

According to [8], the global ERP market is expected to reach $41.69 billion by 2020, with manufacturing & services being the highest revenue generating segment. Also, forecasts indicate that new business functions and on-premise deployments will be the highest income generating segments shortly. North America is also forecast to be the highest revenue generating geographic region. According to Panorama's annual independent analysis of the titans of the ERP market from October 2015 to November 2016 [9], the distribution industry represents 35% of the ERP market, followed by the manufacturing industry (29%) and the education sector (23%). They are mostly used by organisations with at least $50 M in annual revenue. A total of 17% of the companies tend to implement ERPs to improve business performance, 14% to ensure compliance, 14% to make employees' jobs easier, and 13% to better integrate systems across locations. An important number of organisations (67%) implement on-premise ERPs, 27% implement them on demand (SaaS), and only 6% implement cloud-based ERPs. This limited implementation of cloud-based ERP solutions is mainly due to the perceived risk of data losses (72%) and security breaches (12%). 70% of organisations are reported to have customised 26–50% of the software code in their ERPs. 27% hired consultants to manage implementation, 22% to provide organisational change management support, and 19% to conduct unbiased software selection. While more than 70% of organisations focused on organisational change management, about 75% improved all their business processes. Despite the overall excitement and interest in ERPs at all levels, little effort has been done to organise the large bulk of ERP literature in a way that can facilitate research and enable a better understanding of the role of ERP systems in production. Thus, the purpose of this study is to provide an overview of our current body of literature on ERPs and to propose a structured classification framework that accurately depicts the state of ERP adoption and use research in production. The research objectives are set as follows:

1. Develop a classification framework to categorise the articles dealing with ERP adoption and use in production research;
2. Use the classification framework to classify and summarise all relevant articles;
3. Propose future research directions where the implementation and deployment of ERPs are likely to have significant impacts.

In the following section, we present the research materials and implemented research method. The results are then presented in a subsequent section. Finally, the results are discussed while we present their implications for research and practice, and provide future research directions.

2 Methodology

The methodological approach adopted for this study is a systematic literature review. The review process was developed based on those used by [10] on Big Data, [11, 12] on ERP-related topics. The review process consisted of three steps: (i) developing a classification framework; (ii) conducting the literature review; and (iii) classifying and analysing the relevant journal articles. This classification framework focuses on journal articles dealing with topics related to the adoption and use of ERP in supply chain, production, and manufacturing. Specifically, seven dimensions related to ERP were used to build the framework: (i) research approach; (ii) system vendor; (iii) deployment type; (iv) implementation outcome; (v) benefits; (vi) risk factors and effects; and (vii) critical success factors. In this study, research approach refers to the *plans and the procedures for research that span the steps from broad assumptions to detailed methods of data collection, analysis, and interpretation* [13]. System vendor refers to the enterprise that manufactures or sells ERP systems or software. Deployment type refers to the hosting option chosen by a company using ERP functionalities to streamline operations. Implementation outcome refers to the effects of deliberate and purposive actions to implement ERP systems [14]. Benefits refers to the added value an organization expects or perceives after an ERP investment. Risk factors and effects refers to factors that create uncertainty in the ERP environment, the effects they may have on the organisation and the decisions made thereafter. Critical success factors refer to the key areas that management needs to focus on to achieve ERP performance goals. A broad literature search was conducted during the month of October 2017 looking for research articles having used the terms *ERP* or '*Enterprise Resource Planning*' in their body. This search was restricted to the International Journal of Production Research because the authors considered it to be highly representative of the research conducted on ERPs in the field of production. Given the journal's fame and age, it is one of the oldest and most cited journals in the domain. At the end of the search, a total of 321 articles were selected, the abstracts and references of which were downloaded into EndNote reference management software while their full texts were downloaded into a computer for sorting, leading to the identification of 61 relevant articles for this study. Articles deemed irrelevant were discarded; and this was the case when ERP was not the main theme of the article or when it was cited superficially. The 61 articles were then classified into the seven dimensions of the framework. The classification process was rigorous but rather subjective. However, each author individually pegged each article into the framework dimensions, while disagreements were discussed during work sessions. Classification disagreements were resolved through votes. After justification, the authors voted on disagreements and the highest vote won. If there was a tie, the final decision was made by the principal investigator.

3 Results

Figure 1 and Table 1 show that publications on ERP adoption and use in production research only started in 1999 with 1 article. In 2002, 5 publications on the topic were recorded, accounting for 8% of the total number of articles reviewed in this study. After a slight decrease in 2003 and 2004, an increase in publication volume was observed in 2005, with 7 articles published in the domain. The highest number of articles was recorded in 2007 (9 articles), which dropped significantly until 2012, where it stood at 8 articles. Since, then, the number of publications in the domain has dropped to 1 article by the end of 2016.

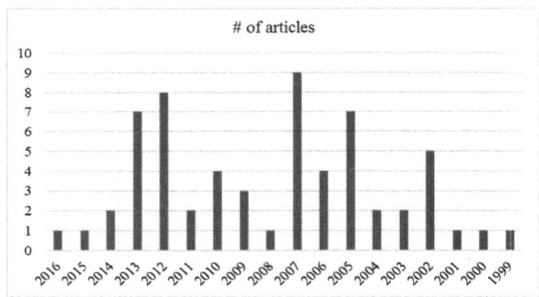

Fig. 1. Year of publication

As shown in Table 1, 28% (17 of 61 articles) of publications on ERP adoption and use relied on a using mixed methods design. 21% of the articles (13) were conceptual while 20% (12 articles) adopted a non-conventional approach (e.g., ethnography, living laboratory…). Authors of 11% of articles (7) used case studies, 8% (5 articles) used literature reviews and experiments, and only 3% (2 articles) approached the topic using surveys.

Table 2 reveals that 74% (45 articles) of the reviewed articles do not focus on any specific ERP, as they only address general issues in relation to ERP and production. However, 15% (9 articles) focus on SAP systems, and 3% (2 articles) focus on Oracle ERPs. Also, 8% (5 articles) of the publications focus on several ERPs for reasons such as comparison or integration. Of the 16 articles that addressed specific ERPs, 13 of them (21% of the total number of articles reviewed) focused on ERPs deployed on premises (Table 3). Two articles (3% of the total number of articles reviewed) dealt with software as a service (SaaS) ERPs, and only one (2% of the total number of articles reviewed) was about cloud-based ERP systems.

ERP benefits were classified (Table 4) according to the acknowledged framework developed by [74]. The analysis revealed that, operational ERP benefits are the most represented (28%) in production research than any of the other benefits. The most prominent operational benefits are cost reduction (8%), productivity improvement (8%) and customer service improvement (7%). Managerial benefits are the second most important category, accounting for 19% of the total number of identified ERP benefits, the most represented benefits being improved decision making and planning (8%) and performance improvement (8%). Strategic benefits (8%), IT infrastructure benefits (4%) and organisational benefits (4%) benefits were the least represented categories.

Table 1. Classification by research approach

Research approaches	Articles	# of articles	%
Mixed methods (e.g. survey + case study)	[15] survey + simulation model; [16]; [17]; [18]; [19]; [20]; [21]; [22] survey + SEM; [23] survey + SEM; [24] Theoretical model & case study; [25] Theoretical model & case study; [26] Formal method + case study; [5] Model + illustrative example; [27] Framework + case study; [28] Framework + case study; [29] Framework + simulation study; [30] Model + case study	17	28%
Conceptual	[31]; [32]; [33]; [34]; [35]; [36]; [37]; [38]; [39]; [40]; [41]; [42]; [43]	13	21%
Others (e.g., ethnography, living laboratory)	[44] literature review + interviews; [45] 'collaborative project between academia and industry'; [46] 'performance evaluation model' + empirical analysis; [47] Algorithm creation + real data test; [48] New framework + numerical example + extensive analysis; [49] Discusses the limitations of SCOR analysis + case study; [50] Ontology and semantic integration in SAP ERP; [51] Fuzzy AHP methodology + case study; [52] Guidelines + case studies as examples; [53] Algorithm creation + case study; [54] Field study; [55] Two-stages approach: development of model & numerical simulation	12	20%
Case study	[56]; [57]; [58]; [59]; [60]; [61]; [4]	7	11%
Review	[62]; [63]; [64]; [65]; [66]	5	8%
Experiment	[67] model + simulation experiment; [68] model + simulation experiment; [69] model + simulation experiment; [70]; [71] simulation experiment	5	8%
Survey	[72]; [73]	2	3%
	Total	61	100%

Note: The texts correspond to the elements referred to in the citation. Each article and corresponding texts are separated by a semicolon. Only articles that need precision have texts next to them

The well acknowledged risk factors and effects framework from [75] was used to analyse our pool of research outlets. Articles were classified in terms of both identified risk factors (Table 5) and risk effects (Table 6). Table 7 regroups risk effects into 'macro' risk classes. The main ERP risk factors that were identified include inadequate change management (8%), inadequate selection (7%), low top management

Table 2. Classification by ERP vendor/system

ERP vendor/system	Articles	# of articles	%
Generic (N/A)	[31]; [24]; [32]; [15]; [16]; [43]; [62]; [67]; [18]; [44]; [63]; [34]; [64]; [68]; [56]; [29]; [35]; [45]; [36]; [37]; [26]; [20]; [65]; [69]; [46]; [71]; [21]; [47]; [48]; [66]; [49]; [39]; [40]; [41]; [22]; [51]; [52]; [70]; [42]; [72]; [60]; [61]; [27]; [28]; [23]	45	74%
SAP	[25] SAP R/3; [38] SAP R/3; [50]; [58]; [53]; [5] SAP R/3; [59]; [55]; [30] SAP[2]	9	15%
Several	[19] SAP R/3, Mfg-PRO, BAAN; [4] Microsoft Navision, SAP, Infor ERP system, Exact Globe ERP; [73] BOPSE, SAP; [54]; [17] SAP, Oracle, Baan, SSA, QAD/MFG PRO, JD Edwards	5	8%
Oracle	[33] Oracle database, RDBMS, Developer/2000; [57]; Oracle AIM	2	3%
	Total	61	100%

Note: The texts correspond to the elements referred to in the citation. Each article and corresponding texts are separated by a semicolon. Only articles that need precision have texts next to them.

involvement (7%), inadequate BPR (7%), ineffective consulting service (5%), and inadequate IT system use (5%). The corresponding risk effects include budget exceeds (10%), poor business performance (8%), time exceeds (7%), project stop (5%), and low degree of integration and flexibility (5%). The classification by macro-level risk classes revealed that process failure, interaction failure and correspondence failure each make up 11% of the risk effects, while expectation failure accounted for 8%.

Table 3. Classification by deployment type

ERP deployment type	Articles	# of articles	%
On-premise	[17]; [25]; [56]; [19]; [57]; [58]; [59]; [28]; [53]; [5]; [30]; [55]; [4]	13	81%
SaaS	[33] P: 2610–2611: 'client/server structures', 'software application'; [27] P: 145/146: 'ERPoutsourced process'	2	13%
Cloud-ERP	[36] p5126: 'web-based ERP component'	1	6%
	Total	16	100%

Note: The texts correspond to the elements referred to in the citation. Each article and corresponding texts are separated by a semicolon. Only articles that need precision have texts next to them

Table 4. Classification by benefits

Benefits	Sub benefits	Articles	# of articles	%
Operational	Cost reduction	[67]; [69]; [48]; [72]; [5]	5	14%
	Cycle time reduction	[24]	1	3%
	Productivity improvement	[57]; [45]; [19]; [5]; [4]	5	14%
	Quality improvement	[19]; [16]	2	5%
	Customer services improvement	[43]; [67]; [45]; [57]	4	11%
Managerial	Better resource management	[43]; [16]	2	5%
	Improved decision making and planning	[56]; [35]; [45]; [47]; [4]	5	14%
	Performance improvement	[20]; [39]; [22]; [5]; [16]	5	14%
	Support business growth	[4]	1	3%
	Build business innovations	[22]	1	3%
Strategic	Build cost leadership	[19]	1	3%
	Build external linkages (customers and suppliers)	[38]	1	3%
IT infrastructure	Build business flexibility for current and future changes	[22]	1	3%
	Increased IT infrastructure capability	[47]	1	3%
Organizational	Support organizational changes	[17] 1	1	3%
	Empowerment	[5]	1	3%
	Total		37	100%

Table 8 classifies the selected articles by critical success factors based on the factors identified by [44, 46]. 23% of the articles identify business process reengineering (BPR), system integration, and minimum software customization as critical success factors for ERP implementation projects. System flexibility and expansibility, and cross-department and cross-region application, are also regarded as critical success factors in 10% and 8% of articles respectively. The following factors was identified by exactly 7% of the reviewed articles: change management program and culture; compatibility between application structure and database; the professional capacity of consulting companies; project management; service quality level of consulting companies; support of top management; and training quality improvement.

Table 5. Classification by risk factors

Risk factors	Articles	# of articles	%
Inadequate change management	[16]; [34]; [45]; [51]; [72]	5	13%
Inadequate selection	[16]; [44]; [5]	4	10%
Low top management involvement	[44]; [34]; [46]; [72]	4	10%
Inadequate BPR	[17]; [45]; [46]; [5]	4	10%
Ineffective consulting service	[56]; [19]; [5]	3	8%
Inadequate IT system use	[16]; [44]; [46]	3	8%
Poor team skills	[16]; [44]	2	5%
Ineffective communication system	[44]; [46]	2	5%
Inadequate training and instruction	[56]; [21]	2	5%
Complex architecture and high number of implementation modules	[34]; [45]	2	5%
Inadequate IT system maintainability	[44]; [56]	2	5%
Low key user involvement	[72]	1	3%
Bad managerial conduct	[44]	1	3%
Ineffective project management techniques	[44]	1	3%
Inadequate legacy system management	[16]	1	3%
Poor leadership	[44]	1	3%
Inadequate IT supplier stability and performances	[16]	1	3%
	Total	39	100%

Table 6. Classification by risk effects

Risk effects	Articles	# of articles	%
Budget exceed	[16]; [44]; [56]; [45]; [71]; [21];	6	24%
Poor business performance	[17]; [19]; [46]; [48]; [22]	5	20%
Time exceed	[44]; [56]; [45]; [21]	4	16%
Project stop	[16]; [45]; [4]	3	12%
Low degree of integration and flexibility	[48]; [40]; [51]	3	12%
Bad financial/economic performance organisation	[40, 48]	2	8%
Low organisation and process fitting	[48]	1	4%
Low strategic goals fitting	[48]	1	4%
	Total	25	100%

Table 7. Classification by risk effect macro-classes

Risk effects – Macro-Classes	Articles	# of articles	%
Process failure	[16]; [44]; [56]; [45]; [71]; [21]; [4]	7	27%
Interaction failure	[17]; [19]; [46]; [48]; [22]; [40]; [51]	7	27%
Correspondence failure	[17]; [19]; [46]; [48]; [22]; [40]; [51]	7	27%
Expectation failure	[17]; [19]; [46]; [48]; [22]	5	19%
	Total	26	100%

Table 8. Classification by critical success factors

CSF	Articles	# of articles	%
BPR, integration, and minimum customization	[31]; [16]; [17]; [44]; [34]; [64]; [36]; [46]; [57]; [66]. [49]; [39]; [51]; [52]	14	15%
System flexibility & expansibility	[24]; [17]; [36]; [46]; [66]; [39]	6	7%
Cross-department & cross-region application	[16]; [67]; [64]; [20]; [46]	5	5%
Change management program and culture	[24]; [16]; [44]; [28]	4	4%
Compatibility between application structure & database	[16]; [67]; [34]; [46]	4	4%
Professional capacity of consulting company	[31]; [16]; [46]; [72]	4	4%
Project management	[31]; [16]; [44]; [38]	4	4%
Service quality level of consulting company	[16]; [46]; [5]; [76]	4	4%
Support of top management	[16]; [44]; [46]; [72]	4	4%
Training quality improvement	[34]; [56]; [46]; [39]	4	4%
Adjustment of the internal organisation structure	[46]; [66]; [54]	3	3%
Software development, testing, and troubleshooting	[44]; [5]; [25]	3	3%
Cost of implementation	[56]; [47]; [72]	3	3%
Information quality	[65]; [5]; [76]	3	3%
Business plan and vision	[16]; [44]	2	2%
Communication with consulting company	[46]; [5]	2	2%
Development of ERP implementation strategies	[64]; [46]	2	2%
Implementation rationality checking	[24]; [46]	2	2%

(*continued*)

Table 8. (*continued*)

CSF	Articles	# of articles	%
IT system quality of the supplier	[46]; [65]	2	2%
Project champion	[16]; [44]	2	2%
System capability	[17]; [46]	2	2%
Technology alignment with business processes and needs	[34]; [45]	2	2%
Choice of software & vendor	[19]; [76]	2	2%
Monitoring and evaluation of performance	[44]	1	1%
Improvement of personnel cooperation and adaptation	[46]	1	1%
Objective management	[46]	1	1%
Teamwork and composition	[72]	1	1%
Implementation time and ROI	[56]	1	1%
Proper resource allocation	[45]	1	1%
System usefulness	[65]	1	1%
Capacity of internal IT personnel	[54]	1	1%
	Total	91	100%

4   Discussion

The first direct observation that can be made from this literature review is that journal publications on ERP adoption and use started in production research by 1999 and became very popular in 2007. Following a rather constant decrease during the four subsequent years, another peak of publications occurred in 2012 and 2013. Given that this study is based on a single journal, it is possible that this contradictory development in the results is due to number of publications accepted by the journal each year. With the proliferation of articles on ERP, many journals became more critical about the articles they accept on the topic to avoid redundancies.

Most of the studies on the topic were conducted using a mixed-methods approach. This research design has the benefit of being able to address confirmatory and exploratory research questions simultaneously and provide stronger inference than a single method [77]. The application of this approach in the study of ERP adoption and use in production research, has helped to develop a deep understanding and to inductively generate new theoretical insights on the subject. The identified articles having relied on such approach opted for a combination of surveys with simulations, case studies and structural equation models (SEM). Others combined frameworks and models with simulations, illustrative examples and case studies. Conceptual papers were the second most represented category. Such studies typically aimed at focusing on identifying and defining ideas related to the topic, thus helping the readers to better understand the principles or generalizations regarding different aspects of ERP adoption and use. A number of papers relying on less 'conventional' approaches such as algorithm creation, performance evaluation models, and fuzzy AHP methodology, were also identified.

Most of the literature that was reviewed did not focus on specific ERP vendors or systems. This may be attributed to the fact that most papers concentrated on factors affecting the adoption and use of ERP and its integration with production units irrespective of the vendor. However, among the articles dealing with specific ERPs, SAP ERPs were the most popular systems under investigation. There were also several publications on different ERP types, especially in the area of the integration of multiple ERPs into companies' production processes. Nowadays, organisations tend to prefer ERP systems to be deployed on-premise or on-demand (SaaS). In this review, most of the ERPs that were studied relied on on-premise deployment even though on-demand solutions have become trendy and very cost-effective compared to on-premise solutions. Data security and customization have remained major concerns regarding the implementation of on-demand solutions [78, 79]. Therefore, the choice to integrate production processes through either on-premise or cloud-based ERPs has remained a matter of business priorities between high levels of customization and security (on-premises) or low operational cost (SaaS) [80].

Most of the reviewed papers did not focus on the implementation outcomes of ERPs in production, addressing only other aspects such as requirements, selection, adoption, integration, and planning. However, all the publications that provided information on ERP implementation clearly indicated positive outcomes in terms of implementation. The main implication that can be drawn from such result is that there is to date no research on failed ERP projects in production. Research efforts in this area need to be encouraged and welcome as they could provide important insights about the other side of the ERP implementation coin.

Our results fully corroborate with [81] who found that the benefits of ERP adoption and use in production are mostly operational and managerial, and that there were no significant benefits in terms of IT infrastructure and organisation. The main operational benefits include product improvement, cost reduction, and customer service improvement. ERPs are very instrumental in Product Lifecycle Management (PLM), providing operational benefits as indicated above [82]. There are also managerial benefits such as performance improvement and improved decision-making planning. ERP vendors today have started adding business intelligence (BI) capabilities to their ERP systems to meet the needs of companies who seek to make the most of their data [83]. This adds substantial value to ERPs since this allows the access of information on production processes directly from ERP modules and provides performance insights in real time [84].

When analysing the risk factors and effects of ERP adoption and use, six main risk factors were recurrently observed: inadequate change management, inadequate ERP selection, low top management involvement, inadequate Business Process Reengineering (BPR), ineffective consulting service, and inadequate IT system use. These factors lead mostly to process, interaction and correspondence failures. The main effects of these risks on a company range from budget exceed, poor business performance and time exceed to project stop and low degree of integration and flexibility. Further studies could be carried out based on these results to more clearly identify the existence of dependencies between these factors [75]. In this study, the most

Table 9. Future research questions for ERP studies

ERP research streams	Relevant theories	Future research questions for ERP in production research
Strategy, culture, leadership, and organization	Resource based theory [89], Competitive strategy [90], dynamic capability theory [91]	How can organizations ensure business alignment, ERP and strategic analytics in the emerging data economy?
		Which ERP architecture will lead to the competitive advantage in the IoT landscape?
		How can organizations develop capabilities in IoT, big data, machine learning and blockchain to leverage digital transformation?
		How can dynamic analytics capabilities be developed using big data to address uncertainty?
Information systems and technology management	Transaction cost theory [92, 93]	What are the key issues related to the design of various interfaces between ERP and IoT-enabled connected devices?
		What is the impact of ERP on lean operations and quality management?
		How can organizations better use insights from ERP and relevant analytics to achieve operational excellence?
		What is the impact of ERP and analytics in various sectors (e.g., healthcare, retail industry, and manufacturing)?
Data quality, cloud infrastructure, privacy and security, blockchain	IT quality theory [94], IS success theory [95, 96], Sociomateriality of IT [97]	What factors influence governance, security, and privacy in the next generation ERP?
		How can a firm leverage ERP to generate, acquire, transform and integrate big data?
		How can a firm leverage a cloud-based platform to produce data and business value?
		How ERP can be used to develop data-driven innovations?
		Should firms continue with the dominant onpremise ERP strategy or move toward ERP as SaaS or a cloud-based ERP system?
Overarching value	IT business value [98], business value of analytics [99]	How do ERP-integrated analytics, machine learning and blockchain influence each other to enhance competitive advantage?
		How do organizations deal with ERP implementation to diversify themselves?
		How do organizations capitalize on ERP to extract value?
		What factors influence ERP implementation at different stages?

represented critical success factors (CSF) are BPR, integration and minimum customization, and system flexibility and expansibility. Indeed, BPR, system integration, and customization are well-known CSFs in ERP implementation [85, 86]. However, system flexibility and expansibility do not appear in a majority of ERP CSF frameworks. This highlights their rather ignored but particular importance in the specific context of production processes.

5 Conclusion and Future Research Directions

There remains a number of limitations that need to be taken into consideration. One is that the study is based solely on articles from the International Journal of Production Research. Our results thus provide a representative but imprecise depiction of ERP adoption and use research in the production field. Furthermore, despite the rigorous sorting of identified papers, their selection and classification remains subjective to some extent. The authors have done their best at mitigating the risks and biases that such relative subjectivity could engender.

Overall, this systematic review offers a clear overview of the current body of knowledge on ERP adoption and use in production. Firstly, this research contributes to research and management perspectives, emphasizing the importance of ERP adoption and use in production and enabling a better understanding of the role and impact of ERPs in production. Secondly, the study presents a general taxonomy for ERP adoption and use and identifies key elements that are relevant to production research. Finally, managers at all level are offered critical insights for the formulation and execution of ERP implementation strategies during operations. The proposed classification framework can be used by companies to address issues ranging from the selection of the right ERP system and the right ERP deployment type to the planning of risk management strategies. The research findings show that managers can implement ERP systems for production operations and have successful outcomes. This research work can eventually help managers to better grasp the most relevant benefits of ERP adoption and use, the related CSFs, and the associated risks to be overcome in the area of production.

Moreover, it is in the interest of managers and researchers to recognise the contribution of ERP systems in production and to assess changes in operational performance at both the modular and the system levels [87]. In fact, present-day ERP system can catalyse the application of lean production practices [88]. Some even suggest that managers should first adopt an ERP as the backbone of company operations before deploying any other enterprise systems (ES), such as SCM systems [81]. Thus, further research is needed on the adoption of modern ERPs to meet their operational requirements in other areas.

One of the major contributions of this paper is to set out a systematic review which results can be used by managers to improve ERP adoption and use in production environments. It shows the current state of research on the topic, proposing other research angles for future studies. Organizations could enjoy several operational and managerial benefits through the successful adoption and use of ERPs for production. They could leverage the information ecosystem created by ERPs to improve their products and reduce cost through supply chain optimization and improved customer services. This study also identified many aspects of ERP adoption and use that can be explored in the area of production and beyond. For example, the development of a comprehensive conceptual framework is needed to fully and efficiently capture the business value that can be derived from the adoption and use of ERPs. Future research may also consider developing explanatory and predictive theories related to BPR, ERP deployment, performance, and decision-making process.

The contribution of this study lies in that it establishes a taxonomy of publications on ERPs in the domain of production, provides a detailed description of core aspects in this regard, and sets out an efficient methodology to be followed. Besides, it identified research gaps and proposed research questions. The review and developed taxonomy should serve as a starting point for the development of more up-to-date and improved insights on the topic. Legacy issues or areas having had limited attention, such as IoT, big data, machine learning and blockchain, are clearly identified and should be the focus of future research. Furthermore, the research perspectives highlighted in Table 9 can be extended and used in the development of a research agenda for future studies in this domain. We conclude by emphasizing the urgent need for more research efforts on ERP deployment types and implementation outcomes, as organisations need such information to replicate best practices and avoid pitfalls. This will be very useful for managers seeking to optimize organisational performance, competitive advantage, and business results during implementation.

References

1. Pan, M.-J., Jang, W.-Y.: Determinants of the adoption of enterprise resource planning within the technology-organization-environment framework: Taiwan's communications industry. J. Comput. Inf. Syst. **48**(3), 94–102 (2008)
2. Dezdar, S., Sulaiman, A.: Successful enterprise resource planning implementation: taxonomy of critical factors. Ind. Manag. Data Syst. **109**(8), 1037–1052 (2009)
3. Momoh, A., Roy, R., Shehab, E.: Challenges in enterprise resource planning implementation: state-of-the-art. Bus. Process Manag. J. **16**(4), 537–565 (2010)
4. Powell, D., Riezebos, J., Strandhagen, J.O.: Lean production and ERP systems in small- and medium-sized enterprises: ERP support for pull production. Int. J. Prod. Res. **51**, 395–409 (2013)
5. Moalagh, M., Ravasan, A.Z.: Developing a practical framework for assessing ERP post-implementation success using fuzzy analytic network process. Int. J. Prod. Res. **51**, 1236–1257 (2013)
6. Chou, S.-W., Chang, Y.-C.: The implementation factors that influence the ERP (enterprise resource planning) benefits. Decis. Support Syst. **46**(1), 149–157 (2008)
7. Esteves, J.: A benefits realisation road-map framework for ERP usage in small and medium-sized enterprises. J. Enterp. Inf. Manag. **22**(1/2), 25–35 (2009)
8. Allied Market Research: ERP Software Market by Deployment (On-premise deployment and Cloud deployment) and Function (Finance, Human resource, Supply chain and Others) - Global Opportunity Analysis and Industry Forecast, 2013–2020 (2018)
9. Panorama, C.S.: 2017 Report on ERP Systems & Enterprise Software (2017)

10. Wamba, S.F., et al.: How 'big data'can make big impact: findings from a systematic review and a longitudinal case study. Int. J. Prod. Econ. **165**, 234–246 (2015)
11. Tarhini, A., Ammar, H., Tarhini, T.: Analysis of the critical success factors for enterprise resource planning implementation from stakeholders' perspective: a systematic review. Int. Bus. Res. **8**(4), 25 (2015)
12. Haddara, M., Zach, O.: ERP systems in SMEs: a literature review. In: 2011 44th Hawaii International Conference on System Sciences (HICSS). IEEE (2011)
13. Creswell, J.W., Creswell, J.D.: Research design: qualitative, quantitative, and mixed methods approaches. Sage Publications, California (2017)
14. Proctor, E., et al.: Outcomes for implementation research: conceptual distinctions, measurement challenges, and research agenda. Adm. Policy Mental Health Mental Health Serv. Res. **38**(2), 65–76 (2011)
15. Koh, S.C.L., Saad, S.M.: Development of a business model for diagnosing uncertainty in ERP environments. Int. J. Prod. Res. **40**, 3015–3039 (2002)
16. Kumar, V., Maheshwari, B., Kumar, U.: Enterprise resource planning systems adoption process: a survey of Canadian organizations. Int. J. Prod. Res. **40**, 509–523 (2002)
17. Gattiker, T.F., Goodhue, D.L.: Software-driven changes to business processes: an empirical study of impacts of Enterprise Resource Planning (ERP) systems at the local level. Int. J. Prod. Res. **40**, 4799–4814 (2002)
18. Craighead, C.W., Laforgej, R.L.: Taxonomy of information technology adoption patterns in manufacturing firms. Int. J. Prod. Res. **41**, 2431–2449 (2003)
19. Ayağ, Z., Özdemİr, R.G.: An intelligent approach to ERP software selection through fuzzy ANP. Int. J. Prod. Res. **45**, 2169–2194 (2007)
20. Gattiker, T.F.: Enterprise resource planning (ERP) systems and the manufacturing–marketing interface: an information-processing theory view. Int. J. Prod. Res. **45**, 2895–2917 (2007)
21. Irani, Z., Sharf, A.M., Love, P.E.D.: Knowledge mapping for information systems evaluation in manufacturing. Int. J. Prod. Res. **45**, 2435–2457 (2007)
22. Schniederjans, M.J., Cao, Q., Ching Gu, V.: An operations management perspective on adopting customer-relations management (CRM) software. Int. J. Prod. Res. **50**, 3974–3987 (2012)
23. Migdadi, M.M., Zaid, M.K.S.A.: An empirical investigation of knowledge management competence for enterprise resource planning systems success insights from Jordan. Int. J. Prod. Res. **54**(18), 5480–5498 (2016)
24. Teltumbde, A.: A framework for evaluating ERP projects. Int. J. Prod. Res. **38**, 4507–4520 (2000)
25. Ioannou, G., Papadoyiannis, C.: Theory of constraints-based methodology for effective ERP implementations. Int. J. Prod. Res. **42**, 4927–4954 (2004)
26. Lian, Y.H., Van Landeghem, H.: Analysing the effects of Lean manufacturing using a value stream mapping-based simulation generator. Int. J. Prod. Res. **45**, 3037–3058 (2007)
27. Zandi, F.: A bi-level constraint-oriented outsourcing framework for orchestration of an ERP system. Int. J. Prod. Res. **52**, 130–148 (2014)
28. Wu, W.-H., et al.: An advanced CMII-based engineering change management framework: the integration of PLM and ERP perspectives. Int. J. Prod. Res. **52**, 6092–6109 (2014)
29. Xu, H.Q., et al.: A Web-based system for manufacturing co-ordination in complex supply networks. Int. J. Prod. Res. **43**, 2049–2070 (2005)
30. Zhang, L.L., Vareilles, E., Aldanondo, M.: Generic bill of functions, materials, and operations for SAP2 configuration. Int. J. Prod. Res. **51**, 465–478 (2013)
31. Ng, J.K.C., Ip, W.H., Lee, T.C.: A paradigm for ERP and BPR integration. Int. J. Prod. Res. **37**, 2093–2108 (1999)

32. Shtub, A.: A framework for teaching and training in the Enterprise Resource Planning (ERP) era. Int. J. Prod. Res. **39**, 567–576 (2001)
33. Zhou, X., et al.: Development of a financial management system in a CIMS environment. Int. J. Prod. Res. **43**, 2603–2613 (2005)
34. Park, K., Kusiak, A.: Enterprise resource planning (ERP) operations support system for maintaining process integration. Int. J. Prod. Res. **43**, 3959–3982 (2005)
35. Gupta, A., Lödding, H., Tseng, M.M.: An approach of capability representation for improving capacity planning. Int. J. Prod. Res. **44**, 3419–3431 (2006)
36. Wang, Z.J., Xu, X.F., Zhan, D.C.: Component reuse based agile reconfiguration for Enterprise Resource Planning (ERP) systems in manufacturing enterprises. Int. J. Prod. Res. **23**, 5107–5129 (2006)
37. Segerstedt, A.: Master Production Scheduling and a comparison of Material Requirements Planning and cover-time planning. Int. J. Prod. Res. **44**, 3585–3606 (2006)
38. Samaranayake, P., Toncich, D.: Integration of production planning, project management and logistics systems for supply chain management. Int. J. Prod. Res. **45**, 5417–5447 (2007)
39. Kahraman, C., Beskese, A., Kaya, I.: Selection among ERP outsourcing alternatives using a fuzzy multi-criteria decision making methodology. Int. J. Prod. Res. **48**, 547–566 (2010)
40. Wu, L.-C., Liou, F.-M.: A quantitative model for ERP investment decision: considering revenue and costs under uncertainty. Int. J. Prod. Res. **49**, 6713–6728 (2011)
41. Feng, K., Rao, U.S., Raturi, A.: Setting planned orders in master production scheduling under demand uncertainty. Int. J. Prod. Res. **49**(13), 4007–4025 (2011)
42. Jodlbauer, H., Reitner, S.: Material and capacity requirements planning with dynamic lead times. Int. J. Prod. Res. **50**, 4477–4492 (2012)
43. Pechoucek, M., et al.: ExPlanTech: applying multi-agent systems in production planning. Int. J. Prod. Res. **40**, 3681–3692 (2002)
44. Loh, T.C., Koh, S.C.L.: Critical elements for a successful enterprise resource planning implementation in small-and medium-sized enterprises. Int. J. Prod. Res. **42**, 3433–3455 (2004)
45. Quiescenti, M., et al.: Business process-oriented design of Enterprise Resource Planning (ERP) systems for small and medium enterprises. Int. J. Prod. Res. **44**, 3797–3811 (2006)
46. Yang, C.-C., et al.: The use of fuzzy measures in a performance-evaluation model for ERP implementation among Taiwanese semiconductor manufacturers. Int. J. Prod. Res. **45**, 4735–4752 (2007)
47. Zobolas, G.I., Tarantilis, C.D., Ioannou, G.: Extending capacity planning by positive lead times and optional overtime, earliness and tardiness for effective master production scheduling. Int. J. Prod. Res. **46**, 3359–3386 (2008)
48. Kim, J.: Activity-based framework for cost savings through the implementation of an ERP system. Int. J. Prod. Res. **47**, 1913–1929 (2009)
49. Wang, W.Y.C., Chan, H.K., Pauleen, D.J.: Aligning business process reengineering in implementing global supply chain systems by the SCOR model. Int. J. Prod. Res. **48**, 5647–5669 (2010)
50. Grüninger, M., et al.: Combining RFID with ontologies to create smart objects. Int. J. Prod. Res. **48**, 2633–2654 (2010)
51. Sarfaraz, A., Jenab, K., D'Souza, A.C.: Evaluating ERP implementation choices on the basis of customisation using fuzzy AHP. Int. J. Prod. Res. **50**, 7057–7067 (2012)
52. Framinan, J.M., Ruiz, R.: Guidelines for the deployment and implementation of manufacturing scheduling systems. Int. J. Prod. Res. **50**, 1799–1812 (2012)
53. Baker, T., Jayaraman, V.: Managing information and supplies inventory operations in a manufacturing environment. Part 2: an order-timing and sizing algorithm. Int. J. Prod. Res. **50**, 1767–1779 (2012)

54. Ifinedo, P., Olsen, D.H.: An empirical research on the impacts of organisational decisions' locus, tasks structure rules, knowledge, and IT function's value on ERP system success. Int. J. Prod. Res. **53**, 2554–2568 (2015)
55. Samaranayake, P.: Improving manufacturing lead time using holistic approach to planning and execution with integrated data structures: numerical simulation and comparison. Int. J. Prod. Res. **51**, 4484–4501 (2013)
56. Dowlatshahi, S.: Strategic success factors in enterprise resource-planning design and implementation: a case-study approach. Int. J. Prod. Res. **43**, 3745–3771 (2005)
57. Liu, C.M., Chen, L.S.: Applications of RFID technology for improving production efficiency in an integrated-circuit packaging house. Int. J. Prod. Res. **47**, 2203–2216 (2009)
58. Lebreton, B.G.M., Van Wassenhove, L.N., Bloemen, R.R.: Worldwide sourcing planning at Solutia's glass interlayer products division. Int. J. Prod. Res. **48**, 801–819 (2010)
59. Chou, Y.-C., Lu, C.-H., Tang, Y.-Y.: Identifying inventory problems in the aerospace industry using the theory of constraints. Int. J. Prod. Res. **50**, 4686–4698 (2012)
60. Cheng, C.-Y., et al.: Application of fault tree analysis to assess inventory risk: a practical case from aerospace manufacturing. Int. J. Prod. Res. **51**, 6499–6514 (2013)
61. Netland, T.: Exploring the phenomenon of company-specific production systems: one-best-way or own-best-way? Int. J. Prod. Res. **51**, 1084–1097 (2013)
62. Koh, S.C.L., Saad, S.M., Jones, M.H.: Uncertainty under MRP-planned manufacture review and categorization. Int. J. Prod. Res. **40**, 2399–2421 (2002)
63. Xu, X.F., et al.: Digital enterprise management in China: current status and future development. Int. J. Prod. Res. **43**, 2593–2601 (2005)
64. Wang, C., et al.: ERP research, development and implementation in China: an overview. Int. J. Prod. Res. **43**, 39153932 (2005)
65. Gunasekaran, A., Ngai, E.W.T.: Knowledge management in 21st century manufacturing. Int. J. Prod. Res. **45**, 2391–2418 (2007)
66. Akyuz, G.A., Rehan, M.: Requirements for forming an 'e-supply chain'. Int. J. Prod. Res. **47**, 3265–3287 (2009)
67. Lea, B.-R., Min, H.: Selection of management accounting systems in JustIn-Time and Theory of Constraints-based manufacturing. Int. J. Prod. Res. **41**, 2879–2910 (2003)
68. Ho, C.J.: Examining dampening effects for alternative dampening procedures to cope with system nervousness. Int. J. Prod. Res. **43**, 4009–4033 (2005)
69. Ho, C.-J.: Measuring system performance of an ERP-based supply chain. Int. J. Prod. Res. **45**, 1255–1277 (2007)
70. Ho, C.-J., Ireland, T.C.: Mitigating forecast errors by lot-sizing rules in ERP-controlled manufacturing systems. Int. J. Prod. Res. **50**, 3080–3094 (2012)
71. Ho, C.-J.: Exploring the compatibility of dampening procedures and lot-sizing rules in MRP systems under uncertain operating environments. Int. J. Prod. Res. **46**, 5097–5120 (2007)
72. Lee, S.M., et al.: Successful implementations of MES in Korean manufacturing SMEs: an empirical study. Int. J. Prod. Res. **50**, 1942–1954 (2012)
73. Olson, D.L., Chae, B.K., Sheu, C.: Relative impact of different ERP forms on manufacturing organisations: an exploratory analysis of a global manufacturing survey. Int. J. Prod. Res. **51**, 1520–1534 (2013)
74. Shang, S., Seddon, P.B.: A comprehensive framework for classifying the benefits of ERP systems. In: AMCIS 2000 Proceedings, p. 39 (2000)
75. Aloini, D., Dulmin, R., Mininno, V.: Risk assessment in ERP projects. Inf. Syst. **37**(3), 183–199 (2012)
76. Migdadi, M.M., Zaid, M.K.S.A.: An empirical investigation of knowledge management competence for enterprise resource planning systems success insights from Jordan. Int. J. Prod. Res. **54**, 5480–5498 (2016)

77. Venkatesh, V., Brown, S.A., Bala, H.: Bridging the qualitative-quantitative divide: guidelines for conducting mixed methods research in information systems. MIS Q. **37**(1) (2013)
78. Purohit, G., Jaiswal, M., Pandey, M.: Challenges involved in implementation of ERP on demand solution: cloud computing. Int. J. Comput. Sci. Issues **9**(4), 481–489 (2012)
79. Peng, G.C.A., Gala, C.: Cloud ERP: a new dilemma to modern organisations? J. Comput. Inf. Syst. **54**(4), 2230 (2014)
80. Bibi, S., Katsaros, D., Bozanis, P.: Business application acquisition: onpremise or SaaS-based solutions? IEEE Softw. **29**(3), 86–93 (2012)
81. Su, Y.-F., Yang, C.: Why are enterprise resource planning systems indispensable to supply chain management? Eur. J. Oper. Res. **203**(1), 81–94 (2010)
82. Gecevska, V., et al.: Product lifecycle management through innovative and competitive business environment. J. Ind. Eng. Manag. **3**(2), 323–336 (2010)
83. Griffin, J.: BI and ERP integration: five critical questions. Inf. Manag. **17**(5), 6 (2007)
84. Chou, D.C., Bindu Tripuramallu, H., Chou, A.Y.: BI and ERP integration. Inf. Manag. Comput. Secur. **13**(5), 340–349 (2005)
85. Ram, J., Corkindale, D., Wu, M.-L.: Implementation critical success factors (CSFs) for ERP: do they contribute to implementation success and postimplementation performance? Int. J. Prod. Econ. **144**(1), 157–174 (2013)
86. Ram, J., Corkindale, D.: How "critical" are the critical success factors (CSFs)? Examining the role of CSFs for ERP. Bus. Process Manag. J. **20**(1), 151–174 (2014)
87. Madapusi, A., D'Souza, D.: The influence of ERP system implementation on the operational performance of an organization. Int. J. Inf. Manag. **32**(1), 24–34 (2012)
88. Powell, D., et al.: The concurrent application of lean production and ERP: towards an ERP-based lean implementation process. Comput. Ind. **64**(3), 324–335 (2013)
89. Barney, J.: Firm resources and sustained competitive advantage. J. Manag. **17**(1), 99–120 (1991)
90. Porter, M.E., Millar, V.E.: How information gives you competitive advantage. Harvard Business Review, Reprint Service (1985)
91. Teece, D., Peteraf, M., Leih, S.: Dynamic Capabilities and Organizational Agility: Risk, Uncertainity, and Strategy in the Innovation Economy. Calif. Manag. Rev. **58**(4), 13–35 (2016)
92. Williamson, O.E.: The economics of organization: the transaction cost approach. Am. J. Sociol. **87**(3), 548–577 (1981)
93. Williamson, O.E.: Transaction-cost economics: the governance of contractual relations. J. Law Econ. **22**(2), 233–261 (1979)
94. Nelson, R.R., Todd, P.A., Wixom, B.H.: Antecedents of information and system quality: an empirical examination within the context of data warehousing. J. Manag. Inf. Syst. **21**(4), 199–235 (2005)
95. DeLone, W.H., McLean, E.R.: Information systems success: the quest for the dependent variable. Inf. Syst. Res. **3**(1), 60–95 (1992)
96. Delone, W.H.: The DeLone and McLean model of information systems success: a ten-year update. J. Manag. Inf. Syst. **19**(4), 9–30 (2003)
97. Orlikowski, W.J.: Sociomaterial practices: exploring technology at work. Organ. Stud. **28**(9), 1435–1448 (2007)
98. Melville, N., Kraemer, K., Gurbaxani, V.: Review: information technology and organizational performance: an integrative model of IT business value. MIS Q. **28**(2), 283–322 (2004)
99. Wixom, B.H., Yen, B., Relich, M.: Maximizing value from business analytics. MIS Q. Exec. **12**, 111–123 (2013)

Solving Location Based Inventory Routing Problem in E-Commerce Using Ant Colony Optimization

Reema Aswani[✉], Arpan Kumar Kar, P. Vigneswara Ilavarasan, and Rohan Krishna

Department of Management Studies, Indian Institute of Technology Delhi, New Delhi, India
reemaswani@gmail.com

Abstract. In the current era of digitization and the rise of e-commerce sector over the past decade, it becomes essential to identify and address issues surrounding e-commerce logistics. The current study addresses the problem of location based inventory routing for delivery from warehouse to various destinations. The study uses a dynamic meta-heuristic approach, Ant Colony Optimization (ACO), to solve this problem in e-commerce. A sensitivity analysis is done to identify the coefficient values to be fixed for the ACO Engine. The longitude and latitude coordinates from Google Maps are mapped to distance metrics between the warehouse and the delivery destinations for orders to be delivered on a particular day. The analysis is conducted for a total of 346 locations and the total distance to be travelled came out to be 690.29 km using the proposed approach. Findings of the study can be applicable in multiple domains of e-commerce logistics and other graph based routing problems.

Keywords: Inventory routing problem · E-commerce
Ant colony optimization · Location inventory problem
Travelling salesman problem

1 Introduction

India has an Internet user base of over 460 Million[1] (as per Statista) with approximately 6 million new users being added every month. This huge inflow of internet users has opened several business avenues. The buying and selling of products and services over the internet is often referred to as e-commerce. The buying and selling of goods have seen some tremendous growth in past decades. The number of e-commerce consumers is exponentially increasing day by day. Further, the growth of smart phones and internet is contributing to this exponential growth in this e-commerce sector. In emerging economy like India, China, Indonesia and Brazil amongst others, the e-commerce presence is expanding every year as the consumer is becoming comfortable in online shopping.

---

[1] https://www.statista.com/topics/2157/internet-usage-in-india/.

S. A. Al-Sharhan et al. (Eds.): I3E 2018, LNCS 11195, pp. 557–566, 2018.
https://doi.org/10.1007/978-3-030-02131-3_48

Apart from online payments made towards these purchases, cash on delivery is a dominating payment method especially in India [1]. The retail market of India is expecting growth of from 2.5% in 2016 to 5% in 2020 [2]. Further, the total valuation of e-commerce market in India was estimated at 27.5 billion USD in 2016 and the expected growth of e-commerce industry is at a CAGR of 31% which can touch 30 billion USD in 2020 [3]. As per the Indian e-commerce industry analysis the e-commerce industry of India is going upward and it is expected to surpass the US in 2034. It is expected to become the second largest next only to China. The growth is triggered by the surrounding ecosystem. Increase in the internet reach and smart phone penetration enables the Indian users to take this leap.

For any e-commerce company, customer satisfaction and service level is deter-mined by three important decisions including facility location decision, inventory decision and transportation decision [4]. The current study, however, caters primarily to the strategic warehouse location and transportation optimization. The study focuses on a combination of location inventory problem, location routing problem and the inventory routing problem. The advancement of information technology with infor-mation capturing as the focus that is available during real-time operations opens several new research directions [5].

Machine learning in the current scenario, is often used in interpreting huge volume of data and is proven to be very helpful in decision making [6]. Thus, the current study also explores swarm intelligence in context of online retail logistic operation opti-mization. Swarm intelligence algorithms are inspired by social insects such as honey bees, bird flocks, ants or any other social animal. For the dynamicity of routing in e-commerce, this study specifically focuses on ant colony optimization for solving the Location based Inventory Routing Problem (LIRP). These swarm based approaches have found applications in domains as varied as energy [7], wireless networks [8], social media content popularity [9] and spam [10], scheduling and resource manage-ment [11] amongst others. The subsequent subsections focus on the review of existing literature, the research methodology adopted and the findings of the study.

2   Related Work

The academic literature illustrates on several approaches that have been proposed for the Vehicle Routing Problem (VRP). These can be broadly classified as classical heuristics, these are exact solutions and were developed mostly from 1960–1990, and meta-heuristics that provide approximate solutions and have become popular over the last few decades [12, 13]. Literature also highlights the emerging importance of vehicle routing and meta-heuristics, specifically in the form of nature inspired and swarm intelligence algorithms.

This section discusses the literature surrounding heuristic solutions to routing problems and applications of swarm intelligence in various domains. The solutions to vehicle routing problems were available as early as 1960s [13]. The classical heuristics follow a merging and assigning process, where the technique merges existing routes using savings criteria where the aim is to minimize the route length followed by the assignment of vertices to routes using insertion cost [14]. Other methods include the sequential improvement [15, 16], the sweep algorithm [17], petal algorithms [18] and clusterfirst, route-second approach [19]. Other existing studies with exact solutions were using mathematical models like spanning tree [20]. Gendreau et al. [21] proposed a Tabu search heuristic approach for solving the same.

The exact mathematical and heuristic solutions for vehicle routing problems were followed by meta-heuristics, probabilistic models like meta-strategy simulated annealing is also used for approximating to a globally optimum solution for the problem [22]. Bio-inspired computing algorithms are being popularly used in various case scenarios including classification, clustering, regression and outlier detection problems [23–26]. Further, literature also has evidences of theories inspired from nature, an ant based system is used for finding the shortest path for the vehicle for routing [27]. The literature has proposed hybrid meta-heuristic approaches to solve hard combinatorial optimization problems like the ones under consideration in this study. Studies also focus on Genetic Algorithms and many of its hybrid variants with and without trip delimiters for solving the problem at hand [28]. Any feasible chromosome sequence is an optimal route that can be used by the vehicle.

This study focuses on using the existing ant colony optimization for routing [29] in the e-commerce domain. With the current explosion in the e-commerce sector, the need to provide an optimal route for delivery through the same warehouse is a great example of the existing Travelling Salesman Problem. This can be used to solve logistic problems optimally. The subsequent section discusses the proposed approach, the dataset used and the findings of the study.

3   Research Methodology

For the purpose of simplicity the current study works on some assumptions that only one vehicle will do the delivery, only Delhi and Gurgaon is used as the location, a warehouse captures the Delhi and Gurgaon location and that the vehicle returns back to warehouse. For capturing the address location as latitude and longitude, the Google Maps API is used. Further, ant colony optimization is applied for the current Travelling Salesman Problem (TSP) [30]. The algorithm is adopted with slight modification for the current vehicle routing problem since routing has to start from the warehouse and not randomly. Figure 1 illustrates the process followed for getting the best route for solving the location based inventory problem in the study.

3.1   Data Description

Online Retail data has been adopted from University of California machine learning repository. The data contain record of 293 days sales record with 541909 entries as represented in Table 1. Further, an extra column has been added to data file with the Delhi and Gurgaon addresses. A total of 468 addresses have been chosen and mapped to online retail data. For Delhi, North, South, East and West Delhi has been considered. Similarly, for Gurgaon, the areas have been divided in urban and rural.

The subsequent subsection discusses the ACO engine and how the routing can be modeled mathematically.

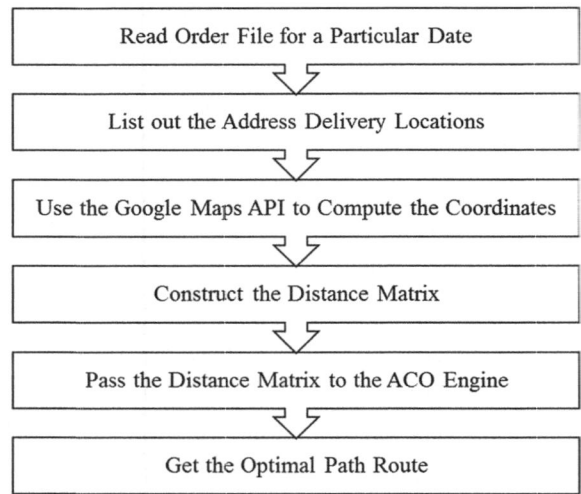

Fig. 1. Diagrammatic representation of ACO based vehicle routing

Table 1. Snapshot of dataset and mapped reference address

Invoice no	Description	Unit price	Reference address
536365	White Hanging Heart T-Light Holder	2.55	Chaukhandi, West Delhi, 110015, Delhi
536367	White Metal Lantern	3.39	Artemis Hospital, Gurgaon, HR
536368	Cream Cupid Hearts Coat Hanger	2.75	Anand Parbat Indl. area, Central Delhi-05, Delhi
536369	Knitted Union Flag Hot Water Bottle	3.39	Kalkaji, South Delhi, 110019, Delhi
536370	Red Woolly Hottie White Heart.	3.39	Sector-46, Gurgaon, Haryana
536371	Set 7 Babushka Nesting Boxes	7.65	Sec-8, Gurgaon, Haryana
536372	Glass Star Frosted T-Light Holder	4.25	Railway Road, Gurgaon, 122006, Haryana
536373	Hand Warmer Union Jack	1.85	Prometric Testing Center, DLF Infinity Tower A, Sec-25, Gurugram, HR
536374	Hand Warmer Red Polka Dot	1.85	Union Public service Commission, Delhi-110069
536375	Assorted Colour Bird Ornament	1.69	Sec-76, Gurgaon, Haryana
536376	Poppy's Playhouse Bedroom	2.1	Sec-89, Gurgaon, Haryana
536377	Poppy's Playhouse Kitchen	2.1	Spazedge, 435-436, Tower-B, Malibu Town, Sec-47, Gurugram, HR

3.2   Mathematical Model

The ACO is a probabilistic meta-heuristic technique which can be used for identifying an optimal path in the graph based on behavior of ants travelling a path between the ant colony and the food source. The current study passes the distance metrics for vehicle routing to the ACO engine and the mathematical formulation/model for the same is elaborated in the current sub-section. The section discusses how ACO's pheromone trail update process can be utilized for seeking an optimal path from the warehouse to different destinations.

For the purpose of analysis, historical data is used to find the area which has received maximum number of orders which is basically the mode in the data. This helps in identifying the location where the warehouse can be established. Now, for the purpose of vehicle routing, the Google Maps API is used to identify the latitude (LAT) and longitude (LNG) of the address location that is further converted in meters for computing the distance between the two address i and j using the Haversine Formula [31] as per Eqs. 1–3.

$$X = \sin^2\left(\frac{\Delta LAT}{2}\right) + \cos LAT_1 \cdot \cos LAT_2 \cdot \sin^2\left(\frac{\Delta LNG}{2}\right) \tag{1}$$

$$Y = 2 \cdot X \cdot \tan 2\left(\sqrt{X}, \sqrt{(1-X)}\right) \tag{2}$$

$$Distance = R \cdot Y, \tag{3}$$

where R is the radius of the earth (Mean Radius = 6,371 km).

After calculating the distance between addresses we need to construct the distance graph so that every demand point is represented by a variable $V_1, V_2, V_3, \dots \dots \dots V_n$ with variable V_i having values $Value_1, Value_2, Value_3, \dots \dots \dots Value_n$. The graph thus constructed would be G = (V, n) and the total number of vertices in the graph becomes n * (n − 1)/2. Each variable V_i vertex $v_{i,j}$ having value $Value_{ij}$. The graph has a single root node (warehouse) from where the routing run is initiated leading to creation of a bidirectional symmetric graph.

The current study uses the ant system algorithm which is the first variant of ACO algorithm [32, 33]. The ant system works on pheromone values that are updated by all the ants completing their tour. The problem comprises of a network flow model where the ants have a probability ($Prob_{x,y}$) that helps them to choose the path to be taken. This path is from a node x to node y in the flow network. Every path has a probability associated with t which is given by Eq. 4.

$$Prob_{x,y} = \frac{\left(\tau_{x,y}^{\alpha}\right)\left(\varphi_{x,y}^{\beta}\right)}{\sum \left(\tau_{x,y}^{\alpha}\right)\left(\varphi_{x,y}^{\beta}\right)}, \tag{4}$$

where $\tau_{x,y}$ is the pheromone amount present on path from node x to node y.

$\varphi_{x,y}$, represents the desirability of the path from node x to node y and is often the inverse of the distance between x and y i.e. lesser the distance (often Euclidean distance), greater is the path desirability as expressed in Eq. 5.

$$\varphi_{x,y} = \frac{1}{dist_{x,y}} \tag{5}$$

Lastly, α is a constant representative of the importance given to a particular pheromone trail and β is a constant which represents the importance given to the vision/ant memory. To find the appropriate values for α and β, a sensitivity analysis is conducted for achieving optimum results.

Further, once the probability for each path is computed, the pheromone trails need to be updated after every iteration depending on the paths chosen by the traveling ants. These trails are updated by the ants that have updated their tour as per Eq. 6.

$$\tau_{x,y} = (1 - \rho).\tau_{x,y} + \sum_{z=1}^{i} \Delta\tau_{x,y}^{z}, \tag{6}$$

where i represents the number of ants in the colony, ρ is the evaporation rate of the pheromone and $\Delta\tau_{x,y}^{z}$ is indicative of the amount of pheromone deposited by z^{th} ant on the path from node x to node y (i.e. edge (x, y) in the flow network (Eq. 7).

$$\Delta\tau_{x,y}^{z} = \begin{Bmatrix} \frac{1}{LenTour_z} & if\ an\ ant\ z\ travels\ path\ x\ to\ y \\ 0 & otherwise \end{Bmatrix}, \tag{7}$$

where $LenTour_z$ is the length of the tour of ant z.

In the current sceanrio of online retail, the source will always be the warehouse and destinations would be the addresses on which the packages are to be delivered. The result of the above ACO engine gives the optimal path for routing which is used for location based inventory delivery. To achive optimal results, certain metrics in the ACO model need to be fixed for which a sensitivity analysis is conducted.

4   Sensitivity Analysis

For the purpose of finding out the optimal vehicle route the ACO is used which is able to find a sub-optimal path. As discussed in the mathematical model, the importance of visibility of pheromone trails can be controlled via Alpha (α), Beta (β) and Rho (ρ), these values need to be identified for optimal results. Further, the ACO engine runs for a particular number of iterations updating the paths in very iteration. The optimization is often directly proportional to the number of ant agents and number of iterations. However, the same needs to be identified and set. This section also explores various combinations of number of ant and number of iterations to achieve the most optimal routing path. Figure 2 represents the plots for all coefficients for sensitivity analysis.

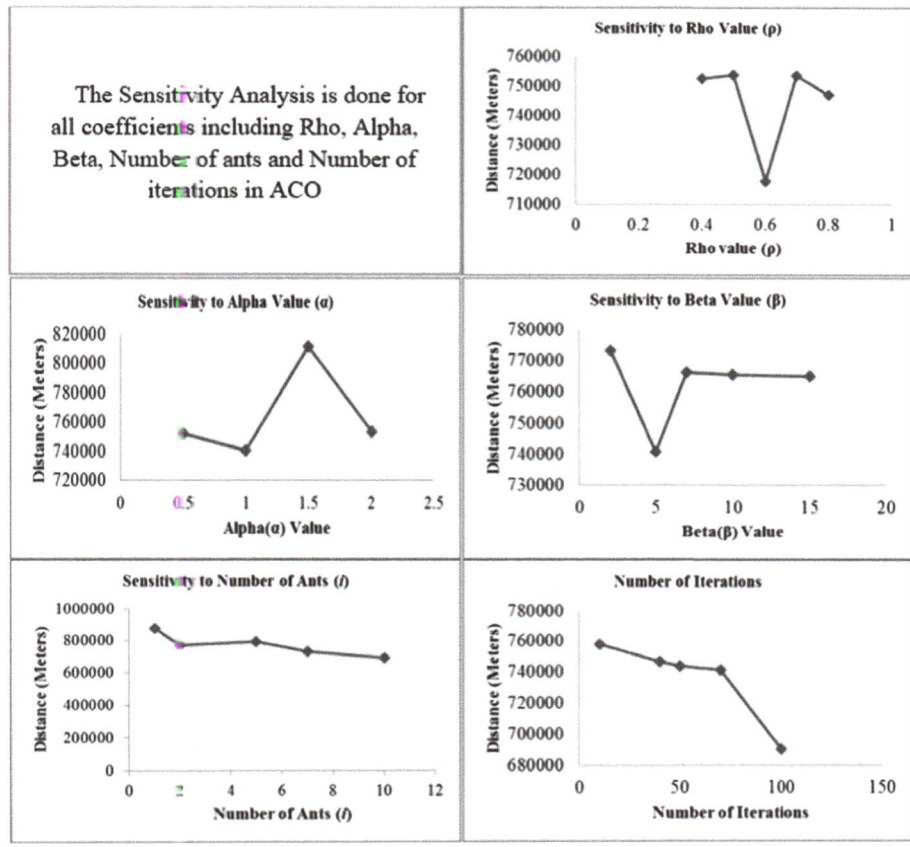

Fig. 2. Sensitivity analysis of ACO engine coefficients

The current study uses ACO to solve the location based inventory routing problem for delivery of packages for an online retail firm. The study uses a sensitivity analysis to identify values for coefficients that result in the most optimal route for delivering the inventory. Table 2 summarizes the coefficients used in the ACO engine to generate the path.

The above variables are fed into the model for routing the vehicle from the warehouse to the destinations. Figure 3 illustrates the optimal path generated from the ACO engine in terms of longitude and latitude coordinates.

The total number of locations are 346 and the total distance to be travelled is 690.29 km as identified through the sensitivity analysis.

Table 2. Coefficient values for ACO engine

Coefficients	Values
Number of iterations	100
Alpha (α)	1.0
Beta (β)	5.0
Rho value (ρ)	0.6
Number of ants	10
Distance	690288.22

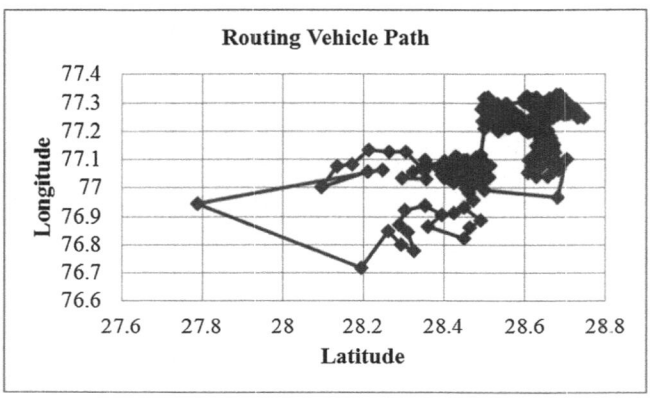

Fig. 3. Optimal routing vehicle path using ACO

5   Conclusion and Future Scope

Ant colony optimization is one of the possible solution of location based inventory routing problem. It is able to find the sub-optimal route in dynamic routing as compared to any static algorithm like Dijkstra, Prim's or Kruskal. This study analyzes ordinal data find the Sub optimal path. The optimization increases as the number of ants and number of iterations increased. The ACO engine can be used in various machine learning applications including both supervised an unsupervised techniques and proves to be reusable in variety of applications. ACO has the ability to adapt to the situation at hand and take corrective action and thus it is well suited for solving problems in dynamic environments like online retail.

This study highlights how powerful ACO is and how the positive feedback system can be used as an optimization tool. ACO can also be used as a broader class of problems. The computation power required for application of the algorithm in case scenarios is quite high. Other possible applications of ACO could be an integration with neural network [34], immune network [35], evolution strategies [36], genetic algorithms [37], job scheduling and project scheduling among others.

We believe there is further scope of the optimization and further work can be done in area of improvement of ACO. The approach can be combined with other static algorithms for taking advantage of the benefits of both for dynamicity of the problems. For a multi-warehouse problem, a clustering algorithm can also be integrated to cluster the delivery locations keeping the warehouse as centroids and then using ACO for generating the routes and assigning suitable delivery agents.

References

1. Hawk, S.: A comparison of B2C e-commerce in developing countries. Electron. Commer. Res. **4**(3), 181–199 (2004)
2. Doger, K., Tarwar, P.: Fulfilled! India's e-commerce retail logistics growth story (2015)
3. FICCI, & KPMG.# Shootingforthestars: Indian media and entertainment industry report (2015)
4. Ballou, R.H.: The evolution and future of logistics and supply chain management. Eur. Bus. Rev. **19**(4), 332–348 (2007)
5. Secomandi, N.: Comparing neuro-dynamic programming algorithms for the vehicle routing problem with stochastic demands. Comput. Oper. Res. **27**(11–12), 1201–1225 (2000)
6. Ali, H., Kar, A.K.: Discriminant analysis using ant colony optimization – an intra- algorithm exploration. Procedia Comput. Sci. **132**, 880–889 (2018)
7. Barbagallo, D., Di Nitto, E., Dubois, D.J., Mirandola, R.: A bio-inspired algorithm for energy optimization in a self-organizing data center. In: Weyns, D., Malek, S., de Lemos, R., Andersson, J. (eds.) SOAR 2009. LNCS, vol. 6090, pp. 127–151. Springer, Heidelberg (2010). https://doi.org/10.1007/978-3-642-14412-7_7
8. Kulkarni, R.V, Venayagamoorthy, G.K., Cheng, M.X.: Bio-inspired node localization in wireless sensor networks. In: IEEE International Conference on Systems, Man and Cybernetics, pp. 205–210. IEEE (2009)
9. Aswani, R., Ghrera, S.P., Kar, A.K., Chandra, S.: Identifying buzz in social media: a hybrid approach using artificial bee colony and k-nearest neighbors for outlier detection. Soc. Netw. Anal. Min. **7**(1), 38 (2017)
10. Aswani, R., Kar, A.K., Ilavarasan, P.V.: Detection of spammers in twitter marketing: a hybrid approach using social media analytics and bio inspired computing. Inf. Syst. Front. **20**(3), 515–530 (2018)
11. Guddeti, R.M, Buyya, R.: A hybrid bio-inspired algorithm for scheduling and resource management in cloud environment. IEEE Trans. Serv. Comput. (2017). https://doi.org/10.1109/tsc.2017.2679738
12. Laporte, G.: The vehicle routing problem: an overview of exact and approximate algorithms. Eur. J. Oper. Res. **59**(3), 345–358 (1992)
13. Laporte, G., Gendreau, M., Potvin, J.Y., Semet, F.: Classical and modern heuristics for the vehicle routing problem. Int. Trans. Oper. Res. **7**(4–5), 285–300 (2000)
14. Clarke, G., Wright, J.W.: Scheduling of vehicles from a central depot to a number of delivery points. Oper. Res. **12**(4), 568–581 (1964)
15. Mole, R.H., Jameson, S.R.: A sequential route-building algorithm employing a generalised savings criterion. J. Oper. Res. Soc. **27**(2), 503–511 (1976)
16. Christofides, N, Mingozzi, A., Toth, P.: The vehicle routing problem. In: Christofides, N., Mingozzi, A., Toth, P., Sandi, C. (eds.) Combinatorial Optimization. Wiley, Chichester (1979)
17. Gillett, B.E., Miller, L.R.: A heuristic algorithm for the vehicle dispatch problem. Oper. Res. **22**, 240–349 (1974)

18. Agarwal, Y., Mathur, K., Salkin, H.M.: A setpartitioning based exact algorithm for the vehicle routing problem. Networks **19**(7), 731–749 (1989)
19. Fisher, M.L., Jaikumar, R.: A generalized assignment heuristic for vehicle routing. Networks **11**(2), 109–124 (1981)
20. Christofides, N., Mingozzi, A., Toth, P.: Exact algorithms for the vehicle routing problem, based on spanning tree and shortest path relaxations. Math. Program. **20**(1), 255–282 (1981)
21. Gendreau, M., Hertz, A., Laporte, G.: A tabu search heuristic for the vehicle routing problem. Manag. Sci. **40**(10), 1276–1290 (1994)
22. Osman, I.H.: Metastrategy simulated annealing and tabu search algorithms for the vehicle routing problem. Ann. Oper. Res. **41**(4), 421–451 (1993)
23. Kar, A.K.: Bio inspired computing–A review of algorithms and scope of applications. Expert Syst. Appl. **59**, 20–32 (2016)
24. Chakraborty, A., Kar, A.K.: Swarm intelligence: a review of algorithms. In: Patnaik, S., Yang, X.-S., Nakamatsu, K. (eds.) Nature-Inspired Computing and Optimization. MOST, vol. 10, pp. 475–494. Springer, Cham (2017). https://doi.org/10.1007/978-3-319-50920-4_19
25. Aswani, R., Ghrera, S.P., Chandra, S.: A novel approach to outlier detection using modified grey wolf optimization and k-nearest neighbors algorithm. Indian J. Sci. Technol. **9**(44) (2016)
26. Aswani, R., Ghrera, S.P., Chandra, S., Kar, A.K.: Outlier detection among influencer blogs based on off-site web analytics data. In: Kar, A.K., et al. (eds.) I3E 2017. LNCS, vol. 10595, pp. 251–260. Springer, Cham (2017). https://doi.org/10.1007/978-3-319-68557-1_23
27. Bullnheimer, B., Hartl, R.F., Strauss, C.: An improved ant system algorithm for the vehicle routing problem. Ann. Oper. Res. **89**, 319–328 (1999)
28. Prins, C.: A simple and effective evolutionary algorithm for the vehicle routing problem. Comput. Oper. Res. **31**(12), 1985–2002 (2004)
29. Bell, J.E., McMullen, P.R.: Ant colony optimization techniques for the vehicle routing problem. Adv. Eng. Inform. **18**(1), 41–48 (2004)
30. Gass, S.I., Fu, M.C. (eds.): Encyclopedia of Operations Research and Management Science. Springer, Boston, MA (2013). https://doi.org/10.1007/978-1-4419-1153-7
31. Robusto, C.C.: The cosine-haversine formula. Am. Math. Mon. **64**(1), 38–40 (1957)
32. Dorigo, M., Maniezzo, V., Colorni. A.: Positive feedback as a search strategy. Technical Report 91–016, Dipartimento di Elettronica, Politecnico di Milano, Milan, Italy (1991)
33. Dorigo, M., Maniezzo, V., Colorni. A.: Ant system: optimization by a colony of cooperating agents. IEEE Trans. Syst. Man Cybern. Part B, **26**(1), 29–41 (1996)
34. Rumelhart, D.E., Hinton, G.E., Williams, R.J.: Learning representations by back-propagating errors. Nature **323**(6088), 533 (1986)
35. Bersini, H.: The immune recruitment mechanism: a selective evolutionary strategy. In: Proceedings of ICGA-91, pp. 520–526 (1991)
36. Rechenberg, I.: Evolutionsstrategie–Optimierung technisher Systeme nach Prinzipien der biologischen Evolution (1973)
37. Goldberg, D.E., Holland, J.H.: Genetic algorithms and machine learning. Mach. Learn. **3**(2), 95–99 (1988)

Machine Learning Approach to Analyze and Predict the Popularity of Tweets with Images

Nimish Joseph[(✉)] [iD], Amir Sultan [iD], Arpan Kumar Kar [iD],
and P. Vigneswara Ilavarasan [iD]

Department of Management Studies, IIT Delhi, New Delhi, India
nimishjoseph@gmail.com

Abstract. Social Media platforms play a major role in spreading information. Twitter, is one such platform which is used by millions of people to share information every day. Twitter with the recent introduction of a feature that helps its users to attach images to a tweet has changed the dynamics of tweeting. Many people now prefer to tweet with images. This study tries to analyse and predict the popularity of such tweets. This study uses learning mechanisms like decision tree, neural networks and random forests to learn the tweets posted by people with a higher number of followers. Image parameters, network variables, transactional, and historical variables of a tweet are identified and are trained for predicting the test data. This study can help businesses to build better social media tools, which allows customers to tweet data at the right time. This study also identifies the contribution of various parameters that may help a tweet to go viral.

Keywords: Twitter image · Neural network · Random forest · Decision tree
Popularity · Machine learning

1 Introduction

Millions of images are uploaded on internet every day and the number keeps on increasing with popularity of social media platforms [1]. Social media platforms like Snapchat, Instagram, Twitter and Facebook are basically used by its users to upload pictures. Various studies show that more than 50% users login to photo sharing platforms like Instagram and Snapchat daily [2]. Majority of the pictures uploaded are ignored by the large share of users. However, certain posts or activities with images gain the attraction of audience [3, 4]. Twitter is one of the most widely used platforms by businesses. Twitter allows its users to share images along with the textual content. This feature of tweets has brought in more users and audience. Further, research shows tweets with media content have much better impressions, engagement, and shareability [5]. Hence, businesses try to incorporate images when they post content in twitter.

The increase in image content usage has brought the attention of academicians, researchers and businesses. Many tweets with image content performs better compared

© IFIP International Federation for Information Processing 2018
Published by Springer Nature Switzerland AG 2018. All Rights Reserved
S. A. Al-Sharhan et al. (Eds.): I3E 2018, LNCS 11195, pp. 567–576, 2018.
https://doi.org/10.1007/978-3-030-02131-3_49

to those without images [6]. However, this is not always true. Various descriptive and content related studies of twitter data [7] explains about popularity with respect to textual data. These studies extract the text related variables in twitter data and perform the analysis. It is therefore necessary to understand that, with the change in tweeting pattern, do we have a change in parameters that will influence the popularity of tweets?

Businesses and individuals try to attach images to their tweets and with the better connectivity, users prefer to get clarity, viewing the image related to textual data [8]. The increase in number of views, viewers retweets, favorites and other activities will enhance the chances for a tweet to go popular. However, popularity also depends on the user profile [9]. A celebrity with a million followers posting a tweet and getting 100 favorites, may not be counted as a popular tweet. Instead a person with 200 followers getting a 100 favorites for a tweet could be counted as popular. Hence, it is necessary to understand the history of users' tweets and its reach to define popularity of a tweet. Machine learning techniques are one of the best ways to perform classification [10] and the tweets in our study needs to be classified to identify the popularity.

This study, tries to identify the features of tweets with images, which could make it popular. This study will also establish a quantitative way to predict popularity of post with images on social media platforms like twitter just before uploading it based on transactional variables, image features, network variables, and historical social activities with the help of various machine learning models.

2   Literature Review

Many of the images that appear in SM goes viral [11]. This has really catapulted the popularity of image focused platforms like Pinterest and Instagram in recent times. For a category of images, studies tries to identify if there is a difference in the various aspects of the images and the content that went popular and that did not [12]. The image resolution, color strength, color combinations are some of these. A study on the effect of thin and heavy weight images in Social Media Users [13] gives an idea of the relevance of understanding the usage patterns of different images in SM users. Virality in Social Media is explained using a SPIN framework [14], where, he demonstrates factors like spreadability, propagativity, integration and nexus. A study done by Garimella et al. [15] show how they used social media image analysis to identify the health related issue of the people in a locality. Certain studies have been done to predict the number of retweets and to obtain values for images in Flickr [16]. Study on the virality of images in Google plus [17] explores the dynamics of the image content that results in virality. Khosla et al., explains how the images become popular and explains it using two factors namely, image content and social context. Deza and Parikh [19], explains how images go viral from the computer vision perspective. However, besides these studies, there hasn't been much of an exploration in this domain of media information propagation in SM.

3   Methodology

The various steps involved in this study are described below

1. Collection of twitter data with images – This process includes the identification of twitter profiles with more than 500 followers. The twitter data with images is collected for a time period of three months ranging from Jan 2018 to March 2018 from these identified celebrity profiles.
2. Cleaning of twitter data. Identifying the tweets with images. Extracting the images to a local path for processing.
3. Performing a descriptive analysis on the extracted tweets to identify the value for various twitter parameters.
4. Performing an analysis on images to identify the value for image related parameters like color detection, strength of the color and normalized value based on its strength.
5. Loading all identified features including transactional variables, network features, image features and user related parameters for learning and analysis. This involves slicing and dicing of data to convert it in the format desired for the modelling.
6. Classify the data as training set and testing set. 75% of the tweets and its parameters will be treated as a training set and the rest for testing.
7. Performing various learning techniques namely - Decision Trees, Random Forest, and Neural Networks to analyze the data and identify the relevance of various parameters in making tweets with images go viral. More techniques are used so as to compare the result of the studies.

4   Data Collection

Twitter data was collected from profile ids which had more than 500 followers. 100 profiles were identified as celebrity profiles. Some of the profiles are listed below:

AskNimesh, AustralianSuper, AwesomityFun, AzharuddinKadri, Bayer, Bayer4CropsUS, BayerSuomi, BeShakespeare, BestLoveNotes, BombayTEXT, Boredwiki, borusanholding, BoschEspana, Bupa, CaIuml5SOS, CapriceHoldings, Cargill, castawaychild, cheth, CloroxCo, ClubSarcasm, coopuk, Djvasava.

Twitter Data was collected from these high profiles for a period of three months starting from January 2018 to March 2018. Python 2.7 was used to extract the data using Twitter APIs. MySQL database was used to store and query for the results. The various parameters extracted include:

tweet_id, source, tweet_text, tweet_favorite_count, tweet_retweet_count, tweet_created_at, listed_count, statuses_count, friends_count, location, favourites_count, name, screen_name, created_at, profile_background_image_url_https, verified, profile_text_color, profile_image_url_https, media, media_url_https, coordinates, hashtags, urls, and retweeted.

4.1 Twitter Data Extraction

Basic building block of modelling exercise is the extraction of tweet (or post) features. The more exhaustive the features are, more accurately we can predict. Feature engineering is considered to have major share in modelling exercise and is therefore the most crucial step. Following section describe various twitter features.

- Tweet_id: Twitter identifies every tweet differently by providing a unique ID; this ID is called tweet_id.
- Source: This is the source through which, a user performs an activity in twitter. This could be a mobile app or a web application. It is also identified at the granular level, for e.g. twitter for mac.
- Text: Tweet shared or posted by a user on twitter platform comes as text field in the API. All content of a tweet including html links, hashtag, etc. is received as part of this tweet text.
- Favorite: Favorite field identifies number of likes received on post. This is an independent variable that we have considered for modelling.
- Retweet: Retweet field identifies number of retweet received on post. This is the second independent variable we have considered for modelling.
- Created at: This is timestamp at which the tweets are created. Timestamp is very important variable for posting on twitter. There are millions of tweets generated every hour, and if tweets are not done in the right timings, that is when your target customers are online, you may miss engagement opportunity.
- Listed: Listed field shows number of times particular person is listed in some other individual's post. This shows how the demand and popularity of a person/celebrity.
- Statuses: This field shows number of tweets posted by the person till now. This is an aggregate variable which shows activeness of a person on social media platform.
- Friends_count: Friends count is the count of people the person is following.
- Location: Location variable shows the places from where the tweets are originating. A diverse location is better for data modelling so as to avoid any kind of bias in the data.
- Favourites_count: This variable shows number of times a person liked tweets of others. This shows social interaction of a person.
- Name: This field shows actual name of a person. A business can use this to identify their target customer like if person is male or female, their religion, region etc. derived from the name.
- Screen_name: Screen name is similar to a user name by which a person is known in Twitter. This not required to be same as the given name.
- created_at: This field shows timestamp on which user created his/her profile on twitter. You can use this variable to calculate age of a person on social media platform.
- Media: This field shows, if tweets have any media content attached to it. This is an important field since it helps us to filter tweets with images.
- Media_url_https: URL linked with media content.
- Retweeted: This indicates if a person shares a post created by his/her own. This it is a very important variable for model building.

Table 1. Data status

	Avg. favorites	Friends count	Favorites count	Text length	Listed count	Status count
Mean	101.92	43912	4406.59	97.09	610.29	14134.91
Std.	323.92	93852.38	12765.5	37.65	1465.09	23852.17
Min.	0	0	0	22	0	73
Max.	1636	705145	187512	318	8980	177862

From the identified profiles the authors extracted 35,721 tweets. Mean average of favorites on the shortlisted posts are 101 whereas the mean of text size is 97 characters. Table 1 gives the status of the data collected.

Location analysis indicates that 17% of the twitter data is from India and rest from other parts of the world. 20% of the profiles did not specify their locations. Tweets were collected from the identified celebrity profiles.

5   Data Analysis

The extraction of tweets and its various other parameters was then followed by the analysis process. Tweets were cleaned to remove noise and other unwanted information. From the downloaded 35,721 tweets only 7,767 tweets were identified to be fit for this study. Other tweets did not have image content attached. Using the Media_url field, images attached to every tweet was downloaded to a local path for faster processing. The tweets with images were then processed for the training purpose. 75% of the data was used for training the model. To identify the success rate of a tweet, following two parameters were used.

- Average likes This shows the average of favorites received by an individual for his past 200 posts.
- Standard deviation of likes: This field shows standard deviation of favorites received by the person in his or her last 200 posts.

If the number of favorites for a tweet exceeds average likes + 2 * standard deviation of likes, then that tweet is considered to be as popular. 75% of the data was labelled as popular and unpopular based on this observation. The image features were then calculated to understand if any of image related parameters are influencing the popularity of tweets.

- Image Feature For this analysis, we have used image features as a quantitative factor. There are two approaches to it, convert colors into a nominal value; other way is to treat color as a continuous variable. This variable will then give a range of continuous vales that can be better utilized in the model.

All set of variables are then grouped into four different sets

i. Historical variables: favorites_count, listed_count, statuses, average historical likes, and standard deviations of likes; are categorized as historical variables.

ii. Transactional variables: Transaction variables are related with the current tweet. Variables like Tweet Creation time (hour), Age of profile (year), tweet_len, retweeted are type of transactional variables.

iii. Network variables: Variables like followers_count and friends_count are counted as network of a person.

iv. Image Features: Colors in an image and strength of colors.

Different learning approaches where then used to learn and identify the importance of these variables with respect to the popularity of a tweet. Decision Trees, Random Forests and Neural Networks were used to understand this problem.

Decision Trees

Decision Tree is a decision based support tool which is often used as a machine learning approach. A graph that looks like a tree is constructed where each intersection or the node acts as a case for a test. The branches denote the outcome of these tests. It includes chance nodes, decision nodes and end nodes. In this study we uses decision tree to identify if a parameter is really contributing in twitter popularity. This is a supervised learning algorithm. This study have used DecisionTreeClassifier package in python.

Random Forests

Random forest is a supervised learning technique, used for regression, classification, etc. Decisions trees habit of over fitting to the training sets are corrected by this mechanism. It works by fitting number of decision trees by dividing samples, on the overall dataset. Generally, sampling works through bagging technique. Average of each decision tree is taken as the final outcome. RandomForestClassifier in python was used for performing this task

Neural Networks

Neural network models are human brain inspired algorithms that are developed to work in the same way our brain process information. Most common used in application form of neural network is multilayer feed-forward network which have several layers, each layer calculate information from its previous layer. Inputs from one node to another are combined through a weighted linear equation. Output is modified based on algorithms before sent as output to the other layer. Weights are generally taken as random values which are passed through several layers. It is recommended to provide pre-learned values to reduce calculation complexity while solving complex problems. MLPClassifier from neural networks in python was used.

6   Results and Discussions

Figures 1 and 2 gives the importance of various features in case of Decision Trees and Random forest separately. It is observed that historical variables contribute more towards popularity. Table 2 compares the result of decision trees and random forests. Tables 3, 4 and 5 gives the confusion matrix.

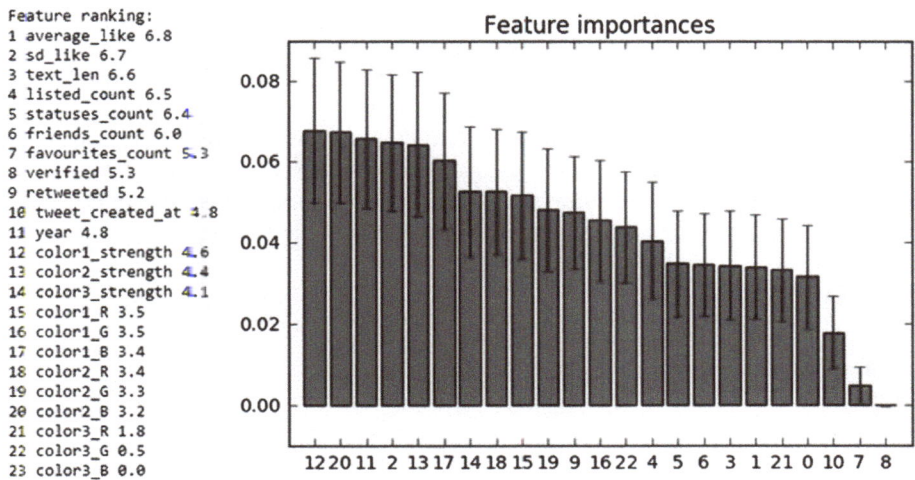

Fig. 1. Feature importance in case of decision trees

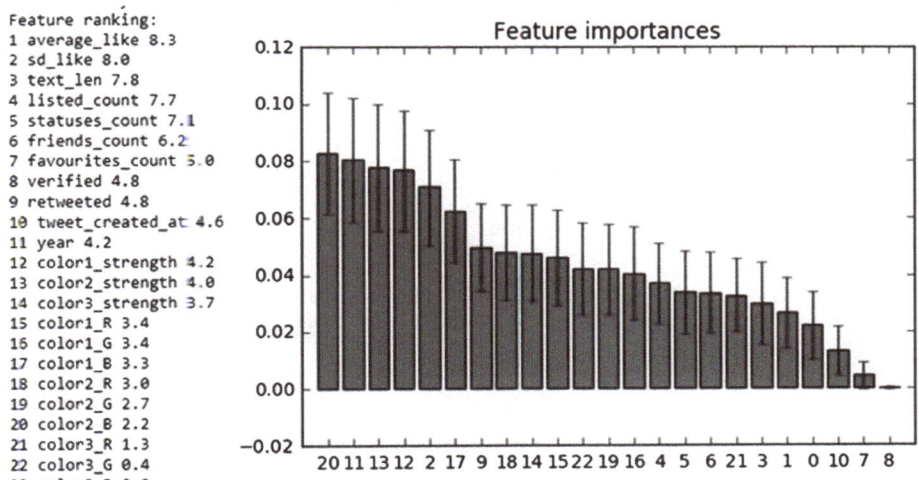

Fig. 2. Feature importance in case of random forest

Table 2. Comparison of decision trees and random forests

Decision trees	Random forests
Historical variables – 34%	Historical variables – 37%
Transaction variable – 26%	Transaction variable – 26%
Network variable – 14%	Network variable – 12%
Image features – 26%	Image features – 25%

Results of the variable importance shows that how random forests are giving higher weightages to the aggregated and real time variables and lower weightages to the network and image features. As historical variables are the function of network variables, random forest is trying to avoid over fit on this data.

In both algorithms, comparatively a lower importance is given to the network variables and image features. In the second part of analysis on confusion matrix, we have seen higher recall for decision tree with less precision, whereas random forest and neural network have higher precision and lower recall (see Table 6).

Table 3. Confusion matrix and prediction for decision trees

Confusion matrix		Predicted	
Decision trees		0	1
Actual	0	1820	33
	1	20	37

Table 4. Confusion matrix and prediction for random trees

Confusion matrix		Predicted	
Random forest		0	1
Actual	0	1,832	21
	1	26	31

Table 5. Confusion matrix and prediction for neural networks

Confusion matrix		Predicted	
Neural networks		0	1
Actual	0	1834	19
	1	25	32

Table 6. Precision and recall

Decision tree	Random forest	Neural network
Precision: 52.9%	Precision: 59.4%	Precision: 62.7%
Recall: 64.9%	Recall: 54.4%	Recall: 56.1%

This study was successful in obtaining, low false negative rates followed by low false positives. Results of confusion matrix is interesting for interpretation and comparisons. Key part of this study is the comparison of results obtained from the decision tree with respect to the random forest method. Decision tree classification is a faster method compared to random forest & neural networks, because it provides a simple interpretation of the dependent variables, which is of interest for many studies.

7   Conclusion

In the light of analysis performed for prediction of tweet popularity based on different factors like - transactional variables, image features, historical variables of the user, and network variables - most important feature obtained was the historical and transactional variables. This behavior has been proven both by decision tree and random forest prediction mechanisms. Image features and network variables did not contribute much to the popularity of the tweet. Increasing the parameters and observations for image and network related parameters might be a problem of future interest. This study will help social media tools to provide capability to automate their process, by helping the businesses and customers to post their content while probability of tweets going viral is comparatively higher. This study was successful in analyzing and predicting the popularity of tweets with images.

References

1. Bakhshi, S., Shamma, D.A., Gilbert, E.: Faces engage us: photos with faces attract more likes and comments on instagram. In: Proceedings of the SIGCHI Conference on Human Factors in Computing Systems, pp. 965–974. ACM (2014)
2. Pittman, M., Reich, B.: Social media and loneliness: why an instagram picture may be worth more than a thousand Twitter words. Comput. Hum. Behav. **62**, 155–167 (2016)
3. Hu, Y., Manikonda, L., Kambhampati, S.: What we Instagram: a first analysis of Instagram photo content and user types. In: ICWSM (2014)
4. Kietzmann, J.H., Hermkens, K., McCarthy, I.P., Silvestre, B.S.: Social media? Get serious! Understanding the functional building blocks of social media. Bus. Horiz. **54**(3), 241–251 (2011)
5. Gupta, A., Lamba, H., Kumaraguru, P., Joshi, A.: Faking sandy: characterizing and identifying fake images on twitter during hurricane sandy. In: Proceedings of the 22nd International Conference on World Wide Web, pp. 729–736. ACM (2013)
6. Toubia, O., Stephen, A.T.: Intrinsic vs. image-related utility in social media: why do people contribute content to twitter? Market. Sci. **32**(3), 368–392 (2013)
7. Joseph, N., Kar, A.K., Ilavarasan, P.V., Ganesh, S.: Review of discussions on internet of things (IoT): insights from twitter analytics. J. Glob. Inf. Manag. (JGIM) **25**(2), 38–51 (2017)
8. Russell, M.A.: Mining the Social Web: Data Mining Facebook, Twitter, LinkedIn, Google+, GitHub, and More. O'Reilly Media, Inc (2013)
9. Abel, F., Gao. Q., Houben, G.-J., Tao, K.: Analyzing user modeling on twitter for personalized news recommendations. In: Konstan, J.A., Conejo, R., Marzo, J.L., Oliver, N. (eds.) UMAP 2011. LNCS, vol. 6787, pp. 1–12. Springer, Heidelberg (2011). https://doi.org/10.1007/978-3-642-22362-4_1
10. Kotsiantis, S.B., Zaharakis, I., Pintelas, P.: Supervised machine learning: a review of classification techniques. Emerg. Artif. Intell. Appl. Comput. Eng. **160**, 3–24 (2007)
11. Mangold, W.G., Faulds, D.J.: Social media: the new hybrid element of the promotion mix. Bus. Horiz. **52**(4), 357–365 (2009)
12. Vinner, S., Dreyfus, T.: Images and definitions for the concept of function. J. Res. Math. Educ. **20**(4), 356–366 (1989)

13. Smeesters, D., Mussweiler, T., Mandel, N.: The effects of thin and heavy media images on overweight and underweight consumers: social comparison processes and behavioral implications. J. Consum. Res. **36**(6), 930–949 (2009)
14. Mills, A.J.: Virality in social media: the SPIN framework. J. Public Aff. **12**(2), 162–169 (2012)
15. Garimella, V.R.K., Alfayad, A., Weber, I.: Social media image analysis for public health. In: Proceedings of the 2016 CHI Conference on Human Factors in Computing Systems, pp. 5543–5547. ACM (2016)
16. Van House, N.A.: Flickr and public image-sharing: distant closeness and photo exhibition. In: CHI 2007 Extended Abstracts on Human Factors in Computing Systems, pp. 2717–2722. ACM (2007)
17. Guerini, M., Strapparava, C., Özbal, G.: Exploring text virality in social networks. In: ICWSM (2011)
18. Wu, B., Cheng, W.H., Zhang, Y., Mei, T.: Time matters: multi-scale temporalization of social media popularity. In: Proceedings of the 2016 ACM on Multimedia Conference, pp. 1336–1344. ACM (2016)
19. Deza, A., Parikh, D.: Understanding image virality. In: Proceedings of the IEEE Conference on Computer Vision and Pattern Recognition, pp. 1818–1826 (2015)

A Critical Review of Empirical Research Examining SMEs Adoption from Selected Journals

S. S. Abed[(⊠)]

Department of Management Information Systems, College of Business (COB),
King Abdulaziz University Rabigh, Rabigh, Saudi Arabia
sabid@kau.edu.sa

Abstract. The purpose of this paper is to review the literature on empirical research examined Small and Medium size Enterprises (SMEs) from selected journals. This has been achieved by reviewing the most examined constructs to identify the key significant factors in the literature. The selected research papers for reviewing are accessed from only high-ranking journals. The review addressed technology adoption in the context of SMEs. The paper attempts to review the studies based on technology-organisation-environment (TOE) framework to identify the relevant set of variables for technology adoption in SMEs. The most significant factors found to be relative advantage and compatibility from the technological context, top management support and size from the organizational context, and external pressure from the Environmental context. This review intended to guide future researchers to improve the predictive power of their examined models.

Keywords Technology adoption · SMEs · TOE · Empirical research

1 Introduction

Small and Medium Enterprises (SMEs) are considered one of most significant sectors to promote nations financial and economic growth [3]. SMEs are defined based on their employment and economy figures as well as fixed assets and sales volumes. They typically employ less than 500 workers. They are known for their major advantages including employment creation at low capital cost, flexibility, and innovation [1, 59, 67]. Economies of most OCED nations comprise nearly 96% to 99% of small and medium enterprises that account for 80% economic growth for those nations. Their existence is evident in all developed and developing countries to the extent that GDPs for North American and European countries today is contributed significantly by SMEs with 99% of all businesses. Apart from that, around 70% job creation is credited to this sector [65]. SMEs are known for their significant role in driving the economic growth. Governments of emerging nations and developed countries support SMEs sector through encouraging public policies [3]. Large corporations, that normally play their central role in country's formal economy, could not effectively operate in absence of SMEs [2]. In fact, they appear more leading where there's a need to rely less on traditional resources and

S. A. Al-Sharhan et al. (Eds.): I3E 2018, LNCS 11195, pp. 577–587, 2018.
https://doi.org/10.1007/978-3-030-02131-3_50

effectively support technology and human intellectual capital as they depends on innovation, change adoption, creation of information and knowledge through strategic disposition of knowledge capital [3, 5, 65].

The existence and growth of SMEs sustain through inter-organizational integration and access to knowledge for which SMEs significantly need resources including Information technology, networking, internet and social media, configurable platforms, and prompt data processing models [1]. Such resources, especially information and communications technology enable SMEs to operate cost-effectively, both at national and international levels [5]. They need to earn and maintain competitive advantage through improved service quality and product expansion, customer evaluations, improved effectiveness and efficiency, cost reduction, and sales forecasting.

Research studies show that SMEs profit heavily by ICT in order to achieve sustainable growth in developed economies [51, 79]. The beginning of last decade observed a huge increase in the use of online platforms by businesses in the US and Europe. It showed similar growth in other parts of the world where online business ventures added billions to aggregate revenues [3]. Certain factors, however, affect SMEs' economic development and weaken their access to global markets, including ICT adoption. This adoption of ICT by SMEs is yet to be explored fully. This study will review the literature based on the TOE framework constructs in order to identify relevant set of variables for technology adoption in SMEs.

2   Technology Adoption

Technology adoption is defined as the choice to obtain and use a new innovation [25]. The mental acceptance of a technology by an individual or an organization, and the decision, by an individual or organization, to implement and utilize a technology [80]. Various models and theories have effectively explained technology adoption as voluntary individual behavior including; TAM, IDT, TRA, TRB, TOE, and UTAUT proposed by [6, 17, 22, 62, 75, 77] respectively.

This technology adoption was categorized at three distinct levels: organization, group, and team [25]. However, some studies show that TRA, TRB, and UTAUT are more aimed at forecasting individual adoption as compared to organizational context. In contrast, the TOE frameworks are mostly used at the organizational level to analyse the technology adoption. In recent years, the TOE frameworks have gained significant value among several authors who employ them to gain theoretical perspective on the ICT adoption as well as to test its variables for acceptance of new technologies [87].

Even though IDT and TOE framework constructs are suitable for examining organizational adoption, TOE frameworks are given more weight due to their addition of new construct (i.e. environmental) in explaining the technology adoption. [87] found TOE framework having more significance than the IDT in their theoretical evaluations. As a result, this research study will consider organization-based research studies established on TOE due to their high significance over other frameworks.

3 TOE Framework

Tornatzky and Fleischer [75] initially developed the TOE framework in order to analyse the organizational-level adoption of a number of information technology products and services. Since then, TOE frameworks have emerged as significant theoretical perspectives by potential researchers studying technology adoption. The addition of various distinct variables including technological, organizational, and environmental in TOE framework has supplemented researchers to test and validate its advantage over other adoption models w.r.t. their ability to technology use, technology adoption, and value created by SMEs sector as a result of technology creation [25, 59]. Therefore, there are many reasons to employ the TOE framework due to its many benefits including; its user adoption of ICT, its influence over value chain undertakings, its implementation, its diffusion among organizations after the adoption, foreseeing obstacles, its ability to develop better organizational competencies using the technology, and other factors impacting business decisions related to innovation-adoption. All three contexts of TOE framework, as explained by [75] influence the technological innovation adoption of the framework and its implementation. The following sections briefly outline those three contexts of Technological, Organizational, Environmental (TOE) framework.

Technological Context: According to [15], technological context is set of those variables that shadow their influence over individuals, organizations, and industries in their process of adopting innovations. [18] Further divided it into five innovation attributes that influence the possibility of adoption. A deep insight into technological context reveals that the adoption relies on various technologies, both inside and outside the organization. Moreover, it depends on application's apparent relative advantage, complexity in terms of learning curve, observability (imagination), compatibility (organizational as well as technical), and trialability (experimentation).

Organizational Context: organizational context comprises of organization's culture, business scope, top management's support, organizational readiness, prior ICT knowledge, owner innovativeness, information intensity, cost, and size [75].

Environmental Context: Factors facilitating or delaying areas of operation are covered under environmental context. [8, 65, 87] have captured a number of significant factors including competitive pressure, socio-cultural issues, readiness of business partners, government support and encouragement, and infrastructures for technology support.

4 Empirical Studies on SMEs Innovation Adoption from Select Journals

Based on the academic journal guide 2015, a literature review was directed to identify the empirical publications conducted on SMEs innovation adoption from high-ranking journals. Thirty-five journals has published empirical studies on SMEs innovation

Table 1. Empirical studies on SMEs innovation adoption from select journals

ISSN	Journal name	AJG 2015 rating	ABS 2010 rating	Articles
0276-7783	*MIS quarterly*	*4*	*4*	[32]
1047-7047	*Information systems research*	*4*	*4*	[73, 84]
0025-1909	*Management science*	*4*	*4*	[86]
0883-9026	*Journal of business venturing*	*4*	*4*	[34, 63]
0022-2437	*Journal of marketing research*	*4*	*4*	[24]
0047-2506	*Journal of international business studies*	*4*	*4*	[27]
0143-2095	*Strategic management journal*	*4*	*4*	[71]
1042-2587	*Entrepreneurship theory and practice*	*4*	*4*	[48]
0090-4848	*Human resource management*	*4*	*4*	[30]
0378-7206	*Information & management*	*3*	*3*	[12 16, 28, 31, 36, 46, 49, 54, 61]
0925-5273	*International journal of production economics*	*3*	*3*	[14]
0921-898X	*Small business economics*	*3*	*3*	[19]
0963-8687	*Journal of strategic information system*	*3*	*3*	[35]
0309-0566	*European journal of marketing*	*3*	*3*	[38, 64]
0960-085X	*European journal of information systems*	*3*	*3*	[53, 85, 87]
0305-0483	*Omega: the international journal of management science*	*3*	*3*	[56, 74]
1086-4415	*International journal of electronic commerce*	*3*	*3*	[70]
0742-1222	*Journal of management information systems*	*4*	*3*	[72]
0266-2426	*International small business journal*	*3*	*3*	[45]
0166-4972	*Technovation*	*3*	*3*	[44, 60, 83]
0047-2778	*Journal of small business management*	*3*	*3*	[10, 78, 81]
1462-6004	*Journal of small business and enterprise development*	*2*	*2*	[21, 25, 39, 40, 58]
0003-6846	*Applied economics*	*2*	*2*	[33]

(continued)

Table 1. (*continued*)

ISSN	Journal name	AJG 2015 rating	ABS 2010 rating	Articles
0955-534X	*European business review*	2	2	[37]
0887-4417	*Journal of computer information systems*	2	2	[47]
1529-3181	*Communications of the association for information systems*	2	2	[52]
1062-7375	*Journal of global information management*	2	2	[76]
0268-4012	International journal of information management	2	2	[43]
1086-1718	*Strategic change*	2	2	[29]
1467-0895	*International journal of accounting information systems*	2	1	[11]
1019-6781	*Electronic markets*	2	1	[7, 8, 41, 54, 82]
1741-0398	*Journal of enterprise information management*	2	1	[9, 13, 23, 59, 65, 69]
0263-5577	*Industrial management and data systems*	2	1	[4, 26, 57, 68]
1741-0401	*International journal of productivity and performance management*	1	1	[50]
Total	**35**			*68*

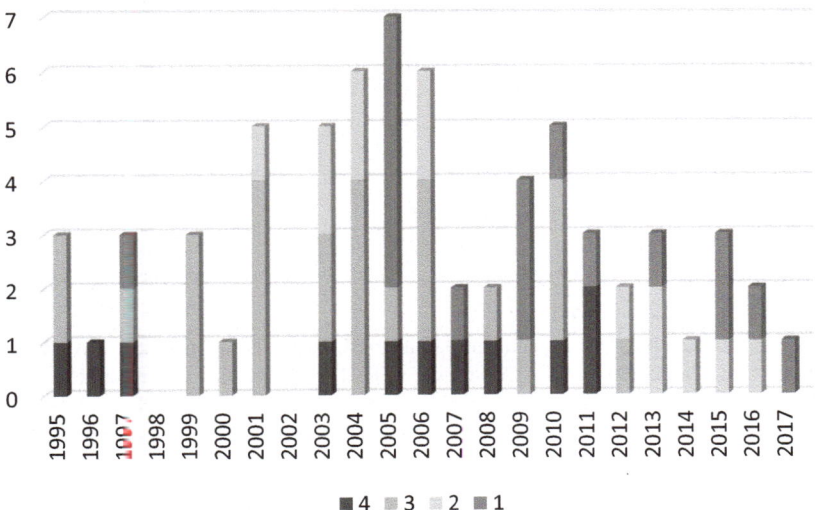

Fig. 1. Empirical studies conducted according to journal rating and year

Table 2. Construct analysis the most significant factors affecting SMEs adoption

IV	Significant	Insignificant
Technological factors		
R A	**DV: BI** [43, 61] **DV:USE** [9, 12, 25, 26, 28, 32, 33, 35, 36, 46, 47, 49, 52–56, 58, 65, 68, 70, 76]	**DV:USE** [7, 8]
C B	**DV:USE** [4, 7–9, 12, 25, 26, 28, 35, 47, 49, 52, 54, 58, 68, 70, 76, 85]	
C X	**DV:USE** [8, 9, 49, 58, 61, 68, 76]	**DV: BI** [43] **DV:USE** [28, 35]
TR	**DV:USE** [9, 35, 58, 59, 68, 82]	**DV:USE** [8]
O B	**DV:USE** [58, 68]	**DV:USE** [8, 35, 59]
SC	**DV:USE** [19, 21, 40, 68, 85]	
Organizational factors		
T M S	**DV: BI** [43] **DV:USE** [9, 12, 14, 47, 49, 54–56, 58, 59, 65, 70, 84]	
O R	**DV: BI** [14] **DV:USE** [28, 32, 36, 46, 47, 49, 52, 58, 59, 82, 86]	**DV: BI** [47]
PK	**DV:USE** [7, 19, 26, 33, 40, 72–74, 76, 82]	**DV:USE** [26, 58, 59]
OI	**DV:USE** [7, 21, 25, 26, 33, 39, 72–74, 76, 82]	
II	**DV: BI** [26, 72, 74] **DV:USE** [26, 37, 41, 54]	**DV: BI** [7, 70]
C O	**DV: BI** [43] **DV:USE** [4, 8, 21, 25, 40, 82, 84, 85]	**DV:USE** [7, 8, 26, 33, 35]
SI	**DV:USE** [7, 9, 13, 19, 31, 49, 56, 58, 59, 69, 72–74, 76, 84, 87]	**DV:USE** [26, 33]
Environmental factors		
EP	**DV:USE** [14, 19, 26, 28, 32, 36, 46, 52, 56, 58, 76, 82, 84–87]	**DV: BI** [43] **DV:USE** [7, 9, 33, 37, 47, 49, 59, 70]
CP	**DV: BI** [43] **DV:USE** [21, 26, 39, 41, 53, 65, 82, 87]	
IS	**DV:USE** [9, 14, 21, 31, 53, 54, 58, 69]	**DV:USE** [59]
MS	**DV:USE** [9, 33, 37, 58, 59, 84, 87]	**DV:USE** [13, 86]
ES	**DV:USE** [9, 26, 65, 82]	**DV:USE** [7, 58, 59]

IV: Independent variable, DV: Dependent variable, BI: Behavioural Intention, RA: Relative advantage, CB: Compatibility, CX: Complexity, TR: Trialability, OB: observability, SC: Security, TMS: Top management support, OR: Organizational readiness, PK: ICT/IS Prior knowledge, OI: Owner Innovativeness, II: Information Intensity, CO: Cost, SI: Size, EP: External Pressure, CP: Consumer pressure, IS: Industry sector, MS: Market Scope, ES: External ICT Support.

adoption, ranging from 4* to 1* rating, and a total of sixty-eight studies was identified (Table 1). These studies were conducted from 1995 to 2017, the highest number of studies has took place in 2005 (Fig. 1).

Based on TOE framework, a construct analysis has conducted to identify the most significant factors affecting SMEs adoption from the studies that has been identified in Table 1. From the technological factors, six constructs has been identified including relative advantage, compatibility, complexity, trialability, observability, and security. From the organizational factors, seven constructs has been identified including top management support, organizational readiness, prior ICT/IS knowledge, owner/entrepreneurial innovativeness, information intensity, cost, and size. From the environmental factors, five constructs has been identified including external/competitive pressure, consumer pressure, industry sector, market scope, and external ICT support (Table 2).

5 Summary and Conclusion

The current study makes a significant contribution for academics by reviewing the literature of the empirical studies on SMEs innovation adoption from high-ranking journals. A total of thirty-five journals have presented empirical research papers on SMEs innovation adoption with sixty-eight different studies. The identified studies has been conducted from 1995 to 2017. Based on the TOE framework, a review of the constructs has directed to identify the most significant factors affecting SMEs innovation adoption from the selected journals. The study found that the most significant factors found to be relative advantage and compatibility from the technological context, top management support and size from the organizational context, and external pressure from the environmental context. This analysis intended to guide future researchers to improve the predictive power of their examined models.

References

1. Abed, S.S., Dwivedi, Y.K., Williams, M.D.: SMEs' adoption of e–commerce using social media in a Saudi Arabian context: a systematic literature review. Int. J. Bus. Inf. Syst. **19**(2), 159–179 (2015)
2. Abed, S.S., Dwivedi, Y.K., Williams, M.D.: Social media as a bridge to e-commerce adoption in SMEs: a systematic literature review. Market. Rev. **15**(1), 39–57 (2015)
3. Abed, S.S., Dwivedi, Y.K., Williams, M.D.: Social commerce as a business tool in Saudi Arabia's SMEs. Int. J. Indian Cult. Bus. Manag. **13**(1), 1–19 (2016)
4. Ainin, S., Parveen, F., Moghavvemi, S., Jaafar, N. I., Mohd Shuib, N.L.: Factors influencing the use of social media by SMEs and its performance outcomes. Ind. Manag. Data Syst. **115**(3), 570–588 (2015)
5. Ajmal, F., Yasin, N.M., Norman, A.A.: Critical success factors influencing e-commerce adoption in SMEs: a review and model. Int. J. Adv. Appl. Sci. **4**(7), 159–172 (2017)
6. Ajzen, I.: The theory of planned behaviour. Organ. Behav. Hum. Decis. Process. **50**(2), 179–211 (1991)

7. Al-Qirim, N.: An empirical Investigation of an e-commerce adoption-capability model in small businesses in New Zealand. Electron. Mark. **15**(4), 418–437 (2005)
8. Al-Qirim, N.: A research trilogy into E-commerce adoption in small businesses in New Zealand. Electron. Mark. **17**(4), 263–285 (2007)
9. Alshamaila, Y., Papagiannidis, S., Li, F.: Cloud computing adoption by SMEs in the north east of England: a multi-perspective framework. J. Enterp. Inf. Manag. **26**(3), 250–275 (2013)
10. Aragón-Sánchez, A., Sánchez-Marín, G.: Strategic orientation, management characteristics, and performance: a study of Spanish SMEs. J. Small Bus. Manag. **43**(3), 287–308 (2005)
11. Azmi, A., Sapiei, N.S., Mustapha, M.Z., Abdullah, M.: SMEs' tax compliance costs and IT adoption: the case of a value-added tax. Int. J. Account. Inf. Syst. **23**, 1–13 (2016)
12. Beatty, R.C., Shim, J.P., Jones, M.C.: Factors influencing corporate web site adoption: a time-based assessment. Inf. Manag. **38**(6), 337–354 (2001)
13. Buonanno, G., Faverio, P., Pigni, F., Ravarini, A., Sciuto, D., Tagliavini, M.: Factors affecting ERP system adoption: a comparative analysis between SMEs and large companies. J. Enterp. Inf. Manag. **18**(4), 384–426 (2005)
14. Chan, F.T., Yee-Loong Chong, A., Zhou, L.: An empirical investigation of factors affecting e-collaboration diffusion in SMEs. Int. J. Prod. Econ. **138**(2), 329–344 (2012)
15. Cindy Claycomba, C., Iyerb, K., Germainc, R.: Predicting the level of B2B e-commerce in industrial organizations. Ind. Market. Manag. **34**, 221–234 (2005)
16. Cragg, P.B., Zinatelli, N.: The evolution of information systems in small firms. Inf. Manag. **29**(1), 1–8 (1995)
17. Davis, F.D.: Perceived usefulness, perceived ease of use, and user acceptance of information technology. MIS Q. **13**(3), 319–340 (1989)
18. Dedrick, J. and West, J.: Why firms adopt open source platforms: a grounded theory of innovation and standards adoption. In: Proceedings of the Workshop on Standard Making: A Critical Research Frontier for Information Systems (2003)
19. Dholakia, R.R., Kshetri, N.: Factors impacting the adoption of the internet among SMEs. Small Bus. Econ. **23**(4), 311–322 (2004)
20. Dwivedi, Y.K., et al.: Research on information systems failures and successes: Status update and future directions. Inf. Syst. Front. **17**(1), 143–157 (2015)
21. Fillis, I., Johansson, U., Wagner, B.: A qualitative investigation of smaller firm e-business development. J. Small Bus. Enterp. Dev. **11**(3), 349–361 (2004)
22. Fishbein, M., Ajzen, I.: Belief, Attitude, Intention and Behaviour: An Introduction to Theory and Research. Addison-Wesley, Reading, MA (1975)
23. Gangwar, H., Date, H., Ramaswamy, R.: Understanding determinants of cloud computing adoption using an integrated TAM-TOE model. J. Enterp. Inf. Manag. **28**(1), 107–130 (2015)
24. Gatignon, H., Xuereb, J.M.: Strategic orientation of the firm and new product performance. J. Market. Res., 77–90 (1997)
25. Ghobakhloo, M., Tang, S.H.: The role of owner/manager in adoption of electronic commerce in small businesses: the case of developing countries. J. Small Bus. Enterp. Dev. **20**(4), 754–787 (2013)
26. Ghobakhloo, M., Arias-Aranda, D., Benitez-Amado, J.: Adoption of ecommerce applications in SMEs. Ind. Manag. Data Syst. (8), 1238–1269 (2011)
27. Golovko, E., Valentini, G.: Exploring the complementarity between innovation and export for SMEs' growth. J. Int. Bus. Stud. **42**(3), 362–380 (2011)
28. Grandon, E.E., Pearson, J.M.: Electronic commerce adoption: an empirical study of small and medium US businesses. Inf. Manag. **42**(1), 197–216 (2014)

29. Hamad, H., Elbeltagi, I., Jones, P., El-Gohary, H.: Antecedents of B2B E-Commerce adoption and its effect on competitive advantage in manufacturing SMEs. Strateg. Change **24** (5), 405–428 (2015)
30. Hayton, J.C.: Strategic human capital management in SMEs: An empirical study of entrepreneurial performance. Hum. Resour. Manag. **42**(4), 375–391 (2003)
31. Hong, W., Zhu, K.: Migrating to internet-based e-commerce: factors affecting e-commerce adoption and migration at the firm level. Inf. Manag. **43**(2), 204–221 (2006)
32. Iacovou, C.L., Benbasat, I., Dexter, A.S.: Electronic data interchange and small organizations: adoption and impact of technology. MIS Q. **19**(4), 465–485 (1995)
33. Jeon, B.N., Han, K.S., Lee, M.J.: Determining factors for the adoption of e-business: the case of SMEs in Korea. Appl. Econ. **38**(16), 1905–1916 (2006)
34. Keh, H.T., Nguyen, T.T.M., Ng, H.P.: The effects of entrepreneurial orientation and marketing information on the performance of SMEs. J. Bus. Ventur. **22**(4), 592–611 (2007)
35. Kendall, J.D., Tung, L.L., Chua, K.H., Ng, C.H.D., Tan, S.M.: Receptivity of Singapore's SMEs to electronic commerce adoption. J. Strateg. Inf. Syst. **10**(3), 223–242 (2001)
36. Kuan, K.K., Chau, P.Y.: A perception-based model for EDI adoption in small businesses using a technology–organization–environment framework. Inf. Manag. **38**(8), 507–521 (2001)
37. Kula, V., Tatoglu, E.: An exploratory study of Internet adoption by SMEs in an emerging market economy. Eur. Bus. Rev. **15**(5), 324–333 (2003)
38. Laforet, S.: Effects of size, market and strategic orientation on innovation in non-high-tech manufacturing SMEs. Eur. J. Market. **43**(1/2), 188–212 (2009)
39. Laforet, S., Tann, J.: Innovative characteristics of small manufacturing firms. J. Small Bus. Enterp. Dev. **13**(3), 363–380 (2006)
40. Lawson, R., Alcock, C., Cooper, J., Burgess, L.: Factors affecting adoption of electronic commerce technologies by SMEs: an Australian study. J. Small Bus. Enterp. Dev. **10**(3), 265–276 (2003)
41. Levenburg, N.M.: Does size matter? Small firms' use of E-business tools in the supply Chain. Electron. Mark. **15**(2), 94–105 (2005)
42. Lin, H.F., Lin, S.M.: Determinants of e-business diffusion: a test of the technology diffusion perspective. Technovation **28**(3), 135–145 (2008)
43. Maduku, D.K., Mpinganjira, M., Duh, H.: Understanding mobile marketing adoption intention by South African SMEs: a multi-perspective framework. Int. J. Inf. Manag. **36**(5), 711–723 (2016)
44. Massa, S., Testa, S.: Innovation and SMEs: misaligned perspectives and goals among entrepreneurs, academics, and policy makers. Technovation (7), 393–407 (2008)
45. McAdam, R., Moffett, S., Hazlett, S.A., Shevlin, M.: Developing a model of innovation implementation for UK SMEs: a path analysis and explanatory case analysis. Int. Small Bus. J. **28**(3), 195–214 (2010)
46. Mehrtens, J., Cragg, P.B., Mills, A.M.: A model of Internet adoption by SMEs. Inf. Manag. **39**(3), 165–176 (2001)
47. Mirchandani, A.A., Motwani, J.: Understanding small business electronic commerce adoption: an empirical analysis. J. Comput. Inf. Syst. Spring, 70–3 (2001)
48. Moreno, A.M., Casillas, J.C.: Entrepreneurial orientation and growth of SMEs: a causal model. Entrepreneurship Theor. Pract. **32**(3), 507–528 (2008)
49. Oliveira, T., Thomas, M., Espadanal, M.: Assessing the determinants of cloud computing adoption: an analysis of the manufacturing and services sectors. Inf. Manag. **51**(5), 497–510 (2014)
50. O'Regan, N., Ghobadian, A.: Innovation in SMEs: the impact of strategic orientation and environmental perceptions. Int. J. Prod. Perform. Manag. **54**(2), 81–97 (2005)

51. Orser, B.J., Riding, A.: The influence of gender on the adoption of technology among SMEs. Int. J. Entrep. Small Bus. **33**(4), 514–531 (2008)
52. Pearson, J.M., Grandon, E.: E-commerce adoption: perceptions of managers/owners of small and medium sized firms in Chile. Commun. Assoc. Inf. Syst. **13**(1), 46 (2004)
53. Poon, S.: Business environment and internet commerce benefit—a small business perspective. Eur. J. Inf. Syst. **9**(2), 72–81 (2000)
54. Poon, S., Swatman, P.: An exploratory study of small business Internet commerce issues. Inf. Manag. **35**(1), 9–18 (1999)
55. Poon, S., Swatman, P.M.: Internet-based small business communication: seven Australian cases. Electron. Market. **7**(2), 15–21 (1997)
56. Premkumar, G., Roberts, M.: Adoption of new information technologies in rural small businesses. Omega **27**(4), 467–484 (1999)
57. Puklavec, B., Oliveira, T., Popovič, A.: Understanding the determinants of business intelligence system adoption stages: an empirical study of SMEs. in: Industrial Management & Data Systems, (just-accepted), 00-00 (2017)
58. Ramdani, B., Chevers, D., Williams, D.A.: SMEs' adoption of enterprise applications: a technology-organisation-environment model. J. Small Business Enterp. Dev. **20**(4), 735–753 (2013)
59. Ramdani, B., Kawalek, P., Lorenzo, O.: Knowledge management and enterprise systems adoption by SMEs: predicting SMEs' adoption of enterprise systems. J. Enterp. Inf. Manag. **22**(1/2), 10–24 (2009)
60. Rhee, J., Park, T., Lee, D.H.: Drivers of innovativeness and performance for innovative SMEs in South Korea: mediation of learning orientation. Technovation **30**(1), 65–75 (2010)
61. Riemenschneider, C.K., Harrison, D.A., Mykytyn Jr., P.P.: Understanding IT adoption decisions in small business: integrating current theories. Inf. Manag. **40**(4), 269–285 (2003)
62. Rogers, E.: Diffusion of Innovations, 4th edn. The Free Press, New York (1995)
63. Rosenbusch, N., Brinckmann, J., Bausch, A.: Is innovation always beneficial? A meta-analysis of the relationship between innovation and performance in SMEs. J. Bus. Ventur. **26**(4), 441–457 (2011)
64. Salavou, H., Baltas, G., Lioukas, S.: Organisational innovation in SMEs: the importance of strategic orientation and competitive structure. Eur. J. Market. **38**(9/10), 1091–1112 (2004)
65. Scupola, A.: SMEs' e-commerce adoption: perspectives from Denmark and Australia. J. Enterp. Inf. Manag. **22**(1/2), 152–166 (2009)
66. Soto-Acosta, P., Colomo-Palacios, R., Popa, S.: Web knowledge sharing and its effect on innovation: an empirical investigation in SMEs. Knowl. Manag. Res. Pract. **12**(1), 103–113 (2014)
67. Sunday, E. Z. E.: Examining information communication technology (ICT) adoption In SMEs: a dynamic capabilities approach. J. Enterp. Inf. Manag., (just-accepted), 00-00 (2018)
68. Tan, K.S., Chong, S.C., Lin, B., Eze, U.C.: Internet-based ICT adoption: evidence from Malaysian SMEs. Ind. Manag. Data Syst. **109**(2), 224–244 (2009)
69. Tan, K.S., Chong, S.C., Lin, B., Eze, U.C.: Internet-based ICT adoption among SMEs: demographic versus benefits, barriers, and adoption intention. J. Enterp. Inf. Manag. **23**(1), 27–55 (2010)
70. Teo, T.S., Tan, M., Buk, W.K.: A contingency model of Internet adoption in Singapore. Int. J. Electron. Comm., 95–118 (1997)
71. Terziovski, M.: Innovation practice and its performance implications in small and medium enterprises (SMEs) in the manufacturing sector: a resource-based view. Strateg. Manag. J. **31**(8), 892–902 (2010)
72. Thong, J.Y.: An integrated model of information systems adoption in small businesses. J. Manag. Inf. Syst. **15**(4), 187–214 (1999)

73. Thong, J.Y., Yap, C.S., Raman, K.S.: Top management support, external expertise and information systems implementation in small businesses. Inf. Syst. Res. **7**(2), 248–267 (1996)

74. Thong, J.Y.L., Yap, C.S.: CEO characteristics, organizational characteristics and information technology adoption in small businesses. Omega Int. J. Manag. Sci. **23**(4), 429–442 (1995)

75. Tornatzky, L., Fleischer, M.: The process of technology innovation. Lexington Books, Lexington, MA (1990)

76. Van Huy, L., Rowe, F., Truex, D., Huynh, M.Q.: An empirical study of determinants of e-commerce adoption in SMEs in Vietnam: an economy in transition. J. Global Inf. Manag. (JGIM) **20**(3), 23–54 (2012)

77. Venkatesh, V. et al.: User acceptance of information technology: toward a unified view. MIS Q. **27**, 425–478 (2003)

78. Verhees, F.J., Meulenberg, M.T.: Market orientation, innovativeness, product innovation, and performance in small firms. J. Small Bus. Manag. **42**(2), 134–154 (2004)

79. Widyastuti, D., Irwansyah, I.: Benefits and challenges of cloud computing technology adoption in small and medium enterprises (SMEs). Bdg. Creative Mov. (BCM) J. **4**(1), 241–246 (2018)

80. Williams, M.D., Rana, N.P., Dwivedi, Y.K.: The unified theory of acceptance and use of technology (UTAUT): a literature review. J. Enterp. Inf. Manag. **28**(3), 443–488 (2015)

81. Wolff, J.A., Pett, T.L.: Small-firm performance: modeling the role of product and process improvements. J. Small Bus. Manag. **44**(2), 268–284 (2006)

82. Wymer, S.A., Regan, E.A.: Factors influencing e-commerce adoption and use by small and medium businesses. Electron. Market. **15**(4), 438453 (2005)

83. Zeng, S.X., Xie, X.M., Tam, C.M.: Relationship between cooperation networks and innovation performance of SMEs. Technovation **30**(3), 181194 (2010)

84. Zhu, K., Kraemer, K.L.: Post-adoption variations in usage and value of ebusiness by organizations: cross-country evidence from the retail industry. Inf. Syst. Res. **16**(1), 61–84 (2005)

85. Zhu, K., Dong, S., Xu, S.X., Kraemer, K.L.: Innovation diffusion in global contexts: determinants of post-adoption digital transformation of European companies. Eur. J. Inf. Syst. **15**(6), 601–616 (2006)

86. Zhu, K., Kraemer, K.L., Xu, S.: The process of innovation assimilation by firms in different countries: a technology diffusion perspective on e-business. Manag. Sci. **52**(10), 1557–1576 (2006)

87. Zhu, K., Kraemer, K., Xu, S.: Electronic business adoption by European firms: a cross-country assessment of the facilitators and inhibitors. Eur. J. Inf. Syst. **12**, 251–268 (2003)

Advantages and Drawbacks of Social Network Sites Utilization in Travel and Tourism

Jaroslav Kacetl[(⊠)] and Blanka Klimova

Department of Applied Linguistics, Faculty of Informatics and Management,
University of Hradec Kralove, Rokitanskeho 62, 500 03 Hradec Kralove,
Czech Republic
{jaroslav.kacetl,blanka.klimova}@uhk.cz

Abstract. The article explores how social network sites (SNSs) are used in travel and tourism. Another objective is to find out and summarize whether or not SNSs are beneficial for the travel and tourism industry. This study was based on literature review that was employed to determine the most popular SNSs in travel and tourism. Then, selected widely used SNSs were compared and evaluated. The advent of Web 2.0 brought about significant changes in tourism. There are currently a lot of platforms that can be utilized in travel and tourism for various purposes. Some of these platforms focus on providing solely travel related content. However, the most popular SNSs used in tourism are still Facebook and Twitter, which do not specialize in tourism. The findings suggest that the tourism related SNSs provide their users predominantly with travel information and/or facilitate contacts. Advantages include an easy access to various content twenty four hours seven days a week regardless the time zone. Among their drawbacks belong a lack of lower control over content and difficulties with sorting the valuable from the worthless among loads of various platforms and messages.

Keywords: Travel and tourism · Advantages · Drawbacks
Social network · Sites

1 Introduction

Social network sites (SNSs) are becoming an inseparable part of people's everyday activities, both for business and private purposes. There are now many definitions of SNSs. One of the most cited is provided by Boyd & Ellison [1] who define social network sites as follows: SNSs are web-based services that allow individuals to construct a public or semi-public profile within a bounded system; articulate a list of other users with whom they share a connection; and view and traverse their list of connections and those by other within the system. They also put the main emphasis on their social aspect since these social network sites enable users to articulate and make visible their social networks (cf. [2]).

SNSs are now on their rise. The most popular social network site is undoubtedly Facebook, followed by Twitter. Since SNSs penetrate in all human activities, they also play a considerable role in travel and tourism business, which is closely connected with the new information and communication technologies. In fact, Werthner & Ricci [3] claim that

S. A. Al-Sharhan et al. (Eds.): I3E 2018, LNCS 11195, pp. 588–595, 2018.
https://doi.org/10.1007/978-3-030-02131-3_51

travel and tourism industry is at the head of the Internet use and online transactions. In travel and tourism industry SNSs are part of other social media platforms such as blogs, forums, wikis, video and photo sharing, virtual communities, chat rooms and podcasts (cf. [4]).

For example, Lange-Faria & Elliot [5] state that travellers use SNSs in order to plan their trips and holidays. SNSs are important in their information search about the place, its attractiveness or accommodation possibilities. All this information is influenced by age, gender, culture and other demographic and sociographic features. In addition, travel and tourism industry is based on the use of word-of-mouth recommendations and SNSs such as Facebook or Twitter enable their users to share their travel experiences. As Nielsen's report [6] presents, 84% of consumers trust these recommendations. Furthermore, Bennett [7] states that 64% of non-US travellers use social networks while travelling, 85% of leisure travellers use their smartphone abroad and 30% of them have already used mobile applications to find hotel deals. In addition, 52% of Facebook users have been inspired in their holiday planning by their friends' photos or 76% of travellers have posted their holiday photos to a social network site. Overall, SNSs enable travellers to have more control over their travel decision making process (cf. [8]).

Therefore, the purpose of this article is to explore those social network sites that are most frequently used in travel and tourism and discuss and summarize their benefits and limitations for the travel and tourism industry.

2 Materials and Methods

Firstly, a method of literature search of available sources exploring the issue of social network sites in the field of travel and tourism was applied. A search was conducted in the world's acknowledged databases such as Web of Science, Scopus, Springer and ScienceDirect. Furthermore, other sources cited in the analysed studies were also examined. Secondly, on the basis of evaluation of these literature sources, the researched issue was explored. The research studies were classified according to their relevancy.

Although there are not many research studies on the issue of SNSs in travel and tourism, there is a noticeable increase in the number of these publications (Fig. 1).

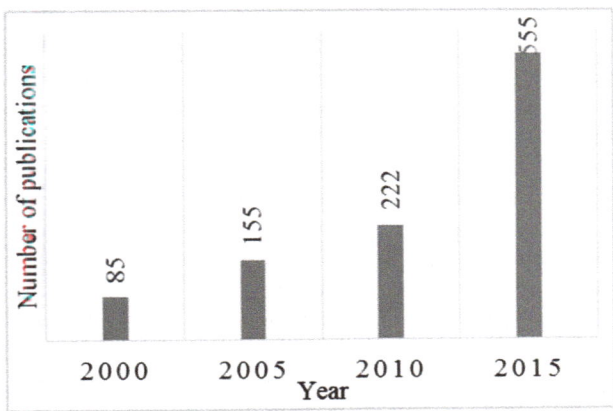

Fig. 1. A number of publications on SNSs in travel and tourism (authors' own processing, based on the data from [9])

3 Social Network Sites and Their Use in Tourism

The existence of SNS is enabled by the fact that ordinary people could start to use the Internet and it has become the mainstream and therefore truly social. It coincides with Web 2.0, the second generation of web-based services, which enables large-scale sharing. According to [10], the SNS take-off point can be identified between February 2005 and August 2006. It was important that the Internet has enabled anyone not only to access information, but also to communicate with other people, become a member of online communities, and to create and share content of various kinds. Web 2.0 is not only social and extremely dynamic, but also hard to understand. As Ali & Frew [11] maintain, it is impossible to make an exact taxonomy of Web 2.0 tools and applications.

According to the website Tourism Boost [12], there are a few monitoring services specializing in social media like Hootsuite [13], which enables its customers to manage up to a hundred social networks, or Sprout Social [14]. These monitoring services can gather messages for their customers, usually businesses, from multiple channels in one place and thus enable these businesses to communicate freely with their customers, understand the customers' feelings about the brand, and instantly react if necessary to any negative trends among any particular group of customers. These services can also monitor conversations happening elsewhere on the Internet, including blogs, forums, and other public sites, social networks and platforms.

Most SNSs are used by both individuals and businesses in order to network and then stay in touch with other people and/or customers, and to gather a wide variety of information about them. SNS usually allow their users to exchange messages both publicly and privately, form groups, create public pages as well as events, share and tag photographs, audio and video, and much more. According to [10], as of January 2014, 74% of online adult Americans use social networking sites, whereas as of February 2005 it was only 9% of all American internet users. The same source [10] provides information on most popular SNSs among Americans as of September 2014: 71% of online adults use Facebook; 23% of online adults use Twitter; 26% use Instagram; 28% use Pinterest; 28% use LinkedIn.

Ali & Frew [11] made a list of most popular Web 2.0 sites, topped by Facebook and YouTube [15], both with 800 million users, followed by Qzone (480 million), Twitter (300 million), Renden (160 million), LinkedIn (120 million), Vkontakte, currently called VK (111 million) and others. The same list [11] also features several sites aiming at travel and tourism – WAYN [16] (travel and lifestyle, 10 million), Couchsurfing (traveller-community interaction site, 2.9 million), Travelbuddy (linking travel, 1.6 million), Travellerspoint (travel community blogsite, 0.3 million). All of the most popular SNSs contain information that may be exploited in travel and tourism – Facebook as well as other top sites like Twitter or LinkedIn are full of travel-related ads and help all kinds of travellers to find what they are looking for [17].

Of course, the above mentioned most popular SNSs may be used for promoting travel and tourism. However, they do not focus on travel and tourism like some other sites. One of the rankings of the best SNSs in the field of travel and tourism [15] features at the top two general SNSs (Facebook and Twitter), which are followed by

WAYN, Airbnb.com and TripAdvisor. Ali and Frew [11] list among the most popular travel-related SNSs WAYN, Couchsurfing, Travelbuddy and Travellerspoint. Figure 2 below illustrates the five best network sites used in travel and tourism.

Fig. 2. Five best social network sites used in travel and tourism [15]

WAYN [16] was initially an entirely travel-related SNS connecting people who happened to be in the same location. Later, however, it widened its scope to dating and other activities [17]. Its users create their profile and upload photographs. WAYN users can ask for travel recommendations by posting questions to other users. WAYN also helps its users plan their trips. If one looks for a destination, WAYN provides relevant information about accommodation, best photos, top questions and answers, travellers tips, tours and attractions and much more. Alternatively, one can look for top destinations for various kinds of activities or attractions, such as hiking, cycling, beautiful architecture, or beautiful scenery, based on WAYN users' votes. WAYN users may view their destination list, or share with other users memories of a place they all visited in the Who's Around section. It is also possible to add images to one's destinations. Last but not least, WAYN's members and experts also determine Top Places in several categories.

Airbnb.com [17] originally offered short-term living quarters, breakfast and a unique business networking opportunity [15]. Airbnb is still mainly for those who are looking for accommodation in various places around the world. In order to become a user, one must sign up and create their own personal profile. The Airbnb official website [17] says Airbnb host network covers 190 countries and 34,000 cities. Its users may check photos of offered accommodation, host profiles, and reviews. Airbnb users can narrow their search according to the type of accommodation, its price, and location. The site makes it easy to contact hosts and book one's stay.

TripAdvisor [18] is rather a travel website than an SNS [15]. It enables anybody to book hotels, flights, and vacation rentals, to find restaurants and things-to-do in one's destination. It updates travellers about the weather forecast for particular destinations, offers forums, reviews, traveller articles, travel guides, it also shows maps, calls the traveller's attention to most popular places, traveller photographs, and much more.

Couchsurfing [19] seems to be very similar to Airbnb as it is a service that connects its members who sign in and complete their profiles featuring their home base, lifestyle, mission and what they consider important. Couchsurfing members make up a global community of travellers who share their homes with other couchsurfers. They can also create local communities by means of Place Page. Locally, they hold and attend more or less regular events. Globally, they choose places to visit and look for potential hosts there by sending Couchrequests. Members may become hosts themselves.

Travelbuddy [20] is a website whose users look for people to travel with. It is possible to set specific search criteria, like sex and age of a potential travel buddy, destinations one wants to visit, and travel dates.

Travellerspoint [21] is another travel community website. It offers highlights, where anybody can create their own travel blog or find advice on trip preparation. There is also a forum for those who want to ask or inform others about virtually anything. Users can join various groups or upload travel photographs. It is possible to look there for accommodation tips, users can create maps of their travels and use a travel planner. The website also features travel guides for various regions, subregions, countries and territories.

All in all, travel and tourism can be promoted by means of both general and traveland-tourism-orientated SNSs. The general ones usually contain travel ads. Companies active in travel and tourism have their fan sites there. SNSs promoting travel and tourism can be divided into two categories. The likes of WAYN, TripAdvisor, Travellerspoint provide their users with information about destinations and enable them to exchange their experience and knowledge about places, attractions and activities. SNSs like Airbnb.com, Couchsurfing, or Travelbuddy focus on facilitating contacts among people as they put together those who look for and provide accommodation and/or company on trips.

4   Discussion of the Findings

As the findings show, there is an increasing number of successful SNSs used for the travel and tourism purposes. However, the most popular SNSs are still Facebook and Twitter. A case study by Buted et al. [22] also shows that the most popular SNSs for tourism industry in Batangas province, Philippines, are Facebook, Twitter and You-Tube, which serve as good tools for the dissemination of information very fast and at low costs. On the contrary, the negative aspect is that travellers' opinions are not well presented, which leads to bad impressions and unfair criticism.

In addition, online communities have a strong impact on travellers' decisions and on the overall image and marketing of a particular destination (cf. [23]). As Kiralova & Pavlicek [24] state, social network sites can help destinations to remain competitive if they present attractive content, exploit creativity and support and stimulate interactive communication. However, to have an influence on travellers' decisions, they must be excellent in a sense of resembling the most glossy and popular magazines. Moreover, they should address travellers as individuals, i.e., they should be personalized. But they should also be dynamic and interactive and provide travellers with s unique experience (cf. [25]).

Karnstedt et al. [26] list seven benefits SNSs might have for travel and tourism destination organizations, which include: (1) solicit endorsements; (2) maximize revenue per seat; (3) bond with guests; (4) manage reputation; (5) reach out to new customers; (6) recruit new staff; and (7) build a buzz.

Table 1 below then summarizes the main benefits and limitations of SNSs for travel and tourism industry.

Table 1. Benefits and limitations of SNSs for travel and tourism industry

Benefits	Limitations
• They are able to address a big number of global travellers at relatively low costs and higher level of efficiency;	• They can spread a negative review of some destinations like a wildfire; information does not have to be credible, objective or useful; they can be abused by travellers and employees in exposing an employer's trade secrets or business proprietary information [26];
• They enable to build and maintain a community of interest;	
• They enable twenty four hours operations regardless different time zones;	
• They enable to post and present travellers' current photos, videos, opinions, experience or experiences;	
• They are valuable source of word-of-mouth recommendations;	• It is difficult to orientate among loads of various platforms and messages;
• They help to build brand equity;	
• They provide feedback for destination management organizations;	• There is no control over the word-of-mouth.
• They enable businesses to instantly react to emerging trends.	

(Source: authors' own processing)

5   Conclusion

Currently, social network sites have a tremendous influence on how tourists create, organize and share tourism experiences (cf. [27]). And since tourism is the main source of revenue in many countries and regions, tourist destination organizations should bear this fact on their mind and take a challenge to promote their places via SNSs because SNSs represent strategic importance for tourism competitiveness [28]. Moreover, SNSs can lower costs, increase operational efficiency and improve service quality and customer experience [29].

Acknowledgments. This study is supported by the SPEV project 2104/2018, run at the Faculty of Informatics and Management, University of Hradec Kralove, Czech Republic. The authors thank Ales Berger for his help with the data collection.

References

1. Boyd, D.M., Ellison, N.B.: Social network sites: definition, history and scholarship. J. Comput.Med. Commun. **13**(1), 210–230 (2008)
2. Poulova, P., Klimova, B.: Social networks and their potential for education. In: Proceedings of the Computational Collective Intelligence 7th International Conference, ICCCI 2015, pp. 365–366. Spain (2015)
3. Werthner, H., Ricci, F.: E-Commerce and tourism. Commun. ACM **47**(12), 101–105 (2004)
4. Universal McCann on social media (2008). http://www.scribd.com/doc/3836535/Universal-Mccann-on-Social-Media#scribd. Accessed 30 May 2018
5. Lange-Faria, W., Elliot, S.: Understanding the role of social media in destination marketing. Tourismos: Int. Multidiscip. J. Tour. **7**(1), 193–211 (2012)
6. Nielsen: The Paid Social Media Advertising Report 2013 (2013). http://www.nielsen.com/us/en/insights/reports/2013/the-paid-social-mediaadvertising-report-2013.html. Accessed 19 July 2018
7. Bennett, S.: The impact of social media on travel and tourism (2012). http://www.adweek.com/socialtimes/social-media-travel-hospitality/466163. Accessed 30 May 2018
8. Cox, C., Burgess, S., Sellitto, C., Buultjens, J.: Consumer Generated Web-based Tourism Marketing. CRC for Sustainable Tourism Pty Ltd., Australia (2008)
9. ScienceDirect: Social network sites in travel and tourism (2016). http://www.sciencedirect.com/science?_ob=ArticleListURL&_method=list&_ArticleListID=-&_sort=r&_st=13&view=c&md5=4d1729d3e570ed33e1c63419424b6a99&searchtype=a. Accessed 10 Jan 2016
10. Pew Research Center: Social networking fact sheet (2016). http://www.pewinternet.org/factsheets/social-networking-fact-sheet/. Accessed 30 May 2018
11. Ali, A., Frew, A.J.: Information and Communication Technologies for Sustainable Tourism. Routledge (2013)
12. Tourism Boost (2016). https://www.smallbusiness.wa.gov.au/TourismBoost/marketing-tips-andtricks/social-media/. Accessed 15 Jan 2016
13. Hootsuite (2016). www.ubervu.com. Accessed 30 May 2018
14. Sprout Social (2016). www.sproutsocial.com. Accessed 30 May 2018
15. The Five Best Social Networking Sites for Travel (Undated, 2013). http://www.worldluxurytourism.com/featured/the-five-best-social-networking-sitesfor-travel.html. Accessed 30 May 2018
16. WAYN (2016). http://www2.wayn.com/help/using-wayn. Accessed 30 May 2018
17. Airbnb.com (2016). https://www.airbnb.com/help/getting-started/how-to-travel. Accessed 30 May 2018
18. TripAdvisor (2016). http://www.tripadvisor.com/. Accessed 30 May 2018
19. Couchsurfing (2016). https://www.couchsurfing.com/. Accessed 30 May 2018
20. Travelbuddy (2016). http://www.travel-buddies.com/. Accessed 30 May 2018
21. Travellerspoint (2016). http://www.travellerspoint.com/. Accessed 30 May 2018
22. Buted, D.R., Gillespie, N.S., Conti, J.B., Delgado, B.A., Marasigan, R.M.P., Rubico, S.K. A., et al.: Effects of social media in the tourism industry of Batangas province. Asia Pac. J. Multidiscip. Res. **2**(3), 123–131 (2014)
23. Miguens, J., Baggio, R., Costa, C.: Social media and tourism destinations: the TripAdvisor study. IASK Proceedings, pp. 1–6. Portugal: Aveiro (2008)
24. Kiralova, A., Pavlicek, A.: Development of social media strategies in tourism destination. Proced. Soc. Behav. Sci. **175**, 358–366 (2015)

25. Morrison, A.M.: Marketing and Managing Tourism Destinations. Routledge, England (2013)
26. Karnstedt, M., Rowe M., Chan, J., Hayes, C, Alani, H.: The effect of user features on churn in social network. In: Proceedings of the ACM WebSci'11, pp. 1–8. Germany: Koblenz (2011)
27. Rathonyi, G.: Influence of social media on tourism – especially among students of the University of Debrecen. Appl. Stud. Agribus. Commer. 7(1), 105–112 (2013)
28. Leung, D., Law, R., van Hoof, H., Buhalis, D.: Social media in tourism and hospitality: a literature review. J. Travel Tour. Market. 30(1–2), 3–22 (2013)
29. Law, R., Leung, R., Buhalis, D.: Information technology applications in hospitality and tourism: a review of publications from 2005 to 2007. J. Travel Tour. Market. 26(5–6), 599–623 (2009)

Raising a Model for Fake News Detection Using Machine Learning in Python

Gerardo Ernesto Rolong Agudelo[1], Octavio José Salcedo Parra[1,2(✉)],
and Julio Barón Velandia[1]

[1] Faculty of Engineering, Universidad Distrital "Francisco José de Caldas",
Bogotá, DC, Colombia
gerolonga@correo.udistrital.edu.co,
{osalcedo, jbaron}@udistrital.edu.co
[2] Department of Systems and Industrial Engineering, Faculty of Engineering,
National University of Colombia, Bogotá, DC, Colombia
ojsalcedop@unal.edu.co

Abstract. Fake news has been spreading in greater numbers and has generated more and more misinformation, one of the clearest examples being the United States presidential elections of 2016, for which a lot of false information was circulated before the votes that improved the image of Donald Trump overs Hilary's Clinton (Singh et al. n.d.). Because fake news is too much, it becomes necessary to use computational tools to detect them; this is why the use of algorithms of Machine Learning like "CountVectorizer", "TfidfVectorizer", a Naive Bayes Model and natural language processing for the identification of false news in public data sets is proposed.

Keywords: Fake news · Machine learning · NLTK · Sklearn

1 Introduction

With the arrival of the technological era and with it inventions such as radio, internet and television; Information media such as the written newspapers were left aside and the world opened the doors to new ways to find out about the events, most of the news content on television and radio is reviewed and controlled but the content of the internet is hardly supervised and even more so when this does not violate any law (Gu et al. 2017), this is how false news has become a place in today's society, from apparently harmless publications on social networks (2017) to pages web completely dedicated to the production of false information, but made in such a way that they manage to imitate with mastery some of the most recognized newspapers and news channels, besides the fact that it is not possible to make a formal definition of a false news (Mauri et al. 2017).

© IFIP International Federation for Information Processing 2018
Published by Springer Nature Switzerland AG 2018. All Rights Reserved
S. A. Al-Sharhan et al. (Eds.): I3E 2018, LNCS 11195, pp. 596–604, 2018.
https://doi.org/10.1007/978-3-030-02131-3_52

2   Related Work

Because the problem addressed is very relevant in this information age, several previous works have been carried out from different perspectives, focused in different ways and using different techniques, but ultimately all seek to combat misinformation, some of these Studies will be presented below.

In Rubin et al. (2016) they make an approach to the detection of false news based on satire, for this they first made a conceptual description of the satirical humor about twelve satirical humor news and compared it with its real counterpart. For the classification process, they used an SMV (Support Vector Machine) algorithm with five characteristics to predict; absurdity, humor, grammar, negative sensations and punctuation, being the algorithm tested with 360 news achieving 90% accuracy to find satirical news using the combination of absurdity, grammar and punctuation.

In Bourgonje et al. (2017) they make a study of the news regarding its owner and the relevance with its content, focusing mainly on the detection of clickbait, that is, news in which its heading does not have any relation with its development. The methodology was applied on a public data set and achieved a success of 89.59. In the study they seek to provide a tool that helps to check the news coming from traditional and non-traditional media. In the study separate parts of the content of the news, analyzing them separately and determining their veracity, later if they find that some of them are false or contradict another part of the information, you can guess that it is a false news. This method can also be useful for detecting news with political bias that is, showing a political position favorable to a position.

On the other hand in Shu et al. (2017) present a review of several existing methods for the detection of false news, on the one hand there are works focused on the processing of news content and its form, those based on knowledge use external sources to verify the information exposed in the news. Those based on style seek to find within the news signs of language that demonstrates subjectivity or disappointment.

The author of Wang (n.d.) publishes a dataset called "LIAR" which brings together in total twelve thousand eight hundred fragments of declarations of the page "POLI-FACT.COM" manually tagged; being one of the largest public datasets in this topic, with which you can do fact checking analysis and allow automation studies to detect false news. In addition, the study used neural networks to demonstrate that by combining meta-data with text, a great improvement in the detection of false news is achieved.

The study done in Shao et al. (2017) makes an analysis of how bots have been used to spread false news on social networks like twitter and facebook.

In Bajaj (n.d.) they present a study of Deep Learning using natural language processing for the detection of false news; thus, different models are presented, and an assessment is made of which may be the best option to obtain adequate results.

In Farajtabar et al. (n.d.) present a framework for the detection of false news combining learning and a model of network activities providing the possibility of doing a real-time analysis in social networks such as twitter.

3   Methodology

In the study carried out natural language processing (PLN) is used as a Python computational tool; This programming language uses different libraries and platforms, among them its PANDAS natural language processing library (Python Data Analysis Library) which is an open source library with BSD license that provides data structures and data analysis tools. Additionally, NLTK was used, which is a set of libraries and programs oriented to natural language processing and Scikit-learn which is a specialized machine learning library for classification, regression and clustering. The three libraries mentioned above have been designed to operate in conjunction with the other Numpy and Scipy libraries which were also included in the program.

To obtain news for the study, a public data set located in a github repository was used https://github.com/GeorgeMcIntire/fake_real_news_dataset compiled in equal parts for ten thousand five hundred and fifty-eight (10558) news items collected in total between the years 2015 and 2017 written in English with their title, full text and false or true label which were taken from different media, making scrapping processes in news web portals for half of real news and news from a published dataset in Kaggle conformed only by false news.

So once having the dataset, the methodology consisted of three fundamental stages; the pre-processing that involved transforming the dataset from a .csv file to a Python object belonging to Pandas; a data frame to be able to deal with it efficiently. Subsequently, for processing, the data was changed so that the first half of the data with false label and the second half with a true label were not simply what would cause impartiality when applying the machine learning methods. Once this is done, groups of data are taken to make training and test sets with which tokenisation algorithms are executed so that the result is processed by the Multinomial Naive Bayes algorithm of the Scikit-Learn package and finally an array was made in analysis. of confusion to make analysis of the results obtained (Fig. 1).

4   Design

To begin with the processing of the data, it was necessary to use the read_csv () function of the Pandas library, passing the path of the file in which the .csv file is located, which converts to the Data Frame format. For the creation of the test and training sets, the train_test_split () function of the sklearn library was used, which takes as parameters the column with which the learning will be done, the type of classification that must be determined, the size with which will be the test set and a random to scramble the data.

Subsequently, sets "bags" of features are gathered, which are words or subsets of words with which you can extract the frequencies that have the word within the paragraphs belonging to the news texts with two different functions CountVectorizer (), but first it is necessary to do a new cleaning, since at the time of applying machine learning one looks for to see a relation between the veracity of the news and the words that more frequently appear in this one; as is logical there will be many occurrences of "stop words" is words like "that, in, on" these words that serve as connectors and to

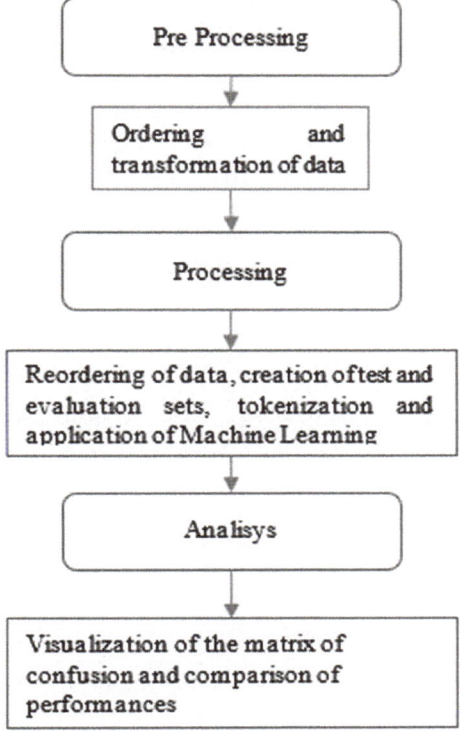

Fig. 1. Source: Own design

give structure to the sentences but semantically does not have a great meaning, so it becomes necessary to get rid of those "stop words" and then if you can proceed to build structures made up of all the words that are part of the news.

Having the sets of words conformed, the NaiveBayes () function is sent as arguments so that it makes the process of determining from the word bag and the training sets if the news should be classified as false or true and subsequently an open source function is used to graph a confusion matrix in which the main diagonal shows the quantity of correctly classified news and the ones that are not seen outside the diagonal.

5   Implementation

The first thing that was done so that the program functions correctly is to import the necessary libraries so that all the functions used are recognized by the interpreter:

```
import pandas as pd
from sklearn.model_selection import train_test_split
from sklearn.metrics import accuracy_score from
sklearn.metrics import confusion_matrix from
sklearn.feature_extraction.text import CountVectorizer
from sklearn.feature_extraction.text import
TfidfVectorizer
from sklearn.naive_bayes import MultinomialNB
import pickle import nltk import numpy as np
import matplotlib.pyplot as plt import
itertools
```

The file is then imported into a DataFrame from the Pandas library and formatted to make it easy to manipulate the data using the following commands.

```
features =
pd.read_csv("fake_or_real_news.csv",usecols=['text',
'label'])
```

Thus, the parts that we will be using for this study of the news, the text and its actual classification have been stored in features; First, mixing them is done to avoid that the classification is affected by the order of the news. These two columns are separated and used to create the training and test sets.

```
features.sample(frac=1)
trainig_set = features.text[:1900]
label_train = features.label[:1900] test_set
= features.text[1900:]
label_test = features.label[1900:]
```

The following commands make the word arrays to be generated do not contain stop words.

```
count_vectorizer = CountVectorizer(stop_words='english')
tfidf_vectorizer = TfidfVectorizer(stop_words='english',
max_df=0.7)
```

Then other counVectorizer functions are used to do a tokenization and frequency count of the tokens and the result is put into matrices made up of the tokens of the test set and the evaluation set.

```
count_train = count_vectorizer.fit_transform(trainig_set)
count_test = count_vectorizer.transform(test_set)
```

To contrast, another way of counting the frequency of the tokens is used and again applied to the test and training sets.

```
tfidf_train = tfidf_vectorizer.fit_transform(trainig_set)
tfidf_test = tfidf_vectorizer.transform(test_set)
```

The algorithm chosen for the automatic learning process was NaiveBayes which works with conditional probability to determine the relationship of one of the tokens with the truth of the news. Thus, the algorithm was run using both forms of tokenization previously named.

```
clf = MultinomialNB()
clf.fit(tfidf_train, label_train) pred = clf.predict(tfidf_test) score =
accuracy_score(label_test, pred)
```

Once the score is set, which is the percentage value of the degree of certainty that the algorithm had when making the classification. It was displayed using the following command:

```
print("certeza %0.3f" % score)
```

Later an open source function was used to graph a confusion matrix and to visualize the results of the process

```
cm = confusion_matrix(label_test, pred, labels=['FAKE',
'REAL'])
plot_confusion_matrix(cm, classes=['Falas', 'Reales'])
```

6 Discussion and Results Analysis

After running the Naive Bayes algorithm with the two forms of tokenization CountVectorizer and TfidfVectorizer the following percentages of certainty were obtained:

- Count Vectorizer: certainty: 0.881
- TfidfVectorizer: certainty 0.848

Likewise, the Confusion Matrices Were Plotted with the Results of Both Classifications, Producing the Following Results:

TfidfVectorizer:

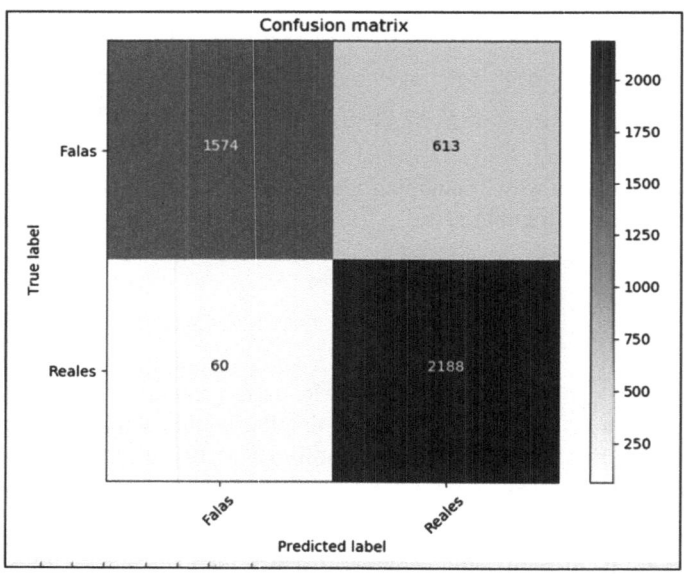

Fig. 2. Source: Own design

Count Vectorizer:

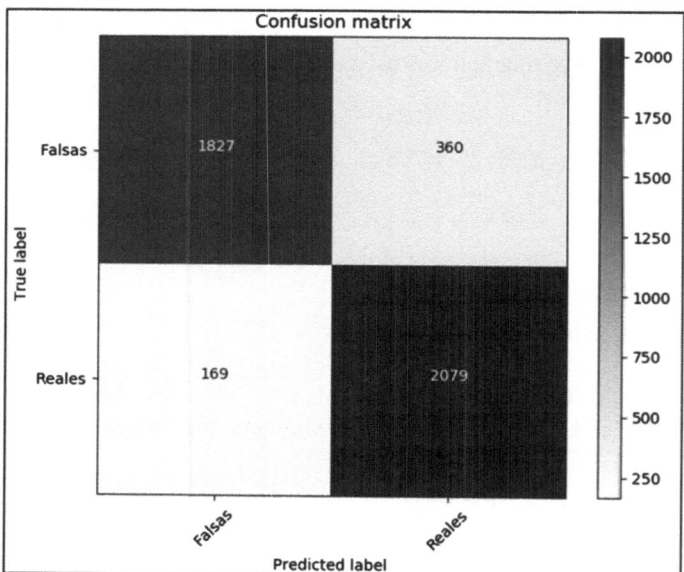

Fig. 3. Source: Own design

This shows that it was more effective to use CountVectorizer as a classification method, since it successfully classified 89.3% of the news correctly classified as false 1827 and as true 2079 (Figs. 2 and 3).

The model used, however, proves not to have the same effectiveness as others, since in Chiu et al. (n.d.) for example they use a model based on Support Vector Machines and achieve an average success rate of 95% and in Chaudhry et al. (n.d.) make an approximation using deep neural networks and achieve a certainty of up to 97.3% in the classification process.

7   Conclusions

Addressing an objective such as the classification of news is a complex task even using a standard procedure of classification of texts, since the news has a large number of characteristics that can be evaluated and to achieve a certainty greater than 95% it is necessary to consider them.

References

Allcott, H., Gentzkow, M.: Social media and fake news in the 2016 election. J. Econ. Perspect. **31**(2—Spring), 211–236 (2017). http://doi.org/10.1257/jep.31.2.211

Bajaj, S.: The Pope Has a New Baby! Fake news detection using deep learning (n.d.). Retrieved from https://web.stanford.edu/class/cs224n/reports/2710385.pdf

Bourgonje, P., Schneider, J.M., Rehm, G.: From Clickbait to fake news detection: an approach based on detecting the stance of headlines to articles, 84–89 (2017). Retrieved from http://www.aclweb.org/anthology/W/W17/W17-4215.pdf

Chaudhry, A.K., Baker, D., Thun-Hohenstein, P.: Stance detection for the fake news challenge: identifying textual relationships with deep neural nets (n.d.). Retrieved from https://web.stanford.edu/class/cs224n/reports/2760230.pdf

Chiu, J., Gokcen, A., Wang, W., Yan, X.: Classification of fake and real articles based on support vector machines (n.d.). Retrieved from https://pdfs.semanticscholar.org/05be/61a7726916644e49e578378d4faa7aa5f4ce.pdf

Farajtabar, M. et al.: Fake news mitigation via point process based intervention (n.d.). Retrieved from http://proceedings.mlr.press/v70/farajtabar17a/farajtabar17a.pdf

Gu, L., Kropotov V., Yarochkin, F.: The fake news machine: how propagandists abuse the internet and manipulate the public. Trendlabs research paper. Trend Macro (2017)

Mauri, M., Jonathan, G., Tommaso, V., Michele, M.: A fiel guide to fake news (2017)

Mele, N., et al.: Combating fake news: an agenda for research and action, May 2017

Rubin, V., Conroy, N., Chen, Y., Cornwell, S.: Fake news or truth? using satirical cues to detect potentially misleading news. In: Proceedings of the Second Workshop on Computational Approaches to Deception Detection, pp. 7-17 (2016). Retrieved from https://www.researchgate.net/profile/Victoria_Rubin/publication/301650504_Fake_News_or_Truth_Using_Satirical_Cues_to_Detect_Potentially_Misleading_News/links/571fed4c0aeaced788acd8e/Fake-News-or-Truth-Using-Satirical-Cues-to-Detect-PotentiallyMisleading

Shao, C., Ciampaglia, G.L., Varol, O., Flammini, A., Menczer, F.: The spread of fake news by social bots (2017). http://doi.org/1707.07592

Shu, K., Wang, S., Sliva, A., Tang, J., Liu, H.: Fake news detection on social media: a data mining perspective. ACM SIGKDD Explor. Newsl. **19**, 22–36 (2017)

Singh, V., Dasgupta, R., Sonagra, D., Raman, K., Ghosh, I.: Automated fake news detection using linguistic analysis and machine learning (n.d.). Retrieved from http://sbp-brims.org/2017/proceedings/papers/challenge_papers/AutomatedFakeNewsDetection.pdf

Wang, W.Y.: Liar, liar pants on fire: a new benchmark dataset for fake news. Detection (n.d.). Retrieved from https://www.cs.ucsb.edu/ ~ william/papers/acl2017.pdf

Design of a System for Melanoma Detection Through the Processing of Clinical Images Using Artificial Neural Networks

Marco Stiven Sastoque Mahecha[1], Octavio José Salcedo Parra[1,2]([✉]),
and Julio Barón Velandia[1]

[1] Faculty of Engineering, Universidad Distrital "Francisco José de Caldas",
Bogotá, DC, Colombia
mssastoquem@correo.udistrital.edu.co,
{osalcedo,jbaron}@udistrital.edu.co

[2] Department of Systems and Industrial Engineering, Faculty of Engineering,
National University of Colombia, Bogotá, DC, Colombia
ojsalcedop@unal.edu.co

Abstract. Skin cancer is one of the most important challenges in modern medicine, especially skin melanoma, being the main causer of deaths for this disease. Images analysis is one of the most transcendental techniques for Melanoma early detection as a prevention method. Artificial neural networks are one of the many developed techniques for images digital processing and characteristic similarities detection. In this work a graphic processing unit (GPU) is developed for clinical skin images analysis getting through an artificial neural networks system for similar patterns detection through processing in a collection of modules tasked of silhouette detection of the object to analyze into the image, and tasked to study borders or contour to determinate a final diagnostic, the dataset used for the training of the artificial neural network designed is gotten from the MED-NODE project and project of international skin images collaboration (ISIC) with 730 images of positive and negative cases as full, the proposed system presents finally an accuracy level of 76.67%, with a level of success of 78.79% in melanoma specific cases, and 74.07% in benign lesions cases.

Keywords: Neural networks · Deep learning · Clinical diagnosis
Patterns recognition

1 Introduction

In last 40 years the progressive increase of people affected by cutaneous melanoma in the world has been seen, because of this, the interest in the study of this disease has evolved to become the focus of a large number of scientists around the world. Cutaneous melanoma is supposed as the leading cause of death from skin cancer actually, producing 3 of every 4 deaths due to such, and representing the 1–2% of all death causes in the world [1]. In Colombia there is not specific statistical data official on the affectations of neoplasms or cutaneous abnormal formations associated with melanoma on the population of the country, although cancer is a disease of priority concern, as set out in the Act 1384 of 2010 [2].

S. A. Al-Sharhan et al. (Eds.): I3E 2018, LNCS 11195, pp. 605–616, 2018.
https://doi.org/10.1007/978-3-030-02131-3_53

Medicine is one of the elements that most beneficiaries can see by near interaction with computer systems, different computing algorithms have been developed with the aim of preventing the cutaneous melanoma disease, besides a lot of methods have been developed in dermatology for skin cancer prevention as ABCD (asymmetry, borders, color, diameter) rules that describe a set of general elements for recognition of positive cases of melanoma, or the seven points of Glasgow [3] which determines a set of criteria for the detection of skin cancer, it's used as a method of complementation to the analysis made by the use of the ABCD rules.

This paper proposes a deigned system in base of artificial neural networks for melanoma detection through the processing and analysis of clinical images, the main objective is to develop an automated system using computation tools for to do diagnostics associated with skin cancer. In the previously raised context, it's designed a structure for the analysis of skin lesions based on investigations made by different institutions and the progress made on the issue until today.

2   Related Works

In recent years there is a significant number of works focused on the detection of Melanoma and techniques of image processing to prevent skin cancer, different models of analysis have been developed on different platforms and with different approaches to the treatment of medical information.

Joseph and Panicker [4] propose a system of analysis of skin lesions for quick melanoma detection with an effective method of segmentation through techniques of image processing and mobile technologies, they develop a series of stages of image preprocessing, subsequent to the detection and extraction of the hair to make a direct analysis on the skin, with the obtained information in the processing of images designed, a rating system for the results obtained is done in a set 3 possibilities (benign, atypical and melanoma) producing results with a high degree of effectiveness. A very similar work is made by Soumya et al. [5] where they propose an algorithm of early detection of melanoma through the use of a system of description and colour analysis, here the develop a set of phases for the image processing which includes different filters and segmentations for the analysis of them, finally they conduct tests with a set of 200 images with highly effective results (91.5%) on the implemented system.

Lugo, Maldonado and Murata [6] perform an study of artificial intelligence to assist clinical diagnosis, within the research made a brief overview of the uses of different systems of machine learning in the history of medicine, they also do a study related to the advantages offered by these systems to the traditional statistics, within the work an specific section is made to refer to the use of artificial neural networks in medicine, foregrounding the flexibility and dynamism offered by these systems and explain generally the operation.

Mentioned related works have a high interrelation with the work of the proposed investigation of this document, there is a lot of progress in image processing, however the most common method, thanks to its effectiveness over several years are neural networks, in this context, different scanned works provide a set of tools associated with the management of this technique in areas of medicine as [6, 7], other revised research papers analyze different characteristics associated with the identification of cutaneous melanoma, and determining techniques of segmentation of images for the recognition and classification, allowing the production of a more effective final result, in conclusion, the literature review provides an important set of tools that allow to make a work guided as a full element of possibilities, and where it's possible to explore different techniques to maximize the efficiency of the project.

3   Proposed System Design

There are many methods for Melanoma detection through images processing through the determination of characteristics, Barata et al. [8] do a work for the detection of Melanoma through the use of two systems based on the analysis of the characteristics of texture and color respectively, within the work is taken as a fundamental base the analysis of the features provided by the ABCD criteria, from which information can be fully relevant for the early detection of skin cancer [9].

Measurement of the ABD (asymmetry, borders and diameter) criteria can be obtained through the analysis of the generation of the mask at the binary level of the analyzed image, however to obtain an image with a high amount of information is required a preprocessing phase allowing to improve quality through a set of filtering techniques that enable to obtain a better result of the characteristics seeking to analyze, and at the same time eliminate the noise of photography [10].

In Fig. 1, can be seen the scheme of the structure for the stage of analysis and classification of the analyzed image.

Fig. 1. Scheme of the main stages of the system. Source: Authors

3.1   Preprocessing

For the development of the system a preprocessing phase is performed which seeks to apply a set of fixes to the image before the phase of analysis conducted with the expert system, the target is to make the generation of a mask from the image that allows to define the texture of the lesion in a base of white and black that can be represented in binary form (0 and 1) to ensure the elimination of noise in the image and obtain the texture defined edges is used the Canny's method, an algorithm developed with the aim of achieving the elimination of noise by three mathematical threads that involve the calculation of the magnitude and orientation of the gradient vector at each pixel within the first phase known as the obtaining of the gradient, the thinning of the width of edges obtained with the gradient until edges of a pixel of width within the second phase known as non-maximum suppression, and the application of a function of hysteresis based on two thresholds in the final phase known as threshold hysteresis; This process is intended to reduce the possibility of appearance of false contour [11].

Figure 2 shows the stage of preprocessing the image with the help of software MATLAB R2016a and its Toolbox for image processing [12], where applies corrections series based on the phases of input, correction of lighting, step to grayscale and generation of mask in black and white for the segmentation of the image serving the process specified in Fig. 1.

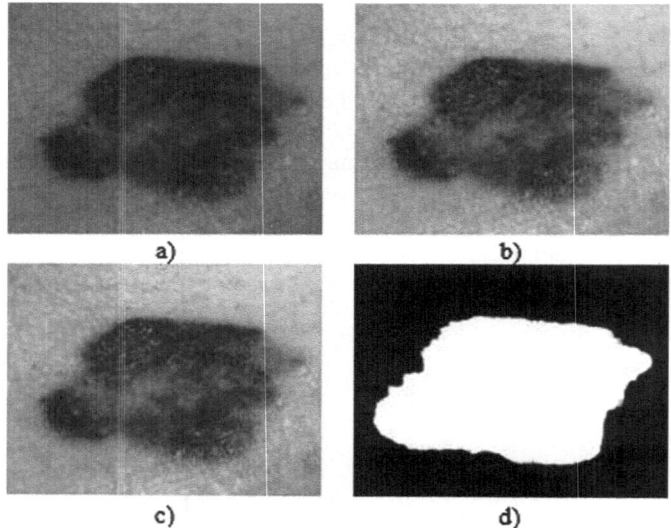

Fig. 2. Preprocessing of the image. a) Input image.   Source: [13] b) Illumination correction. c) Grayscale. d) Gaussian filter and mask generation

3.2 Artificial Neuronal Network Architecture

For the image processing is necessary use a convolutional neural network system, these systems are designed for machine vision tasks, and have a high degree of efficiency in the recognition of characteristics in digital images and their subsequent classification [14].

The neural network Convolutional posed to implement for the recognition and diagnosis of Melanoma consists of six layers, each layer has an output consisting of a set of images or drawings, which is commonly awarded them the name "features maps", which are composed of sets of neurons, neurons located within a map of features connect with neurons hosted on the following maps only through connections called fields of projection also normally known as convolution masks [15].

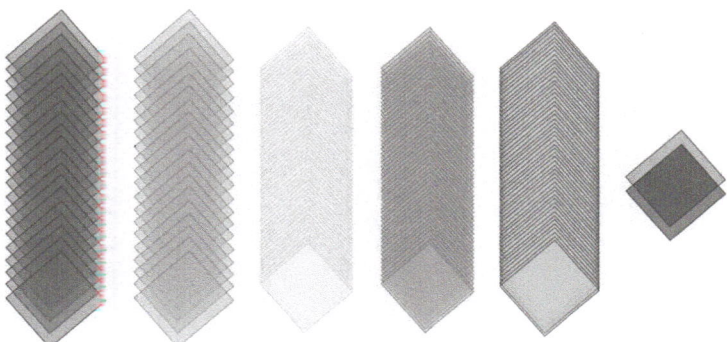

Fig. 3. Convolutional neural network architecture. Source: Authors

In Fig. 3 can be seen the scheme of the layered architecture in the convolutional neural network designed for Melanoma detection system.

The first layer of the convolutional neural network (C1) has twenty five features maps, each unit present in twenty five maps of features are connected with a set of 20 units or pixels in the input image represented by neighborhoods of 5 × 5, each connection with the elements of the image has a trainable and shared weight for each of the units on the map each map feature consists of a set of 255 × 255 units, within this first layer is made using Gabor filters that allow the segmentation of texture and is often the first stage of processing of images within convolutional neural networks systems [16], After the first layer follows a stage of subsampling, also known in some cases as a grouping layer, belonging to this stage, next layer (S2) has fifteen maps of features with a size of 60 × 06 units, the connections of this stage are carried out with a set of 20 units of the previous layer formed by a neighborhood of 5 × 5 elements, subsampling layers have functions of averaging, in this layer each unit is responsible for calculating the sum of the four pixels corresponding stage or layer above (C1), the number of connections between the S2 and C1 there are not trainable elements or changes or functions on images.

4   Results and Discussion

When the stage of training is done nest is to determine the proper functioning of the network and a respective percentage of accuracy, for the realization of these tests it's used a processor Intel core-i5 3337U, with RAM memory 6 GB and graphics processing (GPU) with NVIDIA GeForce GTX graphics card unit.

To perform the test on the implemented system of neural networks used a random number generator that selects the sample used in initial tests of efficiency on the network, so the images are tested within the system in a non-concurrent order and with uniform distribution by simulation of the system in accordance with the Royal field of data entry the algorithm used for the selection of the images is the congruential mixed method, this method is the most widely used for the generation of random numbers,

Table 1. Results of test on designed neural network.

(*continued*)

Table 1. (*continued*)

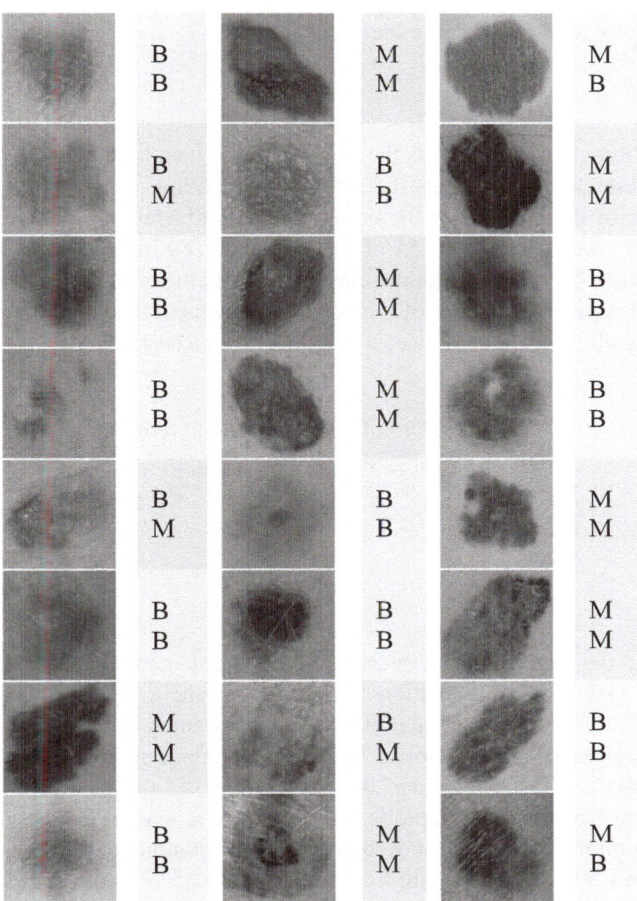

and most suitable to use with the necessary parameters to each test image is assigned an index that is associated with the number obtained through generator.

The generator based on mixed congruential used the following equation:

$$X_i = (aX_{i-1} + b)mob(m) \tag{1}$$

Where m = 256, b = 191, c = 31, and seed Xo = 255, these values are defined, since they meet the basic conditions for the achievement of a maximum period, which ensures the non-existence of repeated numbers.

In Table 1 can be seen some of the images used for the analysis with the order given by the random number generator, with their respective test within the network mounted, and the evaluation of the result on the basis of the actual values of classification, the set of test images is obtained from the project MED-NODE [7] and the international collaboration of melanoma images project (ISIC) [17].

The notations used in the table are

- M: Malignant
- B: Benign

The first abbreviation represents the classification given by the system to the image, the second abbreviation represents the actual classification.

The results of the analysis of the network show efficiency of 77.50% of analyzed images, with a correct result in 155 of the 200 analyzed images, in this context, the Internet presents a good average in the classification of the images, however the results present a level of less than some of the work effectiveness as detailed later defined in Table 2 results obtained with respect to the level of success for each classification:

Table 2. Percentage of accuracy in results

	# Images	# Correct classification	% Accuracy
Benign	89	67	75,28%
Malignant	111	88	79,27%
Total	200	155	77,50%

Comparing the level of effectiveness of the implemented neural network with techniques as Delaunay triangulation [18] arises where a percentage of success of 66.7% for Melanoma images, greater efficiency is presented in the accuracy of records of melanoma, about to the approach by natural computing technique [19], similar results are gotten, with a percentage of success of 80%, the detection of melanoma through geometric characteristics project [20] obtained a level of success to 89% with a rate of success higher than the proposed project, the technique of color correlogram [5] has a level of 91.5% efficiency with the use of a Bayesian classifier, as same than the segmentation technique for classification of the nearest neighbors [21] presenting even a level of highly superior efficiency compared to other work of the project and the proposed system, however these projects are analyzed only with efficient lighting condition images, leaving in doubt the level of efficiency in other conditions.

Figure 4 expresses the results in base of images of melanoma and benign on the proposed system, and works taken as help, next notations used are described:

- TD: Delaunay triangulation
- CN: Natural computing
- CG: Geometric features
- CC: Color correlogram
- VC: Nearest neighbors
- RN: Neural networks.

In the presented context, results obtained in the study presented a suitable percentage of approximation of 77.50% through the structure of the proposed network,

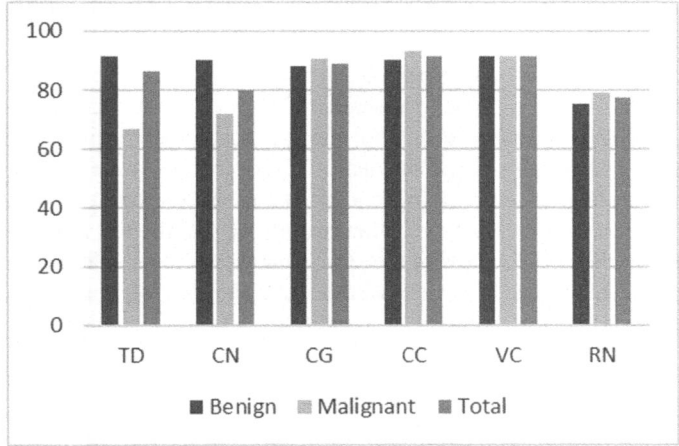

Fig. 4. Accuracy percentage in images classification. Source: Authors

however, other techniques far outweigh it, being necessary to specify that performance tests are performed using different conditions and ideal illimunation states, artificial neural networks are one of the techniques of most renowned for the digital processing of images, every cay new techniques and models based on different algorithms that can exceed the normal functioning of these and their efficiency in the classification of images appear.

5 Future Works

Deep learning trends have allowed to develop new techniques aimed at improving the capacity of the systems in the accuracy of the results, one of the elements that emerged recently within the study of artificial intelligence systems is the concept of auto-organization which represents through unsupervised learning process which will let discover features relations, significant patterns or prototypes in the dataset used [22], within the framework of convolutional neural networks, the concept of auto-organization is an important approach in processing images in convolutioa neural networks systems, as it allows to increase the level of representation of the features extracted by the expert system through the use of maps features auto-organized [22]. Currently it is a littleknown, still under development and under research model, however its implementation can be a key element to improve the level of accuracy of the systems of images processing, which could represent future work with significant influence within the study of medicine.

6   Conclusions

Image use dermatological as element base for medical studies of skin cancer has allowed dealing with large property diseases of high relevance and care through tel-emedicine, making it an essential tool for the creation of new replacements trends in conventional medicine. This work has dealt with a complex method of deep learning based on clinical images getting a percentage of success on the analysis of images of 77,50%, the factor in conditions of illumination in the figures has been the main element affecting the effectiveness of the system, however the results are satisfactory in a large percentage, in Fig. 5 can be seen some examples of images with incorrect results, in them is shown illumination conditions that affected the efficiency of the system.

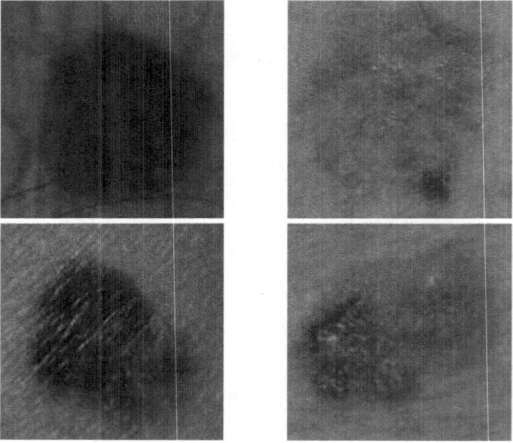

Fig. 5. Incorrect results images. Source: Authors

Features extraction method used in the proposed project is implemented Convo-lutional neural network task, while in all projects related, the characteristics of the lesions are extracted data direct, which represents an important advantage over the related work, however most of the works used in the comparison of results have a higher level of accuracy based on the metric used However in the case of melanoma detection system presents a broad improvement over method of Deulanay's triangu-lation and natural computing, which represents an important element considering that these cases are those who represent the real cause of the alert in the context where the project develops.

In Table 3 we can see a quantitative comparison of the obtained results with other related works.

Having in mind the problem with the illumination conditions of the images and their negative effect on the analysis of them, work to assess such as improvement of the

Table 3. Quantitative comparison of results

	Benign	Malignant	Total
TD [18]	91.5%	66.7%	86.6%
CN [19]	90%	72%	80%
CG [20]	88%	90.5%	89%
CC [5]	90%	93%	91.5%
VC [21]	91.5%	91.5%	91.5%
RN	75.28%	79.27%	77.50%

current system proposed must focus fully on image preprocessing stage, rather than in the network architecture, this implementation would increase the accuracy of the system.

References

1. López Sánchez, R.: Melanoma cutáneo en áreas con índice de radiación ultravioleta elevado (2016)
2. Cormane, J., Rodelo, A.: Epidemiología del cáncer no melanoma en Colombia. Rev. Asoc. Colomb. Dermatol. Cir. Dermatológica, 20 (2012)
3. Abbasi, N.R., et al.: Early diagnosis of cutaneous melanoma: revisiting the ABCD criteria. JAMA **292**(22), 2771–2776 (2004)
4. Joseph, S., Panicker, J.R.: Skin lesion analysis system for melanoma detection with an effective hair segmentation method. In: 2016 International Conference on Information Science (ICIS), pp. 91–96 (2016)
5. Soumya, R.S., Neethu, S., Niju, T.S., Renjini, A., Aneesh, R.P.: Advanced earlier melanoma detection algorithm using colour correlogram. In: 2016 International Conference on Communication Systems and Networks (ComNet), pp. 190–194 (2016)
6. Reyes, S.O.L., Colín, G.M., Murata, C.: Inteligencia artificial para asistir el diagnóstico clínico en medicina. Rev. Alerg. México **61**(2) (2014)
7. Dermatology database used in MED-NODE." [Online]. http://www.cs.rug.nl/~imaging/databases/melanoma_naevi/. Accessed 04 Apr 2017
8. Barata, C., Ruela, M., Francisco, M., Mendonça, T., Marques, J.S.: Two systems for the detection of melanomas in dermoscopy images using texture and color features. IEEE Syst. J. **8**(3), 965–979 (2014)
9. Zaballos, P., Carrera, C., Puig, S., Malvehy, J.: Criterios dermatoscópicos para el diagnóstico del melanoma. Med. Cutan. Iber. Lat. Am. **32**(1), 3–17 (2004)
10. Cuevas, E., Zaldívar, D., Pérez-Cisneros, M.: Procesamiento digital de imágenes usando MatLAB y Simulink (2010)
11. Rebaza, J.V.: Detección de bordes mediante el algoritmo de Canny. Esc. Académico Prof. Informática Univ. Nac, Trujillo Perú (2007)
12. Gonzalez, R.C.E., Woods, S.L., Gonzalez, R.E.R.E.R.C., Woods, R.E., Eddins, S.L.: Digital image processing using MATLAB (2004)
13. Giotis, I., Molders, N., Land, S., Biehl, M., Jonkman, M.F., Petkov, N.: MED-NODE: a computer-assisted melanoma diagnosis system using non-dermoscopic images. Expert Syst. Appl. **42**(19), 6578–6585 (2015)

14. Rodriguez Castello, D.: Extracción de cráneo en imágenes de resonancia magnética del cerebro utilizando una red neuronal convolucional 3D. B.S. thesis, Universitat Politècnica de Catalunya (2017)

15. Pérez-Carrasco, J.A., Serrano-Gotarredona, C., Acha Piñero, B., Serrano-Gotarredona, T., Linares-Barranco, B.: Red neuronal convolucional rápida sin fotogramas para reconocimientos de dígitos (2011)

16. Aznar-Casanova, J.A., Casanova, J.A.: Análisis multiescala y multiorientación de imágenes mediante un banco de filtros de Gabor-2D. Rev. Cogn. **12**(2), 223–246 (2002)

17. ISIC Archive. [Online]. https://isic-archive.com/. Accessed 25 May 2017

18. Pennisi, A., Bloisi, D.D., Nardi, D., Giampetruzzi, A.R., Mondino, C., Facchiano, A.: Melanoma detection using delaunay triangulation. In: 2015 IEEE 27th International Conference on Tools with Artificial Intelligence (ICTAI), pp. 791–798 (2015)

19. Dumitrache, I., Sultana, A.E., Dogaru, R.: Automatic detection of skin melanoma from images using natural computing approaches. In: 2014 10th International Conference on Communications (COMM), pp. 1–4 (2014)

20. Moussa, R., Gerges, F., Salem, C., Akiki, R., Falou, O., Azar, D.: Computer-aided detection of melanoma using geometric features. In: 2016 3rd Middle East Conference on Biomedical Engineering (MECBME), pp. 125–128 (2016)

21. Satheesha, T.Y., Satyanarayana, D., Giriprasad, M.N., Nagesh, K.N.: Detection of melanoma using distinct features. In: 2016 3rd MEC International Conference on Big Data and Smart City (ICBDSC), pp. 1–6 (2016)

22. Palomo Ferrer, E.J.: Arquitecturas Flexibles, Crecientes y Jerárquicas para Sistemas Neuronales Autoorganizados (2016)

Author Index